The Modernization of China and Japan

文章山斗

GEORGE M. BECKMANN

THE MODERNIZATION OF
China and Japan

HARPER & ROW, PUBLISHERS

New York, Evanston, and London

To Jean

Preface

Both fascinating and momentous is the rapidity with which, in today's world, the old and tradition-bound societies of Asia and Africa are being transformed by their acceptance of Western ideas, institutions, and technologies—innovations which were the fruits, slowly matured, of Europe's Renaissance, Reformation, and Enlightenment as well as its more recent scientific and political revolutions. In the long run, each of these non-Western societies will achieve a synthesis of its own traditional ways and those which have their roots in the West. In this book I have tried to analyze within a historical framework the modernization of the societies of China and Japan, a process which, beginning in the age of sailing ships, continues in this second half of the twentieth century.

While recognizing the important differences between the two societies, not only in their traditional backgrounds but in their development in the past century and a half, I have found it convenient to divide the book into three main parts, as follows: (1) The Traditional Society of China and Japan, (2) The Beginnings of Modernization in China and Japan, and (3) The Transformation of China and Japan—to date.

In Japan the process of modernization began as early as the middle of the nineteenth century because Japanese feudal society was receptive to innovations based on Western ideas and institutions. In fact, Japan underwent such a remarkable transformation that her strength as a new industrial nation altered the power structure, first in East Asia and ultimately in the world as a whole. Although the feudal heritage remained an important force, Japanese society under the impact of industrialization began moving in the direction of an Open Society; and this trend was given added momentum after World War II by the reforms of the American occupation.

China, on the other hand, resisted change in the nineteenth century, except in a limited way, and consequently fell prey to foreign imperialisms, including the Japanese. But China was changing under the impact of the West, albeit slowly; and revolutionary elements that were determined to transform society ultimately emerged at the turn of the century. After World War I the Nationalists and the Communists combined forces to carry out such a revolution, but the split between them prevented its consummation. For almost two decades the Nationalists were the strongest element on the Chinese political scene, but the Communists ultimately triumphed; and today, controlling all of China except Taiwan, they are attempting to modernize within the framework of a Closed Society.

In addition to developing the main theme of the book—the modernization of Chinese and Japanese society—I have tried to relate East Asia to important international developments, including the colonial expansion of Europe during the nineteenth century, the attendant rivalries among the imperialist powers, the two world wars, and the contemporary ideological and power struggle between the Communist and Western power blocs.

I wish to express my thanks to Professor George Jenks of the University of Kansas for providing the end-paper maps. My indebtedness to the many scholars whose research has provided the foundation upon which this book was written cannot be individually acknowledged here, but I have called attention to some of their contributions in the six bibliographies. I wish also to express my appreciation to four great teachers: John K. Fairbank and Edwin O. Reischauer, both of Harvard University; Thomas C. Smith, of Stanford University; and Arthur F. Wright, of Yale University.

GEORGE M. BECKMANN

Lawrence, Kansas
March, 1962

Contents

PART

CHINA AND JAPAN IN TRANSFORMATION

The Traditional Society
of China and Japan

PART

The Traditional Society of China

Together with northern India and the Near East, China is one of the oldest birthplaces of civilization in the world, and her culture, like the other two, spread rapidly. From its original source in north China it was disseminated to surrounding areas, and ultimately it exerted a profound influence on the nascent cultures of neighboring Korea and Japan.

The history of the development and diffusion of Chinese culture can be divided into two major chronological sequences. The major theme of the first sequence is the transition of Chinese society from tribalism to feudalism, from feudalism to petty states, and lastly from petty states to the imperial system based on the philosophical foundations of an eclectic Confucianism. This whole process took place gradually during the Shang (1523–1028 B.C.), Chou (1028–221 B.C.), and Han (206 B.C.–220 A.D.) dynasties. The second sequence has as its focal point the growth and development of the Chinese empire after its re-establishment during the Sui (590–618) and T'ang (618–906) dynasties. Despite changes in dynasties caused by rebellions and nomad conquests, Chinese society remained under the imperial system until the twentieth century, a fact which can be attributed in large part to the ability of strong emperors to restore a high degree of social and economic equilibrium at the beginning of a new dynasty and to the enduring strength of Confucian foundations.

Yet Chinese society was often subjected to the impact of forces for change, both material and spiritual, and during the long course of its history it was not the static society so often described by nineteenth-century Europeans and Americans. But, although Chinese ideas and institutions were

2

modified from time to time, there were no changes of a revolutionary nature. Dynasties followed each other in something of a cyclical pattern, and this amazing cultural continuity, unparalleled in other parts of the world, led many foreign observers to emphasize stagnation.

The cultural level reached by China in the seventeenth and eighteenth centuries was probably in every way equal, if not superior, to that of the emerging nations of western Europe. But the very thing which gave China her strength—cultural continuity—proved in modern times to be a fundamental source of difficulty, for when, in the nineteenth century, in the wake of the great technological and political revolutions of Europe, China began to feel the impact of Western imperialism as well as Western ideas and institutions, she was unable to absorb the cultural shock. The overwhelming majority of Chinese intellectuals were simply unable to think in terms of changes that were in fact revolutionary. What was especially unfortunate for China was the circumstance that the impact of the West reached its peak when Chinese society was entering a period of decline in the pattern of the so-called "dynastic cycle."

1   The Origins of Chinese Civilization

The origins and early development of human activity in China cannot be traced with great accuracy. Discoveries of unpolished stone implements prove the existence of Paleolithic cultures in northwest China and Mongolia, but it is not known whether these artifacts were used by ancestors of the modern Chinese. Of greater significance are the skeletal remains of a Paleolithic hominid found in 1927 in a collapsed cave dwelling five miles south of Peking. This "Peking Man," who lived several hundred thousand years ago, was a distant cousin of the Chinese people. He stood erect, used fire, and hunted and fished; and he shared his environment with such animals as the horse, bison, and rhinoceros. Not until much later (6000–2000 B.C.) are we on much safer ground. In that period north China was the home of various Neolithic cultures, the sites of which are fairly numerous. These "Chinese" lived in tribal communities, hunted and fished, and engaged in a primitive agriculture; moreover, excavations have revealed the existence of rectangular cities surrounded by walls of pounded earth. Archeological evidence indicates that Neolithic culture was probably indigenous to China, but there is evidence, though it is not conclusive, that elements of this early civilization, such as pottery techniques, were additions through cultural diffusion from western Asia.

Shang Society

The historian is on slightly more solid ground when he describes the society of the Shang dynasty (1523–1028 B.C.). The earliest Chinese records relate myths of even more ancient dynasties and hero-emperors, but the Shang is the first verifiable dynasty. The central territory of the Shang people, the descendants of Neolithic culture, was an easily defended area in the northwestern part of modern Honan Province, adjacent to the mountains of Shensi Province and extending into the alluvial plain formed by the Yellow River. The physical environment was indeed favorable. The fertile loess soil was easily prepared for planting, there was water for irrigation and for cattle and sheep, and nearby lay broad pasture and mountains for wood and game.

Shang society was a union of clans and tribal states under the hegemony of the Shang king. The central domain, with its capital at Anyang, was under his direct rule, but the larger surrounding territories were inhabited by conquered peoples who paid tribute and rendered military service in exchange for protection. Still farther from the center, on the periphery of the Shang culture area, were independent tribes, some probably nomadic, who offered occasional tribute to the Shang king. In some cases the tribute states had the function of defending the frontiers against the raids of nomad "barbarians" living beyond. Significantly, there was already a clear distinction between "Chinese" and "barbarian," based on a sense of cultural, not racial, superiority. While the Shang king did not have direct power over the chiefs in the surrounding territories, he was their leader in war and their high priest. Shang supremacy was based on the military power of its noblemen charioteers and auxiliary peasant foot soldiers and on the important religious functions of the king.

Occupation or function determined the class structure of Shang society. In his own domain the Shang king was assisted by an administrative class that lived in the walled capital city. The administrators—originally recruited from the slaves in order to thwart the development of an aristocracy—practiced divination, kept records, assisted in religious sacrifices, and collected and stored the tribute and taxes in grain that were needed in time of war. In Anyang also lived the highly skilled artisans who fashioned bronze weapons and chariots or produced the stores of wealth, like jade jewelry and bronze ritual vessels. The peasantry lived in villages and worked under the direction of their tribal chiefs, and in most cases the land was owned by the tribal community as a whole. Cultivation was of the shifting type, i.e., the peasantry burned and cleared the land, and, when its fertility began to be exhausted, the group moved on to a new tract. The main crops, in order of importance, were native millets, wheat introduced from the Near East, and rice from India, while domestic animals included cattle, sheep, dogs, horses, and fowl. Hunting and fishing remained as subsidiary occupations, and household handicrafts made the peasant community economically self-sufficient. Silk was already in use, but hempen cloth was probably more common. Although some money circulated and some goods came from afar, there was no extensive trade in commodities or widespread use of money.

Chou Feudalism

The Shang hegemony was terminated by a rebellion led by the Chou state, located some three hundred miles to the west near the modern city of Sian in the basin of the Wei River. As a frontier dependency, it had slowly assimilated Shang culture, but at the same time it maintained its military vigor and increased its power while that of the Shang declined. In 1028 B.C. the army of the Chou state fought its way across the Yellow River and destroyed the Shang forces, and, according to traditional accounts, the last Shang king set fire to his palace and threw himself into the flames. The conqueror became the first king of the Chou dynasty (1028–221 B.C.).

The task of ruling the conquered territories posed difficult problems for the Chou conquerors. Direct rule was impossible because of poor communication and transportation; moreover, the victorious chiefs had to be rewarded. The Chou king retired to his homeland in the west, where he ruled directly over his royal domain. Part of the conquered territories was distributed to Chou chiefs and allies, but much land was left in possession of chieftains who had either been conquered or had voluntarily submitted. Even the Shang royal family continued to rule over a small state. China was divided into over a thousand states, each with its walled-city capital, but most of these were separated from one another by mountains, marshes, or uncultivated lands over which no one had specific jurisdiction. The largest states were located on the frontiers, where their rulers could more easily expand their holdings; and during the period of the Chou dynasty the frontier lords extended the area of Chinese civilization into the entire North China Plain and the Yangtze River Valley.

The Chou political system was feudal to the extent that political-military contractual relations existed between a lord and his vassals. In a feudal system the lord bestows land which the vassal holds as a fief, and the lord recognizes the vassal's right of income and jurisdiction in his fief. In exchange, the vassal performs services, largely military, for his lord. This contractual relationship existed between the Chou king and the rulers of states. The latter had to provide military aid in time of need, to appear at court at intervals to do homage, and to offer tribute in the form of valuable products from their territories. Sometimes they were called upon for special services, such as the supplying of men and materials for repairing the walls of the royal capital. In return, the Chou king invested them with land and delegated to them sovereign rights over it. At first the fiefs were not hereditary, but, as his vassals became more powerful, the Chou king was compelled to invest their heirs automatically.

5

Even this formality was eventually ignored. Within their fiefs the rulers appointed their own officials, maintained their own military force, levied taxes, and exercised justice. They granted part of their land to officials and relatives, and these holdings became the hereditary property of the recipients. For all practical purposes this was subinfeudation, especially since the landed proprietors functioned as members of the feudal hierarchy.

The descendants of the Chou conquerors and the Shang chieftains constituted an aristocratic ruling class which lived according to a moral code, considered to have been decreed by Heaven, that applied even to war. The virtuous man was moderate in victory; the ruthless victor, violating the moral code, would ultimately experience Heaven's displeasure. When not engaged in warfare, the nobles amused themselves by feasting, games, and hunting. Many of them were well educated, and at diplomatic meetings and court assemblies they could support their arguments with appropriate literary quotations.

The economic basis of the feudal system was a peasant agriculture. The entire region was thinly populated, and farming was still based on the temporary cultivation of fields under the supervision of inspectors. There were fixed boundaries beyond which the lord had no right to send his peasants to burn brush and clear land. In the winter the peasants lived in villages on ground high enough to afford protection from seasonal floods, and in the spring and summer they lived in large communal huts on cleared ground. The nobility imposed what amounted to a labor tax—actually, work on the lord's land—on the peasants, and later an additional tax in kind was levied on the fields allotted to them for the maintenance of their families. The peasantry also owed military and personal service to the lord. For example, in time of war a company of 120 foot soldiers recruited from the common people accompanied each chariot. In return, the peasants were guaranteed protection and grain relief in time of famine. Artisans and merchants were of relatively little importance since no fixed system of metal coinage yet existed and trade consisted largely of barter; both of these groups lived in the walled towns of the great lords or were attached to the courts of the landed proprietors in the countryside.

Religious Foundations

The ideological foundation of Shang and Chou society was largely religious. As high priests the Shang and Chou kings were responsible for sacrifices to Heaven, conceived of as a Supreme Lord who controlled all the natural forces and human fortune. The well-being of the state and the people was thought to depend on the proper conduct of rites. Heaven's will was regarded as a righteous power, and knowledge of it was sought by various types of divination. The origins of the concept of Heaven are not known, but Shang Ti, its anthropomorphic form, may have been regarded as a supreme ancestor by the Shang kings. Many Chinese believed that originally he may have been a god of vegetation in human shape who guided all growth and birth. In some parts of China Heaven and Earth were apparently conceived of as a married couple who were separated by one of their children; the husband ascended to Heaven, and rain was his male seed that created life on Earth.

Since it was the function of the Shang king to sacrifice to Heaven and Earth, the Chou conqueror was required to show that he was eligible to perform these rites. The Chou formulated the idea that Heaven appointed rulers who were responsible to Heaven for the welfare of the people. As a corollary, rulers were entitled to rule only so long as they met this condition. When they did not, Heaven chose a line to replace them. The Chou king applied this theory to the fall of the Shang to justify his conquest and his right to reign. The ritual function of the king was recognized by all the Chou feudal lords, and throughout later dynasties sacrifices to Heaven to maintain harmony remained the supreme duty of the ruler. Every new dynasty assumed "the mandate of Heaven."

The people of China also engaged in a nature worship, the central feature of which was a fertility cult; and of the numerous nature deities, Earth was the most highly venerated. At the royal capital there was an altar dedicated to the Earth goddess at which the Chou king made sacrifices, and each vassal at the time of his investiture was presented with a clod of earth for his own altar. The peasantry celebrated seasonal festivals and sacrifices at sacred earth mounds, which were phallic representations, to guarantee the abundance of crops and the fecundity of women. The spring festival before planting season was also the occasion for the young people of neighboring groups to mate, and these affairs became formal marriages in the autumn if the girls were pregnant. On the whole, Chinese nature worship was a religion of community utility since customs and taboos had to be followed with due propriety if the life of the community was to be kept in harmony with nature and enjoy its blessings.

The Chinese worship of ancestors, probably originating as part of the fertility cult, was also concerned with securing abundant crops and family succession. Local chieftains and feudal lords worshipped their ancestors in special temples, and by Chou times they were believed to rule by virtue of the assistance of powerful noble ancestors. Thus a kind of supernatural power helped to protect the privileges of the aristocracy. Originally the tribe or clan as a whole took part in this worship of a common ancestor, but it is doubtful whether in Chou times the common people could afford the cost of sacrificing to ancestral spirits. It was generally believed that each human being had two souls, the *p'o*, or animal soul, produced at the time of conception, and the *hun*, or spirit soul, which was joined to the *p'o* at birth. At death the *hun*, or higher soul, ascended to Heaven to dwell as a nobleman at the court of Shang Ti, and in return for sacrifices at the ancestral temple this spirit helped to provide for the well-being of its descendants. Success in agriculture and war as well as continuance of the family line depended on the will of the spirits. The *p'o*, which remained in the tomb of the deceased, also required sacrifices to prevent it from leaving the tomb and reappearing as a malevolent spirit (*kuei*). It was popular belief that *kuei* were the cause of many misfortunes and could be neutralized only through potent charms and magical utterances. Much later, when ancestor worship became a common practice among the people, the family made daily and seasonal offerings which enabled the ancestral spirit, represented by its funeral tablet in the home, to take part in the life of its own kinship group. Even the modern Chinese peasant has held firmly to the belief in the power of his ancestors to bestow blessings on his home and to protect it from misfortune.

Chinese religious practices did not lead to the development of a priesthood, for the conduct of rites was the responsibility of the lord or the officials of his administration. There were, however, experts in ritual who assisted the lord and officials in their duties, but the ritualists constituted a professional group which was generally recruited from the lesser nobility. There were also shamans, who were popular with the peasantry; these medicine men claimed to possess psychic powers of divination or special charms for dealing with the numerous malevolent spirits of the unseen world.

The Contending States

By the middle of the Chou dynasty the feudal system had begun to disintegrate as powerful lords proceeded to annex the fiefs of their weaker neighbors and rule them directly. The new and larger combinations of fiefs took on the form of centralized states, whose rulers governed through a bureaucracy directly responsible to them. In the western state of Ch'in, for example, a new administrative system arose, based on prefectures and commanderies directly controlled by the state government through state-appointed officials who were, at least in principle, nonhereditary. In many areas the feudal nobility lost its political prerogatives as men of lowly families rose to positions of administrative power. There was always, however, the tendency for posts in local units of government to become hereditary. Since this tendency was not always checked, not all the states succeeded in maintaining the supremacy of their central governments. The feudal nobility also lost their monopoly of military power when warfare changed from heroic combat between rival feudal camps to struggles between mercenary and later peasant armies under the direct control of the state.

The Chou king eventually lost effective control as overlord in the feudal system. When he attempted to interfere in the affairs of the powerful new states, their rulers resisted him, often forming antiroyal alliances. By 771 B.C. the states were so concerned with their own aggrandizement that the Chou king was unable to organize them to repel a barbarian attack, and the Chou capital had to be moved two hundred miles to the east, near the modern city of Loyang. Thereafter the Chou kings were hardly more than puppets in the hands of their most powerful vassals. It became customary for the Chou king to unite with the ruler who was strongest at the time, and this lord became something like a military dictator assigned to keep the peace. On occasion these dictators convoked assemblies of the leading rulers, who signed treaties pledging themselves to maintain the peace and "assist the royal house." Within a century, however, it was apparent that none of the states was strong enough to coerce all the others. State rulers began to take for themselves the title of "king," and even the fiction of Chou unity was lost. Wars between states became more frequent, and the victors were ruthless as the code of chivalry went unheeded. Finally, only thirteen states remained of the original one thousand and more. The stability of the Chou feudal system gave way to turbulent life-and-death struggles between large contending states; moreover, the danger of nomadic invasion from the Northwest was at times great. It was fortunate for China that the strength of the nomads was usually dissipated in their alliances with Chinese against Chinese, for, had the nomads joined forces, they might have been able to overrun China.

Important economic and social developments also undermined the foundations of the feudal system. States sought to possess as many soldiers as possible, and peasants were mercilessly conscripted into military or labor battalions. Large families and immigration were encouraged in order to increase population and production so that more powerful armies could be supported out of larger tax returns. In Ch'in, where the changes were most sweeping, a system of private landownership with the right of alienation emerged as the basis for a state-wide land tax system. On state lands each family was allotted about four acres, which were inherited by the eldest son, and additional allotments were made to each younger son upon marriage to support a new family. In return, the proprietors paid a land tax in kind to the state. The numerous feudal nobles became simply proprietors of landed estates, although often without the obligation of paying taxes; and their cultivators became tenant farmers paying a rent in kind.

Agricultural production expanded for other reasons. The iron plow drawn by animal power was introduced, and irrigation, flood control, and drainage systems were improved by the state. Some specialists, especially Karl Wittfogel, suggest that flood control and irrigation may have been the basic reason for the replacement of fiefs by the larger states, since the latter were capable of mobilizing and directing the manpower required to maintain water conservation on an extensive and practicable scale. The marshes of the northern plain and the Yangtze Valley had to be drained and dikes had to be built, not for a few miles, but often for hundreds; and for projects of this magnitude centralized control was essential. New areas were brought under cultivation in the south and northwest, where the indigenous population was expelled or absorbed; but when Chinese peasants penetrated the northwest, they had to be protected against the sudden raids of nomads. In some areas great walls were built to fix the frontier between settled agriculture and grasslands.

The process of political centralization, especially in its effect upon warfare, stimulated the development of commerce and the use of money in the form of metal coins. Roads and canals, built to transport supplies for great armies, became arteries of interstate trade; and cities, which were originally administrative centers, became markets for rural surpluses and for luxury items fashioned by skilled craftsmen throughout China. Even along the northwest frontier, markets were held at which Chinese bartered with nomads. On the whole, however, trade was not an essential function in an agrarian society where household crafts provided the major supplementary needs of rural families. Merchants emerged from the ranks of artisans or from the peasantry; and as money came into wider use, merchants amassed capital which they could use to expand their trading activities or to invest in land. Land was a particularly attractive form of investment, for it was difficult to hoard large sums of money safely; and it was the safest form of investment, since conquerors could not confiscate land without seriously disrupting the local order, to their own disadvantage.

This age of political and economic changes, ruthless and opportunistic war, moral decline, and popular oppression was also one of remarkable intellectual achievements. From the lower ranks of the aristocracy, many members of which had become impoverished during the interminable wars, arose a new class of politicans and educators, who often wandered from state to state in the hope that some ruler would implement their ideas. Others were tutors and operators of small schools catering to the educational demands of the sons of the rich. These Chinese thinkers were still preoccupied with the old problem of harmony between man and nature, but they had begun to question the efficacy of religious sacrifices to secure it. Instead there was a growing belief in the power of human attitudes and actions. They rejected the influence of spiritual forces upon human life and sought to persuade man to look to himself to lay the foundations of an ideal society in harmony with the universe. Two schools of thought, Confucianism and Taoism, have made a particularly lasting contribution to the development of Chinese civilization.

Confucius

Confucius (551–479 B.C.) was the son of an impoverished petty noble in the state of Lu, which was located in the southern part of the modern province of Shantung. He demonstrated an early interest in scholarship and, entering government service, achieved high official rank by the age of fifty. His reputation as a scholar attracted a number of students, but in middle age he was forced from office into exile as a result of political intrigue. Thereupon he and his disciples began their travels through China in search of some ruler who would practice Confucius' principles of government and bestow high office upon the philosopher. Failing in his search, Confucius in old age returned to his native state and resumed his teaching and study until death. Most of his ideas must be derived from later works written by disciples; only the *Analects* have been judged to be the words of the master.

As a scholar, Confucius transmitted the literary and intellectual heritage of ancient China, seeking to provide a moral code based on the wisdom of the past for the rulers and scholar-administrators of his own day. He and his disciples reacted against the contemporary decline of moral values, and they believed in a golden age associated with mythological sage-kings who proclaimed and practiced basic truths. It is generally believed that Confucius edited the Chinese Classics: the *Book of Poetry*, the *Book of History*, the *Book of Rites*, the *Book of Music* (which was subsequently lost and replaced by the *Book of Changes*), and the *Spring and Autumn Annals*. In the process, he idealized rulers of old as models of conduct.

Confucius' goal was the establishment of a lasting social harmony with earthly happiness for all mankind. He advised man, both ruler and subject, to follow a fixed code of conduct that would integrate him into the harmonious order of the universe (*tao*). The thought of Confucius was essentially humanistic, casting aside theological premises or mystical speculation. He sought to provide a rational and ethical basis for moral conduct at a time when people, particularly rulers, were still using religious sanctions; and although he concluded that Heaven followed a universal law, as seen in the movement of the sun, the moon, and the stars, he discounted the spiritual power of Heaven as an active moral will, cautioning: "The wicked often prosper and the efforts of the good sometimes come to nought."

It is likely that Confucius held to the premise, common in his time, that man was fundamentally good, for he stressed the need for personal cultivation of inherent virtues. Accepting the premise that man must follow the highest instincts of his own human nature within a framework of social responsibility, Confucius felt compelled to standardize and adjust human relations according to correct forms of conduct. He explained that these forms were simply the outward expression of an inner morality. The primary unit of social responsibility was the family, and beyond were the community and the state. Each individual had a definite status with concomitant duties, based on morality, in relation to other members of the family and society. Within the family the virtuous son respected his father, the wife her husband, and the younger brother his elder brother, and in society as a whole the individual had obligations to friends and to his ruler. Actually Confucius was simply providing a new kind of sanction for what the Chinese already regarded as practical virtues. The social organization of the Chinese was founded on the patriarchal family, and filial piety was not merely a moral but even a legal obligation for the masses. Children gave service and support to their parents and grand-parents in the same way that the latter worshipped ancestors; moreover, the family formed an economic unit, and its livelihood generally depended upon common understanding and solidarity. Thus Confucius approved of ancestor worship because it helped to inculcate filial piety in the living children; how-ever, in his mind the ritual was not effective in itself since ancestral spirits were not the basis of the moral sanction of human conduct. He believed that the constant thought of never disgracing one's sacred inheritance from parents was sufficient as a guide to human action. As stated in Confucian doctrine, "The filial son never moves a step without thinking of his parents, and never utters a word without thinking of his parents."

Confucius made no distinction between politics and ethics, and rulers of states were no exceptions to his system. In his view, their social responsibilities were all the greater since social harmony depended in large part upon virtuous rulers helping to provide for the welfare and happiness of their people. In return, personal example would induce the people to pay allegiance to their rulers. Confucius wanted to make the right to govern wholly dependent upon character and ability without regard to birth, and the moral qualities which he emphasized were three: wisdom, compassion, and courage. He believed that a man who understood these qualities and lived in harmony within his family would be able to rule men and states, and he advocated that such men be entrusted with the business of government regardless of their origin. Confucius did not demand that hereditary rulers vacate their thrones, but he did advise them to "reign but not rule" by handing over their administrative authority to ministers chosen on the basis of merit.

The philosophy of Confucius can best be summed up by his concept of the "rectification of names," which was more fully developed by later disciples. Confucius meant that individuals bearing relationship designations like ruler, subject, father, son, husband, and wife should fulfill the responsibilities and duties that the names implied; if every individual acted according to his posi-tion, then society as an ideal hierarchy would achieve peace and harmony. For later Confucianists the "rectification of names" was a means to preserve the harmony and equilibrium that should exist between the acts of man and the movements of nature.

Confucius held no important government post in his later years, and, although many of his disciples were later employed by states, the Confucian emphasis on the social responsibility of rulers was generally ignored. War re-mained the preoccupation of the petty rulers, who began to dream of a single Chinese empire under their direction. In this situation, appeals to moral codes went unheeded. But Confucian concepts were transmitted from genera-tion to generation by Chinese scholars; and landlord families, the new rural aristocracy, practiced his moral code. The more active of the Confucian thinkers advocated the replacement of selfish despotisms with government by the enlightened, that is, by scholarly ministers. Since the philosophy of Confucius was under constant attack by proponents of other systems, scholars who defended it were often forced to modify and enlarge upon certain elements. Mencius and Hsun Tzu were two of the most important of these disciples who took up and developed much that was merely suggested by Confucius.

Mencius and Hsun Tzu

Mencius' life (371–289 B.C.) was similar to that of his master. He was not content with being just a scholar, and like Confucius he traveled in vain from state to state in search of a ruler who would adopt his ideas. Finally he retired and with the aid of his disciples composed the treatise which bears his name, *The Book of Mencius*.

For Mencius there was a close relationship between politics, economics, and ethics. Basic to his philosophy was the premise that human nature is essentially good and that virtue is inherent in all men; but, like Confucius, he did not carry this notion to its logical conclusion, which would have rid man of all authority in the form of rules. Mencius reasoned that the cause of evil was environment, since hungry people cannot cultivate goodness; thus he argued that it was important for the ruler to make the environment as favorable as possible to permit the people to develop their nature and keep it from degenerating into evil. Mencius meant that the ruler should guarantee the people economic security; and since he would gain political stability in return, his own virtue would bring success. The ruler who treated his people well would command their loyalty, and militarily he would be as invincible as the power of his peasant soldiers. Mencius reinforced the Confucian emphasis upon the importance of the people, and he declared that, if the ruler failed to provide for the welfare of his people, he should be removed by popular rebellion. Mencius reduced the "mandate of Heaven" to the consent of the governed, but he was not a revolutionary. He supported the existing political institutions, wishing to maintain the Chou king and the state rulers. He merely thought that the administration of the states should be turned over to those who had studied the art of government—presumably to the Confucian scholars. Mencius accepted also the idea of a social hierarchy, insisting that each person, from the scholar down to the basest individual, had his proper place according to his training and ability. His ideas on landholding and taxation reflected the development of private property, and he seems to have envisaged a system in which land would in theory be the public property of the state but would in practice be transferred to private ownership. In return, the owner would work part of his land as "state land," the produce of which belonged to the state as a tax.

Mencius seems to have had a metaphysical justification for the cultivation of virtue. He was something of a mystic in suggesting that through the full development of his nature man could know the universe and become one with it. He believed that the moral principles inherent in human nature were also the principles of a moral universe. How then did man achieve this unity? Mencius answered: Through compassion one's egoism and selfishness are gradually reduced, and when they are completely reduced, one will feel that there is no longer a distinction between himself and the universe. According to Mencius, one became identified with the universe as a whole and realized that all things were complete within himself. This important concept was developed more systematically by Confucian scholars of the eleventh and twelfth centuries, but it was at least suggested by Mencius.

Hsun Tzu (298–238 B.C.), a Confucian scholar who served as an official in one of the contending states, defended Confucianism against the increasing challenge of rival philosophies and in the process gave it greater coherence. Hsun Tzu synthesized many of the conflicting currents of interpretation within Confucian circles in his day, and, although many of the basic premises of his own thought were later condemned, much of his teaching became part of orthodox tradition. In later ages Confucian scholars accepted Hsun Tzu's emphasis on education and authority but rejected his premise for it, accepting instead Mencius' more attractive doctrine of the goodness of human nature. As late as the early years of the twentieth century, Chinese school children began their education with the three-character classic which begins thus:

> Man is originally
> Endowed with a nature which is all good.
> And therefore by nature people are all alike.
> It is practice that makes the divergence.
> If they are not properly taught,
> Their nature will be thwarted.

According to Hsun Tzu, man's nature is evil, and his inherent instincts, if unchecked, will lead to a state of violence. To curb these unfortunate natural instincts it is essential that man's nature be transformed by rules of conduct. In general he reached the same conclusion as Mencius: that human nature needs constant cultivation. He reasoned that a moral code should set limits upon individual desires so that social order would emerge from social conflict. Hsun Tzu derived morality from the models of wisdom and virtue of China's earlier rulers as described in the Classics and interpreted by Confucian scholars. According to him, wise rulers and their scholar-administrators should guide the people by decree, instruct them with proclamations, and restrain them by punishments based on law. Hsun Tzu thus glorified the Confucian scholar as the ideal servant of the state and as the logical interpreter of ancient standards, but he also raised law to a position of nearly equal prominence.

Taoism

Taoism provided an alternative to authoritarian government, which curtailed the independence of the individual by law, and to Confucianism, which checked his spirit by a series of moral rules and obligations. The basic tenets of Taoism are derived from two small books, *Tao Te Ching*, or *Lao Tzu*, probably written in the fourth century B.C., and *Chuang Tzu*, which reached its present form in the second century B.C. It is doubtful that there was a man named Lao Tzu, although tradition holds that he was a contemporary rival of Confucius; but Chuang Tzu was an actual Chinese official who died shortly after 300 B.C.

Taoism probably developed out of a nature mysticism which instilled a longing to be in harmony with the natural order of the universe (*tao*). The *tao* was conceived of as a natural process—"natural" in Chinese literally meaning "being so of itself." While the Confucianists taught man to observe a moral code to insure social harmony, the Taoists asked him to follow his instinctive primitive qualities derived from the *tao* and not those enjoined by social sanctions and education; for to them the natural was the ideal, and in the state of nature men lived at peace with one another. They believed that a positive morality such as the Confucianists proposed interfered with the natural order of things, and they argued that man-made morality corrupted man's natural purity while the *tao* effortlessly produced harmony. This exaltation of nature and the natural produced an individualism which placed freedom above everything else. Thus, in Taoist terms, "To live a full life is the best; to live with only incomplete satisfaction of one's legitimate desires is next; to live without freedom or under degrading bondage is worse than death."

Taoism on its religious side prepared man for death. In the case of Chuang Tzu it became a philosophic fatalism, for he regarded life, death, pleasure, and pain as part of the cosmic process—all derived from the *tao*. The Taoists sought spiritual contentment by breaking the bonds of human emotion and adapting themselves to the creative and destructive forces in nature. They cared nothing for worldly honors or position but aimed only at achieving a state of union with the surrounding universe. To Chuang Tzu this was an experience of mystical ectasy, for he grasped the ultimate secret of the universe—the unity of all being.

Taoism was applied in various ways to government. At one extreme it was the basis of an ideal anarchy—a primeval Eden. In more moderate form it was a check against excessive government and doctrinaire programs. "Govern a state as you would cook a small fish," i.e., hardly at all, advised those Taoists who believed that government should confine its activities to a minimum. At the other extreme Taoism could be used as a justification for despotism, for the ruler who was one with the *tao* was beyond man-made concepts of good and evil. Finally, the Taoist emphasis upon natural order paradoxically stimulated the development of law in Chinese society.

Confucianism and Taoism have both helped to mold the character of the Chinese intellectual. Confucianism, especially as Mencius interpreted it, did not neglect the worth of the individual, but it did emphasize his social responsibilities and sought to achieve the harmony of man among masses of men. Taoism, on the other hand, looked to the harmony of man immersed in nature and stressed personal freedom. As an official or family head, the Chinese would think and act as a Confucian, but as an individual he sought inner peace and resignation, often expressing his feelings in poetry and painting. Both of these forms of expression in Chinese hands exude vitality and spontaneity, and both emphasize man's unity with nature.

The Ch'in Dynasty and Legalism

In the third century B.C. the struggles between the contending states finally came to an end when one of them, Ch'in, succeeded in overcoming the others and uniting China under a centralized regime. In 256 B.C. the last Chou king died. A relative did manage to maintain nominal authority until 249 B.C., but he in turn was defeated by Ch'in. The whole process of subjugation and unification was completed by 221 B.C., and the Ch'in ruler took the title "Shih Huang Ti" (First Emperor).

The rise of Ch'in was the result of the successful application of an authoritarian philosophy of statecraft that the Chinese called "Legalism." The Legalists were the practical-minded administrators of Ch'in who were determined to enlarge the power and domains of the state, and their ultimate aim was the conquest of all China. They promoted policies to increase agricultural production and military power and enforced them by a system of rewards and punishments based upon law. In contrast, they restricted commerce because they thought it was unproductive and because merchant fortunes were regarded as a potential danger to the state. Under Legalism the Ch'in state abolished feudalism and established a centralized bureaucratic state, encouraged large families and immigration, established a unified system of land taxation and peasant proprietorship, engineered large-scale irrigation projects, conscripted labor into the *corvée*, and developed a large army based on universal military service. Ch'in, like several of the frontier states, introduced the use of mobile cavalry, which was an advance over the clumsy war chariot; and in war Ch'in ruthlessly added the domains of the vanquished to its own. In the process, Ch'in imposed Legalist controls and destroyed cultures and records.

The Ch'in dynasty lasted only fifteen years (221–206 B.C.), but it gave China political and economic unity under a centralized bureaucratic government. The new regime abolished the remnants of feudal states and reduced the nobles to commoners, forcing them to live in the capital. It divided China into thirty-six and later forty-two commanderies headed by civil and military officials directly responsible to the central administration of the emperor, and the commanderies were in turn subdivided into districts under lesser bureaucrats. Ch'in extended the land tax system based on private property to the entire country. There is no record of land tax rates, but we do know that taxes taken as a whole—the land tax, the poll tax, and state monopoly taxes such as iron and salt—were extremely heavy for the peasantry; moreover, the amount of forced labor due the state was increased from the customary three days a year to ninety days in some cases. The government also restricted the activities of the merchants, who as a class had continued to prosper at the expense of the peasantry and the state.

The Legalists also sought to give China a cultural and intellectual unity. They tried to unify the Chinese written language by establishing a standard written style, and they also vainly attempted to root out and destroy loyalties to local states and rival systems of thought, particularly Confucianism, which was popular with the educated class. The Confucianists openly opposed the military despotism of the Ch'in, and on one occasion a Confucian scholar demanded the re-establishment of feudalism. The Ch'in classified books and burned subversive literature, including the Classics, histories of states, and philosophic tracts. Some copies were entrusted to official scholars, but other persons who concealed proscribed books were put to death. Books that were useful, as in the fields of medicine and agriculture, were also spared. The short life of the dynasty did prevent the "burning of the books" from being a success; however, it should be noted that a large number of books were destroyed when rebels burned the Ch'in capital in 206 B.C. In the following dynasty scholars had to reconstruct many of them from memory, and this process of recovery gave rise to eternal academic controversy.

The Ch'in dynasty expanded the territory of Chinese control. In the north the Ch'in deprived the nomads of some of their frontier pasturage, and the threatened nomad tribes, the Hsiung-nu or Turkish ancestors of the Huns, banded together for protection and retaliation when possible. It was necessary for the Ch'in to maintain a large permanent army in the north, and in addition the government rebuilt the existing frontier walls into a single system, 1,400 miles long. This feat was accomplished by the forced labor of tens of thousands of Chinese, including exiled criminals. For later dynasties the Great Wall served to mark off the steppe culture of the nomads from the intensive agriculture of the Chinese, separating "barbarian" from the "civilized." To the south, Canton became a distant colonial outpost of the new empire.

Although Shih Huang Ti had hoped that his descendants would rule China for generations to come, the decline and fall of the Ch'in came rapidly. A pitiful weakling succeeded the first emperor, who died in 210 B.C., and the imperial court was unable to cope with the rise of discontent and rebellion among the oppressed peasantry, which grouped around former nobles and ambitious generals. The second emperor committed suicide, and the empire broke up into contending areas. Outwardly there seemed to be a re-establishment of the former states, but actually there was simply a struggle between various power groups for control of the united empire. Finally, in 206 B.C. the commoner general, Liu Pang, succeeded to the "mandate of Heaven." He fought his way into the capital, dethroned the nominal emperor, proclaimed a new dynasty—the Han (206 B.C.–220 A.D.)—and proceeded to pacify the rest of China.

The Han Dynasty Imperial System

The political organization of China under the early Han emperors was a compromise between decentralized government, like feudalism or regionalism, and the empire. The framework of the Ch'in bureaucratic administration was retained by Liu Pang, but in practice he divided two-thirds of his empire into landed estates worked by tenant farmers, agricultural laborers, and slaves and owned by military associates, members of his family, and former nobles who had helped him subjugate his opponents. The political history of the early decades of the Han dynasty is the story of a running battle between the forces of centralization and regionalism, the climax of which was reached in 154 B.C. with the suppression of the rebellion of seven fiefs under the leadership of a powerful vassal whose wealth rivaled that of the emperor himself. Thereafter the emperors were able to relegate the nobles to positions of honor without political power, and administrative officials, including first ministers at the courts of the fiefs, were ultimately all appointed directly by the throne. By 106 B.C. the empire, including the landed estates, was divided into thirteen circuits each headed by an inspector who acted for the central government, and below this unit the commanderies and districts were maintained and gradually extended. Over a period of time the fiefs were divided and weakened by mandatory multiple inheritance, which replaced primogeniture; and when there was no heir, the fief reverted to the throne. During the reign of Liu Pang there were 143 sizable fiefs, but by the middle of the Han dynasty there were only 20 with hereditary rights of limited political control and several hundred petty lordships with revenue rights only. The nobility, to be sure, lived lives of great luxury, but the real administrative power lay in the hands of the imperial bureaucracy.

It would be a mistake to describe the machinery of government of the Han empire as a highly centralized system, for there was probably a conscious effort to achieve a balance between centralization and local autonomy. The ministers at the capital were concerned primarily with the organization of palace life and the flow of supplies and taxes to the imperial court. It is true that civil and military governors and district officers were appointed by the central government, but their staffs were normally chosen from among local friends and landlords. In most cases the commandery had a fully developed government with several departments, and each had a separate military organization. Purposeful or not, this system provided an important element of political stability, since administration could continue locally even if the connection with the central authority was interrupted by war or disorder.

The rural landlords, or gentry, became the dominant class in what continued to be an agricultural society. The Han emperors accepted the status of the landlords, many of whom were former nobles, as they were useful unofficial representatives of the government in the numerous villages of China. Yet, while the gentry supported monarchs against unruly peasants, they also often stood as buffers between the government with its oppressive demands and the local populace. Quite naturally it was to their interest to protect the peasantry from excessive taxes and injustices. The gentry's paramount position was based on the fact that they were at the same time bureaucrats, scholars, and landowners; moreover, through education, which was expensive and the monopoly of the rich, they were able to provide careers for sons in the bureaucracy in order to enlarge and protect family holdings. Gentry families rose and fell over a period of generations, and multiple inheritance was a constant threat to the landed base of the family. Often gentry families profited from subsidiary economic activities, such as credit, pawnshops, trade, and handicraft production; and new gentry were likely to emerge out of the merchant class through the investment of surplus capital in land.

Politically the gentry operated at two levels. Locally, the gentry subordinates of imperial officials hoped to curry favor in order to advance their interests from a local to a higher level; and in the capital, cliques of gentry families, often allied by marriage, maneuvered to gain control of ministerial posts and governorships. In theory the important official posts were granted on the basis of merit, but favoritism and nepotism were common practices. Governors generally selected candidates for service in the bureaucracy from sons in their own clique, and since the scholar-examiners were usually involved in the general political maneuvering, it was certain that only candidates who were to the liking of the dominant groups were appointed to office. Surrounded by cliques, emperors often became powerless figures and on occasion were driven from the throne; the Han dynasty was brought to an end in this manner. On the other hand, energetic rulers, assisted by loyal advisers, were sometimes able to play off the various factions against each other and maintain their personal power.

The Confucian Orthodoxy

During the Han dynasty an eclectic Confucianism became the orthodox philosophy of the state and society, since it was attractive to both vigorous emperors and the gentry as a moral justification for authority, agrarianism, and social inequality. Politically the new orthodoxy was a philosophy of en-

19

lightened despotism since the gentry, as Confucian scholar-bureaucrats, endeavored to check the natural inclination to tyranny on the part of emperors. But in the hands of an able and ambitious ruler like Wu Ti (140–87 B.C.) Confucianism became the moral basis for personal absolutism and ministers became mere agents of the throne. Throughout Chinese history the Confucianist has insisted that the ruler rely on the advice of his ministers and that authority be exercised for the benefit of the people, and the most sincere among them have always spoken out fearlessly for what they have believed to be right, even at the risk of death.

Confucianism gradually achieved political supremacy and became the ideological foundation of the state. The early Han emperors relied on the advice of Confucian scholars, who were familiar with ritual and the precedents of history, and used them in administration along with Legalists and Taoists. Confucian scholars were also made responsible for the education of the heir-apparent to the throne. Early in his reign, after dismissing the Legalists from government, Wu Ti made Confucianism the official philosophy of the state, and thereafter the Han emperors selected ministers and governors, in theory at least, for their learning and virtue. They periodically called upon the units of local government and the great estates to send candidates for office to the capital to take examinations administered by Confucian scholars; moreover, they instituted annual examinations for students wishing to attend an imperial academy in the capital which had developed out of the gatherings of disciples around Confucian masters. Finally, in 53–51 B.C. a great assemblage of scholars worked out a canon of standardized interpretations of the Classics and the major works of the Confucian philosophers, and this became the basis for a large portion of the state examinations. The Confucianists succeeded in elevating their tenets to a position of orthodoxy which was alone deserving of government patronage and support.

During the Han dynasty Confucianism tended to assimilate many of the traditional beliefs and superstitions of ancient China which were still popularly accepted by the masses and rulers alike. Wu Ti engaged in many occult practices which he left to the scholars to justify on the basis of precedents in history, and he was the patron of the renowned scholar Tung Chung-shu, who attempted to give Confucianism a cosmological foundation derived from several schools of thought. Tung's philosophy may be summarized as follows. Lying behind the physical universe is an impersonal first cause, the *tao*, from which all being is evolved. The *tao* operates through the interaction of two principles: *yang*, the principle of activity, light, heat, and masculinity, and *yin*, the principle of quiescence, darkness, cold, and femininity. *Yang* and *yin* act to give birth to the five primary elements—fire, water, earth, wood, and metal—and these elements in turn produce all things: Heaven (the personal Shang Ti becomes a mere materialization of *yang*), Earth (along with the minor gods, a materialization of *yin*), animals, and man. The *tao* also operates to produce social harmony through the interaction of *yang* and *yin*, for each of the five proper relationships—ruler-subject, husband-wife, father-son, elder brother–younger brother, and friend-friend—is a correlation embodying *yang* and *yin*. Proper relationships in turn depend on the five virtues cultivated by the individual: compassion, righteousness, propriety, wisdom, and sincerity. On the question of human nature, Tung concluded that man is not wholly good in himself but only contains the "basic stuff" of goodness. Thus, according to him, the emperor is charged by Heaven with the duty of "teaching" the people to bring out their potential for goodness, and in this task he is a force co-operating with cosmic forces making for goodness. Should the emperor ignore his function, he will be warned by Heaven in two ways: natural disasters such as earthquakes or floods, or strange anomalies such as eclipses. Tung believed that it was the function of the Confucian scholars to interpret these warnings; but, more important, by their knowledge of right conduct they could properly advise the ruler in his role of maintaining harmony between man and nature. A vast literature devoted to the science of detecting and interpreting the meaning of catastrophes and abnormalities in the heavens and on earth was an outgrowth of Tung's philosophy.

In later years Confucian scholars sought to purge their philosophy of its cosmological religious elements. For example, Wang Ch'ung (27–100 A.D.) vigorously attacked the theory that an interaction existed between nature and man. Knowledgeable in the astronomy of his day, Wang pointed out that eclipses were regular occurrences having no relation to political action, and he defined man's place in the universe as follows:

Man is like a little flea underneath one's clothes, or a little ant that is in an underground cave. The flea may jump about and the ant may climb or crawl, but can they change the atmosphere of their hiding places? Now heaven is vast and man is very small. How can a man hope to affect the "air" of the heavens with his little body? I am sure that it is a hopeless ambition indeed.

Wang Ch'ung was also the precursor of a Taoist revival, largely because of his attacks on what he regarded as a Confucian doctrine of the purposeful existence of man. He stated:

The forces of Heaven and Earth merely combine and accidentally man is born. . . . Parents never purposely bear children, nor does nature purposely produce man. Man lives just as fish live in water or fleas on the animal body. They all come from the "air" and reproduce according to their kind of species. This is true of all things in the universe.

In the two centuries following the death of Wang Ch'ung, Taoist naturalism gradually came to be accepted by a large number of intellectuals. They put a new emphasis upon freedom from social and political restraints, and many of them longed for a free life in the idealized world of the Taoist immortals, who were thought to move about in the clouds and on the winds and who were never subject to limitations of matter and man-made institutions.

The Han Dynasty Economic and Social Order

Han China remained an agricultural society based upon intensive cultivation of the land by the peasant masses. Those peasants who tilled their small holdings on state land were liable for military service and *corvée* and paid taxes in kind and in money. At the outset of the dynasty the government set the land tax at a fixed rate of one-fifteenth of the estimated productivity of the land, which was thought to approximate the traditional rate under Chou feudalism of a percentage of the harvest as a labor tax. Occasionally the land tax was reduced to one-thirtieth, and for a time, when it was suspended, revenues were provided by selling honorary titles for grain and by accepting grain for the remission of penalties. The state also raised additional revenues by adjusting the rates of the various poll taxes levied on the entire population; and this tax, not the land tax, was usually a heavy burden for peasant families. Tenant farmers, agricultural laborers, and slaves worked the large private estates of the landlords, and estate owners were obliged to pay the land tax when there was no exemption granted by the government and to guarantee payment of the poll taxes that fell upon peasants resident on their lands. There were two forms of slavery in Han times: state slaves sentenced for crimes, who served as frontier guards or as menials in government buildings, and private slaves, sold into bondage in times of famine, who worked as household menials, prostitutes, and agricultural and mine laborers. By the middle of the Han dynasty slavery as an institution was legally abolished, although it continued in practice, particularly in the cases of household labor and prostitution.

The increasing concentration of land in the hands of the rich and powerful was the outstanding characteristic of Han dynasty economic development. The individual peasant proprietor had a difficult time making ends meet. On the one hand, he was constantly at the mercy of the elements since rainfall in north China was very inconsistent, with resulting alternation of flood and drought; famine was a common occurrence, but, conversely, bumper crops depressed prices in markets glutted with grain. The peasant also faced numerous man-made difficulties. He was at the mercy of the merchant who ultimately marketed surplus grain, and he had fixed tax obligations, particularly the onerous poll tax. Multiple inheritance constantly fragmented the land, and to have more than one son often meant impoverishment unless the peasant family engaged in some other economic activity to provide funds for the purchase of additional land. Social obligations, such as marriage and funeral expenses, were also weighty burdens. Thus it was easy for the peasantry to get into debt. Credit was readily available from rich neighbors, landlords, or merchants, but interest rates were high, often over 100 per cent a year. When the peasant defaulted on his debt, he lost title to his land and usually became a tenant farmer. There is also evidence that officials often forced peasants to sell land at low prices. The displaced proprietor could become an agricultural wage laborer or tenant on the lands of the great estates; or, if he was enterprising, he could emigrate to parts of the country where land was more abundant. Emigration was a common solution since north and east China already supported a large population. It is true that there were large tracts of uncultivated land, but most of these required drainage or irrigation which the state was unwilling or unable to provide. Officials who were genuinely concerned over the plight of the peasantry wanted the government to limit the size of landholdings, but they could not succeed in face of the selfish interests of powerful gentry.

The family, which remained the basic unit in society, was of two types: the marriage group, which included husband, wife, and children; and the extended family, in which several generations and brothers lived under the same roof. In either case the individual had to subordinate himself to family interests, and conduct was regulated by the Confucian ethical code. From earliest childhood each individual was taught the correct form and ceremony for every circumstance, and departure from the rule meant loss of face and dignity. Marriage was a family matter arranged by the elders since its primary purpose was to provide sons to carry on the family name, cultivate its fields, and sacrifice to its ancestors. Monogamy was the general practice, although concubinage existed among the rich, particularly the merchants. Within the family, and in society in general, women held an inferior position. Male children were honored above girls since boys had a functional importance to the family, both economically and religiously. A girl entered her husband's family upon marriage as a virtual servant under the dominance of her mother-in-law. Under the pressures of birth control and family hardship, girl infants were subject to infanticide, and girls were apt to be sold into household slavery or into prostitution; in such a society it was quite natural that they were also discriminated against in education.

Beyond the family the clan often had important social and economic functions. In clan villages, which were communities of blood relations, village affairs were essentially the affairs of one big family; and, as in the family village, authority was paternalistic. Families rented land from the clan, and in times of hardship the clan treasury was available to all. The term "clan" is also used to designate larger groups having a common ancestry and surname but living apart, perhaps even in different sections of the country. They were usually united through the functions of the ancestral temple, and some members of the clan usually gathered annually to participate in ceremonies that insured the welfare of the dead and the living. The clan also exercised what might be considered normal functions of the government: settlement of disputes among members, financial relief of members in distress, and maintenance of schools for promising sons. Both the family and the clan constituted a kind of mutual protective association, but the degree of cohesion naturally varied with size.

The relationship of the individual and the family to the state was determined in part by a penal code—a heritage of Legalism and earlier feudal practice. Penalties based on a less severe version of the laws of Ch'in still remained applicable to the masses, but the scholars, having inherited the privileges which once had belonged to the nobility, were not subject to codes. The family was responsible for the actions of its members, and families were often joined together in larger responsibility groups. The severity of justice was tempered by the fact that in theory the codes were administered by wise and virtuous men. Trials were investigations by the magistrate into the facts of the case and into the circumstances, and final decisions were rendered in light of the code, customs, and all the circumstances. Of significance also is the fact that many disputes in which the state was not involved were settled through arbitration on the village level or through the initiative of clans.

The Confucian bureaucrats shared the Legalists' contempt for the merchants as a disruptive force in an agrarian economy, and both groups regarded them as economic parasites living off the body of the peasantry. Confucian economics held that ideally the main division of labor was between the scholars, whose function was to rule, and the peasants, whose role was to support the rulers. Since the merchant was regarded as unproductive, he was demeaned socially and ranked below peasants and artisans among the common people. In fact, local merchants were ordinarily regarded as outsiders by their fellow-villagers unless they acquired land and took up an agrarian role to some degree. Yet merchants continued to grow rich at the expense of the masses, and at times they established exceedingly profitable monopolies over the distribution of various commodities like salt, iron, fish, pickles and sauces, liquors, silks, and lacquerware.

In the period 120–112 B.C. the Emperor Wu Ti introduced legislation to restrain the merchants, curb their wealth, and crush certain monopolies in trade. The state taxed the personal property and income of merchants and shopkeepers and on occasion confiscated commercial wealth, with the result that merchants with surplus capital hastened to invest in land in spite of provisions which forbade their ownership of agricultural holdings. Wu Ti also declared a state monopoly over two basic commodities, iron and salt, entrusting the production and distribution of them to commercial officials of the state, and for a time there was state control over the brewing and sale of liquors. The government also engaged with indifferent success in the wholesale trade of commodities in order to realize a profit and to equalize prices for the masses by influencing supply and demand. The system was based on state purchase and storage of grain in times of abundant harvests and sale or distribution in times of famine. During the Han dynasty a close relationship developed between the bureaucrats and the merchant class because any large commercial undertaking needed official patronage and support. The merchants became a class subordinate to the bureaucracy, and together they extracted the surplus from agriculture and commerce. Theoretically the merchant was an inferior person, but in fact some of the most powerful members of Chinese society were merchants. However, their power was derived not from their economic function but from their ability, through their wealth, to manipulate the legitimate, high-prestige positions.

The Nomad Problem

The borders of Han China were continually threatened by nomads, especially the Hsiung-nu, who consolidated their empire in the northwest prior to the accession of Liu Pang. When drought exhausted the water holes and burned the grass of the steppe, bands of nomads descended on the farmlands of China in well-organized raids. During his rise to power, Liu Pang was trapped in a fortified town by foraging Hsiung-nu, and he secured his freedom only after granting the Hsiung-nu chieftain a Chinese princess in marriage in addition to large stores of silks, wine, grain, and food. The Hsiung-nu menaced China until the reign of Wu Ti, who risked sending an expedition to attack them in their own territory. His general defeated them and captured more than eighty of their chieftains. This campaign firmly established the authority of the Chinese in the northwest at that time, but frontier defense remained a constant responsibility.

The defensive techniques against the Hsiung-nu that Wu Ti and his successors worked out remained basic to Chinese civilization for the subsequent one thousand and more years. Chinese emperors continued to send punitive expeditions into the steppe, and they maintained military garrisons with agricultural colonies to keep order among the Hsiung-nu and other tribes. At times, however, Chinese efforts caused a reaction in the steppe, hastening the growth of political organization among the nomad tribes. In most cases the Chinese preferred to place the nomads in a tribute status, whereby the nomad chieftain accepted a badge of office in the form of a seal furnished by the Chinese emperor and in return sent tribute to the imperial court and contributed troops to Chinese military campaigns in other theaters. Chinese emperors also bestowed wives on vassal rulers and educated their sons, held as hostages at the imperial court.

Down to the nineteenth century the inner Asian frontier was the center of the struggle between China and the nomads since for both it was an important area, not only from the standpoint of defense but also for the control of trade. The nomad way of life was not totally self-contained, and nomads traded their surpluses of animals, wool, and hides for the agricultural products of their Chinese neighbors. Competition for control of the trade took political forms, and the relative strength of the two sides was decisive. At times the nomads became fixed territorial rulers, but generally the Chinese exercised authority over the border tribes.

The Cyclical Pattern in Chinese History

The Han dynasty was a great period of consolidation in the history of China. During a period of over four hundred years many of the political, economic, and social institutions of imperial China, which endured until the twentieth century, were integrated into a unified whole and given a philosophic foundation by an eclectic Confucianism. The history of the rise, development, decline, and fall of the Han dynasty is a kind of history of China in microcosm, for the main theme in the course of Chinese history to the end of the empire in 1912 appears to be the rise and fall of a series of similar and lengthy dynasties, some of which were of nomadic origin. This is indicated in the following table:

CHINESE DYNASTIES	DISUNION	NOMAD DYNASTIES
Ch'in and Han, 221 B.C.– 220 A.D.		
	220–589	
Sui and T'ang, 590–906		
	906–960	
Sung, 960–1279		Yuan (Mongol), 1260–1368
Ming, 1368–1644		
		Ch'ing (Manchu), 1644–1912

This view has been reinforced by the recurrence of Confucian ideas in the various dynastic histories, which in essence simply record the rise and fall of separate dynasties. One observant Westerner, Thomas Meadows, commented in the nineteenth century, "Of all the nations that have attained a certain degree of civilization, the Chinese are the least revolutionary and the most rebellious." He meant that a change of dynasty was not a revolution; it was merely a change of governments. For Chinese scholars hastened to enlist in the service of a new emperor provided he was willing to use them and to carry on the system of government they understood; and the rulers of China have been almost irresistibly drawn to Confucianism to justify authoritarianism and to maintain the stability of their rule.

The cyclical pattern can be explained by an analysis of certain common elements that caused dynastic decline. Decline depended in part upon personal and administrative factors. The imperial line was often weakened because of the personal degeneration of individual rulers, or else emperors became powerless pawns in the struggles between factions at court, particularly gentry cliques and the palace eunuchs. Emperors relied increasingly upon harem eunuchs as administrative assistants and advisers, since eunuchs were not so directly involved in family politics. Moreover, the families of the empress and the more favored concubines constantly intrigued to influence or control the emperor because he generally appointed to key offices relatives from the maternal or wife's side of the family. Some families went so far as to try to seize the person of the emperor as a hostage for their fortunes, for the death of the empress or a favorite concubine might mean extermination of her relatives to pave the way for the relatives of the new empress or concubine. In the long run, factional strife weakened the central authority; and corruption, particularly nepotism, usually spread throughout the bureaucracy. Local officials often became *de facto* rulers over large areas, and civil governors or military officials of frontier satrapies ultimately emerged to contend for the "mandate of Heaven." And on occasion the nomads took advantage of Chinese weakness and disunity to overrun the north and sometimes the whole of China.

Dynastic decline can be attributed also to economic instability resulting from oppression of the peasantry. The state, the gentry, and the merchants were supported by the surplus produced by the peasantry: the state by taxes, the gentry by land rents, and the merchants by profits derived from the distribution of commodities. But over a period of time economic stability usually gave way to imbalance. Taxes tended to increase to meet the mounting expenses of government caused by wars of imperialism, court luxuries, and famine relief. Emperors, moreover, often assigned tax revenues to favorites as gifts, ranging from the taxes of three hundred families for lesser courtiers to as much as ten thousand families for princes; they also exempted from taxes the estates of many of the gentry and, later, those of Buddhist temples and monasteries. The free peasantry on the declining area of state land had to bear the burden of increased taxes. Quite naturally, many of them commended their land and entered the service of the gentry as tenant farmers to escape taxes and the duties of military service and the *corvée*. When the position of the peasantry was further depressed by famine, banditry became common and local revolts broke out against the tax collectors and rent agents of absentee landlords. Under able peasant leaders local uprisings often broadened into general insurrections, but after initial successes peasant leaders had to rely more and more on local gentry for trained personnel. Peasant rebellions usually did not topple dynasties. On most occasions the government put them down with the power of local military officials or even nomad troops, although the saviors often attempted to gain the throne.

In most cases dynastic change resulted from the interaction of all three forces: peasant rebellions, militarism, and the nomads. The fall of the Han dynasty fits this pattern well. The central government was weakened by the struggles and intrigues of court cliques, and local centers of power arose to challenge the ruling house. The expenses of administration mounted, and the tax base contracted. By the reign of Wu Ti the state had to resort to financial expedients to increase revenues: higher taxes on artisans and merchants, government monopolies in salt, iron, and liquor, and forced contributions by the rich. The peasantry provided the bulk of the budgetary requirements of the state through higher taxes, but, when it could bear the burden no longer, it rebelled. In the ensuing chaos the weakness of the regime became apparent, and local warlords unfurled their banners of insurrection. Finally, the collapse of unity enabled the nomads to pour across the northern frontiers into China. The emperor was dethoned, and China passed into an era of contending states of native and nomad origin.

2 The Development of Imperial China to 1644

Since many of China's basic institutions and their ideological foundations were established by the end of the Han dynasty, there is a great temptation to think of the subsequent history of the country until recent times as the history of a static society. The theory of the dynastic cycle reinforces this view, and there is much to justify some emphasis upon the conservation of ancient forms and the slow tempo of change. Yet over the centuries Chinese ideas and institutions were refined and modified, and much that was new was introduced and assimilated. The Chinese expanded their empire, and Chinese civilization, pre-eminent in East Asia, was the source of much of the culture of its neighbors.

Political Institutions

During the T'ang dynasty (618–906) the institutions of government were more fully developed. Emperors were advised by councils of high court officials, and administration was the responsibility of the ministers of six departments—civil service, finance, rites, defense, law, and public works—a functional division which remained in force until the twentieth century. For purposes of local administration China was divided into ten provinces based on natural geographic divisions, but in practice provinces were really groupings of prefectures, about 350 in number, which were directly responsible to the central government. The duty of the provincial governor was to supervise administration on the local level only, but during subsequent centuries the province supplanted the prefecture as the most responsible unit of local government. The lowest unit in the administrative system was the district, or *hsien*, whose number varied from 1,000 to 1,500. The district magistrate, appointed directly by the emperor, had authority over the villages, usually twenty to thirty in number, in his district, and he was assisted by a battery of clerks, tax collectors, bailiffs, and police in his three functions of collecting revenues, supervising public works, and maintaining law and order. Influential local gentry were his unofficial representatives in the separate villages, which were self-contained units headed by village elders chosen in an informal election by the influential persons in the community and confirmed in office by the district magistrate. Village government, which was communal and largely invisible, was the moral domain of elders and was based on established patterns of authority and the corporate spirit of the family system. Mutual responsibility for legal purposes, based upon groups of five and ten families, was probably the origin of modern China's *pao chia* system, in which ten families constituted a *p'ai*, one hundred a *chia*, and one thousand a *pao*, and all members were responsible for each other's actions. Families of each unit nominated their leaders, but these were confirmed by a magistrate to whom they were responsible. Many villages, particularly in the south, were clan villages with a common ancestry and common surname, and the head of the clan was usually the senior elder, who had full control over his clansmen. The imperial government did not interfere in village and clan affairs except for the protection and general interests of the province and empire. Vigorous and intelligent district magistrates could accomplish a great deal, but not without the co-operation of the village dignitaries. They achieved results commensurate with the strength of their own personalities since Chinese government tended to be a government of men, not law. Honest and capable officials could render great service, but, conversely, the incompetent and corrupt could do much harm.

An important link between the central government and the local administration were the censors or inspectors. In feudal times some of the states had used inspectors to check on the work of officials, and this practice was given permanent institutional form during the Ch'in and Han dynasties. The censorate remained as a regular service in subsequent dynasties, reaching its modern form under the Ming emperors. With encouragement from the imperial court, the T'ang censors were outspoken critics of misconduct and maladministration by officials. They impeached officials no matter how high their rank and commended or refuted memorials from officials of all ranks. Perhaps their basic function was to maintain efficiency in government and to minimize corruption, but at times they were used as an instrument of imperial despotism and control. For example, provincial administrators above a certain rank acted as censors of their colleagues to effect for the capital a closer scrutiny over local government. Another function of the censorate was to express public opinion and make necessary criticisms of the imperial regime.

29

During the T'ang dynasty and earlier, censors were expected to be critical of imperial edicts or memorials of high officials, but in later dynasties this function declined and ultimately passed from existence, indicating the increasing power of the emperor and the court.

Although emperors appointed favorites to positions in government, a civil service examination system became the chief means of recruiting able men into government. In the reign of the founder of the T'ang dynasty, T'ai Tsung, high office was largely in the hands of a hereditary aristocracy consisting mainly of leading families of the previous dynasty, but within a century these families had been replaced for the most part by scholars who were products of the examination system. This was the result of a deliberate policy on the part of the dynasty to weaken the old aristocracy and to find support among the gentry. An imperial college in the capital, Ch'ang-an, was the training ground for the new civil service, and there several thousand students studied under Confucian masters. Examinations were held regularly in the capital and in localities, and by the Ming dynasty there was a series of four separate examinations. The first was held in the district and prefectural cities twice every three years; at this level only some 2 per cent of the candidates were permitted to pass, and these were admitted a few weeks later to the prefectural examinations, where somewhat more than 50 per cent were likely to be successful. The fortunate examinees were then eligible for appointment to minor posts and to take provincial examinations, held every three years in the provincial capitals. Success at the provincial level qualified scholars to take the imperial examinations at the capital. Those who passed these examinations, about 6 per cent, were eligible for appointment to high office, and about one-third of this total, by a climactic palace examination in the presence of the emperor himself, were admitted to membership in the most exalted fraternity of Chinese scholarship, the Hanlin Academy, from which were selected the historiographers and other high literary officers. At first the examinations were somewhat flexible, with emphasis upon the Confucian Classics but including also practical subjects like law, mathematics, and political affairs. On occasion, when Taoism was fashionable at the imperial court, its influence was felt; for example, new civil service examinations were introduced in 741 which enabled candidates who had a Taoist schooling to be tested in Taoist instead of Confucian texts. Gradually the examinations became more concerned with literary style and Confucian orthodoxy, and by the Ming dynasty they were hardly a realistic test of ability. The examinations perpetuated Confucian traditions by encouraging reliance upon the wisdom of the past, and there is no doubt that through this device education helped to cement the social and political order.

Often China was troubled by what might be called an overpopulation of scholars, as there were too many of them and too few posts. One important cause of this was nepotism. Many candidates from the provinces were given posts without examinations upon the recommendation of friends and relatives; for example, in Sung times, for every examination which selected three or four hundred talented scholars there were eight or nine hundred others who were exempt. The civil service ministry, moreover, could recommend as many as two or three hundred candidates, and there were others recommended by military officers and relatives of the imperial household.

Although Chinese government and society were based upon the moral principles of Confucianism, law codes continued to buttress philosophy with authority. The principal rules were statutes inherited from preceding dynasties or newly formulated by the reigning dynasty. The T'ang code, for example, defined the status, rights, and duties of family members, offenses against the lives and property of individuals as well as against the emperor and his officials, and judicial procedure. Law codes tended to support tradition and to sustain the social and political foundation of the empire. Their basic purpose was not to provide justice for individuals but to support imperial rule and class inequality.

It was not until the Sung dynasty that the system of separate military administration was brought to an end and the entire administration of the country was placed in the hands of civil officials. From the Han dynasty on, a military wing had paralleled the civil branch of government, and militarism reached its peak during the decline of the T'ang dynasty, when generals controlled entire provinces and refused to remit taxes to the central government. During the T'ang dynasty the imperial army had become a professional career service, with the peasantry, relieved of general military service, paying higher taxes for the support of soldiers; but in times of crisis Chinese armies could be formed from the peasant militia. After 750 the empire consisted of large areas under powerful military governors who often were able to hand down their posts to their sons. The first Sung emperor, a military man himself, terminated the system of independent military administration, placing the army directly under civil officials, and his successor instituted a local militia system which has continued in practice, with minor exceptions, down to the present communist regime. The government grouped families into tens, fifties, and five hundreds, and regular army officers trained the headmen of these units. Each family with more than one adult male provided recruits to fill the ranks of the militia.

The system of taxation that supported the government varied somewhat from dynasty to dynasty, but, so long as the economy remained basically agricultural, the land tax was the foundation of the system. At the beginning of the T'ang dynasty the tax system was based on the equalization of landownership, and a land redistribution was implemented so that, as far as possible, all peasants would own the same amount of land and pay the same amount of taxes, namely: a fixed land tax, which would be remitted or lessened in times of hardship; labor service or its commuted money equivalent; and a household tax paid in silk or other cloth. The government exempted officials, scholars, and particular favorites from such taxes, but it did tax merchants according to their income. To prevent the formation of large estates, the alienation of land was forbidden. The estates of officials and favorites, however, were exceptions to the land redistribution, and over a period of time the T'ang government was unable to prevent the process of land concentration. Because of loopholes in the land regulations, local officials and men of wealth were able to exert pressures on the peasant to give up his title to the land; and they also seized land that was vacated temporarily because of war or famine. Free peasants were turned into tenants and disappeared from the land registers even if they remained on their holdings.

By 800 the landowning families constituted hardly more than 5 per cent of the population, and there was no longer any correlation between land-ownership and equal ability of the cultivators to pay taxes. The government was forced to establish a new land tax system based on the amount of land possessed, and taxes varied from year to year according to the revenue needs of the state. The central government determined a budget and assigned revenue quotas to units of local government, which actually determined the tax rates. The land tax was supplemented by a progressive income tax that extended not only to merchants but to officials.

Later dynasties modified this tax system in only minor ways, adding additional levies, such as an inheritance tax, or separating the land and poll tax again. During the Sung dynasty, for example, the basic land tax was light, amounting to only approximately one-twenty-fifth of the produce, but a general property tax on land and other properties rested heavily on the wealthy. Taxes were paid in kind and in money, first in copper, then in silver; and by the latter part of the Ming dynasty the land tax, into which most other taxes had been amalgamated, was paid in silver, with a set rate for converting grain into specie. Under this so-called "single-whip" taxation, which remained in effect until the end of imperial rule in 1912, the land tax and *corvée* were imposed on the total amount of land and the total number of male adults, and thus every unit of land had its share of taxes and labor service. Taxes were generally collected twice a year, but in some cases on three different occasions. The state supplemented tax revenues with the grain tribute, which was imposed on land in rice-surplus areas, particularly the lower Yangtze Valley provinces of Kiangsu and Chekiang.

The Economy

The migration of the Chinese people to the south was one of the most important developments in the centuries between the Han dynasty and modern times. With the Chinese settler went the strong cultural heritage that has given the Chinese people an amazing cultural continuity; in fact, this was perhaps the most important contribution of Confucianism as a social philosophy.

As early as the reign of Shih Huang Ti the Chinese had established a military colony on the southeast coast as a buffer protecting the empire, and, in addition, the first Ch'in emperor forced the emigration of some half-million agricultural colonists into the provinces south of the Yangtze River. The first voluntary mass migration of Chinese to the south came between 298 and 307, when drought, lawlessness, political chaos, and war caused approximately two million people to flee from China north of the Yangtze River into the south. When the north was overrun by nomads, a steady stream of emigrants pushed into the southern reaches of the Yangtze Basin (the modern provinces of Chekiang, Kiangsu, and Hunan), where enormous estates were developed by gentry capital. Under the impact of Chinese expansion, the cultures of the non-Chinese inhabitants of the south gave way to that of the Chinese, and soon these people were indistinguishable from the immigrants.

The continued migration of the Chinese to the south resulted in the shift of the economic center of China to the Yangtze Valley, and dynasties were often almost wholly dependent upon the Yangtze Delta and the central Yangtze Plain for tax revenues and grain tribute. For example, the T'ang central administration derived nine-tenths of its support from these areas. As early as the Sui dynasty the government constructed out of existing smaller canals a five-hundred-mile artery which linked the Yangtze Valley from Yangchow in Chekiang to the area near the capital, Loyang, on the Yellow River. This Grand Canal facilitated the transport of grain tribute to the capital and provided access to markets for producers in the north and south. Later, when the Mongols established their capital at Cambulac, near modern Peking, they extended the canal to the north.

Over the centuries Chinese jurisdiction was extended further south. The capture of the Sung dynasty capital at Kaifeng in 1125 by the nomadic Jurchen invaders set off a second mass exodus to the south. At this time the Chinese moved into the thinly settled regions of Kwangtung, Fukien, and Kwangsi. Further expansion had to wait until the Ming dynasty, when Chinese administrators sponsored the extensive settlement of Kweichow and Yunnan. Large armies recruited in south China were sent to pacify the region, and after them came civil servants, peasants, and merchants in great number. Prior to the Ming dynasty probably only 20 per cent or less of the Yunnan-Kweichow plateau was accessible to the Chinese, but by the end of the dynasty 60–70 per cent of the area was in Chinese hands.

The displaced tribal peoples were pushed further south into the more sparsely settled frontier lands where the unfavorable environment promised to deter the advance of the Chinese. The Thai went to the humid, hot, malarial valleys, where they continued their rice culture; and the Miao, Lolo, and Yao fled to the mountains of the border regions and beyond to practice their shifting cultivation. The various racial groups formed tribal protectorates, which paid tribute to China to preserve their own autonomy. Geographical factors made it difficult for the Chinese to extend direct administration over the tribes, and local taxation was insufficient to support direct rule. During the Ming dynasty there were over a thousand units under Chinese protection, and many of these were charged with the defense of the frontier. Since there was actually no definite political boundary on the south until the nineteenth century, there was virtually no difference between tribal units within Chinese territory and those beyond the border, and in many cases tribal chiefs in the neighboring states were invested in the same manner.

While Confucianism has given a cultural continuity to China, north and south, geography has created two distinct regions. North of the Tsingling Mountains and the Huai River rainfall is usually sufficient for dry grains such as wheat and millet, but, when there are significant variations in rainfall from year to year, flood or drought cause famine. In the north the farms were about five acres in size on an average—double those of the south—since the northern climate limits cultivation to one growing season. In the south rainfall is more consistent and is sufficiently abundant for rice to be the major crop, and, since the growing season is long, two or three crops are generally possible. In both north and south cultivation was intensive, requiring the heavy application of human labor; in fact, it was closer to gardening than to farming. Topographically there are also significant differences between north and south. The north is a plain and plateau area; consequently, transportation is relatively easy. In the south, which is rugged and hilly, level land is confined to river valleys, and transportation and communication are much more difficult. Geography has also affected language. In the north there is a general uniformity of language, with Mandarin as the spoken dialect, while in the south there are several dialects.

Trade gradually became a more important part of the economy. Trade was essentially the domestic distribution of handicraft products with specialization by localities, but from the Sung dynasty on a fairly extensive foreign commerce developed through the southeast ports, first with Indochina, then overseas to south and western Asia. A list of the various domestic products and localities would constitute a lengthy catalogue, but, to name a few, there were rugs from the northern parts around Peking, iron from Shansi, ivory and bamboo from the south, and lacquer and porcelain from the coastal provinces. Locally, cities and towns held bazaars where the wares of artisan specialists and regional rural surpluses were sold, and merchants, wholesale and retail, organized guilds on national, provincial, and local levels for protection against ruinous competition and official oppression. The units of handicraft production were small, being owned and operated for the most part by families or family partnerships, and craft guilds were formed locally to regulate prices, wages, rules for apprenticeship, and even to serve as mutual assistance societies.

Improvements in transportation and communication facilitated centralized control over the empire and the expansion of commerce. The river systems, supplemented by roads and canals, provided the basis of an extensive transportation network, but there were some important limitations and difficulties. Roads were not adequately maintained, and the vehicles of transportation were crude. In the north the cart and various beasts of burden were the common carriers, and in the south the canal boat, the wheelbarrow, and porters were utilized most commonly. Trade was handicapped to the extent that it was unprofitable to send items of great bulk and little value overland, and it was often difficult to relieve famine even when adjacent provinces had grain surpluses. The government inaugurated a postal system in the Yuan dynasty, but it was limited to official mail and official shipment of funds. By the nineteenth century there were several thousand postal stations along the five main and various subsidiary routes. With mail transported at the rate of 250 miles a day, communication between Canton and Peking took three weeks, and between Shanghai and Peking one week. There were also private postal systems, but their services rarely operated beyond more than one or two provinces.

The development of banking practices and improvements in currency facilitated the expansion of trade, but there remained serious limitations inherent in both. Copper cash became the basic money in China, but it was an obstacle to trade since it was expensive to transport. Regions suffering from deflation when they lost copper through an adverse balance of trade would sometimes prohibit the export of copper, but trade was then curtailed. To overcome this problem, both government and private agencies issued certificates to merchants who deposited copper cash, and these circulated as legal tender. The cash was in turn loaned out at interest or put into general circulation. The government also issued certificates against tax payments or the deliveries of commodities under state monopoly. In the Sung dynasty the increased production of silver led to its being used as money in the form of ingots, which varied locally in weight and purity, and in large transactions the weighing and assaying of silver was necessarily performed by experts for a fee. The government at times issued paper money to meet increasing expenditures, but bills depreciated quickly when the government was unable to resist the temptation to print currency without sufficient backing. During the Sung dynasty private banks were established, but their operations never became extensive as they were usually family concerns or partnerships. In the case of the Shensi bankers, their capital was originally derived from the coal and iron trade. Despite all these advances, credit did not become general, and most transactions were for cash.

The Chinese merchant did not become a powerful force in the economy, nor did handicraft production advance to capitalist forms. China did not share the experience of Europe, where the merchant and industrialist developed as a force for all sorts of political and social change. It is difficult to explain why the Chinese merchant class was not able to break away from its

35

dependence upon officialdom and create an independent entrepreneurial and industrial power. The merchant seems to have been more concerned to profit through control over the distribution of products than through increased production. Trade, moreover, was limited by a number of factors. The economic self-sufficiency of peasant families and the high cost of transportation impeded national commerce and helped to foster the development of local or regional economies, with the administrative walled cities constituting market hubs for the neighboring villages. The complex currency system, which varied locally to the advantage of the money manipulators, was another hindrance. Finally, the guild system, particularly in the case of the crafts, preserved monopolies of technical processes and productive rights.

The merchant was strongly motivated to invest in land. So long as land-owning remained a criterion of social position and success, the surplus capital of merchants found its way into land either directly, or indirectly through moneylending. So great was the distinction between the merchants and the other classes that they and their descendants were sometimes even excluded from eligibility for the civil service examinations. Land was also an attractive investment in itself, since it was secure; fluid capital was liable to confiscation, and commercial and industrial capital was subject to state controls and heavy taxation.

National commerce fell under strict government regulation and taxation, as in the case of commodities like salt, iron, tea, and later tobacco and opium. In theory this was for the benefit of society as a whole, but in practice it caused collusion between officials and merchants at the expense of the masses. During the T'ang dynasty, for example, tea-drinking became a general habit, spreading from Tibet to all of China, and after 783 the state attempted to make it a source of revenue. The government established the tea bureau to buy tea from producers in Szechwan and southeast China and supply it to licensed whole-salers, who created a monopoly through bribery of the officials. It is significant also that rich merchants with unmarried daughters were usually anxious to negotiate generous marriage settlements with the successful examination candidates.

The Social System

A simple but effective way to describe the social structure of China is to divide the population into two broad categories: the dominant groups and the masses. Among the former were the gentry, scholars, officials, merchants, and militarists; among the latter were the peasants, artisans, and the base groups like servants, actors, and prostitutes. The basis of this division is multiple: power, wealth, and literacy. Throughout Chinese history the peasants and artisans have produced the surplus that has supported the dominant groups, enabling them to conserve and perpetuate Chinese culture.

The peasantry, living in family or clan groups in small villages, constituted 80 per cent of the population. Life was exceedingly hard, and the standard of living for tenants, laborers, and most owner-cultivators rarely rose above the subsistence level. To supplement income derived from agriculture, peasant households generally produced handicraft goods like silk and pottery or engaged in trade, but even then they found it difficult to raise their level of living. Ever-increasing taxes and social expenses connected with marriages and funerals kept families impoverished; moreover, the system of multiple inheritance generally meant a constant parcelization of the family's land among the several sons. Infanticide and abortion were commonly practiced to keep down the size of the family, as there was a limit to the number of people that the land could support. War, disease, and famine insured that life-expectancy was short, not exceeding twenty-six years on the average. Thus the nuclear family was a small one, averaging slightly over five persons.

This social division into dominant groups and the masses, particularly in view of the preponderant number of peasants, had an actual physical basis, reflected in an urban-rural dichotomy. There were in reality two Chinas: the numerous semiautonomous agricultural communities of the peasantry, and the towns and cities inhabited by absentee landlords, merchants, and officials. Towns and cities had developed primarily as administrative centers and secondarily as hubs of commerce, but by the T'ang and Sung dynasties they were also centers of amusement and culture where the dominant leisure class had access to the pleasures and refinements of the teahouses, restaurants, brothels, and theaters. The development of printing, the consequent spread of education, and the rise of a new type of popular literature in the form of novels, plays, and short stories broke the monopoly over culture that the society of the capital had formerly enjoyed.

The social consequences of printing and the spread of education came only gradually, but they helped to increase social mobility since the examination system was the means to official position. From the Sung dynasty on, local academies or colleges flourished, and to them flocked young scholars to prepare for the examinations. An analysis of lists of successful candidates during the Sung dynasty indicates that over half had no officials among their ancestors, and during the Ming dynasty this reserve of scholars helped to satisfy the demands created by the enlarged empire and the increased population. Some scholars have called such officials and scholars an intellectual middle class, but, as Wolfram Eberhard has observed, it had no distinctive existence economically or politically. The new "middle-class official" usually made a career when he became subservient to one of the powerful gentry families. Corruption in government seems to have become more common, since salaries were still not adequate and the new "middle-class officials" were often in debt after a long period of preparation for the examinations.

37

According to estimates based on the dynastic histories, population remained fairly stable from the Han to the Ch'ing dynasties. The following table gives a representative set of figures based on the research of Chen Ta:

DYNASTY	YEAR	POPULATION
Han	156	56,487,000
T'ang	755	52,919,000
Sung	1102	43,822,000
Yuan	1290	59,847,000
Ming	1578	60,693,000

This stability is usually explained by such population checks as famine, disease, and war and by the fact that the high birth rate of the Chinese brought population back to normal levels after each decline. Population may have followed a cyclical pattern similar to the dynastic cycle, but it is hard to accept figures which indicate no absolute increase for this long period of history, especially when the same source lists the following two figures for the Ch'ing dynasty:

Ch'ing—1783		284,033,000
Ch'ing—1851		432,164,000

How can this amazing increase be explained? One important answer is that the figures hide the truth. Until the Ch'ing dynasty, population estimates were closely related to the number of taxable cultivators and did not include the entire population. Chen Ta has suggested that Chinese population may have reached the total of 150,000,000 by the end of the Ming dynasty, considering the extent of new land under cultivation. After 1712, however, population figures were no longer related to taxation, and local officials reported actual population, even boosting totals to please the throne. Thus population growth during the Ch'ing dynasty may not have been as dramatic as Chinese figures indicate. Further research may aid the historian, but for the present the matter remains a controversial enigma.

The Origins of Buddhism

Prior to the nineteenth and twentieth centuries the introduction of Buddhism presented the only great challenge to the Chinese way of life, for all Chinese, whether they accepted or rejected Buddhism as a religion, felt its impact, and for many their attitude toward life and their view of the world and the universe were completely changed.

Buddhism was founded as a religion in ancient India during the sixth century B.C. in reaction to the polytheism and priesthood of Brahmanism, the dominant religion of the time. Buddhism emerged as a stepchild of Brahmanism, and there was much in common between the two religions. The ancient Indians worshipped the images of numerous deities, probably manifestations of nature gods who were thought to merge into one pantheistic godhead, called Brahma, and they believed in the transmigration of souls, or reincarnation. Each life, regarded as one in an infinite series of lives, was conditioned by acts of previous existences and could take various forms: animal, human, and divine. Good deeds transported the individual to the abode of the gods in heaven; conversely, evil degraded him to the life of a beast. It was thought that rebirth in the heavenly world could be won by sacrificial rites performed by properly trained priests. The latter, who charged a fee for their services, explained that the universe was regulated by a permeating principle that could be apprehended by sacred science and controlled by the use of methods known only to them. Each existence, however, came to an end, and the process of reincarnation continued without real happiness in heaven or on earth. Happiness existed only in deliverance from rebirth, since the fate of infinite future existences was regarded not as a form of immortality but as repeated death. Thus the Indian sought release and lasting repose in some changeless state, called nirvana and often considered as union with Brahma.

The founder of Buddhism was Gotama (560–480 B.C.), the son of a wealthy noble of the Sakya clan whose territory lay on the frontier of modern Nepal and India. According to the legends surrounding his life, while still a young man he left his wife and son to search for religious truth, a common practice in his day. First he studied with religious leaders, but, finding them inadequate, he turned to asceticism in the hope of obtaining divine knowledge and inspiration by the suppression of desires and the voluntary endurance of tortures. It is said that

he gradually reduced his food to a grain of rice a day. He lived on seeds and grass, and for one period literally on dung. He wore haircloth or other irritating clothes. He plucked out his hair and beard. He stood continuously. He lay upon thorns. He let the dust and dirt accumulate until his body looked like an old tree. He frequented a cemetery—that is, a place where corpses were thrown to decay or be eaten by birds and beasts—and lay among the rotting bodies.

According to Buddhist tradition, he commented on his experience as follows: "When I touched my belly, I felt my backbone through it and when I touched my back, I felt my belly . . . and when I rubbed my limbs to refresh them, the hair fell off." Asceticism did not provide Gotama with spiritual enlightenment, but it has influenced Hindus and Buddhists to this day. Both groups agree that ideally all gratification coming from the senses must be avoided and the mind kept under rigid discipline. The body must be subdued by physical training before the mind can apprehend the higher truths. Gotama finally succeeded in his quest when one day he experienced a vision of his previous births and the hundreds of thousands of his existences with all their details of name, family, and caste. Then came a revelation of religious truths, and a deity appeared before him urging that he preach this wisdom to others. Gotama was now a *buddha*, "an enlightened one," and he began the task of teaching his faith to others.

The Buddhism of Gotama accepted the principle of transmigration and endeavored to secure individual release from it and lasting peace. Gotama explained that the cause of existence was a force or desire for life, something comparable to lust or craving for pleasure. He explained that there had been no single act of divine creation that produced the stream of existence. It simply was and always had been what it was. Even the gods in the Buddhist heavens were attached to the process of life and death and were not its creators. Gotama also denied the existence of the soul, insisting that no soul passed from body to body. Instead he explained that desire created new bodies or individuals. Nothing was permanent. How then would one remove or pacify desire? Gotama answered that one practiced self-purification in preparation for his own enlightenment or Buddhahood. In other words, the acquisition of religious merit through morality and good deeds prepared the individual for the perception of religious truth through knowledge and contemplation. The individual would begin to discriminate between good and bad thoughts, to develop one and suppress the other. Accumulating such religious wisdom and experiencing the same enlightenment as Gotama, he would understand that life is an illusion, that nothing belonging to it has an enduring quality or nature of its own. When the individual annihilated sensual ties and the lust for life, he would escape from the stream of existence. Most Buddhists believed that enlightenment was not just an experience of the mind but also an intuitive realization of truth by all of the senses.

There were other important differences between Buddhism and its Brahman antecedent. Gotama taught that all sacrificial and sacramental acts were irrelevant. Instead of relying upon the assistance or mediation of a priesthood, the individual worked for his own salvation. Gotama ignored the question of Brahma, or God, and he did not describe nirvana beyond a state of peace to be attained in this life. He steadfastly refused to explain its nature after death, and he felt that speculation about what lay beyond death was not truly part of religion.

Monkhood has given Buddhism a permanent institutional foundation. Indians, renouncing lay life in their eagerness to achieve nirvana in their own lifetime, accepted Gotama as their teacher, and religious groups were formed by increasing numbers of disciples as the gospel spread. When these groups accepted rules to help govern themselves, they became communities of monks within a religious system. In the monastic community the individual was able to reduce his passions to a minimum (he begged his only meal in the morning), he meditated, and he enjoyed religious discussion and instruction. There was no work, no code of obedience, and no worship; nor were the monks the priests of the people. They served as teachers, but they had no duty to make the people conform. During Gotama's lifetime women were permitted to form and join monastic orders, but in subsequent periods nuns were merely unordained lay leaders.

What did Gotama offer the laity? He taught that, because laymen were involved in worldly affairs, they were unable to achieve nirvana in their present existence but that they could insure birth in a higher state or possibly in some few cases reach nirvana on their deathbed. Gotama enjoined the laity to live according to a moral code which emphasized moderation in pleasures and consideration of others. His five essential commandments were abstinence from such sins as taking life, drinking intoxicants, lying, stealing, and unchastity, and he urged the laity to earn religious merit by observing three other precepts: use no garlands or perfumes, sleep on a mat spread on the ground, and refrain from eating after midday. Today, in some Buddhist countries, pious laymen observe these eight rules on religious days and often make a vow to observe them for some special period.

In the centuries following the death of Gotama, Buddhism split into two general schools, both of which spread to the rest of Asia. That school which seems closer to the original teaching of Gotama is called "Hinayana" or "Theravada," and today it is the religious foundation of society in Ceylon, Burma, Thailand, and parts of Indochina. The second school is called "Mahayana," and it has played a major role in the history of Central Asia, China, Korea, and Japan. The terms themselves are creations of the Mahayanists. Hinayana is usually translated as "Lesser Vehicle," and Mahayana, "Greater Vehicle." A Mahayana scripture explains this implied superiority as follows: Gotama at first taught only the Hinayana doctrine because men were not ready for the superior truth of the Mahayana. A description of Mahayana Buddhism, which is more pertinent to the study of China and Japan, follows below.

Mahayana Buddhism, first and foremost, is a religion of idealistic compassion. It emphasizes a code of altruistic ethics which teaches that everyone should do good in the interest of the whole world. In the words of the Japanese historian, Anesaki Masaharu, "The central idea in Buddhist teaching is the gospel of universal salvation based on the idea of the fundamental oneness of all beings." Man does not seek his own salvation; he seeks to help others. According to Anesaki, "Individuals may purify themselves and thereby escape the miseries of sinful existence, yet the salvation of anyone is imperfect so long as and so far as there remain any who are not saved." Instead of keeping his great discovery to himself, Gotama devoted the rest of his life to helping others to achieve enlightenment. In Mahayana Buddhism the enlightened one defers entrance into nirvana because he feels a spiritual unity with others and makes over to them whatever merit he may possess or acquire, offering himself and all of his possessions, moral and material, to make possible the salvation of all beings. Such a person is called a *bodhisattva*.

Under the influence of Indian systems of idealistic metaphysics, the Mahayanists conceived of one permanent reality or Buddha-nature underlying all phenomena and all individuals and working in all ages and in innumerable worlds for the salvation of all beings. Nirvana meant escape from the impermanence of life and union with this unchanging reality; however, nirvana was not merely an understanding of pantheism but a realization with all the senses of a personal identity with the universal spirit. In the words of E. A. Burtt,

This *nirvana* becomes a state in which compassionate oneness with others has transcended all thoughts of oneself as a separate, distinguishable entity. Thus, the *bodhisattva* becomes aware that just by being a *bodhisattva* he is already in *nirvana* as it is truly understood. Paradoxically put, the spiritual insight here is that to renounce *nirvana* for oneself, in love for others, is to find oneself in *nirvana* in its real meaning.

It was easy to transform these concepts into a doctrine of vicarious merit and salvation through a savior. Indians fashioned beautiful images of bodhisattvas who refused nirvana's bliss that they might alleviate the sufferings of others. Chinese called upon Kuan Yin (Sanskrit: Avalokitesvara; Japanese: Kannon) to save them from shipwreck, execution, and robbers or to deter them from passions of lust or hate. Kuan Yin was a merciful bodhisattva who heard the cries of suffering which rose up from the earth and vowed to postpone her own eternal peace until every living creature had been saved. Mahayana believers also worshipped Buddhas who were regarded as particular manifestations of the ultimate reality or all-pervading Buddha. Some believers sought to invoke their power through elaborate ritual or magical formulas, but others had faith in their power to cause rebirth in paradise.

Buddhism in China

Buddhism was introduced into China during the middle of the Han dynasty; it became a powerful religious force during the period of dynastic decline; and it won general acceptance during the period of interregnum that followed. Buddhism spread at the expense of traditional values. For example, the pressure of economic and social difficulties caused peasants to seek solace in a religion that gave hope for the future. The various barbarian dynasts also embraced Buddhism, extending favor to Buddhist monks and even using them as scholarly assistants. Most of the Confucianists had fled south, and those that remained were not favored by the invaders, who rightly suspected them of secret loyalties to Chinese rulers. In the case of the kingdom of the Toba Wei (386–534), Buddhism had the status of an official religion, with the emperor appointing a monk as head of the church, to which he granted large endowments of land. The monks on their part regarded the ruler as a Buddha. By the beginning of the fifth century probably 90 per cent of the people of the north were Buddhist, but in most cases the dogma and theory of the new faith were little understood. By the beginning of the sixth century Buddhist rites and ceremonies were practiced everywhere, temples and monasteries had arisen in almost every district, and monks and nuns were numerous and highly respected. While all Chinese could not renounce lay life and enjoy the asylum of temples and monasteries in troubled times, Buddhism did offer salvation to everyone.

Taoist speculations prepared many Chinese intellectuals to accept the doctrines of Buddhism. By the end of the Han dynasty, Taoist philosophy was greatly in favor as a form of protest and escapism, and in these chaotic years intellectuals took refuge in a kind of nihilism and philosophy of naturalism which ultimately gave way to Buddhism once translations of its tracts were widely circulated. Taoism apparently could not fully satisfy the speculative interests it had aroused or suggest solutions for the problems it had raised, and the revival of Taoism thus facilitated the victory of Buddhism. Taoist terms were used to translate Buddhist concepts, some of which were strikingly similar to the Chinese philosophy. For example, the *tao* was described as "unnameable," and the ultimate reality of the Mahayana idealists was characterized as something that could not be explained in words. In some cases Buddhism simply disarmed intellectuals and triumphed over Taoism. Although the increasing vogue of Buddhism was opposed by Confucian scholars, their hostility grew feeble as the empire crumbled and interregnum followed.

Buddhism won popular acceptance because it was tolerant of Chinese religious practices and lent new support to them. The local Buddhist clergy not only offered solace and formulas of easy salvation but also participated readily in local earth and fertility cults since they reasoned that there was no conflict between their faith and the functions of nature deities. Buddhist monks also served as exorcists and engaged in magical practices, including alchemy. Most important, Buddhism provided more effective observances for ancestor worship, for it maintained that the average man stood in danger of rebirth in hell in retribution for his past deeds, that even such a being had the power to struggle upward through the acquisition of merit, and that the living could assist by acts of worship, including rites, prayer, and magic, or by offering votive objects to bodhisattvas who could release the tortured soul. The devout could also earn merit for living family members. It is significant that the Buddhist concept of transmigration did not conflict with the Chinese idea that ancestral spirits traveled about with lightning speed in the ethereal realms. The Chinese continued to believe that the spirit of a great man lived eternally, moved anywhere at will, and at times came to rest in ancestral halls or in its grave. The spirit of a common man, on the other hand, evaporated and dwindled, disappearing entirely with the course of time.

The prestige of Indian science and art helped Buddhism to engulf China. Chinese medicine and astronomy were enriched, and Chinese sculpture and painting took on new and deeper forms. Buddhism not only offered Chinese artists new subjects, but, as a modern specialist has noted, "It offered a creed and ideals suited to the artistic temperament; peace and beauty reigned in its monasteries; its doctrine that life is one and continuous is reflected in that love of nature, that sympathetic understanding of plants and animals, that intimate union of sentiment with landscape which marks the best Chinese pictures." Finally, the appeal of towering pagodas and temples impressed even the unbeliever.

When China was reunited under the Sui and T'ang dynasties, Buddhism flourished under the patronage of the court, becoming established as a national religion. There were monasteries in all the towns and cities, and numerous monastic retreats existed in the countryside. Many of these establishments were tied to the state, and ceremonies on its behalf were conducted on orders from the government. For example, monks prayed for deceased and even living emperors or performed rituals invoking divine help against disease and natural calamities. The integration of church and state was strongest in the capital, where two sets of seven monks constantly read scriptures as a standing precaution against any spiritual mishap to the state. The emperor bestowed titles and honors on favored Buddhist monks as if they were court officials, and he often sponsored the pilgrimages of monks to India. The government also regulated the church by restricting ordinations to prevent too many able-bodied men from entering the tax-exempt ranks of the clergy and by limiting the number of tax-free monastic estates. Enforcement of these regulations, however, depended on the whims of the emperor and the bureaucracy. On the other hand, Buddhism remained free from government control in the sense that the state rarely passed judgment on religious beliefs or interfered with religious practices.

Although Buddhism was regarded by the government as a national religion, it was divided into numerous sects, three of which deserve particular attention: Ch'an, T'ien-t'ai, and Pure Land. The Mahayanists said that Gotama preached many creeds and codes at different periods of his life, and each sect claimed that its own teaching was closest to Gotama's ultimate beliefs.

Ch'an Buddhism derived much of its theory and practice from philosophic Taoism, and the Ch'an masters emphasized that spiritual cultivation did not require special religious acts. Asceticism, good works, ritual, faith in Buddhas and bodhisattvas, psalms, charms, and spells were considered useless. Although many Ch'anists engaged in meditation as a practice, others believed that religious cultivation need not interfere with the simple affairs of daily life. Salvation was simply the awareness by the individual of the unity of man and the universe, or its only reality, the all-pervading Buddha. The basic principle of Ch'an was that the Buddha-nature was in the heart of every man; all that man had to do was to turn his gaze inward to see his relationship to the universe. Some believed that this came suddenly, while others felt that the "awakening" came gradually. In reality, Chinese rationalism transformed Ch'an into something that was no longer Buddhism, for to many Chinese Ch'an taught emancipation from all untruthful seekings after nirvana or rebirth in paradise. There was no Buddhahood to attain, no magical powers to acquire, and no salvation in heaven. One simply found resignation and peace in the concept of spiritual unity.

T'ien-t'ai, named after a celebrated mountain monastery in Chekiang, emphasized gradual spiritual development according to levels of Buddhist teaching in an attempt to reconcile the contradictory creeds of the various sects. Dividing Gotama's life into various periods, each with a different doctrinal emphasis, this sect provided principles suited to all believers. It is likely that this theory reflected the Chinese predilection for harmony and the desire of Chinese rulers to minimize division and conflict. T'ien-t'ai gave both China and Japan many outstanding religious thinkers, but by 900, with Buddhism in decline, it became concerned largely with magical formulas and the worship of Omitofo.

The Pure Land sect ultimately became the most popular of all among the masses, reaching its peak in the late T'ang and in the Sung dynasties. Pure Land was the cult of Omitofo (Sanskrit: Amitabha; Japanese: Amida), which held that simple faith in the grace of this Buddha and invocation of his name could take the place of moral, contemplative, and intellectual efforts. It was thought that Omitofo was so compassionate that he refused to become a Buddha except on condition that he could apportion his vast store of accumulated merit to others as he chose. For the believer, faith and prayer to Omitofo were the means to rebirth in the Pure Land, or paradise. Originally, worship of Omitofo was acknowledged by other sects to be, if not the most excellent way, at least a permissible shortcut to enlightenment, since rebirth in the Pure Land assured steady, rapid progress toward the goal of Buddhahood. This was true in the case of T'ien-t'ai, but eventually the strong devotional character of the act of faith gave rise to a separate sect.

As Buddhism grew more powerful and influential, it unavoidably incurred the hostility of the Religious Taoists, described below, and the Confucianists. The Taoist church, modeled in large part on Buddhism, sought to weaken if not destroy religious competition, and the Confucian rationalists branded Buddhism as a superstitious and alien creed, incompatible with Chinese society. To the Confucian scholars Buddhism was antisocial, since the ideal of monkhood and celibacy took precedence over family life and transgressed the popular Chinese view that to have a son was not only a duty but was essential for those sacrifices without which the departed ancestral spirit could not have peace. They reasoned that celibacy would, if practiced on a national scale, cause the destruction of the state and society. The Confucian bureaucracy also deplored the increase in the number of tax-free monastic estates, sheltering great hordes of monks, who were lost to the labor force of the country. The state also objected to the accumulation by temples and monasteries of large quantities of gold and copper, the two principal monetary metals, stored in the form of images and bells, a practice which, by the middle of the T'ang dynasty, had brought about a general scarcity of money. The situation deteriorated to the point where it cost the government more than a penny to make a penny. This put a limit on the amount of money that the state could afford to mint, and the only remedy was to confiscate the copper of the Buddhist church and forbid nonmonetary uses of the metal.

These and other factors precipitated a great persecution in the period 842–845 which permanently crippled the Buddhist church. There had been persecutions earlier, during the interregnum (220–589), but the T'ang effort was the first on a general scale. It was ordered by a fanatical Taoist emperor who went so far as to call upon all scholars to take up his religion. The scholar-bureaucrats did not heed his request, but they did side with the emperor against the Buddhist church. In addition to the various reasons cited above, there were also more immediate political considerations. The persecution of Buddhism was related to the struggles of the bureaucrats and the palace eunuchs. Many bureaucrats who were not unsympathetic to Buddhism as a religion hated the eunuchs and welcomed an opportunity to attack those among them who were believers. During the persecution the government destroyed tens of thousands of monasteries, melted down statues, including those in private possession, defrocked and returned to lay life several hundred thousand monks and nuns, confiscated much of the private wealth of the remaining clergy, and expelled foreign monks from the country. The persecution came to a halt as suddenly as it had started. The emperor died in 846, and in the same year a general amnesty was declared. The state returned to its normal policy of regulation, but the damage to the church was decisive. Buddhism continued to expand as a popular religion, reaching its peak in the Sung dynasty, but the organization and power of the church never recovered.

In the subsequent development of Buddhism in China the distinctions between sects tended to be obliterated. In most cases all salient differences of doctrine and practice died out, but the older monasteries continued to present variations in details and to honor their own line of teachers. On the whole there was a general toleration of all rites, scriptures, and deities (although a particular bodhisattva might be singled out for reverence in one locality, or some religious practice might be specially observed). Every large temple, regardless of its sect, had a meditation hall, accepted faith among its practices, and adhered to T'ien-t'ai philosophy. Yet, for the mass of Chinese, Ch'an meditation degenerated into habitual quietude instead of the search for enlightenment, and T'ien-t'ai philosophy was largely unintelligible. The recitations of Omitofo's name expressed some degree of devotion, but even this was often pure formalism. Chinese visited temples for materialist purposes; and in return for ceremonies which involved neither moral nor intellectual effort the worshipper expected good luck, offspring, or other material blessings. The monkhood was generally lax and corrupt, and only in well-disciplined monasteries did Buddhism have any vigor.

Religious Taoism and Neo-Confucianism

The major popular alternative to Buddhism was Religious Taoism. Based on nature worship, the cosmology of *yin* and *yang*, and certain of the ideas of early Taoist philosophy, Religious Taoism was a cult of immortality and spirit worship which included a priesthood, ritual, and iconography. Its practices were thought to control the spirit world, which influenced every act of man, and herein lay the power of the Taoist priest to determine the fortuitous time and place for building a house or placing a grave. The secret healing power of herbs, revitalization through aphrodisiacs, and the wonders of astrology and alchemy were his stock in trade. In some areas, during the disintegration of the Han empire, the priests took the place of civil officials and assumed the functions of government. These theocratic leaders emphasized the traditional conception of the close relationship between the actions of men and the supervision of the gods.

Under foreign influences, largely Persian and Buddhist, Religious Taoism developed a church organization which reached its height in the thirteenth century. Its complicated pantheon of deities was headed by the Jade Emperor, a god probably derived from the Persian creator, Ahura Mazda, or else an adaptation of Shang Ti. The Jade Emperor controlled the spirit world through a hierarchy of bureaucrats which extended from celestial ministers down to local tutelary gods, descendants of the classical gods of the soil, and the family gods, chief of which was the kitchen god. Like Buddhism, Religious Taoism was based on a theory of retribution. Familiar deities, like the kitchen god or guardian spirits, watched over the acts of individuals and reported them to celestial record-keepers. On the basis of this information, the Jade Emperor rewarded or punished individuals on earth or after death in heaven or hell. Although pre-Buddhist China had no well-defined conception of heaven and hell as places of dwelling or of judgment after death, Buddhism supplied thirty-three heavens and eighteen hells, and Religious Taoism accepted them all, giving them names and assigning Chinese deities to preside over each one. Taoist monasteries, temples, and rites were patterned after their Buddhist counterparts, and monks and nuns took vows similar to the

Buddhist vows. Even a Taoist canon was written in the form of Buddhist psalms. Religious Taoism also provided for lay masters or priests who made their living by calling upon the celestial hierarchy to defeat the machinations of devils. In the popular mind maladies and calamities of all kinds, including blindness, disease, fire, flood, and drought, were blamed on the actions of malevolent spirits, and to combat their evil purposes it was necessary to enlist the aid of the gods. This was the function of the lay priest, who was ready for a fee to drive away malignant spirits with the necessary charms, ceremonies, and drugs; and if the first attempt was unsuccessful, he always had more expensive remedies.

The majority of Chinese ultimately followed a syncretic religion often called "the religion of the masses." At its foundation was the ancient nature cult; Buddhist and Taoist elements were included as secondary features. The masses worshipped thousands of idols of various origins, making special offerings to whatever deity they believed able to influence their lives at the time. They believed in astrology, almanacs, geomancy, fortunetelling, and all sorts of magic and superstitions, and in most of its practices this religion of the masses aimed at earthly blessings. And, although most Chinese believed in some sort of reincarnation, they thought that salvation was open to everyone since human nature was fundamentally good and the Buddha-nature or the Taoist pure-nature existed in all men.

Although many scholar-bureaucrats were influenced by Buddhism and Religious Taoism, most of them still clung to the intellectual heritage of Confucianism. Even during the interregnum following the collapse of the Han empire, the study of the Confucian Classics continued; and when China was again unified under the Sui and T'ang dynasties, the bureaucracy came to be recruited in considerable part by competitive examinations based principally on these works. The second T'ang emperor ordered scholars to prepare an official edition of the Classics and to select commentaries to elucidate them. The same emperor also sponsored the construction of a Confucian temple at the Imperial University in the capital, and this became the cornerstone of a cult of Confucius and scholarship that was supported by the state civil service and the scholar class. Large temples were built in the name of Confucius, and they were filled with images and great works of art. Veneration was not limited to Confucius himself but was extended to his disciples, old and new, and many scholars were honored in these temples, which became something like modern halls of fame. Commemoration in them was the greatest posthumous honor for scholars and public servants, and the practice continued down into the twentieth century. Even in this activity, however, Confucianism was hardly a religion.

Buddhism and Religious Taoism stimulated Confucian scholars to provide a broader metaphysical foundation for their philosophy. Specifically, they undertook, first, to match the Buddhist and Taoist cosmology, second, to explain the world and Confucian ethics metaphysically, and, finally, to vindicate man's right to find happiness in the ordinary pursuits of normal life. This body of thought, which sought to make objective and self-evident reason the root of everything, is called "Neo-Confucianism." Its formulators condemned both Buddhist and Religious Taoist subjective philosophy, which denied the existence of objective reason.

One of the earliest of the Neo-Confucianists was Han Yu (768–824), who bitterly attacked Chinese Buddhists for their alien, superstitious faith and for their retirement from the world as monks, thereby destroying the human relationships so prized by Confucianism. Like other Neo-Confucianists, he taught that the perfection of the individual was never an end in itself but only the beginning step for the ordering of the family, the state, and the world. Each individual must aim to improve society. Buddhist schemes of salvation seemed to Han Yu to be selfish and antisocial because each man endeavored to become a bodhisattva or Buddha or to be reborn in paradise at the cost of forsaking duties to the family and the state. Yet Neo-Confucianism provided a means to achieve a Confucian type of Buddhahood. Li Ao (died *ca.* 844) emphasized a process of self-cultivation lying within the range of ordinary human conduct and social relationships, but by "self-cultivation" he meant the fulfillment of man's good nature and the nullification of passions. In his view salvation was the achievement of a personal harmony in which the baser instincts of man were brought under the control of his higher nature. The sage "shares the attributes of Heaven and Earth" and "assists the transforming and nourishing activities of Heaven and Earth"; he has gained union with the universe, and thus his experience is no longer merely ethical but religious and mystical as well. It is clear that the thought of both Han Yu and Li Ao was in large part derived from the philosophy of Mencius, for they reflect his mystical tendency, his discussions on mind and human nature, his statement that "All things are complete within us. There is no greater delight than to find sincerity when one examines oneself," and his method of self-cultivation through "nourishing the mind" and "making fewer the desires."

The great synthesizer of Neo-Confucianism was Chu Hsi (1130–1200), who blended the ideas of many of his predecessors into one all-embracing system which was not successfully challenged until the introduction of Western philosophy in recent decades. Chu Hsi came from a literary family, studied philosophic Taoism and Buddhism, became a firm Confucianist, and held posts of considerable importance in government. He had many students and wrote extensively, and his commentaries on a number of the Classics became standard and were considered as correct in government examinations from the 1300's to 1905, when the examination system was finally abolished.

Chu Hsi summarized the cosmological foundation of Confucianism as follows: In the beginning, when no single physical object yet existed, there was nothing but the regulative principles of nature. These principles, which existed for all things in the universe, were contained in a single whole, the supreme ultimate. Under the principles governing movement and quiescence, substance underwent phases of movement and quiescence in the course of which it operated actively to become *yang* substance and congealed to become *yin* substance. By this division into *yang* and *yin*, heaven and earth were formed and the whole process of evolution was set in motion. When the *yang* substance and the *yin* substance were mingled together and obscure, heaven and earth were still in a state of chaos and were not differentiated from each other. Like everything else, human creation was simply the union of principle (human nature) and substance (bodily form). On the basis of these premises, the products of human reason, Chu Hsi concluded that reality was progressively evolved and that the universe was a harmonious system because of the co-operative functioning of principle and substance.

Chu Hsi applied this metaphysical explanation to politics and the social order. He explained that for the state, as an organization having a concrete existence, there was a principle of government which the intellect could apprehend. When actual government corresponded to principle, it was good, and, when it did not, it was bad. Thus, principle was nothing more than the *tao* or moral order stressed in early Confucianism as a means of bringing good government to society and peace to the world. Confucian political philosophy was man's reasoned statement of principle. In the social field, according to the Neo-Confucianists, there were also principles of class distinction and social relationships like ruler and subject, father and son, and husband and wife.

Chu Hsi also believed that he had solved the problem of the quality of human nature that had been so hotly debated in Confucianism since the time of Mencius and Hsun Tzu. According to Chu Hsi, principle or human nature was the same for all men, but unfortunately their substance was not. If a man's substance was impure, he was foolish and bad. Thus, each individual was enjoined to get rid of the impediment and recapture his original virtuous nature. But how was this to be accomplished? Chu Hsi answered: By the exercise of earnestness and the extension of knowledge through "the investigation of things." He meant that the individual could comprehend the principles of everything that existed in the universe and thereby gain an understanding of his own nature, since this, like other principles, was contained in the supreme ultimate and thus constituted a unity.

Chu Hsi gave religious feeling a rationalistic orientation, for he denied the power of deities and spirits over human beings and he urged man to establish his fate by fulfilling his nature. Like other Neo-Confucianists, he helped to provide a philosophy for an active life and directed religious instinct toward social and ethical purposes. There was no belief in reincarnation or search for immortality, and death was regarded as a normal occurrence, as a time to rest. Nor was existence equated with suffering; on the contrary, life was to be happy for all men. Neo-Confucianism did not include the idea of retribution, reinforced by belief in reward and punishment in heavens and hells, which had such powerful effect on the masses; the Neo-Confucianist felt that the doer of good enjoyed happiness and the doer of evil suffered from sorrow even if only in his own mind. There was no worship to placate Heaven or to seek favors. The Neo-Confucianist simply paid respect to Heaven, ancestors, and teachers like Confucius, and he performed rites before ancestral altars, not to seek blessings or to supply deceased parents with material needs, but to demonstrate the proper feeling of filial piety and respect. Particular ancestors were often ideal moral examples worthy of emulation. The goal of Neo-Confucianism was the perfectibility of the individual and mankind, and this was the way to serve Heaven.

Chu Hsi's precept for "the investigation of things" leads inevitably to some discussion of the Chinese failure to develop scientific knowledge and technology. The Chinese have contributed to mankind such significant inventions as paper, gunpowder, printing, porcelain, and the compass, but Chinese thinkers have never developed a body of scientific principles. For example, the Neo-Confucianists established their ethereal premises without concern for facts about nature and relationships based on empirical evidence. In the Western world, science and technological advances were the result of man's eagerness to conquer and harness the forces of nature. In China man has sought to live in harmony with nature, and Chinese philosophers have been more concerned with man and with problems of social harmony, the solutions of which were contained in the Confucian Classics. Scientific and technological failures were also related to the nondevelopment of industry beyond the handicraft and household levels of production. The basic self-sufficiency of localities in an agrarian economy and the abundance of manpower worked against the introduction of labor-saving devices; moreover, state monopolies and official restriction of commerce were inimical to the development of private enterprise on a large scale. There were these other reasons as well: China lacked an adequate logical method for testing ideas, education emphasized orthodoxy through memorization, and intellectuals spurned physical experimentation.

3   *The Manchu Conquest and the Coming of the West*

In 1644 China's last dynasty, the Ch'ing, was founded by the Manchus, originally a nomadic people of northeast Asia who had settled in north and central Manchuria, where they formed a number of tribal states having a tribute relationship to the Ming emperors of China. Nuerhachi (1559–1626) united the several tribes under his personal rule and established a bureaucratic administration based on the registration of adult males, about 150,000 strong, into military units called "banners." In 1616 he proclaimed himself emperor of north Manchuria and set up his capital at Mukden. When he died in 1626, he had already laid the foundations of Manchu power, and his descendants ruled as emperors of China for almost three centuries. Nuerhachi and his immediate successor, his ninth son, Abahai, patterned their state after China. They promoted the study of Chinese, hired Chinese officials, and utilized Confucianism to support centralized political authority.

Under Abahai the Manchus pushed into south Manchuria, subjugated Korea, and formed an alliance with the Mongol tribes to protect their western flank. In 1636 Abahai proclaimed the Ta Ch'ing (Great Pure) dynasty, and by the 1640's the Manchus were a threat to the weakened Ming dynasty. China was the scene of widespread rebellion, and in 1644 one of the rebel leaders, Li Tzu-ch'eng, claimed for himself "the mandate of Heaven," marched on Peking, the capital, and seized it. The Ming emperor hung himself as the city fell. At this point a Chinese general, Wu San-kuei, whose father was murdered by Li and whose favorite concubine was given to a rebel officer, joined forces with the Manchus to destroy the usurper. The Manchus drove Li from Peking; but instead of helping to restore the Ming dynasty, they began their own conquest of China. The adherents of the Ming cause fought long and stubbornly, and it was not until 1683 that the Manchus were able to complete the subjugation of the entire country.

The Manchu Political System

All conquerors of China have faced the same problem, namely, how to govern and still maintain their own political, military, and social identity. In other words, how can a dominant alien minority keep from being absorbed or overthrown by China's millions? This problem confronted the Manchus as it had the Mongols (1260–1368) and other conquerors. The Mongols had failed to rule China longer than a century because they had been unable to maintain their power position or win the support of the Chinese gentry and peasants. The Mongols ruled as conquerors, making few concessions to Chinese institutions or the Chinese way of life. They used foreigners in administration, replaced Confucianism with a degenerate form of Buddhism, and generally exploited the country. When their military power declined, their regime collapsed before the challenge of peasant rebellion.

The Manchus succeeeded as rulers of China in large part because they were able to maintain their administrative control and at the same time give prestige and opportunity to Chinese men of ability. The Manchus ruled China in the Chinese way with the co-operation of the Chinese, adding a system of checks to protect their own position. Manchu emperors instituted a series of court reforms to prevent factional struggles for the throne between rival candidates and their supporters. They abolished the designation of crown prince, excluded all princes from civil and military positions, pensioned maternal and matrimonial relatives and barred them from politics, and treated court stewards and eunuchs as domestics only. Under the emperor, as the source of authority, the highest organs of government at the capital were the grand secretariat, established by the Ming dynasty in 1382 as a substitute for the office of first minister, and the grand council, especially introduced by the Manchus in 1729. In the grand council, Manchu officials outnumbered the Chinese by two to one, and membership in the grand secretariat was increased in order to make additional places for Manchus. Later, members of the grand council were simultaneously grand secretaries, and by the late 1700's the office itself was merely an honorary one conferred upon outstanding high officials, its authority having by that time been absorbed by the grand council. The ministerial posts were shared by Manchus and Chinese, but, on the whole, Manchu officials outnumbered their Chinese colleagues by about two to one. Local government, under the direct control of the emperor, remained largely in Chinese hands. The largest units of local government were the provinces, eighteen in number, which were in turn subdivided into circuits, prefectures, and districts. Provincial governors enjoyed a large measure of autonomy so long as their actions did not run completely counter to Peking's general instructions and so long as the appropriate revenues were forwarded to the capital. Associated with the governor in provincial administration were a treasurer; a judge, who considered appeals from prefectural and district courts; a salt commissioner, who controlled both the production and sale of that commodity; a grain commissioner; and a literary chancellor, who supervised the civil service examinations. The officials of the lesser units of local government were subservient to their provincial superiors, and on the lowest level was the village, which continued to be a largely self-governing unit.

The Manchus were careful to exert certain traditional controls over local government, and they added others. In some provinces a new official, the viceroy, acted as a check upon the governor. Both of these officials, who were usually of a different race, had the right to report directly to the throne; and when there were differences of opinion between them, both reported their views to the emperor for his decision. Later most of the provinces were paired, the governor of one being a Manchu, who was also viceroy over the pair. The viceroys were the outstanding figures in the system of local government, and the viceroy of Chihli, in which Peking was located, was generally the most powerful of them all. All officials down to the district magistrate were appointed personally by the emperor in order to inculcate greater loyalty, and all officials were circulated regularly in office, being limited to three to six years in the same post. As they moved to their new posts, they visited the capital, where they were interviewed again by the emperor. No official was permitted to serve in his native province, since it was thought that the claims of family might impair his service; and officials sent to a particular provincial capital were likely to be chosen from various factions in order that each might check upon his colleagues. Censors also kept a constant surveillance over local administration, and both governors and viceroys were associated with the censorate and could perform impeachments, even of each other.

The Manchus won favor with the Chinese scholar-bureaucrats because they were patrons of literature, and this was particularly true of the emperors K'ang Hsi (1662–1722) and Ch'ien Lung (1736–1796), both of whom sponsored enormous projects of criticism and compilation to absorb the energies of Chinese scholars. During Ch'ien Lung's reign, scholars edited the twenty-four dynastic histories and collected all extant Chinese literary works in the great publication, the *Complete Library of the Four Treasuries*, in 3,462 titles. By means of these projects the Manchus were also able to conduct a literary inquisition, one of their objects being to suppress all works that reflected on alien rulers. Some 2,230 works were banned, including studies of military problems, antibarbarian criticism, and items which extolled the Ming dynasty.

The Manchus were careful to preserve their military supremacy over the Chinese. Their central force was organized into eight banners composed of Manchu, Mongol, and Chinese troops, most of which were stationed in a cordon of garrisons around the capital and on the northwest frontier, with the remainder distributed throughout the various provinces under the command of Manchu generals who ranked above the viceroys and governors. Each general was, however, dependent on funds allocated from the provincial treasury by the governor, who had direct command over an additional five or six thousand men in his own home guard. The dynasty tried to make military service more nearly equal in dignity and prestige to the corresponding grades of civil service than had been customary during Chinese dynasties, and thus the Manchu bannermen constituted a hereditary, privileged class. It is difficult to estimate with accuracy the number of Manchus in the banners, but it seems that out of a total of approximately 170,000 adult males the regime selected one-third for duty. With sizable Mongol and later Chinese additions, the banners totaled over 300,000 men in the eighteenth century and thereafter. To help keep order in the provinces, local officials recruited small units of Chinese volunteers, who were nominally under the Manchu provincial commander; this militia force, scattered throughout the provinces, probably numbered about 600,000 men. On the whole, the Manchu emperors pursued a policy of dividing local military power to prevent insurrection against the dynasty, and they constantly shuffled military leaders among the garrisons in the provinces. Yet the result was that the various commands did not cooperate well, and in times of crisis, like rebellion, governors or provincial commanders found it difficult to amass a large force except by recruiting new soldiers. The cost of the over-all military establishment was very great, and it has been estimated that the dynasty spent one-third of its total revenue on the military.

The Manchus were also able to preserve their identity as a separate racial group. They banned intermarriage between Chinese and Manchus, and they fostered different customs between the two races. For example, Manchu women did not bind their feet; Manchus did not engage in commerce or in common labor; and Manchu clan organization was carefully preserved. Manchuria, regarded as a sort of homeland, was for a long time closed to Chinese immigration and remained under special military government. The southernmost part, the territory of Liaotung, became the home province (Shenking) of the dynasty, with Mukden as an auxiliary capital. Except for the southern basin of the Liao River, which was opened to Chinese settlement in the eighteenth century, Manchuria remained sparsely populated until the twentieth century.

The Empire and the Tribute System

During the Ch'ing dynasty the Chinese empire reached its greatest territorial limits. This was the result of a conscious attempt by the Manchus to secure their borders from attack. Mongolia, Tibet, and Chinese Turkestan (Sinkiang) became dependencies of the Manchus, and beyond these territories lay the tribute states, which recognized the overlordship of China.

During the reign of Emperor K'ang Hsi the Manchus were able to impose a colonial administration over the Mongol tribes of the steppe. Peking placed governors and military garrisons at Urga and Kobdo and compelled the Mongol princes to visit and reaffirm their allegiance to the emperor every three years. The vast grasslands of Mongolia were ruled by hereditary princes and their armed retainers, and their subjects were serfs who provided the labor power necessary for the support of the ruling class. The Mongol economy was based largely upon animals—sheep, cattle, horses, camels, and goats. There was some agriculture in the south and east, but crops were limited to barley, oats, summer wheat, millet, buckwheat, and rape. On the whole, the tribal estates of the nobles were self-sufficient, but there was some trade with China. Mongols exchanged wool, camel's hair, and hides for Chinese silk, cotton fabrics, salt, tea, and rice. In religion, many Mongols had been converted to Tibetan Lamaism, others were Moslems, and a large number continued to practice a primitive shamanism. Among the Lamaist Buddhists the living Buddha, or Hutukhtu, who resided at Urga, exerted a kind of spiritual leadership similar to that of the Dalai Lama of Tibet.

The character of Tibetan life and institutions was determined almost completely by religion and geography. Mahayana Buddhism had spread to Tibet in the seventh century and joined with native shamanism to produce Lamaist Buddhism, a syncretic faith emphasizing divination, magic, and the ability

55

to invoke the aid of supernatural beings. Tibetans organized powerful monastic orders, and gradually the clergy was able to supplant secular tribal government with theocratic rule. Over the centuries, however, the monasteries grew lax and corrupt, but midway through the eleventh century a reform movement critical of shamanistic practices and the degeneration of the clergy split the church into two factions. The dominant sect continued to reject the traditional monastic rules of celibacy and abstinence, and not until the fifteenth century did the reformers, known as the Gelugpa, or Virtuous, sect, predominate in the ecclesiastical struggle. This sect produced the Dalai Lama, who resided at Lhasa, as religious and temporal head of the state. It was relatively easy to control the state religion through the monastic hierarchy, but in civil affairs a high degree of local autonomy was granted to tribal leaders because of the nomadic life of the people in the vast, isolated mountain regions. On the slopes of the high plateau, ranging from 14,000 to 20,000 feet above sea level, herders tended their flocks of sheep, goats, and yaks. Topography, poor soil, and cold climate restricted agriculture to a few areas and to crops like wheat, beans, and barley, but, like the Mongols, the people overcame some of their foodstuff deficiencies by trade with China and India. By modern times the population of Tibet was 3,000,000 people, and of this total about one-fourth of the male population were celibate monks. Families generally dedicated one son to the church, and this practice had the unfortunate effect of limiting population, causing a serious shortage of manpower.

The Manchus maintained cordial relations with Tibet so that, through Lamaism, they could more easily control the converted Mongols. As early as the Yuan dynasty, Lamaism had become the religion of many of the Mongol princes. In 1577 Altar Khan, a Mongol ruler, proclaimed the Gelugpa teaching to be the official religion of his people and conferred upon the head of this sect the title of Dalai Lama; and in 1587, when the incumbent died, his reincarnation was found in a Mongol baby. Thereafter the converted Mongols were increasingly involved in Tibetan politics; in 1641, for example, they invaded Tibet to maintain the supremacy of the Dalai Lama. The Manchus sided with the lamas against secular princes who were often allied with the unconverted Mongols, and in 1720 Emperor K'ang Hsi was forced to intervene directly in Tibetan affairs to restore order after a Mongol tribe had deposed the Dalai Lama. The Manchus placed their own candidate in the office and established a protectorate over Tibet, appointing two Manchu resident commissioners to assist the Dalai Lama in foreign and domestic affairs, including the choice of his successor. During the reign of Emperor Ch'ien Lung, when the Dalai Lama displayed too much independence, the Manchus retaliated by strengthening the position of the Panchen Lama at Tashilumpo, for he was second only to the Dalai Lama in the esteem of the Tibetans.

Chinese Turkestan (Sinkiang) was also a protectorate of the Manchus.

The numerous nomadic tribes which inhabited the mountainous areas remained autonomous under the rule of their chiefs, but the agricultural and town population was governed indirectly by China through a local administration modeled on the Chinese provincial system. A Manchu governor was responsible for the transmission of taxes to Peking and for matters of foreign relations, and he had direct control over the Chinese minority, which numbered about 200,000 by the twentieth century. The total population is today about 2,500,000, divided among at least fourteen different races. Racial diversity is so great that Chinese Turkestan has been called a living ethnological museum. The region was economically self-sufficient, and its trade was slight. Wool, long-staple cotton, camel's hair, and some of the exotic ingredients of Chinese medicines like elk horn and bear paws were exchanged for rice, silk, tea, and sugar. In religion the area was divided between Buddhists and Moslems, the latter faith introduced after the year 1000 by Turkish tribes which settled in the west. The Moslems ultimately became more powerful, and they controlled the largest part of the trade.

Until the expansion of European commerce and Christianity in the sixteenth century, China's international relations were largely confined to her neighbors in Asia. In this part of the world China had produced the dominant civilization from which the peripheral states derived much of their culture. From earliest times the Chinese had the attitude that the peripheral peoples were civilized only to the extent that they accepted Chinese ideas and institutions. In the tributary relationship which usually developed between China and her neighbors, Confucian family morality was followed as a guide for the preservation of harmony as decreed by Heaven. The same degree of inequality that existed in the family was true of interstate relations; thus China, the superior "Middle Kingdom," was surrounded by inferior tribute states, which were considered as younger brothers or children. By the beginning of the Ch'ing dynasty these lesser states included Korea, the Liu Ch'iu (Ryukyu) Islands, Annam, Laos, Siam, and Burma. The closer the proximity to China, both geographically and culturally, the more important was the relationship to China; in the case of Korea, for example, China exercised close supervision, but with Burma and Siam the tribute relationship was largely ceremonial. In theory the system was morally justified by China's supremacy and the voluntary submission of the lesser state, but in many cases force was the ultimate sanction, although this, too, was justified on moral grounds, e.g., force was necessary to secure recognition of some new dynasty as truly holding the mandate of Heaven or to chastise some state which had strayed from the proper rules of conduct and had allowed disorder to rise among its people.

The forms which governed the relations between China and the tribute states were not always uniform, but certain common elements can be summarized. The core of the system was the periodic exchange of visits of state

57

envoys. In the case of the lesser states these were regarded as tribute missions, which offered presents and paid homage to the emperor. The imperial audience included the kowtow ($k'o\text{-}t'ou$)—three kneelings and nine prostrations before the emperor—which was considered as nothing more than polite behavior in the circumstances. The frequency of these missions depended on the degree of acculturation and proximity to Peking. In the case of Korea it was yearly or even more often, but at the other extreme, as in the case of Burma or Laos, it was once in ten years. Usually the ruler of a lesser state accepted investiture in office by the Chinese emperor and used the Chinese calendar to date all official documents. Sons of lesser rulers were accepted at the imperial court for their education, and, as a special favor, women of the imperial household were bestowed upon lesser rulers as wives. Finally, the lesser states usually contributed men and supplies to Chinese military expeditions.

The tribute system was also a mechanism of trade and aid. Chinese regimes never regarded foreign commerce as a means of enrichment and consequently never sponsored it. The lesser states, however, did seek trade, and they were willing to pay tribute in return for commercial privileges. The Chinese permitted the tribute missions to bring products for exchange and to purchase goods through Chinese officials; and Chinese merchants and local officials in the areas traversed by the missions were anxious to trade. Viewed in this light, the tribute system can be regarded as a subsidy by the Chinese government in the form of privileges of greater value than the offerings of the lesser states, and it was, in fact, used as an incentive for other areas to come into the Chinese orbit. Beyond the tribute states were the "barbarians," a term which the Chinese used with little discrimination.

The Confucian concept of international relations differed greatly from its counterpart, developing in Europe. As the basis of social order the Confucianists replaced law with rules of proper conduct, sanctioned by social disapproval or shame, which sought to regulate man's inner nature so that actual laws were unnecessary or used minimally. We have seen how the Chinese applied this to international relations in the tribute system, and tributary relations were the only form of international conduct officially recognized by the Chinese. The Chinese developed no concept of the nation-state or of sovereignty. China was the center of a world system lacking competing states or authority. Her control was through ideas, and there was no place for the legal concept of the state or of sovereignty. Chinese thought in terms of international unity based on homogeneity of ideas and culture and not on forced obedience to a common body of law. Relations between China and her vassal states rested on custom, and there was no treaty or agreeement of any sort at the foundation of these relationships. Nor would Chinese accept the idea of the legal equality of nations, for this would imply an equality of virtue which to them was incomprehensible. The Chinese system of international relations was thus sharply at variance with the emerging international law of Europe, and there was little common ground on which relations between China and the Western world could be based.

Relations with the Western World

Relations with the West did not become continuous until the commercial expansion of Europe that followed the voyages of Columbus and the Portuguese navigators. The silk trade with Rome through Near Eastern merchants, the Arab trade along the southern coast, and the revival of trade and the introduction of Christianity during the Yuan dynasty were sidelights in the history of Chinese civilization. But when Portuguese merchants initiated trade with China at Canton in 1514 and established a permanent commercial base at Macao in 1557, the modern impact of the West began. Hardly of great significance at first, it became a determining factor by the nineteenth century. At Macao the Portuguese purchased Chinese silks, wood carvings, porcelain, lacquerware, and gold, and they sold nutmeg, cloves, and mace from the East Indies, sandalwood from Timor, drugs and dyes from Java, and cinnamon, pepper, and ginger from India. It was the profits they earned as carriers and brokers in Asia that sustained the commerce of Portugal and not the sale of European products, for which there was no market in China. While the Portuguese were developing Macao, Chinese merchants at Canton began to press for foreign trade, and they finally persuaded the local authorities to permit the Portuguese to send two ships a year to that city, beginning in 1578. Although the Portuguese expanded the Canton trade in later years, Macao continued to be the more important base for them.

The Dutch and the British ultimately followed the lead of Portugal and destroyed her monopoly in the China trade. In 1604 representatives of the Dutch East India Company arrived at Canton, but the Chinese denied them permission to trade. In 1607 a second mission met with a similar reception, and in 1622 a Dutch naval force attacked Macao but was driven off. The Dutch were able to establish bases first in the Pescadores and by 1624 on the west coast of Formosa. From these points the Dutch attacked Portuguese shipping and maintained an irregular trade with the Chinese mainland. In 1662 Cheng Ch'eng-kung (Koxinga) drove the Dutch from Formosa during his attempt to set up an independent state which would include the Chinese mainland opposite the island. As a reward for their assistance to the Manchus against this rebel, the Dutch were permitted to trade at Amoy, but they soon abandoned the venture since it proved unprofitable. The first British expedition did not reach Canton until 1637, and although it was permitted to exchange a small cargo for food, no permanent foothold was secured. The British, like the Dutch, were forced to trade irregularly along the south China coast. In 1685, after several Dutch missions to Peking, the Manchu emperor opened all Chinese ports to foreign commerce, but by the third decade of the eighteenth century the China trade was centered at Portuguese Macao and more importantly at Canton, where the English, Dutch, and French East India companies maintained factories; in fact, in 1757 the dynasty decreed that all foreign trade would be confined to Canton and Macao. The extent of the trade was about as follows. Figures for 1741 indicate that five British ships called that year with a total displacement of 2,600 tons. They took cargoes of tea, silk, and porcelain. There were also two French and two Dutch ships. By the end of the century the number of British ships had increased to an average of twenty-five a year, but there was no similar increase in Dutch and French activity. Occasionally ships of other nations, like Denmark and Sweden, traded at Canton, and after the American Revolution Yankee ships from Boston, New York, and Philadelphia made the long voyage and returned with silk, tea, and porcelain.

Coincident with the expansion of western Europe by sea was the Russian movement into Siberia following the end of Mongol domination (1237–1480). As the Mongols retreated over the Ural Mountains, the Russians advanced and built a chain of forts. But the first sustained eastward expansion into Siberia did not begin until the reign of Ivan the Terrible (1533–1582), when Cossacks, who lived along the Dnieper River, fled east to avoid czarist oppression. Some of them were employed by the commercial firm of Stroganov, whose charter gave it the right to raise troops and administer justice. In return, the firm agreed to develop the resources of Siberia. At the end of Ivan's reign, the Russian government financed the drive to the east in order to impose a fur tribute on the various tribes, and by the middle of the seventeenth century there was a well-fortified trade route between Moscow and the Lake Baikal region. Active in this advance were hunters and trappers, but of greater importance were large numbers of peasants who continued to seek relief from oppressive government.

The Russian drive ultimately reached the Pacific slope. In 1646 Poyarkov led an expedition down the Amur River and wintered at the mouth of the Ussuri River, and in 1650 the Cossacks founded the frontier fort of Albazin on the upper Amur near the Yaksa River, after the Manchu town on the same site had been attacked and razed. A year later the Cossack leader Khabarov sailed down the Amur from the Shilka River, plundering native villages and exacting tribute as he went. He built a fort at the mouth of the Ussuri River but was forced to abandon it under Manchu attack. When it became clear that the Manchus were determined to defend the Amur region, Khabarov returned to Yakutsk to raise a force of 6,000 men. The Russian government now began to support this adventurer and dispatched 3,000 troops for his use, and border warfare along the Amur was thereafter increasingly common though indecisive. By the 1680's, however, Manchu military strength in this region was appreciably greater.

Meanwhile the Russians were endeavoring to open trade relations with

China. They had sent missions to Peking as early as 1618, but these failed because the Russian envoys refused to acknowledge Chinese superiority by performing the kowtow. Not until 1659 was Peking satisfied with the Russian attitude; after that, tribute was received and gifts were sent to the czar. Relations between the two countries were finally regularized in 1689 by the Treaty of Nerchinsk, which was negotiated with the assistance of the Jesuit fathers, Gerbillon and Periera, as interpreters. The terms of the agreement were as follows: the Amur region boundary was set north of the river, with the Russians excluded fom the area; Albazin was destroyed; extradition of subjects was arranged; and commercial relations were to be in the hands of merchants who were to be provided with official letters by both countries. The exchange of ratifications was effected at Peking in 1693, at which time the Russians also obtained the right to send caravans directly to the Chinese capital. The caravans were to be a royal monopoly, while the border trade was opened to individual Russians.

In the decades that followed, however, Russian-Chinese relations were still characterized by border disputes, particularly in the area of Mongolia, and the trade was not stable. Both sides realized that further agreement was necessary, and after preliminary talks at Peking a draft treaty was approved in 1727 by the Russian envoy at the Mongolian frontier town of Kiakhta. The Treaty of Kiakhta defined the boundary between Siberia and Mongolia except in those places where topographical information was not available; adjusted relations of both China and Russia with the Mongol tribes; permitted commercial caravans every three years to Peking, where a Russian community of two hundred might build a church and maintain a priest, three curates, and several language students; and designated Kiakhta, Selinga, and Nerchinsk as frontier forts where commodities might be exchanged. The caravan trade was never extensive, probably because the long trip—from the border at Kiakhta to Peking—covered 1,100 miles and took 45 days; between 1728 and 1762 only six caravans reached the Chinese capital. According to some sources, the Chinese at times insisted that the caravans halt at Kiakhta. For one reason or another, by the middle of the eighteenth century the Russian-Chinese trade was confined largely to the border and mainly to Kiakhta, where the Russians exchanged furs, leather goods, textiles, cattle, horses, and glassware for Chinese silks, tea, lacquerware, and porcelain. On the whole, commercial relations were satisfactory, although on three occasion—in 1764, 1769, and 1785—the Chinese suspended trade in order to rectify certain misunderstandings.

The Jesuits in China

The only extensive cultural contact between China and the Western world in this period centered upon the efforts of the Jesuits to spread their religion and knowledge in China. One of the founding fathers of the order, Saint

Francis Xavier, followed the expansion of Portuguese power in India, Ceylon, the Indies, and Japan, and he took upon himself the gigantic task of converting the Chinese to Christianity. In 1552 he arrived at Shang-ch'uan, then the center of a small Portuguese trade near Macao, but died before he was able to risk a visit to the mainland. In the two centuries following his death over four hundred Jesuit fathers labored in China to advance the Christian religion. The Jesuit order was convinced that its missionaries had to prove to the Chinese intellectuals that Christian doctrine was, if not superior, at least compatible with the religious and social customs of China. Realizing that the normal means of conversion by preaching among the masses would not be effective in a country with an advanced culture like China, the order instructed its missionaries to work from the ruler and bureaucracy down by undermining the Chinese intellectual tradition.

Matteo Ricci and Michael Ruggerius were the first of many priests who impressed the Chinese with their abilities as scholars of both Chinese and Western culture. In 1582 they were permitted to reside in Canton, and twenty years later Ricci made his way to Peking, where he served the dynasty in various capacities. His knowledge of mathematics and astronomy was of great value to the Ming bureaucracy. When at last he ventured to discuss religious matters, he argued that Christian tenets were supported by the moral principles of Confucianism. Although he did not win large numbers of converts, Ricci did gain the respect and admiration of Chinese intellectuals. His successors, priests like Schall, Verbiest, and Gerbillon, continued to be useful agents of the Ming and Manchu emperors as technicians, tutors, and diplomatic agents. Jesuit fathers helped the Chinese cast their first cannon, and they were instrumental in negotiating the first Chinese treaty with Russia. They were not offensive in the propagation of Christianity, and slowly a church took form. By the eighteenth century they had converted over 300,000 to their faith.

The Jesuits' accommodation to Confucianism led to controversies with other Catholic orders and to the ultimate proscription of the faith in China. The most famous of these disputes was the "rites controversy," in which the compatibility of the Chinese practice of ancestor worship with Christianity was at issue. The Jesuit order held that ancestor worship was only a civil rite, intended to preserve the continuity of family tradition; but its opponents, the Dominicans and Franciscans, were convinced that it was a heathen religious ceremony, incompatible with Christianity. From 1645, when the question was referred to the pope for his decision, one argument and refutation followed another until 1745, when the pope, under pressure from the other orders, ruled against the Jesuits.

Emperor K'ang Hsi's patience was tried by this bickering and by the insolence of the papal legates who appeared from time to time at his court. He supported the Jesuit position, but after his death his successor proscribed the activities of missionaries in China. This ban, the papal decision against the Jesuits in 1742, and the dissolution of the order in 1773 led to the decline of Christianity in China. But more important, the Jesuit experiment in bringing European cultural influence to bear upon China ended in complete failure. Jesuit scholars acquainted their Chinese colleagues with the best of Western learning but with no effective results. For almost a century following the papal decision there was no intellectual contact between China and the West.

It was in this period—from the mid-eighteenth to the mid-nineteenth centuries—that the Western world began to be transformed by a series of "revolutions" in agriculture, industry, and transportation which provided it with an unprecedented technological superiority over China. This fundamental difference ultimately altered the basis of China's relations with the Western powers; moreover, it was one of the roots of many of modern China's most important problems.

Bibliographical Notes

There are many bibliographies of works concerning China, but perhaps the most comprehensive is Yuan Tung-li, *China in Western Literature* (New Haven: Yale University Press, 1958), which is a continuation of Henri Cordier, *Bibliotheca Sinica* (Paris: E. Guilmoto, second edition, 1904–1908), and the supplement to it published at Paris in 1924. Of special value to students are Charles O. Hucker, *Chinese History: A Bibliographic Review* (Washington: Service Center for Teachers of History, American Historical Association, 1958), and L. C. Goodrich, *A Syllabus of the History of Chinese Civilization and Culture* (New York: China Society of America, sixth edition, revised, 1958). The most comprehensive annual bibliography, especially with regard to periodical literature, is published by the *Journal of Asian Studies* (formerly the *Far Eastern Quarterly*).

The best works on China's geography are George B. Cressey, *China's Geographic Foundations: A Survey of the Land and Its People* (New York: McGraw-Hill, 1934), and his more recent *Land of the 500 Million: A Geography of China* (New York: McGraw-Hill, 1955). Important also is Albert Hermann, *Historical and Commercial Atlas of China* (Cambridge, Mass.: Harvard University Press, 1935).

There are a number of good general histories of China. The most detailed, although in need of revision, is Kenneth Scott Latourette, *The Chinese: Their History and Culture* (New York: Macmillan, third edition, revised, 1946), and the best for the premodernization period is Edwin O. Reischauer and John K. Fairbank, *East Asia: The Great Tradition* (Boston: Houghton Mifflin, 1960).

C. P. Fitzgerald, *China: A Short Cultural History* (London: Cresset Press, revised edition, 1950), is uneven but contains excellent essays on Chinese thought, literature, and art. L. C. Goodrich, *A Short History of the Chinese People* (New York: Harper & Bros., third edition revised, 1959), treats in detail the period from the end of the Han dynasty to the founding of the T'ang dynasty and includes information regarding China's material development. Although it describes many colorful incidents, René Grousset, *The Rise and Splendour of the Chinese Empire* (Berkeley: University of California Press, 1953; translated by A. Watson-Gandy and T. Gordon), is quite superficial. *China*, edited by H. F. MacNair (Berkeley: University of California Press, 1946), is a collection of essays by specialists on all phases of China's development as well as her history; and *Chinese Social History*, edited and translated by E-tu Zen Sun and John De Francis (Washington: American Council of Learned Societies, 1956), contains twenty-five essays by modern Chinese scholars covering the period from the Chou dynasty to the Ch'ing dynasty.

There are a number of stimulating and provocative works that have had varying degrees of influence in the field of Chinese studies. Owen Lattimore, *Inner Asian Frontiers of China* (New York: American Geographical Society, second edition, 1951), analyzes the formation and development of Chinese society in terms of relationships with its nomadic neighbors. Karl A. Wittfogel has outlined his views in many articles, but his *Oriental Despotism: A Comparative Study of Total Power* (New Haven: Yale University Press, 1957), is the most complete statement of his theory of "hydraulic society" and bureaucratic despotism. Chi Ch'ao-t'ing, *Key Economic Areas in Chinese History* (London: Allen & Unwin, 1936), describes water-control measures and the shift of China's economic center from the north to the south. Wolfram Eberhard, *History of China* (Berkeley: University of California Press, 1950; translated by E. W. Dickes), presents a sociological interpretation emphasizing the continuity of gentry domination, and his *Conquerors and Rulers* (Leiden: E. J. Brill, 1952) is highly critical of Wittfogel's thesis.

Li Chi, *The Beginnings of Chinese Civilization* (Seattle: University of Washington Press, 1957), surveys the origins of the Chinese people with an emphasis on anthropological features, and Cheng Te-kun, *Archaeology in China* (Cambridge, Eng.: Heffer, 1959), is the best work in its field.

Among the more important early historical sources, the *Book of History* (*Shu Ching*) has been translated by James Legge in volumes three and four of his *The Chinese Classics* (Oxford: Clarendon Press, eight volumes, second revised edition, 1893–1895) and by Bernhard Karlgren, *The Book of Documents* (Stockholm: Museum of Far Eastern Antiquities, 1950). Legge also translated the *Spring and Autumn Annals* (*Ch'un Ch'iu*) and the detailed commentary, *Tso Chuan*, in volumes seven and eight of *The Chinese Classics*. Arthur Waley, *The Book of Songs* (London: Allen & Unwin, 1937), is a fine translation of the classical anthology of poetry (*Shih Ching*). The Annals of Ssu-ma Ch'ien's *Shih Chi*, the standard early Chinese work on the Chou period, has been translated by Édouard Chavannes in *Les mémoires historiques de Se-ma Ts'ien* (Paris, five volumes, 1895–1905). A critical study of the historical work of Ssu-ma Ch'ien is Burton Watson, *Ssu-ma Ch'ien, Grand Historian of China* (New York: Columbia University Press, 1958).

The most readable and comprehensive survey of China's early history, in the Shang and Chou dynasties, is Herrlee G. Creel, *The Birth of China* (New York: F. Ungar, reissued in 1954). A stimulating analysis based on a sociological interpretation of early literary remains is Marcel Granet, *Chinese Civilization* (New York: Barnes & Noble, 1951; translated by Kathleen E. Innes and Mabel R. Brailsford). Derk Bodde, "Feudalism in China," in *Feudalism in History*, edited by Rushton Coulborn (Princeton: Princeton University Press, 1956), is the most satisfactory description of a controversial subject; and Richard L. Walker, *The Multi-State System of Ancient China* (Hamden, Conn.: Shoe String Press, 1953), describes the relations between the various Chou states. Derk Bodde, *China's First Unifier* (Leiden: E. J. Brill, 1938), and his *Statesman, Patriot, and General in Ancient China* (New Haven: American Oriental Society, 1940), present studies of four key figures in the Ch'in dynasty. H. H. Dubs, *History of the Former Han Dynasty*, of which three of the five projected volumes have been published (Baltimore: Waverly Press, 1938–1955), is a translation of Pan Ku's *Ch'ien Han Shu*. Nancy Lee Swann, *Pan Chao, Foremost Woman Scholar of China* (New York: Century, 1932), provides an account of the family of Pan Ku. Her *Food and Money in Ancient China* (Princeton: Princeton University Press, 1950) is a carefully annotated translation of the treatise on economics in *Ch'ien Han Shu*. C. Martin Wilbur, *Slavery in China during the Former Han Dynasty* (Chicago: Field Museum of Natural History, 1943), is a useful study in socioeconomic history. Hans Bielenstein, *The Restoration of the Han Dynasty* (Stockholm: Museum of Far Eastern Antiquities, two volumes, 1954–1959), analyzes the political impact of peasant discontent caused by natural calamities.

E. R. Hughes and K. Hughes, *Religion in China* (London and New York: Hutchinson's University Library, 1950), and Karl L. Reichelt, *Religion in Chinese Garment* (New York: Philosophical Library, 1951; translated by Joseph Tetlie), are surveys that include descriptions of early religious practices; and Lewis Hodous, *Folkways in China* (London: Arthur Probsthain, 1929), is the best introduction to popular religion.

The most comprehensive and detailed work on Chinese philosophy, including political theory, is Fung Yu-lan, *History of Chinese Philosophy* (Princeton: Princeton University Press, two volumes, 1952–1953; translated and edited by Derk Bodde). Of the shorter works, Fung Yu-lan, *A Short History of Chinese Philosophy* (New York: Macmillan, 1948; translated and edited by Derk Bodde), provides the best coverage, but Herrlee G. Creel, *Chinese Thought from Confucius to Mao Tse-tung* (Chicago: University of Chicago Press, 1953), although more selective, is more analytical and readable. Lin Mousheng, *Men and Ideas: An Informal History of Chinese Political Thought* (New York: John Day, 1942), is a satisfactory popular survey of fifteen influential thinkers and statesmen. Arthur Waley, *Three Ways of Thought in Ancient China* (London: Allen & Unwin, 1939, and New York: Doubleday, paperback, 1956), is an excellent introduction to Mencius, Chuang Tzu, and Legalism. *Sources of the Chinese Tradition* (New York: Columbia University Press, 1960), compiled by W. T. de

65

Bary and others, is a useful collection of readings with an emphasis on intellectual history.

S. Kaizuka, *Confucius* (London: Allen & Unwin, 1956; translated by Geoffry Bownas), and *Wisdom of Confucius* (New York: Modern Library, 1943; translated and edited by Lin Yutang), are conventional accounts, while Herrlee G. Creel, *Confucius, The Man and The Myth* (New York: John Day, 1949), is more analytical but controversial. There are numerous translations of the sayings of Confucius, but Arthur Waley, *The Analects of Confucius* (London: Allen & Unwin, 1938), is by far the best. The *Book of Mencius* is translated, along with an account of his life, in the second volume of Legge's *The Chinese Classics*. Hsun Tzu has been translated by H. H. Dubs in *The Works of Hsuntze* (London: Arthur Probsthain, 1927), and Dubs has also analyzed his thought in *Hsuntze, The Moulder of Ancient Confucianism* (London: Arthur Probsthain, 1928). The best introduction to early Taoism is Arthur Waley's translation, *The Way and Its Power: A Study of the Tao Te Ching and Its Place in Chinese Thought* (London: Allen & Unwin, 1934, and New York: Grove Press, paperback, 1958). *Wisdom of Laotse* (New York: Modern Library, 1948) is a good standard work. A translation of *Chuang Tzu* is included in James Legge, "The Texts of Taoism," Volumes 39 and 40 of *Sacred Books of the East* (Oxford: Clarendon Press, 1891; edited by Max Muller), and in *Chuang Tzu, Mystic, Moralist, and Social Reformer* (London: B. Quaritch, second edition, revised, 1926; translated by Herbert A. Giles). Holmes Welch, *The Parting of the Way: Lao Tzu and the Taoist Movement* (Boston: Beacon Press, 1957), is an interesting recent contribution. J. J. L. Duyvendak, *The Book of Lord Shang: A Classic of the Chinese School of Law* (London: Arthur Probsthain, 1928), and W. K. Liao, *The Complete Works of Han Fei Tzu*—only Volume 1 of which has been published (London: Arthur Probsthain, 1939)—are translations of important Legalist works.

The political development of the Chinese empire is surveyed in Paul Linebarger, Djang Chu, and Ardath Burks, *Far Eastern Government and Politics, China and Japan* (Princeton: Van Nostrand, second edition, 1956). Important detailed studies include Woodbridge Bingham, *The Founding of the T'ang Dynasty: The Fall of the Sui and the Rise of the T'ang* (Baltimore: Waverly Press, 1941), Edwin G. Pulleyblank, *The Background to the Rebellion of An Lu-shan* (London: Oxford University Press, 1955), E. A. Kracke, *Civil Service in Early Sung China, 906–1067* (Cambridge, Mass.: Harvard University Press, 1953), and James T. C. Liu, *Reform in Sung China* (Cambridge, Mass.: Harvard University Press, 1959). Yang Lien-sheng, *Money and Credit in China: A Short History* (Cambridge, Mass.: Harvard University Press, 1952), and Harold J. Wiens, *China's March toward the Tropics* (Hamden, Conn.: Shoe String Press, 1954), are both excellent studies.

An interesting and valuable approach to the T'ang and Sung dynasties is through the following biographical studies: C. P. Fitzgerald, *Son of Heaven: A Biography of Li Shih-min, Founder of the T'ang Dynasty* (Cambridge, Eng.: Cambridge University Press, 1933); C. P. Fitzgerald, *The Empress Wu*—a concubine who usurped the throne in 682 and ruled for twenty years (Melbourne:

Australian National University, 1955); Arthur Waley, *The Poetry and Career of Li Po, 701–762* (London: Allen & Unwin, 1950); Arthur Waley, *The Life and Times of Po Chu-i, 772–846* (New York: Macmillan, 1949); William Hung, *Tu Fu, China's Greatest Poet* (Cambridge, Mass.: Harvard University Press, two volumes, 1952); Howard S. Levy, *Biography of Huang Ch'ao*—a rebel leader during the T'ang dynasty (Berkeley: University of California Press, 1955); Edwin O. Reischauer, *Ennin's Diary* and *Ennin's Travels in T'ang China*—concerning the wandering of a Japanese monk from 838 to 847 (New York: Ronald Press, 1955); H. R. Williamson, *Wang An-shih, A Chinese Statesman and Educationalist of the Sung Dynasty* (London: Arthur Probsthain, two volumes, 1935–1937); and Lin Yutang, *The Gay Genius: The Life and Times of Su Tung-po*—the eminent poet who opposed the reforms of Wang An-shih (New York: John Day, 1947).

Charles Eliot, *Hinduism and Buddhism, An Historical Sketch* (New York: Barnes & Noble, three volumes, 1954), is a good introduction to the origins and development of Buddhism in India and its spread to China. A. F. Herold, *The Life of Buddha, According to the Legends of Ancient India* (Rutland, Vt.: Charles Tuttle, 1954), and *The Path of the Buddha* (New York: Ronald Press, 1956; edited by Kenneth M. Morgan), are also useful in this regard. *Buddhist Texts through the Ages* (New York: Philosophical Library, 1954; edited by Edward Conze), and J. Takakusu, *The Essentials of Buddhist Philosophy* (South Pasadena: Perkins, second edition, 1949), are valuable as introductions to the doctrinal aspects of the religion. *The Teachings of the Compassionate Buddha* (New York: New American Library, 1955; edited by E. A. Burtt), is an adequate popular work. Edward Conze, *Buddhism, Its Essence and Development* (New York: Philosophical Library, 1951), is an excellent brief survey, and Arthur F. Wright, *Buddhism in Chinese History* (Stanford: Stanford University Press, 1960), is the best analysis of the historical and intellectual development of the religion in China. René Grousset, *In the Footsteps of the Buddha* (New York: Barnes & Noble, 1932), provides an account of a Chinese who traveled overland to India in search of religious truth.

In the field of intellectual history there are a number of important symposia: *Studies in Chinese Thought* (Chicago: University of Chicago Press, 1953; edited by Arthur F. Wright); *Chinese Thought and Institutions* (Chicago: University of Chicago Press, 1957; edited by John K. Fairbank); *Confucianism in Action* (Stanford: Stanford University Press, 1959; edited by David Nivison and Arthur F. Wright); and *The Confucian Persuasion* (Stanford: Stanford University Press, 1960; edited by Arthur F. Wright). The thought of Chu Hsi has been analyzed by J. P. Bruce in *Chu Hsi and His Masters* (London: Arthur Probsthain, 1923), and *The Philosophy of Human Nature by Chu Hsi* (London: Arthur Probsthain, 1922). A new contribution is Carsun Chang, *The Development of Neo-Confucian Thought* (New York: Bookman Associates, 1957). The scientific development of China is the subject of an ambitious project, Joseph Needham, *Science and Civilization in China,* of which three of the projected seven volumes have been published (Cambridge, Eng.: Cambridge University Press, 1954–1959). Of special interest is T. F. Carter, *The Invention of Printing in China and Its Spread Westward* (New York: Ronald Press, 1955; revised by L. C. Goodrich).

There are three useful reference works in the field of Chinese literature: J. R. Hightower, *Topics in Chinese Literature: Outlines and Bibliographies* (Cambridge, Mass.: Harvard University Press, revised edition, 1953); Martha Davidson, *A List of Published Translations from Chinese into English, French, and German: Literature, Exclusive of Poetry* (Washington: American Council of Learned Societies, 1952); and Martha Davidson, *A List of Published Translations from Chinese into English, French, and German: Poetry* (Washington: American Council of Learned Societies, 1957). Among prose translations, the following are useful in understanding Chinese life and attitudes: *All Men Are Brothers* (New York: John Day, 1933, and New York: Grove Press, 1957; translated by Pearl Buck); *Chin P'ing Mei* (New York: G. P. Putnam's Sons, 1940), an expurgated edition of the love saga; *The Golden Lotus* (London: G. Routledge, four volumes, 1939; translated by Clement Egerton); *Monkey* (New York: John Day, 1943, and New York: Grove Press, paperback, 1958; translated by Arthur Waley); *Dream of the Red Chamber* (New York: Twayne, revised edition, 1958; translated by Wang Chi-chen); *Famous Chinese Short Stories* (New York: John Day, 1952, and New York: Pocket Books, 1952; translated by Lin Yutang); and *Traditional Chinese Tales* (New York: Columbia University Press, 1944; translated by Wang Chi-chen). Two good introductions to Chinese poetry are Arthur Waley, *Translations from the Chinese* (New York: Alfred A. Knopf, 1941), and Robert Payne, *The White Pony* (New York: John Day, 1947).

Chinese art is best surveyed and illustrated by Laurence Sickman and Alexander Soper, *The Art and Architecture of China* (Baltimore: Penguin Books, 1956). Of interest also is William Willets, *Chinese Art* (Pelican Books, two volumes, 1958). The best of the shorter surveys are Hugo Munsterberg, *Short History of Chinese Art* (New York: Philosophical Library, 1949), and Dagny Carter, *Four Thousand Years of Chinese Art* (New York: Ronald Press, 1948).

Karl A. Wittfogel and Feng Chia-sheng, *History of Chinese Society, Liao (907–1125)* (Philadelphia: American Philosophical Library, 1949), includes an analysis of the nomad problem as well as a complete description of a "barbarian" dynasty. Michael Prawdin, *The Mongol Empire: Its Rise and Legacy* (London: Allen & Unwin, 1940; translated by Eden and Cedar Paul), is the best short work in its field, and B. Vladimirstov, *Genghis Khan* (Paris: Maisonneuve, 1948), and H. D. Martin, *The Rise of Chinghis Khan and His Conquest of North China* (Baltimore: Johns Hopkins Press, 1950), are useful. Although there is no general survey of the Yuan dynasty, Sung Lien, *Economic Structure of the Yuan Dynasty* (Cambridge, Mass.: Harvard University Press, 1956; translated by H. F. Schurmann), is an excellent contribution from the economic side. The most authoritative work on Marco Polo is Henry Yule, *The Book of Ser Marco Polo* (London: John Murray, third edition revised by Henri Cordier, two volumes, 1921), but there are many other translations available, including those of Marsden (1948), Komroff (1933), and Benedetto and Ricci (1931). Henry H. Hart, *Venetian Adventurer* (Stanford: Stanford University Press, third edition,

1947), makes interesting comparisons between Europe and China. The basic work on the Manchu conquest is Franz Michael, *The Origin of Manchu Rule in China* (Baltimore: Johns Hopkins Press, 1942). *Eminent Chinese of the Ch'ing Period (1644–1912)* (Washington: Government Printing Office, two volumes, 1943–1944; edited by A. W. Hummel), is the most important reference work for the period. L. C. Goodrich, *The Literary Inquisition of Ch'ien Lung* (Baltimore: Waverly Press, 1935), is a description of one aspect of Manchu rule.

The best general short survey of China's early contacts with the West is G. F. Hudson, *Europe and China: A Survey of Their Relations from the Earliest Times to 1800* (London: John Murray, 1930). More specialized works include C. R. Boxer's *Fidalgos in the Far East, 1550–1770* (The Hague: Martinus Nijhoff 1948) and Chang T'ien-tse, *Sino-Portuguese Trade from 1514 to 1644* (Leiden: E. J. Brill, 1934). Gaston Cahen, *Some Early Russo-Chinese Relations, 1689–1703* (Shanghai: "The National Review" Office, 1914; translated and edited by W. Sheldon Ridge), can be supplemented by several surveys, including Ch'eng T'ien-fang, *A History of Sino-Russian Relations* (Washington: Public Affairs Press, 1957), and David Dallin, *The Rise of Russia in Asia* (New Haven: Yale University Press, 1949). The impact of the Jesuits on China is evaluated by A. H. Rowbotham, *Missionary and Mandarin: The Jesuits at the Court of China* (Berkeley: University of California Press, 1942), and *China in the Sixteenth Century: The Journals of Matteo Ricci, 1583–1610* (New York: Random House, 1953; translated by Louis J. Gallagher) provides a firsthand account. The problem of Japanese piracy in China during the Ming dynasty is described in Wang I-t'ung, *Official Relations between China and Japan, 1368–1549* (Cambridge, Mass.: Harvard University Press, 1953).

The Traditional Society of Japan

The history of traditional Japanese society is significantly different from that of China. In making comparisons between the two countries, one must always keep this basic conclusion in mind, especially when one is considering the way in which each responded to the impact of the West in recent times; for they entered the modern period, with its central theme of Westernization, from completely different points of departure.

The long period of Japanese feudalism which preceded the impact of the West in the nineteenth century is perhaps the most important feature that distinguishes the development of Japanese society from that of China. Japanese feudalism had its origins in the transformation of tribalism into a fixed territorial political order that resulted from the adoption of settled agriculture following the introduction of rice cultivation and iron implements from China during the early centuries of the Christian era. An attempt (the Taika Reform) during the seventh and eighth centuries to create a centralized imperial political and economic system on the model of T'ang dynasty China postponed the emergence of a feudal order for several centuries, but its ultimate failure was almost inevitable.

The period of the Kamakura shogunate (1192–1333) represents the first stage of Japanese feudalism, since the bulk of the land came under the control of a military power structure, separate from the imperial system and based upon the personal loyalty of vassals to one lord, the shogun. But unlike European feudalism, there was no concept of the fief; instead the vassal was usually rewarded by rights to a percentage of the agricultural production of small manors. During the several centuries of warfare that followed the collapse of the Kamakura shogunate, the emergence of great territorial lords,

70

or daimyo, *with their own vassals, and, at least for part of this period, the bestowal of fiefs, characterized what may be called the second stage of Japanese feudalism. Not until the establishment of the Tokugawa shogunate in 1603 was the suzerainty of a single lord (the shogun) returned to a firm and lasting footing. The period of the Tokugawa shogunate (1603–1868), with its long duration of peace, may be regarded as the third stage of Japanese feudalism, in which the transition to a nation-state was already under way.*

4   *The Origins of Japanese Civilization*

A complete scientific determination of the origins of the Japanese people has yet to be made, but it is evident that the early inhabitants of Japan were a mixture of races, including Mongoloids from northeast Asia and the Ainu, a primitive proto-Caucasoid group, some descendants of which still live in parts of Hokkaido and on the islands to the north. Migrations from the Malay world may also have occurred, but the evidence for this, drawn largely from the field of comparative mythology, is disputed. An alternative theory for the influence of a "southern strain" in the formation of the Japanese people emphasizes the diffusion of racial elements from southern China. In any event, it is clear that the dominant racial strains were those from northeast Asia. From the Ainu the Japanese have derived their tendency to have more body and facial hair than their Asian neighbors, and the possible existence of a "southern strain" may explain why they are generally shorter in stature.

Early Japanese Society

Only a few Paleolithic artifacts have been found. Neolithic remains are, however, numerous and date back to as early as 5000 B.C. This Neolithic culture, like its counterparts throughout the world, was based largely on hunting and fishing and in its later stages included a primitive agriculture. The typical dwelling, a shallow pit covered by a high thatched roof, was probably occupied by a single family—already an important social unit within the tribal organization. There was some trade between tribes, particularly in ornaments made from obsidian and jade, many of which were used in shamanistic rites.

This early Neolithic culture, called *jomon** by the archeologists, was overwhelmed in a series of invasions by a mainland people called *yayoi,*† whose

---

* In reference to the rope pattern on the hand-molded pottery that is typical of this culture.

† In reference to a street in Tokyo where the first site of this culture was discovered. The term is used to designate a kind of wheel-made pottery which lacks the surface design of **jomon** pottery.

culture was very similar to the Neolithic cultures of Manchuria, Korea, and the Maritime Province. In the first century of the Christian era the last of these invaders brought bronze and iron to Japan. The people of Japan continued to hunt and fish, but by this time there was much greater emphasis on agriculture, particularly irrigated-field rice cultivation, introduced from China. Since this crop gave rise to permanent settlements, property assumed a new importance, and tribal leaders set about annexing land and increasing their labor forces. Over a period of time there appeared a class of landowners who effectively controlled large tracts. The old society based on co-operative organization gave way to one marked by class distinctions based on property. Most important of all, the tribe gave way to smaller units, called *uji*, which were communities formed of a number of households. The head or chieftain of the uji was usually the most powerful family head among a group of landowners who, for purposes of solidarity, claimed common ancestry. Leadership was hereditary. Each chieftain was, moreover, the priest in charge of the uji guardian or god.

Each uji was essentially a self-contained unit, and the people were organized corporatively by households according to their hereditary occupations. The corporation was, for the uji, family, or person who controlled it, an important form of property, especially when it was engaged in making some valuable product or its members were skilled in some essential craft. The most common corporations were those composed of agricultural workers and owned by uji chieftains and other landowners. However, some corporations enjoyed substantial autonomy under their own hereditary leaders; the head of the corporation of arms, for example, rivaled the uji chieftains in power. Some corporations were later national in scale, like the Imibe, the imperial ritualists, who had dependent branches which furnished them clothing, food, and other requirements.

Through aggrandizement three uji became more powerful than the others, one in northern Kyushu, another in the area around Izumo (in the modern prefecture of Shimane), and a third in the area of Yamato (the modern prefecture of Nara). Each of these uji often sent missions to Korea and China, superior centers of culture, to increase its own strength. In fact, much of our knowledge of early Japan is derived from Chinese sources. By the end of the fourth century Yamato began to establish its hegemony over the other uji, and its chieftain ultimately became the emperor of a more unified state. He served also as high priest, since his uji god became the most important national deity. A number of uji chieftains and heads of corporations served as central and local officials of the imperial court, and because their positions were hereditary they tended to constitute an aristocracy.

The creation of the imperial Japanese state is described in the first "histories" of Japan, the *Kojiki*, dated 712 A.D., and the *Nihongi*, dated 720. Both are works based on oral tradition, and only the facts after the year 500 A.D.

are considered to be accurately recorded. According to these early chronicles, all objects, both animate and inanimate, were the offspring of the gods. For example, from the union of the god Izanagi and the goddess Izanami were born the islands of Japan. Other gods and goddesses were the progenitors of the Japanese people. It is claimed that the sun goddess, Amaterasu, sent her grandson from heaven to pacify the people and establish a divine rule; as tokens of his ancestry, he was given a mirror representing the sun, a jewel representing the moon, and a sword representing lightning, and these have remained to this day the imperial regalia of Japan. His great-grandson completed the subjugation of the country and founded the Yamato supremacy in 660 B.C. This mythical account of the origins of Japan and the imperial family may reflect historical events, but the dating and details are pure fabrication. The importance of the myth lay in its providing a religious foundation for the position of the Japanese emperor and the important court officials, both of which had their origin in the uji system. For this reason the early chronicles placed great emphasis on divine birth. All of the powerful families claimed descent from the gods.

Shinto

The religion of the ancient Japanese was for the most part a simple worship of the power of nature, but there were also elements of shamanism and ancestor worship. Later, after the introduction of Buddhism, the conglomeration of early religious practices and beliefs was given the name Shinto, the "way of the gods." The Japanese, living in an agricultural society richly endowed by nature, did not approach religion in fear but with love and gratitude, and their religious rites were designed more to praise and thank than to placate particular gods. For example, the food god, Inari, was considered a beneficent deity, and his festivals were usually gay and joyous. The manifestations of nature, great and small, were thought of as harboring a divine presence, but there were no anthropomorphic forms. And demons of disease and calamity were for the most part obscure and nameless.

Fertility rites were important in Shinto. Agricultural fertility rites reached their climax in the harvest, and the autumn thanksgiving was the great religious festival. Human fertility rites were practiced to guarantee family continuity, and phallic symbols were worshipped as aids to procreation. As a corollary, growth and life were regarded as good, decay and death as bad.

Shinto, however, did not have a moral code, and there was no idea of a soul or recognition of a future state beyond life. Great emphasis was placed on ritual and personal cleanliness, a trait still common to the people of Japan. Since unclean people could not participate in religious observances, it was general practice to bathe and put on fresh clothing on such occasions. Much later, symbolic forms were substituted for this cleansing. Menstruation, sexual intercourse, and childbirth were regarded as defiling, not morally, but from the standpoint of ritual uncleanliness, and the pollution had to be removed before a man or woman could resume his normal place in the life of the community. After a death, houses were often burned, and when an emperor died, a new palace had to be built.

Worship was generally communal and at first took place at natural sites, but later simple shrines were constructed. Prayers and offerings of food and drink or even war booty, such as the heads of enemies, were devoted to the deities concerned. Special liturgies were recited by priests, who also served as mediums for the transmission of messages from the gods and even from the ruler. When an individual wanted to consult the gods for his own private purposes, he had recourse to women who acted as shamans; in fact, religious power was the quality most valued in women. Eventually, pilgrimages to famous shrines became common practice, at least for the wealthy.

The cult of the sun goddess, ancestress of the imperial family, was organized and supported by the state. Amaterasu became the chief deity of the nature-worshippers and the ancestor-worshippers, and she came to be regarded as the dispenser of fertility, both human and agricultural. The emperor was regarded as a high priest, and the very word for government, *matsurigoto*, meant "religious matters." The center of the cult of the sun goddess was at Ise, where the shrine has been rebuilt almost every twenty years throughout the course of Japanese history. Some of the most important of the court families functioned as hereditary liturgists, diviners, and abstainers; the Nakatomi, for example, recited twice a year the "Great Purification Prayer," calling upon the gods to cleanse the people from the pollution that they had accumulated, and the Imibe engaged in abstention rites, particularly the observance of taboos, on behalf of the entire country in order to maintain the ceremonial purity of worship.

The Impact of Chinese Culture

By the latter half of the sixth century A.D., after the unification of China by the Sui dynasty and the founding of the cosmopolitan T'ang dynasty, Japan was increasingly influenced by the superior civilization of the mainland. Buddhism, introduced from Korea, paved the way for the introduction of all things Chinese; and students, teachers, craftsmen, and monks, passing back and forth between the mainland and Japan, were a constant source of useful knowledge for change.

The introduction of things Chinese was not unattended by difficulties, as is illustrated by the struggle between the Soga and the imperial family. The Soga family, which had acted as champions of the Buddhist faith, had gradually emerged as a political force comparable to the imperial family, over which it exercised great influence. Among those who were fearful of this development was the imperial prince, Shotoku (573–621), who propagated a philosophy of exclusive rule by the emperor and bolstered it with Shinto and Buddhist doctrines. In spite of Shotoku's efforts, the Soga virtually dominated the imperial court until 645, but in that year they were overthrown by Shotoku's son, Prince Naka no Oe, and the head of the family of Shinto ritualists, Nakatomi Kamatari, who under the new surname of Fujiwara, given in reward for his assistance, became the founder of a line of courtiers that later completely dominated the imperial court. The victors immediately set about establishing a state in which the authority of the imperial family over the land and its people was unquestioned.

The Taika Reform, dating from the year 645 and implemented during the course of the following century, was the attempt in Japan to create a centralized state on the model of T'ang dynasty China. The reformers sought to effect a redistribution of political and economic power in favor of the central government of the imperial family. In accordance with Chinese principle, they nationalized all land in the name of the emperor in order to terminate the uji system and to establish the basis for a national tax system.

The political content of the reform emphasized centralization of the administrative structure. Within the central government the supreme organ under the emperor was the council of state (*dajokan*), below which was a series of eight administrative departments with an official hierarchy based on titles and corresponding privileges, while in the rural areas the uji chieftains were replaced by officials more directly responsible to the emperor. The country was divided into provinces and districts ruled by governors and magistrates who derived their power from the central regime. Their basic functions were to keep the peace, collect taxes, and recruit labor for the *corvée*. The lowest administrative unit was the township of fifty families under a headman responsible to the district magistrate, and at this level law and order were enforced by the Chinese system of family-group responsibility.

The economic content of the reform emphasized the systematization of landholding by actual cultivators. The imperial government allotted land to peasant households according to the number of members in each one and on a scale adjusted for sex, age, and status, a distinction being made between freemen, serfs, and slaves; adjustments were to be made every five years for changes in the size of families. The owner-cultivators were responsible for the payment of a land tax, regarded as a rent payable in rice; a labor tax, especially dreaded when it took the form of military service, which deprived the family of labor; and a produce tax, levied on nonagricultural products.

In both the political and economic realms the Taika Reform had to be modified to suit Japanese circumstances. The fact that Japan was dominated by a hereditary aristocracy forced important alterations which ultimately caused the collapse of the entire system. From the beginning, the Chinese practice of selecting officials on the basis of merit through examination gave way in Japan to aristocratic privilege. The emperor continued to reign by right of divine birth, not by virtue; and in an edict of 682 the imperial court stated bluntly that in selecting men for office the considerations were to be, first, birth, then character, and lastly ability. Thus the old aristocracy was appointed to new offices of status and authority. On the economic side, the large landholdings of the uji chieftains were perpetuated for the most part. In some cases this was the price paid for their support of the reform; in other cases, particularly when they became officials in the central and local administrations, they kept their lands as income for service and as gifts for rank. These landholdings were usually tax-exempt and became in fact manors (*shoen*)—outside the system of local administration—which were worked by serfs subject to the authority of the resident owner or managers. Later, when the political power of the imperial court declined, these units, the manors, provided the economic basis for the first stage of Japanese feudalism.

The Nara Period

The center of Japan's centralized imperial system was the city of Nara, the first permanent capital. The so-called "Nara period" lasted from 710, when the city was built on the model of the great T'ang dynasty capital of Ch'ang-an, to 794, when the seat of the emperor's government was moved to the nearby site of Kyoto, where there was river transportation to the sea. The politics of the central administration in this period were characterized by constant intrigue among the Buddhist clergy and important aristocratic families for the purpose of dominating the emperor. Quarrels over succession to the throne reflected the ambitions of rival factions representing the claims of various imperial princes. There was no fixed law of succession, and the murder of individual princes was common. Emperors themselves, finding the responsibilities of office dangerous as well as time-consuming in ritual activities, began to retire to Buddhist monasteries for safety and privacy and in some cases sought to exercise power from behind the scenes. In the rural areas the manors began to encroach upon state or imperial lands and upon the lands of each other.

Not only were Chinese institutions introduced and adapted by the Japanese, but the philosophic foundations of much of Chinese society were absorbed as well. Confucianism became part of the heritage of the educated Japanese, and over the centuries its doctrines permeated various aspects of Japanese life. Modifications had to be made with regard to the divinity of the emperor and the hereditary position of important families in Japanese society, but the emphasis upon family was welcomed. In fact, one of the earliest Chinese works to be studied at Nara was the *Classic of Filial Piety*. Familism was already part of Shinto, at least in the sense that the people held religious ceremonies for the spirits of the dead, but it was Confucian doctrine that defined the concepts of ancestor worship and the obligations of individuals within the family group.

By the time of the Nara period, Buddhism had become the religion of the emperor and the court aristocrats. Korean and Chinese missionaries first instructed the Japanese, and in turn scores of converts went to China to learn more of the new faith, which raised questions well beyond the simple frames of reference of the various Shinto cults. Returning from the continent, these Japanese student monks took the lead in transmitting to Japan the various Mahayana tenets and many other aspects of Chinese civilization. Because of the tendency among the Nara sects to emphasize Buddhism's philosophical aspects and because there was no missionary effort made to win large numbers of converts, the common man was little touched by the new religion. Even the imperial court aristocracy was, in the beginning, more interested in the organizational and ritual side of the religion, but it soon began to understand fundamental principles and to appreciate the emphasis upon mercy and compassion. Sir George Sansom has noted that the Buddhist concept of change was not very different from the Japanese sense of the transitory nature of the very things they most admired—beauty, splendor, and power.

During the Nara period Buddhism became the state religion of Japan. It was regarded as a new and powerful influence which could protect the state and people, particularly from disease. Buddhist ritual became part of imperial court ceremonials, and in the year 749 the emperor declared that the laws of Buddhism and the imperial laws were to be regarded as identical. The emperor and the court aristocrats sponsored the construction of temples in Nara and in the provinces, and they gave monasteries tax-free lands and large numbers of sustenance households for their support. These endowments usually were made to honor parents, living and dead; less important people dedicated images or made votive offerings.

An excellent example of the relationship between state and church was the building of the huge temple, the Todaiji of the powerful Kegon sect. Following a smallpox epidemic in the year 735, the Emperor Shomu decided to support the casting of a large image of the Buddha Roshana, the central deity of the Kegon sect. In its idealistic metaphysics, Kegon conceived of Roshana as the universal Buddha, the basis of cosmological harmony, of which Gotama was only a manifestation. As a Buddha of infinite compassion, the heart of Roshana remains unsatisfied so long as one human fails to realize his eternal love, the spark of which exists in even the worst sinner.

After a few false starts, the casting began in 747, with the emperor himself in attendance. The image, finished in 749, is negligible as a work of art, but its scale is tremendous. The Japanese claim that it is the largest bronze statue in the world. The 53-foot image of Roshana, estimated to weigh over 500 tons, sits on a throne of 56 lotus petals 65 feet in diameter. Originally it was gilded, but over the centuries the coat has worn and the image now displays the richness of the bronze. The Todaiji, which houses the statue, was built several decades later on a scale fitting the intention that the temple serve as the administrative hub of a network of provincial monasteries. The present great hall is 284 feet long, 166 feet wide, and 152 feet high, but at this it is only two-thirds the size of the original structure, which burned in the twelfth century.

Buddhism also began to absorb certain elements of Shinto in the Nara period, but the process of reconciliation was not completed until much later. The relationship between Shinto and Buddhism at this time can be seen in a story associated with the casting of the image of Roshana. According to the historical chronicles, Hachiman, the Shinto war deity, delivered an oracle promising to assist in the casting and to urge other Shinto deities to join in this endeavor. He also expressed a wish to visit Nara, so an escort of soldiers brought his emblems to the capital from Beppu, on the island of Kyushu. These were installed in a special shrine at the Todaiji, where forty Buddhist monks recited prayers for seven days. Thereafter Hachiman was regarded as a protector of Buddhism, and in one nearby shrine he was actually represented as a Buddhist monk.

The Imperial Court at Kyoto

The growing power of the Buddhist clergy was one of the reasons for the transfer of the capital from Nara to Kyoto, which was also modeled on Ch'ang-an. A symmetrical city, it was a rectangle three and a half by three miles, at the center of which stood the imperial palace, measuring one mile by three-quarters of a mile. Around the palace stood the mansions and offices of the various court aristocrats, and beyond, in the countryside and on the mountainsides, were the shrines and temples. Kyoto was soon a thriving city with a population of almost 500,000 people.

At Kyoto the central government underwent several important changes. A new administrative system replaced the old one, which had grown too cumbersome. Many old offices had lost their authority and existed only in the hereditary titles associated with them. But perhaps the chief reason behind most of the administrative changes was the attempt by the Fujiwara family, descended from Nakatomi Kamatari, to consolidate its control over the emperor.

The Fujiwara had for some time advanced its interests through marriage with the imperial family; in fact, Fujiwara grandfathers were often the regents of boy emperors. From the end of the Nara period on, more and more offices and land fell into the hands of this powerful family, and at Kyoto the office of *kampaku* (chief adviser to the emperor), which developed out of the Fujiwara regency, became the highest office in the state. It was, in effect, a dictatorship exercised by the head of this family, which not only thus dominated politics, but men and women of Fujiwara lineage were also the leading scholars, poets, writers, and artists of their day. Many of them owned tax-exempt manors, and the most powerful among them were, in addition, political protectors of other manors in return for a share of the manors' produce. Since the emperor had the right of confiscation, the power and influence of the Fujiwara family worked like an insurance policy.

Until the end of the twelfth century Kyoto was the cultural center of Japan. During this so-called "Heian period" (795–1185) one of the world's most highly developed aesthetic societies emerged at the imperial court, and artistic and intellectual abilities determined social prominence. Women achieved a status never again equaled in Japanese history, some of them becoming the greatest literary figures of their day. Court life is delightfully described in Lady Murasaki's famous early-eleventh-century novel, *Tale of Genji*, which is typical of a great number of romantic works of fiction that circulated among the court aristocrats. Although it is largely a story of amorous adventure, Confucian and Buddhist influences are important. Family status and relationships are emphasized, and the entire plot is dominated by a sense of the impermanence of human life and social position. All phenomena seemed to the authoress to be an illusion seen best in the transitory beauty of nature and love. Much of Japanese poetry of this era gives the same feeling. However, the *Tale of Genji* and Japanese poetry present another, not so pleasant, picture of a society grown effeminate and devoted almost exclusively to the pursuit of aesthetic and sensual pleasures. This degeneration, which worsened in the next century, was, of course, a factor that contributed greatly to the ultimate transfer of political power from the imperial court to new strong forces originating in the rural manors.

In Buddhism two important new sects were founded in the ninth century. The Tendai sect, its doctrines derived from the T'ien T'ai sect of China, was established by the monk Saicho (767–822). Eclectic like its Chinese counterpart, it could, by its very comprehensiveness, gain ground at the expense of the more rigid sects. This characteristic of strength was, at the same time, a source of weakness, since many adherents broke away and founded new sects of their own; in fact, Tendai gave birth to most of the later forms of Japanese Buddhism. The monk Kukai (774–835), better known by his canonical title of Kobo Daishi, founded the Shingon sect. Derived from Indian and Chinese sources, Shingon was the cult of Dainichi, an eternal Buddha, present everywhere and in everything, from which all other Buddhas emanated. Shingon had its ethical side, but its main emphasis was on magic, particularly incantations, through which the believer could understand the spiritual unity of the universe.

The creation of the Tendai and Shingon sects accelerated the movement by which Shinto deities were reconciled with Buddhist divinities. Earlier it had been common to regard Shinto gods as protectors of Buddhas; now the process of amalgamation was encouraged, and it ended, by the close of the tenth century, in Dual (Ryobu) Shinto. The two religions were believed to be different forms of the same faith, and Shinto deities were regarded as local manifestations of supreme Buddhist gods. For example, according to Shingon doctrine, all gods were manifestations of Dainichi and could thus be invoked by acts of worship. It was commonly believed that the two religions operated on two levels: local and familiar, and universal and supreme. With the development of Ryobu Shinto the native shrines were taken over by Buddhist monks and lost much of their original character. Even so, among the common people the Shinto cults continued to be more important than Buddhism, and a popular form of Buddhism was not developed for several centuries.

5 *Japanese Feudalism to 1603*

The growth in the number of manors undermined the attempt by the imperial court aristocracy in the Taika Reform to adopt Chinese political and economic institutions and ultimately caused a basic shift in the power structure. Although the modified Chinese system worked effectively for a long span of time, there were simply too many forces at work transforming Japanese society. Topography also made it difficult for the central regime to maintain effective control over the rural areas; and since rural life offered none of the refinements that could be enjoyed at Kyoto, many provincial governors increasingly delegated their powers and responsibilities to local subordinates. Important local families and Buddhist temples were always hungry for land and ready to seize it by force. They were also willing to bring new land under cultivation so long as the incentive of tax-exemption was maintained. At court the Fujiwara generally condoned these actions so long as they received their share of revenues as political patrons or protectors. When the peasant owner-cultivators, living on the dwindling area of state land, felt that the burden of increased taxes was too much to bear, many of them fled to the northern frontier areas, won in battle from the retreating remnants of the Ainu (in the vicinity of the modern city of Sendai and beyond), or commended themselves and their land to manors. In this way they were able to avoid taxes and gain protection, but in the process they became serfs. At times the central government tried to check the growth of manors through edict, but it was unable to support law with force. Consequently, by the end of the twelfth century, state land, or tax-paying land, amounted to only 10 per cent or less of the total cultivated area. In these circumstances, provinces and districts became meaningless units of administration. Locally, power was in the hands of the owners and managers of the manors.

The Rise of the Rural Warrior Aristocracy

Although the manorial system of Japan was not uniform throughout the country, some generalizations can be made regarding it. In contrast with western Europe, the fields of manors were usually scattered and in no way corresponded to village units; moreover, there was a greater discrepancy in their size. Japanese manors varied from a few acres to huge landholdings of several tens of thousands of acres spread over more than one province, and manors owned by a single family were often widely separated. But in all cases the manors provided the basic economic support of the various classes or social groups in Japanese society. The peasants who worked the land as serfs received a mere subsistence share of the land's production. The surplus that remained belonged to the owner—a powerful local family, a court aristocrat, or a monastery; but, if he was an absentee owner and lived at Kyoto, a certain percentage of his revenue went to the estate managers. The remaining shareholders in the productivity of the manor were its patrons, usually a member of the Fujiwara family at the imperial court and a powerful neighbor in the countryside. As this system became more formalized, individuals within each social group had legal rights, called *shiki*, which entitled them to a fixed proportion of the manor's produce. And, with the exception of peasants, they could hold shiki of more than one type and in more than one manor. Shiki, moreover, could be inherited by women and freely divided since there was no rule of primogeniture.

The continuing expansion in the number and size of manors gave rise to a rural aristocracy—the resident owners and managers who actually controlled the land. Many of them were descendants of the old uji chieftains, some were offshoots of the imperial court who sought to utilize service in provincial administration for their own advantage, and a few were even descendants of imperial princes who founded new families with new surnames. But in each instance they actually remained or settled on landholdings and, over the years, extended them. Others came from lesser families whose heads served as district magistrates and were thus in a good position to promote their own interests, since administrative powers were often delegated to them by absentee provincial governors. In a third category were the managers of manors owned by absentee court aristocrats; this group often gained control of the land at the expense of apathetic owners who were satisfied as long as

81

they received their share of the production. Finally, there were the military commanders of the troops that fought the remnants of the Ainu in the north and in return received grants of tax-exempt land.

The new rural aristocracy also became dominant militarily. The Taika Reform established at least on paper an elaborate peasant conscript army on the principle that all males between the ages of twenty and sixty were subject to call; however, the system required conscripts to furnish their own weapons, equipment, and food without any relief from the regular tax burden. Under these conditions it proved impossible to maintain an army, and the whole scheme was abandoned in 739. Those military posts that had been created in government became sinecures, generally filled by effeminate court aristocrats. In the campaigns against the Ainu the government used volunteer forces recruited largely from among the rural aristocrats, who had become mounted warriors for purposes of self-defense and aggrandizement. In fact, in the next century even the capital guards were recruited from the same source. Over the next several centuries rural military power continued to grow beyond the needs of the campaigns against the Ainu, and, with the collapse of the system of imperial administration, the responsibility for the preservation of order in the rural areas fell to leaders of coalitions of warriors.

Alliances were formed by warriors of a number of manors in the same locality or by warriors of a kinship group, and in both cases a kind of feudal relationship between leader, or lord, and his retainers, or *samurai* (literally, "one who serves"), began to develop. The relationship was of mutual benefit —the samurai rewarded for loyal service to his lord—but it never became one that was contractual or legal. Instead it was based on an idealized ethic which was in recent times given the name *bushido*, or "way of the warrior." The most important principle was loyalty to one's lord, even to the extreme sacrifice of following him to death in battle. Courage was of course greatly admired, and the warrior's word was supposed to be sacred and irrevocable, but this ideal was often not matched in reality, since spying and treachery were common characteristics of warfare. The basic sanction of the warrior ethic was a sense of honor which caused each man to protect his family name from shame. Important in this respect was the need to remain calm and self-possessed and to keep passion and emotion under rigorous control. The warrior enjoyed special legal and ceremonial rights; for example, he was entitled to regain honor or to atone for criminal actions through *harakiri*, a kind of ceremonial suicide in which the warrior drove a knife or short sword into his abdomen and then into his heart.

With the increasing militarization of Japanese life, women lost much of the practical equality that they had enjoyed earlier. Women of warrior families were taught to sacrifice their own interests for their men, whether father, husband, or son, and chastity became a pre-eminent virtue, respected above life itself, so that its violation was a sufficient reason for their suicide.

By the twelfth century two great competitive alliance systems existed among the rural manors, both headed by families—the Taira and the Minamoto—which traced their origins back to younger imperial princes who had settled on the land in the eastern provinces. In both cases family power increased as new branches were established in various localities, and the alliance system, held together by a community of interest and by strong bonds of loyalty, was also extended to include neighbors who swore allegiance to the family leader. Thus the Taira and Minamoto each came to control the military forces of hundreds of manors.

For a long time the Fujiwara were able to maintain a balance of power by throwing what strength they had to one side or the other, but by the twelfth century they were dependent upon Taira and Minamoto forces for the protection of Kyoto against the raids of warrior-priests. The manors of temples and monasteries had their own armies, which resisted any efforts of the central government to curtail their growth.

Struggles between the Taira and the Minamoto and the Collapse of the Fujiwara Supremacy

Two short military struggles caused the collapse of the Fujiwara supremacy and the establishment of warrior domination of the imperial court. The first was precipitated in 1156 by a personal power conflict between Sutoku, who had reigned briefly and retired, and the Emperor Go Shirakawa, his younger brother. Each was supported by factions of the Fujiwara and by a mixture of Taira and Minamoto forces. Sutoku's cause was backed by a group of Taira and Minamoto warriors, headed by Minamoto Tameyoshi; and Go Shirakawa counted upon the assistance of a band led by Taira Kiyomori and which included Minamoto Yoshitomo, the son and heir of the opposition leader. In the fighting, which involved only a small number of men, Kiyomori's forces were victorious and imposed a harsh settlement upon the vanquished. Sutoku was exiled, and a number of the enemy warriors were executed, including Kiyomori's uncle and Yoshitomo's father.

Fighting broke out again in 1159, when the warriors on the winning side fell out because of jealousies growing out of the division of the spoils of victory. And once again the Fujiwara split into factions supporting the leaders of the two opposing camps—Minamoto Yoshitomo and Taira Kiyomori. Initially Yoshitomo got the upper hand after a successful *coup d'état* at Kyoto during Kiyomori's temporary absence. But in the end the head of the Taira crushed his enemies and established his own personal dominance over the imperial court. Yoshitomo and four of his sons did not survive the fighting; of the four sons that remained, the eldest, Yoritomo, twelve years of age, was exiled to the Izu Peninsula, far to the east, while the other three were permitted to enter monasteries to be trained for monkhood.

83

The period from 1160 to 1181 was dominated by the Taira family under the leadership of Kiyomori. Although he left most of the high offices at the imperial court in the hands of the Fujiwara, he managed them as he wanted from behind the scenes. And like the Fujiwara, he married off a daughter to the emperor, and in 1180 his grandson, Antoku, came to the throne. Kiyomori knew well that power was in reality based on the number of manors and warriors that he could control. Consequently, he secured title from the imperial court to a great number of manors, particularly those in the Inland Sea area, and over these he placed *jito*, or stewards, appointed from among his warriors, to guarantee his family's share of produce. But he was unable to control the manors of the great temples and monasteries in the capital region or of the remaining warrior cliques in other distant rural areas.

The rule of the Taira was arbitrary and severe, and over a period of time the family alienated many of its former allies. Discontent led to several conspiracies against Kiyomori, but in each case they failed. In 1180, for example, Prince Mochihito, second son of the retired emperor, Go Shirakawa, whom Kiyomori had passed over in preference to Antoku, sought to form an alliance with the exiled Minamoto Yoritomo, but the plot was discovered and Mochihito was killed. Yoritomo, however, was successful in rallying many families of Minamoto and even Taira descent against Kiyomori, so much so, in fact, that in the following year, when Kiyomori died, his last order to his sons was that no tomb or temple be erected to his memory until Yoritomo's head had been placed upon his grave.

The revolt of Yoritomo ultimately destroyed the Taira. In his exile on the Izu Peninsula, Yoritomo had made a friend of his jailer, Hojo Tokimasa. In fact, he married the daughter of this new ally and with his help began to form an alliance against the Taira. By 1180, when Yoritomo could count on 25,000 warrior followers, drawn largely from the Kanto Plain, he was joined by his monastery-trained brother, Yoshitsune, who proved to be an extremely capable military leader. He also profited from an uprising led by an ambitious cousin, Kiso Yoshinaka, who had no great love for Yoritomo but saw an opportunity to act independently for his own gain. Thus the fighting became a three-cornered struggle between Yoritomo, Yoshinaka, and the heirs of Kiyomori. In 1183 Yoshinaka gained control of Kyoto, and the Taira fled with the boy emperor to the Inland Sea area, their base of power. In 1184 Yoritomo's forces, under the command of Yoshitsune, crushed Yoshinaka and proceeded to march west to destroy the remnants of the Taira. The last battle of the campaign took place at Dan no Ura at the narrow strait that separates Honshu from Kyushu. Here the Taira forces were annihilated, and the young emperor, just eight years of age, drowned.

Minamoto Yoritomo was now supreme in Japan. The story of the rise and fall of the Taira, as told in the *Heike Monogatari* (*Tale of the Taira Family*), ends as follows: "The things of life are impermanent. One battle follows another, the glories of this world pass quickly away, and all in life is vain and precarious."

The Kamakura Shogunate (1192–1333)

Yoritomo proceeded to consolidate the victory his forces had won on the battlefield. First, to strengthen his personal position, he killed off the members of his own family, including his brother-in-arms, Yoshitsune, who was hunted down as a fugitive and finally died in 1188. And, second, he set about acquiring control of as many manors and warriors as possible. He confiscated the manors of the defeated Taira and granted many of them to his warrior retainers, but those that the Taira had seized during their tenure in power were returned to their rightful owners. Yoritomo also succeeded in getting warriors other than those who were already his retainers to swear allegiance to him. Thus he managed to create a private power structure that was essentially feudal, the initial stage of Japanese feudalism, since it was based on the personal loyalty of vassals to one lord.

Yoritomo's efforts to consolidate power can be seen more concretely in his appointment, from among his retainers, of *jito* (stewards) and *shugo* (constables) throughout most of the manors and provinces of Japan. He appointed jito, to be supported by their own shiki (legal rights to a share of the manor's produce) in almost all of the manors; they performed administrative duties, such as maintaining law and order and judging disputes, and guaranteed payment of the proper share of produce to the owner, in many cases still imperial court aristocrats, and to the other shiki-holders. The jito also collected a small military tax levied by Yoritomo, but this had a greater symbolic than economic significance. The shugo's function was to supervise all of Yoritomo's retainers in an entire province, to maintain law and order among them, and to mobilize them in time of war. Both of these posts became hereditary, and the manors that the jito and shugo controlled began to take on some aspects of fiefs, despite the fact that these officials did not own them. The importance of the system lay of course in the fact that Yoritomo achieved a unified control over the manors and provinces of the country. Its effectiveness varied from area to area, and religious manors were exempted from the system and remained tax-free; but in the important area between Kyoto and Kamakura, Yoritomo's headquarters, organization was strong.

Yoritomo was compelled to define his position vis-à-vis the imperial court, which remained theoretically the source of political power. In 1192 he forced the emperor to make him shogun, or generalissimo, a title that had been conferred on the commanders of the campaigns against the Ainu. This step gave a legitimacy to what had been essentially a private political-military system, for at Kamakura Yoritomo had established what were, for all practical purposes, the organs of a central administration. He had selected this site as his headquarters in order to avoid what he regarded as the debilitating environment of Kyoto and because it was more convenient for overseeing his retainers.

The new military administration of the shogunate at Kamakura came to be known as the *bakufu* (literally "tent government"), a term that was later applied to other feudal governments in Japan. The Kamakura bakufu was composed of several central committees whose basic function was to supervise the complicated land and personal relations of Japanese society. The *mandokoro* was the equivalent of a central policy-making body as well as a board of taxation and treasury. The *samurai dokoro* was responsible for matters concerning the vassals of Yoritomo, such as duties, promotion, rewards, and punishments. Although both committees relied upon consensus for decisions, members of the Hojo family, allied to Yoritomo by his marriage to Tokimasa's daughter, were prominent in both. Lastly, the *monchujo* acted as a court of final decision for suits concerned with land and shiki rights that could not be settled locally by the jito or shugo; its records indicate that it was extremely impartial and provided justice for all. In fact, the bakufu protected the shiki of absentee owners of manors and maintained the collection of imperial taxes on the remaining small area of public land.

Yoritomo died in 1199 at the age of fifty-three, when he was thrown from his horse. In a romantic interpretation of his death, it is claimed that his mount was frightened by the ghosts of Antoku and Yoshitsune. Yoritomo stands out as one of the great figures in Japanese history, and for later generations he embodied the warrior spirit, with its virtues of loyalty, truth, courage, and frugality. But he was cruel and relentless in the destruction of his family, driven as he was by the desire to guarantee the succession of his own sons.

In this he was circumvented after death by his benefactor, Hojo Tokimasa. Each of Yoritomo's two sons lost power to his grandfather as regent; and in 1219, when the Minamoto line failed, the Hojo family set up a Fujiwara baby as a puppet shogun. The only serious challenge to the dominance of the Hojo was led by the retired emperor, Go Toba, who assembled a force of warriors, recruited for the most part from his own imperial manors. But this imperial "rebellion" was quickly put down and actually helped to confirm the power of the Hojo. In fact, although continuing to show great respect for the imperial throne, the Hojo regents maintained a close military control over Kyoto. Their supremacy, which endured for over a hundred years (until 1333), was based upon domination of a series of puppet shoguns (after 1252 chosen from among imperial princes), just as the Fujiwara family had formerly ruled by controlling the emperors.

Popular Buddhism

The decline of the imperial court aristocracy, which had tended to foster Buddhism as an aesthetic cult, paved the way for the development of that religion as a popular faith. The conditions attending the rise of the warrior aristocracy, particularly the disorder and suffering caused by warfare, produced religious leaders who attempted to revive spiritual values. Monks like Kuya (d. 972) and Genshin (942–1017) preached that faith was the only method of salvation. They repudiated the emphases upon philosophic exercise and morality and insisted that faith in Amida's grace was all-sufficient. As Sir George Sansom has written, "Relying upon the strength of another, the believer who desires salvation has only to invoke the name of Amida in simple faith, and then he will be born again in that Western Paradise, the Pure Land, there to attain that enlightenment which by his own efforts he could not reach." This belief in the efficacy of faith was at first accepted by all the sects, but only in relation to other, more important doctrines. Later, distinct Amidaist sects were established, with exclusive emphasis upon salvation through grace.

Jodo (Pure Land), the first Amidaist sect, was founded by the monk Honen Shonin (1133–1212), who preached belief in the mere repetition of the name of Amida, without doubt of his mercy, as the way to achieve salvation. This simple belief opened salvation to all Japanese, since faith was the only essential; and rebirth in paradise (the Pure Land) instead of nirvana became the most important goal of such faith. The monk Shinran (1173–1262), a disciple of Honen, carried these ideas to their logical extreme when he founded the sect of Jodo Shinshu (True Pure Land). He maintained that *one* sincere invocation of Amida's name was sufficient to secure salvation; all further repetitions were merely praise of him. In recognition of Amida's grace, Shinran urged his followers to pursue an ordinary life, since monkhood and celibacy were only evidence of a lack of trust in Amida, and he himself set an example when he married and produced six children. These two sects— Jodo and Jodo Shinshu—remained the strongest in numbers of believers through subsequent Japanese history; in recent times they have claimed over fifteen million adherents.

The founding of the Hokke (Lotus) sect by the monk Nichiren (1222–1282) is another example of the Japanization of Buddhism. Nichiren held that Buddhism was something national and not merely individual. He identified it with national prosperity, relating the spiritual welfare of the Japanese people as a whole to the nation's material fortunes. Like the Amidaists, who cited scriptures predicting that Gotama's teachings would lose their power two thousand years after his death, he believed that the world had fallen upon degenerate days—and there was sufficient evidence that man's depravity was beginning to make itself felt in society. Again like the Amidaists, he felt that the Japanese needed a simple method of worship in order to bring about a revival of spiritual values. He urged the suppression of all other Buddhist sects, arguing that the *Lotus Sutra* was the sole basis of true Buddhism because it emphasized the three forms of Buddha: the universal in Dainichi, the savior in Amida, and the historical in Gotama. Nichiren reduced the essentials of salvation to the simple utterance of the invocation of the *Lotus Sutra*, "Namu myoho renge kyo" ("Homage to the scripture of the lotus of the good law"). Nichiren wanted to establish a Holy See in Japan, for he felt that he was divinely appointed by the universal Buddha to save the nation. The *Lotus Sutra* was to be the means by which Buddhism would enter a new age of faith, and he, Nichiren, was a bodhisattva, reborn to preach the truth. Because of his fanaticism, Nichiren was a menace to the existing sects, and he was a nuisance to the Kamakura authorities, who exiled him from time to time. However, he did win many converts and gained a momentary prestige when a loose prediction regarding a foreign conquest seemed substantiated by the first Mongol invasion; the bakufu consulted him, but, when he urged that the nation adopt his religion, his advice was rejected and he lived the remainder of his life as a hermit. While the Amidaists secularized Buddhism, Nichiren gave it a nationalistic bias that it had not had before.

The third new development in Japanese Buddhism was the founding of the Zen sects. Like Ch'an, its Chinese source, Zen held that enlightenment comes only through direct, intuitive perception. Unlike the Pure Land and Lotus sects, which stressed the need for complete faith in something beyond oneself, Zen insisted that everyone has a Buddha nature and, to realize it, need only look within himself. Zen masters claimed that religious truth cannot be explained by words and that each individual must find his own salvation; the masters could, however, assist the neophyte monk by asking him to meditate upon paradoxical questions or statements called *koan* in an attempt to exclude all logical thought from his mind. Enlightenment was to be experienced intuitively, not reasoned out logically. Masters might also try to jolt the learner into sudden enlightenment by shouting or by a physical blow, but such practices unfortunately led in some cases to simple charlatanry.

The Zen sect Rinzai, brought from China in 1191 by the monk Eisai, stressed *koan*; the Soto sect, introduced by the monk Dogen in 1227, emphasized "sitting in meditation" (*zazen*), a slower, more gradual achievement of enlightenment. As an extreme reaction to the heavy philosophical emphases of some of the Buddhist sects and to the emotionalism of Amidaism, Zen was particularly attractive to the warriors of Japan. It had a simple, practical code of ethics, and it imparted vigorous self-discipline and self-reliance. As in China, Zen had a great influence on art, particularly painting, and in the life of the people generally Zen has given special form to the tea ceremony and to flower arrangement and landscape gardening. Today, in numbers of adherents, Rinzai and Soto rank next to the Amidaist sects.

The Rise of the Great Territorial Lords (Daimyo)

During the Kamakura shogunate Japan suffered invasions by the Mongols. After his conquest of China, Khubilai sent an envoy to Japan (1268) to suggest that the Japanese engage in friendly intercourse with the mainland or face the threat of war. When the Japanese ignored his request, Khubilai sent a series of menacing dispatches, all of which the Japanese refused to answer. In 1274 the Mongols attempted to invade Japan with an expedition of 450 ships and close to 30,000 Mongol troops and Korean auxiliaries. They landed on the western coast of Kyushu and encountered the resistance of the local lords and stewards. After an initial Mongol victory, a great storm swept over the area and destroyed the expeditionary force. Losses were estimated at almost 13,000 men. Later in the same year the Mongols sent six envoys to Japan, and on this occasion the Japanese beheaded them.

Since another Mongol invasion attempt was anticipated, the Japanese continued to strengthen the defenses in the west. In 1281 the Mongols sent their second expedition, and this time it was much larger, comprising two fleets of 150,000 soldiers. After a fifty-day battle, during which the issue was still in doubt, a storm again destroyed the Mongol force. It has been estimated that approximately two-thirds of the Mongol troops were casualties. The Japanese believed their successes were due to the intervention of the gods, and they called these decisive storms "divine winds" (*kamikaze*). Japan was safe, but the menace of invasion lasted until 1300, and defense preparations continued.

The Mongol invasions had an important impact on feudal society under the shogunate because they strained the resources of an economy already seriously dislocated by the development of trade and the growth of a merchant class. Most warriors lived on fixed incomes derived from the sale of agricultural produce, but with the expansion of both domestic and foreign trade the price levels of most commodities rose more than the price of rice and other grains.

Over a period of time many warriors became indebted to brokers and moneylenders and were increasingly forced to mortgage their shiki, or rights to shares of production. As early as 1232 and increasingly thereafter, the Kamakura bakufu issued edicts, known as "acts of grace," which decreed maximum interest rates or a partial cancellation of debts. In the decree of 1297 the bakufu canceled personal loans, prohibited the transfer of shiki, and ordered those that had been transferred to be restored to their original owners unless there had been official approval. In the end, however, these edicts proved to be unworkable, and the condition of warrior indebtedness remained. After the Mongol invasions, moreover, the bakufu found itself faced with claims from vassals and others who demanded rewards for their services and compensation for losses. Lacking the spoils of warfare, the bakufu could not meet these demands. Lastly, since there was no primogeniture, the warrior class was impoverished through the constant division of shiki. In the end, the unity of Kamakura feudalism was broken as a number of warrior aristocrats, largely shugo and jito, emerged as local lords with vassals pledging loyalty and service to them in return for economic assistance and protection.

In these circumstances the imperial court and some of these new local feudal lords allied in order to effect a readjustment of political and economic power in their own interests. They were encouraged to act because the bakufu was controlled by men like the regent Takatoki, who indulged in extremes of luxury and debauchery which offended even his own vassals. After some initial failures, the forces of the retired emperor, Go Daigo, and his allies captured Kamakura in 1333 and destroyed it by fire. Takatoki and two hundred of his followers killed themselves rather than surrender. For the next three years, Go Daigo attempted to restore the effectiveness of imperial rule, but this civil restoration could hardly succeed in face of Japanese militarism.

In 1335 Ashikaga Takauji, a bakufu general who had gone over to Go Daigo, and Nitta Yoshisada, who had destroyed Kamakura, fell into conflict. Yoshisada had the support of the court, but he was defeated by Takauji, who in 1336 established a puppet emperor on the throne at Kyoto. Go Daigo fled to Yoshino, in the mountains to the south, and set up a separate court. In 1338 Takauji had himself appointed shogun in an effort to reunify the country under his personal rule, much like Minamoto Yoritomo before him, but he and his successors were never able to establish effective control over the local military lords. In fact, from 1336 to 1392, when Japan had two emperors and two imperial courts, there was constant warfare between the local military lords in support of each camp. Under this cover the struggle was actually a series of local skirmishes in which these local lords strove to enhance their own power.

In 1392 the imperial line at Yoshino failed, and the court was reunited under the protection of the Ashikaga family, the head of which was reconfirmed as shogun. The power of the Ashikaga, however, was never comparable to that of its Minamoto and Hojo predecessors because they had to bargain with local lords for support. Although their effective rule was confined to their domains around Kamakura, as individuals the shoguns lived at Kyoto in a style of elegance and refinement comparable to that of the old Fujiwara. They continued to hold their title until 1573, but their power declined to a point where it was only nominal.

Local warfare, which continued into the fifteenth century, gave rise to the second stage of Japanese feudalism. It caused the destruction of the manorial system with its shiki and the creation, in turn, of large contiguous territorial domains, called *han*. The Ashikaga were unable to impose the rigid discipline of the Kamakura bakufu, and local lords struggled to control directly as much land as possible. And the emperor and his court, suffering from the loss of shiki, were reduced at times to extreme poverty.

The fortunes of local lords rose and fell with great rapidity, and the successful ones, who seized direct control of great tracts of land and ignored shiki, became territorial lords, called *daimyo* ("great name"). They divided part of their landholdings among vassals, or samurai, of different levels of rank. Thus the feudal relationship between daimyo and samurai depended upon bestowal of a fief. But, in actual fighting, large bodies of foot soldiers replaced the individual samurai as the fighting unit. Military leaders were still mounted warriors with armor, but armies were recruited largely from the peasantry. This circumstance provided a kind of social mobility that had not existed before, and in the fifteenth and sixteenth centuries many a samurai came from humble origins. Lastly, primogeniture became the rule, at least to the extent that any son, natural or adopted, could be designated as full heir. This was important because it prevented constant division of landholdings over a period of time and enabled families to consolidate the economic basis of their power.

During this slow process of land amalgamation, which involved the disappearance of the manor, the agricultural village became the basic administrative and economic unit in the several hundred han. The castle town of the daimyo was the local center of political power, but the villages were largely autonomous so long as they paid their taxes and kept the peace. Peasants worked their own fields on a hereditary basis and paid a tax or rent in kind (usually in rice) to the daimyo or his enfeoffed vassals. They were also subject to labor and military service. Taxation, levied on the village as a whole, kept most of the peasants at a subsistence level and provided the basic support of the daimyo and samurai. But there were some large landowners among the peasants, descended for the most part from manorial managers, and they generally served as hereditary village headmen.

Despite unrest and warfare, the formation of han accelerated the development of trade and a merchant class. Merchants who supplied feudal commanders with the equipment and commodities necessary for their forces formed guilds, usually under the protection of some powerful daimyo or Buddhist temple. Trade centers arose, particularly in the castle towns, and the use of money became more common. Foreign trade, largely with China, was sponsored by the Ashikaga shoguns and by several Zen monasteries. From seaports like Sakai, Hyogo (Kobe), and Hakata (Fukuoka) Japan exported copper, sulphur, fans, lacquerware, and swords to China in return for iron, textiles, pictures, books, and drugs. The Japanese usually maintained a favorable trade balance, which China made up through the export of copper coins.

There were also important cultural developments in this period. Monasteries, particularly those of the Zen sects at Kamakura and Kyoto, provided refuge for artists and men of letters, and, as in feudal Europe, they preserved much of Japan's intellectual and cultural tradition. The daimyo were also important patrons of the arts; such patronage was regarded as a symbol of success and prestige. The Ashikaga family founded a college at Kyoto, and in the han the daimyo provided support for monasteries, which often included local schools (*terakoya*). The *No* and *Kyogen*, two distinct forms of drama, date from this period. The traditions in prose and poetry were maintained, and in works like *Jinnoshotoki* and *Taiheiki* Japanese historians provided a kind of continuity for the institution of the Japanese emperor, despite the fact that the influence of the imperial court probably sank to its lowest level in this period.

The Establishment of Suzerainty

In the sixteenth century unity was forged out of chaos through the careers of three powerful men: Oda Nobunaga, Toyotomi Hideyoshi, and Tokugawa Ieyasu. After a century of constant warfare, these three men were able to establish the supremacy of one lord over the many daimyo. At the beginning of the century Japan was a land divided among several hundred daimyo, by mid-century six of them dominated the rest, and by 1600 or thereabouts the supremacy of one was assured.

Oda Nobunaga (1532–1582) began the process of feudal unification. A descendant of the great Taira Kiyomori, he was the son of a daimyo in the Kyoto area who had acquired considerable land and military power. Nobunaga extended his father's domains until, by the 1560's, through conquest and marriage, he was one of the great territorial lords of Japan. In 1567 he occupied Kyoto and usurped the functions of the Ashikaga shogun. It was Nobunaga's purpose to impose his suzerainty on the other daimyo of Japan, and in this task he had two distinguished allies. One was Hideyoshi (1536–1598), a peasant's son who rose to the rank of general in Nobunaga's service on the basis of ability. The other was Tokugawa Ieyasu (1542–1622), a minor vassal in the Kanto Plain who became a powerful daimyo through his alliance with Nobunaga. By 1573 Nobunaga controlled most of eastern and central Japan. Some of his most difficult campaigns were against independent Buddhist communities which had been formed in the fifteenth century by adherents of the Amidaist sects. After 1573 Nobunaga turned his attention to his enemies in western Japan. These were Mori, daimyo of Choshu han, and Shimazu, daimyo of Satsuma han. In 1582 he defeated Mori, but in that year he fell victim to the treachery of one of his generals. By the time of his death, Nobunaga was master of half of Japan.

Hideyoshi, who succeeded to Nobunaga's power, led the way in establishing the third stage of Japanese feudalism by uniting the country under a single suzerainty. By 1590 he had subdued all his foes, including Satsuma and Choshu, and Japan enjoyed domestic peace for the first time in a century. The daimyo all recognized Hideyoshi as their suzerain, and they were confirmed by him in their landholdings. Anxious to maintain the status quo, which in practical terms meant the stabilization of military power and land control, Hideyoshi effectively carried out a series of measures which fixed landownership and cultivation rights and which froze the class system, so that the daimyo and samurai resumed their former monopoly of military functions and the peasants were tied to the land in order to guarantee an adequate labor force. Merchants, however, acquired a greater degree of freedom as the result of a policy designed to weaken the guilds, which tended to control prices to the detriment of the daimyo and the samurai.

Hideyoshi's thirst for power was not satisfied by his successes in Japan. He was ambitious to conquer neighboring states, including China, and in 1592 sent an expeditionary force of some 200,000 men to Korea. Although it scored some initial victories against the Koreans, it was unable to break the defenses of Chinese reinforcements, and, when a stalemate resulted, he withdrew his forces to Japan. Regarding this setback as only temporary, he sent a second expedition to the mainland in 1597, but his death in 1598 led to its withdrawal.

The death of Hideyoshi precipitated a struggle for power among the more powerful daimyo from which Tokugawa Ieyasu emerged dominant. Prior to the dispatch of his second expedition to Korea, Hideyoshi had sought to guarantee the succession of his son, Hideyori, by naming him regent (1596) and appointing a council of five daimyo, including Ieyasu, to support him. This plan failed when Ieyasu organized a coalition of daimyo to establish his own supremacy within the feudal order. The issue was finally decided in 1600 in Ieyasu's favor on the battlefield at Sekigahara in central Japan, and the victor forced all of the daimyo to take an oath of allegiance to him before confirming them in control of their han. The culmination of the great personal triumph of Ieyasu came in 1603, when the emperor appointed him shogun. For a time, Hideyori, who continued to live in his father's famous castle at Osaka, was a threat to the position of the Tokugawa family, but in 1615 he was destroyed, along with the last of his supporters, in the Battle of Osaka Castle.

6 *The Tokugawa Shogunate*

Tokugawa Ieyasu completed the process of unification begun by Nobunaga and Hideyoshi when he found means to stabilize his own power and to guarantee the succession of his family. Like his immediate predecessor, he formulated policies designed to maintain the status quo in Japan, and to this end he and his heirs utilized Confucianism as the ideological basis of a static society. According to the theory of the Japanese Confucianists, society would preserve a perfect contentment and a perfect peace if every man would be in his proper station and would remain there. Although the Tokugawa shogunate could not prevent change in Japan, for two centuries and longer it did preserve the caste-bound legal and political framework of Japanese society. In addition, it successfully maintained the peace.

The Political System

Ieyasu maintained the institution of the emperor, since its role in legitimatizing power in a given family had a long historical tradition; and at the time of his own retirement as shogun in 1615 he made certain that his son, Hidetada, assumed the same powers that the throne had entrusted to him in 1603. The emperor was provided with revenues for his own support as well as that of a small group of court nobles, but he had no administrative function of any kind. The Tokugawa regime also stringently minimized contacts between the emperor and the daimyo. The latter needed permission to enter Kyoto, and their activities in that city were watched closely by Tokugawa officials. Journeys of court nobles outside the Kyoto area were carefully restricted.

The government of the shogun, or the bakufu, with its headquarters established by Ieyasu at Edo, administered directly the Tokugawa han, estimated to comprise between one-fourth and one-third of Japan's landed area; these were scattered throughout the country and constituted buffers against potentially hostile han. The bakufu also administered directly a number of key cities and ports like Nagasaki, Hakodate, Shimoda, and Kanagawa. The high officials of the regime were drawn from among the personal retainers of the shogun, the heads of branches of the Tokugawa family, and daimyo allies. Minor posts were generally occupied by high-ranking samurai of these same men. By the death of the third shogun, Iemitsu, in 1651, the council of elders (roju), with its rotating chairman, became the supreme organ in the administration. After that date the shoguns themselves, with only a few exceptions, tended to be puppets.

The bakufu devised means to control the daimyo, whose local autonomy depended upon their allegiance, at least nominally, to the shogun; their armed forces were in theory at his disposal in return for his confirmation of their title to their han. Of the 250-odd daimyo, about two-thirds were heads of branch families or allies of the Tokugawa family at the time of the Battle of Sekigahara. The remaining third were regarded as "outside lords" (tozama), and the most powerful among these were the daimyo of the so-called "four western han"—Satsuma, Choshu, Tosa, and Hizen (Saga). Since these four han constituted the greatest potential threat to the shogunate, their daimyo were excluded from all offices in the bakufu, but, along with other daimyo, they were required to reside at Edo at regular intervals and to leave both their wives and heirs as hostages when they returned to their han. This practice, called sankin kotai, was a financial burden on han treasuries since it required the maintenance of an extra residence of some scale and expensive travel. Most of the tozama controlled areas isolated from the heart of the country; and while they had been too weak to withhold their "allegiance" to Ieyasu, they were too powerful for him to deny their autonomy. Ieyasu had been content to redistribute their landholdings in order to place his allies at strategic points from which they could prevent the formation of effective alliances and crush rebellions. The bakufu also limited castle construction and placed restrictions on the number of fighting men that each han could maintain. It used censors (*metsuke*) to keep abreast of local conditions and to ascertain whether the han observed particular orders, such as those regarding public works, another measure designed to reduce the wealth of the daimyo. Lastly, it also carefully checked the movement of travelers from one han to another.

Within the han each daimyo was generally autonomous and had his own administration, which operated at two levels. The central organs were in the castle town, and district magistrates were located throughout the han to collect taxes, administer justice, and maintain peace. In practice the district magistrate was essentially an overseer, since the village communities themselves were responsible for most of the functions of government.

The Economic and Social Order

The bakufu sought social as well as political stability and attempted therefore to create a social order that was rigid and conventional. During the period of Tokugawa supremacy there was, for all practical purposes, a two-class society: the aristocracy and the common people. The aristocrats were for the most part feudal elements, and the common people included the peasants, artisans, and merchants.

The aristocracy of Japan had two main branches. The imperial aristocrats —the emperor and his court nobles (*kuge*) residing at Kyoto—were in theory at the top of the social pyramid, but since they had no power or property and were dependent on the bakufu for support, their position was only honorary. The feudal aristocracy was headed by the shogun and the daimyo, and below them came the samurai in falling ranks. Some of the higher-ranking samurai were given grants of land, but most of the subordinates were paid a fixed annual stipend in rice. The lowest-ranking samurai were usually no better off than a rich peasant, and in the case of several han, e.g., Satsuma, some of them were also farmers. They received land and an additional stipend from their daimyo, engaged in agriculture normally, and took up arms in time of war. This type was the exception since, after the introduction of firearms through trade with the West and the resultant need for strong castle defenses, samurai were generally garrisoned in castle towns, leaving their fields to be farmed by peasants. In the period of Hideyoshi's dominance the distinction between samurai and peasant had been clearly established in most parts of Japan, and during the Tokugawa period, because of the effective maintenance of peace, many of these urbanized samurai became administrative functionaries, and some, intellectuals and scholars. However, a large number became parasites, living at the expense of the underprivileged peasantry.

The well-being of the entire feudal aristocracy was dependent on the rice-producing peasantry. The aristocracy measured its income in terms of rice, and the peasantry provided the labor power to work the land. Most numerous among the village peasants were the smallholders, who were given tenure rights by the daimyo to cultivate the land in return for taxes paid in kind and labor services. The land tax, which generally amounted to 50 per cent of the rice crop, was levied on the village as a whole and apportioned by the village government. Additional levies were applied to local industry and commerce, in part to discourage farmers from abandoning agriculture to enter other occupations. In fact, the han administrations uniformly forbade the peasantry to produce agricultural commodities which would interfere with rice cultivation. Han regulations also prescribed that the peasant rise early in the morning, eat cereals other than rice, not buy tea or rice wine (sake); denied him certain amusements thought to encourage idleness; and forbade him to move without permission.

Within villages there was differentiation among the peasants according to their economic status and hereditary position. In addition to the large number of owners of small and middling holdings, there were landowners of higher social status with tracts ten or twenty times larger than those of the average cultivator and in some cases as much as one hundred times larger. In some areas these large tracts were rented out to tenant farmers, but on the whole such land was cultivated by family members beyond the nuclear group, hereditary and long-term indentured servants, and other persons who were provided with dwellings in return for their labor. Legally it was common to consider as part of the family anyone brought more or less permanently into its farming organization.

Merchants and artisans lived in the large cities of Japan like Edo and Osaka or in the castle towns of the han. The shogun and the daimyo were anxious to attract merchants and artisans to their centers of power, and they established free markets in order to break down the old guild system. Since money became increasingly the medium of payment in society, the most important merchants were the rice brokers and money exchangers of Edo and Osaka. They disposed of the surplus commodities of the feudal ruling class, sent bills of exchange between Osaka and Edo, and provided credit at high interest, usually on the security of next year's income. Since there were many ways in which merchants were of service to the feudal aristocracy, their economic relations were very close, but the merchants had virtually no political rights and no legal protection for their property. Thus it was common for merchants to extend gifts and bribes in order to win the favor and protection of bakufu officials and the daimyo.

The merchants were ultimately able to organize wholesale-dealer associations and trade associations for purposes of security and protection. For over a century the bakufu fought the development of monopolistic guilds, attempts to corner a market, and collusion between merchants and officials for profit. For example, in 1642 bakufu officials discovered a conspiracy between a group of wealthy Edo merchants and important members of the financial department to control the local rice market, raise prices, and make a huge profit. Since this struck directly at the interests of the feudal aristocracy as a whole, the bakufu exiled the merchants, executed their children, and confiscated their property. As merchant activity expanded, however, the bakufu found that merchant organizations could be useful for purposes of economic supervision and control, and thus by the middle of the eighteenth century wholesale-dealer associations and trade associations came to embrace all phases of economic activity, including transportation, inns, and restaurants. Although they were organized chiefly for mutual aid and protection, many of their activities were social, with people engaged in the same economic activity going on outings and even pilgrimages to shrines. These organizations set prices, maintained fair practices, and secured the payment of just obligations; of even greater consequence was their practice of limiting the number of people who could engage in a particular economic activity. Below the wholesale dealers, rice brokers, money exchangers, and proprietors there existed a large number of small independent merchants, managers, clerks, and day workers.

Ideological Foundations

The ideological foundation of Tokugawa society was a brand of Confucianism consciously molded by samurai scholars to suit Japanese peculiarities. Hayashi Razan and others provided a "naturally ordained" philosophic and moral basis for the political administration and for the social hierarchy based upon caste. Of the larger social groupings, the samurai, peasant, artisan, and merchant ranked in that order. Loyalty to one's superior within social groupings and in the hierarchical scale was extolled as the most important virtue, and loyalty to one's lord took precedence over all other obligations. On this principle the bakufu undertook to prescribe standards of behavior for all the people under its direct control, with special attention to the promotion of discipline and obedience among samurai of all ranks. There was a tendency for all the daimyo to follow the bakufu's lead in establishing codes of behavior, and, like the shogun, many of them sponsored Confucian lessons and lectures at their courts.

A Confucian-based family system, modified by Japanese feudalism, also helped to preserve the status quo. In the ideal of the Japanese family, paternal power was absolute and unquestioned, and the unequal social relations of its members were spelled out in greater detail than in China. Even in merchant

97

families and enterprises loyalty and obedience were expected of all inferiors. The subordination of the individual personality to the group produced a sense of group, rather than individual, responsibility. Conformity in extreme forms caused individuals to feel a dangerous amount of inner tension, particularly when there were direct emotional conflicts between duty and desire. The institution of primogeniture, moreover, produced a strong sense of unequal obligations derived from one's status within the family, while the Chinese principle of multiple inheritance, though it did not produce harmony, created a greater spirit of equality. Again in contrast with China, the Japanese family system, especially that of the samurai, was more closely integrated into society because of its subordination to the interests of the shogun or the daimyo.

This "harmony" between the family and the state was of tremendous importance in the modernization of Japan in the nineteenth and twentieth centuries since it provided the psychological and social foundation of modern Japanese nationalism. The Tokugawa experience provided the basis for individual and family loyalty to the emperor in later years when, after the destruction of the feudal system, an effective, centralized imperial regime was established (1868–1871). However, since "harmony" was in reality based upon the subordination of inferiors to superiors, especially of samurai to the shogun or daimyo, there was no foundation of a contractual principle, often associated with feudal relationships in Europe, on which to build the concept of responsible government. It was significant for modern Japan that in the Japanese feudal hierarchy there was no concept of contingent rights and duties.

In the Tokugawa period there were important differences between the samurai family system and that of the peasants and urban workers. The head of the samurai family tended to have absolute power, but among the commoners a much greater economic interdependence of all family members tempered the ideal of paternalism and fostered co-operation and collective understanding. Relationships were more informal, and the individual had more voice in matters that concerned him, although decisions were still unit ones; moreover, the women of peasant and urban working families enjoyed a considerable degree of freedom, probably because of the significant economic role they played.

Although the Tokugawa authorities extolled the Confucian virtue of frugality, the response was uneven among feudal aristocrats and commoners alike. Of particular interest in this regard are the merchants, who were held in contempt by the ruling class in good Confucian tradition. The authorities placed numerous restrictions on their way of life, although, amazingly, merchants were not taxed regularly and were required to make fixed monetary contributions to the bakufu only after the time of the shogun Yoshimune (1716–1745). Among the Osaka merchants a code emphasized the virtues of hard work and sincerity as well as frugality, and wealthy merchant families like Mitsui, Konoike, and Sumitomo lived up to these principles. In general, however, merchant wealth and exuberance triumphed over conformity. In the merchant quarter of Osaka and Edo, restaurants, teahouses, geisha, and prostitutes catered to the fancies of those who could afford their pleasures, and merchant patronage helped to produce new forms of prose, poetry, and drama, e.g., the stories of Saikaku, the poems of Basho, and the plays of Chikamatsu.

The Seclusion Policy

The Tokugawa desire to maintain the status quo was complicated by contacts with the Western world. By the time that Ieyasu had founded his supremacy in Japan (1603), Portuguese, Spanish, and Dutch merchants had established a profitable trade. Religion followed commerce, and Jesuit and Franciscan missionaries were actively propagating the Catholic faith in Japan. This foreign penetration came to be regarded by the Tokugawa authorities as an unsettling factor in society and as a threat to their power.

In 1542 some Portuguese sailors on a Chinese junk were driven off their course and landed in southern Japan on the island of Tanegashima. From them the local daimyo purchased firearms and began to learn how to make guns and gunpowder. The Portuguese followed up this initial contact with several successful trading expeditions, and in 1549 Francis Xavier and other Jesuit fathers landed at Kagoshima, capital of Satsuma, where they were well received and were given permission to preach among the masses of people.

The introduction of firearms was probably the most important result of this early contact with the West. By 1555 the Japanese were producing their own weapons, and in that year they were used for the first time in encounters between the forces of the daimyo Takeda and Uesugi. Han military units organized musket companies, and formation fighting, relying heavily upon foot soldiers, came into vogue, although it did not completely supersede aristocratic single combat for some time. The use of guns, moreover, necessitated modification in the planning and construction of castles, and before long daimyo headquarters were complex citadels of solid rock. Nobunaga and Hideyoshi both were quick to take advantage of the new weapons, and both were pioneers in the building of castles that could withstand gunfire.

In Nobunaga's time the Portuguese penetration, both mercantile and religious, advanced smoothly. Reacting from his difficulties with the independent Buddhist communities, Nobunaga permitted the new faith to make rapid progress in western and central Japan, and he even allowed missionaries to preach in Kyoto. By 1571 the number of Christian converts was estimated at 30,000, mostly in the west; however, in Kyoto there were not more than 1,500. By 1582, just before Nobunaga's death, the total had reached 150,000, with the greater part still in western Japan, where some daimyo had been converted. In Kyoto the total increased to 10,000 and included many of the councilors who assisted Hideyoshi.

It was Hideyoshi who first began to regard with alarm the impact of both trade and Christianity. In Nagasaki, for example, the Portuguese were insisting that they be given the right to administer the city, and they threatened the withdrawal of trade in the event of a refusal. They had already succeeded in forcing the daimyo to offer the revenues of Nagasaki as security for a loan that they had made to him. The militant activities of foreign missionaries were also disturbing, and in 1587 Hideyoshi decreed that all of them must leave Japan. Although Hideyoshi regarded Christianity as subversive of the basic principles underlying Japanese society, the decree was not enforced, chiefly because he and others in power feared that the proscription of Christianity would disrupt trade that was profitable. Thus the Jesuits continued to operate in Japan, though not openly.

Hideyoshi was again disturbed when, in 1593, Spanish Franciscans began to make their way to Japan from the Philippines. With little political sense, they openly flouted the edict of 1587, building churches, preaching, and baptizing, even in Kyoto; however, Hideyoshi was able to use these activities to secure a favorable commercial agreement with the Manila government. The San Felipe affair of 1596 finally brought down the full force of Hideyoshi's wrath upon the foreign missionaries. When the cargo of the Spanish galleon "San Felipe" was confiscated by Japanese officials, a member of the crew boasted defiantly that Spain's method of empire-building was to send out traders and missionaries as advance agents, to be followed by troops who rapidly conquered and annexed territory. Hideyoshi reacted quickly, arresting and sentencing to death many converts and crucifying six Spanish Franciscans. Thereafter Japanese Christians in most parts of Japan were liable to persecution.

Tokugawa Ieyasu was also interested in foreign trade. He permitted the Portuguese to trade duty-free at Nagasaki, and he resumed commercial relations with Spain after a suspension by Hideyoshi. By 1603 ships from Luzon began to call at Uraga every year, and in 1610 the Dutch established a trading base on the island of Hirado. In this same period the British also traded at Hirado, but because of involvement elsewhere they withdrew in 1624. Like Hideyoshi, Ieyasu closely watched foreign activity in Japan and, when it disturbed him, moved quickly to restrict it, for example, when he feared that daimyo malcontents might enlist foreign aid in plotting to overthrow the Tokugawa regime. His suspicions and fears increased as a result of the intense rivalry among the Europeans, who intrigued and curried favor in order to maneuver themselves into the most advantageous positions. For example, in 1611 the Dutch divulged to the bakufu a plot in which a Kyushu daimyo was to be furnished with ships and troops by the Portuguese, and in 1612 a secret Dutch report stated that the Portuguese and Spanish were themselves planning to overthrow the bakufu.

During these years Ieyasu permitted Christianity to prosper. According to estimates made by the Jesuits, the destruction of earlier persecutions had been repaired and the converts swelled in numbers. They put the total of Christians at 300,000 among a population of about 20,000,000. In 1614, however, Ieyasu shifted to a policy of banning Christianity and ordered Japanese converts to renounce their faith; and his successors, son and grandson, fearful of the western han, where Christian missionary efforts were often the most successful, rigidly enforced the ban. They were convinced that missionaries were working to establish an alliance between these han and Portugal or Spain. With the development of the Dutch and British trade, the bakufu was also convinced that the profitable European trade would be preserved without having to put up with missionary activities. If missionaries refused to leave Japan, they were executed. The bakufu used torture to make Christians recant, and it forced every person to belong to a Buddhist temple as a control measure.

It proved difficult if not impossible to draw the line between religious and commercial activities; consequently, the bakufu ultimately excluded all Europeans except the Dutch, who alone had shown no interest in the propagation of Christianity. In 1624 it banned all Spaniards, and after the Shimabara Uprising of 1637, based on local injustices but tainted by the participation of Christians who had been forced to apostasize, it also banned the Portuguese. Only the Dutch and the Chinese were allowed to carry on trade, under extremely restricted conditions on the small island of Deshima in Nagasaki harbor. The isolationist policy also affected the activities of Japanese subjects, who in 1636 were prohibited from going abroad on penalty of death, and ship construction was restricted to permit only coastal trade. The sole exceptions to this policy were the trade with Korea via Tsushima and the Satsuma trade with the Ryukyu Islands. This was the beginning of over two centuries of relative seclusion for Japan, a policy designed to maintain the domestic status quo.

7 Forces for Change

The Tokugawa feudal order depended for its stability on a close correspondence between political and economic power and on continuance of the policy of isolation. As long as land remained the basis of wealth and as long as the bakufu was able to prevent foreign penetration, these conditions were maintained. However, from the beginning, economic and social developments gradually caused fundamental dislocations that affected all groupings in the social hierarchy and gave rise to new domestic forces for change. In some of the han, also, a new economic and social order was emerging.

Domestic advances are, however, only part of the story, for toward the end of the eighteenth century the Western powers renewed their interest in Japan and began to challenge the policy of isolation. This had the effect of causing a number of samurai intellectuals to advocate measures for political reform. Some of them, stimulated by a revival of historical learning, went so far as to advocate the "restoration" of imperial rule.

The Rise of the Merchant Class

The development of commerce and urban centers in the seventeenth century and the subsequent rise of a money economy created new forms of wealth which undermined the correspondence between economic and political power in Japanese society. Although national isolation seriously retarded some commercial activities which had been given great momentum in the relatively brief period of trade with the West, the prolonged peace expanded the requirements of internal markets and stimulated agricultural and industrial production. When barriers to internal trade became less restrictive, surplus produce within the han found its way to outside markets; commercial centers became larger and more numerous as a result; and dealer and trade associations as well as credit institutions grew and prospered. By 1700 Edo was approaching the million mark in population; Osaka and Kyoto stood at around 300,000; and Nagoya and Kanazawa were nearing 100,000. It has been estimated that perhaps 10 per cent of Japan's population lived in cities and towns of over 10,000 inhabitants. Over all, Japan's population increased from 18,000,000 in 1600 to approximately 26,000,000 in 1725. As the demand for commodities increased, merchants and rich peasants began to invest surplus capital in new forms of production, like the domestic, or putting-out, system. They provided materials for peasants and craftsmen, sometimes even equipment like looms, and marketed the finished goods. There are also indications that toward the end of the Tokugawa period industrial production had in some areas reached the point of factory organization. Regional specialization based on available raw materials and local skills was common, and particular areas were known for their textiles, pottery, lacquerware, rice wine, and other products.

These economic changes caused a great many maladjustments, perhaps the most important of which was the mounting indebtedness of the feudal aristocracy to the merchants. The shogun, daimyo, and samurai alike depended on brokers to convert their rice into money, and they depended on merchants in general for their consumption needs. In these transactions, however, they suffered from merchant manipulation of prices through monopolies and from the failure of the rate of exchange (rice to money) to keep pace with the steadily rising prices of other commodities. Having acquired a taste for luxuries and being inclined out of pride to compete with one another in their manner of living, they were quite willing to mortgage their future to the merchants by borrowing at high interest in order to maintain their expensive habits. From the shogun down to the lowest-ranking samurai, the economic position of the feudal aristocrats deteriorated.

By the eighteenth century the bakufu and many daimyo were in serious financial difficulties. They were limits to the degree to which taxes could be increased, and attempts to debase coinage only increased inflation. Production had reached a peak, and restrictions on foreign trade made it impossible for the country to bear the burden of a higher standard of living for a larger population. Traditional calamities like earthquakes, fires, and floods added to the financial woes of the bakufu and daimyo alike. Their treasuries were constantly depleted by funds for famine relief, the rebuilding of Edo and other cities after fires, and additional administrative expenses.

When the financial situation became too desperate, the bakufu was forced to compel money contributions from the wealthy merchants of the large cities, and at times it canceled debts held by brokers who had advanced money to the feudal aristocrats on security of their rice incomes. For example, as early as 1705 the bakufu accused the House of Yodoya in Osaka of ostentatious living not befitting a member of the merchant class and confiscated its entire wealth. Since Yodoya had come to control the finances of many of the daimyo of Kyushu and western Honshu, the confiscation served to cancel the debts of these lords and, at the same time, give the bakufu a nice profit. In 1761 the chief minister of the bakufu, Tanuma Okitsugu, levied forced loans on several hundred Osaka merchants, and thereafter the bakufu resorted to this practice with increasing frequency, especially toward the end of the period. In 1843 about half the rice brokers of Osaka were bankrupted as a result of debt cancellation enacted by the bakufu to pacify the shogun's own retainers, whose allowances it could not pay in full.

The bakufu tried in vain to attack the merchant monopoly system. One of the motives, besides control, for the recognition of dealer and trade associations by the Shogun Yoshimune in 1721 was to secure new sources of revenue in the form of charter fees and regular contributions, but the merchants passed these expenses on to consumers. The bakufu reforms of 1841–1843 ordered the dissolution of monopolies in order to lower prices; however, they caused economic chaos and shortages which gave rise to even higher prices. In 1851 the dealer and trade associations were restored, but by that time local merchants and han mercantile organizations were beginning to compete successfully. The merchant class quite naturally resented these restrictions and confiscations, but it was on the whole too deeply related to the feudal system through commerce and usury to plot its destruction. Only when a potentially successful alternative to the bakufu appeared did the merchants

103

join the political struggle against the old regime. In the case of rural merchants and industrialists, who were just beginning to break down the old monopolies, there was a much greater desire for change.

Individual daimyo faced financial difficulties similar to those of the bakufu. Debt cancellation was often a welcome relief, but daimyo found that, when they did not honor their debts, it was difficult to get credit elsewhere. They found it hard to cut back their level of living, particularly when numerous obligations were imposed by the bakufu, such as the separate residences at Edo, elaborate processionals, and the construction and maintenance of costly public works. Yet there was one means that the daimyo did use to improve their finances. Peace had made many of their retainers superfluous, and in fact the bulk of their samurai had lost their functional basis. Thus many daimyo carried out the policy of reducing samurai stipends by as much as 50 per cent.

The Development of the Economic and Social Order

The samurai, already pressed by a sharp decline in the money value of rice, were forced to engage in new activities which in turn began to destroy their class exclusiveness. In order to make up the difference between their meager incomes and their expenses, many samurai, particularly those of low rank and income, were forced to engage in handicraft production, which was usually carried on as contract work from a merchant. Many of them became makers of fans, parasols, toys, footgear, paper lanterns, rattan wear, and fishnets. Some of them became merchants, tenant farmers, and day laborers, while others went into fishing, horticulture, poultry-raising, and other occupations. A small number were even hired by merchants as bodyguards and by rich peasants and merchants as tutors for their children. In numerous cases samurai gave up their status and became *ronin*, since there was no longer a strong bond between feudal lord and vassal. Ronin originally were retainers of a lord whose lands had been confiscated and who were thus deprived of their income and forced into a life without status; or often ronin were the second and third sons who had no security, since only the eldest son inherited stipend rights under primogeniture. Many ronin went into new occupations, but large numbers became discontented ruffians. Some estimates put the number of ronin near the end of the Tokugawa period as high as several hundred thousand. Most significant is the fact that a small but able group of them provided a force for political intrigue against the bakufu, especially during the turbulent decades of the 1850's and 1860's.

By the nineteenth century, among various solutions for the plight of the feudal order put forward by samurai thinkers, the following two were most common. One was an irrational appeal for a return to agrarianism, with great emphasis placed on the virtues of frugality and self-discipline; this romantic dream entailed the destruction of the merchant class, whose function was crucial in the existing, more sophisticated, economic system. The second solution, which was more practical since it accepted the inevitability of economic and social changes, emphasized state control of commerce and production and an expansion of commercial activities to include foreign trade. For example, Honda Toshiaki (1774–1821), a samurai of Kaga han, advocated that a country with only modest natural resources was incapable of supporting an adequate level of living for a large population unless foreign trade was increased. He proposed state control of commerce, shipping, and industry as well as the expansion of Japan overseas through colonization.

In some han, particularly those in the west, state monopolies in trade and production were instituted with samurai administrators and merchants actively managing the han's business affairs at home and in Osaka and Edo. By the nineteenth century, han monopolists and national wholesalers were working hand in hand. Some han successfully developed monopoly manufacture of wax, silk fabrics, porcelain, paper, iron products, and pottery. Numerous industries, for example silk-reeling and spinning, were begun under han direction and protection. And in some han—Satsuma, for example —the authorities ordered certain portions of land to be utilized for the cultivation of han monopoly crops like sugar, rape seeds, wax, and tobacco. In the case of Satsuma again, its able daimyo, Shimazu Nariakira, developed a sugar trade with the Ryukyu Islands that helped put an end to the han's indebtedness.

The western han increased their economic power by these innovations, and, when they invested surplus capital in the production of military equipment, they created the basis of new military power as well. In 1853, in reaction to foreign threats to the policy of isolation, the bakufu had Hizen undertake to cast two hundred canon for forts guarding Edo harbor. Hizen, in fact, had a research center for military as well as commercial industry, and, on the model of Hizen, Satsuma built a smelting works, which included three small reverberatory furnaces and two blast furnaces for the production of cannon. The technology behind these advances was gleaned from Dutch books imported through the trading base at Nagasaki.

Along with the low-ranking samurai, the peasantry suffered greatly from economic changes and the policies of the feudal rulers. With the increasing use of money, peasants were forced to endure violent fluctuations in the price of rice and other grains and steadily increasing prices on goods that they could no longer obtain by barter, for example, farm implements and fertilizer. They were often forced to borrow from local usurers, usually merchants or rich peasants, in emergencies and in order to meet tax payments, for they rarely had any surplus on which to draw. When a peasant was unable to meet the usurer's terms, he was forced to surrender his land to the usurer, who became officially the cultivator but in actuality the landlord. Since the land in theory still belonged to the daimyo, the new "cultivator" was responsible for the land tax, but in practice the peasant remaining on the land as a tenant farmer had the double burden of the tax to the daimyo and the rent to the landlord. This circumstance was made possible through the higher productivity of the land; consequently, although the burden of rent was added to the land tax, which amazingly remained relatively stable throughout the Tokugawa period, the actual cultivator could still eke out a bare living. But the rise of these "new landlords" was a direct challenge to the daimyo-peasant relationship, and as early as 1643 the Shogun Iemitsu enacted legislation to prevent land alienation. In some cases han governments also took steps against this development; for example, Nabeyama Kanso, daimyo of Hizen, ordered that land-based debt payments cease, and he re-established tenant farmers as owner-cultivators.

Agricultural tenancy increased for other reasons. Rich peasants and merchants invested in the reclamation of wasteland, which they usually rented out on a twenty-five-year tenure. For this and other reasons the land under cultivation doubled in the period from 1600 to 1730. By the latter half of the Tokugawa era, economic and technological changes made tenancy the predominant method of agricultural production on the already existing large landholdings. The rise of cities and towns, the expansion of trade, and the development of new forms of industrial production created serious labor shortages in the rural areas. Landowners simply had to rent land to cultivators as tenants in order to compete with the rising wage rates in urban areas and the countryside. Even the political power of the bakufu and the daimyo was unable to halt the tide of emigration to the cities which caused the rural labor shortage. Only after 1750 did the flow begin to wane because of limits to employment opportunities.

The shift to tenancy in the first half of the Tokugawa period was a gradual transformation from the utilization of the labor of the extended family to *hokonin* (fixed period and payment) labor, from long-term *hokonin* to short, from short-term *hokonin* to wage labor, and finally from wage labor to tenancy. New methods of cultivation, increasing use of commercial fertilizers, improvement of plant varieties, and the extension of irrigation made farm operations more complex and were in part responsible for the transformation, since the nuclear family was more adept at implementing these innovations. It has been estimated that by the end of the Tokugawa period the ratio of tenants to owner-cultivators was probably nearly one to four.

Economic changes also precipitated a kind of struggle between agricultural production and industry, particularly when emigration to urban areas trailed off. The foundation of the feudal economy was the peasants' land tax; thus any large-scale change of occupation which resulted in land being left untilled naturally threatened the revenues of the bakufu and daimyo. In order to alleviate their economic difficulties, many peasants sought to increase their income by engaging in commercial agriculture or by wages from employment in rural industry. For example, village landlords were often industrialists, and, in the case of the sake-brewers, they recruited part of their labor force from their own tenantry and the rest from small owner-cultivators. When this practice had the effect of reducing tax revenues, which were based on agricultural production, the feudal authorities attempted, though without much success, to check the diversion of labor from agriculture.

It is clear that by the decade of the 1830's there was mounting discontent among the rural and urban poor. The economy had matured, but it was not able to keep pace with the birth rate and consequent pressure of population; abortion and infanticide were already commonly practiced as population controls. In the countryside peasant revolts became more numerous. This type of social upheaval was a traditional method of protesting local griev-ances, but the number and intensity of peasant revolts in the nineteenth century sets them apart as indicating a universal discontent. The situation was much the same in urban areas. In the 1830's a series of uprisings took place, the most famous of which occurred in Osaka in 1837 when an enraged, hungry mob rioted for days against the rice merchants because of grain shortages and high prices brought on by the famine of the previous year. A large part of the city was reduced to ashes, and many important buildings and bridges were destroyed.

The Challenge of the West

Conditions in Japan necessitated a change in the organization of the state and society. Whether this change would be orderly or revolutionary would depend on the extent to which the needs and desires of the people could be satisfied and on the degree to which the feudal rulers could control the forces for change. The economic factors described in the previous section were perhaps of prime importance among these forces, but the situation was com-plicated by traditional political considerations, such as the animosity of the western han toward the Tokugawa regime. And there were external factors as well. By the end of the eighteenth century the Western powers had once again turned their attention toward Japan, and this "challenge of the West" accelerated the movement for change and helped to mold its very nature.

During the second half of the eighteenth century Russia made repeated but unsuccessful attempts to open Japan to trade. The Russians used the repatriation of shipwrecked Japanese sailors as a pretext to begin negotiations. Many of these sailors had been pressed into service to teach Japanese to the Russians and to give information regarding their country, and some were taken as far away as Moscow, where they taught in a Japanese-language school. In the decade of the 1790's agents of the Russian-American Company renewed efforts to open Japan as part of expanding activities in the north Pacific, but the missions of Laxman in 1792 and of Resanov in 1804 failed to break the isolation policy of the bakufu. On its part the bakufu began to fear Russian encroachments in the north, particularly with regard to Hokkaido. As early as 1795 the expanding Russian empire had planted a colony on a nearby island, and in 1806 Russia attacked Japanese settlements on Sakhalin and Iturup, creating widespread panic in the area. Since the Russians were using intimidation to secure trade, the Japanese retaliated in one case by the seizure of a Russian survey ship and the detention of its crew until Russia apologized for her actions in the north. Preoccupation with and involvement in the Napoleonic Wars finally forced the Russians to abandon their persistent efforts to open Japan.

By the time that Russian interest had slackened, Great Britain filled the void. British ships began to appear in Japanese waters as early as the 1790's, and during the Napoleonic Wars they raided and destroyed Dutch carriers on the sea route between western Japan and Java. Great Britain also expressed interest in trade with Japan at the time of the Macartney mission to Peking (1793) as a means of encouraging competition in order to lower the prices paid by the British for Chinese products. The acquisition of Singapore in 1819 led to more vigorous British activity in eastern Asia, and British ships began to appear more frequently in Japanese waters. A limited trade was developed with western Japan via the Ryukyu Islands and through offshore meetings of vessels. The bakufu reacted against these developments with the edict of 1825, which ordered forceful expulsion of foreign ships that appeared in Japanese waters and forbade Japanese merchant ships and fishing vessels from approaching and contacting them, and which further provided that foreign landing parties be arrested and killed.

By 1842, however, the bakufu was cognizant of China's failure to resist the demands of the British for trade expansion and, fearing for its own policy of isolation, toned down the severity of the 1825 decree. A new edict suggested that "it is not thought fitting to drive away all foreign ships irrespective of their condition, i.e., their lack of supplies or their suffering of stress of weather. In accordance with the ordinance of 1806, after investigating the circumstances in each case, you should when necessary supply them with food and fuel and advise them to return, but on no account allow foreigners to land."

The United States was also among the powers interested in terminating Japanese isolation. American ships began to appear off Japan in the 1790's after the rapid growth of the Pacific Northwest fur trade, which flourished until about 1820. The fur trade then gave way to whaling expeditions, and occasionally shipwrecked sailors were cast up on the coast of Japan. They were treated inhospitably, and their repatriation was slow, as it was carried out through the Dutch at Nagasaki. Although there was an interest in trade with Japan as early as the War of 1812, the American government waited until 1832 before it commissioned Edmund Roberts, a wealthy New Hampshire shipowner, to negotiate treaties with Siam and Japan. Roberts unfortunately died before he could proceed from Bangkok to Japan. Later, orders were dispatched to Caleb Cushing in China to proceed to Japan with full powers to negotiate a treaty, but the orders arrived after he had departed for home. After further delay the task was finally delegated to Commodore James Biddle, who arrived at Uraga on July 20, 1846, in command of two ships, but his request for trade was denied. By this date the matter of opening Japan had become an important concern to various groups in the United States. An increasing number of ships went into Japanese waters when Shanghai began to establish its commercial dominance among the Chinese ports. Shipping companies began to consider the use of steam vessels for the China trade, and the need for coal spurred their desire to end Japan's isolation. Moreover, public opinion was insisting that Washington take steps to reach a satisfactory agreement with the Japanese government regarding the treatment of shipwrecked American sailors. In 1849 Commodore James Glynn proceeded to Nagasaki and arranged the release of survivors of a shipwrecked American vessel, but he made no attempt to force trade relations upon the Japanese.

The Dutch watched these developments closely, and in 1844 William II of the Netherlands addressed to the shogun a personal letter in which he expressed his anxiety for Japan, explaining that it was impossible for any nation to remain in seclusion without incurring the hostility of other nations. He cited the example of China. Three years later the Dutch monarch again advised the shogun that world events had made the seclusion policy "anachronistic, unwise, dangerous, and untenable." In 1850 the Dutch informed the Japanese of developments in the United States, particularly the settlement of the Pacific Coast. Unfortunately, bakufu officials paid little attention to these warnings.

The bakufu, the daimyo, and their samurai advisers opposed relaxation of isolation, and actually a strong antiforeign feeling began to take hold. Demands for improvement of coastal defenses were numerous, and a defiant attitude toward the "insolent barbarians" became widespread. The bakufu refused a Dutch request that they be allowed to station a diplomatic envoy at Edo, and it placed new restrictions on Dutch books and the study of Dutch in Japan. In the face of a renewed Russian threat in the north, some of the defense proposals put forward by samurai intellectuals went so far as to urge an expansionist policy as one that would best serve the interests of Japan. For example, Honda Toshiaki advocated that Japan should seize not only Hokkaido but also Kamchatka, and he urged that the Japanese capital be moved to the mainland. When American and British pressure was added to that of the Russians, proposals for defense and expansion began to include the southern areas. On the order of the bakufu, the daimyo of Hizen began the manufacture of military equipment for the protection of Nagasaki.

Defense measures, however, presented something of a dilemma for the bakufu. It was clear that foreign incursions would best be prevented if various han combined their defense efforts; yet there was no assurance that newly acquired military strength would not be directed against the shogunate itself. The bakufu decided, none the less, to take a chance on maintaining the continued loyalty of the daimyo and to encourage armament production in various han. The most vocal opponents of intercourse with the West accepted the theory that foreign trade would be harmful to Japan. Confucian scholars among them explained that the weakness of China and her defeat at the hands of Great Britain were the result of corruption that had entered China through Canton. Even those who admitted the inevitability of trade, men like Sakuma Shozan, proposed that Japan should utilize Western methods only to enhance its own strength and preserve its independence.

Ideological Basis of the Emperor Movement

Developments in the field of scholarship were also an important factor working for change in the latter part of the Tokugawa period. From various sources, particularly the revival of Japanese studies by samurai scholars, came the cry that the country be restored to the unitary rule of the emperor. The pursuit of scholarship had been encouraged by the bakufu as a means of keeping samurai intellectuals from meddling in political affairs, but in the course of their studies they learned that the Tokugawa shogunate had been established in the name of the emperor and was based on delegation of political power to the shogun. The emperor had remained the source of all power, and shoguns had never dared challenge the emperor's right to reign. Thus in theory the imperial throne could in its own right intervene at any time in the affairs of state.

Scholars like Motoori Norinaga, who were initially concerned with the need to preserve Japanese literature and history, attacked their counterparts of the classical school who had become so enthusiastic about the Chinese sages and Buddhism that they had nothing but scorn for Japanese studies. Motoori and others who followed his lead labored for the re-establishment of Shinto and the elimination of Buddhist and Confucianist intellectual leadership. Their researches led to the re-emergence of the concept of imperial rule, for in their writings they revitalized the ancient myth of the divine origin of the emperor. When they hinted that the rise of feudal dictators had been achieved through usurpation of imperial power, they sowed the ideological seeds of a movement to establish the emperor as ruler of the state.

Developments within Confucianism in Japan tended to provide an ethical justification for the overthrow of the shogunate and the restoration of the imperial system. The ethical basis of the political administration under the shogun centered on the Confucian doctrine, "Wise men should instruct the people how to behave, and therefore good government depends upon the wisdom of the ruler and the obedience of the people." But orthodox Confucianism also insisted on a correspondence between names and reality in society, and so the difference between the real and nominal powers of both the shogun and the emperor was ultimately questioned. Confucian thinkers like Yamazaki Anzai (1618–1682) regarded the shogun as either a usurper or a mere delegate of the throne. In his philosophy, which was influenced by Shinto national feeling, loyalty to the emperor so supplanted both filial piety and feudal loyalties that to serve the cause of the emperor became the one essential value. In his own time Yamazaki was an exponent of a Shinto-Confucian amalgamation, but in the long run he proved to be a forerunner of the Shinto revival of the eighteenth century, which tended even more to direct loyalties toward the emperor and away from the shogun. An intellectual descendant of Yamazaki was the scholar Hirata Atsutane (1776–1843). His unique contribution to this stream of thought was the notion that every Japanese was a descendant of the gods. Hirata used this idea to strengthen the belief in Japanese racial superiority which was common among his predecessors, and he broadened the scope of racial comparisons to include the Western world.

By the decade of the 1850's restless samurai and ronin began to transform these theoretical conclusions into an ideology of action that advocated the overthrow of the Tokugawa shogunate and, later, the establishment of a centralized national state based on imperial rule. Samurai intellectuals reached the conclusion that, throughout the ages, political change had been effected in the name of the emperor, the one institution that supplied a basic continuity to government in Japan. The fundamental character of the state (*kokutai*) as manifested in the imperial tradition, was, they said, definite and unchangeable. They regarded the imperial family as inseparable from the state; and while they conceded that the forms of administration had changed, they argued that there had been no change in *kokutai*. The emphasis on loyalty, originally thought of as a means of strengthening the bakufu, served in the long run to buttress the *kokutai* concept, since loyalty to the emperor gradually prevailed over the idea of loyalty to the shogun.

Bibliographical Notes

The most useful selective bibliography concerning Japan is Hugh Borton, Serge Elisséef, William W. Lockward, and John C. Pelzel, *A Selected List of Books and Articles on Japan* (Cambridge, Mass.: Harvard University Press, revised and enlarged edition, 1954). Standard extensive works include Friedrich von Wenck-

111

stern, A *Bibliography of the Japanese Empire*, Vol. I (Leiden: E. J. Brill, 1895) and Vol. II (Tokyo: Maruzen, 1907); Oskar Nachod, *Bibliography of the Japanese Empire*, Vols. I and II, covering the period from 1906 to 1926 (London: Goldston, 1928), Vols. III and IV, covering the period from 1927 to 1932 (Leipzig: P. and H. Hiersemann, 1931–1935); and H. Praesent and W. Haenisch, *Bibliography of the Japanese Empire*, in two volumes, covering the period 1933–1937 (Leipzig: P. and H. Hiersemann, 1937–1940). The most comprehensive annual bibliography, especially with regard to periodical literature, is published by the *Journal of Asian Studies* (formerly the *Far Eastern Quarterly*).

The best works on the geography of Japan are G. T. Trewartha, *Japan: A Physical, Cultural, and Regional Geography* (Madison: University of Wisconsin Press, 1945), and George B. Cressey, *Asia's Lands and Peoples, A Geography of One-Third the Earth and Two-Thirds Its People* (New York: McGraw-Hill, second edition, 1951).

There are a number of useful general histories of Japan. A standard single-volume work is G. B. Sansom, *Japan, A Short Cultural History* (New York: Appleton-Century, revised edition, 1944). The same author is currently writing a three-volume history from antiquity to the end of the Tokugawa period, two volumes of which have already been published: *A History of Japan to 1334* and *A History of Japan, 1334–1615* (Stanford: Stanford University Press, 1958–1960). An older work that is still valuable is James Murdoch and Isoh Yamagata, *A History of Japan* (London: Routledge & Kegan Paul, three volumes, third impression, 1949). The best textbook account for the premodernization period is Edwin O. Reischauer and John K. Fairbank, *East Asia: The Great Tradition* (Boston: Houghton Mifflin, 1960); and the most thoughtful popular account is Edwin O. Reischauer, *Japan, Past and Present* (New York: Alfred Knopf, revised edition, 1953).

There is no recent survey of Japan's economic and social development, but two works written before World War II may still be consulted. E. Honjo, *The Social and Economic History of Japan* (Kyoto: Institute for Research in Economic History of Japan, 1935), is the best single volume; and, although it is poorly organized, Takekoshi Yosaburo, *Economic Aspects of the History of the Civilization of Japan* (New York: Macmillan, three volumes, 1930), contains much valuable material. More specialized is Delmer M. Brown, *Money Economy in Medieval Japan* (New Haven: Yale University, Institute of Far Eastern Languages, 1951).

Sources of the Japanese Tradition (New York: Columbia University Press, 1958; compiled by Tsunoda Ryusaku and others) is a useful collection of readings, with an emphasis on intellectual history.

There are three excellent works on the origins of the Japanese people and their civilization: G. J. Groot, S.V.D., *The Prehistory of Japan* (New York: Columbia University Press, 1951; edited by Bertram S. Kraus), Charles Haguenauer, *Origines de la civilisation japonaise* (Paris: Imprimerie Nationale, Vol. I, 1956), and Jonathan E. Kidder, *Japan before Buddhism* (New York: Frederick Praeger, 1959).

Among the important early historical sources, Basil Hall Chamberlain has translated *Kojiki, or Records of Ancient Matters* (London: Kegan Paul, 1932), and W. G. Aston has translated *Nihongi, Chronicles of Japan from the Earliest Times to A.D. 607* (London: "Transactions and Proceedings of the Japan Society of London," Supplement I, two volumes, 1896).

More specialized historical studies and translations include Anesaki Masaharu, *Prince Shotoku, The Sage Statesman* (Tokyo, 1948); K. Asakawa, *The Early Institutional Life of Japan: A Study in the Reform of 645 A.D.* (Tokyo, 1903); Robert K. Reischauer, *Early Japanese History* (ca. 40 B.C.—A.D. 1167) (Princeton: Princeton University Press, two volumes, 1937), a detailed chronology based on original sources; K. Asakawa, *The Documents of Iriki, Illustrative of the Development of the Feudal Institution of Japan* (Tokyo: Japan Society for the Promotion of Science, 1956); Minoru Shinoda, *The Founding of the Kamakura Shogunate, 1180–1185, with Selected Translations from the Azuma Kagami* (New York: Columbia University Press, 1959); Helen Craig McCullough (trans.), *The Taiheiki, A Chronicle of Medieval Japan* (New York: Columbia University Press, 1959); and Walter Dening, *The Life of Toyotomi Hideyoshi (1536–1598)* (Tokyo: The Hokuseido Press, revised edition, 1955).

The most comprehensive general work in its field is Anesaki Masaharu, *History of Japanese Religion, with Special Reference to the Social and Moral Life of the Nation* (London: Kegan Paul, 1930). A useful shorter reference is William K. Bunce, *Religions in Japan* (Rutland, Vt.: Charles Tuttle, 1955). The standard survey in the field of Buddhism is Charles Eliot, *Japanese Buddhism* (London: Arnold, 1935); and more specialized studies include H. H. Coates, *Honen, the Buddhist Saint; His Life and Teaching* (Kyoto: Society for the Publication of Sacred Books of the World, five volumes, reprinted, 1949), Anesaki Masaharu, *Nichiren, the Buddhist Prophet* (Cambridge, Mass.: Harvard University Press, facsimile reprint, 1949), D. T. Suzuki, *An Introduction to Zen Buddhism* (New York: Philosophical Library, 1949), and the latter's *Studies in Zen* (London: Rider, 1955).

Donald Keene, *Japanese Literature, An Introduction for Western Readers* (New York: Grove Press, 1955), is a stimulating brief survey; and his *Anthology of Japanese Literature from the Earliest Era to the Mid-Nineteenth Century* (New York: Grove Press, 1955) is excellent. Kokusai Bunka Shinkokai (ed.), *Introduction to Classic Japanese Literature* (Tokyo, 1948), although not critical, is useful as a reference.

There are a number of excellent translations of Japanese literature, including Arthur Waley's four outstanding contributions, *The Tale of Genji* (London: Allen & Unwin; and New York: Literary Guild, 1935), the first section of which is also available as an Anchor paperback; *The Pillow Book of Sei Shonagon* (Boston: Houghton Mifflin, 1929); *Japanese Poetry, the "Uta"* (London: Lund Humphries, 1945); and *The No Plays of Japan* (New York: Alfred A. Knopf, second impression, 1950, and Evergreen paperback). Other useful works are E. Seidenstecker, "The Kagero Nikki," in *Transactions of the Asiatic Society of*

Japan, Third Series, Volume IV, 1955; Edwin O. Reischauer and Joseph K. Yamagiwa, *Translations from Early Japanese Literature* (Cambridge, Mass.: Harvard University Press, 1951); and Donald Keene, *Major Plays of Chikamatsu* (New York: Columbia University Press, 1961).

Two good surveys in their field are Robert Treat Paine and Alexander Soper, *The Art and Architecture of Japan* (Penguin Books, 1955), and Langdon Warner, *The Enduring Art of Japan* (Cambridge, Mass.: Harvard University Press, 1952, and Evergreen paperback).

In recent years there have been a number of significant contributions by scholars working on various aspects of the development of Japan during the Tokugawa period. The most important of these are Thomas C. Smith, *Agrarian Origins of Modern Japan* (Stanford: Stanford University Press, 1959), and Charles D. Sheldon, *The Rise of the Merchant Class in Tokugawa Japan* (Locust Valley, N.Y.: J. J. Augustin, 1958), both of which emphasize economic growth; John W. Hall, *Tanuma Okitsugu, 1719–1788: Forerunner of Modern Japan* (Cambridge, Mass.: Harvard University Press, 1955); Robert Bellah, *Tokugawa Religion: The Values of Pre-Industrial Japan* (Glencoe, Ill.: Free Press, 1957); Donald Keene, *The Japanese Discovery of Europe: Honda Toshiaki and Other Discoverers, 1720–1798* (London: Routledge & Kegan Paul, 1952); C. R. Boxer, *The Christian Century in Japan, 1549–1650* (Berkeley: University of California Press, 1951); and Joseph J. Spae, *Ito Jinsai: A Philosopher, Educator, and Sinologist of the Tokugawa Period* (Peiping: "Monumenta Serica," Monograph XII, 1948). Useful older works include A. L. Sadler, *The Maker of Modern Japan: The Life of Tokugawa Ieyasu* (New York: Norton, 1941), M. Takizawa, *The Penetration of Money Economy in Japan and Its Effects upon Social and Political Institutions* (New York: Columbia University Press, 1927), and Hugh Borton, "Peasant Uprisings in Japan of the Tokugawa Period," *Transactions of the Asiatic Society of Japan*, Second Series, Volume XVI, 1938.

Howard Hibbett, *The Floating World in Japanese Fiction* (London and New York: Oxford University Press, 1959), is a good introduction to Tokugawa works, and G. W. Sargent, *The Japanese Family Storehouse* (Cambridge, Eng.: Cambridge University Press, 1959), William Theodore de Bary, *Five Women Who Loved Love* (Rutland, Vt., and Tokyo: Charles Tuttle, 1956), and Soji Muzuno, *The Way to Wealth* (Tokyo: Hokuseido Press, 1957), are translations of works by Saikaku. Jippensha Ikku's *Hizakurige* (Tokyo: Charles Tuttle, 1957; translated by Thomas Satchell), is an amusing travelogue. For poetry there is Harold G. Henderson, *An Introduction to Haiku* (New York: Doubleday, 1958). Concerning Tokugawa drama there are a number of useful works, including Earle Ernst, *The Kabuki Theatre* (New York: Oxford University Press, 1956, and Evergreen paperback), and Faubion Bowers, *Japanese Theatre* (New York: Hermitage House, 1952). Two excellent translations and studies of plays are Donald Shively, *The Love Suicide at Amijima: A Study of a Japanese Domestic Tragedy by Chikamatsu Monzaemon* (Cambridge, Mass.: Harvard University Press, 1953), and Donald Keene, *The Battles of Coxinga: Chikamatsu's Puppet Play, Its Background and Importance* (London: Taylor's Foreign Press, 1951).

The art of wood-block printing is described in James Michener, *The Floating World* (New York: Random House, 1954), and is illustrated in the series of booklets published by the Charles E. Tuttle Company of Rutland (Vermont) and Tokyo.

Many aspects of Japanese culture (gardens, music, drama, and architecture, among others) are described in the "Japanese Tourist Library" series published by the Japan Tourist Bureau of Tokyo.

The Beginnings of Modernization
in China and Japan

PART

The Beginnings of Modernization in China

The Beginnings of Modernization in Japan

The Beginnings of Modernization in China

By the nineteenth century the Ch'ing dynasty of the Manchus had entered the phase of decline. The pattern of the dynastic cycle had begun to run the final stages of its course, and by mid-century domestic disorders were sapping the remaining strength of the dynasty. The Western powers, moreover, defeated China in two foreign wars (in 1840 and in 1858–1860); and foreign trade, together with the introduction of Western ideas, began to undermine the very foundations of the imperial system—the self-sufficiency of the agricultural economy, the bonds of the family system, the ideology of the Classics, and the empire-tribute system—which had given Chinese civilization its amazing cultural continuity.

The initial reaction of China's ruling Confucian intellectuals in the decade of the 1860's was to reinvigorate the old social order by reforms in the traditional manner and to strengthen their country against the menace of the Western powers by utilizing the very technological advances that had placed China at the mercy of Western imperialism. These efforts failed miserably, and China's weakness, demonstrated so vividly by her defeat in war at the hands of Japan in 1894–1895, invited the development of foreign spheres of interest and, potentially, actual partition. Proposals for reform, which included important modifications of Chinese institutions, became increasingly common, but not until the dawn of the twentieth century did the dynasty make a serious attempt to implement them. But by that time it was too late, and the last-minute efforts of the Manchu rulers to save themselves failed.

With Confucian ideas and institutions largely in disrepute, an increasing number of Chinese intellectuals began to realize that China had to face up

118

to the long, agonizing task of establishing a new political, economic, and social order, in large part patterned after Western experience, and of maintaining her territory against the pressures of Western imperialism. The activities of radical nationalists like Sun Yat-sen helped to topple the Manchus from power after the outbreak of the revolution of 1911 and to establish the Chinese Republic, but Sun and his supporters were not strong enough to seize power and provide the leadership that China so desperately needed. The revolution was in many ways premature, and the revolutionaries lost power within the framework of republican government to the experienced and opportunistic Yuan Shih-k'ai, who became China's first president. Not long thereafter, following Yuan's sudden death in 1916, the revolutionaries were again unable to act effectively, and political power passed into the hands of selfishly ambitious military leaders—the so-called "warlords."

Thus the Ch'ing dynasty gave way not to a new reform dynasty in the pattern of the dynastic cycle nor to a revolutionary republic bent upon modernization but to the nearly complete decentralization of political power and lack of effective leadership that characterized the warlord era. Meanwhile, of course, foreign imperialism, particularly that of Japan, strengthened its hold on the country.

8 *Western Imperialism and Dynastic Decline*

Trade remained the great link between Europe and China, and Canton continued as the center of commercial activity. From the ports of Europe and the United States came the ships and merchants in search of Chinese products, but after 1750 the largest share of the trade fell to the English East India Company. The Portuguese empire had declined, and its interest in China was limited to a small but lucrative trade at Macao; France, defeated in the colonial wars with Great Britain, did not trade on a large scale; and Dutch energies were absorbed in the Indies. The Russians had no entree into China beyond the border trade and the occasional expeditions to Peking; and in 1806, when some Russian ships arrived at Canton, they were denied trade by the Chinese on the ground that Russia already enjoyed trade on the northwest frontier. Only the Americans provided serious competition for the British. After 1750 China's relations with the West were for the most part with a British commercial company whose superintendent of trade was, to a large extent, spokesman for the entire community of merchants.

The Canton Trade and Its Problems

A group of Chinese merchants known collectively as the *co-hong* conducted the trade and was responsible to the local officials for the security of the foreign merchants. This body had been organized in the early 1700's by Cantonese merchants to control the prices of products like tea and silk, which constituted a large part of the trade, and by 1736 it was general practice to assign every foreign ship to a member of the co-hong, who purchased the inbound cargo and sold the outbound one. Each Chinese merchant was held responsible by his government for the actions of foreigners, and he was the only medium for communication between officials and foreigners. In conjunction with a commissioner of customs, called the *Hoppo*, he levied both import and export duties and collected the numerous ship's fees. The government of China eventually limited the number of merchants in the co-hong to thirteen and sold the lucrative memberships for its own profit. The foreigners objected to the monopoly position of the co-hong, but their profits were still so great that they endured this disadvantage to keep the trade open. The Chinese realized this and used their knowledge to maintain the upper hand in their dealings with the foreigners.

For a long period the trade was one-sided in favor of China. At first the foreigners paid for Chinese products with specie or bullion, but gradually they built up an exchange of commodities. They bartered the furs of Pacific Ocean sea otters, Hawaiian sandalwood, cotton goods, ginseng, and rice for Chinese tea, silks, porcelain, and nankeen cloth (highly durable cotton). Yet China continued to have a favorable trade balance, which the foreigners continued to make up with specie, usually silver. The Western interest in the trade was so great that the Chinese came to believe that the peoples of Europe and the United States were dependent on Chinese products for their well-being, and this conclusion further increased their feeling of superiority in dealing with the foreign merchants. They reasoned that to halt the trade might affect certain Chinese pocketbooks, but it would do the same to foreigners and, moreover, injure their health as well. The government regarded trade as a privilege, not a right, and it realized that a threat to stop the trade was a very effective weapon in controlling foreign merchants.

By the late 1700's the importation of opium into China threw the balance of trade in favor of the foreigners. Opium had been introduced into China as a medicine from India during the T'ang dynasty, and during the 1600's the practice of making it into a paste for smoking became common. As the opium trade grew, it centered first at Macao and later, in the 1700's, at Canton. Many Chinese became addicts, and traders of all nationalities were eager to profit in the vast narcotics market that developed. American and French ships bought Turkish and Persian opium, but the English East India Company monopolized the largest source of supply in India. The Company did not permit its own ships to carry the drug but sold it to private traders, who shipped it to China under special license. Importation of opium increased rapidly, reaching an annual total of about 4,000 chests (133 pounds each) by 1800.

Trade, though profitable to both sides, generated friction. The foreigners objected to the co-hong system, which denied them the liberty to trade with whomever they pleased; and they lamented their inability to seek redress of what they considered legitimate grievances, for the Chinese government did not permit diplomatic intercourse and did not formally recognize the merchant community. Their major complaint, however, concerned tariff irregularities. Peking set moderate tariff schedules, but, since local officials applied them quite arbitrarily, some of the duties were increased by as much as ten times; in addition, it was forbidden to re-export unsold goods duty-free. The foreigners also regarded as intolerable the various social restraints imposed upon them. The Chinese confined foreign living and business quarters to the narrow limits of the warehouses at Whampoa and denied the foreigners access to markets and recreational facilities at Canton. Wives or other foreign women could not accompany the traders to Canton; they remained at Macao. From the standpoint of personal needs and comforts, the foreigners were completely dependent on the good will of the Chinese; even their food and water came from Chinese sources.

Most concerned about these problems, the British dispatched a series of diplomatic missions which sought to put the trade on a treaty basis. In 1787 the British government appointed Lieutenant Colonel Charles Cathcart as special envoy to the emperor of China, but Cathcart's untimely death forced London to postpone the project. In 1793 the British plenipotentiary, Lord George Macartney, was received by Emperor Ch'ien Lung at the summer palace in Jehol, and shortly thereafter at Peking a determined Macartney presented a letter to the grand council requesting the right of residence at the capital for a British minister, the opening of additional ports, the establishment of a British settlement at Peking on the basis of equality with the Russians, cessions of small islands off the coast of China near Chushan and Canton for residences and warehouses, and determination of a fixed tariff schedule. Although Macartney had been received in audience by the emperor without having to kowtow and had been graciously entertained, all his requests were refused. In fact he was reprimanded for his impertinence in making requests that ran counter to Chinese practice. Macartney also encouraged his hosts to employ Western technicians to instruct China in scientific and technological subjects, but his advice was met with indifference.

During the years of warfare with the French Republic and with Napoleon, British merchants at Canton continued to trade under Chinese terms, but in 1816, after the termination of hostilities in Europe, London appointed Lord Amherst as special ambassador to China to seek once again a new basis for commerce. Like Macartney, Amherst sought to put Great Britain on an equal footing with China in their commercial and political relations. At Peking he was not treated as hospitably as Macartney had been, and when he complained, he was ordered to leave the country. It was abundantly clear that the government of China would not accept the Western legal equality of nations but preferred to cling to its Confucian precedents and attitudes; unrealistically, Peking felt that its position was one of strength.

The Background of British-Chinese Hostilities

In 1833 the nature of the relations between Great Britain and China altered significantly. In that year the monopoly privileges of the English East India Company expired, and parliament did not renew them. There had been for some time numerous complaints about the Company's monopoly, and many critics pointed out that American merchants were making great inroads in the Canton trade while many British merchants were prohibited from competing. When the China trade was opened to all British subjects, the economic repercussions were immediate. With an increased demand for Chinese goods, prices rose—raw silk 25 per cent and tea 55 per cent—as did tariffs through manipulation by the co-hong and the Hoppo. There was also an important political change. Prior to 1833 the British merchants at Canton had been represented by a commercial agent of the Company, but now a commissioned officer of the crown was stationed there to protect them and their commercial interests. Chinese-British relations became matters of state concern, and indignities were now considered as insults to the British crown.

In December, 1833, Lord Napier, a Scottish peer, was appointed first superintendent of trade at Canton, and he was instructed to solve outstanding differences by direct negotiations and to establish diplomatic relations on the basis of legal equality between nations. Napier had been ordered by London to announce his arrival to the local Chinese viceroy and to secure direct communication with the imperial court at Peking if possible; yet at the same time he was cautioned not to endanger the trade. He arrived at Macao in July, 1834; and although he lacked adequate credentials, he proceeded to the factories at Whampoa without the permission of the local authorities. When he attempted to communicate directly with the viceroy, his letter was ignored because he had failed to use the required form of petition, and the trade was temporarily suspended by the co-hong, which was blamed by the viceroy for Napier's indiscretion. When Napier refused to accept Chinese procedures, the viceroy formally stopped the trade. Napier insisted that the British king would not tolerate this unjustified pressure, and he ordered two warships to Canton. The viceroy replied through the co-hong that, unless Napier withdrew to Macao, he would use force to counter British actions, but, conversely, should Napier comply, he would revoke the order barring commerce. In September Napier came down with a fever and was ordered by his physician to rest at Macao. On the twenty-first of the month he had the two ships withdrawn, and on the twenty-sixth he retired to Macao. Trade was resumed on the twenty-ninth, but shortly thereafter Napier fell victim to malaria. This affair is recounted in some detail because it raised the curtain on a five-year period of tension which ultimately ended in war.

Napier's successors in the post of first superintendent of trade adopted a conciliatory policy because they were fearful of a suspension of trade. Sir John Francis Davis and George Robinson supervised the trade from Macao, but Charles Elliot, who assumed the post in 1836, announced his arrival in a petition submitted to the viceroy through the co-hong and was permitted to reside at Canton. Although this was a violation of his instructions, he preferred not to press the issue. The problem of diplomatic equality remained unsettled, and British merchants at Canton and at home urged their government to provide Elliot with special authority and adequate military support in order that he might negotiate directly with the authorities at the Chinese capital.

The Chinese government on its part had certain objections to the nature of the trade, especially the importation of large quantities of opium, which was spreading vice and draining China's wealth. As early as 1729 the emperor had prohibited its importation and its sale, but the ban had not been effective so long as Chinese and Western merchants found the trade profitable. In 1796 and again in 1800 the government issued new edicts against the trade and the cultivation of the opium poppy in China. By this time the Chinese were growing their own opium in larger amounts, and in some cases its cultivation interfered with the local food supply. Despite these efforts, the trade continued on a smuggling basis, and its volume increased, even though both the co-hong and the English East India Company ceased to engage in it. By 1829 opium formed 49 per cent of British imports into China, and by 1834 it amounted to 51 per cent. The value of opium exceeded the combined total of all other commodities exported, and the resulting unfavorable trade balance for China reached an annual figure of £2,000,000. Despite a government ban on the use of specie in foreign trade, gold and silver were flowing out of China in steadily increasing amounts, and even copper cash was being hauled away in foreign ships. The following figures give some indication of the increase in the opium trade:

VOLUME IN CHESTS (133 LBS. EACH) (Annual Average)		VALUE IN DOLLARS (Annual Average)	
1800–1810	4,500		
1811–1820	10,000	1818–1819	4,000,000
1821–1830	16,000	1827–1828	10,500,000
1831–1835	18,712	1832	15,000,000
1835	26,000		
1839	30,000		

Chinese smugglers in fast boats met foreign ships offshore, indicated the quantity of opium desired, and paid for it in silver. Local officials were bribed to permit the foreigners to establish storage facilities on Lintin Island, Hong Kong, and other islands in the broad estuary of the Canton River, and drug fleets also operated off the coast, some as far north as Manchuria. Although the trade was a profitable enterprise, the foreign community was not united on the opium question. Some objected to it on moral grounds, while others, of a more practical turn, thought that the opium trade prevented the development of a more normal import business. In the final analysis, the foreigner was responsible for the trade; on the other hand, many Chinese were anxious to profit from it, and, within the country, other Chinese continued to engage in opium cultivation under licenses purchased from local officials.

The problem of legal jurisdiction over foreigners added to the friction between China and the West. The most serious disputes where those in which Chinese officials demanded the surrender of foreigners accused of murdering Chinese. The main problem was the definition of legal standards of fair trial and just punishment. The British objected strenuously to the severity of Chinese punishments, the utilization of torture to extract confessions, and the prevalence of corruption in Chinese courts. In 1784 a bitter jurisdictional dispute arose when two Chinese were accidentally killed during the firing of a salute by the gunner of a British vessel, and not until the local authorities threatened to halt the trade and expel the British from Whampoa did the British surrender him. After a trial that the foreign community considered a travesty on justice, the Chinese court ordered the defendant executed by strangulation. In subsequent disputes the British refused to submit to Chinese justice, and in 1793 Macartney endeavored to secure extraterritorial privileges whereby British subjects would be tried under their own laws. In 1833, when a representative of the British crown began to supervise the trade, the British established a court at Whampoa with criminal and admiralty jurisdiction. While the British refused to concede to China in the matter of jurisdiction, the Americans, their chief rivals in the trade, continued to abide by Chinese law.

After 1835 Great Britain and China drifted toward war. In that year Lord Palmerston returned to head the foreign office, and he was determined to secure direct communication with Chinese officials on terms of diplomatic equality. By 1838 a small British naval squadron was stationed off the south China coast, and the commander was instructed to support, in co-operation with the superintendent, the complaints of British merchants. War was imminent. The British were determined to make China accept the modern practices of diplomacy between nation-states, and the Chinese were equally insistent that, if the British wanted to trade, they would have to respect Chinese hospitality and not venture to reform Chinese attitudes and practices.

The War of 1840 and the First Treaty Settlement

The events of 1839 dramatically exposed the differences in outlook between Great Britain and China and finally brought on the war. For some time the imperial court had been concerned over the flourishing illegal traffic in opium and was considering alternative policies proposed by contending bureaucratic factions. One was to legalize the trade and thus control it more effectively; the other was to enforce the opium ban, with arms if necessary. The latter view won out, and in January, 1839, the central government informed Canton that an imperial commissioner, Lin Tse-hsu, was on his way to terminate the smuggling. Lin reached Canton in March and proceeded to act almost immediately. He ordered the foreign merchants to surrender all the opium in their possession and to give bond, on penalty of death, that they would import no more. Chinese troops and war junks surrounded the factory area, and all trade was suspended. Unless the foreigners complied with the bond, Lin threatened a complete termination of trade. Superintendent Elliot, acting on behalf of the entire foreign community, surrendered more than 20,000 chests of opium, which Lin promptly dumped into the river. The siege was relaxed, but the question of the bond on penalty of death remained unsettled. Elliot feared that, whenever opium was discovered, it would be confiscated and the smuggler executed without trial, so he forbade British merchants to agree to the bond. In May the British merchants, under Elliot's orders, retired to Macao, leaving their business interests in the hands of a group of Americans, who had accepted a slightly modified form of the bond. For a time the Americans did a lucrative business carrying British cargoes to Canton, since British ships were forbidden to enter the river. Opium-smuggling continued; too many merchants, both Chinese and foreign, were anxious to profit from it.

In July, 1839, a jurisdictional dispute arose when a Chinese villager was killed at Kowloon by drunken British sailors. Lin ordered their arrest on the charge of murder; and when Elliot refused to turn them over to the Chinese authorities, Lin cut off the supply of provisions to Macao and proceeded to mass troops nearby. The British evacuated to the island of Hong Kong and prepared for a long siege. In August a British court fined and imprisoned the guilty sailors, but the Chinese were not satisfied. Tension was high, and both sides leaned toward the use of force. Yet war did not break out. The only important military action occurred on November 3, 1839, when two British frigates engaged Chinese war junks along the coast and defeated them. The Chinese retaliated by formally terminating trade with Great Britain, but normal business was continued through American agents, and opium-smuggling thrived.

In February, 1840, the government at London decided to resort to force to improve the conditions of trade in China. William Jardine, member of parliament, head of the largest trading company in the Far East (Jardine, Matheson and Company), and spokesman for commercial and industrial interests anxious to expand the China trade, persuaded Palmerston to demand redress for the seizure of the opium in the form of an apology, an indemnity, and a treaty basis for trade in general. In April parliament passed by a narrow majority a motion urging war with China, and the government ordered the dispatch from India to south China of sixteen warships and transports with four thousand men under the command of George Elliot, cousin of the superintendent. In July this British squadron blockaded Canton, presented a list of demands as the basis of treaty negotiations, and seized one of the Chushan Islands south of the mouth of the Yangtze River.

Because of the dilatory tactics employed by the Chinese authorities, negotiations did not begin at Canton until January, 1841. Charles Elliot represented the British, and the powerful viceroy of Chihli, Ch'i-shan, represented China. Ch'i-shan realistically offered concessions to the British and with Elliot signed a draft treaty which included the following: $6,000,000 as an indemnity for the opium that had been destroyed, diplomatic intercourse on terms of equality, the cession of Hong Kong in return for the restoration to China of Chushan, and the resumption of trade. Peking, however, repudiated the treaty and recalled Ch'i-shan for punishment. Hostilities were renewed, and by May Canton was once again at the mercy of British guns. Chinese merchants, fearful of the potential destruction and loss of life, persuaded Elliot to accept $6,000,000 in ransom for the city, and trade was resumed. This time London dismissed Elliot because of his failure to conclude a more comprehensive settlement and replaced him with Sir Henry Pottinger.

The British were now more determined than ever to force concessions from China. The fleet moved northward along the coast, occupying various ports along the way, but the final blows had to wait until the spring of 1842, when the British were able to bring reinforcements from India. By August of that year Nanking stood defenseless against British attack, and Peking sued for peace. A small army of only seven thousand effectives had humbled the Chinese empire and had destroyed the military prestige of the Manchus.

The Treaty of Nanking, signed on August 29, 1842, by Pottinger and the imperial commissioner, Ch'i-ying, was the price that China had to pay for losing the war. It terms, including those of several subsidiary agreements, may be summarized as follows:

1. Five ports were opened to foreign trade and residence with the right to appoint consular officials in each. These ports were Canton, Amoy, Foochow, Ningpo, and Shanghai.

2. A uniform and moderate tariff on exports and imports was established. [This amounted, as worked out in negotiations at Shanghai, to a 5 per cent ad valorem tariff, which could not be increased except by mutual consent.]
3. The co-hong was abolished, and the British were permitted to trade with individual Chinese merchants.
4. China paid an indemnity of $21,000,000: $6,000,000 for the opium that had been turned over to Lin, $3,000,000 for debts of the co-hong to British merchants, and $12,000,000 for the expenses of the war.
5. Correspondence between British and Chinese officials was to be termed a communication and not a petition.
6. The Island of Hong Kong was ceded to Great Britain in perpetuity.
7. There was provision for extraterritorial jurisdiction in criminal cases in which British nationals were involved. [Civil cases were added in the American-Chinese Treaty of 1844.]
8. The British were to be entitled to most-favored-nation treatment, i.e., if concessions were granted by China to nationals of another state, they would automatically accrue to the British.

The Treaty of Nanking made no provision for the opium trade. In the British view, China was free to legalize and control imports or to prohibit them, but enforcement of any ban would be China's responsibility. During the course of the negotiations China made it clear that she would not legalize the trade. Finally, there was no agreement as to the exchange of diplomatic officials.

The rights conferred in the Treaty of Nanking were soon extended by China to other foreign nations and their nationals. In October, 1843, Commodore Kearney of the United States Navy asked the viceroy of Kwangtung to grant to Americans rights and privileges equal to those conceded to the British on the basis of most-favored-nation treatment. The initial reaction of the imperial court, when it was consulted, was adverse to extending the Treaty of Nanking as the basis of relations with other nations, but it finally decided to continue to apply the principle of the equality of commercial interests. American-Chinese relations were put on a more solid footing, however, with Caleb Cushing's Treaty of Wanghia in July, 1844. Because of its clarity of expression, the American treaty superseded the Treaty of Nanking as the legal basis of Chinese foreign relations with the West until the negotiation of new treaties in 1858. Similar treaties were concluded with France in October, 1844, and with Norway-Sweden in March, 1847. Belgium was granted the same rights in a dispatch of July, 1845. Portugal tried to take advantage of China's weakness to demand full sovereignty over Macao, but China refused, although she granted most-favored-nation status to the Portuguese in the five ports. Acting unilaterally, Portugal declared Macao a free port in 1845, and much later, in 1862, China granted it autonomy and in 1887 recognized Portuguese title to it.

China also made several important concessions to Christianity. In answer to a French request, the government granted permission for the construction of Roman Catholic missions in the five treaty ports and promised toleration of Chinese converts as well as foreign Christians. These privileges were extended to Protestants when the British and Americans quickly pointed out that the original grant applied only to Roman Catholics. The Christian missionary was free to come to China again, but he had to confine his activities to the treaty ports.

All these foreign rights and privileges were the foundation of the "unequal treaty system" that the Western powers enlarged in subsequent decades at the expense of a weak and declining China. It is doubtful whether the government of China rightly understood the implications of some of the concessions it made. This was particularly true in the case of the tariff and extraterritoriality. Foreign goods now had free access to Chinese markets, and tariff increases that might be used to protect the development of Chinese industry depended on the approval of the various treaty powers. Extraterritoriality became a vexatious problem with the great increases in foreign population and the development of concession areas under foreign jurisdiction in the treaty ports. The government of China consciously followed a policy of broadening its relations in the hope of maintaining division among the powers. Its policy was safety in numbers, and, despite numerous difficulties, the decision proved wise.

The Causes of Dynastic Decline

By 1840 the decline of the Confucian system was general and not confined to a loss of military power by the Manchus. The imperial court had lost its vigor, a situation reflected in bureaucratic corruption and maladministration, and the economy, which could never withstand serious fluctuations for any extended period, began to disintegrate under numerous pressures. As of old, the peasantry suffered the impact of dynastic decline to the greatest extent, and peasant rebellion loomed as a threat. In the case of the Manchus there was another important consideration. They were an alien, privileged ruling group, and there had always been resentment against them. The memories of land confiscations by the conquerors, the slaughter of tens of thousands during the south China campaigns, and literary persecutions had been kept alive by nationalist-minded intellectuals.

There were numerous symptoms of administrative decline. After the reign of Ch'ien Lung (1736–1796), the Manchu emperors began to degenerate in ability, and factionalism and its attendant intrigue dominated court activities. Much of the inefficiency and corruption was the result of earlier measures taken by the Manchus to strengthen the monarch at the expense of his ministers. For example, the emperor alone had the power to issue orders to the viceroys and the governors; energetic and able rulers like K'ang Hsi and Ch'ien Lung provided effective leadership, but during the reigns of their incompetent successors there was no responsible agency in government to which these powers could be transferred. It was only natural that the central administration became the battleground of personal and family rivalries, which were now intensified as the old regulations against political interference by imperial princes, relatives, and eunuchs were ignored. During the reign of Tao Kuang (1821–1850) the central government pursued a "do-nothing" policy, and the chief minister, Ts'ao Chen-yang, was content to issue stereotyped decrees. In 1850 the Emperor Hsien Feng, aged twenty-two, ascended the throne, and he was more interested in the pleasures of the harem and in the night life of the capital than in the responsibilities of statecraft. Hedged about by attendants, concubines, and eunuchs, he tended to place blind confidence in favored officials.

As a result, local authorities were often equally lethargic and irresponsible. Although their autonomy was not legally recognized, each viceroy or governor was for all practical purposes left alone in governing his territory so long as he transmitted to Peking the required tax revenues and did not openly defy the authority of the emperor. Corruption began to eat away at the efficiency of the entire bureaucracy; and even its very foundation—merit based on the examinations—was often ignored as offices, ranks, and promotions were sold by a government needy of revenue. Officials, often in debt because of the cost of office and lacking security of tenure, were prone to exploit the people for personal and family gain. When censors complained and criticized such corrupt practices, they no longer enjoyed immunity from punishment. When vigorous censorship became hazardous, the institution proved incapable of stemming the tide of corruption. More often the "eyes and ears of the throne" were at the disposal of the highest bidder, and their advice and judgments were made to serve the purposes of factionalism.

By the beginning of the nineteenth century Chinese society faced serious economic problems, which worsened in the following decades. The growing financial requirements of the government placed a heavy burden on the economy, which the peasantry ultimately had to shoulder. In theory, after 1723, when the land and poll taxes were fused into a single payment, no increase in the basic tax was to be permitted, but, because of mounting expenditures, revenues were raised almost immediately through various surtaxes. The corruption of local officials, especially tax collectors, also squeezed the peasants; collectors were by bribed by landlords, and the peasantry had to bear heavier burdens.

A tremendous increase in population also had an adverse effect on the economic position of the peasantry. In the middle of the nineteenth century two competent American observers estimated that the population of China had reached the total of 400,000,000—an increase of about 200 per cent in the period 1700–1850. Dynastic records, however, show a mere 35 per cent increase in the amount of arable land over the same time span. It is difficult to understand how the excess population was supported. New crops were certainly in part responsible, since introduction of the sweet potato, maize, and to a lesser extent the potato made possible the cultivation of lands hitherto unused because they were unsuitable for rice and other grains. Cultivation became even more intensive in order to secure higher yields per acre, as fragmentation of landholdings continued unabated. Population increase caused a decline in the level of living standards, for there were no new forms of production, such as industrialization, to provide new employment and wealth.

Foreign trade also caused significant dislocations in the Chinese economy. The adverse trade balance brought about by the importation of opium and other commodities caused an outflow of silver, which resulted in the depreciation of the basic copper currency. One tael of silver, the standard unit of monetary measurement, jumped in value from one thousand to two thousand copper cash, and in the payment of taxes this worked a hardship on the peasantry, since the amount of tax they had to pay was fixed in terms of silver. On the other hand, labor paid in cash had less purchasing power. The hoarding of silver forced its price still higher, and the final result was a sharp rise in the cost of living for the people as a whole. The widespread use of opium also caused a drain of wealth from the countryside to the towns and led to an alarming contraction of the internal market. Moreover, foreign manufactured goods had an adverse effect upon some types of local handicraft production, which was subsidiary to agriculture. Matches, kerosene, paper, and cotton goods replaced their Chinese counterparts. The case of cotton goods is a good example. When piece goods from the looms of Lancashire began to be sold in China, the production of Chinese woven cloth (nankeens) began to decline rapidly, and Chinese weavers, particularly those in the southern provinces, lost their means of livelihood.

The progressive impoverishment of the peasantry set the stage for rebellion against the dynasty. The peasantry easily fell into inextricable debt in a society where credit was secured only at usurious rates of interest. When the peasant defaulted on his debt, he lost his land and sank to the status of tenant farmer; he was then faced with increasingly higher rents, driven up by intense competition for the land as population increased. In south China, where economic decline and political corruption were particularly acute, Chinese merchants who prospered in foreign trade often invested in land, becoming absentee landlords. Crop failures and widespread famine were perhaps the fatal blows that turned peasants into bandits and ultimately rebels. Between 1826 and 1850 there were frequent floods in many of the provinces along the valleys of the Yellow and Yangtze rivers, and in the 1840's there were serious famines in south China. The floods were in part the result of the refusal of the dynasty to allocate sufficient funds for water conservation.

The dynasty's military forces proved inadequate to meet any serious challenge to its power. During the long period of peace following the consolidation of the empire, the banners had lost their original fighting capabilities, and the provincial forces, drawn largely from the Chinese population, had always been kept weak and decentralized by the dynasty. Governors or provincial military commanders were not able to gather a large force in a given emergency, and at most they could defend only the capital and important cities of a province. In many cases the provincial army was just a paper force, and pay was drawn by officers for soldiers who simply did not exist. Often local troops were more of a menace than a help to the populace, their depradations being worse than those of the local bandits. One basic reason for the decline of the armies was the dynasty's failure to recruit and train competent officers. Written examinations were a farce, and emphasis was placed on feats of strength and skill until the military reform of 1901.

Secret societies rebelled against the Manchus as early as 1774. These organizations, usually led by prosperous peasants, had existed as early as the Han dynasty. In times of economic stability they were nonpolitical mutual aid associations, but in times of hardship they could be transformed into effective insurrectionary instruments by the rural population. Secret societies were often able to organize peasants into a movement directed against the whole ruling class; for example, some of the great popular rebellions of the T'ang dynasty were instigated by secret societies. These uprisings were put down, but they paved the way for the struggles between military commanders that led to the end of the dynasty.

The societies were secret because the imperial regime exercised a regulatory control over public associations; societies and guilds were expected to secure, and often pay for, official sanction. Since meetings that were not under official auspices were presumed to be purposely or potentially subversive, the secret societies were forced to perfect a measure of security and a covert means of communication. The most active of the secret societies which were anti-Manchu were the White Lotus Society and the Triad Society (Society of the Three United: Heaven, Earth, and Man), and their members were mostly poor workers and peasants who united under the slogan "Rebel against the Ch'ing, Restore the Ming." Between 1793 and 1802 the White Lotus Society rose against the Manchus in parts of five provinces—Hupeh, Honan, Szechwan, Shansi, and Kansu—and the dynasty spent 200,000,000 taels before peace was restored. The expenses involved in putting down these revolts added to the tax burdens of the local populace. In 1813 a rebellion led by another secret society actually threatened the capital, and there were at least fifteen other uprisings between 1820 and 1830. Insurgents in Kwangsi wrote on their flags "Officials Compel the People to Revolt" or "Heaven Is Getting Tired of the Manchus." Because of the decay of military power the government usually found it necessary to recruit local militia to augment the banners; but once a rebellion had been suppressed, the Manchus, distrusting militia forces, generally disbanded them.

The Manchus also had their difficulties with the southern minorities. In the case of the Miao peoples there were major suppression campaigns in 1698, 1732, 1794, and 1855. In the revolt of 1794–1795 the Miao overran and sacked numerous towns and cities in the frontier regions and provinces, particularly Kweichow. Although the Manchus had reinvested all the tribal chiefs in their hereditary positions at the beginning of the dynasty, it was ultimately Manchu policy to seize all power from the tribal rulers and bring their lands under the direct control of the state. When a chief gave up his post without rebellion, he was usually given the status of a civil official and was transferred to some other locality where he had no foundation of power. In some cases, after being paid off liberally, he was permitted to remain in his native district as a private citizen.

9   *The Taiping Rebellion and Second Treaty Settlement*

By the 1840's, in the southeast provinces, there were discontented social elements which, when they were fused, produced a rebellion strong enough to shake the Ch'ing dynasty to its very foundations. The defeat in the war with the British had been costly to Manchu prestige, and the incompetence and lawlessness of the bannermen caused the people's sentiments to shift from hating foreigners to despising Manchus. Agitators went among the populace to accuse the ruling dynasty of negligence, stupidity, and corruption; and bad crop years, landlordism, and high taxes made the peasantry a receptive audience. From 1841 to 1850 not a single year was free from uprisings, and because of the prevalence of bandits and rebels, with hundreds of thousands of followers, Peking ordered that the practice of group responsibility be enforced to keep the population under constant surveillance. The provincial authorities knew that the forces of discontent were formidable, and they found it increasingly difficult to suppress banditry and insurrection during their tenure of office.

Hung Hsiu-ch'uan and the Rebellion

A young scholar named Hung Hsiu-ch'uan provided the rebellious masses with a powerful ideological creed. Of Hakka descent, Hung was born in 1814 in a small village thirty miles north of Canton. The Hakkas, or "Guest Settlers," had immigrated from the north several hundred years earlier during a period of rebellion, and their descendants were still regarded as newcomers and were discriminated against by the local inhabitants. Many of them lived in the hilly and mountainous areas and worked hard for their livelihood. At the age of seven Hung was sent to school, where he proved to be a bright, diligent student with a good memory, and at the age of thirteen he qualified in district, or hsien, tests given for admission to the prefectural examinations. At the age of sixteen he took the prefectural examinations and failed. From 1830 to 1843 he was engaged primarily in teaching in the village school, but he never lost sight of his objective, an official post. Candidates who failed at the prefectural level were permitted to try the circuit (tao) examinations, and Hung appeared for these at Canton in 1833 (or 1834), in 1837, and in 1843 but was consistently unsuccessful. After his failure in 1837, Hung fell ill and supposedly had visions which in later years he insisted were revelations from the Christian God.

Hung interpreted these visions, which became the guide to his subsequent career, in the following manner. During a coma which lasted for forty days and forty nights, he was ushered into the presence of God, whom he described as a "man, venerable from all his years, with golden beard, and dressed in a black robe." Following baptism, Hung received a new heart and was told by God, "All human beings in the world are produced and sustained by me; they eat my food and wear my clothing, but not a single one among them has a heart to remember and venerate me . . . they worship demons; they rebel against me, and arouse my anger." Hung was commanded not to associate with them. He was given a sword and urged "to exterminate the demons" but to spare his brothers and sisters. The final vision took place on a high mountain overlooking the depravity and vices of the world, and there God presented him with ensigns of royalty and commanded him to kill all those who worshipped demons and idols.

Hung's third failure in the circuit examinations in 1843 probably made him an anti-Manchu rebel with dynastic ambitions of his own. His visions, which he interpreted by means of Christian missionary tracts that he received in Canton, probably in 1833 or 1834, provided him with a zeal to redeem China for God. He administered baptism to himself and began preaching to others. In 1844, when he lost his job as schoolteacher because of his destruction of Confucian ancestral tablets, he extended his preaching to the towns and cities around Canton. He wrote tracts in defense of his religious views and for several months in 1847 studied the Bible under an American Presbyterian missionary at Canton. He proclaimed a revelation of Christianity for the Chinese people based on a Trinity of the Father, the Heavenly Elder Brother, and—instead of the Holy Ghost—Hung, as the Heavenly Younger Brother. According to Hung, God willed that he exterminate the Manchus and rule the empire as its true sovereign. In the meantime, a close friend and convert, Feng Yun-shan, organized Hung's converts into the Association of God-Worshippers, with its base in Kwangsi, and in July, 1847, Hung took his place as religio-political leader of its three thousand members.

Membership in the Association of God-Worshippers grew rapidly. Converts came largely from poor Hakka farmers and laborers and from Miao tribesmen; but added to the horde were radical scholars, mutinous soldiers, political opportunists, and even discontented merchants and gentry. Since many of these recruits were opportunistic, struggles for leadership gave rise to factionalism. Hung emerged as the only one who could unite the several factions, and he was perhaps the one indispensable leader. Branches of the association became most numerous in the prefectures and districts in eastern Kwangsi, particularly along the river to Canton. Some secret-society members joined, but on the whole their parent organizations acted as independent insurrectionary bodies. Hung pointed out that his aims were basically incompatible with those of the secret societies since he wanted to establish a theocratic dynasty. Moreover, differences in attitude toward morals, theistic practices, and the restoration of the Ming could not be overcome. By 1850 Hung was the leader of an antidynastic movement backed by 30,000 followers, many of whom had already been involved in local uprisings to effect economic and social changes. The true God-Worshippers were already in the minority.

In 1850 the dynasty outlawed the association, accusing it of being a treasonable society, of subverting the established religion and morality, and of fostering rebellion against the government. When Peking began to take measures to break up the association, Hung and his colleagues mobilized an army of 10,000 men with some secret-society help. From November, 1850, to February, 1851, the rebels defeated imperial forces in Kwangsi, and on September 25, 1851, after the capture of Yungan, they proclaimed a new dynasty, the Heavenly Kingdom of Great Peace (T'ai P'ing), and installed Hung as the Heavenly King. The Manchus had overwhelming military superiority both in numbers of men and in equipment, but they were unable to crush the rebels. The viceroy of Kwangsi and Kwangtung had almost 100,000 Chinese garrison and field troops as well as banner reinforcements, and, in addition, he recruited new forces totaling 30,000 men. Manchu military stagnation and inefficiency had taken their toll, and these forces were no match for the fanatical, hard-hitting rebels, who displayed excellent military co-ordination in contrast to the jealousy and suspicion among the Manchu commanders. The rebel officers were often superior strategists, utilizing at times the equivalent of guerrilla tactics, and their troops were better disciplined than those of the government.

Between 1850 and 1853 the rebels scored a series of spectacular military successes. Their armies pushed from Kwangsi into Hunan, the capital of which, Changsha, fell in 1852; and more and more people were won over to the Taiping cause. By 1853, Wuchang, the capital of Hupeh, was taken, and the Yangtze Valley became the center of hostilities, with Nanking as the most important rebel target. In March, 1853, Nanking fell after a direct assault, and Hung changed its name to T'ienching, or Celestial Capital. Although the Manchu armies were near complete collapse, the rebellion began to lose its momentum. In fact, the rebels were never able to mount a major offensive north of the Yangtze River. In May, 1853, they did send a small expedition, which reached the province of Chihli, but it was halted by Mongol cavalry loyal to the dynasty. Had they been more aggressive, the rebels might have seized the north, which was already unsettled politically. Bandits operated widely, and the Moslems of the northwest were on the verge of a major uprising. Instead of following up their initial gains, the rebels let the situation reach a stalemate. In fact, during the next decade, rebel power diminished to the point where Nanking became an isolated garrison, and in 1864 provincial forces loyal to the dynasty erased this last stronghold. In the end, Hung committed suicide, and thousands of his loyal followers, not so fortunate, were brutally massacred.

The Taiping Reforms

After the fall of Nanking the Taiping leaders began to consolidate their control over their new kingdom. Hung was installed in the capital as theocratic ruler, and there he lived, often in religious seclusion, like an oriental potentate attended by a horde of female servants, wives, and concubines. Assisting him in the central government were both civil and military chiefs, bearing the title of "king," who constituted a council of state. A civil and military bureaucracy, selected in theory on the basis of examinations, handled the routine business of administration, but of necessity the military played a more important role in government. The rebels never had an opportunity to inaugurate civil administration on a broad scale because their territory remained under martial law. Administration was based on a military chain of command, descending from the army headquarters (12,500 families) to the commanders of divisions (2,500 families), brigades (500 families), and companies (100 families). Locally, in the villages, families were grouped together in units of twenty-five for co-operative purposes. Each group had its own public storehouse and church and was under the authority of the company officer, who acted as military leader, teacher, tax-collector, and judge. Each family was obligated to furnish one soldier to the army, though orphans, the aged, and the disabled were exempted.

The Taiping regime attempted numerous economic reforms, many of which were rooted in traditional Chinese practices designed to maintain economic balance in society. At first a land redistribution program based on the size of families was planned, and then a form of communalism based on the twenty-five-family group was introduced. Each family was to share in the harvest according to its needs; what remained was to be held in a common granary for emergencies or was to be sent in part to the national treasury. In addition, each family was to have a subsidiary occupation in handicraft production or animal husbandry, and the resulting products were to be similarly shared. It is doubtful whether these reforms were ever widely practiced since the rebels effectively controlled only towns and cities and in the countryside the people were resentful and unco-operative because of the constant military turmoil. In most areas the old economic system based on private property and land taxation continued, and in fact landlord interests were protected and favored.

The Taiping leaders did little to encourage the development of internal or foreign trade, for they held the usual Chinese low opinion of the merchant and would not support commercial activities. In fact, the rebels did not even exploit the opportunity to acquire foreign guns in exchange for tea and silk.

There were other reforms of a social nature that the rebel regime instituted on a limited scale. Women were regarded as the equal of men, and they were encouraged to take civil service examinations and to hold civil and military posts with men. The army even recruited women soldiers, although mostly as auxiliaries. Foot-binding and prostitution were forbidden, and monogamy was promoted, although the Taiping kings had many wives. Marriage based on individual desires rather than family considerations was proclaimed as an ideal, but is extremely doubtful whether this was practiced. The regime abolished household slavery and infanticide and also forbade gambling and the use of opium, tobacco, and liquor. Except in the city of Nanking, these prohibitions were not widely enforced. Finally, in the field of education, the rebel leadership sought to develop a simplified popular form of writing that would help to increase literacy.

The Taiping program also had a strong religious foundation based on Hung's unique form of Christianity, blended with Confucianism, Buddhism, and Taoism. It shared with Christianity a belief in a supreme God, the cultivation of virtue according to the Ten Commandments, a notion of salvation as taught in the New Testament (but perverted by the substitution of Hung for the Holy Ghost), and rites like baptism and observance of the Sabbath. Young boys were to go to church every day to study the Old and New Testaments, and on Sunday everyone was to attend church, where they listened to Taiping pronouncements and prayed to God. Confucianism contributed the concepts of filial piety, loyalty, and obedience; and while the Taipings destroyed idols, they spared Confucian temples. From Buddhism and Religious Taoism Hung borrowed multiple heavens and hells, the belief in fatalism, and the search for longevity and immortality. He stressed the sacrificial offerings to God of rice, wine, fowl, and pigs on such occasions as birthdays and weddings, and he was even superstitious enough to believe in the magical power of the Taoists, who claimed to be able to render human bodies invulnerable to bullets.

The regime sought to make religion a vigorous force in the life of the people. Religious ideas and rites were used to maintain military morale and prevent mutiny, to promote hard labor, and to popularize education, but in the final analysis a stern and cruel law was the ultimate sanction for much of its program. Absence from divine worship was punishable by the horrible sentence of being torn apart by horses, and adultery by being burned to death. It is safe to conclude that the people at large had very little understanding of the deeper matters of faith. Religion was forced on them against their will.

For a time the foreigners for the most part took a neutral attitude toward the Taiping Rebellion. This was certainly true of the diplomatic representatives of Great Britain, France, and the United States. But there was some initial enthusiasm for the rebel cause. Hung's Christian teachings won the favor of some missionaries, and there was a general feeling among many foreigners that a native Chinese dynasty would be more friendly to foreign trade. When the nature of Hung's faith was more fully disclosed, however, the missionaries were repelled; and when the rebel regime actually sought British aid in the form of an alliance in October, 1854, it was refused.

Friction between China and the West

The foreigners tended to watch and wait, and their main concern at this time was getting the Manchus to revise the treaties. Despite the treaty settlement following the Sino-British war of 1840, relations between China and the Western powers had continued to deteriorate. The government at Peking maintained its attitude of superiority, and it was seemingly trying to recover lost ground by delaying the implementation of the treaty provisions. Some of the responsibility for this must be borne by local officials, who enjoyed a large measure of autonomy. In the negotiation of the Treaty of Nanking (1842) the central government had stubbornly refused to permit foreign diplomatic representatives to reside in Peking, and relations between China and the powers continued to be handled in the main by the viceroy of Kwangsi and Kwangtung. He in turn further refined the indirect approach by referring foreign diplomats to inferior officials, even personal servants, and, when he did actually meet with ministers, he treated them with indifference. These practices, which were intended to be humiliating and intolerable for foreigners, prevented Peking from getting a realistic picture of the problems of foreign relations.

China justifiably resented the expansion of opium-smuggling which had occurred after 1842. Estimates of "imports" of opium between that date and 1858 indicate an increase of over 300 per cent. The laws of China still prohibited the opium trade, but merchants on both sides found it a profitable enterprise, and the foreigners, particularly the British, felt that China should legalize and control the trade under fixed duties.

Peking also objected to the traffic in Chinese labor that flourished in the 1840's and 1850's, when foreigners shipped coolies in increasing numbers to the plantations of Cuba, the guano fields of Peru, and the mines and railroads of the American West. For example, by the end of 1851 there were as many as 25,000 Chinese working in California as placer miners, cooks, and manual laborers. At first foreigners hired labor on a voluntary basis; but when news reached China that contractual conditions were not being met, the foreigners and their Chinese agents had to resort to violence and kidnapping in their recruiting. After 1855 the Chinese government issued edicts against the coolie trade, but the ban was ineffective since local officials were often involved in it. The dynasty objected to the trade largely on the ground that it violated laws against expatriation. The Manchus had always sought to prevent Chinese emigration, as they did not want overseas Chinese to become the basis of a movement that might, with foreign aid, stir up revolt at home.

The dynasty also complained about the convoying system which grew out of the need to protect domestic and foreign shipping against Chinese pirates. Armed foreign vessels provided protection for a fee, and at first charges were reasonable. Before long, however, the charges became extortionate, and protection was literally forced upon Chinese coastal shippers.

Finally, there was the problem of extraterritorial jurisdiction. The Chinese complained that the foreigners shamelessly disregarded obligations and responsibilities by failing to provide consular courts and jails. The British were the first to meet these obligations, but they did not act until the late 1850's.

Friction between China and the West was most evident at Canton, where the local officials had purposely developed antiforeignism among the population during the war of 1840. After the war Ch'i-ying was able to obtain a two-year postponement for opening Canton to the British, but, when the stay expired, his successors denied the right of residence, would not permit official intercourse on terms of equality, attempted to keep the trade in the hands of an enlarged monopoly of Chinese merchants, and refused to acquiesce in the extraterritorial provisions of the treaties. Yeh Ming-ch'en, the viceroy after 1852, was arrogant in his refusals to let the British enter Canton and boasted that he himself would "wash off China's humiliation and enhance its dignity." Despite these difficulties, trade in the Canton area expanded.

Trade expanded also with the opening of Shanghai and, within limits, at Amoy, Foochow, and Ningpo. Shanghai's location on the Whangpoo River near the mouth of the Yangtze helped make it China's greatest port, and in fact, when foreign settlement began in November, 1843, Shanghai was already active in China's inland and coastal trade. Its population numbered about 270,000, and its inhabitants were free from the intense antiforeignism of the south. By 1852 Shanghai handled more than half of China's coastal and foreign trade. It was particularly the center of the silk and tea trade, and opium was imported without restriction. A fairly lively trade developed at Amoy, but the volume was limited by the fact that Amoy was a coastal pocket without the easy access to interior markets enjoyed by Shanghai and Canton. Trade at Foochow was negligible until the expansion of the American tea trade after 1854. Foochow was too close to Amoy, the harbor was poor, and the population was hostile. Ningpo was simply too close to Shanghai. While the China trade continued to grow in volume, it was not large enough to satisfy the foreign merchants, and by the 1850's they wanted more ports and direct access to interior markets.

Foreign "concessions" were the centers of commercial activity in the treaty ports. Concessions were grants of land on which foreign merchants erected their residences, offices, and warehouses. They were leased by China to a particular foreign power, which in turn subdivided the land into lots, granting these on long-term leases to its subjects or in some cases to other foreigners. The foreign community of each concession ultimately had its own municipal administration, presided over by its consul, which was responsible for the various services essential to welfare: public works, sanitation, and police. These areas were established under the Chinese land regulations of 1845, which were later revised several times, until by 1881 concessions became virtually autonomous entities within Chinese territory. The treaty ports, which reached a total of nineteen by the twentieth century, contained thirty-three concessions or general settlements. In the case of Tientsin, opened in 1860, there were eventually as many as eight separate foreign concessions.

The land situation at Shanghai was somewhat different. There the local authorities objected to the concession system; instead they permitted lots to be leased in perpetuity (in theory all land belonged to the emperor and could not be alienated by outright sale) by Chinese owners to foreigners. Over a period of time a system developed by which each consul exercised jurisdiction over his own nationals in the common settlement area and at the same time participated with his fellow-consuls in the supervision of settlement affairs. The foreign community at Shanghai came to be known as the International Settlement, and only the French maintained their own concession. When the International Settlement came into being, it was thought that the area would be inhabited exclusively by foreigners; but it soon included a large Chinese population, and by 1854 the number of Chinese residents had increased from an original few hundred to twenty thousand. Of necessity the foreign community was forced to devise a more effective system of local government, since multiple consular jurisdiction was not adequate; and in 1854 the foreign merchants adopted a constitution which placed power in the hands of an elected and exclusively foreign municipal council.

By the 1850's the foreign community in China desired a revision of the treaties. It wanted the Chinese to observe the present treaties faithfully, to extend the trade to more ports and to the interior, and to accept diplomatic representation at Peking on the basis of the legal equality of nations under international law. The demand for revision was based on a provision in the American and French treaties which the British claimed as a right according to the most-favored-nation clause. They held that the Treaty of Nanking was subject to revision after 1854, and, on instructions from London, Lord Bowring, the British high commissioner, presented a list of proposals to Viceroy Yeh Ming-ch'en at Canton. When Yeh failed to reply, Bowring turned to Peking but was informed that the only course was to work through the Canton viceroy. The British were forced to endure Yeh's insolence until after the Crimean War, but in the autumn of 1856 London dispatched a diplomatic and naval expedition to Peking to deal directly with the central government.

War and the Second Treaty Settlement, 1856–1860

Friction between China and Great Britain was intensified by the "Arrow" incident. The "Arrow" was a small ship owned by a Chinese resident of Hong Kong but registered under the British flag and captained by a British subject. It was common practice for foreign consuls to issue registry to native vessels, but this constituted a grave problem for Chinese officials, as they could not be sure whether these craft were engaged in legitimate enterprises or not. In fact, many of them were suspected of smuggling or of supplying Chinese rebels. In October, 1856, a Chinese water patrol boarded the "Arrow" near Canton and arrested twelve of her crew of fourteen on charges of piracy, removing them to a Chinese war junk. The British consul, Harry Parkes, demanded their release on the ground that the "Arrow" was a British ship, that she had been boarded without his knowledge, and that the British flag had been hauled down by Chinese police. Bowring also demanded an apology and guarantees for the future. Yeh, who had been given forty-eight hours to comply or face the consequences, released the prisoners; but Parkes refused to accept them since they were not accompanied by a Chinese officer of rank nor by an apology. British naval forces then destroyed the forts guarding the approach to Canton and occupied the city, but they did not have sufficient strength to follow up their advantage, since the Sepoy Mutiny in India caused the British to transfer troops from China.

The Chinese retaliated for the bombardment of Canton. Yeh, not familiar with the Western idea of the sanctity of flags, felt that China had been unjustly attacked, and he called upon all Chinese to exterminate the British "devils." He even went so far as to offer monetary rewards for every British head brought to him. A Chinese mob set fire to the British commercial area, and the British retaliated in kind against Chinese warehouses. Local tension reached a climax in January, 1857, when it was discovered that a Chinese baker, who supplied foreigners at Hong Kong with bread, was putting arsenic in the dough. Despite evidence to the contrary, the Chinese authorities denied any implication in the plot.

In this period the British were seeking to develop a co-operative policy with the United States and France, since it was in the interests of their nationals, also, to revise the treaties. In general the American commissioners in China supported British policy, and in 1854 Robert McLane had co-operated with Bowring in an effort to persuade the Chinese to accept treaty revision. But when Great Britain proposed a three-power alliance in March, 1857, the United States declined to join. France, on the other hand, was ready for decisive action. French resentment had risen when a French Catholic priest and several of his converts in the interior of Kwangsi had been executed as rebels in February, 1856. The charge of treason was probably based upon the fact that many Roman Catholic converts were being indoctrinated with the idea of France as their supporter and liberator from persecution; the Chinese authorities could also point to the fact that the priest was illegally preaching beyond the treaty ports. News of the execution reached Canton in July, 1856, and by October France agreed to the British policy of a show of force. The British government appointed Lord Elgin to head the diplomatic-military expedition, and France designated Baron Gros as plenipotentiary to co-operate with his British colleague. The United States and Russia were invited to join the expedition, but they declined, although both sent representatives to observe and reap the rewards of the action. War was likely unless the Chinese government proved willing to negotiate with the foreign representatives.

When Yeh refused to comply with an ultimatum demanding revision, the fighting began. In December, 1857, British and French forces bombarded and captured Canton. Yeh was seized and transported to India, where he died as a prisoner of war. Trade was resumed, and Canton was ruled for the next three years by Chinese officials acting under the orders of a British and French commission. The expedition moved northward to the mouth of the Pei-ho, and in February, 1858, the allies demanded that the court at Peking appoint a single plenipotentiary to negotiate with them at Shanghai. After some delay the court appointed the viceroy of Chihli, but the British and French regarded his powers as inadequate. They concluded that only a military advance through Tientsin to Peking would end China's procrastination and bring her to terms. The allied troops stormed the forts at Taku on May 20 and reached Tientsin on May 30. Peking promptly appointed officials whose powers were regarded as adequate, and negotiations were conducted at Tientsin concurrently but separately with the representatives of the four powers.

The Treaties of Tientsin, which by virtue of the most-favored-nation clause may be regarded as a single treaty settlement, extended the scope of the unequal treaty system. They provided for the following new rights and privileges:

1. The right to maintain a resident minister at Peking or the right of a minister to visit the capital. The minister should not be called upon to perform any ceremony derogatory to him as representing the sovereign of an independent nation on a footing of equality with China.
2. The right of travel in the interior under passports issued by the foreign consuls and countersigned by local Chinese authorities.
3. The right of foreign ships to trade and patrol on the Yangtze River, and the opening of additional ports to trade and residence: Chefoo in Shantung, Chinkiang in Kiangsu, Hankow in Hupeh, Kiukiang in Kiangsi, Kiungchow in Hainan, Newchang in Manchuria, Swatow in Kwangtung, Wenchow in Chekiang, and Nanking in Kiangsu. [The opening of these ports was delayed greatly in some cases; for example, Nanking was not a treaty port until 1899.]
4. The right of missionaries to have access to all parts of the interior to spread Christianity and to have protection by Chinese authorities. [Unfortunately, the fact that toleration was forced on China as a result of war caused many Chinese to regard the religion as a political weapon of imperialism.]
5. Two million taels of silver were to be paid as reparation for the losses of British merchants and two million taels as indemnity for military expenses.

Following the Tientsin agreements, negotiations continued at Shanghai, where the tariff schedule was revised to establish an effective 5 per cent ad valorem duty on both imports and exports. In addition, the opium trade was legalized but was subject to a higher duty. Legalization stabilized the trade and provided the Chinese government with much-needed new revenue.

The Treaties of Tientsin were to become effective when ratified copies had been exchanged at Peking, but the imperial court, dominated by a "war party" of Manchu princes, preferred to resume hostilities. When British and French troops attempted to storm the Taku forts again, they were repelled and forced to withdraw. Peking was greatly pleased at this turn of events and foolishly dared hope that the foreigners would not attack again, but the allies organized a new expedition in March, 1860, landed at Peitang, and advanced on Tientsin and Peking. When the allied troops entered the capital in September, the emperor had fled safely to Jehol, leaving the peace negotiations to officials who had earlier urged a policy of moderation. One particularly unfortunate aftermath of hostilities was the allied looting of Peking and burning of two hundred buildings in the summer palaces of the emperor in retaliation for the Chinese execution of twenty allied prisoners of war.

Ratifications of the Treaties of Tientsin were exchanged at Peking in

October, 1860, and new concessions were conceded by China in the Peking Convention, as follows:

1. Tientsin was opened as a treaty port. [This was particularly objectionable to the dynasty because of its proximity to Peking.]
2. Kowloon, the mainland peninsula opposite Hong Kong, was ceded to Great Britain.
3. The French text secured restoration to the Roman Catholic Church of all church property confiscated since 1724. [This was to work great hardship on the Chinese who had acquired the property.]
4. The Chinese text of the French convention also contained a troublesome provision allowing French missionaries to rent and purchase land in all provinces and to propagate Catholicism without hindrance.
5. The British text made more specific the right of a minister to reside permanently at Peking.
6. The coolie trade was legalized as a measure of control. [However, this did not prove workable until the 1870's. British legislation, which made contract labor acceptable under humane conditions, had the effect of driving the trade to Macao, where the Portuguese authorities permitted it. In 1862 the United States barred its citizens from the trade, and by 1870 both Great Britain and the United States were able to put pressure on Portugal to ban it.]

Under the most-favored-nation clause these rights were accorded to other nationals and to the Protestants. By 1860 the unequal treaty system was more firmly established, and the powers accepted the view that their interests lay with the dynasty. On the Chinese side, many of the officials at Peking learned a valuable lesson in defeat. For example, Prince Kung, *de facto* head of state in the absence of his brother, the emperor, and his able assistant, Wen Hsiang, realized that it was foolhardy to provoke the foreign powers. Instead, they sought to strengthen China in order to get on with the task of suppressing the Taiping Rebellion.

The Suppression of the Taiping Rebellion

As early as 1855 the military and political fortunes of the Taiping rebels had begun to decline, and even when the dynasty was embroiled in foreign war the rebels were unable to press their advantage. Their initial drive was spent, and dissensions weakened their cause. The five kings under Hung were mutually jealous and ambitious men, and their quarrels became minor civil wars; after the capture of Nanking, moreover, they often succumbed to licentious living. By 1858 they were all dead, and Hung, feeling that he could trust only the members of his own family, granted the royal titles to his two brothers. Later, when the movement was near to complete disintegration, the title of king was sold to over 2,700 people.

Hung himself retired more and more to the seclusion of his palace, living as a Taoist emperor uninterested in state affairs, and in the last years of his rule the problem of leadership became crucial. Hung was increasingly obsessed with the belief that God would always intervene on his side, and men of ability who did emerge among the rebels found their talents wasted and their policies usually overruled. One of the great failings of the movement was its inability to produce an administrative elite to consolidate its gains, and the likeliest candidates, the Confucian bureaucrats, would hardly have joined the regime.

Popular support of the rebellion was alienated by Taiping bigotry and attacks upon popular beliefs. Particularly disillusioning to the masses were the great inequalities of wealth, which contradicted the movement's doctrine that all land and property were to be enjoyed in common by everybody. In the end, Confucian ideas became more popular than Taiping Christianity.

By the late 1850's there were Chinese forces in the field effectively defending the dynasty. These troops were largely local militia recruited by Chinese officials who preferred to stand behind the traditional system rather than join the rebels. One of the most outstanding of these men was Tseng Kuo-fan, a member of the gentry who could trace his ancestors back to the period of Confucius. At the end of 1852, under orders from Peking, he had begun to recruit and drill village volunteers to fight against the rebels in the province of Hunan; and when the rebels began to threaten the Yangtze Valley, he patiently worked to organize a larger force. In all, he trained ten thousand men—five thousand in a land army and five thousand marines. Financial difficulties prevented him from developing a larger force; and to support what he had, he was forced to use such expedients as selling titles and levying internal transit taxes (*likin*). Tseng took to the field in the Yangtze Valley in 1854, and for the next five years his victories barely outnumbered his defeats. By 1859 Tseng's troops were gaining superiority, but the tide of battle did not turn in the dynasty's favor until the fall of Anking in September, 1861. By 1862, in co-operation with other provincial units under Tso Tsung-t'ang and Li Hung-chang, he was moving on the rebel stronghold at Nanking.

The dynasty also received foreign support against the rebels, although at first this was strictly unofficial. In 1860, when it appeared that Shanghai would fall to the rebels, who had made repeated attacks, influential Chinese and foreign businessmen engaged an American adventurer, Frederick Townsend Ward, to defend it. Ward, who stemmed from a long line of seafaring New England ancestors, was a soldier of fortune who had been associated with the notorious American filibusterer, William Walker, in Nicaragua, had served with the French army in the Crimea, and had been involved in revolutionary enterprises in Mexico and South America. After some initial failures Ward captured the city of Sungkiang with a hundred Filipinos in July, 1860. This was the birth in battle of the "Ever Victorious Army," a title later formally conferred by the Chinese government.

Chinese and foreigners were soon eager to join Ward's army, and so great was his popularity that sailors deserted British and American ships to serve under him. At one time he was actually taken into custody by the United States and charged with encouraging desertion and endangering American neutrality. He escaped and rejoined his army, but he was forced to claim Chinese citizenship to free himself from consular molestation. In September, 1861, with the approval of the Chinese government, he adopted Western methods to organize and train a larger Chinese army. Victory followed upon victory, but Ward was finally killed in an assault on Ningpo in September, 1862. His command fell to Major Charles George Gordon, on loan from the British army, and this was the beginning of an illustrious military career that ended with Gordon's heroic death at Khartoum in 1896.

After 1860 the foreign powers finally gave official support to the dynasty, although as early as August, 1860, British and French troops had helped to defend the Shanghai area. While Great Britain and France were fighting the dynasty in the north, they sought to maintain the status quo in the south, and by February, 1862, the authorities at Shanghai were able to persuade these powers to undertake offensive operations against nearby rebel strongholds. Foreign troops captured many important towns and cities, but it would be rash to conclude that foreign assistance was a decisive factor in the suppression of the rebellion. The largest force, the "Ever Victorious Army," did not at any time number more than three thousand men, and the Chinese placed restrictions on the operations of foreign troops. Tseng Kuo-fan, for example, feared that they might become an entering wedge for foreign control of China.

Early in 1863 the imperial forces launched a three-pronged attack against the rebel stronghold at Nanking. By summer the situation was so desperate that Hung's principal general advised him to leave Nanking with 500,000 men and try to make a fresh start, but Hung refused, declaring that God would take care of him. Within a year, however, Nanking was isolated, and in anticipation of final victory the dynasty disbanded the "Ever Victorious Army" in June. Realizing that the end was near, Hung took poison, and his body was buried behind his palace by one of his wives. His eldest son, Hung Fu, ascended the throne in order to quiet the public, but in July imperial troops stormed the city and captured it after fierce fighting. The retribution was horrible. The remaining members of Hung's family were put to death, and Hung's body was dug up, dismembered, and desecrated. Two hundred of his female attendants were forced to hang themselves in the front garden of the palace, two thousand people were drowned in the moat, and thousands more were slaughtered in the streets. An imperial edict announced the end of the rebellion, although scattered military engagements continued until May, 1865.

The Taiping Rebellion was a symptom of dynastic decline, and it also hastened the process of disintegration. The physical damage alone was tremendous. Hundreds of towns and cities were destroyed, almost every province felt the devastation of war, vast areas of arable land were deserted as people fled the countryside, and tens of millions lost their lives directly or indirectly during the long period of strife. The normal processes of political life had deteriorated, and power gravitated into the hands of local strong men, particularly provincial governors who had helped to suppress the rebels. It is erroneous to think of these men as precursors of China's twentieth-century warlords since central and local officials—Manchu and Chinese alike—were united in efforts to strengthen Confucian institutions. Only with the failure of this policy near the end of the century did the breach between central and local government develop.

The rebellion also affected the economy, particularly state finance, since it prevented the normal collection of taxes in many of the richest provinces. New taxes had to be devised to pay the expenses of suppression and foreign war, and of these, likin, the internal transit tax levied on commodities in China, was the most important. Instituted as a temporary measure to bolster provincial finances, it remained in existence until 1931. Likin stations were farmed out to the highest bidder, who then had the right to collect duties on goods in transit; all the revenue above the amount of the bid was kept by the likin "commissioner," who naturally imposed duties on as many goods as possible in order to swell his private fortune. This form of taxation hindered the development of a national economy, but it did permit the government in the years following the rebellion to reduce the land tax, and after its abolition in 1931 land surtaxes soared.

Likin was also a problem for China in her relations with the powers. Foreign merchants argued that these taxes, applied to foreign goods, were illegal on the ground that they had not been applied generally until after the treaties of 1858, which expressly forbade additional levies on imports. The force of this argument was weakened, however, by the fact that other internal customs duties, similar to likin, did antedate all the treaties. The British treaty of 1858 had established a procedure for commuting these internal levies by a single payment amounting to one-half of the tariff, and it was specified that no further taxes were then to be imposed. However, the breakdown of central authority made it increasingly difficult to force local authorities to observe this arrangement.

The establishment of the Foreign Inspectorate of Customs warrants special attention. In 1853, when a Triad rebel band seized part of Shanghai, the imperial authorities fled, deserting the customs house. The situation was chaotic for a time, but soon the foreigners themselves collected duties on behalf of the dynasty. In 1854, when the rebels were dislodged, the local Chinese officials agreed to formalize the arrangement by the establishment of the Foreign Inspectorate of Customs. By 1858 the agency's authority was extended to all the treaty ports, and under the firm leadership of Sir Robert Hart it was a model of honesty and efficiency. While the personnel of the service continued to be foreign, they served as agents of the imperial government.

10 Confucianism and Modernization, 1861–1894

In the 1860's Chinese scholar-bureaucrats, desiring to restore Confucian stability, began to consider to what extent China's adoption of Western ways would serve that purpose. Actually the question had been raised as early as 1842 by Lin Tse-hsu, who was exiled for his failure to get a satisfactory settlement of the opium problem at Canton. In private letters to his friends Lin conceded China's military inferiority to the West and proposed the purchase and manufacture of Western ships and guns, but he dared not openly advocate these views. After the rebellion and the foreign wars, more and more officials put forward similar proposals, and in the following few decades the government was divided between the bureaucrats who were willing to accept certain of the material accomplishments of the West and those who rejected almost everything Western.

In reality China's problems were not going to be solved by the simple acceptance or rejection of limited modernization. It was not that easy; but the fact that it was considered so by many influential persons prolonged and increased the misfortunes of China. The premise that a revival of Confucian values and institutions, modified or not, could provide strength and stability was erroneous because China was slowly being Westernized in spite of bureaucratic decisions. Dynamic forces for change were beginning to nibble away at the foundations of the Confucian system and were preparing the groundwork for something new in its place.

Reform and Politics

The promoters of Westernization were Neo-Confucianists who had little admiration for Western culture as they understood it. To them Confucianism provided the basis of organized life, while Western culture was nothing more than a matter of military and industrial techniques. In their minds "the Confucian social order, the Confucian political system, and the Confucian ethic were of enduring value, true and right for men in all ages." In brief, they were willing to use Western armor to preserve their Chinese heritage, but they failed to realize that it was difficult if not impossible to

147

accomplish this without causing fundamental social and economic changes.

Outstanding proponents of this view were Prince Kung and Wen Hsiang at Peking and Tseng Kuo-fan, Tso Tsung-t'ang, and Li Hung-chang among the important provincial leaders and literati. These men, Manchus and Chinese, were striving to uphold traditional institutions against internal and external threats, and their co-operation in the 1860's stands in vivid contrast to the later strife between Chinese and Manchus, based on racial difference. Until his death in 1872 the able and indefatigable Tseng Kuo-fan was perhaps the most active and respected among the local leaders, and his efforts were aimed at strengthening the Confucian system at both the central and regional levels. Tso Tsung-t'ang not only was active in the Confucian revival but also served many years in the northwest, first suppressing the Nien rebels and later the Moslems. Li Hung-chang, a protégé of Tseng, was active as an innovator until his death in 1901, although in later years he became increasingly conservative. He held a number of important posts—as viceroy of Chihli, as grand secretary, and as superintendent of trade for the north. In this latter capacity he was responsible for the conduct of China's foreign relations during most of the period from 1875 to 1901. After China's defeat at the hands of Japan in 1894–1895 he suffered the attacks of political opponents, but the empress dowager, Tz'u Hsi, the dominant force at court, protected him. Li was certainly one of the more flexible leaders among the Chinese, but even he never dreamed of a fundamental reform of the Chinese political and social systems.

Wo Jen was typical of the bureaucrat who held that a simple revival of Chinese morality and learning would serve China without recourse to Westernization of any sort. He feared that Western ideas, imported along with Western techniques, would undermine the power of the literati and the dynasty. On one occasion he wrote:

> The only thing we can rely upon is maintenance of our own scholars' ability to delve into Confucian principles, by means of which they keep the minds of the people quiet and harmonious. When these brilliant and talented scholars who have been trained by the country in reserve for great usefulness in the future are converted from their regular course of study to follow the barbarians . . . the multitudes of the Chinese will be tempted to give allegiance to the barbarians.

The views of this grand secretary were supported by many officials at Peking and by the gentry as a whole. The promoters were willing to use Western learning as a means, but Wo Jen and his followers were afraid that it would become an end in itself, destructive of the existing order.

Throughout most of the decade 1860–1870 the central government was controlled by a regency which supported policies of limited Westernization within the framework of a Confucian revival. In 1861 the Emperor Hsien Feng, who had fled from Peking to a hunting lodge in Jehol, died, leaving only a nine-year-old son, known by the reign name T'ung Chih. Thwarting the plans of powerful Manchu officials, who had dominated Hsien Feng by pandering to his sensual desires, Tz'u Hsi, the concubine mother of the boy emperor, joined forces with Tz'u An, the deceased emperor's first wife, and together they acted as regents under the advice of Prince Kung. The central government was purged, and the new power of the moderates gave hope that a restored Confucian state might emerge. After the suppression of the Taiping Rebellion and the stabilization of foreign relations, the alliance of Manchus and Chinese scholars carried out important reforms in the administration. The examination system was revitalized with practical questions, at least in part; semiofficial schools and libraries which had been destroyed during the years of warfare were rebuilt; the Classics and Histories were reprinted; and new books on government were published. It is clear that such measures were designed to create greater social stability by reviving the traditional relationship of the gentry to government, and for a decade at least there was a continual flow of able men from that class. Ability, however, was still weighted down by tradition and compromised by corruption, caused by low salaries. Confucian teaching also penetrated to the lowest ranks of society, but more effective in securing popular support was a program of tax reduction, land reclamation, and grain relief.

In the 1870's the opponents of limited Westernization came into control of the government at Peking. Tz'u Hsi, relying upon strong allies among the palace eunuchs, was able to reduce Tz'u An and Prince Kung to nominal positions in the regency. Upon the ascension of the young Emperor T'ung Chih to the throne in 1873, the regency was terminated; but Tz'u Hsi continued to dominate him under precedents of filial piety and by encouraging his pursuit of pleasure. In November, 1874, T'ung Chih contracted smallpox and became so ill that the regency of the empresses was restored; and after a brief recovery he suffered a relapse and died in January, 1875. Tz'u Hsi, conspiring to control the succession and establish another long regency, successfully persuaded a council of princes and high officials to enthrone a first cousin of the deceased emperor, her own young nephew. By 1881, after the death of Tz'u An, the former concubine was sole regent.

Tz'u Hsi owed much of her success to the assistance of eunuchs. For example, the chief eunuch, Li Lien-ying, dominated palace politics from 1870 until the death of his imperial mistress in 1908. In later years he boasted that he could make or break the highest officials in the empire and defy the authority of the emperor. This was no exaggeration, since high officials of the central government and the provinces were reduced to ingratiating themselves with the favorites of Tz'u Hsi in order to maintain their power and position. In 1887 the emperor came of age, but not until 1889, when he married a niece of Tz'u Hsi, was he permitted to ascend the throne under the name Kuang Hsu. Tz'u Hsi retired to a new summer palace, but she did not relinquish political power. Through Li Lien-ying she continued to appoint and dismiss high officials, and Kuang Hsu still had to report administrative affairs to her for decision. While the emperor appeared to be intelligent, imaginative, and genuinely concerned for the welfare of his subjects, he was powerless. Most officials still looked to Tz'u Hsi as the possessor of power and patronage, and official careers and policies were often undone by the intrigues of the chief eunuch and his satellites. In later life Li Hung-chang was careful to remain in the good graces of Tz'u Hsi and to keep the protection of Li Lien-ying against the plots of his enemies.

This narrative of politics is illustrative of important basic weaknesses in the central government. Tz'u Hsi has been both praised and damned by historians and others. Some credit her with having held the dynasty together during her lifetime, but the majority have zealously catalogued her faults and failures. In any case, it is clear that this remarkable woman did not help to give China the leadership she needed. Tz'u Hsi was concerned with consolidating her own power and wealth, that of her family, and that of the Manchu dynasty against political opponents. She was not sympathetic to Westernization; in fact, there is sufficient evidence to conclude that she strongly opposed it. Without capable government in the capital, initiative was largely in the hands of provincial leaders; and the process of Westernization, limited in concept as it was, had no over-all planning and direction. It is true that some of the provincial leaders were influential at court and served concurrently in capital posts, but the central government, for its part, only occasionally experimented with Western ways in the hope of strengthening itself against growing separatism as well as the foreign menace, real or fancied.

Material Self-Strengthening

The major emphasis of the promoters of Westernization was in the military field. Foreign pressure and internal rebellion had made them feel that military reforms were essential to the preservation of the revived Confucian state. During the Taiping Rebellion, Tseng Kuo-fan, Li Hung-chang, and Tso Tsung-t'ang had made use of foreign guns and ships and had learned to appreciate the superior equipment of the "barbarians." In later years Li, as viceroy of Chihli, and Chang Chih-tung, viceroy at Canton and at Wuchang, organized provincial armies drilled by German officers, who proved that, given proper training, Chinese were first-class soldiers. Li even went so far as to send officers to Germany for training, and after 1885 he brought instructors from Europe to teach his officers at a military academy in Tientsin. Chang also founded a military academy near Canton, where he employed a staff of six Chinese and one German. The promoters also placed great emphasis on the development of arsenals and shipyards in order that China could supply her own needs, and in 1865 Li and Tseng established the Kiangnan Arsenal and Dockyards near Shanghai, which built China's first modern gunboat in

1868. Kiangnan continued into the twentieth century to be the center of ship construction for the Chinese government. There was a printing shop attached to the arsenal, and here over two hundred standard scientific works were translated and published between 1868 and 1882. Tso Tsung-t'ang started the naval yard at Foochow, and between 1867 and 1874 it turned out fifteen ships before it lost official backing. Chang Chih-tung was largely responsible for the establishment of the Hanyehping Iron and Steel works, which comprised an iron foundry at Hanyang, an iron mine at Tayeh, and a coal mine at Pinghsiang.

Despite these advances, the army and navy were not regenerated. The central government did not revitalize the banners, and it was difficult to recruit and train a competent professional officers corps for the provincial forces. The few Western-trained officers stood in vivid contrast to vast numbers who were products of traditional Chinese training. The troops were poorly equipped, and in 1894 the Japanese general staff estimated that only 60 per cent of the Chinese soldiers mobilized against Japan were armed with some kind of rifle; many carried only a pike, spear, or sword. In the interior provinces the percentage armed with antiquated weapons was even higher. The navy was probably in worse condition. During the war with France in 1885 the Chinese fleet was destroyed at Foochow in a little more than ten minutes, and after the war Tz'u Hsi squandered naval appropriations on the construction of a new summer palace. Since both the army and navy were largely provincial services, there was little feeling of national loyalty; consequently, after 1872, when the hold of Confucian ideology weakened, local armies became increasingly the tools of ambitious governors, and during the Sino-Japanese War of 1894–1895 the southern squadron of the Chinese navy simply sat out the war as a spectator.

The industrialization effort also included attempts to improve communications. Some Chinese officials were quick to understand the strategic and economic value of railroads, but they soon discovered that there was a lively popular opposition to them. In fact, an initial project undertaken by foreign capital ended in failure because of an indignant populace. In 1876 a British firm built a short line linking Shanghai and Woosung, but when a Chinese committed suicide by flinging himself under the wheels of a train, public opinion demanded its destruction. Technological unemployment of carters and boatmen and concern for the peace of family graveyards added to the clamor. Moreover, the railroad had been built over the protests of local officials, who lost face when the foreigners openly flouted their authority. The central government finally intervened, purchasing the line and ultimately reselling it to an Englishman who salvaged the materials for use in his home country. In the following years some minor lines were constructed on the initiative of provincial authorities, but the central government failed to act on memorials urging the development of a national rail network. The basic

151

problem was lack of capital and technology, and Peking was unwilling to contract foreign loans which would permit foreigners to penetrate into the interior of the country. Railroads, moreover, required the services of foreign engineers and financial experts who might bring diplomatic pressure to bear whenever any difference arose between themselves and the Chinese government. So long as Peking was determined that no railroads would be built unless they remained under Chinese control, there was no progress.

The China Merchants' Steam Navigation Company, founded by Li Hung-chang in 1872, was China's only venture in this field, and it ultimately proved a dismal failure despite government subsidies in the form of duty and tonnage-dues exemptions. Chinese capitalists preferred investment in foreign shipping, and Chinese merchants were generally reluctant to use CMSNC because the authorities were inclined to single out the largest shippers as targets for extortion while foreign shipping companies, in sharp contrast, kept their records secret, thus protecting their clients. In the final analysis the basic function of CMSNC was to carry tribute grain from the Yangtze Valley to the north. Interestingly, its operation did lead to one of China's first modern mining ventures. To supply the needs of the CMSNC and to provide for a southbound cargo, Li Hung-chang built a railway to bring coal to the coast from the K'aiping mines at Tongshan, some seventy miles north of Tientsin; and the K'aiping Mining Company grew to become the largest and most important mining enterprise in all China. Until 1900 it remained entirely in Chinese hands, but its increasing capital requirements led ultimately to control by British and American investors.

The central government was also interested in developing telegraphic communication as a means of exercising more effective control over the provinces; and in 1881, on the recommendation of Li Hung-chang, Peking financed a line connecting Tientsin and Shanghai, which was later extended to the capital and other cities. The lines were kept under Chinese control and were built and operated entirely by Chinese engineers—graduates of the Imperial Northern Government Telegraph College established by Li at Tientsin in 1879.

In the 1860's the Foreign Inspectorate of Customs started a postal service to care for its correspondence and that of the legations, and by 1878 it had grown to such an extent that China was asked to join the Postal Union. Finally, in 1896, an imperial postal system for all China was established under the direction of Sir Robert Hart.

The political leaders who promoted these enterprises were motivated largely by noneconomic considerations, and in most cases they were not good managers. For example, Chang Chih-tung's industrial plans were rarely based on careful estimates and preparation. While he served as viceroy at Canton, he planned to establish a cotton mill by raising funds from a gambling organization. Transferred to Wuchang and still unable to raise sufficient funds for the project, he nevertheless ordered machinery from London but had to store it at Canton for four years until he could get the necessary capital. When the machinery finally reached Wuchang and was set up for operation, Chang discovered that the skilled workers and subsidiary equipment were not available, and he had to suspend the enterprise once again.

Factionalism in government often crippled projects whose promoters became involved in struggles for power and prestige. For example, the intense political rivalry between Li Hung-chang and Chang Chih-tung blocked for a time the construction of the K'aiping Mining Company railroad. Chang protested against the line on the ground that it would open Peking to invasion by foreign troops, but his real object seems to have been to strike at Li, since the railroad provided Li's steamers with cheap fuel. On the other hand, Li used his official position as superintendent of northern trade to secure for the China Merchants' Steam Navigation Company a monopoly in freighting tribute rice and other government supplies, and he also prevented other Chinese shipping-owners from competing with his steamers in the Yangtze River trade. The Li family, rapidly increasing in wealth in their native province of Anhwei, also came to dominate the rice trade of that important center of production.

Except for projects that would serve a limited and specific purpose, Chinese traditionalists resisted industrialization. Economic development along Western lines would, they surmised, bring in its train the whole transformation of political, economic, and social life which the West had undergone. Unwilling to see the traditional Confucian society undermined, the promoters of limited industrialization continued to regard agriculture as the only possible basis of the people's livelihood and of state finance, and much of their reforming zeal went into the restoration of devastated land to cultivation and the opening of new lands. The dynasty also modified the land tax in the hope that a more equitable system might bear less heavily on the people and still yield adequate revenue. There was some improvement in the peasants' lot over several decades, but the power of the gentry and merchants blocked the government's effort to create a system of peasant owner-cultivators to replace the hordes of exploited tenants and agricultural laborers.

Confucian bureaucrats also exploited the Confucian virtue of frugality as a solution of production and consumption problems; Prince Kung, for example, advised: "Teach the people frugality so that their incomes will suffice." Mary Wright has commented: "No government was ever farther from the notion that increasing production, increasing revenues, and increasing consumption are healthy signs." On the local level the gentry opposed industry because they feared their vested interests in property would be jeopardized. Some scholars went so far as to exclaim that use of industrial machines would tighten the foreigners' hold on China. The mass of the people regarded new industry as a threat to employment and livelihood, and their weapon was rioting. Even merchant groups had their fears. For example, when Chang Ch'ien, one of the few early competent industrial managers, undertook to establish a cotton mill at Shanghai with local merchant financing, several of the Shanghai merchants refused to pay their contributions on the grounds that they feared official interference and that any agreement with the government was unreliable. For most merchants, speculative ventures in commerce or investment in land were more profitable and secure than industrial enterprises.

The Education Experiment

Despite the resistance and inertia of Chinese traditionalism, there were some indications of fundamental change. In the treaty ports Chinese were acquiring foreign tastes and assimilating Western ideas; and missionary schools, wherever they were able to operate, consciously tried to present the merits of Western civilization as a whole rather than those of Christianity alone. Members of Chinese diplomatic missions to foreign countries often became vigorous advocates of Westernization, but perhaps the group of Chinese who best understood that modernization would entail drastic changes in the traditional system were the few young Chinese who had been educated abroad. This was certainly true in the case of Yung Wing.

Yung Wing was born near Macao in 1828 and received an elementary education in mission schools in Canton and Macao. In 1847 he was taken to the United States by a missionary and enrolled in Monson Academy in Massachusetts. In 1850 he entered Yale College and worked his way through, graduating in 1854. This exposure to Western education convinced Yung Wing that China should accept the civilization as well as the technology of the West. He realized that modern military power rested on a much broader basis than the simple application of machine power to the arts of war, and he was convinced that it was the product of a way of life that was decidedly incompatible with Chinese tradition. To begin the necessary transformation of Chinese society, he hoped to persuade his government to send a steady stream of youths to American schools, and for that purpose he returned to China. At first he was hopeful about the Taiping Rebellion, but when he went to Nanking in 1858 he was quickly disillusioned by what he saw and heard. He did not abandon his project, but during the Rebellion he became a tea merchant, trading between Shanghai and the Taiping areas.

A golden opportunity for Yung Wing to cultivate official support came in 1864 when he was invited by Tseng Kuo-fan to go to the United States to purchase machinery for the Kiangnan Arsenal. His visit coincided with the American Civil War, and, since he had become a naturalized American citizen in 1852, he offered his services to the Union Army. This offer was rejected by the American authorities, who did not wish him to interrupt his work for China. Returning home, he was able to interest Tseng and Li Hung-chang in the idea of training Chinese youths in technological fields at American universities. Their memorials to the imperial throne explained the project as a means for acquiring technical knowledge for resisting foreign aggression, but their efforts were attacked by conservatives like Wo Jen, who submitted memorials criticizing the scheme. In 1871 the imperial court finally approved a plan which would send to the United States each year for four years thirty selected youths between the ages of twelve and twenty. They were to study for fifteen years, and at the end of this period they were to return to China and enter government service.

Yung Wing was appointed co-chairman of the project, and a school was established at Shanghai to give preliminary training to candidates recruited locally throughout China. At first no candidates responded to the invitations of local magistrates because the people were either suspicious or unwilling to have their sons abroad for so long a period. Finally, Yung Wing had to recruit personally in the Canton area; prejudice against foreigners was seemingly less there, and Chinese youths who had been educated in mission schools were more numerous. Of the 120 students actually sent to the United States over 80 came from the Canton area and 37 came from Yung Wing's own village. Not a single Manchu volunteered. The first group of students arrived in Hartford, Connecticut, in 1872, and from there they were dispersed to homes and schools in communities in the Connecticut River Valley. Most of the young scholars adjusted well to their new environments, did well at school, and, after completion of their secondary-school education, entered American universities.

This experiment, begun so favorably, did not run its full course. Reports reached Peking that the students were being weaned away from Confucian principles and behavior. Chinese teachers had been dispatched with the mission to provide instruction in the Chinese language and the Classics, but this work was not encouraged by Yung Wing. Some of the students had become Christians, and others had even cut off their queues. Yung Wing himself married the daughter of an American physician. Peking's attitude was also influenced by the rise of anti-Chinese feeling in the United States. In 1868 a bilateral treaty had provided for mutual rights of residence and attendance at public schools by the citizens of both nations, but anti-Chinese outbursts in the American West, based largely on economic factors, were pressuring the American Congress to suspend Chinese immigration. For these reasons conservatives at the imperial court favored termination of the education mission, and Li Hung-chang found it expedient to go along with them. In 1881 some one hundred students were suddenly recalled in the midst of their work; and although most of them were given low official ranks by the government, they suffered the contempt and jealousy of many of the Confucian scholars. In the following decades, however, their technical training and knowledge of the West were increasingly in demand, and they gradually earned positions of trust and responsibility as engineers and business managers. Traditional scholars continued to occupy the titular positions at the head of railway, telegraph, mining, and other technical enterprises, but they depended on these first Western-trained subordinates to undertake the actual construction and management of these projects. Yung Wing himself was ahead of his time, and in 1902 he returned to the United States, where he lived happily until his death in 1911.

The self-strengthening program was weakened by the continuation of rebellion on various fronts. The Nien Rebellion, which had been stimulated by the initial successes of the Taipings and by natural calamities in Shantung, Kiangsu, and northern Anhwei, had grown from simple bandit activity into a general uprising. By 1862 the Nien rebels controlled the entire Huai basin, and efforts to suppress them proved highly embarrassing to a number of military leaders who had won substantial reputations during the Taiping campaigns. For example, Tseng Kuo-fan, Li Hung-chang, and Tso Tsung-t'ang successfully competed for popular support and were able to contain the rebels, but they could not claim complete victory until 1868. The Nien Rebellion had the effect of continuing Peking's reliance upon provincial troops, and this reinforced the shift of political and military power from the central government to the governors and viceroys. Command of troops by provincial authorities became a matter of course.

In Yunnan from 1860 to 1873 the large population of Chinese Moslems was in a constant state of rebellion. The existence of this large religious minority in southwest China was a by-product of Mongol rule, when there had been a steady immigration of Chinese Moslems from the northwest. In the first half of the nineteenth century their discontent had led to four major uprisings in forty years, and by mid-century they were seeking to set up their own state in western Yunnan and to claim jurisdiction over their religious brethren in Szechwan and Kansu. At the same time, they were under pressure from Chinese to defend their economic interests in the mines located in the upper Red River Valley, a region rich in lead, tin, silver, and iron. The Chinese Moslems, though they were a minority group, had, through their vigor and efficiency, acquired the best mining sites and become prosperous. During the thirteen years of rebellion, land was devastated, property was destroyed, and thousands of peasants were murdered on suspicion of complicity with one side or the other. The danger of foreign intervention, unlikely though this was, made Peking redouble its efforts to suppress the rebellion. By 1873 Moslem forces had reached a point of near exhaustion, and the rebellion collapsed. Out of the total regional population of eight million, only three million remained. The rest had fled or died. Ill-feeling between Moslems and Chinese continued to plague China in the years to come.

By 1862 discrimination against Moslems by local officials and proscription of the so-called "New Teaching of Islam" caused uprisings in the northwest in an area extending from Shensi and Kansu into Sinkiang. After initial failures by the dynasty, Tso Tsung-t'ang pacified Shensi in 1869 and Kansu in 1873, but Sinkiang presented more difficult supply problems. There the adventurer Yakub of Kokand had been able to set up an independent Moslem state, proclaiming himself *beg*, or ruler. After a long period of preparation, Tso was ready in 1876 to move against the rebel government. Great Britain, anxious to use Yakub Beg as a buffer against Russian expansion, tried to persuade China to recognize him as a local ruler under Chinese suzerainty, but Tso successfully opposed the plan. In 1877 Urumchi, the rebel stronghold, fell to Tso, and in May of that year Yakub Beg died of fever at Korla. He was succeeded by a son who was forced to flee into Russian territory, and Sinkiang was incorporated into China as a province. For many centuries it had been under Chinese military governors, but, except for collecting taxes and suppressing riots, they had followed a laissez-faire policy. Tso, however, gave the area an active administration based on the policy of assimilation of its Moslem population.

The Powers and the Co-operative Policy

The foreign threat to Chinese sovereignty that underlay the thinking of the Confucian reformers was more imagined than real in the period from 1861 to 1890. The basic policy of the powers toward China was to maintain equal commercial opportunity and to hold her accountable for observance of the treaties. Certainly through the decade of the 1860's, under the leadership of the British government, the powers followed what has been called the "co-operative policy," generally defined as an attempt to secure the peaceful settlement of disputes and the gradual modernization of China. The record indicates, for example, that the British government, particularly from 1865 to 1870, when the anti-imperialist Clarendon served as foreign secretary, effectively prevented its subjects from unduly exploiting Chinese instability. Clarendon and his representatives in China even had little sympathy for the difficulties of the missionaries, whom they regarded as a menace to British interests. Some British officials went so far as to say, "What right have we to be trying to convert the Chinese in the middle of their own country?"

During the crisis of 1860 and thereafter, Peking began to shift to Western concepts and techniques in its diplomacy; instead of making simple but futile assertions of Confucian moral authority, the Chinese diplomats began to meet their Western counterparts on their own ground, appealing to moral arguments based on Western law and justice to protect Chinese sovereignty and endeavoring to use the existing treaty settlement as the maximum line of Western advance. In 1861 the Chinese government created a special office, the *tsungli yamen*, under the direction of Prince Kung and Wen Hsiang, to control foreign relations, and now for the first time a single organ of the administration had charge of all relations with the foreign powers. Appointments to the tsungli yamen were based on experience and ability, but because of a shortage of persons qualified in diplomacy and foreign languages, it established a special school, the T'ung Wen Kuan, at Peking. When this school added astronomy and mathematics to its curriculum in 1867, it came under attack by Wo Jen and his colleagues; and, although these criticisms were rebuffed, the experiment in broadening the education of officials failed ultimately because of its incompatibility with the Confucian philosophic basis of the state.

The basic foreign policy problem in the 1860's was revision of the existing treaties. The Chinese government was anxious to maintain the status quo, but most of the foreign merchants thought that the treaties offered too little. British merchants, particularly, were demanding lower duties, enforcement of the transit-tax clause of the Treaty of Tientsin, and the general opening of the interior to foreign residence, steam navigation, mining, and railways. The British government, however, did not support its nationals in these matters. For example, London upheld the Chinese contention that there was no exemption from likin and that foreign residence and business were to be confined to the treaty ports.

In 1868 Peking did something unprecedented when it invited the retiring American minister, Anson Burlingame, to head a diplomatic mission to the treaty powers to discuss revision. Burlingame had won the friendship and respect of many Chinese officials by his willingness to support the co-operative policy, and like his British colleagues, Hart, Wade, and Alcock, he had urged the Chinese government to strengthen itself through reform. Peking hoped that Burlingame might be able to persuade the powers to show forbearance in the approaching revision of the treaties. He was given a warm welcome in California, and at Washington in July, 1868, he negotiated with Secretary of State Seward eight supplementary articles to the American Treaty of Tientsin. The United States disavowed any intention of intervening, or any right to do so, in the domestic administration of China with regard to the construction of railroads, telegraphs, or other material improvements, and the United States recognized the right of immigration by Chinese but not the right of citizenship through naturalization. The United States was guaranteed a flow of cheap labor, but when, within a decade, unrestricted immigration by Chinese caused economic and social problems, especially in the western states, the American government shifted to a policy of virtual exclusion. In September, at London, Burlingame received assurances from the British government that it would delay asking new commercial concessions and would deal only with the central government in seeking redress of wrongs to British subjects. After similar calls at the major capitals of Europe, Burlingame fell ill with pneumonia and died in Russia in February, 1870. The greatest success of the Burlingame mission was the firm precedent that it established in China for sending envoys abroad. In the matter of treaty revision, the convention negotiated by the British minister, Rutherford Alcock, was of greater importance.

Negotiations between Alcock and the tsungli yamen were undertaken just as Burlingame prepared to depart for the United States, and they were concluded by the formal signing of a convention at Peking on October 23, 1869. Both parties were anxious to reach a satisfactory settlement of outstanding differences. Alcock was determined to protect Chinese sovereignty despite pressure from the foreign merchant community, and his Chinese counterparts were willing to make concessions that did not unduly threaten the security of their country. The most important clauses of the convention were as follows:

1. It is agreed that commodities of the following classes and denominations, viz., cottons, linens, woolens, woolen and cotton mixtures, etc., etc., imported by British merchants shall pay both import duty and transit due simultaneously at the time of importation.

   On the other part, China agrees that the above-mentioned commodities, imported by British merchants and having paid import duty and transit due simultaneously at the time of importation, shall be exempt from all other taxes and charges whatsoever in Treaty-Port provinces.

2. It is agreed that native produce purchased in the interior by British merchants . . . shall pay all inland dues and charges on its way to the Treaty Port.

   On the other part, China agrees that any such native produce, having paid all inland dues and charges on the way to the port from the place of purchase, shall be entitled to the return of any amount that may have been thus paid over and above the Treaty transit due (half export duty), provided exportation by British merchants to a foreign port takes place within twelve months.

   It is further agreed that native produce shipped to another Treaty Port shall not be entitled to such refund.

3. It is agreed that the port of Wenchow in Chekiang shall be opened to British trade and that Kiungchow, named in the Treaty of Tientsin, shall be removed from the list of Treaty Ports.

   It is agreed that Wuhu, in Anhwei, shall be opened to British trade.

The Alcock Convention was not ratified by the British government, and the story of its failure is an interesting sequel to the ratification crisis of 1859. The Chinese government regarded the agreement as a diplomatic triumph, and for the first time it was eager to ratify a treaty. In Great Britain, however, public opinion would not support Alcock's enlightened diplomacy. Despite his insistence that the Chinese had been far more generous than was realized, British business interests were disappointed and put sufficient pressure on the government to block ratification.

Opposition to the convention on the part of the other treaty powers, with the exception of the United States, added support to the contention that treaty revision should be postponed. Even Alcock, who had been recalled for consultation, admitted defeat, and the death of Clarendon and the Tientsin Massacre in June, 1870, sealed the fate of the convention. Unfortunately, Britain's rejection of it increased Chinese mistrust of the West, and in the decades that followed there was no comparable opportunity to strengthen the diplomatic ties between China and the powers.

The Third Treaty Settlement

Missionary activities provided the severest test of the co-operative policy. Missionaries had acquired a legal status in China outside the treaty ports by the toleration clauses of the Treaties of Tientsin in 1858 and by the Russian and French texts, which permitted missionaries to travel with passports in the interior. The Chinese text of the French Convention of Peking, moreover, conceded the right of missionaries to reside in the interior, to acquire land, to build churches and schools, and to propagate Catholicism without hindrance. Over and beyond these rights, some missionaries, especially the French Catholic fathers, assumed a semiofficial position that was annoying to many Chinese officials. For example, they often claimed the right to protect converts from persecution, thus constituting themselves for all practical purposes as arbiters of disputes and judges of wrongful acts, thus removing numbers of Chinese from the control of their own officials. In these circumstances it was quite natural for many Chinese to regard Christianity as the vanguard of imperialism and not as a gospel of salvation.

Christianity, moreover, conflicted with Chinese social practices. Intolerant of the eclecticism of Chinese religion, missionaries and their converts tended to be exclusive and to renounce traditional customs, such as ancestor worship. Resentment, suspicion, and willingness to believe any sort of slanderous tale about Christianity became widespread, and superstition reinforced slander when, for example, missionaries were accused of extracting the eyes of orphan children to compound potions powerful enough to cause conversion. In 1868 on Formosa Chinese mobs destroyed Catholic and Protestant churches near Tainan following circulation of a rumor that mysterious drugs were being used to convert Chinese to Christianity. In general, the decade of the 1860's was one of increasing violence, marked by looting of churches and beating and killing of missionaries and converts. In contrast to these outbursts of mob violence, the majority of Chinese officials were in agreement that Christianity as a doctrine was not important enough to worry about and that the behavior of converts was a problem to be worked out locally, and there is little evidence to prove the charge that Chinese officials provoked or condoned anti-Christian activities.

Anti-Christian agitation came to a head at Tientsin in 1870 when a Chinese mob destroyed the Roman Catholic orphanage and adjoining church, killing the French consul, two priests, ten nuns, seven foreign residents, and a number of Chinese servants. Alarm spread to many of the treaty ports, and French, British, and American warships appeared near Tientsin. Under threat of foreign intervention, the Chinese government executed or banished some of the perpetrators of the outrage, paid an indemnity of 250,000 taels, and sent a mission of apology to France. Even in this case the powers realized that missionary zeal and the folly of the French consul were partially responsible for what had happened. Actually, an earlier crisis at Tientsin had been averted only because France's able minister, M. Berthemy, had informed the missionaries that "their assumptions were not warranted either by treaty right or good policy." British policy was even stronger. Intervention was acceptable to London only if sanctioned by the Chinese central government; and in 1869 the foreign office had made it clear that the British minister was to appeal to Peking for remedy and that it would disavow a resort to force on the part of any consul. London held to this policy even after the Tientsin massacre. Although there were some attempts through negotiation in the 1870's to regulate missionary activity, no solution was found, and another eruption of anti-Christian and antiforeign sentiment appeared inevitable.

The matter of treaty revision came to a head after the Margary affair in 1875. It had become clear that the Chinese government would not negotiate except under coercion, and the death of Augustus Margary, a British subject, supplied a convenient pretext for the threat to use force. For some time the British had been interested in reaching China's western provinces by way of the Burmese frontier, and in 1868 an initial expedition from India had actually proceeded as far as Bhamo on the upper Irrawaddy River. In 1874 a second expedition was organized to enter Yunnan, and Margary, a consular officer, had been detached from duty at Peking to serve as interpreter. In February, 1875, when the expedition left Bhamo, an advance group of Chinese led by Margary was ambushed, seemingly by Chinese, although this was disputed by the Chinese authorities. This was a border area where tribes were often not easily controlled, but the British took the stand that the local Chinese officials must bear the responsibility for the deaths of Margary and his companions.

Wade, the British minister at Peking, used the murder of Margary to force a general settlement with the Chinese government. In August, 1876, Wade met with Li Hung-chang (who, as superintendent of trade for the north, now conducted foreign relations) at Chefoo, and on September 13 they signed an agreement known as the Chefoo Convention. In marked contrast with Alcock's negotiations in 1868, the new treaty was a return to the unilateral pattern of earlier agreements. Its terms may be summarized as follows: an indemnity of 200,000 taels was paid, regulations for a border trade were determined, a third mission from India was approved, and British troops were permitted to be stationed in Yunnan for five years. In the matter of official intercourse between China and the powers, China agreed to invite foreign representatives to consider with her a procedural code and official etiquette designed to insure proper treatment of envoys in Peking and of consuls in the treaty ports. In trade matters the convention provided for the opening of additional ports (Ichang, Wuhu, Wenchow, and Pakhoi), for the stationing of a consul at Chungking, and for the opening of several ports of call on the Yangtze River. Additional clauses defined more clearly the foreign settlement areas in the treaty ports. On the other hand, Li's discussions with Wade did pave the way for considerable increases in the duties on Indian opium. In general, the Chefoo Convention was a substantial addition to the earlier unequal treaties, but because of the opposition of British merchants, who preferred a policy of forcing China to implement existing rights and concessions more effectively, ratification by Great Britain was delayed until 1885.

The opium trade remained as a problem but in a new, interesting context. The Chinese government was still determined to halt the importation of the Indian supply, but now for different reasons. Native cultivation had fallen under the control of Chinese officials, who dreamed of greater profits if the India trade was abolished. For example, after 1880 Li Hung-chang was active in encouraging British and American humanitarians, like the Society for the Suppression of the Opium Trade, to support "China's efforts to escape from the thralldom of opium." Li, on whose own ancestral estates opium flourished, was anxious to consolidate cultivation in the hands of a government monopoly which promised to be even more lucrative than salt production. So long as the foreign trade in opium continued, however, monopoly was impossible, and Li had to be content with his share of production.

11   The Impact of Imperialism on China

While the Western powers showed considerable forbearance with regard to China's domestic situation in the period 1861–1895, their imperialist expansion on China's periphery caused the tribute system to collapse. Between 1870 and 1895 China lost whatever control, *de facto* or *de jure*, she had previously exercised in Southeast Asia, the Ryukyu Islands, Korea, and parts of Central Asia. Most of the Southeast Asian states, despite theoretical dependence on China, were independent in fact, and the powers paid little attention to Chinese claims of overlordship. The tribute relationship to China —implying dependence but no control—was giving place to new legalistic relationships in which these states were recognized by China as the colonies or protectorates of Western powers. Of greater direct threat to China herself were the expansion of Russia in Central and Northeast Asia and the beginnings of Japanese influence in Korea.

Russian Expansion in Asia

Russian expansion into Asia at the expense of the Chinese empire had actually begun earlier than the period now under review. After the Treaty of Nerchinsk (1689), the Manchus failed to consolidate their hold on the Amur Valley, which remained as an uncolonized, undeveloped, and unprotected frontier. The first tangible signs of Russian interest appeared in 1828, when the czar ordered surveys of the region, but it was not until 1847 that Russia undertook seriously to advance the frontier beyond the Nerchinsk line. In that year Czar Nicholas I appointed Count Muraviev governor-general of eastern Siberia with instructions to explore the Amur Valley. Russia desired to establish ports on the Pacific Coast to assist the development of settlements in Kamchatka, expansion of the Russian-American Company in Alaska, and maintenance of the whaling industry in the Bering Sea. The time was fortuitous for Russia since China was embroiled in trade difficulties with the powers. Muraviev sent an expedition down the Amur in 1848, contrary to treaty rights, and in 1849 carried on additional explorations along the Sea of Okhotsk coastline as far south as the mouth of the Amur River. In August, 1850, he founded the city of Nikolaievsk at the river's mouth, and in 1853 he annexed the island of Sakhalin. The government of China paid little attention to the Russian advance since officially the policy of the Russian government was respect for the terms of the Treaty of Nerchinsk. Chinese border authorities were negligent, and most of their troops had been withdrawn to be used against the Taiping rebels.

Russian intentions became clear to China when, during the Crimean War, British and French attacks on Russian coastal bases in Siberia increased the value of the Amur River as a supply line. In April, 1854, on the pretext of defending Kamchatka, Muraviev sent an expedition down the entire length of the Amur, and the Chinese forces made no attempt to stop it. In 1855 he dispatched more troops and munitions down the river. Muraviev held the view that all territory on the left bank must be ceded to Russia, and despite Manchu protests he went ahead and established settlements at Khabarovsk and Blagoveshchensk, moving settlers from the trans-Baikal region. He had authority from the czar to settle all questions concerning the boundary directly with Peking, and, although overtures in 1855 and 1856 failed, he succeeded in bringing the Chinese into a conference at Aigun early in May, 1858. There he forced upon them the Treaty of Aigun, by which Russia not only acquired all the territory on the left or northern bank of the Amur River but also established a condominium over the territory between the Ussuri River and the Sea of Japan (the Maritime Province).

163

Meanwhile, the Russian diplomat, Admiral Putiatin, had been dispatched to Peking to secure from China whatever commercial concessions should be granted to Great Britain as a result of the Arrow War and to seek a settlement on the Amur question. He was a party to the Treaties of Tientsin, but he failed to get agreement on the northern boundary. Peking, moreover, repudiated the Treaty of Aigun. The Chinese court was willing to accept the Amur boundary, but it would not approve the disposition of the trans-Ussuri territory. Early in the summer of 1859 Russia sent General Ignatiev to Peking to exchange copies of the Treaty of Tientsin and to seek outright cession of the Maritime Province. Fortune smiled on Ignatiev when the British-French expeditionary force seized Peking in October, 1860, for in return for his mediation China, by the Treaty of Peking, ceded the disputed territory to Russia and accepted the Amur boundary as determined at Aigun. Three hundred fifty thousand square miles passed under the Russian flag.

During the next two decades the focus of Russian expansion passed to Central Asia and specifically to Sinkiang, one of China's dependencies. As early as 1851, by the Kuldja Convention, Russia obtained rights to trade at Kuldja (Ili) and Tarbgatai (Chuguchak); and by the Treaty of Peking in 1860 Russia and China began the process of delineating their western boundaries and agreed upon the establishment of a trade market in the south of Kashgar. Russian expansion into this area aroused serious concern in Great Britain; in fact, general Anglo-Russian hostility was in part based on London's fears that Russian expansion would eventually endanger India. Great Britain began to penetrate Tibet and showed considerable interest in southwestern Sinkiang, particularly the principal cities of Kashgar and Khotan.

The rebellion of Yakub Beg gave the Russians an opportunity to occupy the Chinese territory of Ili in 1871. The Russian minister at Peking informed the Chinese government that his country had acted in the interest of peace and order and stated that as soon as China was strong enough to extend its authority over Ili, the Russian forces would withdraw. Russia, however, shortly thereafter demanded an expansion of the Central Asian trade as compensation for its losses. After Yakub Beg's defeat by the expeditionary force of Tso Tsung-t'ang, China had the misfortune to send an ineffective diplomat, Ch'ung Hou, who had accompanied Burlingame in his mission to the powers and had served in the tsungli yamen, to St. Petersburg to negotiate the restoration of Ili. By the Treaty of Livadia Ch'ung surrendered to Russia fertile lands along the Tekes River Valley in the southern part of Ili, the strategic passes to Kashgar, commercial privileges, and an indemnity of five million rubles to cover expenses incurred by Russia during her occupation of Ili. Since Ch'ung had not been authorized to cede territory to Russia, the court at Peking was enraged and refused to approve the treaty. He was recalled to Peking, and as soon as he arrived was thrown in jail to await beheading.

Russia considered China's treatment of Ch'ung an insult to her, and relations between the two nations neared a breaking point. Russia dispatched reinforcements to Ili and a fleet to the China coast. Many Chinese officials, including Chang Chih-tung, wanted war, but hostilities were averted. Ch'ung's diplomatic blunder was corrected by the Treaty of St. Petersburg, signed in 1881, which remained the basis of Russian-Chinese relations in Central Asia until the end of the Chinese imperial system in 1912. Russia relinquished the major part of Ili for an increased indemnity of nine million rubles and the right to open consulates in Sinkiang and Mongolia; Russian trade also became duty-free as far as the Great Wall, including all of Sinkiang and Mongolia.

Japanese Expansion and the Concept of Responsibility

During the latter half of the nineteenth century China also faced the challenge of Japan, which was embarking on an expansionist foreign policy directed at the Ryukyu Islands and Korea. After the Manchu conquest China had no official communications with Japan, but in 1871 Li Hung-chang agreed to a trade treaty between the two countries on the basis of legal equality between nations. Before the treaty could be ratified and exchanged, however, trouble broke out over the Ryuku Islands. The land area of the Ryukyus was about 570 square miles, and its population numbered about 170,000, the largest part of which lived on the island of Okinawa. Ryukyu kings had sent tribute to China since late in the fourteenth century and were part of the tribute system; however, Japan also exercised certain political claims. Early in the seventeenth century the feudal lord of Satsuma had attacked the islands and had brought the northern group under his immediate control, and thereafter the Ryukyus sent tribute to both Peking and Satsuma. After the abolition of feudal territories, or han, in 1871, the new Japanese central government moved the Okinawan king to Tokyo and established a branch of the Tokyo foreign office at Naha on Okinawa to manage Ryukyu foreign relations. Shortly thereafter some Ryukyu islanders were shipwrecked on the coast of Formosa, and fifty-four of the sixty-six survivors were killed by aborigines. Japan demanded redress of China for the death of her subjects, and in 1873 the Japanese foreign minister, Soejima Taneomi, journeyed to Peking to exchange ratified copies of the treaty of commerce that had been signed in 1871 and to discuss the Formosan outrage. When China refused to accept responsibility for the action of the Formosans, Japan dispatched a military force to occupy Formosa. Finally, with the help of British mediation, China gave in and accepted a settlement by which Japan established a legal claim to the Ryukyus. In 1879 the islands were incorporated into Japan as Okinawa Prefecture. This dispute can be regarded as a prelude to the more important struggle between China and Japan over Korea because it was the first Japanese effort to break the Confucian concept of state relations and substitute the Western code of responsibility.

The kingdom of Korea, which was the most important member of the

165

tribute system, was politically autonomous but was powerfully influenced by Chinese cultural values. Although aristocratic privileges played a greater role in Korean life, the country's basic institutions were modeled on those of China. The king ruled with the assistance of a bureaucracy selected in theory by examinations, but in most cases successful candidates were the sons of powerful local landowners. In 1863 a boy of twelve succeeded to the throne, and power was wielded by his father, Tai Won Kun, a reactionary isolationist. The country was divided into eight provinces, each headed by a governor appointed by the king. The administration was generally corrupt and oppressive, and rival political factions, tied together by family interests, vied for control through the favor of the king. The military forces of the country were decentralized on the provincial level, but in time of war a central board constituted the high command. The economy was essentially the same as that of China, and inequality of landownership was its most important characteristic. Landlord interests dominated village affairs, and in fact Korean peasants of this time have been correctly described as slaves on the land. The abundance of copper and lead permitted the manufacture of brass items, a particular specialty of the country. Both Confucianism and Buddhism were important, with the former providing social cohesion and the latter, although in decline, spiritual salvation for the individual. The Chinese language was the language of higher education and government, and the Korean language, written by a combination of Chinese characters and native symbols for inflection, was the normal means of communication.

With the exception of her contacts with China, Korea had remained isolated from the rest of the world. Early in the nineteenth century there had been some unsuccessful attempts on the part of Europeans to open trade, and these were renewed, again in vain, in the 1860's when British, Russian, and French ships visited the Korean coast. Christianity, however, had gotten a foothold. Some Koreans had been converted by the Jesuit mission in Peking, and subsequently, in the nineteenth century, French priests secretly entered the country in violation of royal orders. They made several thousand converts, but their zeal caused them to be persecuted and in some cases murdered. When France sought some explanation in 1866, she was informed by the Korean government that Korea was subordinate to China, to whom all questions regarding foreign relations must be referred. But China would not accept responsibility for the persecution, which virtually wiped out the Christian community, and, since the Koreans defeated the French punitive expedition, the matter rested. China again disclaimed responsibility in 1871, when a Korean shore battery fired upon an American naval mission which was seeking to sign a shipwreck convention with Korea. By this time, Japan was beginning to show interest in Korea.

The new government of Japan was anxious to establish diplomatic relations and trade, but Korea, under the regency of Tai Won Kun, remained antiforeign and isolationist. The Japanese overtures were not even accepted, and Tai Won Kun posted notices warning his subjects to have no contact with the Japanese. Similar incidents occurred in the next few years, and anti-Japanese feeling increased. The situation was propitious for Japanese expansionists, and the central issue in Japanese government for some time was whether to embark on a punitive war against Korea. Calmer heads prevailed in Tokyo; but when negotiations with Korea continued to be unsuccessful, the Japanese government became convinced of the need to threaten the use of force. Japan dispatched warships to the Korean coast to engage in a hydrographical survey in preparation for military action that would support the next diplomatic move, and in September, 1875, a Korean shore battery fired on a vessel sounding the area at the mouth of the Han River. In the ensuing battle the Japanese warship destroyed the forts on the bank.

Japan was ready to use this incident as a pretext to force some sort of settlement on Korea, but, recognizing that her success might well depend on the attitude of China, Japan first dispatched a mission to Peking to seek a more definite Chinese disavowal of responsibility regarding Korea. A few years earlier, when the Japanese minister had negotiated with officials of the tsungli yamen on the Formosan question, he had been advised that, although Korea had been China's vassal state, she was completely independent in her domestic and diplomatic affairs. China continued to maintain that the relationship between herself and Korea was one "of dependence yet no control." Li Hung-chang, who had primary responsibility for the handling of foreign relations, assisted Japan in securing a friendly reception at Seoul; but when negotiations in Seoul lagged, Japan presented a virtual ultimatum backed by the threat of war. The Korean government then agreed to a treaty settlement (Kanghua), signed in February, 1875, which opened to trade the three ports of Pusan, Inchon, and Wonsan and established diplomatic and consular relations. Details regarding these concessions were to be negotiated within six months; however, it was not until December, 1880, that agreement was reached on the opening of the three ports and on the exchange of the officials. The Treaty of Kanghua also stated with unmistakable clarity that Korea was independent, and her equality with Japan was emphasized.

Sino-Japanese Rivalry in Korea

China at last recognized that she was dangerously near to losing her ancient Confucian relationship with Korea, and to block Japanese ambitions she urged Korea to conclude treaties with those powers which would be unlikely to have territorial ambitions. The United States was the most willing to conclude a treaty with Korea, and through Chinese good offices she negotiated a commercial agreement in 1882. Yet when Peking asked the United States to include a clause acknowledging Korean dependence upon China, Washington took the position that Korea was in fact independent and that American acceptance of China's friendly aid was in no sense a recognition of her suzerain power. A series of similar treaties with European powers followed— Great Britain and Germany in 1883, Russia and Italy in 1884, and France in 1886—but in each case Korea, while negotiating as a sovereign power, was forced to set forth in an accompanying letter her dependence upon China. Li Hung-chang, moreover, ignored the independence clause of the Treaty of Kanghua and in 1883 had Yuan Shih-k'ai appointed as Chinese Resident in Seoul. Some of Yuan's actions were considered high-handed and arbitrary, and elements within the Korean government began to see in the treaties a way to counteract Chinese influence. China also concluded a trade agreement with Korea, securing discriminatory advantages over other foreigners in matters of duties, travel, and residence; in theory these privileges were extended to China because Korea was a tribute state.

Chinese policy also reacted to the development of pro-Japanese elements in the Korean government. In 1873 the Korean king came of age, and his pro-Chinese, conservative father retired as regent. The queen's family (Min), anxious to exercise power, advocated a modernization program and looked to Japan for help. The first move in this direction was an invitation to the Japanese to help train a new army; and after the Treaty of Kanghua the king, still under the queen's influence, accepted more Japanese assistance. The former regent, who had been losing prestige and power, waited to retaliate, and his chance came in 1882. Discontent had developed in the Korean army because of the embezzlement of funds intended for military purposes and the presence of Japanese instructors. Tai Won Kun incited the troops to seize the imperial palace, where they killed many members of the Min faction and a Japanese military adviser. The unruly mob also attacked the Japanese legation, forcing the Japanese minister and his staff to flee to the coast, where they found safety on a British ship which returned them to Japan. Both China and Japan then dispatched troops to Korea. China moved to settle the matter quickly because she wanted to give no pretext to Japan for commencing hostilities, and, claiming to act in her traditional Confucian capacity, she seized Tai Won Kun and sent him to Tientsin for punishment. Japan, ignoring the Chinese and dealing directly with Korea, exacted an agreement providing for an apology, an indemnity, the right to station a legation guard at Seoul, and the right to travel in the interior.

The opposition between factions within the Korean government was now greatly intensified. At stake was control of the court and administration of national affairs. The struggle was between the Min family—now increasingly conservative and pro-Chinese—and the reformers, who courted Japanese assistance. Yuan Shih-k'ai, the Chinese Resident, supported the Min faction, and by 1884 the Japanese minister at Seoul, Takezoe Shinichiro, was openly criticizing the policies of China, adding that Japan would welcome the complete independence of Korea. An opportunity for Takezoe to act on his own initiative came in 1884 when China was embroiled in war with France over Annam; in December the reform party, with his urging, seized the king, killed many members of the Min faction, began a reorganization of the government, and called upon Japan for military protection. A company of Japanese troops was dispatched to guard the palace, but the Min family countered by appealing to Yuan Shih-k'ai, who sent some two thousand Chinese troops against the Japanese and defeated them. During the fighting, the king managed to escape and seek Yuan's protection, while Takezoe fled to the coast and, with some of the Korean reform leaders, returned to Japan.

The incident was settled when Korea, through negotiation with Japan, agreed to pay an indemnity for Japanese loss of life and property damage. Tokyo, anxious to settle the clash of interests with China, also sent a mission headed by Ito Hirobumi to Tientsin to discuss the Korean situation with Li Hung-chang. On April 18, 1885, they signed the Tientsin Convention, whereby the two powers agreed to withdraw their troops from Korea within four months and, in the case of future disturbances, not to send troops without notifying the other. While she felt this was a victory, Japan was not yet strong enough to force the Korean issue, and China remained confident that propinquity and historical precedent gave her an advantage which she was prepared to exploit.

After 1885 Li Hung-chang so strengthened Chinese control over Korea that the country came closer to being a Chinese protectorate than a dependent state in the Confucian sense. Li was determined to preserve China's influence in Korea against foreign designs—and to do so by Western as well as Confucian techniques if necessary. The Korean government came increasingly under the control of Yuan Shih-k'ai, who directed all Korean commercial and diplomatic relations, obtained for China a monopoly in the Korean telegraph system, and attempted to get control over all future loans sought by the Korean government. However, the Japanese, officially inactive in Korean politics, were careful to look out for their economic interests. When in 1889 the Korean government, at the instigation of Yuan, promulgated a law forbidding the sale of rice to Japanese merchants despite the abundant harvest of that year and in contravention of treaty rights, Japan protested and the action was rescinded. Yet so successful was Li's policy that by 1892 even Japan approached Korea through Peking when seeking satisfaction for losses caused by Korean embargoes on the exportation of beans to Japan. But these circumstances irritated the Japanese government and hastened its preparations for a final reckoning.

After 1885 Russia loomed as the most important challenge to Chinese domination of Korea. The Min family attempted to use Russian military advisers to counteract both Chinese influence and the pro-Japanese inclinations of the reformers, and Russia, interested in Korea's ice-free ports, was

169

ready to occupy Port Lazarov despite Chinese and Japanese protests. Great Britain, however, brought pressure to bear on the Russians by occupying Port Hamilton, an island off southern Korea, which she held until 1887, when it became clear that Russia would not implement her Lazarov intentions. Moreover, in order to check the power of the Min faction, Yuan Shih-k'ai arranged with Peking to return Tai Won Kun to Seoul. Russia finally made her bid in 1888, when she concluded a treaty of commerce with Korea, but her attempt to persuade the Korean government to adopt policies calculated to advance Russian interests was foiled by strong Chinese opposition. Like Japan, Russia was not quite ready to contest with China for control of Korea.

The Sino-Japanese War and the Treaty of Shimonoseki

As long as the struggle for Korea had been with China, Japan had been content to bide her time until she was ready to strike. Russian actions, however, forced the Japanese hand. In 1891, having obtained the necessary financial assistance from French bankers, Russia announced that she was going to build the 3,500-mile Trans-Siberian Railway. Tokyo viewed this announcement with alarm, believing that, if Russia completed the railway, the Russian advance into eastern Asia could not be stopped. Japanese leadership was convinced that Korea must be independent or, preferably, under Japanese control; and to insure these aims, Japan was ready to go to war with China. This decision was based also on domestic considerations. Parliamentary opponents of the Japanese cabinet had forced a series of political crises by blocking budgetary increases necessary to enlarge the army and navy. The temptation to unite the country in a foreign war was great; moreover, nationalist societies and chauvinist writers were demanding a stronger foreign policy.

The circumstance that provided Japan's opportunity to oust China from Korea was the outbreak of the Tong Hak Rebellion. The Tong Hak, or Eastern Learning Society, was originally a religious sect organized in the 1860's in an effort to combine the teachings of Confucianism, Taoism, and Buddhism into a single faith to preserve Eastern learning against the inroads of Western civilization. Later, however, the movement took on a political complexion, advocating the murder of corrupt officials for the benefit of the masses. The Tong Haks won support from a people harassed by misgovernment, and an insurrection which broke out in March, 1894, became widespread during the next few months. When the Korean troops sent to quell it were defeated by the rebels, Li Hung-chang, acting on the advice of Yuan Shih-k'ai, decided, after some delay, to send fifteen hundred Chinese troops into Korea and, in accord with the Tientsin Convention, so notified Japan. The Japanese government had already dispatched seven thousand men and had ordered general mobilization, but Li and Yuan had no idea that Japan intended to use force to get her way. Ironically, by the time that the Chinese and Japanese troops arrived on the scene, the insurrection had subsided in reaction to the foreign intervention. The Tong Haks were brought under control, but two hostile foreign armies faced each other outside Seoul.

Japan moved decisively to gain a position of dominance in Korea. She proposed joint Japanese-Chinese action to effect financial, administrative, and military reforms in Korea, but China replied that she would not interfere in the internal administration of Korea and added that Japan had no right to do so. Japan began to act independently when on June 26 the Japanese minister began to pressure the Korean government to adopt a general reform program. Two days later in Tokyo the Japanese cabinet decided to go to war, if necessary, to drive Chinese troops out of Korea. When the Korean government delayed in accepting the Japanese proposals, Japanese troops on July 23 seized the king and reorganized the government. One of the first actions of the new regime was to ask Japanese aid in expelling Chinese officials and troops. Peking had not been reinforcing its position because it did not believe that Japan would go to war. To the Chinese, the political bickering in Tokyo during the past few years was an indication of Japanese weakness. They failed to understand its alternative significance.

The powers were much concerned about the Korean crisis. Great Britain, having supported the Chinese position for some time, indicated that she would not agree to Japanese annexation of Korean territory and vainly sought to mediate. Russia, too, extended her diplomatic support to China—probably on the theory that it was better to have Korea controlled by a weak China than a strong Japan—and she informed Japan that she would countenance no settlement that would violate Korean independence. Japan assured both powers that she had no designs on Korean territory but was interested only in Korean reform; she added that, in case of war, she would not attack the Shanghai area, since it was the center of European commercial interests. Li Hung-chang, still confident of mediation or intervention by the powers, fought the desires of his critics to dispatch a larger force to Korea, since he felt that reinforcement might cause war. Li's attitude simply made it easier for the Japanese troops to occupy Seoul and all nearby strategic points.

Hostilities began on July 25 when the transport "Kowshing," carrying Chinese troops to Korea, was sunk by the Japanese navy in the Yellow Sea. A few days later the Japanese minister instructed the Japanese commander, General Oshima, to move against the Chinese, and on July 29 Japanese troops engaged and defeated part of the Chinese army in Korea. On August 1 Japan declared war, and China reciprocated. The interested powers declared or implied their neutrality.

The war was a series of spectacular Japanese victories. The Chinese army was crushed in Korea, and at the mouth of the Yalu River the Japanese fleet intercepted and defeated the Chinese force of twelve ships. The Chinese navy fought bravely, but bureaucratic peculation had left it poorly equipped.

Naval supremacy opened the way to further Japanese successes. A Japanese army under General Yamagata crossed the Yalu into Manchuria in October, and a second force under General Oyama landed on the Liaotung Peninsula and by the end of November had seized the important harbor facilities. At Port Arthur and elsewhere Chinese commanders and troops had little stomach for fighting. Great sums had been expended on the naval base at Port Arthur, which German experts had declared impregnable, but it fell almost at the first attack, with the garrison looting its own military stores and the portable property of civilians preparatory to flight. There was no attempt to destroy supplies such as coal and ammunition or to dismantle the fortifications and dockyard facilities. In March, 1895, the Manchurian armies were united and began a drive on Peking, and meanwhile Japanese troops landed in Shantung and occupied Formosa and the Pescadores. A weak China lay prostrate, but only self-concern guided the actions of her officials. Li Hung-chang could not persuade them to commit their soldiers to his command, and the southern naval squadrons regarded the war as one between north China and Japan. Li was limited for all practical purposes to the resources of Chihli.

China had to sue for peace, and as early as November, 1894, Li Hung-chang, who was held responsible by the court for China's failures, began to make overtures to Japan. Fearing a harsh peace, Li worked desperately for European intervention to prevent Japan's despoilment of China. However, the war was prolonged, and nothing concrete was accomplished toward peace until March, 1895, when Li arrived at Shimonoseki in Japan to negotiate with the prime minister, Ito Hirobumi. Despite difficulties created by an attempt upon Li's life by a Japanese fanatic, the negotiations took less than a month, and on April 17 the Treaty of Shimonoseki was signed. Li had to accept most of Japan's demands, but he was careful to keep all the foreign ministers at Peking informed of the negotiations. He continued to hope for their intervention. In the tradition of Chinese diplomacy, he was anxious "to use one barbarian to check another barbarian." The terms of the Treaty of Shimonoseki may be summarized as follows:

1. China to recognize the independence of Korea.
2. China to cede Formosa, the Pescadores, and the Liaotung Peninsula to Japan.
3. China to pay an indemnity of 200,000,000 taels to Japan.
4. China to conclude with Japan a new treaty of commerce, granting Japan a most-favored-nation status, and to open several new ports, including Chungking, Soochow, Hangchow, and Shasi. [This subsidiary treaty was concluded in July, 1896. China agreed to Japanese manufacture of commodities in the interior, and such goods were to be exempted from all taxes. These privileges were automatically shared by all countries by virtue of the most-favored-nation clause.]

The Triple Intervention

The powers followed the Li-Ito negotiations with great concern. On April 2, the day after Japan made known to Li her conditions for peace, the German government obtained and transmitted them to Russia. The latter still desired to acquire a warm-water port in northeast Asia and did not want to lose out in the Liaotung Peninsula as well as in Korea. Russia's policy at this time was being formulated by her finance minister, Count Serge Witte, who believed that the preservation of the status quo in Manchuria would work to the advantage of his country. On April 8 Russia proposed that Great Britain, France, and Germany advise Japan to restore the Liaotung Peninsula to China in the interests of peace. France was ready to support the Russian proposal under the obligations of their Dual Alliance; moreover, France was anxious to claim a reward from China in the form of concessions in the southern provinces, adjacent to Indochina. Germany, under Kaiser Wilhelm II, was eager to join the intervention for different reasons. She sought diversion of Russian energies to Asia to relieve pressure on her own frontiers and to isolate France in Europe. The kaiser, exaggerating the so-called "yellow peril" —the nightmare of China and Japan united in a war on Western civilization —sought to persuade young Czar Nicholas II that Russia was Europe's outpost against the Asiatic hordes. And Germany, like Russia and France, was also ready to ask favors from a prostrate China. The British government and British public opinion, however, were becoming friendly to Japan. To them Japan was a check on Russian expansion, and they preferred to see Japan rather than Russia dominant in Korea and south Manchuria. The efforts of Germany to establish closer relations with Russia also made London begin to see the advantages of working in co-operation with Japan in Asia. In fact, a discussion along this line had already taken place between Foreign Secretary Lord Kimberley and the Japanese minister, Kato Takaaki. The British, in answering the Russian proposal, took the position that no provision of the treaty so affected British interests as to necessitate intervention which might involve the use of force. On the other hand, Great Britain did not oppose the intervention because she feared that a strong stand might jeopardize her position in Europe.

The Triple Intervention of Germany, France, and Russia began informally while the Li-Ito negotiations were still in progress. Russia warned the Japanese government that cessions of territory on the Asian mainland might result in intervention by the powers. At the same time she informed the French and German governments that, if Japan refused to heed this advice, Russia was prepared to carry out a naval blockade to isolate the Japanese troops in China and, after joining forces with the other two nations, to conduct combined military operations against Japan. When its own army leaders insisted that Japan retain the continental foothold in south Manchuria, the civil government of Japan, caught between two conflicting forces, acceded to the wishes of its generals.

After the Treaty of Shimonoseki was signed, the situation became critical; and on April 23 a climax was reached when the diplomatic representatives of Russia, France, and Germany in Tokyo presented to the Japanese foreign minister, Hayashi Tadasu, identical notes which demanded that "Japan restore the Liaotung Peninsula to China on grounds that Japan would be a constant menace to the capital of China, render illusory Korean independence, and be a perpetual obstacle to the peace of the Far East." The ultimatum was backed by the threat to use force, given substance by the presence of thirty Russian warships in Asian waters. Japan could not resist, for she was close to exhaustion militarily and financially; however, the Japanese government did attempt to strengthen its position diplomatically. Feelers were sent out to ascertain if any assistance could be expected from Great Britain or the United States, but there was no success in either case. On May 1 Japan attempted to get a modification of the Liaotung cession by offering to give up all but the southern tip of the peninsula. The powers refused, and on May 5 Japan gave up the entire area, asking that she be compensated by an additional indemnity. The powers agreed to this modification. Finally, in a separate convention signed between Japan and China on November 8, 1895, the Liaotung Peninsula was returned to China for an additional indemnity of 300,000,000 taels.

The Sino-Japanese War and its sequel, the Triple Intervention, are outstanding landmarks in the modern history of East Asia. China's defeat revealed her weakness more dramatically than ever before, and the moribund Confucian theory of international relations was finally buried. Korea was legally independent but was subject to the blandishments and power politics of Japan and Russia. Japan emerged as a new power to be reckoned with, and she made it clear that economically and territorially she proposed to be a party to whatever imperialist pressures were exerted on China. The Triple Intervention left a specific legacy of national humiliation for Japan, and her leaders and people hoped to even the score with Russia and the powers at an opportune time.

Spheres of Interest in China

In the period immediately following the Triple Intervention Russia was the first among the Western powers to advance her own interests by preying upon China's weakness and need for financial assistance. In July, 1895, a Russian-French loan of 40,000,000 francs enabled China to pay the Shimonoseki indemnity to Japan, but this service placed Peking in Russia's debt. In December, 1895, Russia's finance minister, Count Witte, who referred to his policy as one of "peaceful penetration," chartered the Russo-Chinese Bank to act as the agency of the Russian government in northeast Asia. The bank was empowered to establish local governments, collect taxes, coin money, and secure from China economic concessions.

Russia was particularly interested in constructing the line of the Trans-Siberian Railroad across central Manchuria, a route that would save three hundred fifty miles of difficult engineering through the swamplands along the Amur River and which would serve also as the instrument of Russia's economic penetration of Manchuria. The railroad concession was negotiated by Li Hung-chang, Witte, and the Russian foreign minister, Lobanov, on the occasion of Czar Nicholas' coronation in June, 1896. Li, anxious to secure an alliance against Japan, was willing to grant concessions to Russia in a protocol which remained secret for some years. This so-called "Li-Lobanov Agreement" provided for mutual defense against Japanese aggression, the use of Chinese ports by Russia in the event of war, and China's consent to the construction of the Trans-Siberian Railroad across Manchuria.

On September 8, 1896, the Russo-Chinese Bank and the Chinese government agreed to the construction and operation by the Chinese Eastern Railway Company, under a Russian manager, of a line slightly over a thousand miles in length from Manchouli, on the northwest frontier of Manchuria, to Suifenho, near Vladivostok. The line was completed in 1904. China permitted reduced tariffs on Russian goods entering or leaving Manchuria and pledged not to interfere with the movement of Russian troops. The railway company was to have "the complete and exclusive right of administration" over "lands actually necessary for the construction, operation, and protection of the line." Although the Chinese government was to provide protection for the line, the statutes of the company, confirmed by Russia in December, 1896, stated that "the preservation of law and order on the lands assigned to the railway and its appurtenances shall be confined to police agents appointed by the company." The railroad was to revert to China without payment after eighty years, and China could purchase it by paying the capital outlay, with interest, after thirty-six years. The Chinese Eastern Railway Company was to be financed by the Russo-Chinese Bank, which had been established under a Russian charter. Only nominally was the bank a joint undertaking; actually it was a Russian concern in its incorporation and control. The Chinese Eastern Railway Company was the property of the Russian treasury, and the Russian government guaranteed the company's bonds and was its sole shareholder and creditor. The company carried on a number of varied activities, including mining, manufacturing, and commerce. Later, when Germany established her sphere of interest in Shantung Province (March, 1898), Russia reacted within three weeks by pressuring China into leasing for twenty-five years the southern tip of the Liaotung Peninsula, including Port Arthur and

Dairen, and granting to the Chinese Eastern Railway Company the right to build a railroad to those ports. This line, known later as the South Manchurian Railway, was completed in 1900.

For some time Germany had wanted to secure a naval base and commercial outlet in China, and in the summer of 1897 she decided to take Kiaochow Bay in Shantung Province. German designs were assisted in November of that year when two German Catholic fathers were killed by bandits in Shantung. A German naval squadron used this incident as a pretext to secure a convention from China (March 6, 1898) granting Germany a ninety-nine-year lease of Kiaochow Bay, including the Port of Tsingtao as a naval base; the right for a Sino-German Company, in which nationals of both powers might invest, to construct railroads in Shantung (the Tsingtao-Tsinan line was completed in 1904); the right to mine coal within ten miles of the railroads; and the exclusive right to provide China with assistance in the form of personnel, capital, or materials for the development of Shantung.

France, secure in Indochina, desired to extend her influence into south China, and in the period 1895–1898 French gains were extensive. As early as June, 1895, China had granted French manufacturers and engineers a priority in the exploitation of new mines in the provinces of Kwangsi, Kwangtung, and Yunnan. China also accepted in principle the extension of the Indochinese railways into China, and in June, 1896, she agreed to the construction of a French line to Lungchow in Kwangsi. Later in that year China promised never to alienate the strategically located island of Hainan to any other power. In April, 1898, after Russia and Germany had prospered in the north, France secured additional concessions from China, including a nonalienation promise regarding the provinces of south China adjacent to Indochina, the right to construct a railroad into Yunnan (the Haiphong-Kunming line was completed in 1910), and a lease on Kwangchow as a naval base for ninety-nine years.

Great Britain viewed the development of spheres of interest with alarm and took steps to protect its commercial position in China. In February, 1898, she had China promise never to alienate any territory in the Yangtze Valley, and she extracted a pledge that a British subject would be kept as inspector-general of the China maritime customs so long as British trade predominated. British merchants wanted a free and open market for their commerce and capital, for under these conditions Great Britain controlled two-thirds of all China's foreign trade. Since 1897 Great Britain had been casting about for ways to uphold China's territorial integrity and to prevent exclusion of British commerce from parts of China, and in January, 1898, she extended feelers to Russia for an alliance to guarantee most-favored-nation treatment. When nothing came of this, she turned to the United States; but President McKinley, preoccupied with the revolution against Spain in the Caribbean, was not disposed to act with Great Britain in China. In March, Great Britain approached Japan and Germany but suffered similar failures. By this time she found herself caught between Russian and German gains in the north and French successes in the south, and, unable to secure a collective guarantee regarding most-favored-nation treatment or an alliance, she secured a series of important concessions from China during the period March–July, 1898. China leased Wei Hai-wei in Shantung Province as a naval base for so long as Russia remained in Port Arthur and extended Britain's Kowloon holding to include the entire peninsula (New Territories) for ninety-nine years.

The most intense competition between the powers concerned railroad concessions in China. By November, 1898, the British had secured nine concessions totaling 2,800 miles; the Russians three concessions for 1,500 miles; the Belgians one concession for 650 miles; and the French three concessions for 300 miles. This scramble intensified the desire of the powers to define more specifically the limits of the spheres which each claimed, but fortunately, in April, 1899, the Anglo-Russian rivalry over railroads in Manchuria and north China was alleviated by an exchange of notes in which the British agreed not to seek concessions north of the Great Wall while Russia pledged herself not to venture into the Yangtze Valley. Railway concessions were extremely profitable for the foreigners. They loaned money to the Chinese government, less fees and commissions, and, in accordance with loan contracts, Peking placed orders with foreign factories for railroad equipment in the amount of the loan. The railroad, mortgaged against the indebtedness, used its profits to pay off interest and amortization charges on the loan. Railroad concessions meant new business and profits for bankers, manufacturers, shippers, brokers, salesmen, and even insurance agents; moreover, railroad contracts provided for the services of foreign auditors, managers, directors, and engineers.

The Open-Door Policy

The United States had been little concerned over these developments in China until the autumn of 1898, when an interest in maintaining most-favored-nation treatment slowly mounted. The American annexation of the Philippines during the Spanish-American War and the aspirations of American expansionists called attention to the need to preserve China as a free market. The decision to uphold the historic American policy of equal commercial opportunity in China, as formulated by Kearney and Cushing, began to take hold when John Hay became secretary of state in September, 1898. Hay approved of co-operation between the United States and Great Britain to protect China's territorial integrity, and in this he was supported by Senator Lodge of Massachusetts. Prodded by American business and missionary groups, President McKinley called the attention of Europe to the long-standing American interest in equal commercial opportunity and the preservation of existing treaty rights, and in the late summer of 1899 the state department more effectively set forth American policy.

On September 6 Hay dispatched his now famous "Open Door" notes to Great Britain, Germany, and Russia, and he sent similar notes to Japan on November 13, to Italy on November 17, and to France on November 21. Hay recognized spheres of interest as accomplished facts about which the United States could do nothing, but he did ask for equal commercial opportunity within each sphere. Specifically, he asked each power not to interfere with the treaty ports, not to hinder administration of the Chinese tariff, and not to charge discriminatory railroad rates or harbor dues. Hay omitted any references to mining and railroad concessions, and he did not discuss the whole perplexing problem of capital investment. He also avoided the question of territorial integrity because he felt it was still too complex. In reply, Russia virtually rejected the idea of equal commercial opportunity, and at first Great Britain refused to apply it to Kowloon and Wei Hai-wei. British acceptance was made dependent on similar assent by the other powers. On March 20, 1900, Hay announced that the replies, most of which were evasive at best, were "final and definitive." Hay had restated American policy, but he had failed to get multilateral acceptance of it.

China's integrity in this period was protected from a worse fate by her astute reaction to the pressure of the foreign powers. Using balance-of-power tactics, China deliberately exploited existing rivalries and suspicions among the powers to maintain her territorial integrity and often purposely pitted one power against another. When one of them acquired an advantage, the others consoled themselves by wresting similar privileges, and, although this was humiliating and costly to China, it helped her avert her own obliteration. And it was fortunate for China that the intentions of each aggressor were checked by fear of what the others might do.

12 _Reform, Revolution, Rebellion, 1895–1901_

China's defeat at the hands of Japan, followed by the development of spheres of interest, brought home to many Chinese intellectuals the fact that traditional institutions were bankrupt and that adjustment to Western ideas and practices was necessary if China was to survive. Intellectuals who supported change fell into two groups: reformers and revolutionaries.

The reformers, in terms of basic attitudes, fell somewhere between the Confucian self-strengtheners, who wanted to use Western techniques to supplement Chinese tradition, and the pioneer educationalist Yung Wing, who rejected his cultural heritage. Perhaps their most important representative was K'ang Yu-wei, who in 1889 began to propose a program to modernize China within the framework of imperial administration. Like many of his contemporaries, he learned from the example of Japan that modernization meant more than guns and ships, and with his colleagues he worked to develop a synthesis of Chinese and Western ideas that would provide a stable foundation for modern society. The reformers, however, differed among themselves according to the degree of their desire to retain features of Confucianism and their willingness to accept Western values.

The revolutionaries, who were anti-Manchu and antitradition, wanted more drastic change. Politically they were nationalists and proponents of a system of government based more broadly on the will of the people. Sun Yat-sen, who had turned against the dynasty as early as 1885, emerged as one of their outstanding spokesmen.

The period from 1895 to 1898 may be regarded as the beginning of the struggle between reform and revolution, and in this short span of time the reformers were in the ascendant. K'ang Yu-wei was the hope of many Chinese; but with the failure of his reform efforts in 1898, the pendulum began to swing to Sun and the revolutionary cause. Unfortunately, conservative intellectuals and Manchu leaders resisted both the reformers and revolutionaries and in defense of the status quo foolishly supported an attempt to drive the Westerner into the sea by force. In the period from 1898 to 1901 the activities of the Boxer rebels dominated the Chinese scene.

K'ang Yu-wei, the Confucian Reformer

K'ang Yu-wei was born in 1858, in the district of Nan-hai in Kwangtung Province, into a family renowned for its tradition of Neo-Confucian scholarship. His education, directed by his grandfather, was concerned largely with knowledge of Confucius and Mencius, and from 1876 to 1882 the "sage Wei," as he was called mockingly by the village boys, studied under a famous Kwangtung scholar, Chu Tz'u-ch'i, a Neo-Confucianist particularly interested in historical research and problems of political evolution. After the death of his teacher, K'ang lived and studied alone for four years in a mountain retreat, but in 1894 he passed the provincial examinations. En route to Peking via Hong Kong and Shanghai for the metropolitan examinations in 1895, he began to learn about the West, and he was particularly impressed with the efficiency and honesty of Western administration. His inquiring mind led him to purchase and read translations of Western books, and his initial researches brought him to the conclusion that foreigners had their own moral principles as well as knowledge of social and natural sciences. The Chinese historian Li Chien-nung has written of K'ang's education:

K'ang Yu-wei received an old-fashioned and characteristically Oriental education. He was absorbed in abstruse inquiries and was inclined always to examine affairs in terms of comprehensive systems and universal meanings. His acquaintance with Western culture was only indirect. K'ang's opinions, when people first encountered them, appeared to be fresh and original, but actually he never freed himself from traditional assumptions which hampered his power to deal with changing times and new circumstances.

K'ang Yu-wei was in Peking to take the metropolitan examinations when the terms of the Treaty of Shimonoseki were published. After passing the examinations, he was the choice of the candidates to act as their spokesman to protest the treaty and to propose reforms. His memorial, signed by over a thousand young scholars and presented to the throne in December, 1895, urged the Emperor Kuang Hsu to take the lead in a program of modernization, which included the creation of a popularly elected advisory council and a Westernized educational system. Although his memorial was ignored by higher officials, K'ang had already decided to mobilize support for his ideas. In the fall of 1895, together with other intellectuals, including Liang Ch'i-ch'ao, he had formed the Ch'iang Hsueh Hui—called by foreigners the "Reform Club"—with headquarters in Peking and branches in other cities. In 1896 K'ang himself edited a reform journal for a time, and Liang began issuing a modern newspaper at Shanghai. A reformist press of various shades of opinion flourished and penetrated to all parts of China. For a time their activities were encouraged by some officials, as reform talk was fashionable; however, reform was soon denounced by the conservatives, who moved quickly to outlaw the Ch'iang Hsueh Hui and to ban reformist periodicals. But in Hunan Province the viceroy, Chang Chih-tung, and the governor, Ch'en Pao-chen, were receptive to reform proposals, and they co-operated with Chiang Pao, director of studies, and other intellectuals in establishing the Academy of Current Affairs. Later, in 1898, K'ang was able to establish in Peking the Pao Kuo Hui (National Protection Society), with branch study clubs in the provinces, to discuss ways of saving the country from the foreigners.

K'ang Yu-wei's success in winning the support of other scholars may be explained in part by his ability to provide a Confucian theory for modernization on a broad scale. In K'ang's day and earlier, Confucian scholars fell into two groups, the ancient-text school and the modern-text school—designations based on a controversy regarding the Book of History. The so-called "modern text" of this work was recovered after the Ch'in dynasty destruction of the books and was transcribed into the new official script. In the period 317–321, however, the scholar Mei Tzu presented to the throne twenty-five additional sections of this work supposed to have been in the ancient script but regarded by scholars to have been forged by the donor. On the basis of this controversy two antagonistic schools arose which differed in their emphasis on the Classics, in their attitude toward Confucius, and in their interpretations of ancient institutions. The major point of difference was highly pertinent to the development of K'ang's thinking. The ancient-text school pictured Confucius as a historian and conservator of ancient values, and its scholars held that the Classics were written long before the time of Confucius. The modern-text school, on the other hand, maintained that Confucius was the actual author of most of the Classics, or at least utilized them for the specific purpose of proclaiming an ideal social order. To these scholars Confucius was not a mere transmitter of ancient historical documents but a philosopher, statesman, and educator. The supremacy of one or the other of these schools at different periods in Chinese history depended largely upon which way official winds were blowing, and in K'ang's day most of the scholars were of the ancient-text school. K'ang, however, adopted the modern-text point of view and used it to lay the groundwork for reform. He wanted to undermine the conservative opposition to change by showing that it was based on false works which obscured the true picture of Confucius, a man of action deeply concerned with the salvation of society. This was the portrait of the philosopher which K'ang painted in his book *Confucius as a Reformer*, published in 1897. He made Confucius "the prophet of progress to a Utopian Confucian future, toward which the West, with its modern values, was also on its way."

K'ang advanced what he believed to be an evolutionary Confucian concept of progress in three stages: limited peace, great peace, and universal brotherhood. The first was an era of world confusion in which men were governed by force or by rules of conduct which they accepted; the second, an era of greater stability in which the masses were educated and participated in government; and the third, an era of world harmony. A serious problem for K'ang was to harmonize this idea of progress with the concept of a golden age in antiquity. He held that Confucius consciously read his ideas back into a past which he knew had no basis in fact; Confucius was aware that the model emperors were not perfect, but he used their examples in order to convey other, more revolutionary, ideas which otherwise would never have been tolerated. According to K'ang, Confucius used the past only to teach men how to live in his own time and thus told stories about model emperors in a golden age to help make better rulers and better subjects. K'ang's argument assaulted fundamental positions long held by the Chinese as to the value of antiquity. It took issue with ideas that kept them looking backward instead of pressing forward, and it also opened their minds to the idea of historical progress. The majority of classical scholars, however, did not accept K'ang's theory. Chu I-hsin, for example, wrote a letter to him: "Now you call Confucius a reformer in order to facilitate the promotion of your own reform movement. Even though the

Sage Confucius really had a reform intention, he only desired to restore the ancient systems of the Sage Kings of the Three Dynasties; he had no intention of replacing Chinese institutions with barbarian systems."

On January 29, 1898, K'ang submitted to the government his most comprehensive plan for reform. After describing the need for extensive changes, he proposed that, to silence the opposition, the emperor should proclaim his determination to reform China. All high officials should be required to pledge in the presence of the emperor their support and faithful execution of reform policies or else resign from their posts. The throne should encourage people throughout the empire to submit their opinions, and it should establish a committee on institutions, consisting of twelve outstanding scholars, to draw up the master plans for reform, subject to imperial approval. If the existing boards and ministries were inefficient or were hostile to change, they should be replaced by twelve new departments responsible for the administration of reform measures.

By 1898, when spheres of interest had been carved out by the powers, reform became an important issue between the two leading factions in the bureaucracy. For years northern and southern parties had contested for the favor of the empress dowager, but now the situation was different. The Emperor Kuang Hsu, having attained his majority, had ascended the throne in 1889; and Tz'u Hsi, though she was still a powerful force in the central government, had retired to the summer palace. Under the influence of Weng T'ung-ho, his tutor and a leader in the southern party, the emperor had studied about the West and had come to believe that Western education and science were essential for the reconstruction of China. After the war with Japan he showed leanings toward a general reform program; and the southern party, which had been moving away from the empress dowager, began to support him. On the whole, these officials would not go as far as K'ang, but they urged reform as part of the contest for power at court. In mid-summer, 1898, reform was probably given its widest publicity by the little book, A Charge To Learn, by Chang Chih-tung, viceroy of Hunan and Hupeh and a leader in the southern party. Chang insisted that Confucian philosophy be the basis of Chinese society, but he advocated vigorous study of Western institutions. In brief, he was reiterating the point of view of Tseng Kuo-fan and Li Hung-chang, and his proposals, typical of the southern party, were less drastic than those of K'ang Yu-wei. The book was given imperial endorsement, and by 1900 over a million copies had been distributed.

The Reform Attempt of 1898

By the summer of 1898 the proposals of K'ang Yu-wei dominated the emperor's thinking, and on the recommendation of Hsu Chih-ching, Kuang Hsu summoned K'ang for an interview and was impressed by him. K'ang was appointed to serve in the tsungli yamen, the body responsible for considering reform matters, and from that time on he was able to approach the emperor. On June 11, on the advice of K'ang's supporters at court, the emperor issued the first reform edict, a general statement regarding the need to reform along Western lines in order to strengthen China. The famous One Hundred Days of Reform had begun.

Throughout the summer of 1898 K'ang Yu-wei and his aides dominated the emperor and the reform movement. In all, they issued forty decrees, which made the following recommendations:

1. Many sinecures in the imperial administration are abolished—the governorships of Hupeh, Kwangtung, and Yunnan, the director-generalship of the Yellow River, the *taotai* for grain transportation, and many salt *taotai*.
2. The examination system is to be modernized, and examination topics are to be based on current problems.
3. The government is to consider carefully what other posts, civil and military, should be abolished.

In K'ang's mind these were the first of a series of political reforms designed to give new vigor to the dynasty. In addition, he wanted to establish a cabinet which would meet daily to determine general policy and to administer twelve departments, described by K'ang as follows:

1. *Law.* Foreigners in our country are allowed to rule themselves, and our people are not allowed to be on terms of equality. This is a great shame to our country, and arises from foreigners regarding our punishments as too severe and different from their own. We should now take the Roman, English, American, French, German, and Japanese laws and revise them for our own use. They should not be used at once in the interior, but first tried at the open ports.
2. *Revenue.* The area and population of our empire are double those of Europe, but we are much poorer; and our revenue is only like that of small nations, such as Chile and Greece, because we do not know how to manage this department. The modern methods of Western nations, such as duties on checks, banks, stamps, post offices, tobacco, spirits, mines, forests, public debts bring in hundreds of millions. Most of these things do not exist in our country; therefore, a new department should be established to superintend the revenue.
3. *Education.* Peking should have a university. Every provincial capital should have a college, and every prefecture and county should have schools. There should also be special schools, such as naval and military, medical, legal, and normal schools, and books of all kinds should be translated and courses marked out. The Board of Rites cannot superintend this; there should be established a special department for it.
4. *Agriculture.* Arable land, forests, fisheries, herds, require that suitable land should be provided for each, so that every branch may be benefited.

5. *Works.* This is to look after arts and manufactures of the nation; to encourage discoveries and invention, in shipbuilding, in bridges, in embankments, and in roads.
6. *Trade.* All the trade of the nation, commercial schools, chambers of commerce, commercial customs, commercial goods, and commercial law, should be under the control of this department.
7. *Railway.* Trunk railways of the empire should be carefully mapped out and power to act given to this department.
8. *Postal.* Post offices should be established throughout the empire, in every province, prefecture, county, and parish, and the telegraphs should be also under the same control.
9. *Mining.* All the different mines of the empire, mining duties, and mining schools should be under its control.
10. *Traveling.* Statesmen, educators, and religious teachers should travel abroad and see how other nations carry on their respective departments and specially look after the constitution of the Government.
11. *Army.* This is to raise an army throughout the empire and drill it.
12. *Navy.* This is to see about gunboats and naval practice.

K'ang also thought in terms of political reform on the local level. In his own words:

Let each county have a branch "People's Council," and the director appoint a deputy-director to meet with the county gentry in council to carry on reforms, while the district magistrate is only to look after the punishment of crime and the collecting of revenues. All surveying, census, roads, forests, education, agriculture, trade, rearing cattle, and police, to be under the new council's care to be gradually carried out. Have a beginning made in three months, and have good results to show at the end of a year. Thus there will be co-operation in the capital and in the provinces, each will assist the other, like arm and hand, and we shall have an outline of new government. Reform after this will be possible, and its fruit easily reaped

Conservatives, who opposed reform, looked to the empress dowager for direction, and in fact their leaders did not conceal their belief that she should assume power. Tz'u Hsi did not hesitate to interfere in the affairs of state. For some time she had been aware of the leanings of the emperor, and she continued to maneuver her favorites into key positions from which they could thwart his moves. On June 14, just as the reform movement got under way, she was able to secure the appointments of the eunuch, Jung Lu, as viceroy of Chihli with many of the best troops in China under his command, and of Yu Lu, a confidant, as a secretary in the grand council to spy on the activities of the reformers. K'ang Yu-wei, however, was cognizant of the fact that the empress dowager and the conservatives were obstructing the reform edicts. For example, when Huai Ta-pu, president of the board of rites, refused to present reform memorials to the emperor, the emperor dismissed him and five of his colleagues, thus alarming the conservatives, who plotted retaliation.

Reform and foreign policy were closely interrelated. The empress dowager and northern conservatives like Li Hung-chang favored a policy of close collaboration with Russia, while the reformers were pro-Japanese and wanted to imitate that country's modernization program. Thus Li's opposition to reform in 1898 in part was based upon his conviction that it was Japanese-instigated and harmful to China. Li, however, had been stripped of most of his important posts in the aftermath of China's defeat in the war with Japan and was no longer an important force in the government; in fact, only the protection of the empress dowager prevented him from losing his post as grand secretary.

In August, 1898, the reformers, seeking to dominate the administration by packing the grand council, persuaded the emperor to appoint Yang Jui, Liu Kuang-ti, Lin Hsu, and T'an Ssu-t'ung as probationary secretaries in that body. K'ang Yu-wei wanted to transform the grand council into a cabinet; but since the emperor dared not replace its members, he appointed these four persons to take over executive direction of the council. The new functionaries proved so energetic and aggressive, giving the impression that everything was to be changed at once, that they excited the jealousy of the councilors. The emperor did his utmost to persuade the reformers to cultivate friendly relations with their more conservative colleagues, but they were suspicious of the power of the empress dowager and her followers.

The struggle between the reformers and the conservatives reached a climax in September, 1898. The empress dowager and her allies plotted to depose the emperor on the occasion of an inspection of the Tientsin garrison in October. They planned to confront Kuang Hsu with Jung Lu's troops and compel him to abdicate. The reformers, hearing numerous rumors of the empress dowager's plans, urged the emperor to move against her. Their plotting depended on the support of Yuan Shih-k'ai, who was then a judge in Chihli and director of the officer training school which the dynasty had established to train an army along Western lines. The reformers counted on his help because they thought him ambitious and sympathetic to their program, and he agreed, in the presence of the emperor, to proceed to Tientsin to take actual command of the new army of seven thousand men, murder Jung Lu, march on the summer palace, and seize the empress dowager.

Instead of adhering to the plot, Yuan united forces with Jung Lu, and under the orders of Tz'u Hsi they marched on Peking. On September 21, on the pretext of the illness of the emperor, Tz'u Hsi resumed control of court affairs and the entire imperial administration. The conservatives, led by Jung Lu, had petitioned her to conduct all state affairs, and Jung Lu's troops had moved quickly to garrison the palace. Most of the reforms were rescinded by an imperial decree dated September 22, and in the following months all the reforms were terminated.

For a time it appeared that the emperor might be killed or forced to abdicate, but it was finally decided to keep him in confinement. That he was permitted to live was the result of several factors: the intervention of the foreign powers, the opposition of the Yangtze viceroys and Li Hung-chang, and the desire to hide the fact that China was again ruled by a woman. Later, in January, 1900, a child, P'u Chun, from a close branch of the imperial family was named heir apparent. As for the reformers, many of them fled Peking, while others were jailed or executed. K'ang Yu-wei and Liang Ch'i-ch'iao left the country and took up residence in Japan, continuing to campaign for the introduction of reforms. Tz'u Hsi, of course, rewarded the faithful. Jung Lu became a member of the council of state and head of the department of military affairs; Yu Lu was made viceroy of Chihli and assistant commander of the army; and Yuan Shih-k'ai was appointed governor of Shantung. The *coup d'état* by Tz'u Hsi and Jung Lu was welcomed by a majority of Confucian scholars, many of whom had lost sinecures, and by thousands of students who looked with dismay at the introduction of Western learning to replace the Chinese Classics. Officials who continued to support reform were immediately dismissed from office and denied any further employment by the government.

Sun Yat-sen, the Revolutionary

Revolution had its origins in this period, exemplified particularly by the career of Sun Yat-sen. Sun was born to a peasant family in 1866 in the village of Chouyung, situated about thirty miles north of Macao in the delta of the West River. Despite family poverty, he was able to get a few years' education from his uncle; and when he was twelve years of age, an opportunity that altered the course of his life opened up when his elder brother, fifteen years his senior, who had emigrated to Hawaii, invited Sun to come and live with him. In Honolulu Sun attended a Church of England school from 1879 to 1882; there he learned the rudiments of a Western education and also became interested in Christianity, although he was not baptized. In the latter months of 1882 or early in 1883, Sun returned to China, where he continued his education at Hong Kong and Canton. After a short sojourn in his native village, he entered Queen's College, a preparatory school in Hong Kong, to study both Western and Chinese subjects. In May, 1884, Sun interrupted his education to marry according to his parents' wishes, but the bride, now a member of the Sun household, saw little of her husband except when he returned from school on holidays. In the same year Sun also became a Christian. In 1886 he entered a Canton hospital school, paying his way in part by assisting in routine work, but in October, 1887, he transferred to a newly established medical school at Hong Kong and graduated five years later with a Certificate of Proficiency in Medicine and Surgery.

According to his autobiography, Sun became a political revolutionary at the time of the Franco-Chinese War of 1884–1885, when China suffered a humiliating defeat. What disturbed Sun most was Manchu "inefficiency and cowardly diplomacy." At the Canton hospital school he met three other youths who shared his views, and they talked freely, discussing the idea of revolution against the ruling dynasty. To their friends at Hong Kong and Macao they were known as the "Rebel Quartet." After graduation Sun began to practice medicine at Macao, the largest city in the neighborhood of his native village, but his medical career was terminated when the local authorities learned that he lacked a Portuguese diploma; he then went north to secure a government medical post but failed to do so. At this juncture he turned his entire attention to the search for solutions to China's problems and became a leader of a revolutionary group in Canton.

In 1894 Sun did two important things. First, he proposed a program for China. These views, which contained the core of much of his later thinking, were written in a letter to Li Hung-chang, which was later published in Shanghai in the early fall of 1894. Sun maintained that the power and wealth of the European powers was due less to their military strength than to the following "foundations of national strength," which he related to China:

1. *A full development of human talent.* China needs universal free education, vocational guidance, an efficient civil service, and scientific development.
2. *Increased agricultural production.* China should develop a modern agriculture with a modern administration of agricultural affairs.
3. *Full utilizaton of natural resources.* China should adopt policies of technological development, conservation, and regulation of private capital.
4. *Efficient transportation system.* This included abolition of the likin, establishment of free trade, and adequate protection of merchants.

Second, Sun journeyed to Hawaii, where he organized his first political society among the overseas Chinese. It was called the Hsing Chung Hui (Revive China Society), and its basic purpose was to raise money for the revolutionary cause in China. Most of the Chinese who had emigrated lived out hard lives as laborers, and some of them eventually returned to China with small savings. Only a small minority achieved wealth in trade and business. Sun discovered that among many of the expatriates strong nationalist feelings had taken root long before they developed in China, and he sought to make laborers and rich alike the financial and moral support of revolution. Sun, however, had to compete with the ideas of K'ang Yu-wei, and it was not until several years after the failure of the reform movement that he began to win strong support from the overseas Chinese.

China's defeat at the hands of Japan in 1894–1895 spurred Sun and his followers to action. After his return from Hawaii in December, 1894, he established the headquarters of the Hsing Chung Hui in Hong Kong and made his first attempt to organize a revolutionary army in Kwangtung. He and his followers plotted to seize Canton and make it the territorial base for revolution; but before they could act, the government learned of their plans and routed them in a raid on their Canton base of operations in September, 1895. Sun, made notorious throughout China by the press, fled with a price on his head to Macao, then to Hong Kong, and finally to safety in Japan.

During the next few years Sun traveled extensively in the United States and Europe to promote the Hsing Chung Hui, but he found little interest in his revolutionary views. The only time that he received noteworthy attention was in 1896, when he was kidnapped and confined for a short time in the Chinese legation in London. But in this period Sun was exposed to the important intellectual and political currents of his day. In Europe he had direct contact with socialist movements, and he was able to read Marx's *Das Kapital* in the English translation which appeared after 1887; and in the United States he was influenced by the political content of the Progressive Movement and by Henry George, the single-tax advocate, who died in 1897 in the midst of his second mayoralty campaign in New York City.

In the fall of 1899 Sun settled briefly in Yokohama in the sizable Cantonese colony, but he found the Chinese very unresponsive to his ideas and was able to enlist less than a hundred in his cause. Sun was still competing with the reform plans of K'ang Yu-wei and Liang Ch'i-ch'ao, who after their flight from China had settled in Japan, where they sought to win the support of their countrymen. Efforts at co-operation between the revolutionaries and the reformers failed since K'ang felt that association with Sun might jeopardize his own activities. In these years Sun also suffered the contempt of Chinese scholars. In the words of Wu Chih-hui: "At first I despised Sun simply because he was not a man who had passed the high official examinations, nor was he a classical scholar and a man of letters. I suspected that he was illiterate."

In 1900, following the failure of the Boxer Rebellion, Sun and his followers in the Hsing Chung Hui planned uprisings in several parts of China. At Huichou in Kwangtung the rebels scored some initial successes but lacked sufficient military supplies to overcome the local government troops; they also failed in an attempt to assassinate the viceroy. Similar uprisings in the Yangtze Valley at Hankow and Tatung were also quelled by the dynasty. Despite these military failures, Sun's popularity began to grow, and in his autobiography Sun commented: "After my first failure in 1895, the whole nation regarded me as a bandit or a rebel, an unprincipled man guilty of rank treason. . . . But after my failure in 1900, not only did the people stop cursing me, but the progressive elements were actually sympathetic with me in my misfortune." The improvement in Sun's position at this time was indicative of the changing attitude of a great number of Chinese, who were increasingly disillusioned by the policies of the Manchu court.

The Conservatives and the Boxer Rebellion

Tz'u Hsi and her conservative allies defended the old order in China against reform and revolution, and they concentrated their efforts on reorganization and modernization of the army. Following the Sino-Japanese War, the Manchu military and political leader, Jung Lu, had helped to promote the new army under Yuan Shih-k'ai, and after the failure of the reform movement in 1898 the dynasty joined Yuan's troops with other forces to form the Grand Army of the North, to be financed by the central government. The quality and size of China's provincial armies, however, varied considerably, and in most cases they were nothing more than an armed rabble. Many of the governors used military funds—a great source of peculation, since they amounted to 50 per cent of all official revenues—for their own purposes, and their officers regarded their posts as sinecures. Even where there was an efficient military organization, troops could not be used outside the province without the governor's or viceroy's permission.

Peking also tried to curb foreign activity in China by refusing to concede any further privileges and by strictly defining those already extended to the powers. In November, 1898, the central government issued new regulations which stipulated that railroad construction permits did not include mining or other rights along the railroad lines, and in the following year the dynasty established a central bureau for control of railroads and mines throughout China. In December, 1898, the government forbade all further concessions until all the existing ones were exploited, strictly defined the locality of a concession, and required that at least half of the capital of any business was to be Chinese and that control of the enterprise should be in Chinese hands. But, as in the case of military reform, implementation of these regulations depended on effective government. In its absence they were circumvented by the comprador system or were ignored by foreigners and Chinese local officials alike.

Between 1898 and 1900 Peking explored the possibility of relying on Japan to defend China against the Western powers. During the scramble for concessions Japan had been able to elicit a Chinese promise not to alienate Fukien Province, opposite Formosa, to any other power; but with the exception of a few officials like Li Hung-chang, the dynasty ignored the menace of Japanese imperialism and hoped to use Japan for certain immediate benefits to China. In July, 1899, two Chinese commissioners, visiting Japan ostensibly on a commercial mission, discussed the possibility of an alliance with the Japanese government; but when news of the project leaked, Russia informed Peking that such an alliance would have the "most serious" consequences for China, and Tokyo, regarding such an alliance as a liability at that time, did not pursue the matter. This project having failed, Tz'u Hsi threw her support from the pro-Japanese faction in Peking to the pro-Russian faction, which included Li Hung-chang.

Conservatives in government longed most of all to restore the old condition of isolation, and some, like Li Ping-heng, Yu Hsien, and later Tz'u Hsi herself, sought to channel deepening peasant discontent into antiforeignism in an attempt, however ill-conceived and unrealistic, to drive the foreigner out of China. Peasant unrest was due largely to economic factors, particularly to the increase in taxation to pay the indemnity to Japan, the introduction of foreign goods and production methods, and, most important, to the widespread starvation following the Yellow River flood of 1898, which inundated over fifteen hundred villages in Shantung. In some cases no rational kind of motivation at all, but only superstition and mass hysteria, led to peasant disturbances, and the behavior of foreigners was actually only one—and apparently a minor—motivation among others. Yet peasant discontent in the north became organized into the famous Boxer Rebellion, a movement to expel foreigners and to eradicate Christianity.

The Boxers, or the Society of Harmonious Fists, was originally an anti-Manchu secret society that was revived in the villages of Shantung Province as the basis of the movement to expel the foreigners, who were held responsible for the misery of the Chinese people. In 1899 Chu Heng-ting, leader of the society, who was particularly critical of the German politicoeconomic invasion of Shantung in the period 1897–1899, set up the slogan "Protect the Ch'ing and Annihilate the Foreigners." Yu Hsien, governor of Shantung, encouraged the movement, as had his predecessor, Li Ping-heng, who had been dismissed from office in response to a German request following the death of two missionaries in 1897. Taoist and Buddhist priests were also active in the movement from the beginning. One Taoist exclaimed: "I have reverently received a decree from the Jade Emperor ordering me to command the Celestial soldiers and officers in the annihilation of all foreigners; how do I dare disobey His order?"

Boxer attacks on foreigners began in Shantung, and after 1899 the movement spread from there to Chihli, Shansi, and south Manchuria. As a result of the protest of the French minister, Yu Hsien was recalled to Peking in December, 1899, and replaced by Yuan Shih-k'ai, who vigorously suppressed the Boxers, executed Chu Heng-ting, and drove the heart of the movement from Shantung to Chihli. Here the Boxers were supported by the viceroy, Yu Lu, and by the judicial commissioner, T'ing Yung. The movement as a whole, however, remained confined to north China, and, although there were uprisings in the south, they were rarely directed against foreigners and Christians.

The Boxer movement was directed against native Christians even more than against foreigners. Converts were often regarded as traitors, and, if they were not attacked, they were socially ostracized. Officials, antagonized by the efforts of missionaries to extend special protection to their converts, persecuted Christians, arraigning them in court on trumped-up charges and punishing them for crimes not committed. Christians were also accused of practicing strange rites, abandoning Chinese ways, and showing insufficient respect for the teaching of the sages, and those who refused to contribute to village festivals, on the ground that these were pagan and offensive to their beliefs, were singled out for Boxer contempt.

Early in 1900 the Boxers began to spread their ideas in Peking, and from their first appearance they had strong support at court. Although the foreign ministers at Peking protested against their activities, Tz'u Hsi sympathized with the Boxers and urged viceroys and governors to give encouragement to those who resisted the "foreign aggressor." Once Tz'u Hsi showed her support, the movement spread more quickly; and although the Boxers continued to concentrate their attacks on converts, many foreigners were killed. In fact, in Peking and later in Tientsin it was unwise for foreigners to be seen in the streets. Yet as late as June, 1900, the diplomats were still in doubt concerning the dynasty's attitude toward the Boxers. Although they were not quite certain about the meaning of the rebellion, they were fairly well convinced that it was antidynastic as well as antiforeign and that they would therefore be able to obtain the collaboration of the empress dowager. The Chinese government did little to clarify the situation because uncertainty was politically useful and because it delayed foreign intervention.

The strongest supporter of the Boxers was Prince Tuan, the violently jingoistic head of foreign affairs and father of Tz'u Hsi's choice to succeed Kuang Hsu as emperor. The name of the heir apparent was announced on January 24, 1900, but when none of the foreign diplomats sent congratulatory messages, the ultraconservatives were deterred from carrying out their plan to depose the emperor. This particularly infuriated Prince Tuan, who was anxious to see his son enthroned. Yet as late as June, 1900, counsels of moderation could still be heard in the meetings of key officials. For example, Li Hung-chang, who had been appointed viceroy at Canton, branded the Boxer movement a folly and retired to the south. Chang Chih-tung, viceroy at Hankow, telegraphed Peking that the "Boxer bandits" who "resist government troops, kill military officers, stir up riots in the gate of the capital, and destroy the railroads built by the country" must be executed since they "are staging a rebellion on the pretext of anti-Christianity." Other moderates were of the same opinion, and not until the siege of the legations began did the imperial court put its official support behind the Boxers.

The climax of the Boxer movement came in late spring when the railways were attacked, and finally, on May 28, the diplomats appealed to their governments for an immediate increase of legation guards. The Boxers then cut rail and telegraph connections between Peking and Tientsin. Their strategy was to isolate the legation quarter, prevent reinforcements from reaching the scene, and wipe out the foreigners. On June 10 the Boxers entered the capital in force, and on the same day an international body of fifteen hundred troops was dispatched from Tientsin by train only to be defeated and turned back with heavy losses. On June 11 Sugiyama, chancellor of the Japanese legation, was murdered, and on June 13 the Boxers began to attack the legations and the nearby missions. The foreigners were forced to take refuge in the British legation or in the nearby Catholic cathedral, both of which also accommodated as many Chinese Christians as possible. On the following day hundreds of converts, not so fortunate, were attacked and burned throughout the city; moreover, a price was put on the head of every foreigner. On June 17 French, Japanese, British, and German warships destroyed the Taku forts guarding the entrance to the Pei-ho. The Boxers regarded this as the equivalent of a declaration of war and retaliated by striking at the Tientsin concessions; and in Peking on June 20 the German ambassador, Baron von Ketteler, seeking to negotiate a settlement, was shot to death on the street by a Manchu soldier. On the following day Peking declared war on the foreign community, and regular Chinese troops joined the Boxers in a siege of the legations. The entire foreign community of 470 civilians, 450 guards, and some 3,000 converts was left to defend itself. On June 23 an Englishman was savagely tortured and then decapitated, and his severed head was placed on public exhibition in a cage.

Fortunately for China the Boxer attacks were localized. The provincial governors were ordered to drive out all the foreigners, but most of them regarded the undertaking as foolhardy. Officials such as Li Hung-chang, acting viceroy at Canton, Yuan Shih-k'ai, governor of Shantung, and Chang Chih-tung, viceroy of Hupeh and Hunan, would not join the movement, although they did send some second-rate troops to Peking. In fact, they ignored the June 21 declaration of war and urged Jung Lu, who was probably the most powerful military figure in the north, to restrain the Boxers. Jung Lu wavered; although he knew that it was dangerous to precipitate a foreign war, he remained undecided whether he should encourage the Boxers or oppose them. Finally, on June 25, he ordered a cease-fire and attempted to negotiate with the legations, but the effort failed when his soldier-messenger was caught and killed.

Many court officials realized early in the fighting that the foreigners would eventually be victorious and that practical considerations required a policy that would make a reasonable peace possible; however, the regime was caught between the Boxers and the foreigners and between reactionary and moderate officials. Tz'u Hsi carefully left the door open for an understanding with the foreigners by never making clear exactly how far Manchu collaboration with the Boxers went; and in July there was even a short truce, during which time she sent officials to the legations apologizing for the murder of the Japanese and German diplomats and presenting the foreigners with vegetables, fruit, rice, and flour. At other times communications were sent to the powers requesting them to help China out of her difficulties. In fact, on July 15, Li

Hung-chang was ordered to inform the foreign countries that their subjects at Peking were all well and that they need not be worried about their safety.

In the meantime a second allied relief expedition was organized, the main components of which were 8,000 Japanese, 4,500 Russian, 3,000 British, 2,500 American, and 800 French troops. On July 14 the allied force captured Tientsin after several days of bitter fighting. Casualties for the allies were amazingly light, amounting to only 745 killed and wounded; but for the Chinese the total ran to 15,000. The arrival of reinforcements swelled the allied army to 23,000 men, and on August 4 it began to march on Peking. The dynasty then moved quickly to achieve a truce. On August 11 the imperial court appointed the seventy-six-year-old Li Hung-chang, who had been recalled from the south, as viceroy of Chihli with responsibility to negotiate with the powers, but the effort was made too late. On August 12 the allies shattered the last of Peking's defenses, and on the 14th they entered the city and broke the siege of the legations. The cathedral was relieved two days later. The victorious troops then proceeded to loot the city. Perhaps the most organized projects were carried out by the Japanese, who took three million taels of pure silver from the treasury as well as government rice and silk, and by the Germans, who transferred many of the art treasures of the Forbidden City to German museums, not to be returned until after World War I. Interestingly, the foreigners discovered large quantities of modern guns and rifles which had not been used by the Chinese during the attack on the legations.

The imperial court feared to face the unknown demands of the powers, and early on the morning of August 15 Tz'u Hsi and a party of attendants, dressed as peasants and riding in common carts, fled Peking and finally made their way to Sian, where a temporary court was set up. Those who remained behind supported Li Hung-chang in his negotiations with the foreigners, but the settlement of the terms of peace was protracted because of the ambitions and rivalries of the several powers.

Imperialist Rivalry and the Boxer Settlement

Russia was especially anxious to use the Boxer settlement to advance her position in Northeast Asia. During the course of the uprising the Boxers had attacked the Chinese Eastern Railway, forced the Russians out of Mukden and Tsitsihar, and laid siege to the Russian section of Harbin. These actions seem not to have been too unwelcome in some Russian quarters since, from the czar down, Russian leaders continued to be interested in Asian expansion. Differences among them centered around means, but all accepted Russia's mission in Asia as a matter of fact. General Alexei Kuropatkin, minister of war, regarded the rebellion as an excellent pretext for seizing Manchuria, and he was supported by other zealots in the cabinet, though later he became too cautious for the even more intransigent group led by Bezobrazov and Plehve. Witte's policy of peaceful penetration was thus challenged by the use of force. Realizing better than others the extent of Russian weakness in Asia, he had consistently sought to avoid a crisis, particularly in Russian-British relations, and had therefore become increasingly moderate; but when the riots in Manchuria assumed a threatening character, he, too, urged the dispatch of Russian troops from the Amur region into Manchuria. By October, 1900, Russian troops were in complete military control of Manchuria, having occupied strategic positions on the pretext of protecting railroads and other properties, and it appeared that Russia intended to convert her Manchurian sphere of interest into a Russian province.

The powers quite naturally looked with disfavor on Russian territorial designs. As early as July 2, 1900, the French foreign minister, Delcassé, sent a circular to various Western nations outlining a general accord with regard to China based upon the agreement which he claimed existed among many of the powers on the following points: guarantee of the welfare of the foreign nationals in China, maintenance of the territorial status quo, and guarantees against a repetition of uprisings. It was certainly true that Great Britain, France, and Germany preferred a whole to a partitioned China and that American policy had traditionally supported China's territorial integrity. Moreover, John Hay, who had previously taken the lead in seeking multilateral acceptance of the doctrine of equal commercial opportunity, provided the strongest support for Delcassé. On July 3 he declared in a dispatch to American diplomatic representatives in Paris, London, Berlin, St. Petersburg, Tokyo, and elsewhere that it was American policy to preserve China as a territorial and administrative entity, to protect all rights guaranteed to friendly powers by treaty and international law, and to safeguard for the world the principle of equal and impartial trade with the Chinese empire; and he went on to seek co-operative action among the powers by suggesting a collective guarantee of the above principles. Delcassé received acknowledgments, at least, from every nation he approached, but Hay had to be content with only a cursory reply from Great Britain.

The direction of Chinese policy was in the hands of Li Hung-chang, and he concentrated his attention on the Russian problem. He favored dealing with Russia on friendly terms, a decision based not on appeasement but on judicious recognition of necessity. The active anti-Russian faction in the government, which included Chang Chih-tung, wanted to oppose Russia with Japanese help, as suggested by Tokyo; but Li feared Japan's long-range plans more than those of Russia. He felt that, failing some agreement, Russia would stay in Manchuria forever and that the other nations might follow the Russian example elsewhere in China; moreover, he realistically discounted effective outside help. Convinced that China had to come to terms with Russia, he proposed to Witte that Russia should renounce all ambitions in

Manchuria in return for Chinese concessions in Mongolia, but the Russians ignored the proposal.

In Manchuria the Russian commander, Alexeiev, had persuaded the Chinese official, Tseng Ch'i, to sign an agreement which would turn Manchuria into a Russian protectorate, and on February 7, 1901, conversations began in St. Petersburg between the Chinese and Russian governments regarding ratification of this agreement. Russia now proposed an even harsher treaty, which would restrict the sovereign rights of China in Manchuria and create a monopoly in the hands of the Russo-Chinese Bank over the region's economic development. Russian diplomacy was underlined by threats. On February 23, for example, Witte warned the Chinese minister at St. Petersburg that if the Russian proposals were not quickly accepted, the military men in Russia would demand the annexation of Manchuria; and on February 25 the Russian minister in Peking delivered a similar threat to Li Hung-chang.

Despite their discussions concerning principles, the powers showed little determination to oppose Russia in Manchuria. Russian actions had brought Great Britain and Germany into an agreement, signed on October 16, 1900, to uphold the "open door," and both powers disavowed any territorial designs on China and invited other powers to adhere to a similar pledge. Japan, Austria-Hungary, France, Italy, and the United States complied, but Russia offered the reservation that these principles would not perceptibly modify the situation established in China by existing treaties. Multilateral co-operation proved to be impossible, and among its proponents Hay himself was one of the first to be disillusioned. He retreated to the position that Manchuria was no longer an integral part of China but rather a Russian province in which open-door treatment was to be bargained for with the czar's government. He expressed this view privately to President Roosevelt, and was later to explain to the Japanese government (February, 1901) that the United States was "not at present prepared to attempt singly or in concert with the other powers to enforce China's integrity by any demonstration which could present a character of hostility to any other power." In November, 1900, under pressure from the United States Navy, he sought a naval base and territorial concession at Samsah Bay inlet north of Foochow on the coast opposite Formosa. He consulted Japan about this because the latter regarded Fukien Province as its sphere of interest after China pledged in April, 1898, never to cede or lease any part of the province. Japan blocked the move, reminding Hay of his recent efforts to preserve the territorial integrity of China.

Among the powers, Japan actually made the most strenuous efforts to check Russia. On February 5, 1901, the Japanese government proposed to Great Britain that the two countries warn China not to conclude any such agreement as that reported to have been signed by Tseng and Alexeiev. London, wishing to encourage the Chinese to hold their ground, approved of the Japanese plan and sounded out Germany for participation. By

February 17 the three powers warned China against the agreement, and by the end of the month the United States, Austria-Hungary, and Italy acted similarly. But these overtures lost much of their effectiveness when on March 15 Germany declared that Manchuria was out of the scope of her recent treaty with Great Britain. Without German support, London was unwilling to continue support of the Japanese position, and Japan, unaided, was unwilling to risk war with Russia.

Li Hung-chang was finally forced to advise his government to approve the Manchurian agreement signed by Tseng Ch'i because he felt that a Chinese refusal, on the very doubtful chance of support from other quarters, would only irritate Russia. The Chinese government did make one last effort to reduce Russian demands when the emperor wrote the czar expressing fear that the agreement would destroy Chinese sovereignty and integrity and that other powers would be stimulated to make similar requests. This last-ditch attempt can also be explained in part by increasing Chinese resistance to the policy of concession, especially the threat by many provincial officials and a number of Peking bureaucrats to challenge the throne's authority if the dynasty acceded to Russian demands. The Russians were willing to accept some modifications, and Count Lamsdorff, the Russian foreign minister, suggested that Russia would withdraw her troops from Manchuria in stages in return for an increase in the privileges of the Russo-Chinese Bank. Although Li agreed to secure formal approval of such an agreement, he died before he could do so, and the negotiations were then postponed until November, 1901.

Meanwhile, Great Britain, Japan, and the United States took the lead in working for a common and all-inclusive treaty to settle the Boxer troubles. For example, in February, 1901, Hay again circularized the powers, asking that none of them consider a private territorial or financial agreement without the full knowledge and approval of all the negotiating powers. But fears that Russia might gain control of Manchuria and even the province of Chihli led to all manner of attempts by other powers to secure additional concessions, and this rivalry, rather than Chinese unwillingness to reach a settlement, prolonged negotiations into the summer of 1901. Finally, in September, the Boxer Protocol was signed by China and all the powers. Its terms were as follows:

1. China was to pay an indemnity of 450,000,000 taels, or $333,000,000. [This was to be paid in thirty-nine annual installments plus interest charges of 4 per cent on the unpaid principal. The indemnity was secured on the Maritime Customs and the Salt Tax. This amount, far in excess of justifiable claims, seriously complicated the dynasty's financial problems. The United States, which had wanted to keep down the size of the indemnity, remitted substantial portions of its share in 1907 and in 1924, to be used for the education of Chinese abroad; and by 1925 all

the powers had agreed to a settlement by which Boxer payments, in part at least, were to be devoted to educational and philanthropic purposes.]

2. Customs duties would be raised to an effective 5 per cent. [This rectification would help China meet the indemnity payments. It was also provided that the importation of arms, munitions, and materials for their manufacture would be prohibited for two years and the prohibition extended by two-year terms if and as long as the foreigners desired. This latter provision hardly seems consistent with avowals regarding Chinese integrity.]

3. Punishment by death and in other ways of those responsible for the Boxer troubles and suspension of examinations for five years in all the cities where antiforeign outbreaks had occurred. [As early as February, 1901, Tz'u Hsi ordered punishment for those that she claimed were responsible. Some were banished, while others were permitted to commit suicide or were executed. The empress dowager was anxious to give the impression that she repudiated the antiforeign policy.]

4. Permanent quartering of foreign troops in Peking as legation guards, foreign policing of the area from Peking to the sea, and destruction of the Taku forts.

5. Establishment of a foreign office to replace the tsungli yamen, and a revision, in foreign interests, of the ceremonial used in audiences with the emperor.

6. Apologies to Germany and Japan for the murder of the German minister and the Japanese chancellor of legation and erection of a memorial to von Ketteler on the spot where he was assassinated.

The following provisions were included in treaties signed on a bilateral basis but, under the most-favored-nation clause, applied to all nations:

7. The internal transit tax (likin) was to be abolished for foreign goods and replaced by a 7½ per cent surtax which would be paid in addition to the normal 5 per cent.

8. Mining regulations were to be revised in order to attract foreign capital.

9. Mukden and Antung were to be opened to foreign settlement and trade. [In April, 1901, Hay had asked for specific assurances that American enterprise in Manchuria would not suffer discrimination.]

10. All native customs houses were placed under the foreign inspectorate of customs.

After staying at Sian for nearly a year, the imperial court, including Tz'u Hsi, on October 6 started its return to Peking, and it arrived at the capital on January 7, 1902, after several delays en route. The situation created by the Boxer Rebellion was terminated except in Manchuria, where the Russian army still remained.

Chinese authority in Manchuria was legally re-established by the April, 1902, settlement with Russia, which provided that in the future China would be responsible for the protection of Russian interests and subjects, and, if the actions of other powers did not prevent it or if no other disturbances arose, Russia would withdraw her troops in three stages at six-month intervals, completing the task by September, 1903. The development of Russian policy in Manchuria will be told elsewhere in this book (see Chap. 19, pp. 321–24), since it is more significantly related to the history of the Anglo-Japanese Alliance of 1902, which did much to prompt this Russian diplomatic retreat, and to the background of the Russo-Japanese War of 1904–1905. Yet it should be noted here that the Russians did not live up to the agreement, and Russian troops remained on in Manchuria after the 1903 deadline. Technically the Russian position was covered by the blank check, "if the actions of other powers did not prevent it."

Many reasons have been asserted for the failure of the powers to dismember China, but the following seem to be the most valid. First, the interests of the various nations in China were too general and dispersed to make partition feasible. This was particularly true in the cases of Great Britain, Japan, Germany, and the United States. Spheres of interest, moreover, brought adequate advantages, and the thought of having to administer parts of China was more than discouraging. In addition, liberal public opinion was growing in support of China, and it was in this realm that Hay's efforts were psychologically effective. Finally, there was the circumstance that the potential aggressors were fearful of the debacle that would follow, particularly if conflict spread to other areas and possibly to Europe, and each hesitated to make the first move. In the background, of course, were tense European and African situations, and the major European powers wanted to avoid strife.

13 *Reform and Revolution, 1902–1912*

After the Boxer Rebellion, and at a very late date in her life, Tz'u Hsi came to understand that nothing short of new policies could save the dynasty. She was not converted to reform in principle, but she did realize that the dynasty would have to make concessions to reform proposals. From 1902 to her death in 1908, therefore, Tz'u Hsi supported a program that was on the surface strikingly similar to that of K'ang Yu-wei. She did her utmost to maintain Manchu power and at the same time satisfy the conservatives and reformers, and before her death on November 15, just a day following that of Kuang Hsu, she selected P'u Yi, the two-year-old grandson of her lifelong friend Jung Lu, to succeed to the throne. Tsai Feng, the young boy's father, and brother of the deceased emperor, became sole regent and continued the reform efforts of the dynasty, but he was motivated increasingly by anti-Chinese attitudes. Since 1902 the power of Chinese officials at the Manchu court had been gradually reduced, and after the death of Tz'u Hsi the most powerful of them, Yuan Shih-k'ai, was dismissed from office. Yuan, whose military power was especially feared, had strong enemies at court among the Manchu nobles, including the regent. After 1908 the central government was more closely controlled by the Manchu imperial family, and few important positions were held by Chinese.

Politically the dynasty faced two basic problems in this period. One was the need to centralize authority by breaking down the autonomy of the provinces, and the second was to permit some popular participation in government while reserving the supremacy of the throne. Tz'u Hsi, reluctantly accepting a form of constitutionalism, announced that the Chinese people would have to be trained to accept political responsibility and thus proposed an evolutionary reform program. She wanted the dynasty to reorganize the administration and enact practical reforms in various fields, and when popular education and the study of other governments had advanced sufficiently, a form of constitutional government would be introduced. In advancing these aims, the dynasty was caught between the criticisms of the conservatives, who resisted change, and the reformers and revolutionaries, who complained that reform was being implemented only as a means to save the Manchus.

Political Reforms

Political reform began with the appointment in 1905 of a commission of five distinguished scholars to go abroad to study foreign constitutional systems. It was thought that if China could learn the secret strength of Western government she could regain her position in the world; but the commission was also in part the dynasty's reaction to a petition for constitutional monarchy submitted by reform-minded scholars. Like Chinese reform advocates before them, the commissioners were particularly impressed by what they saw in Japan, for it seemed clear to them that Japan's power, as evidenced by her victory in war with Russia, was the result of her adoption of Western institutions, even a constitution, which she had achieved without sacrificing the position of the imperial family. The arguments of conservative Chinese, who were antireform and anticonstitution, gave way before the examples of Japan's successes.

In September, 1906, when the five-man commission returned to China, the government announced that it was preparing a constitution and initiating a reform of the administration. The council of state and the grand secretariat remained unchanged in organization, but appointments to these bodies were to be made from the group of younger men acquainted with Western political institutions. The government boards, however, were reorganized, with these new ministries emerging: foreign affairs, which replaced the tsungli yamen, civil service, interior, finance, war, agriculture-industry, and posts-communications. There was also a major reshuffling of positions in Peking, with almost 1,400 officials discharged from service. The dynasty had promised that there would be no distinctions, as in the past, between Chinese and Manchus in appointments, but it did not hold true to this policy. In important offices Manchus were generally placed in a superior or, at worst, an equal position with Chinese. Only the inferior ranks of the imperial hierarchy were dominated by Chinese, and this was because of an almost complete lack of trained Manchus at these levels.

One of the most important issues between the Manchus and the Chinese was the commission's recommendation that the power of the viceroys and governors be reduced to that of Japan's prefectural governors and that their military commands be transferred to the central government. When the local government system was reorganized in June, 1907, there was no change in the military and financial powers of the viceroys. Shortly thereafter, however, Peking created financial supervisors for the collection of taxes in the provinces in order to gain greater control over provincial revenues; and the dynasty ordered the two most powerful viceroys, Yuan Shih-k'ai and Chang Chih-tung, to Peking for promotion as grand councilors. These steps were regarded as looking toward the gradual elimination of the power of the viceroys throughout China. The issue of centralization *vs.* autonomy was not settled in these last years of the dynasty but remained to contribute significantly to the destruction of the imperial system in 1912. Certain of the military reforms, intended by the dynasty to absorb the power of local officials, deserve special consideration.

Military reform continued to demand a great amount of attention by the dynasty. As early as the Taiping Rebellion, it had been abundantly clear that the banners, largely horsemen and archers, were outmoded, but until the twentieth century army reform had been limited largely to those few enlightened viceroys who followed in the tradition of Tseng Kuo-fan. Yuan Shih-k'ai was one of these men. In 1896 he had organized a force, trained by German officers, which he took with him to Shantung in 1900 and to Chihli in 1901. As viceroy of Chihli from 1901 to 1907, he replaced his German advisers with Japanese officers, established a series of military schools at Paoting, and began sending advanced trainees to Japan for experience. With strong support from Tz'u Hsi and Jung Lu, Yuan was able to create a powerful, semipersonal army of six divisions, and after Jung Lu's death in 1903 he associated himself for a time with influential Manchu princes. Yuan's own subordinates increased their power as the prestige of their master grew, and it is important to note that a number of them subsequently formed the dominant Peiyang (northern administration) military clique. In central

China Chang Chih-tung continued to increase the number of foreign-style troops in his service, and he also strove to raise the social status of the military profession by compelling civil officials to enroll their sons in his military academies; he himself sent three of his own grandsons to Japan to be educated in service schools.

In association with Chang Chih-tung and others, Yuan Shih-k'ai pleaded for greater military unification under a general staff, but the dynasty had to cling to a policy of modernizing China's armed forces within the decentralized political framework. The best that Peking could hope for was the establishment of conditions under which troops of various provinces could be mobilized in time of war and integrated into a unified command. Provincial armies remained controlled by provincial officials, but officers and noncommissioned officers were ordered to Chihli or Hupeh for training at the new military academies. It was hoped that upon their return to their units these officers would supervise local instruction along the same lines; and although the objective of uniformity was never fully realized, this practice did widen the influence of the Peiyang and Hupeh armies. Instruction, however, was generally confined to younger, junior officers because their superiors were often too incompetent or too proud to learn. Yuan Shih-k'ai was also ordered to train a brigade of three thousand bannermen, and after 1905 he helped to establish a military school for sons of princes, imperial clansmen, and senior Manchu and Chinese officials. The superintendent of this school was a Manchu, but the actual director was one of Yuan's subordinates, General Feng Kuo-chang. After Yuan's dismissal from office in 1908—following the death of his patroness, Tz'u Hsi—and Chang's death in 1909, Tsai Feng and his brother, Tsai T'ao, organized a new army of imperial guards to offset the Peiyang Army, whose officers were still loyal to Yuan. The Manchu princes also made preparations to develop a navy that they could control, but they found it impossible to regain command over provincial vessels. Despite all these advances, the balance of power between the central and provincial governments remained basically unchanged, and China still supported a varied collection of military units, most of which were untrained by modern standards.

Popular participation in government began in July, 1908, when Peking issued regulations for provincial assemblies that were to meet within a year. They were conceived of as sounding boards of provincial opinion, and their discussions were to be limited to matters submitted to them by the viceroy or governor, who also had the right to petition the central government to order their dissolution. They were to meet once a year from the first day of the ninth month for a session of forty days; and the right to vote for the electors, who in turn would choose members of the assemblies, was strictly limited by property and educational qualifications. In the first elections 119,549 males voted out of a total population of 38,000,000 in Shantung Province, and

113,233 out of 34,000,000 in Hupeh Province. The provincial assemblies, which existed ultimately in seventeen provinces, met for the first time in October, 1909, and they reflected a considerable amount of public opinion. For example, they agitated for the early convocation of a national parliament, and they attempted to play a positive role in the actual formulation of provincial policy, many times in opposition to the viceroy or governor. By 1911 they were in some instances on the way to establishing themselves in a controlling position; in fact, in October of that year it was the provincial assembly of Hupeh that turned the first province over to the revolutionaries. Finally, the assemblies often checked the central government's efforts to increase its own power, as illustrated by their opposition to the national railway policy of the dynasty.

In 1908 Peking promulgated a nine-year constitutional program which outlined a yearly schedule of civil and military changes in the provinces and in the central government, to be climaxed by the establishment of a parliament in 1917. The parliament was to be a bicameral legislature elected by literate male Chinese subjects who had resided in their neighborhoods for a year and who had no criminal record, but its legislative powers were weak, making it hardly more than an advisory body. It was abundantly clear that the constitutional system was designed to maintain the position of the Manchu imperial family, especially since it was known that the Japanese constitution was the source of most of its principles and that the Manchu commissioners had consulted with Ito Hirobumi, who had emphasized the great authority of the Japanese emperor. And since all legislative, executive, and judicial powers were reserved for the Manchu sovereign, it was logical to conclude that constitutional reform was designed to centralize political control over the empire. Thus the policies of the dynasty earned the opprobrium of reformers, who wanted a constitutional monarchy with strong popular participation in the government; of revolutionaries, who wanted a republic; and of provincial conservatives, who guarded their autonomy.

Peking convoked a central legislative council in October, 1910, to serve as a forerunner of the parliament; of its two hundred members, half were chosen by the throne and the other half by the provincial assemblies from their membership. The council had partial powers of legislation and budget control, but in its first session the central government did not accept its statutes and budget resolutions. Influenced strongly by advocates of constitutional reform like Liang Ch'i-ch'ao, whose Political Information Society criticized the dynasty for not giving up any part of its power, the council did succeed in forcing the government to agree to convoke parliament in 1913 instead of 1917. And after an unsuccessful attempt to impeach the grand council, it demanded and got the government's promise to make the grand council responsible to the entire country or alternatively to appoint a responsible cabinet. Although the assembly was dissolved by the dynasty in January,

1911, it was reconvened in the autumn of that year during last-minute attempts by the Manchus to save the dynasty. In May a cabinet replaced the old advisory bodies, but all of its members—the prime minister, two deputies, and ten ministers—were appointed by the emperor and were responsible to him rather than to the central legislative council. The powers of the cabinet were limited to those the emperor chose to delegate, and its composition reflected Manchu dominance since the prime minister was a prince of the blood and the majority of the cabinet posts were held by imperial clansmen. Only five Chinese were ministers, and of these one was a Chinese bannerman.

Peking also began to implement important judicial reforms in this period in order to secure the abolition of extraterritoriality. In the commercial treaties of 1902 and 1903 the United States, Great Britain, and Japan declared that they would surrender extraterritorial jurisdiction as soon as Chinese laws and courts satisfied them. In 1907 the dynasty approved a new system of courts, separating judicial responsibility from other functions of administration, and in 1911 the central legislative council passed a new criminal code based largely on that of Japan. Two notable legal changes were the termination of family responsibility for individual crimes and the mitigation of numerous punishments. The new code remained in force under the republic, which replaced the dynasty in 1912.

Educational and Economic Reforms

In the dynasty's reform proposals education was regarded as an important prerequisite to progress in other fields, particularly politics and national defense. Thus Peking began to inaugurate a new system of education that included a Westernized curriculum as well as the Confucian Classics. In 1901 an imperial edict called for the building of a national school system, and in 1903 a ministry of education was established. In the following year the new ministry produced a plan for a system based on that of Japan, with kindergartens, primary schools, middle schools, high schools, provincial colleges, and the imperial university at Peking. A board of education was created to seek some uniformity of standards and administration, and in each province it was to be represented by a commissioner of education. At first there was no provision for the education of women, but in 1907 the government decided to establish primary schools and normal schools for them. In 1905 one of the most effective obstacles to the new system was removed with the abolition of the old civil service examinations.

To get these proposals from paper into practice was indeed difficult if not impossible. In the central government there was conservative opposition, which extolled Confucian studies and belittled Western learning, and still greater opposition came from local officials, scholars, and gentry. Even where local feeling was favorable, there were problems of finance. The dynasty of necessity had to leave financial details to the ingenuity of the local communities, which rarely could provide adequate funds. In the larger provincial cities, where funds were sufficient, there was unfortunately a tendency to build schools of higher learning instead of lower schools, since more prestige attached to the former. The quality of instruction was another problem. Because of the shortage of qualified teachers, instructors were often nothing more than relatives of local officials. Missionaries offered some hopeful possibilities, but unfortunately they were barred by a rule forbidding the teaching of religion in government schools. Some teachers did come from Japan. They were willing to work for far lower salaries than Westerners, and culturally they fitted more easily into the Chinese environment. Finally, to stimulate applications for teaching posts, the government gave them official rank. Despite all these problems, significant progress was made, particularly in localities where officials supported the program, as did Yuan Shih-k'ai and Chang Chih-tung, and by 1910 China had over 57,000 schools, almost 90,000 teachers, and over 1,600,000 students. The National University at Peking became the cultural center of the country and a leader of the reform movement. Yet only a beginning had been made, since China's population was in excess of 400,000,000, of whom some 65,000,000 were children of school age.

The central government also urged more students to continue their education abroad in the hope that this would build a new body of public servants capable of strengthening the dynasty and resisting the pressures of the foreign powers. At one time during this period there were about 15,000 students in Japan and another several thousand in Europe and the United States. Ironically, many of them became leaders and supporters of movements far more radical than the reform program of the dynasty, and many were converted to the revolutionary views of Sun Yat-sen. Tz'u Hsi also encouraged Manchus, especially her own kinsmen, to go abroad to study, for she wanted to use them to offset the growing numbers of Japanese-trained radicals.

Railway development was given a high priority in the economic plans of the dynasty. Lack of an efficient national transportation system stood in the way of centralized control over the country and of mobilizing an army to deal with antidynastic disturbances or international crises. In 1908 Peking was able to obtain favorable terms from German, British, and French interests for the construction of a railway from Tientsin to Pukow. The foreign loan was not secured on the railway receipts but on certain provincial revenues, and its terms provided that the construction and control of the railway would be in the hands of the Chinese government. Other railways in which foreign capital was invested on these terms included the Shanghai-Hangchow-Ningpo, the Peking-Hankow, and the Lunghai (from Haichow on the coast of Kiangsu westward to Shensi). In the case of the Hankow-Canton and Hankow-Szechwan lines (Hukuang railways), however, Peking was anxious to avoid additional foreign financing and turned the projects over to provincial companies. These in turn appealed for money on patriotic and economic grounds, and thousands of small shareholders provided the necessary capital. By 1909, however, it was apparent to the government and particularly to Chang Chih-tung, strongest supporter of the plan, that the provinces were unable to complete the projects. In some cases adequate funds were not available, and in others the company officials merely squeezed profits for themselves from the subscriptions.

Peking was finally forced to turn to foreign sources to finance the Hukuang railways, and by this time the political and financial rivalry of the powers was so great that they themselves began to favor pooling certain types of loans to China through an international banking agency called the consortium. Peking was quite willing to deal with the consortium because it was a means of breaking the quasi-monopoly of the British in the Yangtze Valley, and it reached agreement with British, French, and German banking groups for capitalizing the Hukuang railways in June, 1909.

At this point the President of the United States, William Howard Taft, became determined that American capital should actively enter the China field in order to preserve the open-door policy. As early as 1898 American interests, represented by the American-China Development Company, had secured a contract from the Chinese government to build a railroad from Hankow to Canton, but American rights had gone by default to a Belgian syndicate. The construction right was repurchased by J. P. Morgan in 1905, and he promptly sold out to the Chinese government. Under prodding by the American government, an American banking syndicate was organized in 1909, and Taft sought equal participation for this group in every foreign loan floated by China. Washington warned Peking that, unless Americans were invited to share in the Hukuang railways loan, it might reconsider the remission of the Boxer indemnity funds, of which some $12,000,000 had been designated for return to China in excess of amounts claimed for actual American losses. Taft finally had to appeal directly to Tsai Feng, the regent, and in May, 1910, the American banking group was permitted to enter the consortium. In the quadruple agreement of November, 1910, the four banking groups agreed to share equally in all Chinese railway loans. The entry of the United States into the consortium necessitated a new agreement with China, and internal complications delayed the signing of a final contract between the powers and China until May 20, 1911.

The shift to foreign financing was in part the result of Peking's judgment that the establishment of a national system of rail transportation would help to break down provincial autonomy. In May, 1911, the central government announced its plan to nationalize railroads under the board of communications, but provincial governors and local officials, who saw the political motives behind the plan, opposed it and were joined in their opposition by local businessmen and bankers. None of these groups wanted to lose profitable construction contracts, the distribution of enormous patronage, and the power to manipulate rates and service. They insisted on provincial control despite the poor showing made by the first provincial promoters, and they continued to form companies to collect funds for railway construction.

In the face of this strong feeling, Peking was willing to come to terms with the provinces, and for a time it looked as though Chang Chih-tung would be able to make mutually satisfactory arrangements. After his death in 1909, however, Peking aggressively attacked provincial leaders, accusing them of inefficiency and corruption. The local authorities became more convinced that the Manchus were conniving with the foreigners to keep themselves in power, and the governors of several of the central and western provinces started a Rights Recovery Movement to prevent further foreign investment in railways in order to thwart the Manchu design. Peking again shifted to appeasement, promising to exchange interest-bearing government bonds for the full value of local railway shares in Kwangtung, Hunan, and Hupeh provinces. This was particularly generous since most of the railway companies were bankrupt. The Szechwan investors were treated somewhat differently. In this case the government proposed redemption only of the sums actually expended for railway purposes rather than for the amount subscribed or collected by special tax levies; it was simply not willing to make up losses resulting from corruption or speculation. Justly or not, the dynasty reaped a harvest of discontent, and by the summer of 1911 the railroad issue reached a crisis in Szechwan, where general strikes were called on all the railroads and in industries associated with them, and radical students utilized the situation to parade in the streets, calling for the end of Manchu rule. Arrest of some of the ringleaders of these disturbances led to an attack on the viceroy's residence.

The railroad issue and the political significance behind it were typical of the situations that gave rise to criticism and hostility toward the Manchu rule, and they show clearly the assortment of difficulties that the dynasty faced in its efforts to reform and strengthen itself. The consortium loan was finally floated on June 11, but the outbreak of revolution in October delayed actual construction on the lines until 1913, and the political upheavals of the subsequent years prevented the projects from being completed. Not until 1936 was the Canton-Hankow line finished, and then solely by Chinese efforts. The Szechwan line was not constructed.

Finance was another field in which Manchu reform policies were frustrated. Reform had been necessary ever since the middle of the nineteenth century, when the financial demands on the central government far exceeded its income. Costs of suppressing rebellions, indemnities for lost wars, and the expenses of modernization all called for additional revenues, but corruption, nepotism, and lack of budgeting and accounting characterized a finance ministry that had no system at all. Only the imperial maritime customs, staffed with foreign administrators, was run in a businesslike manner. Tz'u

Hsi had not dared to propose drastic reform measures, but in January, 1909, her successors established within the ministry of finance a committee to reorganize the fiscal structure of the empire according to modern budgeting practices. One of the basic problems it was ordered to solve was the financial balance between the provinces and the central regime. But provincial officials, who were concerned about their financial autonomy, opposed the plan and only complied with its minimum requirements. Although an imperial budget was submitted to the central legislative council in 1911, no basic modification of the inadequate financial structure had yet taken place.

The dynasty also began to face up to the chaos of the currency system. Chinese money included copper cash, new-style coins from provincial mints, paper bank notes, bar silver, and the tael, the uncoined unit of value which had variable forms. The problem was further complicated by fluctuations in the value of silver to gold in international markets. In September, 1910, Peking sought a loan exclusively from the United States for the double purpose of currency reform and the industrial development of Manchuria, but the United States was bound by the consortium agreement to share any loan equally with the other three members. In April, 1911, the dynasty signed a contract with the consortium for a currency-reform loan, a small part of which would be used for Manchurian development purposes. Revolution in China and threatening war clouds in Europe prevented the floating of this loan, but it did serve to arouse additional animosity against the Manchus. Peking's intentions became another political issue, since the fluctuations and uncertainties of the value of different coins and notes in circulation were an important source of income to many local officials, small bankers, owners of cash shops, speculators, and merchants.

Opium was another problem that the dynasty attacked with some vigor. Brought under legalized trade after 1858, the importation of opium had continued to increase, reaching a high point of over 70,000 chests (of 133 pounds each) by 1888. After that date, trade declined, but Chinese production, which continued to expand, took up the slack. In May, 1906, Peking first decided on a policy of taxing opium out of production but within a few months shifted to gradual prohibitions. All land under cultivation was to be put to other uses within ten years; all opium-smokers were to be licensed, and restrictions were to be placed on the sale of opium appliances; and government officials were entirely prohibited from using the drug. Opium dens were banned, but retail shops were allowed to remain open during the ten-year period. Finally, there was to be a gradual reduction in the amount of opium permitted to habitual and licensed smokers, with the exception of those over sixty years of age, who could continue to have the same amount.

Moreover, in 1908 the British agreed to annual decreases of its imports of opium into China, proportionate to the annual reduction of cultivation in China. This arrangement would last for three years and was to continue for an additional seven years if Great Britain was satisfied that China had maintained effective measures for suppressing native production. In 1911 Great Britain consented to continue the import restrictions, and later in the same year, at an international opium conference in The Hague, the powers having treaties with China agreed that they would take more effective measures to stop the smuggling of drugs into China, to close shops and dens in the concessions areas, and to prevent opium from passing through foreign post offices in China.

All these measures, domestic and international, represented impressive gains, but success depended ultimately upon the strength of local opinion, the co-operation of officials, and the attitude of the economic interests involved. Ironically, progress was costly in some ways, for the opium policy of the dynasty caused a reduction in the revenues of the government, which was then forced to tax national production and imports; caused serious economic dislocations in many areas where farmers specialized in opium cultivation; and to some extent furthered the use of cocaine and morphine. Later developments, including the revolution of 1911 and its failure, the subsequent rise of the warlords, and the outbreak of World War I, tended to nullify the restrictions against opium and caused both an increase in production, encouraged by greedy, tax-minded officials, and a revival of the trade; but the achievements of the period 1906–1911 did demonstrate what could be done with political direction and enforcement.

The reforms of the dynasty did not stem the tide of discontent with Manchu rule. Paradoxically, they went far enough to alienate the support of the more conservative-minded Manchus and Chinese but did not go far enough to win the support of the advocates of reform, who wanted the establishment of a constitutional monarchy with popular participation in government. And the reforms had little effect on the revolutionaries, who continued their campaign to replace the dynasty with a republic. The dynasty also failed in its efforts to control the provinces. Reform came too late and was too narrow in its conception to protect the regime against the growing conviction among the Chinese that the Manchus had to be overthrown.

Sun Yat-Sen and the T'ung Meng Hui

Sun Yat-sen was developing in this period an organizational framework for the revolutionary forces that opposed the dynasty. Following the Boxer Rebellion there was evidence of mounting revolutionary thought and action in China, e.g., during the two years 1904 and 1905 more than a hundred revolutionary pamphlets, magazines, and journals were published at Shanghai. Although the police power of the dynasty prevented the development of an integrated movement, Sun Yat-sen was able to operate effectively in Japan, where he found a receptive audience among the intensely patriotic young

Chinese. In the spring of 1901 Cantonese students in Tokyo organized a Kwangtung Independence Association, which urged the provincial authorities to issue a declaration of independence from the dynasty. Sun extended his support to these students and formed close relationships with them. After 1902 Japanese schools were congested with Chinese students from all the provinces, and in Tokyo alone there were over six thousand of them, as well as an increasing number of exiled reformers and rebels. Many of these young men, turning their backs on the past, were attracted by revolutionary ideas. In Tokyo they had freedom of speech, and they discussed political questions without fear. They published numerous revolutionary magazines and went so far as to institute secret military training.

In September, 1905, with Sun as the guiding force, several hundred Chinese students, representing seventeen of the eighteen Chinese provinces, organized the T'ung Meng Hui as a revolutionary association. Again from Tokyo, revolutionary influences spread throughout China via magazines, pamphlets, and newspapers. The main propaganda organ of the T'ung Meng Hui was *The People*, which had a circulation of 150,000. The propaganda line stressed the urgency of learning from the West, the corruption and extravagance of the Manchu regime, the insincerity of the promulgated reforms, the stupidity of the regime's dealings with foreign nations, the humiliating wars, the alienation of territory and the imposition of indemnities, the peril of the partition of China, and the advantages of republican government. But perhaps the most effective appeal was to Chinese racial prejudice against the foreign Manchus.

The Manchus reacted to these activities, and in 1906 the Japanese board of education, at Peking's request, began to enforce strict regulations for the control of Chinese students; for example, Japanese police halted the publication of *The People*. The ardor of many of the students diminished, and a large number of them, especially those financed by the dynasty, decided to return home. After 1906 the flow of students to Japan declined, but by this time there were new opportunities for study in China.

By 1906 the T'ung Meng Hui was already well established in China. According to a survey made by the revolutionaries, there were 10,000 enrolled members, and there was not a province without a branch of the association. The membership was made up largely of returned students whose susceptibility to revolutionary propaganda increased when they were unable to get posts in the administration befitting their level of education. Some were influential as teachers in the dynasty's educational reform program. The T'ung Meng Hui also enlisted the support of secret societies like the Triads, who had grand lodges in each of the five southern provinces, and the Ko Lao Hui, which was strong in the Yangtze Valley and the extreme west and northwest. In fact, Sun's success among the overseas Chinese, especially the establishment of T'ung Meng Hui branches in Singapore and the United States, was in part due to the receptivity of the secret societies to anti-Manchu appeals. The T'ung Meng Hui also infiltrated the army, with particular success in the Hankow and Nanking area and among students at military academies in Japan. By 1909 the Manchus became aware of this trend and began to disarm and disband suspected regiments, but by this time the army was already strongly imbued with revolutionary sentiments. Lastly, the T'ung Meng Hui received financial assistance from Chinese merchants and capitalists, particularly in the treaty ports, where, under Western influences, they were beginning to assert themselves more boldly. Nothing showed this more clearly than the active role they played in boycotts against the United States in 1905 because of discriminatory immigration practices and against Japan in 1908 because of the dynasty's concessions after a minor ship accident.

The T'ung Meng Hui also began to develop a basic philosophy of revolution in this period. In 1894, when Sun Yat-sen had organized the Hsing Chung Hui, he had two principles in mind, nationalism and democracy; but during his three years in Europe, from 1896 to 1898, his ideas expanded to include the principle of the people's livelihood. In 1905, speaking before a student group at Brussels, Sun summarized the ideology of the revolution as The Three Principles of the People:

1. To implement the sovereignty of the Chinese people through the establishment of a nationalist regime.
2. To create a republican government, based upon the principles of equality, in which all citizens would be represented and governed by a popularly elected president and legislature.
3. To equalize the ownership of the land so that all the people might enjoy the blessings of modern civilization.

Sun acknowledged that "The Three Principles of the People correspond with the principles stated by President Lincoln—'government of the people, by the people, for the people.' I translate them into *min yu* (the people to have), *min chih* (the people to govern), and *min hsiang* (the people to enjoy)." Sun also explained what he considered to be "the three phases of the revolution":

1. A *period of military rule.* In this introductory period, the country would throw off the evils of monarchical oppression, official squeeze, cruel punishments, heavy taxes, and the badge of subjection—the queue. Slavery, foot-binding, opium-smoking, and ignorant superstitions would be prohibited.
2. A *period of political tutelage.* After three years of military rule every district (hsien) would learn to govern itself. Local councils and all local administrative officers would be elected by the local citizens. A provisional code would be put in force defining the relations of the hsien with the central government, which would still be a military government.

3. *A period of constitutional government.* When this provisional arrangement had been in force all over China for six years, the people would elect their representatives to a national assembly, which in turn would adopt a permanent constitution and organize a government as provided by it. The military government would retire, and the constitutional government would be completed.

Sun's program was not accepted in its entirety by all Chinese who joined the T'ung Meng Hui. Some members objected to "the equal distribution of landownership"; nor did all have genuine belief in democracy. Most Chinese became revolutionaries because of political discontent, but very few of them understood such concepts as republicanism and democracy. It is clear that the only real common ground of the revolutionary movement was its anti-Manchuism.

From 1905 on, the revolutionaries were involved in a series of abortive uprisings that demonstrate many of the weaknesses of the movement. Early in 1905 Huang Hsing organized an insurrection at Changsha, the capital of Hunan Province, which failed; Huang himself was captured but managed to escape and flee to Japan, where he became active in student circles. In 1907 there were four unsuccessful uprisings in Kwangtung and Kwangsi. One of these attempts is particularly instructive. In January, 1907, Peking persuaded the Japanese government to expel Sun from Japan, but he turned up at Hanoi and with French help planned to seize Canton. He was unable to co-ordinate the actions of diverse T'ung Meng Hui elements, and the project failed miserably. Under Manchu pressure, the French banished Sun from Hanoi but assisted him to set up a revolutionary headquarters at Singapore. Sun then continued on to Europe in search of much-needed financial assistance. There were several more failures in the period 1908–1911, and the attempt in April, 1911, was especially costly in lives. This was a courageous but reckless assault upon the viceroy's yamen at Canton by about a hundred revolutionaries, most of them intellectuals. Unfortunately, the supporting units failed to join in, and the central group had to act alone. Using pistols and small bombs, they dislodged the yamen guards, destroyed buildings, and for about five hours resisted the attempts of several thousand government troops to regain the area. When the battle was over, forty-three revolutionaries were dead and twenty-nine were captured and promptly executed. This so-called "Martyrdom of the Seventy-two" captured the imagination of many young men and prompted them to join the movement. In retrospect, all these uprisings seem to have been naïvely ambitious projects. Co-ordination was faulty, and shortages of weapons and ammunition were never overcome.

The revolutionaries also resorted to assassination, but failure was again the common result. The most spectacular action occurred on October 15, 1905, when Wu Yueh threw a bomb at the members of the constitutional commission as they were boarding their train at Peking to go abroad. Innocent bystanders suffered, but the targets escaped. Another notorious attempt was made by Wang Ching-wei, an early editor of *The People* and a confidant of Sun Yat-sen. In 1909 he became so disheartened by the repeated failures of plots and insurrections that he planned a bold move to arouse the country. He went to Peking and with fellow-terrorists plotted to kill the regent, Tsai Feng. Their dynamite and mechanism were discovered, and Wang and an accomplice were arrested. Wang was sentenced to be executed, but Tsai Feng commuted the punishment to life imprisonment in order to gain a reputation for benevolence and also to quiet the rebels.

As the revolutionary movement developed, it gained more and more adherents, but it never became a mass movement. The masses continued their daily pursuits, showing little excitement and frequently no interest, and this was true even in the large urban centers. When the revolution was finally under way, there was occasionally some mass participation locally, but this was more often due to local grievances than to revolutionary sentiments. There was, however, tremendous resentment against the Manchus, and in Sian they were massacred by the local populace. The actual fighting, of which there was relatively little, was done mostly by professional soldiers, attached to one side or the other, and they were joined by bandits, destitute persons, occasional mobs, and idealistic individuals who hardly knew what they were fighting for.

The Revolution of 1911

The revolution actually began as a result of two events that occurred in the cities of Hankow and Wuchang in mid-October, 1911. On October 9 there was an accidental explosion in a house in the Russian concession at Hankow; this house was a revolutionary headquarters where bombs were being prepared for an uprising on the 16th. An investigation by the Russian authorities led to the arrest of many of the rebels, who were extradited to the viceroy, Jiu Ch'eng; but more important, a list of revolutionaries was confiscated and turned over to Jiu. On the following day, revolutionaries in the army across the river at Wuchang decided to take action. Seizing the ammunition dump, they bombed the viceroy's yamen and burned it. When Jiu Ch'eng fled, the military commander, Chang Piao, abandoned the city with his troops. According to Sun Yat-sen:

> The success at Wuchang was accidental and was mainly due to the flight of Jiu Ch'eng; if he had not fled, Chang Piao undoubtedly would have stayed and kept his troops together and in order. At that time most of those in the new army at Wuchang who supported the revolutionary cause had been sent away to Szechwan. The few who remained made up only a very small part of the artillery and engineering battalions, while the other soldiers in the new Wuchang army

had little appetite for the new cause. It was that small group that was prompted by the police discovery of the revolutionary headquarters to make the attempt without much thought for its chance of success.

The revolutionary troops forced a Japanese-trained colonel, Li Yuan-hung, to lead the mutiny. Within the short period of forty-eight hours all of Wuchang, capital of Hupeh, was controlled by Li's forces, and the members of the Hupeh provincial assembly, sitting at Wuchang, went over in a body to the rebels. On October 12 Hankow was occupied by Li's troops, and they created a provisional government with Li as president. The new government issued a Manifesto of Revolution and called on other cities and provinces to rise and drive out the Manchus.

A spark had set off the revolution throughout China. Fighting spread to other large urban areas. Szechwan Province declared its independence, followed by Hunan and Shensi provinces. In Shansi Province local troops assassinated the governor, burned the Manchu section of Taiyuan, the capital, and established a revolutionary government under Yen Hsi-shan. In Canton the Manchu garrison commander was killed, and an independent government was set up under Hu Han-min. Hu, who later rose to prominence in the Nationalist movement, was typical of the revolutionary intellectual. As a scholar who had failed the metropolitan examination, he became a schoolmaster in Wuchow and later edited a Canton newspaper. In 1902 he entered a normal school in Tokyo as a Chinese government student but for some reason returned home after three months. In 1904 he was once again sent to Tokyo with a group of students that included Wang Ching-wei, and there he studied law, politics, and economics. In October, 1905, he was introduced to Sun Yat-sen, and shortly thereafter he became head of the secretariat of the T'ung Meng Hui.

The general outbreak of revolution caused great consternation at Peking, and Tsai Feng was thoroughly alarmed. On October 14 the dynasty issued an edict appointing Yuan Shih-k'ai viceroy of Hupeh and Hunan provinces with military powers to suppress the "bandits." These orders were issued without consulting Yuan, who had been living in forced retirement since January, 1909, but the main concern of the dynasty was to get a strong man in the field. The diplomatic corps at Peking, which was negotiating another loan for the dynasty, seconded this viewpoint. At first Yuan declined the invitation, but, after repeated urging by the Manchu court, he presented Tsai Feng with six demands: the opening of parliament in the following year, the organization of a responsible cabinet, amnesty for all those who were connected with the revolution, legal recognition of the revolutionary party, his own full authority and power to reorganize all the armed forces, and adequate military funds. Yuan wanted the first four points to be the basis of a compromise which the revolutionaries would accept and through which he could achieve power for himself. Military power would secure for him the position of mediator

213

between the dynasty and the revolutionaries, and his popularity would enable him to become prime minister of the responsible cabinet. If the revolutionaries did not accept the compromise, military power, he felt, would guarantee his supremacy. Tsai Feng, reluctant to accede to Yuan's demands, was forced by the worsening military situation in the Yangtze Valley to appoint him imperial commissioner of all the armies on October 27. Yuan still did not come out of retirement, but the imperial army responded to the news of his appointment by fighting its way into Hankow.

Meanwhile, on October 22, in a last effort to win popular support, the dynasty hastily reconvened the central legislative council, which had been adjourned in the spring of 1911, to facilitate the establishment of constitutional government. The council, dominated by the advocates of parliamentary government, made four demands upon the dynasty:

1. A capable and virtuous person to be immediately appointed to organize a responsible cabinet, from which members of the imperial family would be explicitly excluded. [The dynasty had promised to do this earlier but had merely changed the name "grand council" to "cabinet."]
2. Amnesty for all political offenders, including the reformers of 1898.
3. The constitution to be framed only after consultation with representatives of the people.
4. Parliament to be convened immediately.

The council also passed a motion on October 25 demanding the punishment of Sheng Hsuan-huai, whom it regarded as most responsible for the dynasty's efforts to centralize its control over the railways. He was dismissed from office on the following day and fled to Tsingtao.

Pressure on the dynasty increased on the 29th when elements in the imperial army stationed at Lwanchow, halfway between Mukden and Peking, refused to entrain south until the demands of the council were accepted, and on October 30 the dynasty capitulated. It authorized the council to draft a constitution, released political prisoners, including Wang Ching-wei, and on November 1 appointed Yuan Shih-k'ai as premier. Yuan left for the south to assume command of the troops loyal to the dynasty, but when he learned on the 11th that the council had confirmed him in office, he prepared to return to Peking to take charge of the government, leaving his field troops under the command of General Tuan Ch'i-jui. Meanwhile the council, moving into high gear, drew up a set of constitutional principles, promulgated by the dynasty as a constitution of nineteen articles, to transform China into a monarchy on the British model.

In the new government, power gravitated to Yuan Shih-k'ai. On November 8 the council elected him premier, and on the 16th, after returning to Peking, he formed a cabinet of his partisans. Early in December Tsai Feng resigned as regent and was succeeded by Kuang Hsu's widow, who had little interest in politics. The last obstacle to Yuan's power in the capital, the imperial guards, were replaced by a force under the command of his protégé, General Feng Kuo-chang. Realistically appraising the situation, Yuan began to hint that the Manchus should abdicate, and he had already opened negotitions with Li Yuan-hung to achieve this end. Yuan performed like a clever opportunist, "bending or surging with the wind." With superior military forces, he never attempted to push his military advantage to ultimate and decisive victory on the battlefield, for so long as indecision prevailed he was more easily able to impose his will on the dynasty and the council. Yet in negotiations with the rebels he was able to bargain from a position of strength.

As the revolution spread in the period from October to December, 1911, it was clearly revealed as a series of spontaneous revolts rather than a well-planned, co-ordinated, national revolution. Provincial groups acted independently and in most cases established separate "republics" under military governors; the only common objectives of these groups were destruction of the dynasty and some form of political change. In November, however, there were some efforts to establish a central organization and to formulate a common program of action. On the 9th the revolutionary military government of Hupeh requested that the independent provinces send delegates to Wuchang to serve as a revolutionary council, and two days later other elements at Shanghai proposed that a constitutional conference be held at that city. By November 15 the Shanghai group opened a "Conference of the Representatives of the Military Governments of the Provinces," which recognized Wuchang as the seat of the "Central Military Government of the Republic," with Li Yuan-hung at its head; and shortly after the 20th the Wuchang representatives were able to persuade the delegates to journey to their city to establish a provisional government. Since Hanyang had been reoccupied by the imperial forces and Wuchang was under the fire of their guns, the representatives met instead in the British concession at Hankow on November 30. Between December 2 and 4 they elected a committee which drafted an outline for the organization of a provisional government along federal lines and passed a resolution to elect Yuan Shih-k'ai president if he would shift his support to the revolutionary cause. On the 4th Nanking fell to the rebels, and they selected it as the capital of the provisional government.

After the fall of Nanking to the rebels, a truce was signed to work out a settlement in a peace conference at Hankow. The willingness of both sides to negotiate was the result of the military stalemate, their financial difficulties, fear of foreign intervention, the danger of a complete political breakdown, and the ambitions of the various leaders. The Peking treasury was empty, and Yuan had been forced to make the Manchus contribute from their household treasury to pay the troops. The rebels had no treasury, and their funds were confined to contributions from overseas Chinese and such provincial revenues as were at their command. Both sides were prevented from financing themselves from foreign sources by reason of the neutrality agreed to by the powers. When the revolution first broke out, the Japanese thought that every aid should be given to Peking and hoped for joint action with Great Britain under the Anglo-Japanese Alliance. In fact, while the matter was being discussed with the British, Japanese leaders attempted to soften the attitude of the revolutionaries with a view to effecting a compromise settlement within the framework of a constitutional monarchy, which they favored. Great Britain, however, was reluctant to take any action against the revolutionaries that might provoke retaliation harmful to British interests in the Yangtze Valley and elsewhere.

Throughout December negotiations for a settlement continued at Hankow. The revolutionaries were represented by Dr. Wu T'ing-fang, former Chinese ambassador to the United States, who held the post of minister of foreign affairs in the provisional government, and Yuan was represented by an able lieutenant, T'ang Shao-i, who like Wu was an American-educated Cantonese. Wu asserted that the Chinese people would accept no other form of government than a republic, but he was careful to suggest that the Manchus would have equality with the Chinese. The crucial problem, however, was how to end the dynasty. The republicans advocated calling a national convention to discuss what form the government should take, but the method to be used in organizing this body proved to be a stumbling block. Although there was no final agreement, the conference did decide to extend the truce until December 31, pending a complete settlement.

While these issues were being debated at Hankow, Li Yuan-hung, now commander-in-chief of the revolutionary armies, summoned representatives of all the republican groups to Nanking for the purpose of consolidating their interests and organizing a unified regime. It had been decided in the Hankow meeting that, as soon as representatives of more than ten provinces arrived in Nanking, they should elect a president and vice-president. This was not an easy task, for there were many differences of opinion and conflicting ambitions among the numerous military and political leaders; however, out of this conference there emerged, in the early part of December, a fairly coherent political body known as the provisional assembly, to which power tended to gravitate.

The Revolutionary Settlement

Sun Yat-sen finally brought a more complete unity to the revolutionary cause. Sun was in Denver, Colorado, when the revolution broke out in October, and although he was naturally anxious to return to China, he delayed and worked to arouse sympathy for the movement in the United States and Europe. He had been traveling most of the time since 1909, and after a visit to the United States in 1910 he stopped off in disguise in Japan, was discovered, and ejected. After an ill-fated journey to Malaya, where he found himself excluded from British colonies, he turned his attention to Europe and the United States. In Great Britain he sought to block Anglo-Japanese aid to the Manchus and to get revocation of the British exclusion policy. Sun's travels had the salutary effect of keeping him from being identified with any of the groups that were struggling for supremacy at Nanking, and when he returned to China, arriving at Shanghai on December 24, 1911, he was regarded as the only man who could unite the various factions. On December 27 he was urged by a committee representing the Nanking assembly to accept the presidency of the provisional government. He consented to do so on December 29, when representatives of sixteen of seventeen provinces voted for him; and on January 1, 1912, he assumed office. General Li Yuan-hung, who had organized the revolutionary army, became vice-president.

Sun had to face up to the problem of Yuan Shih-k'ai, whose co-operation was necessary to the success of the revolutionary movement. Yuan had shown a willingness to co-operate with the rebels for a price, but he had terminated the negotiations after Sun's election to the presidency. Yuan, who had assumed that he would become president, regarded Sun's election as a breach of agreement, and he schemed to get the Manchu emperor to abdicate voluntarily and to grant him the authority to organize a provisional government. Yuan's actions forced Sun to make a choice between the probable failure of the revolution and the obliteration of his own ambitions in favor of Yuan.

In January, 1912, Sun and Yuan began a series of telegraphic negotiations which ended Manchu rule. Sun suggested that if the Manchus would abdicate and Yuan would swear to uphold a republican constitution, he would step down and urge the assembly to elect Yuan president. Sun also offered generous terms to the imperial family. The emperor was to receive from the republic the respect commonly accorded a monarch plus an annuity of 4,000,000 taels; he was also to be allowed to perform the customary religious rites at the imperial ancestral temples and tombs. Yuan conferred with the court and won its approval of these terms; the opposition that did exist among the younger Manchu nobles melted away before a joint memorial signed by most of the northern generals, who made it clear that the throne could no longer rely on their troops if it stood in the way of the republic.

On February 12 the emperor abdicated and transferred power to Yuan but not to the provisional government at Nanking. Yuan announced the establishment of a republic, but Sun, upset by this turn of events, argued that the republic could not be organized by any authority conferred by the emperor. Yuan gave his assurance that he would co-operate with Nanking, and this cleared the way for his election as president. On February 13 Sun submitted his resignation to the assembly, now composed of the elected representatives of all the provinces, and on the following day Yuan was elected by acclaim. In the final analysis, Yuan was accepted because of his military power, his recognized administrative ability, and his standing with the powers, but he was not wholly trusted. On February 20 the assembly declared that General Li Yuan-hung would remain as vice-president.

By March the republicans had drafted a provisional constitution to supersede the Hankow general outline. The preamble stated that the new government was established by the will of the Chinese people, that sovereignty was vested in all the people, and that supreme authority was to be exercised by the president, the cabinet, the provisional assembly (until a two-house parliament could be elected), and the judiciary. The constitution also included a bill of rights, but all civil rights could be restricted by law in time of emergency in order to maintain the peace. Sun Yat-sen commented: "I have done my work; the wave of enlightenment and progress cannot now be stayed, and China—the country in the world most fitted to be a republic—will, in a short time, take her place among the civilized and liberty-loving nations of the world." The constitution was provisional until the elected parliament drew up a formal, permanent document.

The presidency and cabinet were modeled on the French system. The president was to proclaim the laws, command the army and navy, appoint and remove civil and military officials, receive ambassadors, and concur with the legislature in declaring war and concluding treaties; however, every presidential act required ministerial countersignature. The cabinet, consisting of the premier and the ministers, had to be approved by the legislature so that a responsible cabinet system would be preserved. Although it was the intention of the framers of the constitution to place executive power in the hands of the premier and the cabinet, their wording of the constitutional provisions concerning the relationship between the president and the cabinet was not explicit. The document provided that "Members of the Cabinet shall assist the Provisional President in assuming responsibilities," and Yuan Shih-k'ai interpreted this to mean that the premier and the cabinet were his subordinates. He was able to make this interpretation stick since he was a man of strong personality who wielded tremendous political and military influence.

The legislative system was only a provisional one, with the assembly serving as a temporary unicameral body until elections could be held within ten months for a bicameral parliament. The assembly had the power to pass laws, approve the budget, assent to treaties and administrative regulations, introduce tax measures, and interpellate members of the cabinet. If a bill was vetoed by the president, it could become law if passed again by a two-thirds vote. Finally, the assembly had the right to impeach the president by a vote of three-fourths of its members, and a cabinet minister by a vote of two-thirds.

The judicial system was under the department of justice, whose courts had the right to try all civil and criminal cases but not those pertaining to administrative affairs. For the latter purpose a special administrative court was established in 1914. The revised law codes of the dynasty, which were completed in the period 1902–1911 to Westernize the judicial system, were to remain in effect temporarily, as was the organization of the new courts. There were four types of ordinary courts; and judicial procedure, civil and criminal, generally required three trials. At the district, or hsien, level, trials were held before a judicial official or the local magistrate and, where they had been established, before the courts of first instance under a single judge. Metropolitan courts in a larger administrative area (*fu*) dealt with cases of first instance and appeals from the lower courts, and high courts in each provincial capital were courts of second and third instance. The supreme court in Peking was the highest tribunal and last court of appeals, but it did not have the power of judicial review. This system remained in effect until 1932, when it was slightly modified.

14 *Yuan Shih-k'ai and the Failure of the Republic*

It was soon apparent that Yuan Shih-k'ai had his own ideas about running the government, and he was seldom in agreement with the republicans. The site of the capital of the republic was the first issue that divided them. In his letter of resignation Sun Yat-sen insisted upon the selection of Nanking, but Yuan continued to find reasons for not moving the capital to the Yangtze Valley, where the republicans were strong. He explained that unsettled conditions in the north required his constant attention, and he used the excuse of a short-lived military mutiny by his loyal henchman, Ts'ao Kun, to persuade the assembly to permit his inauguration at Peking. On March 6 the assembly tentatively agreed to the change and requested Yuan to submit the names of his premier and cabinet for its approval. On March 10 Yuan took the oath of office, promising to observe the constitution, which was officially promulgated on the next day by Sun Yat-sen.

The issue of the site of the capital was finally resolved on April 4 when the assembly decided that the government should be transferred to Peking. On this and other issues Yuan benefited from the factionalism that existed in the assembly. One group was conservative and supported Yuan generally, but another was representative of the more radical, republican elements. The remaining assemblymen, holding the balance of power, were moderate and interested in peaceful reform. When allowed to act freely, they were often willing to compromise with Yuan; but when he pressured them, they tended to join the republicans. In general, in the period from 1912 to 1914 the moderates were dissatisfied with the republicans and inclined toward Yuan and his military colleagues.

The Struggle between Yuan and the Republicans

The composition of the cabinet was almost a constant issue. Yuan appointed T'ang Shao-i as premier, and he was careful to appoint his allies to the key ministries—internal affairs, army, and navy—and to appease the republicans by appointments to the less important ministries. Later, in June, when Premier T'ang resigned over the issue of foreign loans, Yuan played the moderates off against the republicans, who wanted a responsible party cabinet, to get the appointment of a nonpartisan, Lu Cheng-hsiang; and when Lu could not get the assembly to approve his cabinet, Yuan came to his rescue with threats to the personal safety of the assemblymen. But because of the persistent opposition of the assembly, Yuan shifted several appointments; and this time, with one exception, they were confirmed. The assembly had objected to the cabinet nominees because they were mostly former officials of the old regime; but when Yuan had his army officers issue a manifesto protesting against the attitude of the assembly, it capitulated to the president. Shortly thereafter, because of illness, Lu appointed Chao Ping-chun to perform his duties, and in September Chao became premier. By this time the cabinet was the secretariat of the president, and all cabinet members took orders from him. Yuan's position was especially strong because he maintained direct control over the armed forces through the general staff board and the army and navy ministries, which continued to be headed by military men. He also created the office of the supreme command in his palace and required the daily attendance of the chiefs or deputy chiefs of the services.

Yuan ultimately had to face up to parliamentary elections. He was not anxious to convene parliament, but the issue was kept alive by the republicans. In August, 1912, the government published electoral laws providing for the indirect election by the provincial assemblies of 274 members of the upper house for six-year terms, with one-third of the members to retire every two years. An additional six members would be chosen by an electoral college of overseas Chinese. Local electoral colleges would vote for the 596 members of the lower house for three-year terms on the basis of proportional representation.

In preparation for the elections Sun Yat-sen and his colleagues Wang Ching-wei, Hu Han-min, Huang Hsing, and Sung Chiao-jen in August joined elements of the T'ung Meng Hui with other republican factions to form a new party called the Kuomintang, or Nationalist Party. They hoped that the republicans, by presenting a united front, might be able to control the parliament, little realizing that, if the party was to oppose Yuan effectively, it would need greater popular support. The Chinese people looked to Yuan to give them peace and security without interfering in their daily lives, and this was not understood by the Kuomintang and the other parties, like the Constitutional Party of Liang Ch'i-ch'ao, which were organs of the intellectuals.

There were also important differences between Sun Yat-sen and his colleague Sung Chiao-jen. Sun preferred to devote the energies of parliament to developing education and industry as a stable foundation for the nation. In fact, Sun had continued to hope than Yuan would make judicious use of his powers as president and in the summer of 1912 accepted a post as director-general of railways, with full powers to reorganize and improve the railway system throughout the country, borrowing the necessary funds from foreign sources. His close friend, Huang Hsing, was given general control of mines and construction of the Canton-Hankow railroad. Sung, on the other hand, wanted parliamentary power to control the cabinet and limit Yuan's power.

In the December, 1912, elections the Kuomintang won 122 of the 274 senate seats and 269 of the 596 seats in the house of representatives. Although the elections were a victory for the republicans, they were a travesty on democracy since votes were openly bought and sold. And the victory was capped by a violent climax on March 20, 1913, when Sung Chiao-jen, who had been publicly demanding control of the cabinet by the majority party, was murdered at a Shanghai railway station by a youth whose deed was generally regarded as having been instigated by Yuan. On April 26 the military and civil governors of Kiangsu, whom Yuan had instructed as a matter of routine to probe into the case, made public findings implicating the president in the murder. Sung's death set the stage for the struggle between Yuan and the parliament over finance.

Finance was crucial to Yuan's position, and like the Manchus he looked to foreign assistance. The national treasury was empty, and tax revenues from the provinces had diminished. With the exception of the customs, which continued to be collected under foreign administration, all sources of revenue were being appropriated by local authorities. Yuan found it impossible to meet foreign obligations and administrative expenses, particularly the payment of his troops. Not wishing to be dependent on the financial power of the assembly, he approached the consortium in February, 1912, for funds secured on the salt tax; and after receiving a few small cash advances, he entered into negotiations with the consortium for a large loan.

Japan and Russia, who had joined the banking group, made special demands. The former insisted that her special rights in Manchuria and in the eastern part of Inner Mongolia be impaired in no way, and the latter requested that her rights in Manchuria, Mongolia, and west China be protected. Actually, Japanese and Russian participation was wholly political. Great Britain and France were to float their shares of the loan, but Japan and Russia were anxious to obtain additional international recognition of their special interests. During these negotiations strong opposition to the foreign loan developed, centering in the assembly. The foreign bankers were demanding that the salt administration be reorganized under their direction; and they also insisted on the right to supervise the expenditure of the loan funds. Even Yuan objected to these provisions, but he failed in attempts to get funds elsewhere on better terms. Opposition to the loan also developed in the United States, and in March, 1913, President Woodrow Wilson withdrew the American banking group from the consortium partly on the ground of the monopolistic character of that body and partly because the loan conditions unduly impaired the administrative integrity of China. The loan agreement between Yuan and the five-power consortium was not put into final form and signed until April 26, 1913. Yuan got $125,000,000, and in return the powers felt that they had provided support for a strong man capable of giving security for their investment and protection to their interests in China.

Yuan clashed with the newly elected parliament over the loan. Both houses convened on April 8 and took the position that, lacking their consent, the loan was unconstitutional. Yuan held that the loan had been approved by the provisional assembly, which was true; but he had accomplished this through intimidation and bribery. Parliament held firm, and this proved to be the most decisive clash between Yuan and the republicans. Parliament did not object to foreign money in principle; it simply opposed Yuan's methods of obtaining it. After all, the followers of Sun Yat-sen were making determined efforts to secure foreign support themselves. After Yuan concluded the loan on April 26, feeling ran high in parliament, and the sessions became disorderly. The senate passed, by a vote of 107 to 64, a resolution that "the action of the government in signing the contract for a loan, without having previously submitted the proposal to parliament [is] unconstitutional, and the contract in consequence [is] null and void." A similar resolution was passed by the house of representatives by a vote of 223 to 149. Sun Yat-sen, thoroughly disillusioned with Yuan, dispatched a telegram to London attempting to persuade the five-power banking group not to carry out the loan, but his protest was ignored. The loan was oversubscribed by May 21.

The loan issue led to violence and insurrection. By the summer of 1913 there was much unrest in the Yangtze Valley, and at the end of June Yuan's removal of several prominent members of the Kuomintang from the military governorships of Kiangsi and Anhwei provinces precipitated a rebellion which was suppressed by Li Yuan-hung. On July 2 Sun Yat-sen sent a telegram to Yuan calling on him to resign, and Yuan retaliated on the 23rd by relieving Sun of his post of director of railway development. Earlier, on July 12, rebels had attacked the government garrison at Kiukiang, and on the 14th Nanking declared its independence and called for a punitive expedition against Yuan, with Huang Hsing as generalissimo. Although five provinces—Szechwan, Kiangsu, Kiangsi, Anhwei, and Kwangtung—nominally joined the revolt, most of the local military governors played politics between the two sides, and the insurrection never generated much power. In fact, the Kuomintang itself split into two factions, the militarists and the parliamentarians. By August Yuan's troops had routed the rebels and their leaders had fled. On August 8 Sun Yat-sen once again landed in Japan, but he managed to keep in close contact with his followers in China during the struggle against Yuan. During this second period of exile, Sun's wife declined to join her husband, giving as her reason her desire to care for her aged parents. Sun divorced this wife and in October, 1915, married the American-educated Soong Chung-ling, the daughter of a Shanghai businessman and close friend.

The Supremacy of Yuan Shih-k'ai

Yuan had defeated the republicans, and the revolution of 1912 had failed to do more than dethrone the Manchus. This failure revealed the fact that the forces behind the ideal of republicanism were not strong enough to realize any program of national interest. Many of the party politicians sought to gain personal advantages. Even the Kuomintang disintegrated into this kind of individualism, and by the eve of the second revolution only about 150 members of parliament still remained in the party.

The revolution also had no mass understanding or support. The people regarded it as essentially anti-Manchu and antiforeign; beyond that they were uncertain of its meaning—a circumstance to which the parties contributed in no small measure, for in some cases members of parliament belonged to two or more parties at the same time, and party programs were not clearly distinct, one from the other. On the other hand, Yuan Shih-k'ai emerged as a strong man. He had the support of the military in the north, and his recognition of local autonomy in the south worked, at least for a time, in his behalf against parliament. He won the co-operation of the majority of the older officials, who abhorred change that was too drastic, and he had the support of moderates like Liang Ch'i-ch'ao and his Chinputang (Progressive Party), which saw in Yuan a force for peace and stability; not until Yuan boldly attempted to implement his own monarchical designs did he offend Liang's sensibilities. Finally, the powers, increasingly alarmed by the nationalism of the republicans, provided Yuan with funds.

Yuan quickly proceeded to consolidate his power. Through adroit maneuvering, which again included intimidation and bribery, he had parliament elect him to the presidency for a five-year term that was no longer provisional, and he took office on October 10, 1913, in a brilliant inaugural which was attended by the entire diplomatic corps. Yuan thus strengthened his position in the eyes of the people, and he continued to receive formal recognition by the powers. Within a month of his inauguration, with the concurrence of the cabinet and the local military governors, Yuan ordered the dissolution of the Kuomintang as a seditious organization. This meant the unseating of all those members of parliament who had been elected as Kuomintang candidates, and, when no steps were taken to fill the vacancies, parliament simply became inactive. In its last days parliament had been discussing drafts of a permanent constitution which contained provisions designed to curtail the powers of the president. The lower house passed a draft on October 26, but Yuan's suspension of parliament in January, 1914, sealed the fate of this constitution. He changed the cabinet into a presidential secretariat under Hsu Shih-ch'ang, and on March 10, to satisfy his military supporters in the provinces, he abolished the provincial assemblies.

Yuan then established his own constitution, which made him a virtual dictator. He appointed a political council, which drew up regulations for the establishment and election of an assembly—the constitutional council—consisting of 56 members elected on a proportional basis from the provinces and dependencies. Actually, the members of the constitutional council were all appointed by Yuan. This body met in February, 1914, and within six weeks drafted a constitution known as the "Constitutional Compact," which, when promulgated by Yuan on May 1, superseded the provisional constitution of the republicans. Under the Compact the central organ of government was a council of state, whose members were appointed by the president and were directly responsible to him for their policy decisions. The council of state met for the first time on June 20, 1914, with Li Yuan-hung as its chairman. Yuan also appointed all heads of departments, who were also directly responsible to him. The Compact, moreover, extended the president's term of office to ten years, with no limitation on the number of terms; and during presidential election years the council of state, if it saw the "necessity, for political reasons," could permit the president to continue for another term without the formality of an election. The Compact did provide for an elected house of legislature, an advisory body which never came into existence. There was no freedom of assembly, and the press was closely censored. Against his political opponents Yuan resorted to terrorist methods, including assassination.

The revolution of 1911 had diverse effects on provincial administration. When the fighting broke out in October, the regular provincial officials in some cases proclaimed their allegiance to the republican cause and thus retained control of provincial administration. In other cases the provincial assembly took control, ousted the imperial officials, and selected the head of the province from among the gentry or officials who declared for the revolution. In general, there was more dislocation south of the Yangtze River, and in the main the officials who did establish themselves in control of the southern provinces were those whose authority was supported by troops. In the northern provinces, which remained loyal to the dynasty, the revolution merely effected a transfer of the personal allegiance of the provincial governors to Yuan as legal heir of the Manchus; however, there, too, military power came to the be most important basis of authority.

Within the provinces, particularly in the south, there was a nearly complete breakdown in administration. Military leaders rendering nominal allegiance to the legal or self-constituted provincial authorities established themselves in control of prefectures and districts. These warlords supported themselves by force and maintained themselves by collecting taxes and by requisitioning supplies from the people. Part of their gains might be turned over to the provincial authorities after the expenses of the local regime had been defrayed, but very little revenue went beyond the province. Peasants joined the armies of these local warlords because of the promise of pay, food, and clothing. The more troops a local warlord had, the larger the area he could control successfully and the more important he was politically.

Yuan Shih-k'ai had realistically sought to take advantage of the breakdown of authority in the provinces. The republicans had made him promise to eliminate the old officeholders and to appoint men fitted for a progressive regime, but Yuan preferred to build up a personal following among the provincial governors and local warlords. With their backing it became possible for him to defy the assembly more easily, to enforce his own decisions, and even to violate the provisional constitution with impunity. On the other hand, he had to confirm these local leaders in their positions of power and in a sense condone their activities. Yuan had little choice in the matter. He did not have the means to disband locally independent troops; nor did he have the financial resources to pay them and their leaders off. In the north Yuan generally had his own followers in high positions, but in the south he was forced to legalize the positions of many warlords who were not his allies. Under the circumstances the only limitations on the power of the military lay, first, in the general requirement of the central government that a measure of peace and order be maintained in the provinces and, second, in such public opinion as could be heard directly or indirectly through the provincial assemblies while such bodies were in existence. In the spring of 1913, with a view to the ultimate restoration of civil government, Yuan used some of the funds provided by the consortium to buy off warlords in the central and southern provinces in order to replace them with others loyal to himself. But he soon had other urgent uses for the money and had to accept the fact of warlordism.

Yuan did ultimately succeed in breaking away from the consortium, whose activities were denounced by almost all Chinese. In their minds it was a weapon of imperialism and a threat to China's integrity; moreover, it was a monopoly which eliminated competition among the powers. Even Yuan had dealt with it only from sheer necessity, and, once he had consolidated his position, he resorted to playing off the powers and met with some success. He got some funds from individual firms like the newly created Banque Industrielle de la Chine, formed by a group of French and Chinese citizens, and from Japan, which was attempting to expand its concessions in China through the notorious Twenty-one Demands. His conspicuous failure was his attempt to get American help for the development of Chinese resources. Americans were promised far-reaching opportunities in developing flood control and water conservation, in petroleum exploitation, and in the marketing of government tobacco. The American minister to Peking, Paul Reinsch, was enthusiastic about these projects as a means of countering Japanese pressures on Yuan, but he could not interest American businessmen in them; in fact, financial records indicate that American interests in China were declining.

By the end of 1914 Yuan Shih-k'ai was monarch in all but name, and he aspired to re-establish the empire, with himself as successor to the Manchus. By the summer of 1915 his family, friends, and advisers, including his chief legal counsel, Frank J. Goodnow, later president of Johns Hopkins University, were all actively urging him to ascend the throne, and the council of state on three occasions memorialized him to do so. Yuan consented, but he wanted the approval of a "convention of citizens' representatives" for a very practical reason. The powers—Great Britain, Russia, France, and Japan— had united in advising him against the step; given the unsettled international situation, they felt it would be unwise to disturb the existing situation by inciting potential opposition. But Great Britain, France, and Russia were willing to recognize Yuan as emperor in return for a declaration of war on Germany. Great Britain and France, especially, wanted to force the last remnants of German commercial activity out of China and to procure Chinese coolie labor for the fighting front in Europe and thus relieve the strain on their own depleted manpower.

This bargain failed because of Japanese opposition to Yuan. The Japanese, judging that the chances of the monarchical movement were slim, had no intention of incurring the resentment of the Chinese people. Japan had no special interest in republican government, but her ruling forces were bent on fishing in China's troubled waters. At the same time Tokyo viewed with displeasure the possibility of a strong central government in China, especially one dominated by her old enemy in Korea. The Allies in the world war were forced to side with Japan, as they needed her help against Germany. The Japanese government informed Yuan that information at its disposal indicated that there would be a revolt in the south if he went ahead with his plans. Despite this warning, Yuan convoked a packed convention in Peking in December, 1915. The delegates—1,834 alleged representatives of the people—voted unanimously for the new dynasty, and Yuan allowed himself to be memorialized three times before reluctantly yielding to the "will of the people." He fixed February 9, 1916, as the date for his enthronement.

Opposition to Yuan's scheme was immediate. Republican sympathizers and other radical reformers saw their hopes of creating a new China threatened with total destruction, and in Japan Sun Yat-sen organized the Chinese Revolutionary Party with secret branches in China. But it was the moderate Liang Ch'i-ch'ao who presented the case for the antimonarchists most ably in a pamphlet which was read throughout the country. He argued that Yuan should accept the republic and make every effort to provide an effective administration. Even the provincial generals, on whom Yuan relied for the perpetuation of his power, balked at a step which might threaten to put restraints on their own activities. In fact, Yuan's attempts to concentrate power in his own hands had already lost him the support of Tuan Ch'i-jui, who resigned as minister of war and returned to Shensi, and of Feng Kuo-chang, who was military governor of Kiangsu. The generals realized that they were the real holders of power, and they preferred to be arbiters in a weak republic than obedient generals in a new empire. Finally, Yuan had lost prestige by his acceptance of some of Japan's Twenty-one Demands.

A revolt in the south began the process of Yuan's decline and fall. In December, 1915, General Ts'ai Ao of Yunnan, supported by members of the old Kuomintang and Liang Ch'i-ch'ao, rose against the government, demanding cancellation of the monarchy plans, restoration of the Nanking constitution as the basic law of the land, and reconvocation of the 1913 parliament; he also ordered the arrest and execution of all monarchist supporters in Yunnan. Yuan sent troops to quell the uprising, and for a time it looked as though he would emerge victorious. Ts'ai Ao, suffering from tuberculosis, succumbed to the rigors of a winter campaign in Szechwan, and Huang Hsing, about to lead the Kwangtung troops, fell ill and died at Canton. But the intervention of Feng Kuo-chang on the side of the rebels turned the tide, and by the middle of March, 1916, the whole country was in open revolt.

Faced with a general civil war, Yuan decided to postpone his enthronement and promised the immediate convocation of the house of legislature provided in the Constitutional Compact. When the rebels demanded Yuan's withdrawal from politics, he canceled the monarchy scheme on March 22, and, seeking to placate his enemies, announced his intention to hand over his political powers to a responsible cabinet. In April he asked Tuan Ch'i-jui, whose support he needed, to organize a cabinet to replace the council of state; however, when it became evident that the southern rebels would continue to insist on Yuan's retirement, Tuan and others of his military colleagues began to desert him. Feng Kuo-chang, for example, sought to organize a conference at Nanking to create a neutral force under his own control to win support from the provincial authorities for his own candidacy for the presidency.

By May, eight central and southern provinces had declared their independence, and on May 12 their representatives, constituting a rival government at Canton, elected Li Yuan-hung as president of the republic. Li, however, declined the honor and responsibility. Shortly thereafter Yuan agreed to retire from office, recommending Li as his successor, but, just when a settlement seemed imminent, the controversy was suddenly terminated by Yuan's death, caused by uremia, in June, 1916.

The Politics of Warlordism

Yuan's death led to a nominal re-establishment of the political situation as of the beginning of 1913. Li Yuan-hung, who succeeded Yuan as president, restored the old constitution of 1912 and reconvened parliament at Peking on August 1, 1916. However, it was impossible for him to unite the various republican, monarchist, and warlord factions. China remained divided politically and was impotent. Actual power rested with the provincial warlords, who would accept the direction of the central government only to the extent that Peking acted in accordance with their views and only if it did not attempt to interfere with their prerogatives in the provinces.

Clashes between the parliament and Premier Tuan Ch'i-jui—appointed because he was regarded as the warlord most likely to maintain peace and order—weakened the Peking regime. Tuan planned to use Li as his puppet and to grasp power in his own hands; he thus objected to the reinstatement of the 1912 constitution, which gave complete control to parliament. He preferred the 1914 Constitutional Compact, but in this matter he was unable to stand against the opposition of both parliament and the southern warlords. Tuan, seeking to strengthen his position, contracted loans from Japanese sources without consulting parliament and then proceeded to demand its approval for his actions. Parliament retaliated by refusing to approve his administrative appointments and continued to work on a constitution that would provide a stronger foundation for its own supremacy. There was a steady stream of threats of impeachment by parliament and counterthreats of adjournment of parliament by Tuan. Finally, in December, 1916, the military and civil authorities of all the provinces, playing the role of mediator, began to bring pressure to bear on Peking. In a joint telegram they advised Li to have confidence in Tuan in his management of state affairs, and they warned parliament to decide on a constitution at an early date and not meddle in administrative affairs.

The issue which hastened the destruction of parliament and paved the way for open warlord domination of the government was China's participation in World War I. Despite the opposition of parliament and President Li, who favored the maintenance of neutrality, Premier Tuan was anxious to enter the war and had been negotiating with the Allies, especially Japan, for loans that would strengthen his hand. And, when the United States broke off diplomatic relations with Germany on February 3, 1917, after Germany announced her intention to use submarines to blockade the Allies, the American minister to Peking, Paul Reinsch, urged Tuan to follow Washington's lead. Japan, moreover, no longer opposed China's entry into the war, since the Allies—Great Britain, France, and Russia—had paid the Japanese price; by treaty they secretly sold out German economic rights in Shantung Province to Japan in return for Chinese participation in the war and Japanese recognition of their own territorial conquests. On February 9 Tuan sent a mild note of protest against Germany's unrestricted submarine warfare, and on February 24 the way was paved for more decisive action when a German submarine torpedoed the French ship "Athos" in the Mediterranean, causing 543 Chinese deaths.

On March 11 Tuan severed diplomatic relations with Germany with parliamentary approval; only Li opposed the move. To declare war, however, was another thing. On May 8 Tuan asked parliament to approve a war bill, and when he resorted to threats, bribes, and the pressure of mob demonstrations, parliament refused and demanded that Li dismiss Tuan as the price for its consent. Tuan refused to retire from office and was supported in his war policy by a conference of warlords that he had convoked in Peking on April 25. When the warlords demanded the dissolution of parliament, President Li told their representatives that the president had no constitutional power to dissolve parliament and that the only way to solve the problem was to ask Premier Tuan to resign. The warlords, recognizing that Li would continue to stand by parliament, began to hold conferences at Tientsin, Hsuchow, and elsewhere.

On May 23 Li made a bold move when he dismissed Tuan from office, but he failed to save the parliament. Tuan's warlord subordinates on May 29 declared their independence from the republic and established a provisional military government at Tientsin. They were willing, however, to renew their allegiance to the republic, but only on condition that the parliament be dissolved. Li invited one of the warlords, Chang Hsun, to come to Peking as mediator between Tuan and parliament; but when Chang reiterated the demands of the warlords, Li bowed to pressure and dissolved parliament. By this time many of its members had already left the city.

Chang Hsun had led a large number of troops from Hsuchow to Peking via Tientsin, and on June 14, supposedly with Tuan's approval, he announced the restoration of the Manchu dynasty. K'ang Yu-wei, who for some time had been plotting the restoration, hurried to Peking to assist Chang. But having successfully used Chang to destroy parliament, Tuan led an army to Peking and put an end to the brief revival of the dynasty on July 12. Chang fled to the Dutch legation, while K'ang Yu-wei took refuge in the Japanese legation. The affair came to an end with the resignation of Li Yuan-hung as president, to be succeeded by Feng Kuo-chang, the Yangtze warlord, who thus realized his ambition; and Tuan was appointed premier.

The declaration of war on Germany, which had almost been forgotten in the political maneuvering, was finally approved on August 14 by a specially convoked, Chinputang-dominated parliament—a move that Tuan and his clique hoped would bring financial aid from the Allies and international recognition that would add prestige to their regime. Later, in October, 1918, Tuan and his Anfu faction (Anhwei and Fukien warlords) further consolidated their position when they were able to replace Feng Kuo-chang, head of the rival Chihli faction, with an official of the former dynasty, Hsu Shih-ch'ang.

Tuan did not get large-scale financial aid from the European powers and thus had to rely increasingly upon Japan for money and weapons to strengthen himself against his enemies. Great Britain, France, and Russia did make some minor concessions, such as a five-year postponement of Boxer indemnity payments and an upward revision of customs duties to an effective 5 per cent, but China paid for them by contributing several hundred thousand laborers for work behind the lines in France and Siberia. China also ultimately liquidated German economic holdings and deported the entire German community from the country. Japan was willing to make sizable loans to Tuan in return for recognition of Japan's gains in Shantung Province at Germany's expense, acceptance of the May, 1915, treaties, which put into legal form some of the Twenty-one Demands, and grants of additional rights and privileges. On May 18, during the height of the declaration-of-war controversy, a British newspaper, *The Peking Daily*, reported that Tuan had just borrowed $100,000,000 from semiofficial Japanese banks for the reorganization of three arsenals by Japanese and for the training of Chinese troops by Japanese officers. It has been estimated that in the years 1917 and 1918 Tuan was able to borrow nearly two billion dollars from Japan. Part of these funds were used in struggles with warlord enemies and part for the training of an army, supposedly for participation in the European war—the so-called "New Army" of three divisions and four mixed brigades. Tuan's real intention was to use the New Army to wipe out enemy warlord cliques.

Chinese society was at this time characterized by a delicate balance of power between provincial warlord factions. Warlords constantly struggled to enlarge their territorial domains, and groups of them fought each other to control Peking. Whoever held Peking dominated such national administrative machinery as continued to exist and thus had a basis for claiming the allegiance of the country. Recognized by the foreign powers, the Peking government could negotiate foreign loans and had access to any surpluses from the customs collections and the salt tax after international obligations had been deducted. Until 1920 the Anfu clique controlled Peking, and its critics maintain that its basic function was to line the pockets of its members with Japanese gold.

Republicanism, even in nominal forms, was at the mercy of warlordism. When President Li Yuan-hung had dissolved parliament under warlord pressure in June, 1917, many of the members gathered at Shanghai, where they met with Sun Yat-sen. There they issued a manifesto declaring the dissolution illegal, branding the convening of any other parliament illegal, and announcing their intention to reconvene themselves at some other place. The provincial authorities of Kwangtung and Kwangsi, having declared their autonomy and opposing Tuan, invited Sun and 250 members of the parliament to Canton to participate in an administration which would claim to be the lawful republic. In August, 1917, the remnants of parliament approved the establishment of a provisional military government at Canton with Sun at its head. Real power, however, rested with the local warlords, T'ang Chi-yao, governor of Yunnan and Kweichow in succession to Ts'ai Ao, and Lu Jung-t'ing, based in Kwangtung and Kwangsi. Actually, Sun and the Canton warlords were united only in the sense that they opposed Tuan at Peking; and since they had very little in common, the outcome of their alliance was not very different from the Peking failures. Factionalism also split the republicans. In May, 1918, the warlords reorganized the military government, setting up a seven-man committee which included the powerful provincial authorities. Sun, giving up the attempt at co-operation, left Canton and went back to Shanghai to reorganize his followers.

The Cultural Revolution

Political failures had an important impact on fundamental cultural changes that were taking place in these years. From the Sino-Japanese War to the founding of the republic in 1912 great numbers of students believed that China would be "saved" by getting rid of monarchical government, but gradually they learned that political changes were not enough and that China's salvation lay in the development of a new culture. What the students of China realized was that the old cultural foundations could not support the new China that they wanted. Much of tradition would simply have to be swept away. This attitude was important, because these students, the new intelligentsia of China, became the leaders of subsequent revolutions, both nationalist and communist.

The center of this cultural revolution was the National University at Peking. Its chancellor, Ts'ai Yuan-p'ei, had studied in both Germany and France, had been the first minister of education under the republic, and in 1917 had become head of the university established by the reformers of 1898. He discouraged students from going to college for the sole purpose of preparing themselves for positions, especially in government. Their goal, as he defined it for them, was rather to discover knowledge from the "storehouse of China's past and from the storehouse of the West," to create programs, and to lead society. Ts'ai refused to become involved in politics, and under his aegis the National University became a center of intellectual freedom and research, inviting scholars of international reputation like John Dewey and Bertrand Russell to its campus.

Active among the faculty were scholars like Ch'en Tu-hsiu, who edited the mother journal of the cultural revolution, New Youth, which began publication in September, 1915. Ch'en stated in his famous article, "An Appeal to the Youth of China": "To have democracy, we cannot avoid a conflict with Confucianism, the older forms of logic, and of government. To have real science, we cannot avoid disagreeing with the old forms of learning, and religion; and, if we are to have both democracy and science, we cannot avoid a conflict with our long-established culture." There were also translators like Yen Fu, who had gone to Europe in 1876 as one of forty-eight students sent by the dynasty. After his return he engaged in a program of translation that introduced Western thought into China: J. S. Mill, Charles Darwin, T. H. Huxley, Herbert Spencer, Rousseau, Montesquieu, and Adam Smith. Moreover, the campus of National University was enlivened by various organizations like the Young China Association, established in July, 1918, by students, scholars, and professors and "dedicated to social service under the guidance of the scientific spirit in order to realize our idea of creating a Young China." Publications poured off the presses. The Young China Association was active with The Young China (1919) and The Young World (1920), and the Renaissance Society, formed in 1918, published The New Tide, the first all-student magazine.

One of the central targets of the attack led by Ch'en Tu-hsiu and the other university critics was Confucianism. After the 1911 revolution a group of conservative scholars, led by Dr. Chen Chung-yan, had founded the New Confucian Association; and after the failure of the republic a group of scholars and officials, under the leadership of K'ang Yu-wei, had tried to get Yuan Shih-k'ai to make Confucianism the state religion of China. K'ang's argument was that only primitive peoples had no religion, and, if China gave up religion, she would be called uncivilized. According to Ch'en Tu-hsiu, however, Confucianism was unable to meet modern needs because it was a morality of inequality and injustice. Ch'en emphasized the following points: first, the principle of filial piety involved the idea of a double ethical standard; second, a woman was enslaved to her husband, father, parent-in-law, and even to her sons. On the latter point, he noted that the emancipation of women, one of the most important social advances in the modern world, was opposed by Confucianists. According to Ch'en, Confucianism should be eliminated or China might just as well maintain autocratic government, and his cry was taken up by others in magazine articles concerned with the family revolution. "The source of all evils," wrote a student, "is the force which destroys our personal individuality . . . and this force is our family." Later, in 1922, women students in both the Government Law School and the Higher Normal Government School in Peking started a Woman's Suffrage Association and a Woman's Rights League. The latter urged equal constitutional rights for men and women; equality between men and women with regard to marriage, inheritance, and property laws; abolition of licensed prostitution, slavery, and foot-binding; and equal pay for equal work.

Criticism of religion, particularly Christianity, was an extension of the attack on Confucianism. This aspect of the cultural revolution, assisted strongly by the thinking of Bertrand Russell, reached its high point after World War I, when Chinese students related Christianity more closely to imperialism. It was part of their post-Versailles nationalism, described below. The attack on religion centered on Christianity because, as one of the leaders stated, "Most of the so-called powers are Christian nations . . . and Christianity in China is one of the most aggressive of all religions." On the occasion of the World's Student Christian Federation meeting at Peking in April, 1922, Chinese critics proclaimed that religion was a superstition which shackled freedom of thought and scientific progress, and they condemned Christianity for the same reasons that they had rejected Confucianism. Marxist-Leninist influences also were clear. Christianity was branded as the "intelligence officer of the capitalists" and "the hireling of the imperialist countries of the world." Many Chinese students and scholars joined the Anti-Religion Movement, which had branches in most of the major cities.

It would be incorrect to give the impression that all Chinese students supported these views. In 1920 a branch of the Young China Association in Paris, where many of its leaders were then studying, decided that persons having religious beliefs would not be accepted as members, but the protests by the general membership against this stand were so numerous that it had to be revoked. Christian students answered the accusations of their critics by emphasizing that religion and science were not conflicting factors in modern society and that Christianity did not support capitalism; they maintained that socialism was in fact the practice of Christian principles. Great numbers of students and scholars remained neutral, taking the position of freedom of choice and toleration. The debate, which filled the pages of the new journals, produced some interesting results. The Mission Book Company of Shanghai reported that it had never before sold so many copies of the Bible, and books on Buddhism and other religions were in great demand. It was reported also that Chinese were taking a greater role in the leadership of Christian churches.

The cultural revolution was also characterized by important advances in Chinese scholarship. The new historians of China no longer wished to judge the past in terms of fixed ethical standards but to cut through Confucian morality and reinterpret events in their original setting. Confucian historians, following the tradition of the ancient masters, were wont to read into history judgments of praise or blame for the instruction of future generations; they regarded history as a mirror not in the sense of giving a faithful reflection of the past but of showing rulers the types of conduct to emulate and to avoid. The new historians, however, subjected the Classics to careful scrutiny, and they reassessed the contributions of Confucius, accepting his own statement that he was a "transmitter, not a creator." They abandoned the quest for absolutes, repudiating the doctrine that the sages handed down in the Classics moral truths which scholarship had to defend and transmit, and they rejected the concept of traditional schools of history, which committed scholars in advance to some ethical theory, type of scholarship, and literary style. In their objective investigations the new historians sought to detect and eliminate forgeries by the application of scientific methods, to recover lost or neglected works, to delineate spheres of specialization according to disciplines (ethics, philosophy, folklore, art, religion), and to emphasize comparative study. For example, archeological research helped to destroy erroneous theories based on the Classics and showed that the Chinese people were a mixture of many races and that their culture had perhaps been akin in prehistoric times to similar cultures in Central Asia.

Language reform was another integral part of the cultural revolution. Particularly active in this field was Hu Shih, who after 1917 was a professor of philosophy at National University. While still a student at Columbia University, he wrote a strong plea for language reform in the magazine *New Youth* (January, 1917) which called for a "living, democratic, and scientific medium of expression." The need to simplify the Chinese language was seconded in an important article in the same journal by Ch'en Tu-hsiu, "A Literary Revolution." Both men advocated abandonment of the archaic classical style in favor of the vernacular Peking dialect *(pai-hua)* as the new national language *(kuo-yu)*. According to Hu Shih, this reform was a necessary prerequisite for the reorganization and re-evaluation of China's entire literary heritage. Journalism was quickly won over to the new language, and by 1919 about four hundred new periodicals were written in the vernacular. It was clear that language reform provided a new and effective means for all sorts of propaganda. Novels, short stories, poetry, drama, and serious and learned books also appeared in the vernacular. The students took to it rapidly, and by 1920 it was made compulsory for the first two years of the primary grades and was shortly thereafter extended to the upper grades and the middle schools as well. In the 1920's, moreover, college and middle-school students began to work voluntarily in the cities, setting up vernacular schools to develop literacy among the general population.

Economic Problems

The downfall of the dynasty, the failure of the republic, and the resulting warlordism added to the misery of the masses of Chinese peasants. The first principle of warlordism was the use of power for personal enrichment, and with only occasional exceptions warlords profited through ruthless exploitation of the people. In some cases they collected taxes years in advance through requisitions, and at worst they compelled peasants to cultivate opium instead of food crops so that they might profit through their own organized opium trade. Furthermore, rival armies plundered the land like locusts. In many instances, landlords fled to the cities, especially to the treaty ports, to escape the disorders, leaving agents behind to collect their rents. Landlords who remained in the countryside and rent agents found that the only way to maintain their interests was to enter into partnership with the military in exploiting the peasantry.

Administrative breakdown caused irrigation and drainage works to decay, and disastrous floods for which there was no relief, unless from foreign sources, became increasingly common. The invasion of villages by cheap manufactured goods continued to put an end to the peasant's old self-sufficiency; moreover, he was at the mercy of the merchant because he could not ship his crop to more distant markets and hope for a large return. The Chinese peasant was also surrendering his position in the world market as a producer of crops like tea and silk because better varieties were supplied more cheaply by foreign competitors who were utilizing more scientific techniques and improving quality.

Invariably new debts were all the peasant had to show at the end of a season, and, when he defaulted on them, he lost his land. China continued to experience an increasingly swift concentration of landownership in the hands of a constantly narrowing section of the population. According to a survey made by the Kuomintang, the big landlords (those owning more than fifteen acres) made up 5 per cent of the population but owned 43 per cent of the cultivated land. Title to land passed to absentee landlords, government officials, and urban capitalists, who generally controlled the commercial capital which penetrated even the remotest villages via the local merchants and usurers. China's commercial wealth lacked the technical knowledge, courage, and proper conditions to invest in industry, and it continued to invest in land. More and more peasants became tenants, surrendering 40–70 per cent of their crops and a substantial additional percentage in special dues, gifts, and labor. The great mass of the peasantry were plunged into what seemed to be a perpetual state of pauperism, and millions crowded into the cities and towns, providing an inexhaustible supply of cheap labor that could not be absorbed by China's limited industry. Others emigrated, mostly to Manchuria, became bandits, or swelled the armies of the warlords. In these circumstances so much land went untilled that China was compelled to import ever-increasing amounts of foodstuffs.

In the field of industrial development China was making progress, but it was not sufficient to balance agricultural decline. When World War I absorbed the full industrial output of the foreign powers, Chinese industrialists and investors began to increase production for the home market. The following figures give some indication of industrial advance. With 100 as the base in 1913, by the end World War I coal production had soared to over 180, cotton spindles to 403, and processed bean exports to over 430. Cotton mills increased in number from 42 in 1916 to 120 in the early 1920's, and spindles from 1,145,000 to 3,550,000. Chinese industrial growth was reflected also in the rise in value of industrial machinery from 4,300,000 taels in 1915 to 55,600,000 in 1920. The Chinese foreign trade deficit also fell, until by 1919 it was only 16,000,000 taels. Along with growth came extensive alterations in the Chinese business structure. Corporate organization was more widely adopted, and the banks multiplied.

The rise of Chinese industry created new problems. First, there was the rivalry between aspiring Chinese capital and entrenched foreign business interests; for despite tremendous Chinese gains during the war period, foreigners still maintained a large share in the ownership of the Chinese industrial economy. In 1920 foreign capital controlled nearly half of China's cotton industry, the largest in the country; it owned a third of the railways outright and held mortgages on the rest; and it owned and operated more than half the shipping in Chinese waters and carried in its bottoms nearly 80 per cent of China's foreign and coastal trade. Second, industrialization brought into being an urban working class. By 1920 there were probably about two million industrial workers in China, many of whom were already organized in modern labor unions as distinct from the old craft guilds, and young Chinese communists were already fomenting class struggle between capital and labor. The Chinese worker who was employed in a foreign-owned factory was also taught that he could help his country economically and politically by opposing the "imperialists."

The cultural revolution extended to serious discussions of China's economic problems, and students and scholars generally felt that the salvation of their country was inseparable from the fate of the peasant masses, who formed over 80 per cent of the population. They believed that any gains made in the upper level of the society, in the modern cities or among the literate few, could not be held so long as the countryside remained unchanged. It was equally clear, however, that mere redivision and redistribution of land was not the answer to the peasant's plight. Any far-reaching transformation of Chinese society would have to include a long-term program for increasing the efficiency of agricultural production; moreover, it would require a program of industrialization to raise living standards.

Communism and Nationalism

It was only natural that along with other varieties of Western thought communism would begin to influence Chinese intellectuals. After 1917 many

Chinese came to admire the Russian Bolshevik Revolution as the first successful blow against monarchism and imperialism, and some of them viewed communism as an instrument to achieve political, economic, social, and cultural progress. For most Chinese who accepted it, communism was two things: a means to judge and criticize the capitalist West from a Western point of view, and a means to transform Chinese society. John Dewey had directed the youth of China to study educational and social problems in accordance with the needs of the individual as well as society, but Ch'en Tu-hsiu for one rejected Dewey's cry "to search for concrete methods to meet concrete problems according to the exigencies of time and place" and embraced communism. His more philosophic-minded colleague, Li Ta-chao, professor of economics and librarian, heeded "the messianic message of the Russian Revolution" and found it easy to replace the Hegelian "world spirit" with its Marxian counterpart.

The interest in the Russian Revolution and in communism was made manifest by the founding of the Society for the Study of Marxism at National University in the spring of 1918. Its membership, never large in number, was made up for the most part of students, many of whom, such as Mao Tse-tung and Chang Kuo-t'ao, were later important figures in the communist movement. In 1920, May Day was for the first time celebrated by students and professors in Peking, and to mark the occasion *New Youth* ran a special number, which discussed various problems of labor in China and the Western countries. The concluding article was a letter sent by representatives of the Russian government, with twenty-five replies by various Chinese organizations. The letter explained the nature and purpose of the Bolshevik Revolution and expressed the hope that Russia and China might become friends. The reply of the National Students' Association included the following:

Representing the students of the whole country we address the dear Russian people and the new Russian Republic with complete sincerity in the following words: Your recent revolution has opened a new chapter in the history of the world revolution, for which we respect you. We hope from now on that your people and our people, in the pursuit of liberty, equality, and the real meaning of co-operation, may work together amicably and sincerely to get rid of "national suppression" and of "national, racial, and social prejudice" in order to create real liberty, equality, and universal love.

A month later, in June, 1920, the Comintern agent, Gregory Voitinsky, with the assistance of Ch'en Tu-hsiu and Li Ta-chao, presided over the organization of the Socialist Youth Corps, a forerunner of the Chinese Communist Party. A year later, for all practical purposes, there were branches of a communist party in Peking, Canton, and Shanghai and in Hunan Province, where young Mao Tse-tung was engaged in organizing labor.

The Chinese student movement, despite intellectual differences, was motivated by a powerful political nationalism, with a special emphasis upon anti-imperialism. This circumstance was rooted in past humiliations—the unequal treaty system, spheres of interest, Japan's defeat of China, and the consortium. Some degree of nationalism had been expressed in the earlier reform movements, in the revolution of 1911, and in sporadic boycotts of foreign goods and business, but it attained an unprecedented emotional peak in reaction to Japanese imperialism during World War I. During the negotiations concerning the Twenty-one Demands, the government and press were flooded with letters, telegrams, and pamphlets demanding resistance to Japanese aggression. Students appealed for resistance, soldiers offered their services, merchants started unofficial boycotts of Japanese goods, and civic organizations advocated higher taxes for defense purposes. Resentment against Japan seemed to be the one point of Chinese unity in these trying years.

The most significant antiforeign eruption began on May 4, 1919, when several thousand students demonstrated in Peking. Carrying placards demanding "international justice" and "self-determination," they marched to the legation quarter to protest the Treaty of Versailles, which gave international sanction to Japan's gains in Shantung Province at Germany's expense. A group of students stormed the houses of pro-Japanese "traitors," singling out Ts'ao Ju-lin, minister of transportation, who had negotiated the September, 1918, treaties with Japan to reconfirm the earlier concessions made under the Twenty-one Demands, and Chang Tsung-hsiang, minister to Japan. Ts'ao managed to escape, but Chang was caught and brutally assaulted. When Chang died the following day, the government sentenced to death thirty-two students who had been arrested and banned all public meetings. In protest National University students refused to attend school until their classmates were released. Everywhere there was great sympathy for the students, and in many cities there were mass demonstrations. Telegrams poured into Peking demanding that the government free the students. On May 7, National Humiliation Day (anniversary of the signing of the 1915 treaties implementing much of the Twenty-one Demands), the government capitulated to popular feeling. Meanwhile, Chinese students in Tokyo attempted to hold a rally on May 7 to voice their discontent, but the Japanese police stymied their efforts. Since the grounds of the Chinese embassy were patrolled by the police, the students assembled before the German embassy, adjacent to the imperial palace, and began to parade. A few hundred Japanese cavalrymen encircled the students, and, when fighting broke out, there were many casualties.

The May 4th movement precipitated a government attack on the students and professors of National University. For some time the government had been unhappy with the situation at the university, and after the disturbances it began to force the resignations of key staff members, including Chancellor

Ts'ai Yuan-p'ei. This action increased the friction between the government and the students, and when the latter continued to resort to strikes and passive resistance, the government retaliated by forceful suppression and mass arrests. On May 20 the Peking Student Union declared a general strike, which spread to Nanking on the 27th, Paoting on the 28th, Anking on the 30th, and Hankow, Wuchang, and Kaifeng on the 31st. And in June the strike spread to southern Chinese cities. The manifesto of the Peking Student Union emphasized the cruelty and insincerity of the government in its dealings with the students, accusing a number of officials and warlords of destroying the spirit of democracy, and it insisted that three officials of the government, classed as traitors, be dismissed and that the delegation at Versailles be told not to sign the treaty. When popular response again supported the students, the government was forced to back down, releasing over a thousand imprisoned students on June 6 and accepting the resignations of the "traitors" on June 11. Anti-Japanese agitation, however, continued, with discriminatory labor strikes called in Shanghai, Nanking, and other cities; and merchants joined boycotts of Japanese goods, partly out of fear to refuse but partly out of conviction.

Bibliographical Notes

The most detailed survey of this period is Li Chien-nung, *The Political History of China, 1840–1928* (Princeton: Van Nostrand, 1956; translated by Teng Ssu-yu and Jeremy Ingalls), and the most analytical is John K. Fairbank, *The United States and China* (Cambridge, Mass.: Harvard University Press, revised edition, 1958). Two important documentary works are H. F. MacNair, *Modern Chinese History—Selected Readings* (Shanghai: Commercial Press, second edition, 1923), and Teng Ssu-yu and John K. Fairbank, *China's Response to the West* (Cambridge, Mass.: Harvard University Press, two volumes, 1954). Another useful compilation of sources is George M. Beckmann, *Imperialism and Revolution in Modern China, 1840–1950* (Lawrence, Kans.: Student Union Bookstore, 1955). P. C. Hsieh, *The Government of China, 1644–1911* (Baltimore: Johns Hopkins Press, 1925), is still useful and can be supplemented by Paul Linebarger, Djuang Chu, and Ardath Burks, *Far Eastern Government and Politics, China and Japan* (Princeton: Van Nostrand, second edition, 1956). F. H. King, *Farmers of Forty Centuries, or Permanent Agriculture in China, Korea, and Japan* (Emmaus, Pa.: Organic Gardening Press, reissue, 1948), is still the best account of agriculture during the Ch'ing dynasty, and H. B. Morse, *The Trade and Administration of China* (London: Kelly & Walsh, third revised edition, 1920), has not been superseded. Chang Chung-li, *The Chinese Gentry: Studies on Their Role in Nineteenth Century Chinese Society* (Seattle: University of Washington Press, 1955), emphasizes the scholarly bureaucratic foundation of the dominant social class, while Fei Hsiao-tung, *China's Gentry: Essays in Rural-Urban Relations* (Chicago: University of Chicago Press, 1953), discusses other factors as well, especially economics.

There are a number of good political studies concerned with this period. Thomas Meadows, *The Chinese and Their Rebellions* (Stanford: Academic Reprints, 1954), provides interesting insights into the process of decline in China, and the best introduction to the Taiping movement is Teng Ssu-yu, *New Light on the History of the Taiping Rebellion* (Cambridge, Mass.: Harvard University Press, 1950). More specialized studies are Eugene P. Boardman, *Christian Influence upon the Ideology of the Taiping Rebellion* (Madison: University of Wisconsin Press, 1952), and W. J. Hail, *Tseng Kuo-fan and the Taiping Rebellion* (New Haven: Yale University Press, 1927). One of the finest recent studies in nineteenth-century history is Mary C. Wright, *The Last Stand of Chinese Conservatism: The T'ung Chih Restoration, 1862–1874* (Stanford: Stanford University Press, 1957). A more specialized work is Chiang Siang-tseh, *The Nien Rebellion* (Seattle: University of Washington Press, 1954). M. E. Cameron, *The Reform Movement in China, 1898–1912* (Stanford: Stanford University Press, 1931), although lacking in analysis, has not been superseded. Chester Tan, *The Boxer Catastrophe* (New York: Columbia University Press, 1955), is the best work on the subject. The origins of warlordism are described by Ralph Powell, *The Rise of Chinese Military Power, 1895–1912* (Princeton: Princeton University Press, 1955). The political development of China under the republic is presented in detail by Franklin W. Houn, *Central Government of China, 1912–1928: An Institutional Study* (Madison: University of Wisconsin Press, 1957), and by H. F. MacNair, *China in Revolution: An Analysis of Politics and Militarism under the Republic* (Chicago: University of Chicago Press, 1931).

Chen Shao-kwan, *The System of Taxation in the Tsing Dynasty* (New York: Columbia University Press, 1914), is still a useful basic work in the field of Chinese economic development; and Liang Fang-chung, *The Single Whip Method of Taxation in China* (Cambridge, Mass.: Harvard University Press, 1956; translated by Wang Yu-ch'uan), is an important recent contribution. More specialized is Harold Hinton, *The Grain Tribute System of China, 1845–1911* (Cambridge, Mass.: Harvard University Press, 1956). One important aspect of China's modernization has been analyzed by Marion Levy and K. H. Shih, *The Rise of the Modern Chinese Business Class* (New York: Institute of Pacific Relations, 1949). A more extensive study of the same problem is Albert Feuerwerker, *China's Early Industrialization: Sheng Hsuan-huai, 1844–1916* (Cambridge, Mass.: Harvard University Press, 1959). Another useful specialized study is Ellsworth Carlson, *The Kaiping Mines, 1877–1912* (Cambridge, Mass.: Harvard University Press, 1957).

Joseph R. Levenson, *Confucian China and Its Modern Fate* (London: Routledge & Kegan Paul, 1958), is a thoughtful introduction to Chinese intellectual history in this period. O. Briere, *Fifty Years of Chinese Philosophy, 1898–1950* (London: Allen & Unwin, 1956; translated by L. G. Thompson), and Chan Wing-tsit, *Religious Trends in Modern China* (New York: Columbia University Press, 1953), are important contributions. Hu Shih, *The Chinese Renaissance* (Chicago: University of Chicago Press, 1934), is indispensable for understanding the spirit of the Chinese cultural revolution, and Chiang Wen-han, *The Chinese Student Movement* (New York: Columbia University Press, 1948), and Chow Tse-tung, *The May Fourth Movement* (Cambridge, Mass.: Harvard University Press, 1959), are detailed studies in the field.

Eminent Chinese of the Ch'ing Period (1644–1912) (Washington: Government Printing Office, two volumes, 1943–1944; edited by A. W. Hummel) is an excellent biographical reference. A. E. Grantham, *A Manchu Monarch: An Interpretation of Chia Ching* (London: Allen & Unwin, 1934), is an uncritical study of an early nineteenth-century emperor; and W. L. Bales, *Tso Tsung-t'ang, Soldier and Statesman of China* (Shanghai: Kelly & Walsh, 1937), and J. O. P. Bland, *Li Hung-chang* (London, 1917), are biographies of nineteenth-century Confucian officials. Thomas E. La Fargue, *China's First Hundred* (Pullman, Wash.: Washington State College, 1942), narrates the career of Yung Wing and the fate of his education experiment. Joseph R. Levenson, *Liang Ch'i-ch'ao and the Mind of Modern China* (Cambridge, Mass.: Harvard University Press, 1953), is a helpful analysis of the career of one of China's most persistent advocates of reform. The best biography of the "founder of modern China" is Lyon Sharman, *Sun Yat-sen, His Life and Its Meaning, A Critical Biography* (New York: John Day, 1934). Bernard Martin, *Strange Vigour, Biography of Sun Yat-sen* (London: Heinemann, 1944), is a good short account. More specialized is Marius Jansen, *The Japanese and Sun Yat-sen* (Cambridge, Mass.: Harvard University Press, 1954). Jerome Ch'en, *Yuan Shih-k'ai* (Stanford: Stanford University Press, 1961), is a recent contribution. Useful for the academic side of the Chinese Renaissance is Ku Chieh-kang, *Autobiography of a Chinese Historian* (Leiden: E. J. Brill, 1931; translated by A. W. Hummel).

The most comprehensive survey of China's modern foreign relations is still H. B. Morse, *The International Relations of the Chinese Empire* (London: Longmans, Green, three volumes, 1910–1918). The best of the textbook accounts is Paul H. Clyde, *The Far East* (Englewood Cliffs, N.J.: Prentice-Hall, third edition, 1958). William F. Mayers, *Treaties between the Empire of China and Foreign Powers* (Shanghai: third edition, 1901), E. Hertslet, *Hertslet's China Treaties* (London: two volumes, third revised edition, 1908), China Maritime Customs, *Treaties, Conventions, etc., between China and Foreign States* (Shanghai: printed for H.M. Stationery Office by Harrison and Sons, two volumes, second edition, 1917), and J. V. MacMurray, *Treaties and Agreements with and concerning China, 1894–1919* (New York: Oxford University Press, two volumes, 1921), are useful reference works. Maurice Collis, *Foreign Mud* (New York: Alfred A. Knopf, 1947), and H. E. Abend, *Treaty Ports* (Garden City, N.Y.: Doubleday, Doran, 1944), are interesting popular works. John K. Fairbank, *Trade and Diplomacy on the China Coast* (Cambridge, Mass.: Harvard University Press, 1954), is an excellent study of Chinese attitudes in

241

the middle of the nineteenth century. Lord Charles Beresford, *The Breakup of China* (New York and London, 1899), and P. Joseph, *Foreign Diplomacy in China, 1894–1900* (London: Allen & Unwin, 1928), are indispensable for study of spheres of influence. William L. Langer, *The Diplomacy of Imperialism, 1890–1902* (New York: Alfred A. Knopf, two volumes, 1935), provides the European background of the turmoil in China.

The only survey of British-Chinese relations is the short work by G. E. Hubbard, *British Far Eastern Policy* (New York: Institute of Pacific Relations, 1943), but there are a number of good special studies, including Earl H. Pritchard, *The Crucial Years of Early Anglo-Chinese Relations, 1750–1800* (Pullman, Wash.: Washington State College, 1936); Michael Greenberg, *British Trade and the Opening of China* (Cambridge, Eng.: Cambridge University Press, 1951); P. C. Kuo, *A Critical Study of the First Anglo-Chinese War* (Shanghai: Commercial Press, 1935); Teng Ssu-yu, *Chang Hsi and the Treaty of Nanking* (Chicago: University of Chicago Press, 1944); W. C. Costin, *Great Britain and China, 1833–1860* (Oxford: Clarendon Press, 1937); Nathan A. Pelcovits, *Old China Hands and the Foreign Office* (New York: Institute of Pacific Relations, 1948), which sheds much light on conflicts between the British government and business interests; S. T. Wang, *The Margary Affair and the Chefoo Agreement* (New York: Oxford University Press, 1940); E. V. G. Kiernan, *British Diplomacy in China, 1880–1885* (Cambridge, Eng.: Cambridge University Press, 1939); R. S. McCordock, *British Far Eastern Policy, 1894–1900* (New York: Columbia University Press, 1931); and E-tu Zen Sun, *Chinese Railways and British Interests* (New York: Columbia University Press, 1954).

There are several surveys of Russian-Chinese relations. Cheng Tien-fang, *A History of Sino-Russian Relations* (Washington: Public Affairs Press, 1957), Aitchen Wu, *China and the Soviet Union* (New York: John Day, 1950), David Dallin, *The Rise of Russia in Asia* (New Haven: Yale University Press, 1949), and M. Pavlovsky, *Chinese-Russian Relations* (New York: Philosophical Library, 1949), are helpful.

Seiji Hishida, *Japan among the Great Powers: A Survey of Her International Relations* (New York: Longmans, Green & Co., 1940), is a good introduction with a Japanese point of view. Tatsuji Takeuchi, *War and Diplomacy in the Japanese Empire* (New York: Doubleday, Doran, 1935), is an objective study with a problems approach. F. H. Harrington, *God, Mammon, and the Japanese* (Madison: University of Wisconsin Press, 1944), and M. Frederick Nelson, *Korea and the Old Order in Eastern Asia* (Baton Rouge: Louisiana State University Press, 1945), are useful for the Chinese-Japanese difficulties over Korea.

Tyler Dennett, *Americans in Eastern Asia* (New York: Barnes & Noble, reprint, 1941), and A. W. Griswold, *The Far Eastern Policy of the United States* (New York: Harcourt, Brace, 1938), although somewhat outdated, still provide the best survey of Chinese-American relations. F. R. Dulles, *China and America* (Princeton: Princeton University Press, 1946), is a good popular account. More specialized studies include Kenneth Scott Latourette, *The History of the Early Relations between the United States and China, 1784–1884* (New Haven: Yale University Press, 1917), Paul H. Clyde, *United States Policy toward China,*

1839–1939 (Durham, N.C.: Duke University Press, 1940), Earl Swisher, *China's Management of the American Barbarians* (New Haven: Far Eastern Association, 1953), A. L. P. Dennis, *Adventures in American Diplomacy, 1896–1900* (New York, 1928), Paul A. Varg, *Open Door Diplomat: The Life of W. W. Rockhill* (Urbana: University of Illinois Press, 1952), Tyler Dennett, *John Hay, from Politics to Policy* (New York, 1933), and C. S. Campbell, *Special Business Interests and the Open Door Policy* (New Haven: Yale University Press, 1951).

The Beginnings of Modernization in Japan

The emergence of Japan as a powerful, modern nation-state with a large empire is the main theme of Japanese history in the period stretching from the chaotic decade of the 1850's to the end of World War I. Politically, this change was embodied in the transition from feudalism to a highly centralized unitary state. On the economic side, Japan became one of the major industrial producers of the world. But socially, although there were a number of important reforms, traditional values remained strong, especially in the rural areas, because they were utilized—in education and the civil code, for example— to maintain the social equilibrium desired by the dominant political and economic interest groups.

The process of modernization had its origins in the movement to establish an imperial regime in place of the Tokugawa shogunate, which culminated in the Meiji Restoration (1868). Although the anti-Tokugawa movement was based in part on popular discontent caused by economic and social changes, the restoration was not the culmination of a class struggle. It was essentially a kind of aristocratic revolution achieved by a small group of samurai intellectuals, the key elements of which came from the han of Satsuma and Choshu. These samurai leaders were motivated largely by concern for Japan's security in face of the menace of penetration by the Western powers, and they initiated, in the name of the emperor, a series of political, economic, and social reforms which strengthened the country. For all practical purposes, the new government was an oligarchy, not in outward form, but in the sense that political power was concentrated in the hands of a few men.

The process of modernization, especially in the economic sphere, gave rise to forces which soon challenged the power of the oligarchs. Ambitious former samurai, especially intellectuals from the han of Tosa and Hizen, landlords, who often also engaged in rural commercial and industrial activities, and, to a lesser extent, urban capitalists—all of whom wanted a voice in the decision-making process—provided the leadership and support of political

244

parties that demanded representative government. The pressure of this movement was so great by the decade of the 1880's that the oligarchs were forced
to compromise with it and share political power with the two-house parliament, or diet, established by the Meiji Constitution (1889). And from 1890 to
the end of World War I the parties and the remaining oligarchs, now better
known as genro (elder statesmen who constituted an informal but influential
group that advised the emperor), continued their political struggles—at times,
of course, reaching necessary compromises. But by the decade of the 1920's
the political parties were on the verge of triumph for a number of reasons. For
one thing, the genro had either died off or, because of advanced age, had lost
influence; but, more important, the parties themselves had been transformed
in character and now comprised an amalgam of politicians, representing the
key economic groups—the large monopolistic trusts, or zaibatsu, and the
rural landlord-capitalists—and bureaucrats, who inherited the idea of "stewardship" or "trusteeship" that motivated the oligarchs or genro.

The social composition of Japanese political leadership in this period—
and this is true of both the oligarchy and the political parties—inhibited the
development of democracy. Neither of these two basic political groupings
spoke for the interests of the great masses of peasants and workers, and together they co-operated to prevent the development of any movement that
would speak for them, e.g., the labor movement and the socialist movement.

Despite the intensity of their domestic conflict, the oligarchs and party
leaders were both intensely nationalistic, especially in the realm of foreign
policy. Although there were some important differences of opinion between
them in the first four decades of the Meiji era (1868–1912), both supported
the drive for expansion in Korea and Manchuria that led to war with China
in 1894–1895 and with Russia in 1904–1905. And both looked to the development of a special position in China, although by the decade of the 1920's
there were significant differences of approach in the policies of the political
parties and the military.

15 The Restoration of Imperial Rule

One of the fundamental differences between Japan and China in the middle of the nineteenth century arose from the circumstance that Japan was a society in motion while China was handicapped by the inertia of traditionalism. In Japan economic and social maladjustments provided the background for revolution, and by the decade of the 1850's samurai, ronin, and court nobles were already plotting the destruction of the shogunate and the restoration of imperial rule. While traditional political animosities and han rivalries played a part in this movement, it is impossible to overlook the fact that its leadership was in the hands of men who desired basic changes. The revolution, however, cannot be explained strictly in terms of internal developments which were leading to some sort of reconstruction of Japanese society, for it was the impact of foreign political and economic pressures that brought matters to a climax.

The Treaty Settlement

The United States led the successful attack on Japan's policy of isolation when in late March, 1852, President Fillmore appointed Commodore Matthew C. Perry as commander of the American East India Squadron and special envoy to Japan. Perry arrived off Uraga with four ships in July, 1853, under instructions, unknown to the Japanese, not to use force except in self-defense. With the decks of his ships cleared for action, he rebuffed the first Japanese officials who approached, announcing that he would receive only a high-ranking dignitary for the presentation of a letter from the President of the United States, which outlined the objectives of his mission.

The bakufu, although it had been forewarned by the Dutch of Perry's impending arrival, was not ready to decide on a course of action. Officials were hurriedly summoned to the shogun's castle in Edo for an all-night conference, in which they decided to ask Perry to go to Nagasaki in order to delay if not discourage him. Perry, however, insisted on presenting his letter and threatened to come ashore to deliver it himself, forcibly if necessary. The bakufu reluctantly sent two commissioners to accept Fillmore's message, but they requested time to deliberate on the matter of concluding a treaty with the United States. Perry, consenting to the delay, left but promised to return early in the following year with a larger force. Immediately thereafter the bakufu embarked on a program of military preparedness, including the construction of forts just south of Edo, and it granted permission to the daimyo of the various han to build large ships, purchase war vessels and guns from Holland, and establish local fortifications.

The bakufu also decided to consult with various groups in Japanese society with regard to the foreign policy problem. In fact, Abe Masahiro, the young senior councilor, had already conferred with those daimyo whom he regarded as able men—Shimazu Nariakira of Satsuma, Date Munemori of Uwajima, Yamanouchi Toyoshige of Tosa, and Matsudaira Yoshinaga of Echizen. In August, 1853, Abe sent translations of President Fillmore's letter to leading officials in the bakufu, the daimyo, important Confucian scholars, a number of samurai who were influential in their han, and even some wealthy merchants. It is important to note that by thus inviting public discussion Abe set a precedent for later demands on the part of leading daimyo for participation in the decision-making process.

The leading daimyo at this time tended to divide into two groups. One saw the need to end isolation, avoid hostilities, and give the nation time to improve its own defenses; the other wished to refuse trade, retain the policy of isolation, and if necessary resort to hostilities to drive the Americans away. Both groups regarded the West as a threat and were concerned to combat it, and they agreed that it was necessary to adopt Western military techniques. The "open-the-country" view (kaikoku) was based on the premise that Japan could not resist the West and would have to make temporary concessions. The "expel-the-foreigner" view (joi) held that Japan was psychologically un-prepared to cope with Western influences and needed reform at home as a preliminary to opening the ports. The bakufu judged the forces of exclusion to be stronger and thus informed the nation that Perry would be sent away without being granted concessions in trade. Realizing, however, that should Perry threaten hostilities, it would have to give in to his requests, the bakufu embarked on a policy of procrastination, requesting him, through the Dutch, to delay his return because of the recent death of the shogun.

The American interest in Japan coincided with a renewal of Russian activity in Northeast Asia. In the late 1840's Muraviev decided that it would be to Russia's advantage to make friends with Japan in order to check British and American influence in East Asia. In 1852 Czar Nicholas I agreed to send an expedition to Japan under Admiral Putiatin, who arrived off Nagasaki with four vessels in August, 1853, to find that Perry had already arrived at Uraga. Putiatin was able to open negotiations for a boundary settlement in the north and for the inauguration of trade, but he was unable to overcome the dilatory tactics of the bakufu officials. In the end he was forced to leave Japan for service in the Crimean War.

Hearing of the Russian mission, Perry lost no time in returning to Japan to resume negotiations. He anchored off Kanagawa on January 16, 1854, with a reinforced squadron of eight ships. The bakufu, realizing that Perry could not be put off, consented to his demand for a formal treaty. The significance of the Treaty of Kanagawa, signed on March 31, 1854, does not lie in its terms but in the precedent it set with regard to the Tokugawa seclusion policy. It was little more than a convention covering the safe return of ship-wrecked sailors and provision of supplies for American ships at the ports of Shimoda and Hakodate. Shimoda, some sixty miles from Edo on the southern extremity of the Izu Peninsula, was a three-day journey from the shogun's capital. It had an exceptionally poor harbor which later (1855) was ruined by a tidal wave, and it was shut off from the roads and markets of the interior by ranges of hills. Hakodate was located in the extreme northern part of Japan, a region largely undeveloped economically. The most significant clauses of the treaty provided for a most-favored-nation treatment and for the exchange of consuls whenever either party thought it necessary after a lapse of eighteen months.

In the following two years the bakufu signed treaties with several other powers: with Great Britain at Nagasaki in October, 1854, with Russia at Shimoda in February, 1855, and with the Netherlands at Nagasaki in January, 1856. The most-favored-nation clause included in each treaty made for a common settlement, which included the following rights: to secure supplies at Shimoda, Hakodate, and Nagasaki; to trade through Japanese officials and under their regulations at these ports; to appoint consuls at Shimoda and Hakodate; and to maintain a limited extraterritorial jurisdiction. The Russian treaty also led to an informal understanding on the northern boundary question. The Kuriles south of Iturup were to be Japanese, while Sakhalin's status was to be left undetermined.

By signing these treaties, the bakufu created a foreign policy debate in Japan that was not stilled even when it secured imperial approval for them in February, 1855. Within the bakufu the treaties became an issue in a struggle for power between two forces, centering on the selection of an heir to the office of shogun. Tokugawa Nariaki of the Mito branch of the family supported the candidacy of his son Keiki, who had been adopted into another branch eligible for the high office of shogun. Nariaki condemned the existing regime for its conciliatory policy toward the foreigners. Not only did he want to advance the interests of his son, but it is clear that he believed that Japan's domestic and foreign crises had been caused by the arbitrary and selfish policy of the bakufu, which he accused of constantly seeking to weaken the daimyo both financially and militarily. But the group under the leadership of Ii Naosuke, daimyo of Hikone, which accepted trade as a means of strengthening Japan, won out and finally, in 1858, managed to get the succession decided in favor of its nominee, Iemochi.

Another Japanese reaction to the treaties was the acceleration of defense measures. The bakufu and various han spent large sums of money on the importation of new weapons and ships and for the construction of foundries, arsenals, and shipyards. By 1857 Satsuma, Hizen, and Mito, as well as the bakufu, had shipyards, and by 1868, the year of the imperial restoration, fourteen han had either repair or building facilities. Improvements in the manufacture of steel cannon and gunpowder were instituted to strengthen the coastal batteries. The bakufu also established a new office for the study and translation of Western books, especially those on military science and technology.

Before these efforts could create the strength necessary to check the Western powers, there were demands for additional commercial privileges. The second assault on Japan's isolation was begun by Townsend Harris, the first American consul. Harris, a former merchant with experience in Asia, arrived at Shimoda in August, 1856, to take up his post under the terms of the Treaty of Kanagawa. At Shimoda he was isolated from the mainstream of Japanese political life and was forced to endure difficult living conditions. For a time he inhabited an old temple infested with rats, and his food was a constant source of irritation. The bakufu, which kept him under complete surveillance, hoped that he would give up and go home in disgust.

Harris was, moreover, isolated from his own country. Fourteen months passed before he was visited by an American ship, and eighteen months before he received additional instructions from Washington. His principal objective was to secure a full commercial treaty, but from the moment of his arrival the Japanese used every device of obstruction and deceit to discourage him. The bakufu even ignored his request to present his credentials at Edo in order to conduct negotiations.

Since Ii Naosuke was still engaged in his struggle with Tokugawa Nariaki, he was unable to concede immediately what Harris wanted, but by June, 1857, he did agree to certain proposals. In the autumn Harris was permitted to enter Edo for an audience with the shogun to present his credentials. In negotiations with bakufu officials, he explained China's difficulties with the West and urged them to take steps to prevent a similar situation from developing. By February, 1858, his persistence, patience, and firmness won the bakufu's approval of a commercial treaty, although it deferred signing for some time. When the bakufu consulted the daimyo, few among them were positively against foreign trade, but almost all suggested that the matter wait upon the emperor's approval. That sanction the bakufu was, however, unable to obtain, largely because of the active opposition of a small group of court nobles who, though supported by the bakufu, had long been eclipsed by the feudal rulers; these men hoped to use the treaty issue to revive their own power in the name of the emperor.

The bakufu was forced to decide the treaty issue unilaterally. Harris, skillfully using the news of the Treaty of Tientsin, brought it to the view that by accepting his treaty it would forestall excessive and unreasonable demands on the part of the other powers. Since the succession issue had recently been decided in his favor, Ii Naosuke, acting as regent (*tairo*), a post established only in times of grave crisis, signed the treaty on July 29, 1858. Its terms were as follows:

1. Ministers and consuls would be exchanged between Japan and the United States.
2. Hakodate, Kanagawa, and Nagasaki would be opened to trade immediately. Other ports would be opened according to specific dates: Niigata on January 1, 1860, and Hyogo (Kobe) on January 1, 1863. Edo and Osaka would be opened to trade and residence on January 1, 1862, and January 1, 1863, respectively.
3. Duties, for the most part 5 per cent ad valorem, to be imposed on imports and exports.
4. Extraterritoriality for American nationals.
5. Freedom of worship for Americans.
6. Revision after July 4, 1872.

The treaty also provided that the United States would act as a mediator between Japan and other foreign powers if necessary and that the Japanese government could purchase or construct in the United States ships of war, merchant vessels, cannon, munitions, and anything else that it might require. Japan also might engage American scientific, naval, and military personnel. The European powers quickly followed up Harris' success and used his treaty as a model for their own. The Netherlands concluded a treaty on August 18, 1858, Russia on August 19, 1858, Great Britain on August 26, 1858, and France on October 7, 1858.

The Civil-Military Amalgamation Movement

The bakufu's decision to sign the treaties without imperial approval precipitated a domestic crisis. Samurai and ronin who for one reason or another opposed the bakufu poured into Kyoto to offer their support to the imperial court, and some Choshu elements plotted with ambitious court nobles to effect a *coup d'état*. Under Ii Naosuke's leadership the bakufu was determined to crush any movement that sought to weaken if not destroy its authority. Thus it arrested and imprisoned a number of court nobles, some of whom were later executed, and it forced several daimyo to turn over their han to their sons. Nariaki, who had continued to conspire with the imperial court in order to advance the interests of his son, was placed under house arrest and died in September, 1860. Finally, the bakufu was able to get the emperor to agree not to oppose the treaties; to gain this concession it had to promise to rid Japan of foreigners within a fixed period, reportedly five years.

After the murder of Ii Naosuke in March, 1860, by a band of Mito samurai in revenge for Nariaki's political demise, the bakufu relaxed the purge and adopted a policy of compromise based on union of the imperial court and the shogunate. This concept came to be attractive to many of the han which, like Satsuma, were traditional enemies of the Tokugawa family, for they saw in the union a chance to extend their influence in a new national administration. Even in Choshu, where anti-Tokugawa sentiment was very strong, samurai disciples of the bakufu's archenemy, Yoshida Shoin, broke with him on the ground that his plotting would bring disaster to their han. By 1861 the dominant clique in Choshu decided that it should seek to mediate between the imperial court and the shogunate. As part of the shift in bakufu policy, Tokugawa Keiki, Nariaki's unsuccessful candidate, was made guardian of the young shogun, Iemochi, who had assumed office in August, 1858. As far as the treaties were concerned, the bakufu reiterated its promise to cancel them through negotiation or to expel the foreigners by force. In this case, expediency triumphed over judgment.

The marriage of Emperor Komei's sister to the shogun in January, 1862, was conceived of as the beginning of the compromise union between the court and the shogunate. In fact, the bride used her title of "imperial princess" instead of the customary designation, "shogun's consort." In October of the same year the bakufu relaxed the hostage system which forced the daimyo to pass alternate periods of residence in the han and in Edo. Thereafter they were required to spend only one hundred days every three years at the capital of the shogun. They were also permitted to enter Kyoto and have access to the emperor, and the resulting scramble among the most important daimyo for quarters in Kyoto was spectacular. In 1863, under the prodding of ambitious court nobles who were looking for every opportunity to increase the political power of the emperor, the imperial court established a bureau of state affairs to supervise its administration and policies. Later in 1863 the shogun went to Kyoto for the first time in two hundred and fifty years in compliance with an imperial summons to discuss the treaty situation, and when Iemochi entered the city, he found it saturated with antiforeign and antibakufu sentiments.

The treaties remained a problem, since they were constantly being exploited by samurai who detached themselves from han service and congregated in Kyoto. Essentially conservatives who desired a return to agrarian self-sufficiency, they hoped, by influencing the imperial court, to force the bakufu to terminate the treaties. The more radical among them conspired with court nobles like Sanjo Sanetomi to fabricate antiforeign imperial edicts, and they plotted to intimidate and assassinate bakufu officials and merchants profiting from trade. In reaction, the bakufu reinforced its police in Kyoto, and daimyo forbade their samurai from detaching themselves and engaging in terrorist acts. For example, Shimazu Hisamitsu, father of the new daimyo of Satsuma and the real power in the han, repudiated the activities of unattached samurai at Kyoto, and among those samurai within his jurisdiction he banished Saigo

Takamori, later one of the key leaders of the restoration movement, and executed Arima Shinshichi.

The intensity of much of the antiforeignism was based on material considerations. Gold was rapidly being drained from Japan, and prices rose as a result, causing a marked increase in living costs which further aggravated the difficulties of the people, particularly those on fixed incomes like the samurai. The large outflow of gold was induced by the disproportionately high price of silver in Japan. The bakufu had set a silver-gold exchange rate which varied from 6:1 to 10:1 while abroad it was 15:1 and 20:1. It was not until 1860 that the rate was adjusted upward; in the meantime Japan was drained of sizable amounts of gold by foreigners who made huge, easy profits. Moreover, a large volume of exports created a scarcity of goods, especially consumer items, thereby also increasing prices. In the period from 1859 to 1867 the price of raw silk, the dominant export, trebled; tea doubled, cotton quadrupled, rice increased as much as twelvefold but fluctuated tremendously; salt went up tenfold, soybeans fivefold, and wheat trebled. Conversely, the sudden importation of cheap manufactured goods, especially yarn and cloth, cut deeply into markets normally supplied by household production. There is much evidence that price increases and the decline of domestic handicrafts were important causes of peasant uprisings and riots of the urban poor. Certainly there was a steady rise in their number in the last years of Tokugawa rule.

Discontent often took the form of terrorist attacks upon foreigners. Between 1859 and 1861 a Russian naval officer and two sailors were slain at Yokohama; Townsend Harris' aide, the Dutch Heuksen, was cut down in Edo; and the newly arrived legation secretary and consul were wounded during an attack on the British legation in Edo by ronin and samurai. Later, in 1863, the British legation was burned to the ground.

The bakufu was quick to settle these incidents by indemnities, but it was unable to guarantee protection to the foreign community. In the spring of 1861, therefore, it decided to negotiate the postponement of the opening of the two ports, Hyogo (Kobe) and Niigata, and the two cities, Edo and Osaka. The foreigners, informed that these concessions were necessary if the treaty system was to be preserved, accepted a five-year delay, and the bakufu presented this diplomatic triumph to the imperial court and antiforeign groups as evidence that it was serious in its declaration of resistance to foreign encroachment. The terrorist outbreaks, however, did not cease. In September, 1862, C. L. Richardson, an Englishman visiting from Hong Kong, was killed near Yokohama by samurai heading the procession of the daimyo of Satsuma, and his companions were wounded. The British demanded an indemnity, part of which was to be paid by Satsuma, as well as the trial and execution of the murderers. The bakufu paid £100,000, but the British insisted on an apology also and an additional £25,000 to be paid directly by the daimyo of Satsuma. When the latter did not comply, the British decided to deal directly with him.

In the meantime, the shogun obeyed the imperial summons and journeyed to Kyoto to discuss the treaty situation with the emperor. Despite the bakufu's protests, on June 5, 1863, the emperor ordered that all ports be closed to foreign commerce within twenty days. On June 24, when the bakufu paid the Richardson indemnity, it notified the powers of the exclusion decree. When the powers insisted that the treaties must be enforced, the bakufu acknowledged that it would not enforce exclusion. In July, having returned to Edo, the shogun sent a memorial to the emperor asking that the expulsion of foreigners be postponed, and the imperial court agreed reluctantly. The Richardson affair was settled shortly thereafter; in August a British squadron bombarded Kagoshima, and in December Satsuma paid the indemnity and agreed to execute the culprits in the presence of British officers. In Choshu, however, there were still difficulties for the foreigners. After June 25, the date originally set by the emperor for the termination of trade, Choshu shore batteries began to fire on foreign ships passing through the Shimonoseki Straits. When the bakufu sent an official envoy to rebuke those responsible for these rash acts, Choshu replied that it was acting on orders from the imperial court. In defiance of the bakufu, Choshu executed the envoy and seized the ship on which he arrived.

In 1863 and 1864 Choshu was the most important threat to the success of the union plan. The han administration was dominated by anti-Tokugawa sentiment and by the desire to challenge the increasing influence of Satsuma, which was actively participating in the negotiations between the imperial court and the bakufu. Choshu jealousy of Satsuma's new prestige and potential power was an important motivating force in the determination of han policy. But when Choshu made repeated efforts to increase its influence at Kyoto, a Satsuma-led coup in the summer of 1863 expelled Choshu and other antibakufu samurai from Kyoto on orders from Emperor Komei. In the following year Choshu attempted a countercoup, which failed. The upshot of these actions was that Choshu was declared "an enemy of the imperial court." The bakufu dispatched a punitive expedition to Choshu, and by late autumn, 1864, it had succeeded in surrounding the han. Shortly before this, in September, a combined naval expedition of the Western powers destroyed the shore batteries of Choshu at Shimonoseki and forced the han leaders to agree to open the straits, not to repair the forts or build new ones, and to pay an indemnity covering the costs of the expedition.

These two factors, the bombardment and the imminent attack of the bakufu, brought conservative elements to power in Choshu which ordered the suicide of three councilors held responsible for the attack on Kyoto and disbanded the militia. In fact, however, the greater part of the militia retired to isolated areas in the han, along with its antibakufu samurai leaders. Only a few samurai, e.g., Kido Koin and Takasugi Shinsaku, were forced to leave the han. Following these events, the bakufu forces withdrew, but shortly thereafter Choshu was plunged into civil war from which the antibakufu clique emerged dominant and committed to a policy of restoring the emperor to power. But antiforeignism as a policy was not revived. Choshu began engaging in foreign trade, and many of its samurai went to Nagasaki or even abroad for study.

During 1864 the plan for the amalgamation of the imperial court and the shogunate moved closer to conclusion. The shogun visited Kyoto again, and with helpful mediation by Satsuma made further concessions, which were made public. The emperor's ultimate right to rule was recognized, but the conduct of state affairs was entrusted to the shogun, who agreed that in the future each new shogun would visit Kyoto to receive investiture from the emperor. The same was to hold true for daimyo succession. It was also agreed that certain of the daimyo—Satsuma, Tosa, Echizen, and Aizu—should be advisers of the emperor; however, Keiki, speaking for the shogun, refused to admit them into bakufu councils. On his part, the emperor compromised on the treaties issue. In the formal statement issued on March 5, 1864, the emperor no longer insisted upon immediate and forcible expulsion but instead declared a preference for the day when Japan should establish its independence.

In the following year the imperial court was made to feel the power of the foreigners. After the bombardment of the Choshu batteries, the bakufu assumed responsibility for the $3,000,000 indemnity on the ground that it could not permit foreign powers to negotiate with a single han. The powers, realizing that this amount was a huge burden for the bakufu, attempted to use it as a lever to hasten the opening of Japan's ports; and when the bakufu refused to take the bait, in November, 1865, an allied naval force, under British leadership, assembled near Osaka, where pressure could be most effectively brought to bear upon the imperial throne. The powers promised to remit two-thirds of the Shimonoseki indemnity if Hyogo (Kobe) and Osaka were opened immediately, if the emperor gave his approval to the treaties, and if the tariff were reduced to a general 5 per cent ad valorem. It is clear that the foreign representatives realized that, although the shogun continued to manage the administration, the point had been reached where his acts required the formal approval of the emperor to make them effective. The emperor agreed to ratify the treaties and to reduce the tariff, but he preferred to pay the full indemnity if Hyogo's opening could be postponed until 1868. The emperor's decision signaled the end of the expulsion movement, although there was still much fear and hatred of the foreigners.

The Meiji Restoration

By 1865 the bakufu had apparently checked the opposition; its successes had been due, however, to the support of several leading han, particularly Satsuma, which had been a prime mover in the efforts to unite the imperial court and the shogunate. But in Satsuma there were also strong anti-Tokugawa elements under the leadership of samurai like Okubo Toshimichi, who on various trips to Kyoto had met with antibakufu court nobles and samurai of other han. Saigo Takamori, after his recall from exile in 1864, began to negotiate with similar groups in Choshu, Tosa, and Hizen, and Shimazu Hisamitsu began to harbor doubts about the bakufu's intentions with regard to the union plan. It was becoming clearer that the bakufu had no desire to broaden the base of the national administration and that in fact it had shifted its policy.

The bakufu decided to rely on an offer of French support to strengthen itself militarily and financially, and it decided to unify the country under the shogun by confiscation of the han. In May, 1865, it began to mobilize an expeditionary force against Choshu, whose daimyo and administration were now controlled by anti-Tokugawa samurai, and the shogun himself went to Osaka to supervise the preparations. These had to be delayed, however, because of the crisis in foreign policy over the opening of Hyogo and Osaka.

In Choshu, Takasugi and Omura Masujiro reorganized the militia, composed of all classes and trained in Western techniques, and prepared to meet the bakufu attack. And Choshu soon got assistance from other quarters. In March, 1866, Sakamoto Ryoma, a Tosa samurai, was instrumental in concluding an anti-Tokugawa alliance between the revolutionary samurai of Satsuma and Choshu, who increasingly dominated the councils of their han, with the daimyo becoming mere figureheads. It was his hope that such an alliance would prevent civil war and foreign intervention. The consequences of this act followed immediately. In July, 1866, when the bakufu finally put its forces into the field against Choshu, Shimazu Hisamitsu, on the advice of Saigo and Okubo, refused to allow Satsuma troops to join the expedition.

The death of Iemochi in August, 1866, postponed settlement of the struggle between the bakufu and its enemies. Iemochi was succeeded as shogun by Tokugawa Keiki, whose family had long been supporters of imperial power. The new shogun, looking for a way to resolve the bakufu's difficulties, received help from the imperial court, which ordered the bakufu to demobilize its forces out of respect for the deceased shogun. Keiki complied promptly, as it gave him an opportunity to recall the expedition without suffering too great a loss of face. Thereafter he worked vigorously to reform bakufu administration and to strengthen its military industries.

The death of Emperor Komei (February, 1867), who had earnestly desired unity between the bakufu and his court, worked against Tokugawa interests. A young boy, Mutsuhito, aged fifteen, who assumed the reign name of Meiji, came to the throne, and as a minor he was dominated by his advisers, drawn largely from anti-Tokugawa court nobles like Iwakura Tomomi. Finally, in the spring, Shimazu Hisamitsu openly acknowledged the alliance with Choshu, and Saigo Takamori led Satsuma troops into Kyoto and placed them at the disposal of the young emperor. They were soon joined by other anti-Tokugawa forces, but Choshu troops did not participate, since their banishment from Kyoto remained in effect.

By summer the nation was faced with the immediate threat of civil war. Of the powerful four western han, only Tosa, whose administration checked antibakufu plotting largely because of the close personal relationship that had developed between its daimyo and the Tokugawa family, continued to seek a peaceful settlement. It proposed the creation of a national federation of han based on a deliberative assembly of han representatives. It wanted the shogun to resign his commission and participate in a new government as an equal among the vassals of the emperor.

The Tosa proposal was a logical extension of the idea of union of the imperial court and the shogunate, but its emphasis on the establishment of a deliberative assembly was in large part the result of the diffusion of Western ideas of parliamentary government. Japanese translations of Dutch books in the early nineteenth century had introduced the concept to a limited few. About the middle of the century another source of knowledge appeared in the form of Chinese works on Western government and politics, which reached a larger audience of educated Japanese. Finally, the termination of the Tokugawa seclusion policy in the 1850's opened a third source of information in the form of travel and study abroad as well as firsthand observation of the workings of Western political institutions.

As knowledge of parliamentary government spread among samurai intellectuals, they modified its theory and transformed its practice into concrete political programs to reform the feudal system. Yokoi Shonan, a samurai from Kumamoto, who was an early advocate of the restoration of imperial rule, urged the establishment of a bicameral assembly as a means of achieving national unification. Under his influence Matsudaira Shingaku, daimyo of Echizen, argued the need for an assembly in which even rich peasants and townsmen would be represented in the lower house. Okubo Tadahiro, a bakufu official who was sympathetic to Yokoi's views, memorialized the bakufu in 1862 for the establishment of a bicameral assembly composed of an upper house of great daimyo to discuss national affairs and a lower house of lesser daimyo for local affairs. According to his memorial, both bodies would meet once every five years, or oftener in cases of national emergency, and in the interim the administration of the country would be conducted by a standing committee of five great daimyo. In 1863 Akamatsu Kosaburo, an Ueda samurai, made a similar proposal, which outlined a system of imperial rule based on a six-man administrative board chosen from among the court nobles and the daimyo. In addition, he advocated the establishment of an upper house of daimyo, court nobles, and direct retainers of the shogun, totaling thirty, and a lower house of one hundred thirty samurai chosen from the various han to debate and decide national issues. The decisions of the assembly would become law after imperial assent, and, should the emperor not give his consent to a particular measure, the matter would be debated again, with the assembly having the power to enforce its decision as law. Later, Matsudaira Noritaka, a high councilor in the bakufu, argued along the same lines. But perhaps the most prominent bakufu advocate of an assembly was Nishi Amane, who submitted the first of his several memorials in 1866 in an effort to counter the pro-French policy shift. In fact, Nishi ultimately submitted what amounted to a draft constitution based on a separation of powers, "to create law," "to execute law," and "to protect the law."

The bakufu did not act on these proposals, but some Tosa samurai saw in them a possible means to avert civil war and to gain greater influence in the national scene for their han. For example, early in 1867 Sakamoto Ryoma proposed a system of government in which no one han would dominate. He suggested instead that with the restoration of imperial rule a bicameral assembly be established, together with an administrative council of samurai. Sakamoto's ideas became the political program of Tosa when it became clear, in the summer of 1867, that the samurai leaders of Satsuma and Choshu were determined to destroy the bakufu by force. Sakamoto and Goto Shojiro, another Tosa samurai, realized that to avoid civil war it was absolutely necessary to get the shogun to resign voluntarily. A memorial to that effect was drafted by Goto, signed by the daimyo, Yamanouchi Toyoshige, and presented to the shogun on October 29, 1867. Along with the restoration of political power to the imperial court, the memorialists proposed the establishment of a bicameral assembly "of honest and good men, with their selection ranging from high-ranking court nobles and great daimyo down to rear vassals and commoners." This formula did not intend to eliminate the shogun from the political scene; quite the contrary, he would retain considerable influence as head of the assembly and thus provide a powerful obstacle to the arbitrary seizure of power by either Satsuma or Choshu.

The increasing strength of the anti-Tokugawa coalition tended to make the bakufu receptive to some sort of political compromise by which the Tokugawa family could maintain its pre-eminent position. This receptiveness had been evident as early as the autumn of 1866, when, after canceling the expedition against Choshu, the new shogun, Tokugawa Keiki, had made tentative overtures to the leading daimyo for the creation of a national government based on a council representing their han. Since that time the position of the shogunate had become more precarious, and Keiki thus saw in the Tosa proposal a means of making a strategic withdrawal that might block the plan of the anti-Tokugawa coalition to destroy the shogunate by force. He decided to return full power to the emperor, but at the same time he was determined to become the leading figure, perhaps president of the assembly, in the new government, which would have the support of all the han.

After consulting and winning the approval of samurai representatives of several of the largest han—Komatsu Tateki of Satsuma, Goto Shojiro and Fukuoka Kotei of Tosa, and Tsuji Shiso of Aki—Keiki tendered his resignation as shogun in the form of a memorial to the emperor, who accepted the restoration of power to the imperial court. It was made clear in subsequent correspondence, however, that the emperor would permit Keiki to remain responsible for the administration of the nation until a council of leading daimyo could meet at Kyoto to help form a new government. One point deserves special attention. The imperial rescript that accepted Keiki's resignation asserted that the territories under bakufu control belonged to the emperor, although for the present they would remain in bakufu hands.

While these developments were taking place, the more ardent antibakufu elements continued their plotting. The daimyo of Tosa, Yamanouchi, had made an effort to dissuade them through the good offices of Goto and Fukuoka, but these emissaries met only with rebuff. The two influential Satsuma samurai leaders, Saigo Takamori and Okubo Toshimichi, with the co-operation of a court clique led by Iwakura Tomomi, persuaded the young emperor to issue a secret rescript commissioning an expedition against the bakufu. When Keiki's resignation caused the emperor to revoke this order, Saigo and Okubo reluctantly canceled their plans for the expedition, for they remained convinced that the bakufu had to be crushed by force. They were suspicious of any compromise that would leave the Tokugawa family any vestige of power, and they showed no sympathy for a deliberative assembly, especially as the idea had become associated with an attempt to assist the Tokugawa interests. So, in consultation with their Choshu allies, they continued to make arrangements for military action against the bakufu. The number of anti-Tokugawa troops in Kyoto grew larger, and finally, on January 3, 1868, the coalition of samurai and court nobles, led by Saigo of Satsuma, seized power in the name of the emperor. It ordered the bakufu administration to cease operation, and it formed a new provisional government, the structure of which had been planned late in 1867 by Saigo, Okubo, and Iwakura. Choshu was pardoned for its earlier attack on Kyoto, and soon a large contingent of Choshu troops entered the city and joined the Satsuma forces in support of the new government.

The Imperial Regime

The formal organization of the provisional government was modeled on the imperial system that had existed in Japan before the development of feudalism. It consisted of the office of supreme administrator (*sosai*), the supreme council, the associate council, and seven administrative departments, namely, Shinto, home affairs, foreign affairs, war, finance, judicial, and legislative. Prince Arisugawa Taruhito was appointed sosai, and his deputies (*fukusosai*) were Iwakura Tomomi and Sanjo Sanetomi. These appointments were calculated to emphasize the importance of the throne and the imperial court, whose power the military class had for so long usurped. The councils were composed of court nobles, daimyo, and samurai; their main function was to deliberate matters of importance and suggest measures to the sosai, who was theoretically responsible for the entire administration. The departments were headed by princes of the blood or court nobles, who were at the same time members of the councils.

The whole organization was in reality a great council, the members of which not only discussed and formulated policy but administered the resulting decisions through their conduct of the various departments. And, although most of the high offices were held by princes, court nobles, and daimyo, actual power tended to gravitate to the samurai leaders of the western han like Kido Koin of Choshu, Okubo and Saigo of Satsuma, Goto of Tosa, and Okuma Shigenobu of Hizen, who held lesser positions strategically located with the office of the sosai and in the various administrative departments which enabled them to formulate and guide policy. In fact, Kido, Okubo, and Saigo constituted a triumvirate because they were able to transfer their positions of leadership in their han to the new imperial government. This was facilitated by the fact that the new regime was dependent for the most part upon the support of Satsuma and Choshu.

In their first conference the leaders of the new government discussed the status of the former shogun and the disposition of his lands and wealth. A majority agreed to strip Keiki of all power and resources, but there was a group led by Yamanouchi of Tosa which proposed to invite the former shogun to assume an important position in the government. Keiki was informed that his resignation would hold and that he was to surrender his lands and revenues to the provisional government. When his Tosa supporters continued to be unable to reduce the government's demands, Keiki left Kyoto (January 6) and retired to Osaka. But further efforts on his behalf bore fruit, and Keiki was informed (January 18) that a general conference was to be held to apportion the expenses of the new government among the various daimyo on the basis of the han rice yields; perhaps he would not lose his lands, and Iwakura went so far as to suggest that he be made a senior councilor. These last efforts at compromise were defeated, however, by a series of incidents perpetrated by Satsuma and Choshu samurai that led to armed clashes.

In February the imperial court stripped Keiki of his court rank, and a month later a punitive expedition was on its way to Edo. The loyal supporters of the shogun were determined to fight to the end, but Keiki, who wished to avoid a bloody civil war, succeeded in restraining them. He retired to a temple in Edo to await imperial orders, while his retainers negotiated the surrender of the city with Saigo (April, 1868). The terms imposed included the re-

259

linquishing of all arms and the punishment of those who had conspired against the emperor. In Keiki's case the penalty was commuted from death to a life of house arrest in Mito. Keiki accepted the terms, but many of his followers felt that a great injustice had been done and resumed fighting. By June, however, the Tokugawa opposition had been effectively contained by the forces of the provisional government, and by autumn the last large contingent of troops had surrendered. Thereafter, only the Tokugawa naval forces in Hokkaido remained, and they finally surrendered in the summer of 1869. Despite this background of hostilities, many former officials of the bakufu accepted posts in the new government, thereby providing greater administrative continuity.

During the period of civil war the samurai leaders of the imperial government felt that to maintain the loyalty and support of the han it was necessary to establish some sort of national assembly; moreover, Tosa elements argued that the return of political power to the emperor had been predicated on the convocation of an assembly of daimyo or their representatives. During January, 1868, Goto Shojiro and Fukuoka Kotei petitioned for the formation of a bicameral assembly in which all the han would be represented by their daimyo and samurai. Shortly thereafter the government began to convoke such a body, the organization of which was based on a draft proposal that had been appended to the petition. The assembly (*gijisho*) consisted of an upper house of court nobles and daimyo and a lower house of samurai representing all the han, apportioned on the basis of three representatives for the large han (no less than 400,000-koku rice income), two for the intermediate (400,000–100,000 koku), and one for the small (less than 100,000 koku), and an unspecified number of appointed representatives, to include commoners— a concession to the wealthy merchants, who were helping to finance the new government and the civil war.

The famous *Charter Oath*, issued in April in the name of the Emperor Meiji, was also consciously designed to unite the han on some general principles. Yuri Kimimasa, an Echizen samurai, wrote the first draft of this document. As finance minister well aware of the revenue needs of the government, Yuri urged that all people express their loyalty to the new regime and asked that "all things be decided by public discussion." In his revision Fukuoka Kotei placed a much greater emphasis upon broadening the basis of government. He began his draft thus: "An assembly of daimyo shall be established and all matters shall be decided by public discussion." Kido Koin made the last revision, and he gave particular emphasis to a provision which would make clear to both the Japanese people and the foreign powers that Japan was prepared to utilize the vast knowledge of the Western world. Earlier the new government had informed the powers that it intended to respect the treaties and that it planned audiences with the emperor for the leading foreign diplomats. In its final form, the *Charter Oath* reads as follows:

1. Deliberative assemblies shall be established on an extensive scale, and all measures of government shall be decided by public opinion.
2. All classes, high and low, shall unite in vigorously carrying out the plan of the government.
3. All classes of people shall be allowed to fulfill their just aspirations so that there may be no discontent.
4. Uncivilized customs of former times shall be broken through, and everything shall be based on just and equitable principles of nature.
5. Knowledge shall be sought throughout the world so that the welfare of the empire may be promoted.

On April 7, 1868, Sanjo Sanetomi read the *Oath* aloud in the presence of the emperor and other dignitaries; in a brief ceremony that followed, the court nobles and daimyo who were present affixed their seals to a document in which they swore to uphold the *Oath*. Its proclamation was to coincide with the attack against the shogun's forces at Edo, with the emperor, at least nominally, in command.

In June, 1868, with Tokugawa resistance largely crushed, the government issued a new plan of organization called the *Seitaisho*. This political reorganization, proclaimed as the fulfillment of the *Charter Oath*, clearly demonstrates the determination of the samurai leaders of Satsuma and Choshu to consolidate their positions of power. These men made a general claim for the supreme authority of the imperial government by declaring that each han was subordinate to it. On the other hand, since they were aware of the need to maintain the support of the han, particularly Satsuma and Choshu, they continued to bestow high offices on a few daimyo and made no move against the daimyo in general as hereditary rulers of their han. The nomenclature of the government was still modeled on the ancient imperial system, but organization was in theory based on the doctrine of separation of powers among the executive, legislative, and judiciary. While all authority was actually centered in the council of state (*dajokan*), it was in theory divided among its constituent bodies. The executive included the administrative departments of Shinto, war, finance, and foreign affairs, and a council in which the chief minister of state (*dajodaijin*), his deputies (*dainagon*), and the key samurai leaders, e.g., Kido and Okubo, met to decide matters of policy.* The legislative branch was represented by a bicameral assembly (*giseikan*), while the judiciary was confined to the department of justice, which was responsible for the administration of the court system.

The actual operation of the system resulted in the concentration of power in the upper house (*jokyoku*) of the assembly, which had comprehensive powers including "the establishment of the constitution; the enactment of

* Additional departments were later added: home affairs in the spring of 1869, public works in the winter of 1870, and education in September, 1871.

laws; the decisions on questions of policy, the selection of men to fill the offices of the three higher ranks, and supreme judicial power; the conclusion of treaties; and the power to make peace and war." The centralization of authority was carried a step further, since the upper house was usually manipulated by its samurai members—especially Kido, Okubo, Saigo, Goto, Yuri, and Fukuoka—who also had fairly effective control over departmental administration, since the heads of departments were their colleagues in the upper house and they were also able to appoint samurai friends to the office of deputy minister or to some other key position within each department. Since the ministers were usually court nobles or daimyo who were mere figureheads, the samurai appointees were able to manage the actual workings of the administrative system. Thus, for all practical purposes, a small group of samurai intellectuals with administrative experience in their han was able to control the government. The upper house functioned until July, 1869, when its duties were taken over by an executive committee of the dajokan, a further step in the concentration of power. This change coincided with the government's success in breaking down the local authority of the han.

The lower house (*kakyoku*) of the assembly, on the other hand, was nothing more than an advisory body to reflect han opinion and to satisfy the political demands of those samurai who continued to advocate some form of government in which all the han would be represented. At first it consisted exclusively of samurai delegates from the han, but soon representation was extended to the cities of Kyoto, Osaka, and Edo (shortly thereafter the seat of government was moved from Kyoto to Edo, which was renamed Tokyo, or "Eastern Capital") as well as to former Tokugawa territories, which were being reorganized into prefectures under the administration of the central government. The basic functions of the lower house, as determined by the upper house, were confined to mere discussion of national affairs and to the settlement of disputes between the han. The lower house actually met several times, but the limited nature of its power and the inexperience of its members kept it insignificant politically. It was given no encouragement by the samurai leaders of Satsuma and Choshu, who desired a strong government unhampered by legislative limitations. Okubo Toshimichi especially felt that the useless discussions of a deliberative assembly would ultimately hinder the workings of the government and the plans of its leaders. The meetings of the lower house were soon abandoned, and in the autumn of 1868 it was officially abolished by an imperial decree.

The assembly idea, however, persisted among the leaders of the lesser han. Yamanouchi Toyoshige, daimyo of Tosa, proposed (October 26, 1868) a system of indirect representation through the establishment of local assemblies which would in turn send representatives to a national body. The government once again reluctantly agreed, but its official spokesman, Iwakura Tomomi, stipulated that the principle that the emperor have the final decision in affairs of state must in no way be abrogated. The government appointed an investigative committee which was headed by Yamanouchi and included two young officials, Sameshima Naonobu and Mori Arinori, both of whom had been sent to Great Britain and the United States for study by Satsuma han. After a long series of discussions, highlighted by frequent conflicts of opinion, the committee finally proposed the convocation of another assembly and submitted a draft law for its organization. The draft was approved by the government in January, 1869.

The new assembly, the *kogisho*, was convoked in the spring of 1869. Its members, representing the various han, were selected by the imperial court from among han officials and were appointed by the central government for a term of four years. Half of the total membership was to be chosen every two years, and no limit was placed on the number of terms that a member was eligible to serve. Its chief function was the enactment of laws, and all bills required at least a three-fifths majority to pass. To facilitate its work, which was organized on a committee system, the assembly was granted the power to summon administrative officials for questioning.

The life of the kogisho was confined to but one session, in which a variety of bills were introduced and debated, e.g., the abolition of forced loans, the abolition of limitations upon interest charges, the abolition of *harakiri*, and the abolition of the samurai privilege of wearing two swords, except for civil and military officials. The kogisho was useful to the government as a sounding-board, but most of its members were insufficiently experienced in parliamentary practice to carry on legislative discussion and debate, and much prolonged and useless arguing took place.

A few months later (August 18, 1869) the kogisho was replaced by another assembly, called the *shugiin*. Its regulations were similar to those of its predecessor, but its functions and powers were further limited by a provision that the small executive committee of the dajokan would propose measures for its consideration. The nature of the bills discussed, however, tended to become more important, because the government desired to ascertain han opinion regarding bolder reform measures. For example, the government introduced bills calling for the expansion of the army and navy, the establishment of an administrative election law, reform of the education system, and the abolition of the han; but when the discussions of the shugiin proved to be inconclusive, the government ordered the representatives to return to their han. After October, 1870, there were no more meetings, and finally, in 1873, the shugiin was formally abolished.

The failure of these assemblies to become an integral part of the government can be explained in large part by the lack of encouragement given them by the samurai leaders of Satsuma and Choshu, who were intent on establishing an efficient centralized government. Confronted by considerations of national defense as well as serious national economic and social problems, these men desired a government capable of reforming and strengthening the Japanese state. That they found it expedient to turn to the examples of the absolutist administrations of their own han was only natural; moreover, leaders like Okubo tended to regard the assemblies as useless organs or as mechanisms which political opponents might use advantageously. Until the abolition of the han in 1871, however, the assemblies did help to maintain the stability of the government by satisfying the demands for broad representation, but thereafter the assemblies were of no appreciable use to the government and were replaced by organs more closely compatible with the workings of a centralized political system.

It is clear that the demand for a representative assembly had no mass basis in these early years of the Meiji period. The tradition of authoritarian government, based on a rigid class and family system, had left the people of Japan with no equalitarian ideals and little sense of individual rights. Japanese law had no provision for rights as well as duties, and even the feudal bond between daimyo and samurai was one-sided in favor of the former. There was no mass understanding of the principle that government be responsible to public opinion. The demand for a national assembly actually represented the interests of han like Tosa, which feared the domination of Satsuma and Choshu samurai like Okubo, Saigo, and Kido; and the membership of these early assemblies was made up of samurai who had little experience in politics and whose interests were more local than national.

16   The Abolition of Feudalism

The han had remained intact after the Meiji Restoration because the objective of the coalition of the western han had been limited to the destruction of the Tokugawa shogunate. The samurai who became the leaders of the new imperial regime knew that they were dependent on the continued support of the han; consequently, they made no attempt to interfere with han administrations. Before long, because of the pressure of problems national in scope, they became aware of the need to subordinate the han to a strong central government and ultimately to abolish them, but they moved slowly and cautiously to insure domestic peace and to prevent the coalition of supporting han from dissolving. That their objectives were accomplished peacefully is an indication of the able statesmanship of men like Kido, Saigo, Okubo, and their Tosa and Hizen colleagues, who utilized their positions as influential retainers of their daimyo to persuade the western han to accept their program.

The Abolition of the Han

The reorganization of the administration of the Tokugawa lands in June, 1868, was the starting point in the creation of a unitary political system. The new imperial government, which had confiscated these lands during the civil war, converted them into prefectures (*ken*) and at the same time organized the cities of Osaka, Kyoto, and Tokyo as special administrative districts called *fu*. It appointed governors, among whom were outstanding samurai like Ito Hirobumi and Yuri Kimimasa, to manage the affairs of these units. In an area comprising approximately one-fourth of the entire country the imperial regime was able to establish completely subservient local governments. The rest of the country remained divided among the han, which continued to exercise local autonomy.

During this period the leaders of the central government were beginning to discuss the need to abolish the han in order to centralize political power under the supreme authority of the emperor. As early as 1867 the samurai Terashima Munemori proposed to the daimyo of Satsuma "that to make loyalty to the emperor a complete reality the fiefs and their inhabitants must be restored to the jurisdiction of the imperial court and everyone accept the status of a common subject." Kido Koin suggested to Iwakura Tomomi and Sanjo Sanetomi in early 1868 that the daimyo "should be caused to surrender their subjects all at one time," and, "immediately unifying the energies of the empire thereby, we must utilize the resources of the entire country, including naturally the armed forces and government, to strengthen the nation." Although the government received many memorials urging the conversion of the han into prefectures by imperial order, Kido and his colleagues did not think it wise to attempt an outright confiscation because the success of such a venture would depend ultimately upon the attitude of the daimyo and their advisers. They preferred to work through han administrations in an effort to persuade the more powerful daimyo to restore their lands, in theory at least, to the emperor. Kido won over Lord Mori of Choshu, and Okubo was similarly successful with Lord Shimazu of Satsuma. The consent of the daimyo of Tosa and Hizen was secured through the joint efforts of Okubo, Itagaki Taisuke, and Hirosawa Sanetomi.

These efforts culminated in the March 5, 1869, memorial, signed by the daimyo of Satsuma, Choshu, Tosa, and Hizen—the four western han—in which these four lords formally recognized the supremacy of the central government and offered their lands to the emperor. This document, thought to have been written by Kido, stated the attitude of the leaders of the imperial government that "there must be one central authority which must be preserved intact" and added that "all laws, decrees, and military regulations, extending even to military dress and accoutrement, will be issued by the central government, so that all matters of state will be decided by one and the same authority."

On the following day the dajokan issued a statement approving the request of the four western han, and soon other daimyo submitted similar petitions and received the same reply. But when the central government began to consider whether it should proceed further toward the abolition of the han, it was divided between two opinions. A minority advocated the immediate extension of the prefectural system to the han, but the majority, including Kido, Okubo, and Iwakura, felt that the government was not yet strong enough to carry out such a measure, especially in face of the potential opposition of large numbers of samurai who still dreamed of a return to their ideal of the good old days of feudalism. The majority preferred to maintain the han as territorial units, with the daimyo and their administrators as imperial officials. It correctly concluded that the daimyo for the most part had proposed the return of their lands only as a formal gesture of recognition of the supremacy of the emperor and that they expected only a nominal change in local administration. Moreover, the discussions of the kogisho, used in this case to sound out opinion, indicated that han representatives opposed the establishment of prefectures.

In an imperial decree issued July 25, 1869, the central government announced the policy it proposed to follow. The surrender of land by the four western han and others was officially accepted, and the remainder of the han were ordered to do the same. At the same time, the daimyo were appointed as han governors and were to have a hereditary annual allowance of one-tenth of their former income; as imperial officials they were expected to reside in Tokyo three months each year and to take part in a special convocation once every three years, and their senior councilors would reside in Tokyo six months each year and would serve as members of the assembly. All samurai were given a fixed income corresponding to a fraction of their former stipends, and those who still held fiefs from daimyo were required to surrender their holdings and accept a fixed income. The central government assumed the financial obligation of maintaining the former feudal aristocracy, but for its part it had secured control of the power to tax.

Throughout 1869 and 1870 the leaders of the central government continued to discuss the status of the han, since it was increasingly apparent that some change was necessary. On April 20, 1870, Kido, Okubo, and two other Choshu samurai, Inouye Kaoru and Yamagata Aritomo, met secretly with Iwakura and Sanjo and decided to replace the han with prefectures. In their view it was impossible for the central government to direct han administrations effectively so long as the daimyo and their retainers remained as officials; moreover, the people as a whole acted as if they still lived under the feudal system. There was also a conspicuous tendency for the han to lag behind the prefectures in efficiency of administration, and in some cases the larger han purposely opposed reforms ordered by the central government. On the other hand, many of the smaller han were unable to maintain a stable financial position and either petitioned for relief or became prefectures voluntarily, with their daimyo and samurai resigning administrative control in return for a guarantee of their incomes.

Whether all the han would be abolished peacefully depended in large part on the attitudes of the daimyo of Satsuma and Choshu and their advisers. Throughout most of 1870 the leaders of the central government, particularly Okubo and Kido, who were themselves of Satsuma and Choshu background, were unable to win the consent of these important daimyo. But early in 1871, they conferred directly with Lords Shimazu and Mori and succeeded. And shortly thereafter they also won over the daimyo of Tosa.

Since they were still uncertain of the reaction of the other han, in April the samurai leaders of the central government had the emperor order Satsuma, Choshu, and Tosa to provide an armed force which in total strength would number ten thousand men. Finally, they issued a decree in August in the name of the emperor which stated simply, "The han are abolished, and prefectures are established in their places." The central government then quickly removed the daimyo from their posts as governors and ordered them to live in Tokyo, and it proceeded to apply the prefectural system to the entire country.

The personal diplomacy of the samurai leaders of the central government goes a long way in explaining the consent of Satsuma, Choshu, and Tosa to the application of the prefectural system. But other factors were at work as well. These han were increasingly guided by a sense of national prestige that had developed from the feeling of loyalty to the emperor and the desire to meet the foreign powers on terms of equality, and they were fearful that another civil war would result from an attempt by any one of them to seize power. All the han, moreover, had specific economic advantages to gain by consenting to the policy of the central government. As early as 1869 the former daimyo had been granted one-tenth of their normal revenues and at the same time were relieved of the expenses of administration and samurai stipends; and in 1871, when their annual income payments were commuted into bonds issued by the government, which also assumed much of their personal indebtedness, many of them used their capitalized pensions to buy large tracts of land and to enter business as large-scale investors. Lastly, of great importance was the fact that many younger samurai, particularly in Satsuma and Choshu, desired a national government in which they could find employment for their talents.

Many samurai, however, did not fare so well as their daimyo. Their annual incomes, the payment of which had been assumed by the government in 1869, were in general computed at one-fourth of their former allotments, and in individual cases reductions were more severe, ranging from a maximum of

250 koku for 9,000–10,000-koku stipend recipients to a minimum of 8 koku for 30–40-koku recipients. And under the pressure of financial difficulties the government was finally forced to repudiate the pension scheme, which was costing 25 per cent of its annual budget. In December, 1873, it announced a voluntary system of pension commutation to encourage samurai, paid off in bonds and cash, to use their capital to enter business and buy land. When this voluntary plan failed, the government in 1876 put into operation a compulsory commutation scheme, by which its annual payments to the samurai were halved, and a claim without term was reduced to a twenty-year lump-sum obligation. For thousands of samurai this settlement did not provide sufficient income for the support of their families.

The Unitary Political System

After the abolition of the han in August, 1871, the central government began an immediate reorganization of the system of local administration in order to consolidate its control over the entire nation. The han were all converted into prefectures, and by amalgamation the number of prefectures was reduced from 302 in August to 72 by the end of the year. Prefectural administration was entrusted to governors appointed by Tokyo. In 1873 the department of home affairs was re-established, and in 1874 it was given control over the entire local government system. The power of this ministry, headed by Okubo Toshimichi, helps to account for the peculiarly centralized nature of Japanese government. Local authorities had to bring every matter of importance to the attention of the department of home affairs and receive instruction as to what action to take. The prefectures were divided into districts (*gun*), cities (*ku*), towns (*machi*), and villages (*mura*), the officials of which were appointed by the prefectural governor and were responsible to him for the local administration.

The abolition of the han paved the way for the reorganization of the central government by its samurai leaders according to a modification of the separation-of-powers principle. The dajokan was divided into three boards: the central board (*seiin*), an executive body presided over by the dajodaijin; the right board (*uin*), which included only the heads of administrative departments; and the left board (*sain*), a legislative branch that replaced the shugiin.

As the supreme organ of the government the seiin was entrusted with the general management of the affairs of state, which it discussed and settled in the presence of the emperor. Besides the dajodaijin, its members included the dainagon—later replaced by the minister of the right (*udaijin*) and the minister of the left (*sadaijin*)—and an undetermined number of councilors (*sangi*), an office monopolized by a few samurai leaders. At first, at the suggestion of Okubo, only Saigo and Kido, representing Satsuma and Choshu interests, respectively, were appointed as sangi; however, two other samurai, Itagaki Taisuke and Okuma Shigenobu, soon thereafter joined their ranks in recognition of the support of Tosa and Hizen and as a symbol of the theoretical equality of the four great han.

The uin, whose members included the ministers of departments and their deputies, drafted departmental ordinances and regulations, handled the collective business of the departments, and discussed general administrative problems. The following departments were included in the government by the 1871 reorganization: foreign affairs, finance, war, public works, imperial household, education, Shinto, and justice.* In theory the uin was a separate body in the dajokan, but in practice it became a mere adjunct of the seiin, since there was a tendency for the court nobles and the daimyo to be replaced as ministers of departments and deputy ministers by samurai leaders who were concurrently councilors of the seiin. Thus by a system of dual control the samurai leaders were able to maintain effective supervision over both the formation of policy and its administration.

The legislative functions of the government were in theory vested in the sain, whose members were appointed by the emperor to represent public opinion; but because of strict limitations upon its powers and functions, the sain was nothing more than an advisory body under the complete control of the seiin. All measures that it considered were proposed by the seiin, which also had the power to appoint and dismiss its members in the name of the emperor. That this body was created at all can only be explained by the desire of the samurai leaders of the government to have in existence an assembly which they could use to counter complaints against the concentration of power in their hands. It was for this reason that its basic function after 1873 was to discuss the need for a written constitution.

The abolition of the han and the concentration of political power in the hands of an oligarchy were accomplished in the name of the emperor. The oligarchs were determined to create a strong national state, and for this purpose the institution of the emperor was an important asset. They were determined to transfer the emphasis on loyalty in *bushido* ("way of the warrior") and in Japanese Confucianism into a patriotism based on loyalty to the emperor. Thus the government decided on a policy of revitalizing Shinto at the expense of Buddhism, which had dominated the religious scene throughout the Tokugawa period. That aspect of Shinto which emphasized the sun goddess and the divinity of the Japanese emperor and people was given the status of a state religion. A Shinto ministry was established in the government,

---

* The following changes occurred in the next few years: the department of Shinto, abolished in April, 1872, was replaced by the department of religion, which in November, 1872, merged with the department of education; the department of war was abolished in February, 1872, and was replaced by the department of the army and the department of the navy; in November, 1873, the department of home affairs was re-established, having been formerly merged with the department of finance.

and Shinto shrines, which in many cases had fallen under the domination of Buddhist priests, were organized into various grades and ranks under state control. When the government established the department of religion and education in 1872, it also converted Shinto priests into officials supported by local administrative offices; and in an effort to replace the Buddhist parish system, the emperor decreed that each Japanese subject must register at a Shinto shrine.

By these measures the government hoped to inculcate greater respect for the Shinto deities and a more whole-hearted acceptance of "high moral principles" so that the people would serve the emperor with deeper feelings of loyalty. Although these policies stimulated some anti-Buddhist outbursts, the government had no intention of letting the separate existence of Shinto develop into a general anti-Buddhist movement. Religious freedom was accepted as an important aspect of modernization, and in 1873 even the proscription against Christianity was lifted. The popular faith continued to be a mixture of Buddhism and Shinto, but all Japanese were indoctrinated to some extent in the religion of the state.

After the Meiji Restoration, one of the principal aims of the samurai leaders of the imperial regime was to develop a national army for purposes of political stability and national defense. In 1870 they sent Yamagata Aritomo and Saigo Tsugumichi to Europe to study military organization, and in April, 1871, preliminary to the abolition of the han, they established a national guard of troops from Satsuma, Choshu, and Tosa and, at the same time, ordered the disbandment of han military forces. After the abolition of the han, the leaders of the government, now for all practical purposes an oligarchy, moved toward the creation of a national army based on the French system, having rejected Yamagata's advocacy of the German system. In February, 1872, the war department was divided into the department of the army and the department of the navy, and in the following year universal conscription was proclaimed.

Conscription represented a triumph for Yamagata (Choshu), the first army minister, since both Saigo Takamori (Satsuma) and Itagaki Taisuke (Tosa) preferred a volunteer army. Yamagata had not the slightest doubt concerning the fighting qualities of the Japanese peasants, for he had seen Choshu build a militia out of raw recruits from all walks of life. Under the new system, which reached its final form in 1883, all able-bodied males seventeen years of age and over were to be conscripted for compulsory military service for a period of three years, after which they were to remain in the first reserve for four years, the second reserve for five years, and the standby reserve until they reached the age of forty. The conscription law did provide for the exemption of teachers, students, heirs, only sons, acting heads of households, only grandsons, and anyone who paid 270 yen, but these exemptions were later abolished. The country was divided into six military districts,* each with

---

* Tokyo, Sendai, Nagaoya, Osaka, Hiroshima, and Kumamoto.

a garrison of 40,000 men at peacetime strength and 70,000 at wartime strength.*

The government also began to develop a modern navy and as a first step created a naval academy staffed largely by British officers. The Japanese navy had to rely on foreign shipyards for its warships, and from a force of 17 vessels, totaling slightly over 13,000 tons, in 1873 it expanded by the eve of the Sino-Japanese War to one of 28 vessels, totaling 57,600 tons, and an additional 24 torpedo boats.

For some time the new army of Japan was not a popular institution. Many samurai were outraged at the destruction of a monopoly they had enjoyed for centuries, and, to add insult to injury, they were forced to serve in the army along with commoners. The peasants, on the other hand, objected to military service since they felt that their labor was needed on the land. In fact, peasant opposition had forced postponement of earlier attempts to inaugurate conscription. For a time the government was embarrassed by its inability to secure the necessary quota of conscripts. In 1875 the combined strength of the standing army was only 31,400 men plus 42,000 reserves, and after 1877 only 15,000 men were drafted each year. This situation was not corrected until the government conducted a nationwide educational campaign through the new prefectural administrations.

Social and Economic Reforms

In these early years of the Meiji period the central government abolished feudal customs and practices that tended to obstruct or retard national development. By 1872 the rigid class system based on occupation and birth had given way to the practice of legal equality. Every Japanese was granted the freedom to select his occupation and place of residence, and this was true even in the case of social outcasts like the *eta*, who engaged in butchery and other "unclean" occupations and who for centuries had lived under segregation. Although new distinctions like *kazoku* (peer), *shizoku* (samurai), *sotsu* (foot soldier), and *heimin* (commoner) were used for purposes of family registration, they were historical and genealogical identifications rather than distinctions conferring legal privileges.

Many social reforms were designed to destroy the anachronistic privileges enjoyed by samurai. In the autumn of 1871 the government issued a decree making the wearing of swords optional, and a few days later it revoked the samurai right to cut down a commoner for real or fancied insults. In June, 1872, the samurai lost the right to have two names (a popular name and a dignified name given at birth by the father), while the commoners were granted the right to adopt surnames. In 1873 the time-honored practice of vendetta was abolished, and in 1876 the discontinuance of sword-wearing was made mandatory.

---

* Later, in 1886, the garrisons were replaced by divisions, as follows: two at Tokyo and one each at the five other headquarters.

271

On the other hand, the government did much to assist samurai. It appointed many of them to positions in the central and local administrations, and at one time more than 80 per cent of its employees—bureaucrats, policemen, and teachers—came from that class. It inaugurated land-development programs, the largest of which was on the island of Hokkaido, to encourage thousands of samurai to enter agricultural pursuits, and it even went so far as to establish training centers to develop occupational skills and to provide loans for business opportunities. Despite this help, many samurai found it difficult to adjust to the new times, and many were disappointed at their failure to get official posts or to receive patronage. A good number tried their hand at business or farming, but generally they failed and lost everything, including their pension bonds.

Discontent mounted among that large number of samurai who had participated in the restoration movement in the hope that it would revitalize the feudal order. They dreamed of a return to a warrior-dominated agricultural society and never accepted the policies of the new government. Some were spurred to assassinate the innovators,* and ultimately their discontent expressed itself more broadly in a number of uprisings that culminated in the Satsuma Rebellion (1877).

It would be incorrect to assume that the establishment of the legal equality of classes changed the traditional social attitudes. The feeling of social hierarchy remained strong, and social position continued to correspond to official position and, to a lesser extent, to wealth. Although feudal class barriers were abolished, there was no strong equalitarian trend in the early years of the Meiji period. The case of the *eta* is a good example of this. These outcasts, numbering approximately 400,000 in 1871, found little change in their actual social and economic status. A new designation, "the new commoners," was widely used to identify them, and socially they were not conceded practical equality. Intermarriage with them was frowned upon, and many social functions were closed to them. Their economic activities were limited to their traditional occupations and to handicrafts, tenant farming, peddling, and day labor.

The individual, moreover, generally remained subordinate to the interests of the family. The Confucian notion of status and Confucian virtues, reinforced by feudal notions of loyalty and obligation, regulated behavior not only within the family but also in economic and political organizations. Relationships between landowner and tenant, manager and clerk, capitalist and worker were all imitative of the family pattern with its emphases on paternalism, inequality, and obligation. Later, when political parties were formed, relationships between party leaders and subordinates had the same characteristics.

---

* For example, Omura Masujiro (Choshu), one of the founders of modern military thought in Japan, was a victim of his own clansmen in 1869; Yokoi Shonan (Kumamoto) was killed in the same year because of his political views; and Hirosawa Sanetomi (Choshu) was murdered in February, 1871.

It is also important to note that male dominance continued as a basic feature of Japanese society; for example, the attempted liberation of geisha and prostitutes in 1871 proved to be a useless gesture and had no effect, since there was universal acceptance of the double standard of morality for men and women.

The rapid industrialization of Japan became the primary economic objective of the oligarchs. They considered it a prerequisite not only to the creation of a strong Japan but also to the solution of a number of economic problems, especially the pressure of deficit balances in foreign trade and the devastating effect of imported manufactured goods on handicraft production. Private capital was unable to undertake an industrial program of the magnitude contemplated by these men. Denied profits from overseas adventures and colonialism and limited to a market restricted by the overlapping of agriculture and household industry, it was simply too weak, and available funds were largely in the hands of former guild merchants, many of whom lacked the understanding and willingness to participate in a program of industrialization. Most of the merchants who did not succumb to bankruptcy —which was common under the chaotic conditions of these years—were cautious and, for the most part, unwilling to adopt new ideas, learn new techniques, and take the great risks that industrialization demanded. The wealthy urban merchants preferred to remain in trade and banking operations, especially in the safe and lucrative field of government loans, while their rural counterparts had no inducement to leave the countryside, where profitable trade, usury, and, above all, land rents averaging from 50 to 60 per cent of the tenant's crop prevented capital from flowing into industrial channels.

The government was compelled to develop heavy industry and communications and to encourage private capital to expand consumer industries. After 1870 it brought under its control arsenals, foundries, mines, and shipyards owned by the bakufu and the various han.* The shortage of capital forced the government to accept some foreign loans, although its policy was to hold these to a minimum. In the winter of 1869 it negotiated a loan from Great Britain, and work was begun on the Tokyo-Yokohama Railway line early in 1870 under British supervision. Later, construction of a main railway line for the island of Honshu was initiated. Although private capital ultimately came into the railway field, the government continued to operate numerous lines. In the field of communications it inaugurated the postal service, telegraph service, and later the telephone.

The government also established model factories, supplied technical assistance, and granted generous loans and subsidies to a few enterprising individuals and companies. For example, the government established silk-reeling factories at Maebashi and Tomioka on French and Italian models, the

---

* For example, the bakufu's foundry and shipyards at Yokosuka, its Nagasaki iron foundries, and Satsuma's shipyards at Kagoshima were taken over and developed by the government until they reached a high level of technical efficiency.

Shirakawa White Tile Works, the Fukugawa Cement Works, and the Senji Woolen Web Factory. Some of these projects necessitated the hiring of foreign advisers and the sponsoring of the technical education of young Japanese abroad. Foreign experts were welcome so long as they were needed, but as soon as possible they were replaced by Japanese graduates of foreign or national technical schools.

The great modern Japanese family trusts like Mitsui and Mitsubishi had their origin in these years. The Mitsui Company, which derived from the wealthy merchant and banking firm of the Tokugawa period, was an underwriter of government loans and through its commercial subsidiary, the Mitsui Trading Company, acted as the purchasing and sales agent of the government in foreign countries. Through its close relationship with the leaders of the government, especially Inouye Kaoru of Choshu, it obtained possession of various han and bakufu properties, including what was to become the important Miike Coal Mining Company. The Mitsubishi Company was founded by the young samurai Iwasaki Yotaro, who had been active earlier in Tosa trade associations. The foundation of its great subsidiary, the Nippon Yusen Kaisha (Japan Steamship Company), was laid in 1874 when it acted as the supply agent of the government during the Formosan expedition and its small fleet of ships was supplemented by the addition of thirteen steamers purchased abroad by the government.

The creation of a national army and the beginnings of industrialization strained the financial resources of the government; and since Japan was predominantly agricultural and lacked tariff autonomy under the "unequal treaties," the land tax remained the major source of revenue. A system of private landownership with the right of alienation formed the basis of a new tax structure in which there were no unexpected fluctuations resulting from variations in the size of the harvest. In October, 1871, the government decreed the right of private ownership and after a land survey, carried out in 1872, issued title deeds to peasant proprietors. At the same time it recognized the claims of local landlords, who had been acquiring land by mortgage and forced sale, and abolished restrictions on the amount of land that could be held by any one individual. These measures consolidated the position of the landlord class, and when the government guaranteed at least part of the pre-restoration debts of the old feudal aristocracy to landlord-usurers, the added capital was usually invested in commerce, industry, or the acquisition of more land.

Locally the activities of commerce, industry, banking, and landlordism continued to be interlocking. The new land system, especially the characteristic of the right of sale and purchase, also tended to stimulate the penetration of urban capital into rural areas. In the early 1870's about 20 per cent of Japan's arable land was worked by tenant farmers, who usually rented fragmentary strips of land from a number of landlords. The typical landlord, moreover, leased small and scattered holdings to a large number of tenants. Finally, in 1873, the government decreed that the land tax was to be paid in money by the holder of the title deed at the rate of 3 per cent of the assessed value of the land. This actually amounted to about 35 per cent of the value of an average crop, which was comparable to the high rates maintained during the Tokugawa period. The government stated frequently, however, that it thought the land tax could be reduced to approximately 1 per cent as soon as taxation could be levied on other commodities. This promise was never kept, and throughout the modern period the land tax provided the greatest share of taxes for the government. In the period from 1875 to 1879, 80 per cent of the taxes collected were derived from agriculture; this figure declined in subsequent years, but it was generally over 60 per cent.

The new landownership and tax systems did not lighten the difficulties of the peasant. Confronted with a fixed tax obligation and, as agriculture became increasingly commercialized, vexed by problems of marketing and price fluctuation, the peasant found it difficult to keep title to his small holdings. Moreover, since the average peasant was usually forced by circumstances to sell his rice as soon as possible after the harvest, he was exposed to the perils of price fluctuations which did not similarly affect the landlords, who could store rice in granaries and sell at opportune times. Peasant handicrafts, vitally necessary to supplement agricultural income, were also facing new competition from manufactured goods, both foreign and domestic. This new hazard was lessened to some extent by the demand for silkworm eggs and silk as a result of the outbreak of silkworm disease in Europe, and between 1868 and 1883 exports of both items doubled. On the other hand, crop failures, illness, and social obligations like weddings and funerals took their toll.

The old self-sufficiency of the peasant also declined because of the loss of village common lands. During the Tokugawa period the feudal authorities had permitted the peasant to use meadow and woodland for grazing and for the collection of fodder, fertilizer, fuel, and timber in return for "thank-you money," but after the land survey most of the common land became state property and was sold cheaply to daimyo and landlords. The peasant was now forced to buy those commodities which he had formerly obtained so easily. Year after year there was a constant increase in concentration of landownership; and population pressure, since industrialization could not absorb the surplus, caused insecurity of tenure and consequent rack-renting. The peasant also had difficulty in adjusting to many of the reforms of the early years of the Meiji period. Conscription, introduction of the Western calendar, legalization of Christianity, vaccination, and the establishment of schools were upsetting to the life of the peasant community.

All these factors help to explain why peasant rebellions were still common after the restoration. In the first decade of the Meiji period there were over two hundred uprisings, each of which was suppressed by the power of the state.

17   *The Emergence of Factional Struggles*

The samurai leaders of the new central government had co-operated among themselves in order to carry out the abolition of the han and to implement a number of economic and social reforms; shortly after 1871, however, this unity broke down, and they tended to divide into factions. The issues that led to division were (1) whether or not to engage in foreign war for expansion and (2) whether or not to establish a representative system of government. The differences of opinion regarding these issues cannot be judged merely on the merits of particular policies, for often the personal ambitions of the various factional leaders complicated the situation. The war issue was settled in favor of those who advocated the priority of domestic reform, and this result contributed to the discontent of large numbers of former samurai and to rebellion by them. The second issue was not settled in any clear-cut manner, but it also had the effect of creating an antigovernment movement—the so-called "democratic movement."

The War Issue

The desire to expand overseas was a significant element in the Meiji Restoration. As early as the 1850's a school of thought had developed among some samurai intellectuals which considered foreign expansion a correlate of both the antibakufu movement and the achievement of national power. Some of the leaders of the restoration movement were schooled in this point of view, and soon after their successes against the bakufu they made Korea the target of their overseas ambitions. They had strong grass-roots support among large numbers of discontented samurai who, although they did not think in terms of the long-range interests of the state, wanted satisfaction in foreign war. As early as 1869 the imperial government made several attempts to open normal relations with Korea; and when Korea stubbornly refused to comply, the intensity of the expansionist sentiment in Japan increased.

The crisis over Korea began to come to a head when several of the important leaders of the central government were abroad. In December, 1871, Iwakura, Kido, Okubo, and many of their subordinates departed on a travel mission to the United States and Europe. They planned to initiate preliminary discussions for revision of the unequal treaties in accordance with the terms of the American treaty of 1858, and at the same time they intended to observe and study conditions in the countries they visited. Since the mission would be abroad for a long period, Okubo and Kido were concerned about problems that might arise at home in their absence, and they secured from their colleagues, Saigo, Itagaki, Goto, Eto Shimpei, and Soejima Taneomi, a pledge not to institute any major reforms or make any new political appointments at high levels. Should some action be imperative, the leaders at home were to act only after consulting the group abroad. Despite this gentlemen's agreement, several major domestic measures, including the appointment of new councilors, the land-tax reform, the military conscription law, and a banking law, were decreed without such consultation. These actions created feelings of suspicion and jealousy between the leaders at home and those abroad, and when Saigo pressed for war with Korea, the mission made plans to return home.

Saigo, who had not gone along with most of the revolutionary changes that followed the Meiji Restoration, felt that war with Korea would provide a satisfactory means of employing large numbers of former samurai who wanted to regain their old social standing. He was able to persuade his colleagues in the dajokan to send him as head of a mission to negotiate the establishment of diplomatic and trade relations with Korea. He felt that the mission would almost certainly be insulted or even attacked, thereby providing a just cause for war. The emperor approved of the plan but only on condition that no action be taken until Iwakura's return from abroad. Saigo waited, confident that he had strong support among other samurai leaders in the dajokan and in other offices of the central government; for example, Itagaki Taisuke and Goto Shojiro, both former Tosa samurai, formed what amounted to a political clique which still demanded some form of representative government and which saw in the war issue a way to weaken the power of Okubo and Kido. Eto Shimpei, a former samurai from Hizen, saw the social need for war, and Soejima Taneomi, another former samurai from Hizen, who was a leading official in the department of foreign affairs, had long been an outspoken champion of expansion.

By late spring, 1873, opposition to war began to take form. Okubo returned home in May and urged the government to await consultation with Iwakura before making any final decision; and when Kido returned in July, he added the weight of his support to Okubo's position. Finally, Iwakura arrived in September and in a dajokan session on October 14 urged the priority of domestic reform and modernization over military expansion. His arguments were vigorously supported by Okubo and Kido, but the session came to a close with heated expressions of disagreement, some of which dramatically divided han groups. In the case of Satsuma, Saigo and Okubo stood opposed to each other, and in the case of Hizen, Eto and Soejima clashed with Okuma Shigenobu. In the dajokan meeting on the following day Saigo won majority support for his plan. Two days later (October 17) Kido, Okubo, and Okuma submitted their resignations in protest, while Iwakura, professing illness, refused to attend further sessions of the dajokan and announced his intention of resigning. Saigo's last hurdle was to secure imperial approval through Sanjo Sanetomi, the dajodaijin; but Sanjo, caught between the two factions and in a state of nervous exhaustion, resigned. This proved to be the turning point, for Iwakura was appointed acting dajodaijin and was able to use his prestige to win the emperor to his point of view. Finally, on October 23 the emperor ordered Iwakura to proceed with a program of extensive domestic reform, and he refused to accept the resignations of Kido, Okubo, and Okuma, among others.

The leaders of the war party, outwitted by the astute political maneuvering of Iwakura and his group, found it impossible to remain in the government. Saigo, Itagaki, Goto, and Eto resigned from the dajokan, and Soejima left the foreign office. Kido and Okubo, leaders of the peace party, proceeded to consolidate their power by appointing a number of their followers as councilors. These included Ito Hirobumi (Choshu), Okuma Shigenobu (Hizen), Oki Takato (Hizen), Yamagata Aritomo (Choshu), Katsu Awa (former bakufu official), and Terashima Munemori (Satsuma). Moreover, since it was decided that councilors could serve concurrently as ministers of departments, Okubo became minister of home affairs; Kido, education; Okuma, finance; Oki, justice; Katsu, navy; Ito, public works and industry; Terashima, foreign affairs; and Yamagata, army.

Despite Kido's resignation in 1874 in protest against the Formosan expedition, which he criticized as a sop to the war party and as a diversion of national attention from domestic politics, the Satsuma-Choshu balance within the government was maintained because of the abilities and new prestige of Ito and Yamagata. Choshu influence was also strong within the army, since the resignation of Saigo and many of the Satsuma officers forced its reorganization by Yamagata, thereby paving the way for its domination by the Choshu clique in subsequent decades. On the other hand, Okubo held the key post of minister of home affairs, which enabled him to dominate the entire system of local government, and Satsuma officers remained in control of the navy.

The Assembly Issue

The issue of war with Korea was closely related to demands for political reform. While the Iwakura mission was abroad, Itagaki, Goto, and their Tosa followers continued to agitate for a system of representative government, and the sain became a center of lively political discussion. This body petitioned the executive committee of the dajokan (September, 1872) to draft a constitution and convoke a popularly elected bicameral assembly, although for the time being it suggested that the sain itself constitute the upper house and the uin, joined by prefectural officials, the lower house. In order to transform this provisional assembly into an elected representative body, the petition included detailed election laws and a suggestion that a meeting of prefectural officials be held in the closing months of 1872 to discuss the convocation in the following year of an elected assembly which would meet each year for a three-month period. This petition had no significant impact on the government, for the executive committee refused to consider it on the pretext that many of its members were still abroad.

But the issue of war with Korea did force the leaders of the peace party, who emphasized the need for domestic reforms, to consider seriously the matter of a constitution and an elected assembly. For example, in his plea for peace, Kido Koin emphasized the need to establish a constitutional monarchy as part of the program of modernization. He felt that the *Charter Oath* and the *Seitaisho* were no longer suitable as political guides and that the government needed to formulate a more detailed constitution as a legal foundation for its power and structure. In a memorial to the emperor he explained the advantages of constitutional government in which the people participated, but he pointed out that, "if the people are still insufficiently enlightened, it becomes necessary, at least for a time, that the sovereign should by his superior discernment anticipate their unanimous wishes and entrust to officials the execution of them." Kido concluded that the political limitations of the Japanese people as a whole necessitated a gradual transition toward popular participation in government. The ultimate constitutional system he envisaged was one in which imperial power would be limited generally by strict adherence to the basic law of the land and specifically by a system of qualified responsibility to a parliament. In the final analysis, Kido regarded a constitution as a means to secure and maintain harmony between the powers of the emperor's government and the rights of the people.

Okubo Toshimichi, who assumed the key post of home minister, also conceded that the Japanese people were becoming more and more concerned with politics and that the establishment of a constitution was inevitable. But he felt that because Japan was in a period of transition from the decentralized political system of the Tokugawa period to a modern national state, some form of imperial absolutism was essential for the time being to protect the nation against foreign pressures and to enable it to reach a position of equality with the great powers. Okubo was particularly attracted by Prussian political thought and by the dynamic leadership of Bismarck, and he was convinced that absolute government, dominated by men of ability, was in keeping with Japanese tradition as well as with the conditions of the times. He regarded constitutional monarchy as the ultimate form of government for Japan, but he did not think in terms of a responsible parliamentary system. He was convinced that democratic, representative government was not suited to the customs and needs of Japan. He would establish a legislative body, but it would be appointive and merely advisory. In his mind the basic function of a constitution was "to establish harmony between the ruler and the people by fixing the powers of the emperor and limiting the rights of the people."

While the leaders of the government were discussing the matter of a constitution along these conservative lines, Itagaki Taisuke and Goto Shojiro agitated for popular rights and a national representative assembly. They helped to organize the Aikokukoto (Public Society of Patriots), a small political association of discontented Tosa samurai, which on January 17, 1874, presented a memorial to the emperor criticizing the arbitrary methods of the administration and warning that Japan needed a national representative assembly to limit the power of officials. The signers opposed the government's emphasis on "gradualism" and argued that the people would gain political experience only by having an active voice in the affairs of state. They based this view in large part on the demands of nationalism: "The establishment of a council chamber chosen by the people will create community feeling between the government and the people, and they will mutually unite into one body. Then and only then will the country become strong." This opposition group took on the name "the democratic movement" (*jiyu minken undo*), but it used the Western theory of natural rights not to enhance individual liberty but to increase the power and prestige of the state. Representative government in its view did not require a popular assembly; instead it thought in terms of a limited electorate. This is not to say, however, that Itagaki, Goto, and their followers were not assisted by a number of writers and intellectuals who were genuinely moved by European and American political doctrines and sincerely desired to see democracy planted in Japan. They advised, wrote speeches, and published long articles in newspapers extolling democratic rights.

The government referred the Aikokukoto memorial to the sain, which accepted in qualified form the principles put forward in the document. The sain, in a statement dated January 23, suggested that local assemblies be established in the immediate future; but with regard to a national representative assembly, it recommended that this matter be discussed by a meeting of prefectural governors which was then under consideration.

A more direct answer to the Aikokukoto memorial was made by Kato Hiroyuki, president of the government college that became the nucleus of Tokyo Imperial University. Kato objected to the immediate establishment of a national assembly, and he based his arguments on similarities to Japanese circumstances that he found in the history of Prussia. Institutions, he thought, must bear a close resemblance to the stage of progress reached by a people; and he felt that since the Japanese people had little political consciousness, they must continue to be ruled by a body of officials acting arbitrarily but for the best interests of the nation. Kato defended the policy of "gradualism," cautioning that, "if it is desired to introduce reforms suddenly, it is impossible not to fall into the evil of rash progress. There is nothing like steadily nourishing the intelligence and acting as far as possible in a gradual way."

Kato's views indicate the beginning of a fundamental change in the intellectual-political outlook of the leaders of the government. Men like Okubo and Kido, who had been abroad, no longer justified their power solely in terms of *kokutai* (the uniqueness of the Japanese state and the emperor system). They began to see a defense for absolutism in German theories of the supremacy of the state; and in the following decade, when government leaders, or the oligarchs, actually faced the task of writing a constitution and establishing a parliament, they relied increasingly on German thought to justify their power and to provide techniques for sustaining it.

Itagaki and his followers persisted in their attack on the oligarchs, and in April, 1874, they organized the Risshisha in order to mobilize the former samurai of Tosa more broadly behind the demands for a national assembly, local self-government, and democratic rights. The Risshisha, however, was something more than a political association. The name itself, properly translated, means "self-help," in the sense of the rehabilitation of former samurai in face of their deteriorating economic, social, and political circumstances. The Risshisha provided former samurai with opportunities to get training in trades, and it even sponsored co-operative action for such purposes as securing lower rates of interest. The Tosa experience was duplicated in other parts of Japan as schools and associations similar to the Risshisha began to spring up. Finally, at Osaka, in February, 1875, some forty representatives of local groups organized the Aikokusha (Society of Patriots) and adopted the Tosa political program.

Samurai Discontent and Rebellion

Samurai discontent also began to take violent forms. In January, 1874, nine samurai attempted to assassinate the court noble Iwakura, and in the following month Eto Shimpei, who had resigned over the Korean issue, led a revolt of former samurai in Hizen. Eto had expected Saigo, who had retired to Kagoshima, and Itagaki to organize similar uprisings, but they did not respond. The Hizen revolt was put down by government forces, and Eto, denied sanctuary by Saigo and Itagaki, was executed. Despite Eto's failure, there was still the threat of a unified armed opposition under the leadership of the popular Saigo. Okubo, worried over the lack of Satsuma support, renewed efforts to get both Saigo and Shimazu, the ex-daimyo, to resume office in the central government. While the latter did return to Tokyo and took an official post in compliance with an imperial order, he attacked the policies of centralization and modernization. Saigo remained at Kagoshima, where he conducted a private school to train former samurai in administration and military science.

Under these circumstances, the leaders of the government were forced to make compromises. Okubo wanted to persuade Kido and Itagaki to resume office in order to get a maximum of support for the imperial regime. In January, 1875, he confided his intention to Ito Hirobumi, a young protégé of Kido, who proposed an administrative reorganization with emphasis upon the gradual development of constitutional government. Ito's plan provided for the establishment of an appointed senate (*genroin*) and a conference of prefectural governors (*chihokankaigi*) in preparation for a national parliament, the creation of a supreme court (*daishinin*) as the nucleus of an independent judiciary, and a functional division of the dajokan into an executive council responsible for the formulation of policy and the various departments responsible for its administration. Kido and Itagaki met with Okubo in February and on the basis of Ito's proposals agreed to resume office.

By March 28 a committee made up of Okubo, Ito, Kido, and Itagaki completed a plan for the reorganization of the government, and on April 14 their draft was made official by an imperial rescript which cautioned the people against seeking rash progress and promised that "constitutional government would be established in gradual stages." The rescript also stated that a compromise should be made between Western forms of autocracy, constitutional monarchy, and republicanism so that a modified system of government, suitable to Japanese conditions, would be created. The sain and uin were abolished, and only the sein was retained as the executive committee of the dajokan. In theory, the government was based on the separation of powers, with the dajokan as the supreme executive body exercising power in the name of the emperor, the genroin and the chihokankaigi as a bicameral legislature, and the daishinin as the judiciary. However, the dajokan was scarcely changed and remained the focal point of power; through it Okubo and his Satsuma-Choshu colleagues continued to determine basic policy and laws.

The genroin proved to be nothing more than an advisory body whose main function was to deliberate on bills submitted by the dajokan, which had the power to indicate whether such bills were for decision or simply for study and discussion. The dajokan, moreover, continued to have the power to enact legislation on its own authority, having only to submit its measures to the genroin for inspection. The genroin did become the forum, however, for political controversies between the various factions that composed the dajokan. Itagaki and his followers worked for the transformation of the genroin into an effective legislative organ, but their opponents, with Kido as their spokesman, defended gradual political reform through the expansion of popular education and the development of local self-government. The more conservative Iwakura considered the genroin to be incompatible with the system of imperial government and consequently opposed the whole reorganization plan, did not attend the sessions of the dajokan, and offered to resign his official post. In his letter of resignation, which the emperor refused to accept, Iwakura concluded that "the genroin would destroy the great accomplishment of restoring the imperial system."

The meetings of the chihokankaigi were mere convocations of prefectural governors in routine administrative conferences under the control of the home minister. After it was convened in June, 1875, Goto Shojiro, vice-president of the genroin, criticized the chihokankaigi as "merely participating in the emperor's power to frame laws and not being a legislative body in any sense." Ito replied to the charge by insisting that "the chihokankaigi was a step on the way to popular representation in a national assembly." The concept of an independent judiciary met a similar fate, since the daishinin was placed under the control of the dajokan through regulations which directly subordinated it to the department of justice.

During 1875 and most of 1876 the main stumbling block to political harmony within the government concerned the dajokan. Kido and Itagaki had resumed office on condition that the executive and administrative functions of the dajokan be separated. They had objected to the practice by which councilors of state were at the same time ministers of the various departments; however, their objections were ignored and the majority of the councilors continued to serve in key administrative posts. In a memorial to the emperor Itagaki protested that this was a violation of the agreement that he had made with Okubo, but only Shimazu Hisamitsu, the former daimyo of Satsuma, who had taken office in the imperial government in 1874, sided with him. Okubo had used the excuse of a crisis with Korea to postpone action on the matter, but finally (October 19, 1876) the emperor stated that there would be no division of dajokan functions. On the very day that the government promulgated the imperial decision, Shimazu presented a memorial criticizing the councilors for their modernization policies. In the end, both Itagaki and Shimazu presented their resignations; and though the government feared the loss of both men, it accepted their resignations on October 27, 1876. Thus the attempt by Okubo and Ito to broaden the basis of the government's support ended in failure. They suffered an additional blow in the following year when Kido died after a long illness.

The political settlement of 1875 failed to stem the tide of opposition, and by 1876 discontent among the former samurai, increased by the compulsory bond-commutation scheme, again erupted in armed rebellion. In October two hundred former samurai in Kumamoto took up arms and carried out a surprise attack on the local prefecture office and garrison, killing the commanding general and fatally wounding the civil governor. The uprising was quickly put down, but not before it had stirred other groups into action elsewhere. Four hundred former samurai rebelled in Fukuoka, and a similar uprising broke out in Yamaguchi. Again the government was able to suppress these outbursts with little difficulty. The rebels had been confident that similar discontented elements in Satsuma would join them and that rebellion would spread rapidly to all parts of the country. The government was aware of such a possibility, for it had secret agents at work gathering information. In the case of the Yamaguchi revolt, it knew the leaders well in advance and anticipated their acts.

When the government began to take measures in the autumn of 1876 to strengthen its control over Kagoshima, the former capital of Satsuma and center of discontent, it provoked the Satsuma Rebellion. On January 29, 1877, a group of Satsuma extremists attacked the army munitions depot and the navy yard and succeeded in carrying off sizable quantities of rifles and ammunition. Saigo, who was off on a hunting trip, hurried back to Kagoshima, but when it was impossible for him to check the violence, he cast his lot with the rebels. The Satsuma Rebellion was supported by an armed force of about 150,000 men, of which not more than 40,000 were effective combatants. The government garrison was no match for the rebels until reinforcements arrived, but by the middle of March the tide of fighting swung in its favor. By early June Satsuma forces were in flight, and by August the issue was decided in the government's favor. Saigo and his most devoted followers, hardly more than four hundred in number, made a last desperate stand at Kagoshima; and when Saigo was critically wounded, one of his lieutenants mercifully killed him. Not more than two hundred men lived to surrender. In battle the new conscript army displayed superior generalship, training, and equipment, all of which proved necessary to overcome the fanaticism of the former samurai. In all, 11,000 men were killed and 36,000 wounded.

This rebellion proved to be the last armed revolt by the former samurai, who soon disintegrated completely as a separate class. In subsequent decades discontent was expressed by individual acts of violence. The suppression of the rebellion, however, did not terminate demands for a positive foreign policy of expansion, and the next several decades saw the formation of a number of nationalist societies which urged such a policy and which had their roots in the discontent of former samurai.

The Satsuma Rebellion also marked a definite change in the leadership of the government, for by the spring of 1878 the original triumvirate of the Meiji Restoration—Okubo, Kido, and Saigo—were no longer alive. Kido had died on May 26, 1877, Saigo perished in September of that year, and Okubo fell at the hands of an assassin on May 14, 1878. Ito, Okuma, Yamagata, Inouye Kaoru, and Matsukata Masayoshi (Satsuma) emerged as the most important leaders in the government, and Iwakura remained as the spokesman for an intensely conservative political philosophy which resisted any political reforms that would impair the power of the emperor. Despite the rebellion, the new leadership, with its strong Choshu base, maintained something of the old balance of power between Satsuma and Choshu men, but this does not mean that a feeling of rivalry did not continue to exist or that there was not a great deal of maneuvering for political power. In fact, after the assassination of Okubo, Satsuma elements sought to form a coalition with Okuma and his followers, for the most part lesser officials in the central government. When this failed, Matsukata, who assumed leadership of the Satsuma clique, hurried home from Paris to prevent Inouye Kaoru from taking office as minister of finance. Since Ito was minister of home affairs, the Satsuma clique felt that another key post should not fall to a Choshu man. Inouye's appointment was blocked, and the office went to Okuma, who continued to ignore requests from Satsuma men for a political alliance.

The "Democratic Movement"

Armed rebellion came to an end with the suppression of the Satsuma Rebellion and the death of Saigo, but Itagaki and the other leaders of the "democratic movement" continued to criticize the authoritarian nature of the government and worked constantly to make their opposition more effective by developing mass support. On the whole, the leaders of the "democratic movement" took a neutral position during the Satsuma Rebellion because Itagaki insisted on working through the pressure of public opinion; but he did use the rebellion to press the government to accept the demands of his group, and in June, 1877, the Risshisha petitioned the emperor to establish a national parliament in accordance with the *Charter Oath* of 1868. The signers complained that the political disunity of the country was caused by the "despotism of the government oligarchy, which carried on the administration without reference to the opinion of the nation." They also criticized the government for its failure to implement the separation of powers outlined in the imperial rescript of 1875, its failure to revise the unequal treaties, and its favoritism in the economic development of Hokkaido. Occupied with the Satsuma Rebellion, the government tried to ignore the memorial, while Itagaki had it printed and circulated throughout Japan.

By this time, the "democratic movement" began to generate greater pressure for political reform because its leadership, at least locally, passed into the hands of important economic interest groups—rural landlords, merchants, and industrialists. Just as important was the fact that mass support was gained among discontented peasants and to a lesser extent among wage earners. The former objected to the high land tax and to excise taxes on many of the by-products of agricultural production which were under their control, like sake, soy sauce, and bean paste; and the latter agitated for reduction of taxes, land rents, and interest rates. The Risshisha memorial of June, 1877, took note of the feeling that the government favored the urban economic interests at the expense of the rural communities:

The taxes of the fu and ken are collected and sent directly to the department of finance. This causes great scarcity of money in the country and cripples its powers of production. The government shows great activity in promoting schemes for agricultural industries, in opening up Hokkaido, and in establishing manufactures, but the officials appointed to take charge of such matters utterly mismanage whatever is entrusted to their care and interfere with just rights and powers of the merchants. Hundreds of thousands of yen are spent assisting certain companies, or in founding new ones, but such benevolent acts of the government are confined to certain persons or associations and in no way exercise any benefit for the public good.

The principal organ of the "democratic movement" was the Aikokusha, formed at Osaka in September, 1878; and within a short time thereafter numerous local affiliates, which worked to stir up the peasantry, arose on the village level. In order to co-ordinate the activities of the various local political associations, the leaders of the Aikokusha in March, 1879, called a national convention at Osaka, and in November a second convention resolved to petition the emperor to establish a national assembly. By the time that the third convention met in April, 1880, political agitation had reached such proportions that the leaders of the government decided to take action. On April 5 they passed a law restricting public meetings and issued a decree ordering the convention to disband. Forewarned of the ban, the Aikokusha resolved to continue its activities until its aims were achieved and sent two deputies to Tokyo to submit the petition for an assembly to the emperor. The government refused to accept it and informed the bearers that all petitions should be submitted to local prefectural governments, which would transmit them to the genroin. In 1880 at least fifty-five petitions urging the establishment of an assembly were presented to the government.

During these years when political opposition was nearing its peak, the government vainly attempted to meet the demands of the opposition by establishing local assemblies. In 1875 the representatives of thirteen prefectures met and submitted a memorial to the chihokankaigi requesting the formation of prefectural assemblies on a national scale. They argued that such institutions would provide forums to develop popular experience in government. During the session of the chihokankaigi which was opened by the emperor in June, 1875, the government submitted a draft of regulations for prefectural and urban assemblies and asked the chihokankaigi to decide whether members of such bodies should be local government officials or elected representatives. After a lively discussion a vote of the chihokankaigi was taken, and a majority recommended the establishment of local assemblies composed of local government officials. Before the government was able to effect this recommendation, it was confronted by rebellions by former samurai in 1876 and 1877, but after their suppression it submitted a draft of regulations for popularly elected prefectural and urban assemblies to the second session of the chihokankaigi, which convened in April, 1878. A majority of that body approved the government's draft with one modification, namely, reduction of the voting qualification, based on the land tax, from ten yen to five yen. In July, 1878, these regulations were promulgated by the government.

Shortly thereafter the government established prefectural and urban assemblies which would be convened for one month each year and on special occasions. Male subjects over twenty-five years of age who had paid a land tax of at least five yen became eligible to vote.* Those who had paid a land tax of at least ten yen were eligible for assembly membership in the prefecture or fu in which they resided. These assemblies were permitted to deliberate on bills submitted by governors, who had veto power over their decisions. By 1880 the assemblies proved to be the scene of numerous conflicts between local governors and the members, who struggled for increased power. In an attempt to lessen friction, the government provided for mediation by the home minister and, in the case of money matters, by the minister of finance. Finally, in 1881, a board of adjudication was established in the dajokan to settle disputes, and because of the increasing intractability of several assemblies, the governors were empowered to put measures into operation on the approval of the home minister.

Although these prefectural assemblies were criticized widely because they were powerless to check the local bureaucratic controls of the central government, they did serve as forums for political agitation by the leaders of the "democratic movement," and the government did make new concessions. In 1880 it extended the establishment of local elected assemblies to cities, towns, and villages; but these bodies, since they were modeled on their prefectural precursors, were no more acceptable to the government's critics. They could not initiate debate but could only discuss matters submitted to them; their decisions were subject to revocation by local officials; and their meetings could be suspended or dissolved by the prefectural governors. When an assembly was thus suspended or dissolved, local officials were empowered to enact legislation, which was then subject to the governor's approval.

During this period the government restrained the organs of public opinion, especially the press. Modern Japanese newspapers began to be published shortly after the Meiji Restoration, and they soon became politically important. By 1873 the press had begun to take sides in the issues that divided the government and the "democratic" Tosa faction. In that year the government enacted a press law which required newspapers to secure official authorization to publish and which prohibited editorial attacks upon government policies, discussion of laws, or attempts "to cast obstacles in the way of the working of national institutions by persistent advocacy of foreign ideas." The press was also forbidden to comment on officials during their term of office.

When this measure proved ineffective, Okubo replaced it in 1875 with a more drastic law that made criticism and slander of the government and its officials a crime punishable by fine or imprisonment. Under the new law the editor of the newspaper as well as the writer could be held responsible for libel

---

* Excepted were public schoolteachers, military men, lunatics, and criminals.

or subversion of the state "in every case where the discussion turns upon foreign or domestic politics, finance, feelings of the nation, the aspect of the times, learning or religion, or matters affecting the rights of officials or the people." During 1875 and 1876, as a direct result of the application of this law, the government arrested sixty editors and newspapermen, and between 1876 and 1880 fines and jail sentences were increasingly common since the press continued to protest the limits imposed on the legislative power of the newly created local assemblies.

By 1880 the government also moved to restrict public meetings and to hinder, if not prevent, the development of political parties. Permits were required for public political meetings or discussions, and the police were authorized to control such meetings and even to disperse them. Political associations were forbidden to combine or communicate with each other; and men in the armed forces, teachers and students, and policemen were prohibited from attending political meetings or from becoming members of political associations.

The enforcement of these laws required vigorous action by the Japanese police, who were organized under the control of the home minister. Local police were placed under the administration of governors, but in Tokyo the metropolitan police were placed directly under the home minister. By 1877 both the national police and the Tokyo police were subject to the orders of a chief inspector in the department of home affairs, who did not hesitate to use them against political agitators; for example, he directed the Tokyo force "to search out and punish those guilty of political offenses." The government was especially concerned about the spread of political thought in the army; and when a unit of the imperial guards mutinied in 1878 because of an arrears in pay, it suspected that the troops had been influenced by its opponents. Shortly thereafter, to reinforce military discipline, General Yamagata issued a warning to members of the army to abstain from discussion of politics, and in 1881 he formed a gendarmerie (*kempeitai*) to enforce the directive.

The Constitutional Issue

In the period from 1876 to 1880, when the political pressure of the "democratic movement" was mounting, the leaders of the government did not overlook the problem of drafting a constitution. As early as September, 1876, the emperor ordered a committee, under the chairmanship of Prince Arisugawa Taruhito, president of the genroin, to draft a constitution "based on the system established at the time of the founding of the nation and which gives consideration to the laws of various nations." Between September, 1876, and May, 1878, the committee, placed under the jurisdiction of the genroin, compiled four draft constitutions, the last of which was submitted to the leaders of the government for their consideration. On the whole, the draft constitution made important concessions to the democratic movement by providing for constitutional checks on the imperial power. The emperor would continue to conduct the administration through his ministers, with the power to command the army and navy, to declare war and make peace, and to conclude treaties, but with responsibility to parliament in specific cases. For example, "treaties which would involve expenditures or changes in the national boundary would require the approval of both houses of parliament." The draft constitution also restricted the financial independence of the imperial institution by providing that "the annual income of the emperor would be decided by law." With regard to the legislative process, the draft constitution placed important checks on absolutism, for it declared that the legislative power would be "shared by the emperor and the parliament." While bills would be submitted to parliament by the emperor, who would have the ultimate power of veto, they would require the consent of both houses. The only exceptions would be budget and tax measures, both of which would require the consent of the lower house only. Parliament would also participate in the process of constitutional amendment, for the draft stipulated that "amendments would require the consent of both houses expressed by at least a two-thirds majority." The parliament would consist of the genroin and a house of representatives (*daigishiin*). The former would be for the most part a continuation of the body already in existence, with its members chosen from among princes, nobles (*kazoku*), officials, and individuals who had performed some meritorious service. Besides its role in the framing of laws, the genroin would have the following specific powers: the prosecution of high officials in impeachment proceedings and the right of ministerial interpellation. The daigishiin, on the other hand, would be a popularly elected chamber, the members of which would serve for four years, with elections for half the total every two years. The draft constitution also contained a bill of rights which guaranteed all the basic freedoms but with the sweeping qualification that they could be modified by law.

The leaders of the government did not react favorably to the draft constitution submitted by the genroin committee. Ito Hirobumi, for example, feared a parliamentary check on the powers of the government and objected to parliamentary control of the annual budget and the imperial income; the provision that the emperor and parliament "share equally" the legislative power was, he said, a step in the direction of parliamentary supremacy, and he cited the decline of the power of the British monarchy. Iwakura, who had only reluctantly accepted the decision to establish a constitution, was even more apprehensive. Since 1875 he had been worried about the possibility of parliamentary limitations on the imperial power, and he was so concerned about the work of the genroin committee that in March, 1878, he proposed the establishment in the dajokan of a bureau to compile a constitution which would "fortify the imperial power." Iwakura simply did not want to accept any official organs for the expression of public opinion, and later (1882) he went so far as to submit a proposal for the abolition of local assemblies. Ito and Iwakura took the lead in suggesting that the genroin draft be revised to make it conform more closely to the traditional imperial system. In December, 1879, at the prompting of Iwakura, the emperor asked Ito, Yamagata, Okuma, and the other councilors of state to comment upon the advisability of establishing a constitution and a national parliament. All complied, with the exception of Okuma, who did not answer until the spring of 1881, at which time he precipitated a crisis in the government. While the opinions of the councilors differed in detail, all agreed that a constitution which placed sovereignty in the person of the emperor should be established in the future and that the government should take gradual steps toward the establishment of a national parliament.

In December, 1880, the genroin committee completed its revision of the draft constitution and submitted it to the throne. The committee had endeavored to reach some sort of compromise between the imperial system and parliamentary government, but the only significant changes from the 1878 draft were a modification of the wording regarding the legislative functions of the emperor and parliament and a clearer statement of the power of impeachment, which would rest with both houses instead of solely with the genroin. The revised draft again omitted any definite statement regarding sovereignty, but it was inferred that sovereignty was to be shared by the emperor and parliament.

The members of the genroin, who were permitted to append their private opinions to the draft, were enthusiastic supporters of it. The attitude of Fukuoka Kotei, long an advocate of representative government, is especially noteworthy. He expressed a strong desire for parliamentary initiation of legislation and cabinet responsibility to parliament and not to the emperor. But the leaders of the government received the revision no more favorably than they had the original draft. As a group they regarded it as a dangerous compromise with the theory of parliamentary supremacy, and Iwakura, who remained the most apprehensive, again proposed that the dajokan establish its own constitutional committee. The government finally rejected the revision in March, 1881, and at the same time abolished the genroin committee.

The Political Crisis of 1881

By the spring of 1881 the democratic movement had achieved such momentum that the government found it increasingly difficult to ignore its demands; moreover, there were signs of a new split among the councilors of state when Okuma Shigenobu threw his support behind the demand that parliament be established immediately. In a memorial to the emperor submitted in March, 1881, Okuma asked that parliamentary representatives be elected by the end of 1882 and that parliament be convened early in 1883. He emphasized that "constitutional government is party government" and that "when a party's program wins the support of the majority of the nation, that party should come into power." He added that "the leader of a party possessing a majority of seats in parliament should be entrusted with the conduct of public affairs, but he should retire when his party falls into a minority."

There is no clear explanation of the motives behind Okuma's action. The genuineness of his conversion to parliamentary government is difficult to assess, but it is clear that he wished to overcome the Satsuma-Choshu oligarchy and to assume leadership of the government. His stand may be regarded as the culmination of struggle for power between Ito Hirobumi and himself that had developed since the death of Okubo in 1878. Ito, who succeeded to Kido's leadership of the Choshu faction, had been able to get along well with his Satsuma colleagues. Okuma slowly gained supporters among the more liberal-minded young university graduates who had entered government service; and while he was an important official, his ambition was held in check by the powerful forces of the Satsuma-Choshu oligarchs. Thus it seems that Okuma was taking advantage of the increasing pressure of the democratic movement's demands.

The constitutional issue was not, moreover, the only source of the political crisis. Early in the summer of 1881 a difference arose between Okuma and the other councilors concerning the sale of government-owned nonstrategic industries to private capitalists in order to economize the financial and technical resources of the state. Okuma objected to the sale of certain enterprises on the island of Hokkaido, valued at 14,000,000 yen, to a private company, in part owned by the councilor and commissioner of colonization and development of Hokkaido, Kuroda Kiyotaka of Satsuma, for approximately 380,000 yen (just slightly more than an estimate of one year's profits), this sum to be paid over a thirty-year period without interest. Despite Okuma's objections, the dajokan tentatively approved the sale on July 30.

News of the proposed transaction was disseminated widely in July, when the Tokyo press began attacking it. The leaders of the democratic movement used the disclosure to attack the Satsuma-Choshu oligarchs and blamed the scandal on the lack of ministerial responsibility to a national parliament. Despite the fact that Okuma, who was on tour with the emperor, played no direct part in the agitation against the government, Ito and his colleagues blamed their difficulties on him. They had evidence that Okuma's followers and agents of the Mitsubishi Company were spreading the report that Okuma was the only councilor who opposed the sale. There were even rumors that the Mitsubishi Company was paying Tokyo newspapers to support Okuma. Although the company president, Iwasaki, denied these activities, it was generally recognized that the new enterprise would seriously challenge the

Mitsubishi trading interests in Hokkaido. When Okuma finally returned to Tokyo, he opposed the sale in sessions of the council and turned against the whole Satsuma-Choshu group.

The climax of the political crisis came on October 11 when the members of the dajokan met without Okuma and decided to cancel the inopportune Hokkaido transaction, to dismiss Okuma from the dajokan, and to issue an imperial rescript proclaiming the establishment of a national parliament. Their discussion on the parliamentary question was based on a proposal that Iwakura, the conservative court noble, had submitted in July as a refutation of Okuma's demand for parliamentary government. Iwakura's proposal was actually drafted by Inouye Kowashi, a lesser official who had been influenced by a German professor of jurisprudence, Hermann Roessler, who had arrived in Japan in 1878. Iwakura again proposed that the dajokan establish its own committee to draft a constitution, and, as a guide for the task, appended the following fundamental principles:

1. The constitution shall emanate from the emperor and the policy of a gradual approach toward constitutional government shall prevail.
2. The emperor shall have supreme command over the army and navy, declare war, make peace, conclude treaties, etc.; moreover, the emperor shall direct the national administration.
3. The organization of the cabinet cannot be subjected to the intervention of parliament. Except for those administrative affairs that are of fundamental importance to the state, for which all ministers shall be jointly responsible, each minister shall only be individually responsible for administrative affairs under his official jurisdiction. Ministers shall be responsible to the emperor and not to parliament.
4. Parliament shall consist of two houses: an upper house composed of members appointed by the emperor and members elected from among the ranks of peers and former samurai, and a lower house of popularly elected representatives.
5. The election law for the lower house shall include a property qualification for the suffrage, while the electors for the peerage and ex-samurai shall not be subjected to property qualifications.
6. All legislative bills shall be initiated by the government.
7. When parliament does not pass an annual budget bill, the government may execute the provisions of the budget of the previous year.
8. With regard to the rights of citizens, constitutional provisions of other nations shall be consulted.

Iwakura also expressed his views regarding the adaptability of foreign systems of government. He felt that the British system of parliamentary government was unsuited to Japan's needs because it was incompatible with the institution of the emperor; and, like Ito earlier, he cited the fact that the British king had lost his power to parliament and had become a mere figurehead. On the other hand, Iwakura looked with favor on the Prussian system because the kaiser selected his own cabinet, which remained responsible to him. The councilors agreed that Japan might be able to adapt Prussian ideas and institutions to its own special needs and conditions.

After the meeting Ito called on Okuma at midnight and asked him to resign. On the following day, October 12, Okuma and many of his followers in the central administration left their posts; the dajokan canceled the sale of the properties in Hokkaido; and Sanjo Sanetomi, as dajodaijin, promulgated an imperial rescript which pledged the establishment of a parliament in 1890 and threatened reprisals against agitation for immediate action. As a postscript, Kuroda Kiyotaka resigned when the dajokan refused to meet his demands regarding financial support for the Hokkaido colonization and development project, and in March, 1882, the project was terminated. Finally, in February, 1883, Hokkaido was given a prefectural status.

18 *Political Parties and the Constitutional Struggle*

The imperial rescript of October 12 did not silence the "democratic movement." On the contrary, it stimulated the formation of national political parties, which put forward their own platforms concerning constitutional systems of government, with special emphasis on the nature of the proposed parliament. These parties were also greatly interested in economic policy—a consequence not only of the interest groups that they represented but also of the economic stabilization program of Finance Minister Matsukata Masayoshi, which was being implemented by the government at this time.

Matsukata sought to put an end to the inflation, caused by commodity shortages and a constantly depreciating paper money, and to the mounting official expenditures. He effected a retrenchment in the national budget by terminating a number of official enterprises, some of which were operating at a considerable loss, and by turning over to private capital others which, though profitable, were not of strategic value. He also increased government revenues by levying new taxes and raising existing excise taxes on commodities, like rice wine (sake), soy sauce, and tobacco, which were consumed in Japan. By these measures he was able to reduce the number of paper notes in circulation and to increase the specie reserve. National banks were required to transfer their reserves to the Bank of Japan, which was established in 1882 to provide greater financial control, and to make annual payments into a fund to be used for the redemption of their notes. Within four or five years both government paper money and national bank notes were exchanged at par with the convertible silver notes of the Bank of Japan. For all practical purposes, Japan had a silver standard, but her economy was influenced by fluctuations in the world price of silver, especially since two-thirds of her foreign trade was with gold-standard nations. Japan wanted to adopt a gold standard, but she was unable to amass a large gold reserve until China paid the huge Shimonoseki indemnity. In March, 1897, Japan went on the gold standard, and her monetary position was placed on a firm footing.

These policies and others, such as government loans and subsidies, assisted the emerging financial-industrial combines (*zaibatsu*) at the expense of local economic interests. Although both small and medium business occupied an important position in over-all production, the most important characteristic of Japan's industrialization was the concentration of financial control in the government and in the powerful zaibatsu. Each of the three largest combines, Mitsui, Mitsubishi, and Sumitomo, was a family enterprise based on a holding company which controlled a network of subsidiaries and affiliates through intercorporate holdings, interlocking directorates, management agreements, and bank loans. For example, the Mitsui trust was managed by a council representing eleven branch families, and its control extended over the Mitsui Bank, the Mitsui Trading Company, the Mitsui Mining Company, and, later, interests in textiles, shipping, metals, and machinery. Other zaibatsu included Asano and Okura in industry and Yasuda, Kawasaki, and Shibuzawa in banking and finance.

The Formation of Political Parties

The most important of the political parties that were formed at this time was the Jiyuto (Liberal Party)—an outgrowth of the Aikokusha—which was organized in October, 1881, at Tokyo by representatives of local political associations. They elected Itagaki Taisuke as president and adopted a platform based on the goal of responsible parliamentary government. On the whole, the Jiyuto was the most liberal of the parties in that its political philosophy was based on the principle of popular sovereignty. Yet it sought to make party government compatible with the imperial system by advancing the thesis that the wishes of the people and those of the emperor were one and the same. In its economic policies the party reflected the interests of landlords and small industrialists, who were critical of the fiscal measures of the government, particularly Matsukata's reforms.

A second political party, the Rikken Kaishinto (Constitutional Reform Party), was formed on March 15, 1882, by a group of former bureaucrats led by Okuma and a number of intellectuals from Keio University. The Kaishinto has often been called an urban business party, in contrast to the rural character of the Jiyuto, because its platform supported Matsukata's economic and fiscal policies and because it derived some of its financial backing from enterprises like the Mitsubishi Company, which sought to use the party to advance its own interests. Most urban merchants and industrialists, however, remained aloof from the party movement. The Kaishinto was essentially a party of urban intellectuals, and its mass support came from student groups. Its platform reflected the thought of Fukuzawa Yukichi, who was anxious to transplant the basic concepts of nineteenth-century British liberalism into Japan. On the matter of sovereignty, the Kaishinto advocated the "king-in-parliament" theory of the British, and it urged the establishment of a greater degree of local self-government, the gradual extension of suffrage, and the convocation of a constitutional convention representative of the people.

The conservatives, both in and out of government, attempted to counterbalance the formation of the Jiyuto and Kaishinto by forming the Rikken Teiseito (Constitutional Imperial Party) in March, 1882. The Teiseito drew its members from the ranks of young bureaucrats, including the officials of prefectural and local governments, Shinto priests and Buddhist monks, public schoolteachers, and businessmen closely connected with the government. While the party did not gain a mass following, it was an important instrument for the popularization of the political views of the ruling oligarchy. Its platform was approved in a private meeting attended by such councilors as Ito Hirobumi and Inouye Kaoru, and specific planks were based on Iwakura's 1881 recommendations. The basic theme was that sovereignty rested with the emperor but that its exercise would be governed by a constitution which would establish imperial supremacy over parliament by such means as absolute veto power. The Teiseito was championed by several conservative newspapers, which defended the government and made the opposition parties appear treasonable. They quoted at great length from Edmund Burke, and almost all preached the German doctrine of state autocracy to combat liberal and democratic principles.

Confronted by two opposition parties which gained increasing strength, the government felt compelled to restrict their activities by a new ordinance (June, 1882) which required political associations to register their constitutions, by-laws, and the names of all their members with the police and to notify the police of every new entry and resignation. If an association desired to hold a meeting for the study, debate, or discussion of political topics, it was required to secure permission from the police three days in advance. The ordinance forbade associations to advertise the nature of political meetings, to excite the public by agents or circulars, or to correspond or join with similar groups; and it directed the home minister and the police to disband any meeting which they considered a menace "to the preservation of public peace and order." The government also revised the press law (April, 1883) to place harsher restrictions on the activities of opposition newspapers, particularly the highly critical *Jiyu* of the Jiyuto and *Yubin Hochi* of the Kaishinto, and in one year (1883) it suspended publication of forty-nine newspapers.

The government also successfully maneuvered the two opposition parties into a quarrel and thus prevented the formation of a united movement. In 1882 Ito and Inouye lured Itagaki and Goto from the Jiyuto by the prize of a trip through Europe. Inouye tried to get the funds for the trip from the Mitsubishi Company but failed; however, he was successful when he approached the rival Mitsui Company, which was rewarded by an extension of an important army contract. The two Jiyuto leaders came under heavy criticism from their own party members, even though Itagaki explained that they were leaving to study constitutional matters. When they refused to alter their plans, several of the critics resigned from the party. When the *Tokyo-Yokohama Mainichi,* an important Kaishinto newspaper, published an editorial condemning Itagaki and Goto and intimating that the government was financing the trip, the Jiyuto denied the charge and used its own press organs to attack the Kaishinto as the tool of the Mitsubishi Company, labeling it as "a profit-making organization parading as a political party." On the other hand, the Jiyuto counterattack was in part formulated by an editor who was a close friend of one of the founders of a new shipping company organized by the Mitsui Company and the government to compete against Mitsubishi's Japan Steamship Company. The net effect of this controversy was to widen the existing differences between the two parties and their leaders. Whatever basis there had been for a common front against the government was lost; moreover, both parties were seriously harmed by the fact that they were discredited in the eyes of the general public.

The Jiyuto was also weakened by a growing radicalism within its own organization. After 1881 the government's deflationary economic policy caused a general depression in the rural areas. The peasants were hurt by the price declines of many agricultural products, and they had to bear the burden of many of the new taxes. Japan's industrialization also had an unfortunate impact upon the peasantry; this was particularly true of the modern textile mills, which turned out excellent thread and cloth at low prices, to the detriment of handicraft production. Finally, the peasantry suffered several poor crops caused by floods in 1881 and again in 1883 and 1884.

The resulting discontent led to the organization of local peasant associations which demanded lower rents, taxes, and interest rates, and before long many of them came under the leadership of a radical wing of the Jiyuto which advocated social and economic reform as well as political change. When these associations began to resort to violence to achieve their aims, a fundamental cleavage developed within the party. Violence reached an alarming climax in the years 1883 and 1884, when attempted assassinations and bombings became increasingly common. For example, in Chichibu in October, 1884, under slogans of "reduce land taxes," "cancel debts," and "amend conscription laws," a mob of thousands attacked government offices, police stations, and wealthy homes, seized and divided up goods, and terrorized landlords. Only after days of rioting were law and order restored.

Tax relief was a cardinal point in the Jiyuto program; but when local affiliates attacked landlordism, the conservative elements in the party were disturbed. Although it had made efforts to impose discipline on the peasantry, the party found it impossible to quash the demand for radical reforms. In fact, the extremists urged that everything be risked, and even plotted to overthrow the government by force. Although the majority of Jiyuto members opposed direct action, they could not control the party branches. In the end the Jiyuto organization began to break down from within. Funds for party activities became scarce, for men of wealth, fearful of government retaliation and opposed to the waves of terror, refused to make contributions. On October 29, 1884, shortly after the Chichibu Uprising, a convention of the Jiyuto voted formally to dissolve the party.

The Kaishinto did not disband, but it became a virtual nonentity in December, 1884, when, after a disagreement among its leaders on economic policy, Okuma and several of his close friends resigned. The government, in anticipation of the collapse of the political opposition, forced the dissolution of the conservative Teiseito; Ito notified the party authorities that the party was no longer needed, and they proceeded to disband its organization.

Preparations for the Constitution

During the national debate regarding the nature of the proposed parliament, precipitated by the imperial rescript of October 12, 1881, and the subsequent formation of political parties, the oligarchs began to implement measures to reorganize the administrative structure and to draft a constitution which would safeguard the imperial system, through which they dominated the government. On March 3, 1882, the emperor ordered Ito Hirobumi to lead a mission of investigation to Europe to observe the operation of various systems of government. Ito recruited a committee of nine assistants, the membership of which represented a compromise to prevent domination by Choshu interests, and on March 14 the group embarked from Yokohama. Upon arrival in Europe, Ito dispatched Saionji Kimmochi and several others to Paris to study the constitution of the Third Republic. The remainder of the mission proceeded to Berlin, where Ito, his assistants, and Aoki Shuzo, minister to Germany, attended a series of lectures by Rudolph Gneist, a professor of jurisprudence.*

Gneist based his lectures on the general principle that constitutions should be firmly rooted in national history. He compared the history of Japan to that of Prussia, and he urged Ito to adopt a Prussian-style constitution. He stressed the need to protect the supreme powers of the emperor as exercised by his

---

* The lectures lasted from May 27 to July 29. Aoki acted as interpreter for Ito, while Ito Myoji took notes on the lectures in Japanese. Supplementary lectures by Albert Mosse, a disciple of Gneist, were also attended by Ito.

ministers. Specifically, he emphasized that ultimate control over foreign affairs, military matters, and legislation be entrusted to the emperor. With regard to the decisive matter of finance, Gneist recommended a clause which had been inserted in the Prussian Constitution which assured to the government the previous year's appropriations should parliament refuse or be unable to pass a budget bill. He also told Ito to be certain that the financial resources of the imperial family would in no way be controlled by parliament. Finally, he cautioned his listeners against convoking a constitutional convention and advised that they establish a property qualification to limit suffrage.

From Berlin Ito and his party journeyed to Vienna, where they attended lectures by the famous jurist Lorenz von Stein, who outlined an authoritarian system of government called "bureaucratic constitutionalism," in which the state and the monarch were synonymous. Opposed to universal suffrage and party government, he urged Ito to establish a constitutional system not with cabinet responsibility to parliament but with paramount power in the hands of the ministers as representatives of the sovereign emperor. With regard to legislation, he advised that only the cabinet should have the right to initiate bills and that the emperor should have the power of absolute veto. Finally, he suggested that the management of the imperial household should be kept separate from the regular administration. Stein justified authoritarian government by a theory of society which he felt was applicable to both Germany and Japan. According to him, the chief purpose of the state was to resolve the clashing interests and remove the social tensions that resulted from the nineteenth-century victory of industrialism over feudalism.

Ito and his party did not return directly to Japan. They stopped off at Paris, where Ito met Clemenceau; and they visited England, where he heard Herbert Spencer lecture on the theory of representative government. Much later Ito wrote of his tour in a rather misleading fashion, claiming that he had made "an extended journey in different countries to make as thorough a study as possible of the actual workings of different systems of constitutional government, on their various provisions, as well as theories and opinions actually entertained by influential persons on the actual stage itself of constitutional life." From London the mission went to Russia to attend the coronation of the czar, and from there to Naples, where in May it departed for Japan. The homecoming was marked by a note of sadness, occasioned by the death of Iwakura.

In March, 1884, the dajokan established a special committee to draft a constitution within the imperial household department in the hope that a small group could work in secret with virtual immunity from public criticism and at the same time create the illusion of personal supervision by the emperor. Ito was appointed minister of the department and chairman of the drafting committee. He selected nine assistants, the most influential of which were Ito Myoji, who had accompanied him to Europe, Inouye Kowashi, who was familiar with the Prussian Constitution, and Kaneko Kentaro, who had studied in the United States. They did not begin their task immediately, however, because Ito first wanted to enact several administrative reforms which would facilitate the shift to a constitutional regime.

Ito's first move in this direction was the creation by imperial ordinances (July, 1884) of a new peerage to provide the basis for membership in the upper house of parliament as a check on the popularly elected lower house. The new nobility was modeled on the German system and was divided into five ranks—prince, marquis, count, viscount, and baron—which were bestowed on five hundred individuals selected from among the court nobility, former daimyo, and former samurai who had rendered meritorious service to the state. Ito, Yamagata, and Inouye became counts, and the heirs of Kido and Okubo were made marquis. That the government intended to create a body favorable to its policies was evident from the fact that Itagaki, Goto, and Okuma, leaders in the restoration who now were political opponents, were overlooked. The establishment of the peerage was a very practical political maneuver, for the oligarchs thus institutionalized the support of many of Japan's conservatives.

The second major reform was the formation by imperial decree (December, 1885) of a cabinet to replace the dajokan. Sanjo, the retiring dajodaijin, explained the change as a return to ancient Japanese theory under which the emperor personally ruled—receiving reports from his ministers and deciding matters by and with his ministers' advice—but there were actually more practical reasons. The leaders of the government felt it necessary to strengthen the base of their personal power before the convocation of parliament in 1890. Only two of the ten posts in the new cabinet were awarded to men "outside" of Satsuma and Choshu. The eight, who for all practical purposes constituted the ruling oligarchy, were, from Satsuma, Matsukata Masayoshi (finance), Oyama (army), Saigo Tsugumichi (navy), and Yamada Akiyoshi (justice), and, from Choshu, Ito Hirobumi (prime minister), Inouye Kaoru (foreign affairs), Yamagata Aritomo (home affairs), and Mori Arinori (education). The exceptions were Tani Kanjo (Tosa), minister of agriculture, and Enomoto Takeaki (Hizen), minister of communications.* Under the new system the prime minister was responsible to the emperor for the administration of the entire country and its affairs; moreover, all ministers were subject to his direct supervision and were at the same time accountable to him for all the affairs of their respective ministries.

The last major reform enacted by the Satsuma-Choshu oligarchs in

---

* Essentially, this was the same administration as the cabinet in office at the time of the promulgation of the constitution in 1889. The only changes were as follows: Kuroda Kiyotaka (Satsuma) became prime minister, replacing Ito, who was appointed president of the privy council to facilitate ratification of the constitution by that body, and Okuma became minister of foreign affairs, replacing Inouye, who became minister of agriculture and finance.

preparation for constitutional government was the formation of the civil service (December, 1885). This act initiated a shift in the appointment of officials below the two highest bureaucratic ranks from a "spoils system" to a merit system based on examinations, although present officeholders were frozen in their positions. The graduates of Tokyo University were also exempted from the examination requirement. By 1881 this school, which had been founded in 1877, had already become the preferred institution for the training of prospective bureaucrats. In 1881, when it was reorganized, its president was made an appointee of the government, directly responsible to the minister of education, and the faculty became civil servants. In March, 1886, Tokyo University became Tokyo Imperial University, with its announced purpose to investigate those fields of science and learning which were of practical service to the state. Although the university remained the most important center for the training of conservative officials, the examination exemption was withdrawn in 1893 because of criticism by political parties.

By 1886 Ito and his committee were at long last ready to turn to the problem of drafting a constitution that would provide legal sanction for the newly reorganized imperial government and that would limit the powers of parliament. As a guide for the members of the committee, to whom he delegated most of the work, Ito outlined a basic policy, viz., that "in accordance with the development of Japanese history, the emperor would remain as the source of political power in the state." He conceded that in form the constitution should be based on those of Prussia and the various German states, but he insisted that the spirit behind it should be Japanese. He advised them to draft a short document—simple, broad, and free from statements of theory, as had been advised by Stein—and to work out the administrative details separately in an Imperial House Law, a Law of the Houses, an Election Law for the House of Representatives, and an Ordinance for the House of Peers. In its work the committee consulted with two German specialists, Hermann Roessler, who had been in Tokyo for some time, and to a lesser extent Albert Mosse, whom Ito had invited to Japan as an adviser on local government.

In June, 1887, the committee moved to a village hotel in Kanagawa Prefecture and then to Ito's summer home on the island of Matsushima near Yokosuka. Ito felt that greater secrecy was needed to avoid adverse criticism or interference caused by premature publicity. Because Ito's home was very small, Ito Myoji, Inouye Kowashi, and Kaneko Kentaro resided in a nearby town; but when a briefcase containing a draft prepared by Roessler was stolen in early August, the three men also moved to Matsushima as a security measure. These secret deliberations were criticized by liberals and conservatives alike. The liberals, fearing an authoritarian regime, called Ito a Bismarck, while the conservatives claimed that Ito was drafting a constitution on the British model. Throughout the summer of 1887 the committee discussed draft constitutions prepared by Roessler and Inouye, but their work was interrupted in the autumn when Ito departed on a tour of Kyushu and Okinawa.

Deliberations were resumed early in 1888, and finally, in April, drafts of the constitution and of the Imperial House Law were completed and ready for ratification. The ratification procedure to be used was determined in large part by a revival of political agitation against the government. In the summer and fall of 1887 Itagaki and Goto organized mob rallies in Tokyo and submitted petitions to the government demanding freedom of speech and assembly, reduction of the land tax, and particularly revision of the unequal treaties.

For over a decade the government had worked without success to remove the stigma and disadvantages of the unequal treaties. After initial failures, negotiations were at a standstill until 1884, when a new British minister intimated that revision would be acceptable when Japanese law codes reached the same standards as those in the various nations of the West. Shortly thereafter the government hired a number of foreign legal experts to assist in the compilation of codes. Negotiations were reopened in April, 1886, by Foreign Minister Inouye Kaoru, and between May, 1886, and April, 1887, a long series of meetings was held in Tokyo. While the representatives of the powers were willing to concede the principle of treaty equality, they insisted that Japan agree to the unrestricted residence of foreigners and the temporary acceptance of foreign judges in cases involving foreigners. It was these demands that prompted Itagaki and Goto to make the revision issue a major basis of their opposition to the government. The popular agitation was so great that Inouye was forced to terminate the negotiations and resign his position. It is ironic that a strong nationalist sentiment should be used against the very officials who had been responsible for its development.

When the antigovernment clamor increased in volume in the autumn and winter of 1887, Home Minister Yamagata ordered the police to enforce regulations restricting the right to present petitions and to hold public meetings; and on December 14 he issued new regulations forbidding government employees to attend political gatherings. When these measures proved inadequate, the government promulgated the drastic Peace Preservation Law on December 25, which forbade secret societies and political meetings, authorized the police to disband the latter at their own discretion, and, most important, empowered the police to banish the political opponents of the government from Tokyo. Over five hundred persons deemed "dangerous to the public peace" were ordered to leave the city immediately. The government also made several shrewd political maneuvers. It induced Okuma to join the cabinet in February, 1888, as foreign minister to take over the revision negotiations, thereby shifting responsibility to a prominent leader of the opposition, and it persuaded Goto to become minister of communications.

The Meiji Constitution

It was against this background that Ito had to decide on a method of ratification for the draft constitution and the accompanying laws. He understandably rejected the opposition's demand for a constitutional convention of delegates elected by the people, but at the same time he refused to accept the conservative suggestion that approval by the emperor would be sufficient. Although he considered the possibility of ratification by the genroin, he finally selected the privy council, which had been established by imperial ordinance on April 28, 1888. On April 30 Ito became its president, resigning the office of prime minister, which was bestowed upon Kuroda Kiyotaka. Membership in the council, the highest advisory body on constitutional and foreign policy matters, was by imperial appointment and was confined in practice to members of the imperial family, peers, and cabinet ministers.

The ratification deliberations, which began in May, 1888, and lasted until January, 1889, were conducted in secret, with every effort being made to prevent information from leaking out. There is evidence that some of the sessions were spirited and that differences of opinion were aired at great length, but a comparison of the draft and the final text reveals few significant changes. Parliament was permitted to initiate legislation, and both houses were given equal power with regard to finance. The constitution was promulgated by the emperor on February 11, 1889, the anniversary of the founding of the dynasty in 660 B.C., and the occasion was made one of national celebration. In order to minimize public criticism, the government suspended publication of several Tokyo newspapers and issued warnings to others.

The government had made important concessions to those groups that demanded a national parliament, but the Meiji Constitution* was essentially a carefully formulated legal justification for a regime in which power was held by a small number of men with minimal responsibility to the people. Their power continued to stem from the doctrine that sovereignty rested in the person of the emperor, not by divine right but by divine descent. The government made certain that this basic principle was beyond the possibility of constitutional change by providing for uninterrupted imperial succession to the sovereignty of the state in the Imperial House Law, which was regarded as superior to ordinary legislation and could not be amended or supplanted by such. The constitution conferred on the emperor the following broad executive powers: to command the army and navy; to declare war, make peace, and conclude treaties; to confer titles of nobility, ranks, and orders; and to declare an amnesty or commutation of punishment. He was empowered to determine the organization of the administrative branches of the government and the salaries, appointment, and dismissal of civil and military officials. Every law required the consent of both the house of representatives and the house of peers, but the emperor had effective veto power; if a veto was inappropriate, the government could delay publishing the act in the *Official Gazette*, or it could fail to provide enabling funds for it in the budget. The emperor had

* See Appendix 1.

the power to convoke, open, adjourn, and prorogue the diet; to convoke extraordinary sessions and determine their length; and to order the diet to hold secret meetings. Cabinet ministers or their delegates could bring in bills and claim precedence for them, and they had the right to speak in either house and in committee meetings. The emperor also had ordinance power of an extensive nature. He could issue ordinances with the force of law in case of national emergencies when the diet was not in session, but each action required the consent of that body at its next session. More important from an ordinary legislative standpoint, however, was his power to issue administrative ordinances "necessary for the carrying out of the laws, or for the maintenance of the public peace and order, and for the promotion of the welfare of the subjects."

The oligarchs secured the paramount political power of the emperor and his officials by providing for a maximum of financial independence from the diet. Although the constitution required that the annual budget be approved by the diet, it stipulated that "those already fixed expenditures based by the constitution upon the powers appertaining to the emperor, and such expenditures as may have arisen by the effect of law, or that appertain to the legal obligations of the government, shall be neither rejected nor reduced by the imperial diet, without the concurrence of the government." These expenditures included ordinary administrative expenses, salaries of officials, expenses arising from treaties, interest on the national debt, and subsidies and pensions. In case the diet failed to pass the budget, the cabinet was authorized to carry out the budget of the previous year; thus the government was not dependent on the diet for an annual vote of revenues, with the exception of budgetary increases. It did, however, need the consent of the diet to modify existing taxes or to levy new ones. The Imperial House Law gave the emperor and his family financial independence by stipulating that "no landed property or other property, that has been fixed as imperial hereditary estates, shall be divided up and alienated." Since 1882, at the suggestion of Iwakura, the government had been increasing the resources of the imperial family. In 1881 the imperial lands consisted of only 634 *cho*,* but by 1890 they comprised over 3,500,000 *cho*. In 1882 the imperial family held private funds totaling 1,700,000 yen, and by 1887, with the addition of valuable securities, they amounted to over 7,500,000 yen. Besides its income from land and investments, the imperial family was granted an annual appropriation of 3,000,000 yen, which, according to the Imperial House Law, "shall not require the consent thereto of the imperial diet, except in case an increase thereof is found necessary."

While the Meiji Constitution invested supreme political power in the person of the emperor, he did not actually take part in administration. For all

---

* One **cho** equals 2.45 acres.

practical purposes a small number of men controlled the government through their positions in the cabinet, the supreme command, the privy council, and the imperial household ministry, all of which constituted the actual repositories of executive power. This group tended to become institutionalized as an extraconstitutional informal advisory council known by 1900 as the *genro*, or elder statesmen. Their number included those former samurai who had participated in the Meiji Restoration and who had succeeded to political power after the deaths of the so-called "triumvirate"—Kido, Okubo, and Saigo—which had dominated the scene in the 1870's. Ito, Yamagata, and Matsukata were perhaps the most important genro and of course were the architects of many of Japan's modern policies and institutions. The genro never constituted a large body, although later a few important additions were made, e.g., Saionji Kimmochi, an influential civil political leader, who became the so-called "last genro," and Katsura Taro, the military-political protégé of the army boss, Yamagata.

With several executive agencies advising the emperor independently, the genro proved to be the only body able to make final decisions; the genro also provided a basic continuity among the several executive agencies by virtue of their dominant position in each. Until 1918, with only one exception, they controlled the cabinet through their monopoly of the prime ministership, and they also controlled the privy council through their near monopoly of the office of president, their domination of the cabinet, and their role in approving the appointment of members. Finally, in the military-naval sphere, the most important men were genro: Yamagata Aritomo, Matsukata Masayoshi, and Oyama Iwao.

With regard to the cabinet, the constitution provided that "the respective ministers of state shall give their advice to the emperor and be responsible for it" and recognized the legality of the imperial decrees which enumerated its functions and its powers. While the constitution was not absolutely clear regarding ministerial responsibility, in practice the cabinet recognized responsibility only to the emperor. According to Ito Hirobumi:

> He alone can dismiss a minister who has been appointed by him. Who then is it, except the sovereign, that can appoint, dismiss, and punish a minister of state? The appointment and dismissal of them having been included by the constitution in the sovereign power of the emperor, it is only a legitimate consequence that the power of deciding as to the responsibility of ministers is withheld from the diet.

Ito did concede that,

> although the emperor reserves to himself in the constitution the right of appointing his ministers at his pleasure, in making an appointment the susceptibilities of the public mind must also be taken into consideration. This may be regarded as an indirect method of controlling the responsibility of ministers.

Evidently Ito had in mind a dual responsibility, primary to the emperor and secondary to the people. He denied the principle of the joint responsibility of the cabinet, insisting that ministers individually were responsible for the conduct of their departments, for he feared the development of party control through this back door; however, in reality the cabinet did become closely unified, with results equivalent to those obtained by recognition of joint responsibility.

The supreme command, consisting of the ministers of the army and the navy as well as the two chiefs of staff, was also independent of legislative and popular control; in many matters it was even beyond the control of the cabinet. According to an imperial ordinance promulgated in December, 1889, and revised in 1907, the chief of the general staff had the power to report directly to the throne without having to go through the cabinet on matters pertaining to military command and military secrets. During wartime the operational plans of the armed forces and the execution of those plans were functions of the imperial headquarters, consisting of the general staffs of the army and navy, which had direct access to the emperor and was independent of the cabinet. This division between civil and military in government had been supported for some time by General Yamagata, who served as chief of staff of the army at different periods and who dominated the post, since on other occasions it was filled by one of his loyal subordinates. In 1879 Yamagata and his protégé, Katsura Taro, who had studied in Germany from 1871 to 1874 and had served as military attaché in Berlin, effected the creation of the general staff office with direct access to the emperor and sole responsibility for carrying out military commands. In 1879 the government also established the position of inspector-general to improve military education. As far as the navy was concerned, the head of that department exercised a general supervision over administration and command together.

Although these practices were not written into the constitution, they were accepted by its framers and were not questioned thereafter. Later, in 1894, an imperial ordinance decreed that the army and navy cabinet ministers were to be officers of high rank in their respective services; this provision gave the military the power to interfere in the formation of the cabinet and in the determination of its policies.

The privy council was sanctioned by the Meiji Constitution in much the same manner as the cabinet. "The privy councilors shall, in accordance with the provisions for the organization of the privy council, deliberate upon important matters of state, when they have been consulted by the emperor." These matters included constitutional problems and amendments, legislation, treaty-making, and affairs of the imperial family. The oligarchs maintained their control of this body in a number of ways. Most important was their near monopoly of its presidency. Ito, Saionji, Kuroda, Oki, and Yamagata held the post, the latter from 1905 to 1922. Members were appointed by the prime minister in consultation with the genro, and cabinet ministers automatically became privy councilors.

The oligarchs also kept close control over the imperial household ministry. Such posts as lord keeper of the privy seal and grand chamberlain were especially important in their eyes since these officials were the personal confidants of the emperor. It was through these men, who were not part of the cabinet or subject to cabinet control, that policies and decisions were reported to the emperor. From the outset, the imperial household ministry was dominated by officials of Satsuma and Choshu background who were usually privy councilors or members of the house of peers.

The Meiji Constitution contained a bill of rights, which superficially resembled those of liberal Western constitutions, but none of its basic rights and freedoms were unconditionally guaranteed. Laws restricting any fundamental right or freedom, like freedom of the press or freedom of association, were not directly prohibited by the constitution; and in the absence of any legal process like *habeas corpus*, individual freedoms were limited. The rights of Japanese subjects were also curtailed by the lack of legislative control over the police ordinance power. According to the constitution,

no suit which relates to rights alleged to have been infringed by the illegal measures of the executive authorities, and which should come within the competency of the court of administrative litigation, especially established by law, shall be taken cognizance of by a court of law.

Nationalism and Education

The overthrow of the Tokugawa regime, the abolition of feudalism, and the ultimate creation of the imperial system under the Meiji Constitution did not resolve the underlying struggles in Japanese society; in fact, the process of modernization intensified them and gave rise to others. Agrarian reactionaries clashed with advocates of an urbanized, industrial society, while on another level the new monied interests of the countryside objected to government policies that favored their urban rivals. Peasants opposed high rents charged by the landlords and high taxes levied by the government, while urban workers, often recruited from rural poverty, fell victim to industrial exploitation.

Stein had suggested to Ito that only the state could resolve these clashes through reforms carried out by the government. But a government dominated by intense nationalists, determined to compress a lengthy historical process into several decades, had to favor certain interests over others. Thus the genro felt that, so long as fundamental social clashes continued to exist, to broaden the base of government might jeopardize their whole program. They held to the conclusion that their leadership was indispensable.

Nationalism was the instrument by which the leaders of Japan sought to reconcile divergent interests. Their policies had created the Japanese national state, and in these early decades of the Meiji period they were seeking to transform the old feudal loyalty into a patriotic devotion of individual Japanese subjects to their emperor. They continued the revival of state Shinto and even utilized a blending of Confucianism and statism much like the one conceived by their predecessors in the bakufu. The imperial rescript on education issued in 1890 exhorted the people:

Be filial to your parents, affectionate to your brothers and sisters; as husbands and wives be harmonious; as friends true; bear yourselves in modesty and moderation . . . always respect the constitution and observe the laws; should emergency arise, offer yourselves courageously to the state; and thus guard and maintain the prosperity of our imperial throne co-equal with heaven and earth.

The emperor was the father of the nation; consequently, political obligations were equated with filial piety. There could be no conflict between state and family, for loyalty to the state and filial piety were one and the same. Even the leaders of the political opposition never questioned the emphasis on nationalism; however, they tended to equate national interests with their own.

The government's concern for education indicates clearly the relationship between nationalism and modernization. The economic environment of Tokugawa Japan had favored an expansion of educational facilities for the urban and rural rich, while the masses of peasants and workers remained illiterate and ignorant. After the Meiji Restoration Japan's new leaders set out to create an educational system that would accelerate national development. In 1871 they established the department of education, which in the following year put into effect a system of compulsory education based on French experience. The country was divided into 8 university districts, which were subdivided into 32 middle school districts, each comprising 210 elementary school districts, which gave the country one elementary school for every six hundred persons. School attendance was compulsory for all children, male and female, six years of age or older. In the beginning the period of compulsory instruction was only sixteen months, but this was extended to three years in 1880 and four years in 1886; it was finally extended to the full six-year period of the elementary school in 1907. By 1899 middle schools (five years) had been established in all the prefectures of Japan, and beyond this level there were various educational institutions. *Kotogakko* (three-year higher schools) provided university preparation, but in addition there were professional schools in vocational fields like agriculture, forestry, engineering, mining, and fisheries. Normal schools trained teachers, and the needs of business and industry were met by commercial and industrial institutes. The capstone of the system were the universities (three years). By the end of the century the government was supporting imperial universities at Tokyo and Kyoto, and later it established others at Sendai (1907), Fukuoka (1910), Sapporo (1918), Osaka (1931), Seoul (1923), and on Formosa (1928). Private universities also played an important role in training men for careers in politics, law, medicine, and business. One of the oldest and most famous was Keio University, founded by Fukuzawa Yukichi as a small private school in the 1850's; another was Waseda University, founded in 1882 by Okuma Shigenobu.

Educational opportunities came more slowly for women than for men. Traditionally the education of women was restricted to those types of training which fitted them to be good wives and mothers. Some women learned the bare essentials of reading and writing, but generally their education went no further than the necessary household arts and skills, such as weaving, spinning, sewing, and cooking. For daughters of the rich there was additional training, intended to give graceful manners and refinement, which included the tea ceremony, flower arrangement, and music and dancing. Since this view of female education continued over into modern Japan, it was Christian missionaries who pioneered in establishing schools for girls. Although some girls' middle schools and normal schools were founded in the first decade of the government's program, the first girls' higher school was not established until 1882. At the turn of the century, Tsuda College for Women and a medical school for women were opened, and in 1913 the imperial university at Sendai accepted for the first time a small number of women students.

For a time American influences were strong in Japanese education. By the middle of the 1870's, the government began to shift from the French system to one based on the American principle of decentralized control. In 1877 normal schools, which had been established and administered by the central government, were turned over to the prefectures, and in 1879 the entire system was remodeled on American lines, with recognition of the principle of local autonomy in educational administration. Finally, in 1880, Japan began to organize locally elected boards of education. In this period the English language was the required foreign language in the middle schools and in the institutions of higher learning; later, in the 1880's, the ministry of education introduced English into the elementary school curriculum.

The system reached its final form in the 1880's, when, under German influence, the administration of Japanese schools was recentralized under the control of the ministry of education; moreover, a revision of the educational code placed morals courses in a far more prominent position in the school curriculum and made moral character an essential qualification for teachers. While Confucianism had been discredited in the years immediately following the Meiji Restoration because of its close association with the bakufu, the leaders of the government ultimately realized that a more widespread acceptance of Confucian principles would help create the kind of ideological unity they desired and would tend to weaken the Western liberal principles that caused them so much anxiety. Students were also taught that to improve their skills meant to increase the strength of the nation. The enrichment of the lives of individual students was only a secondary purpose of education. Even the goals of imperial universities were defined as "the offering of instruction in carrying on thorough investigation in the arts and sciences to meet the needs of the state." The government also introduced military drill, both for its practical and moral benefits, into the school curriculum and utilized retired army officers to teach it.

Nationalism was, for the most part, geared to the modernization program by both the government leaders and their critics in the opposition parties, but there were elements that wished to direct nationalism toward military expansion. Samurai had supported the demand for war with Korea in the 1870's, and in subsequent decades they inspired a number of ultranationalistic, expansionist societies. The history of one of these, the Genyosha,* is particularly enlightening. It supported a militant Korean policy and the democratic movement, but by the middle of the 1880's it abandoned the cause of popular rights and turned its attention almost entirely to the expansion of national power. Like other nationalist societies, it urged the government to increase the size of the army and navy and to adopt a more "positive" foreign policy. It had allies in leaders like General Kuroda, who wanted to attack China before she became too strong. Although these views were successfully opposed by Ito Hirobumi and Inouye Kaoru, who argued that Japan was not yet ready for such a course, some responsibility must be given to the Genyosha for the ultimate declaration of war on China in 1894.

Japanese nationalism was not just the creature of the state or the expansionist societies. In the 1880's and after, many intellectuals espoused nationalism in a reaction against what they regarded as indiscriminate acceptance of Western principles; for example, a group of Tokyo intellectuals began to publish a magazine called Nihonjin (The Japanese), which was noted for its vigorous opposition to all Western ideas and customs and for its demand that the "Japanese national essence" be preserved. Such efforts as this made the Japanese re-examine their own culture in a more critical spirit. In art, for example, there was a reaction against prevailing Westernism and a return to traditional forms. In the first two decades of the Meiji period Japanese artists had become almost completely absorbed by artistic styles, forms, and techniques dominant in the West, and they seemed to lose interest in their own tradition. But with government support there emerged what has been termed a national art movement. In scholarly fields like history, intellectuals began to concern themselves with studies of Japanese ideas and institutions and to give less attention to foreign cultures; and they shared with their Westernized colleagues a belief that knowledge should serve the interests of the state.

---

* Founded in Fukuoka in 1881 by Hiraoka Kotaro, a mine-owner and former samurai who had taken part in the Satsuma Rebellion.

Parliamentary Struggles

After the promulgation of the Meiji Constitution in February, 1889, political conflict was renewed with an intensity reminiscent of the early 1880's. The platforms of both the Jiyuto and Kaishinto, which were re-established in anticipation of the parliamentary elections of 1890, advocated that a party cabinet be formed on the basis of the election results. But the oligarchs denied the applicability of the principle of party government and insisted that since the cabinet derived all its power from the throne it could not presume to represent anything less than all the emperor's subjects. Ito, one of the most influential of the genro, explained this view as follows:

It cannot be helped if, as the people acquire advanced political ideas, political parties grow, and if there are political parties there will be conflicts in the diet. But it is absolutely necessary for the government to have no connection whatever with any political party. The sovereign power of the state resides in the emperor; its exercise therefore must be absolutely independent and impartial to all parties; so, to every subject, there will be equal recognition and equal benevolence. If the ministers of state who assist the emperor and conduct the government with all its responsibilities have any relation with political parties, it is impossible for them to maintain this impartiality.

And his colleague, Yamagata, who succeeded Kuroda as prime minister in October, 1889, strongly endorsed this view.

The elections for the house of representatives were held on July 1, 1890; and out of a population of approximately 40,000,000 people, about 460,000 had the right to vote. The Jiyuto, Kaishinto, and antigovernment independents, all of whom advocated cabinet responsibility to the house of representatives, won over 200 of the 300 seats that were contested, while the cabinet, which had not participated actively in the election, could count on less than 90 supporters. Of the total number of representatives, the largest bloc, 129, came from the landlord class and only 19 from commercial and industrial interests. This breakdown can be explained in part by the fact that Japan was still essentially an agrarian nation; moreover, the political strength of the landlords had been increased by the suffrage qualification, which restricted the electorate to those who had paid a direct national tax (land, business, or income) of not less than fifteen yen for a period of at least one year prior to the time that the election lists were drawn up. However, landlord political strength, which continued into the first two decades of the twentieth century and on a declining scale thereafter, must be explained also by the political indifference of urban businessmen, many of whom were dependent upon the government and who tended to confine political activities to behind-the-scenes operations which involved less risk and promised greater results; for businessmen claimed that when they entered politics openly, they invited attack upon their persons and jeopardized their business interests. About one-third of the electorate and a substantial number of representatives were former samurai, and their political credos ranged from democracy to reactionary nationalism. While the cabinet fared poorly in the election, it was able to control the house of peers by appointing its 250 members from among the nobility, scholars, payers of high taxes, and individuals who had performed some meritorious service for the state.

When the first diet was convened on November 25, 1890, Prime Minister Yamagata faced the opposition of the political parties. Although he referred to the need for complete unity and implicit trust in the cabinet in his introductory speech to the house of representatives, he soon found himself on the defensive. The house financial committee cut the government's budget by about 10 per cent, hoping thus to reduce taxation but also to strike at the opponents of party government among the civil and military bureaucracy. The most important reductions were in official salaries, retirement pensions, social allowances, residence allowances, and travel expenses. The cabinet, however, would not give way. It cited the provision of the constitution which prohibited the reduction of already fixed expenditures and claimed that the house had exceeded its powers. To make his position clear, Yamagata prorogued the house for a week. The cabinet also hired *soshi* (bullies) to intimidate its political party opponents and in other cases resorted to bribery in an effort to split the Jiyuto. Yamagata even threatened to dissolve the house, but his colleagues objected that such a drastic step in the very first session of the diet might cause adverse criticism abroad. Negotiations regarding the unequal treaties had continued, and the cabinet was not anxious to weaken its case. In the end Yamagata succeeded in getting 2,500,000 yen of the 6,000,000-yen cut restored, but his success was the result of bribery, intimidation, and his own promises to make certain administrative reforms. When Ito criticized his handling of the first diet, Yamagata resigned as prime minister.

Matsukata Masayoshi, who became prime minister in May, 1891, faced another hostile diet when it convened in November. A coalition of the Jiyuto and Kaishinto slashed military and naval expenditures in the appropriations bill, which was reduced by nearly 8,000,000 yen, including an increase of 6,500,000 yen over the budget of the previous year. In retaliation Matsukata dissolved the diet and took the offensive in the subsequent election campaign. His cabinet used every possible repressive measure against party candidates, including personal arrest and destruction of their property. Both Itagaki and Okuma were prosecuted under the assembly and political-association ordinance. Local police and prefectural officials were ordered to assist progovernment candidates, and on election day voters were molested by bullies. The brutality of the campaign and the election resulted in at least twenty-five deaths and over three hundred wounded.

In spite of the violence directed against them, the parties emerged from the February election with a clear majority of 163 seats in the house of representatives. At most, the cabinet could count on the support of about 100 members. Ito once again was critical, and with the support of the house of peers he forced Matsukata to demand the resignation of Home Minister Shinagawa Yajiro, who had directed the antiparty operations. Yamagata, who had supported the use of terror, regarded this as a personal affront and was instrumental in arranging protest resignations by the ministers of the army and navy.

The political conflict was renewed in the special diet session of May, 1892. The house of representatives passed a resolution, concurred in by the house of peers, condemning and censuring the cabinet for its election interference, but the genro simply ignored it. The parties again attacked the budget. After the dissolution of the second diet, the budget of the previous year had automatically gone into effect; but when the special diet session considered a supplementary budget, the parties made new cuts, particularly in expenditures for the military and for official enterprises, which amounted to one-third of the total. When the house of peers refused to uphold all the cuts, the matter was referred to the privy council, which ruled that a compromise should be effected by a joint committee of both houses. This was a disappointment to party leaders, for they had hoped that on budgetary matters decisions of the house of representatives would be final. In August Matsukata resigned, and Ito, who had been so critical of others, became prime minister. This shift was largely the result of a split within the cabinet. When Home Minister Kono Togama attempted to transfer or dismiss governors who had been involved in the election scandals in order to restore public confidence in the cabinet, some of them objected and won support from the military. Since Kono refused to compromise, the cabinet split, and Matsukata resigned.

The struggle between the cabinet and the parties reached a climax during Ito's ministry. The fourth diet convened on November 25, 1892, and once again the parties cut budgetary increases, including a large naval building program. When the cabinet continued to object to the reductions, the parties secured 146 signatures on a memorial to the emperor impeaching it. Ito ordered a fifteen-day suspension of the house of representatives, but when it reconvened in February, 1893, the memorial was passed by the house and delivered to the emperor on February 8. Two days later the emperor answered by rescript after consulting with the cabinet, the privy council, and certain leading members of both houses of the diet. He strongly supported the cabinet on the matter of naval appropriations, and he personally promised to curtail the expenses of the imperial household and for six years, every year, to give 300,000 yen to maintain Japan's naval strength. He also ordered the civil and military officials of the country to donate one-tenth of their annual salaries for the same purpose.

This imperial foray into politics put the parties in a difficult position. The emperor had appealed to their patriotism, and their response would be subject to close public scrutiny. Party leaders, though angered by Ito's tactics, could not, under the circumstances, continue to oppose the increase in naval appropriations; they did, however, try to salvage some of their prestige by securing promises of administrative reform while conferring on the budget with the cabinet. The most important result of this affair was perhaps the realization by many party members, particularly those of the Jiyuto, that they had better compromise with the cabinet; Hoshi Toru, for example, an important Jiyuto leader, concluded that such a course was the only road to political power.

The fifth diet, which convened in November, 1893, was the scene of party attacks on the government's conduct of foreign policy, particularly its attempts at revision of the treaties; the session was also marked by intraparty squabbles based on charges of corruption. Ito was forced to prorogue the house of representatives twice, and in January, 1894, he ordered its dissolution. Despite cabinet efforts to hamper the campaign activities of political parties, the May, 1894, elections returned another house hostile to Ito. In the new diet session the parties passed a nonconfidence motion based largely on criticism of foreign policy and presented it to the emperor on June 1, 1894. After consulting Yamagata, Ito on the following day again dissolved the diet.

The problem of treaty revision had been a constant embarrassment to the government. In February, 1888, Okuma began secret negotiations with the powers, especially the British, hoping to conclude new treaties without the interference of public opinion. But when a news item in *The Times* (London) in April, 1889, disclosed that a draft treaty provided for the temporary use of foreign judges in cases involving foreigners, the enemies of the cabinet, liberals and reactionaries alike, opposed the treaty for their own purposes. In fact, one outraged fanatic attempted to assassinate Okuma. The tumult forced the cabinet to reject the treaty, and a few days later Prime Minister Kuroda resigned. Although opposition to the treaty can be explained in large part by the realities of practical politics, much of the mass support for it was stimulated by genuine nationalistic sentiment.

The government continued to negotiate for revision of the treaties, and its persistence finally brought success. In November, 1892, Foreign Minister Mutsu Munemitsu resumed negotiations for a settlement that would give Japan equality after a five-year period. In the meantime new civil and commercial legal codes could be put into final form. For the next several years negotiations were conducted through the various foreign offices by Japanese diplomats, with the strongest efforts being made to win over Great Britain and the United States, since Mutsu felt that the other powers would follow their lead. Success was assured when in July, 1894, the negotiations of Aoki Shuzo in London resulted in a treaty in which the British agreed to relinquish extraterritorial jurisdiction in Japan by July, 1899. In November the United

States signed a similar treaty, and by December, 1897, the last of the major powers, Austria-Hungary, gave up extraterritoriality. During this same period the powers also began to recognize Japan's tariff autonomy, but this goal was not completely achieved until the signing of the Treaty of Commerce and Navigation with the United States on February 11, 1911.

The political conflicts in Japan were a factor helping to determine the decision to go to war with China over Korea in 1894. The cabinet's opponents were demanding a stronger foreign policy. Although treaty revision was the basic concern of most of them, others concentrated on Korea. Nationalist societies and chauvinist writers took up the cry for war, and even some moderate newspapers joined in. In the general election of 1892 the Matsukata cabinet assured the Genyosha that it would pursue a stronger policy and would increase military appropriations. The Genyosha, one of the more active ultra-nationalistic societies, terrorized antigovernment candidates in the Fukuoka area, working closely with Home Minister Shinagawa, and it also organized a small subsidiary group, the Tenyukyo (Society for the Celestial Salvation of the Oppressed), to further the activities of the rebellious Tonghaks in Korea. When war with China over Korea did break out, the news was received enthusiastically in Japan.

The constitutional crisis in Japanese government was also an important factor in the decision to go to war. With the house of representatives dominated by the political parties, whose opposition to the government was unrelenting, a number of the genro, especially the military component, welcomed a foreign war that would unite the home front. The war did bring temporary stability to Japanese politics, and when the seventh diet met in special session at Hiroshima in October, 1894, it passed without a dissenting vote a huge war budget. The eighth diet was equally peaceful, and again the budget bill was passed without modification. But after Japan's victory in the war with China the struggle between the parties and the cabinet was renewed.

19 *Japanese Expansion in Asia*

Much of the glitter of Japan's victory over China was erased by the Triple Intervention of 1895. The popular reaction, which included ceremonial suicides by several ultranationalists, was so great that the government was forced to suspend publication of many leading newspapers. The intervention became a domestic political issue, since the entire country was enraged not only at the powers but also at the Japanese officials who had yielded to their demands.

The difficulties of the government, moreover, were increased by its failures in Korea.

Japanese-Russian Rivalry in Korea

In 1894 Japan had sought to lay the foundations of a protectorate over Korea. Immediately after the beginning of hostilities with China, a provisional agreement was signed at Seoul between the Japanese minister and the Korean government stipulating that the latter would carry out domestic reforms on the advice of Japan. Under the supervision of Tai Won Kun, now a tool of Japan, the king proclaimed a series of reforms, punished the members of the queen's family (Min faction), and renounced the Sino-Korean treaties. But when the reform measures proved ineffective, Tokyo dispatched a new minister, Inouye Kaoru, to prod the Korean government. After securing the formation of a new cabinet, Inouye returned to Japan for discussions regarding policy in Korea.

Korean conservatives looked to Russia for assistance against Japan, and in Inouye's absence the queen became increasingly friendly with the Russian minister. Under her influence the king stiffened his attitude toward Japan, and in October, 1895, the reform cabinet gave way to a conservative one which had the support of the Russians.

Then, early on the morning of October 8, Tai Won Kun, who succumbed to the blandishments of Miura Goro, Inouye's successor as minister, led Japanese-trained Korean soldiers and heavily armed Japanese bullies into the palace and killed the queen. He imprisoned many members of the Min faction and forced the king to form a cabinet of officials who were friendly to Japan. For a time the king was virtually a prisoner of the reform cabinet, but on February 11, 1896, he and the crown prince escaped from the palace and found asylum in the Russian legation. From this vantage point the king ordered the dismissal of the pro-Japanese cabinet and severe punishment for those responsible for his wife's murder. In the blood purge that followed, the prime minister and several ministers were murdered. Since Miura had acted on his own initiative, he was recalled by his government and tried by court martial, but he was acquitted.

These events caused widespread resentment against Japan, and Russian influence superseded that of Japan in the Korean government. The Japanese-trained army was disbanded, and Japanese resident merchants as well as fishermen along the coast left Korea for Japan. This second defeat at the hands of Russia was almost more than ardent Japanese nationalists could bear, but despite their demands for a stronger policy, the nation was not prepared for another war. The Japanese government had to be content to salvage through diplomacy what influence it could in Korea.

In June, 1896, Japan and Russia reached a compromise with regard to Korea. Yamagata, who was in Moscow for the coronation of the czar, proposed

315

that Korea be divided at the thirty-eighth parallel between a Russian sphere in the north and a Japanese sphere in the south. The Russians rejected his proposal, since they hoped in the long run to dominate the whole peninsula, but they did suggest the establishment of a joint protectorate. Yamagata and Foreign Minister Lobanov signed an agreement by which both powers would support the Korean king's efforts to restore and maintain order, guarantee foreign loans for the development of a police force, abstain from interfering in the Korean police and army, and seek to secure equal treatment in matters of economic rights and privileges. In a secret article they pledged that, should it become necessary to send troops into Korea, the two powers would fix a neutral zone between their spheres of action.

Russian actions, however, did not coincide with Russian diplomacy. Shortly after the signing of the Yamagata-Lobanov Protocol the Russian government dispatched military advisers and instructors to assist the Korean army; it also secured timber concessions on the Yalu River and mining concessions on the Tumen River. Although the Korean king returned to his palace in February, 1897, Russian influence continued to increase. His government granted more lumber and mining concessions, approved a request for a coaling station at Pusan, and accepted a Russian financial adviser and superintendent of customs. Lastly, a Russo-Korean bank was opened in Seoul with authority to manage the government's currency and accounts.

In 1898 Russian policy became conciliatory once more. For one thing, Russian actions in Korea invited a reaction much like that which Japan had provoked against herself.* More important, Russia was in the process of establishing a sphere of interest over Manchuria, and the czar had been persuaded that, if he expected to avoid antagonizing Great Britain and Japan, it would be better to withdraw from Korea. The Japanese reaction to the Russian leasehold in the Liaotung Peninsula was loud and strong, and even the cry of war was heard in some press quarters. Thus at Tokyo in April, 1898, the Russian ambassador, Baron Rosen, and Foreign Minister Nishi Tokujiro, reaffirming the principles of the Yamagata-Lobanov Protocol, recognized the sovereignty and independence of Korea and agreed not to assist her in the reorganization of her army and finances without previous consultation and agreement. The Russian advisers were withdrawn, and the Russo-Korean Bank was closed.

Domestic Politics

The struggle with Russia over Korea had important repercussions on politics in Japan. The "strong foreign policy group," comprising Kaishinto members

---

* E.g., in March, 1898, the Russian envoy, Alexis Speyer, asked the king to oust a number of persons in the government who opposed Russian interests and threatened to withdraw Russian military instructors in case he refused. When the king called his bluff, the officers departed.

and numerous ultranationalists, denounced the cabinet for its failures, but the Korean issue led to an alliance between the cabinet and the Jiyuto. In November, 1895, Itagaki, Jiyuto president, and Kono Hironaka, one of the party's leading members, pledged their support of the Ito cabinet and helped to beat down efforts of the opposition to impeach it, and at the close of the diet session the Jiyuto was rewarded when Itagaki was appointed home minister. Actually, the *rapprochement* between the Jiyuto and the cabinet had been in the making for some time. Many Jiyuto members were disillusioned by their experiences in fighting a succession of cabinets, while some of the genro, Ito, for example, realized the need for party support. Ito had come to the conclusion that the establishment of a progovernment party was necessary to bring order to internal politics, and even the militarists, who liked to think that they could ignore the parties, were in practice compelled to find supporters among party members.

The Kaishinto took steps to counteract the Jiyuto-government alliance. First, it effected a merger with other antigovernment elements in the house of representatives to form a new party, the Shimpoto (Progressive Party), and elected Okuma as president (March 1, 1896). The new party then found allies among the Satsuma men in government, namely, Matsukata and Admiral Kabayama. Iwasaki, head of the Mitsubishi economic empire, was evidently instrumental in working out this *rapprochement*; like many businessmen, he found it expedient to have friends at the top among both government and party figures. Ito, anxious to get a maximum of political support for his cabinet, invited Okuma and Matsukata to join it; but when Itagaki, head of the Jiyuto, who had accepted the post of home minister, threatened to resign, Ito had no alternative but to withdraw himself.

Matsukata succeeded Ito as prime minister in September, 1896, and was dependent on Okuma and the Shimpoto for support in the house of representatives. He appointed Okuma as minister of foreign affairs, agreed to conduct a more vigorous foreign policy, and promised to appoint a large number of Shimpoto members to subordinate bureaucratic posts. The Shimpoto tried to impose the principle of responsible cabinet government, but Matsukata would not go that far; and when he did not live up to Shimpoto expectations with regard to foreign policy and official appointments, Okuma resigned (November, 1897). The oligarchs' approach to government in this period is wonderfully illustrated by Matsukata's subsequent efforts to revise his cabinet and seek the support of the rival Jiyuto. His overtures were rejected, and a vote of nonconfidence would have carried had he not first dissolved the house of representatives. Lacking party support and thus having no hope for victory in a general election, Matsukata resigned as prime minister in favor of Ito.

Ito also failed to secure party support. His new cabinet, organized in January, 1898, was dominated by Choshu elements which refused to make concessions to the parties. Prior to the general election of March 15, 1898, which once again returned party majorities to the house of representatives, Ito promised to admit Itagaki, head of the Jiyuto, into the cabinet, but he was unable to keep the commitment because of the opposition of Inouye Kaoru and Yamagata Aritomo, both of Choshu and two of the most influential genro. When the Jiyuto announced angrily that it was severing all connections with the administration, Ito attempted to woo Okuma and the Shimpoto but failed in this effort also. When the diet convened in May, he faced the withering blasts of party criticism. The heaviest attack was launched against the cabinet's foreign policy, but in the end the crucial issue was taxation. The cabinet's proposal for increases in land, sake, manufacturing, and income taxes was defeated, and another deadlock between the parties and the cabinet ensued.

The political parties were disillusioned by their experiences in co-operating with cabinets and their genro leaders, who, it was clear, attached no real importance to parties as such. For the first time the leaders of the two most important parties came to a full realization that the genro could be checked only through their effective co-operation, and in June, 1898, the Jiyuto and Shimpoto joined to form a new party, the Kenseikai (the Constitutional Party), with a platform emphasizing the principles of cabinet responsibility to the house of representatives and advancement of local self-government.

This unification so amazed and alarmed the genro that they called a special conference to discuss countermeasures. Prime Minister Ito stated that it was impossible to keep in office a cabinet that was unresponsive to the opinions of the house of representatives, and he outlined two alternatives: that he organize a political party to support the policies of the genro or that he turn the administration over to the Kenseikai. Yamagata, supported by the army, refused to accept either course and advocated temporary suspension of the constitution. When the conference proved unable to reach a decision, Ito resigned; and when no successor as prime minister could be found among the genro, the Kenseikai was invited to form a cabinet. On June 30 Okuma assumed the posts of prime minister and minister of foreign affairs, and Itagaki became minister of home affairs.

Ito's proposal during the special conference reflected a growing conflict between the civil and military components in government—for all practical purposes between their two Choshu leaders, Ito and Yamagata. The influence of the military had been increasing in recent years for several reasons. The Triple Intervention and the rivalry with Russia in Korea were convincing evidence of the need to expand military power, and the upsurge of nationalism, particularly the activities of the expansionist societies, further strengthened the hand of the military. The national budget for 1896 was nearly twice that of the preceding year, with the largest increase going to military appropriations; and in 1897 military expenditures amounted to almost half the total budget. Because of the direct control it exercised over such a large proportion of national expenditures, the military achieved a strong voice in the general management of national affairs. The civil leaders, moreover, accepted the practice by which the cabinet ministers for the army and navy were selected from the top two ranks of officers on active duty. Thus, in the Kenseikai cabinet, General Katsura Taro and Admiral Saigo Tsugumichi continued to hold the army and navy portfolios. Ito, frustrated by the mounting power of the military, saw in the Kenseikai the only alternative to direct military control.

The Okuma-Itagaki cabinet was, however, a complete failure. In fact, it fell from office even before the opening of the diet session, despite the fact that it continued to hold approximately 260 seats in the house of representatives. The Kenseikai cabinet was pledged to conduct a more aggressive foreign policy and to expand the size of the military establishment, but the factions within the party could not agree on a supporting tax program. They also fought over the spoils of office. Unable to resolve these differences, the cabinet resigned after a tenure in office of just four months, and the Kenseikai split into two separate parties. Jiyuto members formed the Kenseito (the Constitutional Party), while the Shimpoto members organized the Kenseihonto (the True Constitutional Party).

Yamagata and the army formed a new cabinet on November 8, a day after Ito arrived at Nagasaki from a tour in China. Yamagata, who became prime minister, won legislative support by resorting to systematic bribery of the house of representatives, particularly its Kenseito members. In this way he succeeded in raising land and residence taxes for a five-year period to pay for the expansion of the army and navy. To counter the previous cabinet's liberalization of civil service requirements, a measure they had taken to increase the spoils of office, Yamagata had the great majority of high offices placed under an examination system, which he hoped would prevent party infiltration of the bureaucracy. The civil service was in fact stabilized and underwent no major change until after World War II because Yamagata also secured acceptance of a provision whereby all revisions of civil service regulations were made subject to privy council inquiry.

Yamagata did make one important concession to party demands. Bills designed to reform and extend the election law had been passed since 1894 by the house of representatives, only to be voted down each time by the house of peers, the genro's staunch ally. Faced with continued party agitation and with a public opinion that clamored for extension of the suffrage, Yamagata felt obliged, despite his own personal wishes, to support a new election law which increased the electorate by three times the original total. The new law provided for a secret ballot, reduced tax qualifications to ten yen, made the whole prefecture the election district, and increased the number of representatives to 369, or one for each 130,000 people.

A *rapprochement* between Ito and the Kenseito brought about the fall of Yamagata's cabinet. Disappointed by Yamagata's refusal to admit its leaders into his cabinet, the Kenseito sought out Ito in order to form an alliance with him to its advantage. Ito agreed to co-operate, but only on terms which included the formation of a new party with a membership obedient to his orders. The Kenseito accepted this condition, and the Rikken Seiyukai (Association of Constitutional Friends) was inaugurated on September 13, 1900, with Ito as president. His hope of establishing a political party to support the government was thus realized, while the Kenseito members looked ahead to political success, although for the time being they had to commit themselves to a leadership which planted the imperial interpretation of the constitution squarely at the heart of the party movement.

Perhaps the most significant result of this political alliance was the fact that the new party was infiltrated by a growing number of Ito's followers in the bureaucracy, many of whom were strong opponents of liberalism, but Ito was disappointed in his hope that the new party would create a national political unity. The Kenseihonto criticized the Kenseito for its act of "servile submission," and Yamagata's militarist faction viewed Ito's move with great alarm and hostility. Both were forced to accept Ito as prime minister after Yamagata's resignation on September 26; but although the Seiyukai enjoyed a majority in the house of representatives, Ito encountered effective political opposition. He pushed an unprecedentedly large tax bill through the house of representatives, but the house of peers, under the influence of Yamagata, blocked it. He appealed in vain to his genro colleagues, especially Yamagata and Matsukata, and finally had to persuade the emperor to instruct the peers to pass the legislation. Ito also found it difficult to control the members of his own party and to harmonize the conflicting elements within it. He finally quit office after a party dispute on matters of finance and threw the problem of governing back to Yamagata, who elevated his Choshu military protégé, General Katsura Taro, to the prime ministership.

Japan achieved a remarkable degree of political stability during the long tenure of the Katsura cabinet, which assumed office in June, 1901. For example, when the parties clashed with Katsura over his proposal to expand the army and navy by permanent retention of the tax increase that had been established for a five-year period, Ito, who supported the military on this issue, was able to effect a compromise whereby the new expenditures would be made but would be financed through loans. And when the Kenseihonto introduced a motion of nonconfidence against the prime minister, the Seiyukai majority voted it down.

The success of the Katsura cabinet, which remained in office until 1906, must also be explained by its ability to diminish Ito's political power. Although they were thankful for Seiyukai support, Yamagata and Katsura objected to Ito's dual position as a supposedly impartial adviser of the emperor, a role he shared with other genro, and as president of a political party. Ito promised unqualified support of whatever cabinet the emperor might appoint, but the militarists were fearful of his antagonism toward them and of the policies of his party. They demanded that Ito make his own position clear by choosing either the party presidency or his place among the genro; and when Ito refused, they brought the issue to a head with Katsura's resignation in July, 1903. On the advice of Yamagata and Katsura, the emperor ordered Katsura to remain in office and Ito to give his undivided attention to the throne by accepting the presidency of the privy council. Ito's subsequent resignation from the Seiyukai did not return its leadership to the original Jiyuto members, however, for in his last official act Ito made Saionji Kimmochi, his friend and protégé, its president. Many of the experienced politicians like Itagaki and Ozaki Yukio left the Seiyukai, and the party could no longer be sure of an absolute majority in the house of representatives. But perhaps the most important cause of the relative stability of Japanese politics in these years was the increased tension in Japan's relations with Russia.

The Anglo-Japanese Alliance

Japan continued to look for means to counter a Russian East Asian policy which had come to be dominated by advocates of forcible expansion. It was clear that Russia was anxious to control Manchuria and to secure a position in north Korea from which she could eventually overrun the entire peninsula. As early as 1899 the Russian government purchased some of the lumber concessions along the Yalu River and sent into them an advance force of 20,000 men masquerading as lumberjacks. Great Britain was also apprehensive about Russian expansion; and after some attempts at seeking Germany's co-operation against the Russian threat to the interests of both in China, she turned her attention to an alliance with Japan.

Opinion within the Japanese government was divided concerning these developments. One group, led by Ito and Inouye, favored *rapprochement* with Russia in the belief that it was impossible to drive Russian influence from East Asia. It hoped to preserve the independence of Korea, the first line of Japan's defense, by conceding Russia's paramount interests in Manchuria. A second group, which included Yamagata and Katsura, maintained that agreement with Russia would at best be a temporary expedient. It was convinced that Japan would eventually have to come to grips with Russia and that, to prepare for this struggle, Japan should seek an alliance with Great Britain.

Although much of the groundwork for an alliance was actually laid by the end of the century, the debate over policy continued in Tokyo. In March, 1898, in discussions with Ambassador Kato Takaaki concerning Russia, the British colonial secretary, Joseph Chamberlain, underscored the identity of British and Japanese interests and expressed surprise at Japan's not having approached London on the subject of co-operation in East Asia. However,

Kato's hands were tied, as were those of his successor in London, Hayashi Tadasu, because of the hesitancy of the government in Tokyo.

Finally, in July, 1901, Foreign Secretary Lansdowne notified Hayashi that the time had come for consideration of an alliance and asked what Japan's demands would be. In Tokyo Prime Minister Katsura won the consent of his genro colleagues, but only after lengthy discussions. Ito remained skeptical and did not abandon the idea of an agreement with Russia. In fact, in the autumn of 1901, while visiting St. Petersburg on a world tour, he privately initiated preliminary negotiations, but he found that the Russian government would make few concessions to the Japanese view regarding Korea.

Ito's strange dealings made the British very uneasy over the possibility of a Russian-Japanese alliance, and London moved rapidly to conclude a treaty with Hayashi. The Japanese cabinet approved a draft treaty on December 19, and the matter was referred to the emperor, who asked the advice of the privy council. When the latter returned a favorable report, the emperor approved the alliance. Even Ito, having given up hope for an accord with Russia, expressed his concurrence. On January 30, 1902, Hayashi and Lansdowne signed a formal treaty in London, the terms of which were announced simultaneously in London and Tokyo on February 11 as follows:

1. Both powers pledged to maintain the status quo and general peace in East Asia.
2. Both recognized the independence of China and Korea as well as their territorial integrity. And both pledged themselves to maintain equal commercial opportunity.
3. Both recognized each other's special interests in China and the special interest of Japan "politically as well as commercially and industrially in Korea." The alliance was to safeguard these interests if they were threatened either by the aggressive action of any other power or by disturbances arising in China or Korea.
4. Each pledged to maintain its neutrality if the other was at war unless the other was attacked by more than one power.
5. The alliance was to run for five years, at the end of which period it could be terminated.

The alliance was a diplomatic triumph for both powers. The British regarded it as recognition by Japan of their interests in China and as an instrument to diminish the Russian menace to them. In Tokyo the alliance was considered tantamount to British recognition of Japan as a world power and of her aspirations in Korea; moreover, the genro felt that they could plan and carry out a war against Russia without fear of interference by a third power or of a combined action like that of the Triple Intervention. The alliance, however, did not make the Russo-Japanese War inevitable, for it did not exclude the possibility of a settlement with Russia, which was desired by both Japan and Great Britain. Finally, although the alliance paid lip service to the open-door principle, it was a denial of Hay's co-operative policy. Great Britain needed Japanese power in Asia, not American ideals.

During this period anti-Russian sentiment reached a fever pitch in Japan, especially among the expansionist societies. For example, the Kokuryukai (Black Dragon Society or Amur River Society), founded in 1901 by Uchida Ryohei, had as its avowed aim the extension of Japan's sphere of influence as far north in Manchuria as the Amur River. Before 1902 the Kokuryukai talked of the weakness of Russia and of the ability of Japan to resist Russian aggression, but with new confidence stemming from the alliance the society began to engage in espionage for the army and in other activities which anticipated the defeat of Russia and the acquisition of new territories by Japan.

Opposition to Russia was also linked to Japanese Pan-Asianism. In November, 1898, the Toa Dobun Kai (East Asian Common Culture Society) was established to sponsor studies of conditions in Korea and China with a view to bringing about reforms in those countries and to revive interest in Japan's "proper role in Asia." With the support of influential businessmen, politicians, and nationalists, the Toa Dobun Kai opened branches in China with the mission of "saving her from the predatory Western powers." Even such a prominent political leader as Okuma held the conviction that a modernized Japan had a duty to protect China from Western aggression and to aid her in adopting political, economic, and social reforms. The society regarded war with Russia as an opportunity to strike a blow against a Western power that inflicted injustices upon Asian peoples.

The Japanese government, however, thought in terms of protecting specific interests in Korea. Japanese subjects had recently obtained permission to build railroads between Pusan and Seoul and between Inchon and Seoul as well as to purchase land around most of the important harbors, and the Bank of Japan had acquired special whaling, fishing, and mining rights. Japan hoped to extend these interests, but she was faced with a renewal of Russian activity in 1902 and 1903. Russia occupied a Korean port near the mouth of the Yalu, built telegraph lines and roads from north Korean ports to her military posts in Manchuria, and tried to obtain a concession for a railroad from Seoul to the Yalu River. And although Russia agreed in April, 1902, to evacuate her troops from Manchuria within eighteen months, she merely shifted them from one area to another.

Japan was quite willing to recognize Russian gains in Manchuria, but she wanted Russia to reciprocate by recognizing Japan's "unique status" in Korea. Anxious to negotiate along this line, Japan was prepared to resort to war should negotiations fail; in fact, in the spring of 1903 the Japanese government succeeded in obtaining a loan from the Rothschilds in London for military expenditures. In July, 1903, Japan opened direct negotiations with Russia for an understanding on both Manchuria and Korea. Katsura's cabinet proposed the following:

1. Chinese sovereignty and integrity would be respected.
2. The administration of Manchuria would be restored to China, with Russia retaining only railway guards.
3. Japan would recognize Russian rights in Manchuria based on ratified treaties.
4. Russia would recognize Japan's political as well as commercial and industrial interests in Korea as already set forth in the Anglo-Japanese Alliance.

Not only was Japan seeking to safeguard her Korean interests, but under the principles of the open door and territorial integrity she was attempting to confine Russian interests in Manchuria within the narrowest interpretation of a sphere of interest.

Despite the fact that the expansionists had increased their influence at the Russian court, the czar's government did not answer the Japanese proposals until October, 1903. The delay was caused by policy debates behind the scenes; at one moment concession was favored and at another resistance. The Russian counterproposals proved to be unsatisfactory to Japan. Russia was willing to have Japan advise Korea on reforms if the advice did not jeopardize Korean independence, but she insisted that no Korean ports were to be used for strategic purposes and that no coastal defenses be built along the Korean straits. She suggested also that a neutral zone be established north of the thirty-ninth parallel, a line just south of Wonsan and Pyongyang. Finally, Russia demanded that Manchuria and all of its coast be completely outside the Japanese sphere of influence.

Although some last-minute negotiations were carried on in early January, 1904, the Japanese cabinet was committed to a policy of war. On December 28 it had issued an emergency imperial ordinance providing for special military expenditures, and it had created a supreme war council. On January 12, 1904, with the emperor presiding, a conference of the cabinet, genro, and military and financial experts decided on Japan's minimum terms. These included recognition of Manchuria as outside Japan's sphere providing Russia respected China's territorial integrity and permitted legitimate activities of Japan and other powers in Manchuria. In return, Russia would have to promise not to interfere with Japan's interests in Korea. When no satisfactory reply from Russia was received, the issues were settled by war.

The Russo-Japanese War and the Treaty of Portsmouth

Hostilities broke out in early February. After an imperial conference on February 4, the Japanese government severed diplomatic relations (February

6) and immediately dispatched fleet forces and a military expedition to Korea. On February 8 a division landed at Inchon, and on the following day Japanese warships defeated a Russian cruiser and gunboat outside the harbor. And on the evening of the 8th a flotilla of Japanese torpedo boats struck at Port Arthur and effected a blockade of that base. By the time that Japan formally declared war on February 10, she had control of the seas and was able to speed up the flow of troops into Korea.

These events caught the powers, including the Russian enemy, by surprise, for no one had been sufficiently aware of Japan's determination to settle the Korean question by force if necessary. Great Britain wanted to see Russian influence driven from Manchuria and Korea, and American sympathies, especially those of President Theodore Roosevelt, were unofficially but unmistakably on the Japanese side. Most important, American bankers cooperated with their British colleagues to help finance Japan's war needs. On the other hand, the French government provided Russia with moral support, and Parisian bankers loaned funds largely to protect the already heavy French investment in Manchurian development schemes. The German kaiser hoped for a Russian victory and wanted to share with the czar the partitioning of north China in return for concessions to Russia in central Europe and the Near East. The Chinese declared their neutrality and refrained from any military activity, despite the fact that thousands of Chinese lives were lost and extensive damage was inflicted on Chinese property in subsequent fighting in south Manchuria.

Japan won a quick and decisive victory in Korea. Japanese troops under General Kuroki advanced northward from the Inchon-Seoul area and defeated a Russian force at Pyongyang. Additional units landed at Rashin on Korea's northeastern coast. In mid-April, in a major battle along the Yalu River, the Japanese army drove the Russians out of Korea completely. Japan then proceeded to consolidate politically what she had won on the battlefield. In fact, as early as February 23, 1904, she forced the Korean government to sign an agreement in which it promised to place full confidence in Japan and to adopt her advice with regard to improvements in administration. The Korean government also pledged not to conclude with any third power an agreement contrary to these commitments. Under another accord, signed under duress in August, 1904, Korea accepted Japanese advisers in her departments of foreign affairs and finance; moreover, Japanese became advisers to the Korean royal household department. By the beginning of 1905 Japan had assumed responsibility for policing Seoul and had placed a Japanese police inspector in each province. She also took over the communications system as a matter of security. Korea was well on the way to becoming a Japanese protectorate.

The main theater of the war was Manchuria. On May 1, 1904, General Kuroki's army crossed the Yalu River, a second Japanese army under General

Oku landed in south Manchuria a week later, and another army under General Nogi disembarked near the Russian leasehold on the Liaotung Peninsula. Oku quickly seized Chinchow and Dairen, but General Nogi had great difficulty in capturing Port Arthur, which Japan needed as a base for landing reinforcements and supplies, as there were no rail connections into south Manchuria via Korea. Japan was also anxious to force the surrender of the remnants of Russia's Far Eastern Fleet. It was not until May that Nogi seized high ground from which he could direct fire on the harbor below and on the ships at anchor, and after six months of fierce fighting, which cost Japan 20,000 men, Port Arthur finally fell on January 1, 1905. Shortly thereafter the veterans of this bloody siege, numbering 50,000 to 60,000, began moving north to join a larger force near Mukden under General Oyama. Between February 23 and March 10 two huge armies were locked in battle, but Japan's numerical superiority, amounting to approximately 350,000 men, turned the tide against Russia, and her army withdrew from Mukden to Tiehling. The Russians had lost approximately 150,000 men, killed or wounded, which was three times the number of Japanese casualties.

The last major engagement of the war was fought between the Japanese fleet under Admiral Togo and a Russian fleet which was attempting to run the Tsushima Straits to Vladivostok after its long voyage from European waters. On May 27, 1905, the Japanese sank the Russian flagship and three other battleships, and before noon of the next day the issue was decided. In two days of running battles Russia lost six battleships, five cruisers, one converted cruiser, five destroyers, and four special-service vessels. Two battleships and a destroyer were captured by the Japanese. One cruiser and two destroyers reached Vladivostok, and several other ships escaped but were interned at Shanghai and Manila. Out of a total of 18,000 Russian sailors, nearly 12,000 lost their lives. Japan lost only three torpedo boats, and her casualties amounted to but 116 men killed and 538 wounded.

Despite this series of victories, Japan took the initiative in making peace, largely because her economy could no longer support the war. The government was already burdened by prodigious war debts, and it could borrow no more funds. In the field, moreover, the Japanese army had failed to crush Russian resistance completely. In fact, in March, 1905, after the Battle of Mukden, General Kodama returned to Tokyo and insisted that the cabinet make peace. After hints and preliminary discussion, the Japanese government on May 31 formally invited President Roosevelt to act as mediator, and on June 6, after much urging by the German kaiser, the czar agreed to terminate the war. Russia, too, had exhausted her funds in a war that was never popular with the Russian people, and French bankers were not disposed to extend further credits. In fact, on April 5 the French foreign minister intimated to the Japanese ambassador that Russia was ready to consider peace terms.

The peace conference opened on August 10 at Portsmouth, New Hampshire, with the Japanese represented by Foreign Minister Komura Jutaro and Baron Takahira Kogoro, minister to Washington, and the Russians by Witte and Rosen. The latter were willing to recognize Japanese supremacy in Korea and to transfer to Japan the Liaotung Leasehold as well as economic rights in south Manchuria, including the railroad between Changchun and Port Arthur; but they stubbornly refused to consider Japanese demands for an indemnity, the surrender of Russian war vessels interned in neutral ports, the limitation of Russian naval power in East Asia, and the cession to Japan of Sakhalin. In order to break the deadlock, Roosevelt persuaded the czar to agree to a division of Sakhalin and payment of a "substantial sum," but Witte, who knew of Japan's financial difficulties, refused to consider any monetary payment and threatened to break off negotiations. When the Japanese government decided to yield, the delegates signed the Treaty of Portsmouth on September 5, 1905.

The treaty made Japan an Asian continental power. She acquired from Russia, subject to the consent of China, the Liaotung Leasehold, the southern section of the Chinese Eastern Railway, and the coal mines which were worked by the Russians. Although both powers agreed to evacuate Manchuria within eighteen months after the treaty became effective, they reserved the right to maintain guards to protect their respective railway lines, the number not to exceed fifteen men per kilometer. They promised "to exploit their respective railways in Manchuria exclusively for industrial and commercial purposes and in no wise for strategic purposes, with the exception of the leasehold" and "not to obstruct any general measures, common to all countries, which China might take for the development of the commerce and industry of Manchuria." They agreed also to restore to China administrative rights usurped by both powers during the war. With regard to Korea, Russia acknowledged that Japan possessed "paramount political, military, and economic interests" and pledged not to obstruct such measures as Japan might take to protect them. Lastly, Russia ceded the southern half of the island of Sakhalin to Japan in place of an indemnity and granted fishing rights in certain territorial waters off the Siberian coast. An annex to the Treaty of Portsmouth delineated the fishing areas and defined the conditions under which Japanese could bid on equal terms with Russian subjects for leases of them and under which they could build depots and canning stations in Russian territory.

The victory in the war with Russia was a tremendous stimulant to the development of Japanese nationalism. The people were thrilled by the knowledge that Europeans, Americans, and Asians alike recognized Japan's military might and were ready to assign her a proper position among the world's great powers. Victory tended to transform a nationalism based on feelings of inferiority into one characterized by greater confidence. This psychological change was in part responsible for the Japanese people's disappointment in the terms of the Treaty of Portsmouth. Because of rigid censorship, the public had not been given an accurate picture of the war or even of the strained conditions at home; nor was it kept informed of the treaty negotiations. Victory seemed more complete to the Japanese people than it really was. When the peace treaty was finally published, they felt they had been betrayed by the government, especially since they had been led to expect a large indemnity. Public demonstrations denounced the cabinet; and despite the proclamation of martial law, rioters burned or wrecked over a hundred and fifty police boxes, burned thirty-eight homes, including the official residence of the home minister, destroyed ten Christian churches, and killed or severely wounded over a thousand persons, about half of whom were police officials. Despite numerous arrests, an enraged public continued to agitate against the Katsura cabinet and forced the resignation of the prime minister in January, 1906, in favor of Saionji, leader of the Seiyukai.

Japan in Korea and Manchuria

After the war Japan secured international recognition of her protectorate over Korea. In conversations at Tokyo with William Howard Taft, the American secretary of war, in July, 1905, Katsura obtained approval, later confirmed by President Roosevelt, of Japanese suzerainty over Korea and in return disavowed any aggressive Japanese designs on the Philippine Islands. Roosevelt's administration simply recognized that the United States could do nothing for Korea, especially when her people could not strike a single blow on their own behalf. Katsura achieved British recognition of Japan's "paramount political, military, and economic interests in Korea" and her right of "guidance, protection, and control" in the renewal of the Anglo-Japanese Alliance in August, 1905. The alliance was also transformed into a mutual defense pact, since it provided that, in the event of attack or aggressive action on the part of any power or powers against the territorial rights and special interests of either Great Britain or Japan in the regions of Asia and India, each was obligated to come at once to the assistance of its ally and to conduct the war and make peace in common. Japan not only gained recognition of her position in Korea but also protection against a Russian war of revenge or a repetition of 1895.

In the autumn of 1905 Japan moved quickly to define its protectorate in Korea. In November, Ito Hirobumi negotiated an agreement with the Korean government which established Japanese control over Korean foreign relations and the right to appoint a resident-general at Seoul. When the Japanese foreign office in Tokyo took over the conduct of Korean foreign relations, the powers closed their legations in Seoul and transferred diplomatic representation to their ministers at the Japanese capital. Ito, who resigned as president of the privy council to become the first resident-general, began to implement a comprehensive reform program designed to modernize Korea for Japan's purposes; but his powers were largely advisory, and many of his proposals were hamstrung by Korean opposition. Ito could control the appointment of Korean officeholders, but he had little influence among the palace advisers, through whom the king plotted with Koreans in Russia and China.

In the minds of Japan's leaders the protectorate concept soon gave way to that of outright annexation. In 1907 the Korean king precipitated a crisis when he dispatched an official delegation to the Hague Peace Conference to make known "the violation of Korean rights by the Japanese." Although neither the conference nor the Dutch government would receive the mission, the Japanese cabinet reacted promptly by sending its foreign minister, Hayashi Tadasu, to Seoul to confer with Ito. While both agreed that annexation might be the ultimate solution, they decided that such a step was not yet possible. They did force the king to abdicate in favor of his son, with the resident-general as virtual regent. Despite this arrangement, Ito was still confronted on every occasion by stubborn Korean opposition to his plans; and by July, 1909, when he resigned, he was convinced that annexation was necessary to preserve Japan's interests and to bring about efficient administration.

Ito, who intended to return to office in the privy council, was assassinated at Harbin by a Korean patriot on October 26. His untimely death aroused public opinion in Japan, and demands for immediate annexation were heard among the people as well as in high government circles. In June, 1910, the Japanese cabinet informed the press of its intention to annex Korea, and four days later, on June 22, it created the imperial colonial board, with the prime minister as its president, for the administration of Formosa, the southern half of Sakhalin, the Kwantung Leasehold (formerly Liaotung), and Korea. On June 24 the Korean police were placed under the command of the resident-general; and a month later, on July 23, when the army minister, General Terauchi Masatake, arrived at Seoul to assume that office, he placed the entire country under control of the army. Finally, by the treaty of annexation, which was signed on August 22, 1910, all rights of sovereignty were transferred to the emperor of Japan. A new administrative system was organized under a governor-general, and Korea became an integral part of the Japanese empire.

During the subsequent decades Korea was developed according to Japan's national interests. Agricultural production was steadily increased, and more and more grain flowed to Japan. The fish catch in Korean waters was quadrupled, primarily to meet the demands of the Japanese market. Japan also undertook extensive exploitation of Korean resources and built industries based on them, with special emphasis on war production, including iron and steel, light metals, chemicals, machine tools, and transport vehicles. More than 75 per cent of all industrial production was owned by Japanese corporations, and in mining 93 per cent of the capital was Japanese-owned. Much of the demand for consumer goods in Korea was supplied by Japan. Militarily Korea became an outpost for Japanese defense and a springboard for future expansion; for Japan built numerous army, navy, and air bases, and she planned the railway and highway systems primarily with an eye to military needs.

Japan also sought to "Japanicize" the Korean people by making the Japanese language compulsory in schools, discouraging all religions except Shinto, and establishing law codes modeled on her own, with little concern for Korean customs. Discrimination against Koreans was common. All important jobs, political and economic, were reserved for Japanese. Children of the Japanese were given adequate schooling, but Korean children were restricted even in the primary grades; and among the labor force a double standard of wages was maintained, one for the Japanese and another for the Koreans.

After signing the Treaty of Portsmouth, Foreign Minister Komura secured Chinese consent to the transfer of Russian rights and interests in south Manchuria by the Treaty of Peking, signed by Yuan Shih-k'ai on December 22, 1905. It provided for the following:

1. China agreed to open sixteen cities in Manchuria to international trade and residence.
2. Japan agreed to withdraw her troops and railway guards (if Russia did likewise) when "China shall have become herself capable of affording full protection to the lives and property of foreigners."
3. Japan secured the right to maintain the military railroad she had built from Antung to Mukden for a fifteen-year period. [By a new agreement signed on August 19, 1909, Japan was permitted to reconstruct the line as a standard-gauge road. In 1915 the provision regarding control was extended to ninety-nine years.]
4. China agreed to the formation of a Sino-Japanese corporation to exploit the Manchurian forests adjacent to the Yalu River.

In Manchuria Japan took steps to stabilize her political position. Although the administration of Manchuria was Chinese, Japan and Russia had broad powers within the so-called "railway zones." Earlier agreements had defined these zones as lands "actually necessary for the construction, operation, and protection of the Chinese Eastern Railway." As broadly interpreted, first by Russia and then by Japan, political power within railway zones included ordinary rights of administration pertaining to sovereignty, taxation, police, and transfer of real property; employment of a number of guards to protect the railways; and the exercise of ordinary police power and of customary functions of municipal and local government. Within the Kwantung Leasehold Japan established an administration under a governor-general, who was of high rank in the Japanese army. This official owed his appointment to the prime minister in Tokyo and was responsible in questions relating to foreign affairs to the foreign minister, in matters of military administration to the minister of the army, and in matters of mobilization and operations to the army general staff. As the ranking officer he commanded the Kwantung garrison and the police in the railway zones. The only exception to Japan's control over the leased territory was the port of Chinchow, where the Chinese retained general administrative rights.

By the summer of 1906 it was clear that the Japanese government was to dominate, if not monopolize, the economic exploitation of south Manchuria. It formed the South Manchuria Railway Company to own and manage all Japanese industries and railroads; and because it owned half of the capital stock, it controlled appointment of the president and vice-president of the company. In subsequent decades the company engaged in numerous activities, including mining, water transportation, electric power, warehousing, and many others; moreover, it possessed broad administrative powers, which included the right to collect taxes within the railway zone. The company obtained from China new concessions for coal mines, telegraph lines, lumbering operations, and other commercial and industrial undertakings; but in the case of the Russian-worked coal mines at Fushun and Yentai near Mukden, Japan was unable to get Chinese consent to their transfer until 1909, when she promised to pay a tax to China on the coal. By another agreement Japan was granted the right to develop the coal mines at Penhsihu along the line of the Antung-Mukden Railway.

Because of the proximity of her interests in south Manchuria to those of the Russians in the north, Japan was anxious to reach some sort of understanding with her former enemy. The situation following the Treaty of Portsmouth was naturally one of tension between the two nations, but within several years the Russian government was ready to forget old wounds. Accordingly, it sought a *rapprochement* with Great Britain through the good offices of France, and in East Asia it was desirous of maintaining the peace through an agreement with Japan.

Negotiations were initiated in secret by the Japanese minister at St. Petersburg, and by February, 1907, a draft agreement was ready for signature. The Japanese cabinet hesitated, however, because of an article in the Anglo-Japanese Alliance which provided that neither of its parties would, without consulting the other, enter into separate arrangements with another power to the prejudice of the objects described in the preamble of the treaty. But when Great Britain raised no objection, Japan and Russia entered into a series of agreements. On June 13 they signed a convention providing for through traffic at the junction of the Russian and Japanese railroads at Changchun, and on July 28 they signed a treaty of commerce and navigation as well as a convention which defined Japanese fishing rights in the Sea of Japan, the Bering Straits, and the Sea of Okhotsk. On July 30 they signed two political

331

conventions, one of which was made public and the other kept secret. The former subscribed to the open door, both in the sense of trade and the territorial integrity of China, and the latter—finally published by the Soviet government in 1918—established a line of demarcation between the Russian and Japanese spheres in Manchuria, with each power promising not to interfere in the other's interests. Russia confirmed Japan's domination of Korea, and Japan recognized the special interests of Russia in Outer Mongolia.

In June Japan also signed a treaty with France, which defined their respective spheres of interest in Asia and acknowledged their roles as guardians of peace within them. France had been anxious to reach an accord with Japan in order to help bring Great Britain and Russia closer together in Europe, while Japan was interested in getting a French loan to help finance her Asian economic program. Finally, in August, 1907, Great Britain and Russia settled their outstanding differences, thus paving the way for the Triple Entente in Europe against Germany and Austria-Hungary.

Japanese-American Difficulties

Since Great Britain tended to concede Japan's economic dominance in south Manchuria in deference to the Anglo-Japanese Alliance, American diplomacy offered the only challenge to Japanese ambitions. The administration of President Theodore Roosevelt complained, as early as March, 1906, that Japanese military authorities were seeking to establish Japanese commercial interests in the principal towns and to acquire property rights for Japanese in all available quarters so as to leave little or no opening for other foreign trade by the time the territory was evacuated. It pointed out also that the Japanese were employing practices for which they earlier had criticized the Russians. For example, the Kwantung military administration closed Dairen to all but Japanese vessels and goods, and throughout south Manchuria the railway discriminated against foreigners by paying rebates to Japanese firms. Moreover, Japanese goods were being transported over the railroad to interior towns, though transportation facilities were supposedly being used only for the evacuation of troops and for other military purposes. However, President Roosevelt found it difficult to complain too vehemently, handicapped as he was by the mounting intensity of American agitation against Japanese immigration.

Until the 1890's there was a very small number of Japanese in the United States, although in Hawaii Japanese had begun to enter in large numbers as contract laborers. In the decade of the 1890's, however, Japanese immigration into the United States and to Hawaii was fairly extensive, and by 1900 there were over 80,000 Japanese residents in Hawaii, constituting about 40 per cent of the total population. Most of this latter group had entered Hawaii under the terms of a labor convention signed in 1886 in the interests of sugar-growers, but in March, 1897, a new Hawaiian government refused entry to over a thousand Japanese immigrants. When Japan protested, the flow of contract laborers continued until the last of the contracts expired in June, 1897. By 1900 there were over 24,000 Japanese in the United States, an expansion of 22,000 over the 2,000 of 1890. When American immigration officers protested in 1892 about the importation of Japanese laborers to the Pacific Coast, the Japanese government took steps to discourage such movement, but it had no control over immigrants entering from Hawaii after her annexation by the United States in August, 1898. In the American-Japanese Commercial Treaty of 1894 the United States made its position clear by stipulating that, while in matters of residence and travel the Japanese were to enjoy all the privileges of the most-favored nation, nevertheless such rights were in no way to affect the laws, ordinances, and regulations with regard to trade, the immigration of laborers, police, and public security which were already in force or which might thereafter be enacted in either of the two countries.

By the early 1900's there was strong agitation, especially in the Pacific Coast states, for restriction of Japanese immigration by application to the Japanese of the Chinese exclusion laws. Although the Japanese cabinet said that, for the present, it would entirely suspend emigration of laborers to both the United States and Canada, agitation continued because of the flow of Japanese from Hawaii. In fact, President Roosevelt had to veto discriminatory legislation passed by Congress, but he could not prevent local discrimination against the Japanese, such as the October, 1906, San Francisco school board resolution, which directed school principals to segregate Chinese, Japanese, and Korean children in the public schools. Since the Chinese were already segregated, the resolution was obviously aimed at Japanese subjects, who were branded as vicious, immoral, and unfit to associate with white children. The school board also claimed that the Japanese were overcrowding the system, while in fact there were only 93 enrolled, of whom 25 were American-born. This action was condemned by responsible San Franciscans and Californians as well as by Americans in general; and on October 25 the Japanese government protested, pointing out that the segregation of Japanese children on the basis of nationality was "an act of discrimination carrying with it a stigma and odium which it is impossible to overlook."

President Roosevelt sought to find a solution to the problem that would be satisfactory to the agitators and to Japan. In effect, he began waving his big stick but speaking softly behind the scenes. In a message to Congress in December, 1906, he threatened to use the Army to protect Japanese persons and their treaty rights and asked that they be admitted to citizenship through naturalization; at the same time, he promised the San Franciscans to end the immigration of Japanese laborers if their school board would rescind its resolution. He succeeded in blocking the flow of immigrants from Hawaii,

Canada, and Mexico by an amendment to the 1907 Immigration Law, and he proposed to Japan that she sign a treaty prohibiting the emigration of laborers to the United States.

Japan agreed, provided the United States would recognize the right of naturalization of immigrants other than laborers; but Roosevelt, since he could not commit the Congress, followed Secretary of State Root's advice that Japan herself impose the restrictions desired by the United States. On February 24, 1907, the Japanese cabinet indicated that it would continue the policy then in force of not issuing passports to laborers except to those who sought to resume residence in the United States or to join a parent, wife, or child residing there; and on March 13 the San Francisco school board rescinded the objectionable resolution in so far as it applied to Japanese. Details of the so-called "Gentlemen's Agreement" were completed in the following year, and by October, 1908, Japanese departures from the United States for the first time began to exceed arrivals. Later, in 1911, when the 1894 commercial treaty was renewed, the United States omitted the provision regarding her right to legislate the exclusion of laborers; but this was only a gesture, since Congress could act regardless of treaty provisions.

Despite the formulation of the Gentlemen's Agreement, diplomatic tension, particularly in the summer of 1907, led to talk of war. When irresponsible Japanese ultranationalists, including elements in the army, threatened to interfere in the Philippines, Roosevelt sent special instructions to General Leonard Wood for meeting a Japanese attack. It is ironical that the President had to admit that the Philippines were like "an Achilles heel to our foreign policy in the Far East . . . that makes the present situation with Japan dangerous." Roosevelt also sent his secretary of war, William Howard Taft, to Tokyo in October, 1907, and he reported that the Japanese were anxious to avoid war. The Japanese government was extending no aid or support to Filipino revolutionaries. It became clear that much of the war talk was the result of sensational journalism on both sides of the Pacific.

Yet once again Roosevelt waved the big stick but spoke very softly. He sent an American fleet on a world cruise between March, 1908, and February, 1909, to show the Japanese that the United States was developing naval supremacy. When the fleet visited Tokyo in October, 1908, it received an extremely warm welcome. And on November 30 the Root-Takahira notes were exchanged at Washington. Thereafter there was little talk of war. Both countries firmly resolved to respect the territorial possessions of each other in East Asia and the entire Pacific region, and both declared support for the status quo in those regions, the open door, and China's independence and integrity. In the case of a threat to these principles, the two powers agreed to communicate with each other in order to reach an understanding. Unfortunately these commitments were stated vaguely, and there was subsequently no agreed interpretation of them. The United States held that the exchange was an acceptance of its policy in full, while Japan felt that she had given a pledge not to attack the Philippines in return for a free hand in Manchuria. Legally, the American interpretation seems accurate; but the timing of the note exchange tends to support the Japanese view.

Since the old balance of power in East Asia, which China had regarded as beneficial, had been destroyed by the Russo-Japanese and Franco-Japanese agreements of 1907, Peking sought to establish a new balance of power through the creation of a Chinese-American-German entente and hoped to invite American capital into Manchuria and China proper. The latter idea was very attractive to the American consul-general at Mukden, Willard Straight, who was convinced that the weakness of American policy in East Asia was due to the relatively small American investment in the region. From 1906 to 1908 his Mukden office was a high-pressure sales agency for American commerce in south Manchuria, and he personally sought to reawaken Averell Harriman's interest in railroad construction in Manchuria.

After the signing of the Treaty of Portsmouth, Harriman had gone to Tokyo with the idea of buying the South Manchurian Railway as a link in an American round-the-world transportation system, and he hoped also to purchase the Chinese Eastern Railway from Russia and to obtain trackage rights over the Trans-Siberian Railway. At first the Japanese cabinet was favorable, and in fact a preliminary understanding was signed by Prime Minister Katsura, which provided for a syndicate to share with the Japanese government ownership and operation of the railroad and mining rights. However, the plan fell through when objections were raised within the Japanese government and when Japan was able to get a British loan to put the South Manchurian in working order.

In the summer of 1907 Straight succeeded in reaching an understanding with the Manchurian viceroy, T'ang Shao-i, for an American loan of $20,000,000 to construct a Hsinmintun-Aigun Railway and to develop Manchurian commerce and industry. Harriman was interested in providing the funds, but he was prevented from doing so because of the financial panic of 1907. Temporarily, at least, Straight was unsuccessful in mobilizing American capital to combat the growth of Japanese interests in south Manchuria, but Peking sent T'ang to Washington to discuss the possibility of the entente and a loan. When he passed through Tokyo in the autumn of 1908, T'ang was advised that Japan was China's best friend and that an alliance between China and any other power would be regarded by Japan as an indication of China's distrust.

The Japanese cabinet, moreover, instructed Ambassador Takahira to reach some understanding with the United States which would frustrate China's plans. The Root-Takahira exchange was made on the very day that T'ang arrived in Washington. T'ang did attempt to secure a loan for Manchurian development purposes, but Roosevelt did not want to take any steps regarding Manchuria which would give Japan cause to feel that the United States was hostile or a menace to Japanese interests. A few years later Roosevelt, reviewing the American open-door policy in a letter to his successor, President Taft, stated:

The open-door policy in China was an excellent thing, and I hope that it will be a good thing in the future, so far as it can be maintained by general diplomatic agreement; but as has been proved by the whole history of Manchuria, alike under Russia and under Japan, the open-door policy, as a matter of fact, completely disappears as soon as a powerful nation determines to disregard it, and is willing to run the risk of war rather than forego its intention.

China's tenacity in attempting to combat Russian and Japanese economic expansion in Manchuria was finally rewarded by a shift in American policy during the Taft administration. The new American secretary of state, Philander C. Knox, attempted to interest American financiers in Manchuria and China proper for the purpose of strengthening the principles of the open door and China's integrity. He enlarged the commercial machinery of the department of state and appointed Willard Straight as chief of its Far Eastern division. By this time, also, Harriman had revived his international transportation scheme and with Straight was anxious to win the support of New York City bankers. In fact, Harriman had already gone to Europe and in June, 1909, had entered into negotiations with the Russian finance minister, Kokovtsov, who seemed willing to sell the Chinese Eastern Railway to an international syndicate. Meanwhile, the State Department organized a banking group, which it designated as "the official agent of American railway financing in China," and Straight became its Peking representative.

At Peking Straight concentrated on securing a concession for a Manchurian railway that would provide a broad field for the investment of American capital. He worked closely with Harriman, who wanted to build a line parallel to the South Manchurian from Chinchow to Aigun on the Amur River; but when Harriman died in September, 1909, the entire project lost much of its impetus. Straight remained active, however, and was able to secure from the Manchurian government in October, 1909, a preliminary agreement to finance and construct the Chinchow-Aigun line. He hoped that the project would be financed by the American banking group and constructed by Pauling and Company, a British firm that had been denied support by its own government in 1907 for a similar undertaking because of Japanese objections. When Harriman's death made it difficult for Straight to mobilize American capital, Secretary of State Knox finally made two striking proposals to Great Britain in November, 1909. He suggested that "the foreign-owned Manchurian railroads be both neutralized" by providing China with funds to purchase them through a multipower loan, during the life of which the railroads would be under international control, or that Great Britain join with the United States in supporting the Chinchow-Aigun project and in inviting other powers to participate. The British government approved the general principle of the neutralization proposal but told Knox that it would be wiser to postpone any consideration of its application. When Knox went ahead and approached China and other powers, Russia and Japan quickly consulted each other and with British approval rejected Knox's plan in almost identical notes signed on January 23, 1910. In February, 1910, they protested to Peking against the Chinchow-Aigun project and demanded that they be consulted before foreign capital was employed in any such railway enterprises. Since the Chinese government had ratified Straight's Manchurian agreement on January 21, 1910, it turned to Washington for advice. Knox recommended that it should wait until the reaction of all the powers was known and in the meantime should be "firm and patient but not aggressive." When Great Britain and France gave public notice that they would not support the United States, the failure of Knox's neutralization scheme was complete.

Knox's efforts actually caused a tightening of Japanese and Russian control in Manchuria. On July 4, 1910, the two powers signed conventions much like those of 1907. The public convention announced their intention to perfect their connecting railway service in Manchuria and, without any mention of the open door or China's integrity, stated that in case the status quo was menaced they would decide what measures were necessary to maintain it. The secret agreement reaffirmed the line of demarcation drawn between their spheres in 1907 and strengthened their special position by recognizing the right of each, within its own sphere, freely to take all measures necessary for the defense of its interests. Neither power would hinder the consolidation and further development of the special interests of the other, and each would refrain from all political activity within the other's sphere. They also pledged common action in defense of their special interests.

Knox, though discouraged, did not give up the game. In April, 1911, the Manchu regime signed a contract with the four-power consortium for a currency-reform loan, part of which would be used to undertake Chinese industrial development of Manchuria. To Knox this offered another chance to bolster the government of China and restore its authority over Manchuria. The loan was never floated, but the negotiations aroused the Japanese and Russians, who regarded it as an attempt to frustrate their own ambitions. In fact, they persuaded Great Britain and France that their claims to special rights in Manchuria went beyond railroads. Finally, in 1912, Japan and Russia once again defined more specifically their spheres of interest and agreed upon methods of close co-operation in defense of their special rights; moreover, they made it clear that they considered that their spheres of influence in Manchuria were outside the purview of the consortium.

20 *Industrialization and Political Development*

War and expansion had a tremendous impact on Japan's economy. The mounting costs of both activities were reflected in the increases in annual state expenditures from 80 million yen in the early 1890's to between 250 and almost 300 million yen in the period 1900–1904. They were paid for out of revenues derived from higher excise, land, income, and business taxes; from profits earned by newly created government monopolies like tobacco; and from foreign and domestic borrowing. Of special importance was the fact that the Japanese government created long-term credit facilities like the Hypothec Bank of Japan (1896), the Industrial Bank of Japan (1900), the Bank of Taiwan (1899), and the Bank of Chosen (Korea) (1906). The national debt held at home and abroad rose from 207 million yen in 1894 to 539 million yen in 1903. During the Russo-Japanese War annual state expenditures reached a high of 600 million yen, part of which was met by increases in tax revenues based on a higher national income. The balance was added to the national debt, which rose to 2,244 million yen by December, 1907. By 1914 the government's general indebtedness was reduced to 1,832 million yen, most of which was foreign-held because of lower interest rates; but its railroad indebtedness increased from 117 million yen in 1906 to 729 million yen in 1914, largely because of the nationalization of many of the lines.

The Economic Transformation

During this period Japanese industrial productivity grew slowly at first, but after the Russo-Japanese War the country was well into an industrial revolution. The fact that Japan remained on a war footing for such a long time accelerated this process, but there were also other factors that acted as stimulants. As a result of the huge Chinese indemnity, Japan was able to go on the gold standard, thus strengthening her currency and establishing closer relations between the domestic and international money markets. Her ability to regain tariff autonomy had a significant impact on domestic industrial production, while she had new sources of raw materials and markets in Formosa, Korea, south Manchuria, and China. In the period from 1895 to 1905 there was steady progress in industrial fields previously favored, such as silk and paper, copper, electricity, gas, clothing, and other consumer industries. Shipping and railroads made substantial gains, as did iron and steel; but, in general, heavy industry remained subordinate to light industry. The follow-

ing set of figures indicates increases in the total capitalization of Japanese
companies (employing over ten men) by category (all figures are in yen):

CAPITAL ASSETS

YEAR	Industrial	Communications	Commercial
1894	44,590,000	82,560,000	20,015,000
1897	105,380,000	164,684,000	53,512,000
1903	170,000,000	262,380,000	76,994,000

Production techniques were also improved as more and more factories
were mechanized. By 1899, 42 per cent of the factories employing more than
ten persons used power-driven machines, and the number of workers in
power-equipped plants amounted to 71 per cent of the total. After 1905 the
most spectacular increases occurred in heavy industry: shipbuilding, iron and
steel, and the chemical and machine-tool industries; for example, iron and
steel production quadrupled between the years 1905 and 1914, and coal
production doubled. Among consumer industries the cotton-yarn and cotton-
weaving industries made great progress, doubling their production and exporting to ready markets in Korea and China. Banks, insurance companies,
and other financial institutions underwent a similar expansion. The following table provides a general quantitative picture of Japan's industrial development in the period from 1905 to 1914:

Year	Number of Industrial Companies	Capital Assets (In 100,000 Yen)	Number of Factories (Over 10 Men)	Percentage Using Power	Number of Workers
1905	2,449	189	9,776	44.3	587,851
1908	3,065	441	11,390	49.3	649,676
1911	3,921	629	14,228	54.5	793,885
1914	5,266	833	17,062	60.6	853,964

Despite substantial progress toward self-sufficiency, Japan's industrial
economy suffered from serious deficiencies. Although iron production rose
from 26,000 tons in 1896 to 145,000 tons in 1906 and to 243,000 tons in 1913,
the general demands of industry also increased. Domestic smelting plants were
able to meet only 48 per cent of requirements. The same situation held true in
the case of steel, where the bulk of the output was supplied by a single large
concern, the Yawata Iron Works in Kyushu. Production increased from
69,000 tons in 1905 to 255,000 tons in 1913, but this total supplied only one-
third of the nation's demand for steel. In 1913 domestic ore output of 153,000
tons, supplied largely by the Kamaishi mines, comprised only 27 per cent of
ore consumption; the difference had to be imported from China and Korea.

For some time Japanese coal reserves were sufficient, but since her coal was low-grade bituminous, she had to begin importing metallurgical coal. Petroleum, commercial salt, and cotton were other raw-material deficiencies that had to be met through foreign trade.

It is important to remember that handicraft production was still a substantial part of the Japanese economy. Although the silk industry had gradually been modernized in order to meet export standards, small hand-reeling establishments accounted for 22 per cent of silk filatures, which supplied domestic weavers. Despite the development of power weaving in the cotton-cloth industry, only half of the 2,000 factories had power, and at the same time half a million households continued domestic weaving. Moreover, Japan's traditional occupations, like the manufacture of paper and *tatami* (straw floormats) accounted for about 40 per cent of the total nonagricultural labor force, and most of the workers were employed in shops with less than five operatives.

Japan's industrialization, despite raw-material deficiencies, made the country dependent on a high level of foreign trade. The following table indicates Japanese progress in this field (all figures are in millions of yen):

Annual Average	Imports	Exports	Balance
1888–1893	73	77	4
1894–1898	223	139	—84
1899–1903	270	244	—26
1904–1908	441	375	—66
1909–1913	544	496	—48

During this period the character of the trade changed along with the process of industrialization, and by the end of the period there was a marked decline in the import of finished goods and an increase in the import of raw materials, like cotton, and of machines and tools. On the other hand, Japan became a leading exporter of manufactured and semimanufactured goods. She supplied 25 per cent of world exports of cotton yarn and a growing share of cotton cloth, and in these items she displaced American exports to China and began competing successfully with the British. Two other important characteristics of Japan's trade were the unfavorable trade balances and the high dependence on silk exports. Raw silk constituted 30 per cent of total exports by 1914, and textiles as a whole accounted for almost 60 per cent. Lastly, the development of a sizable trade accelerated the growth of Japan's shipping industry. In 1893 about 14 per cent of ships entering her ports were Japanese, and they carried only 7 per cent of exports and about 9 per cent of imports. But after the passage of the Navigation Subsidy Act in 1896, Japanese shipowners were encouraged to build larger vessels, and the share of the trade that they carried gradually increased; by 1913 the proportions had risen to 51, 52, and 47 per cent, respectively.

Population increase was one of the most significant results of the process of industrialization. The expanding economy and urbanization enabled Japan to support a much larger population, which rose from 35,000,000 in 1873 to 45,000,000 in 1903 and to about 50,000,000 in 1913. About 50 per cent of the 1913 population lived in towns and cities. In this period agricultural production was able to supply most of Japan's food needs, and imports of food accounted for only about 5 per cent of total consumption. Rice production increased by 30 per cent because of additions to the cultivated area, greater use of fertilizers, double cropping, improvement in varieties, and a number of other reasons. By the end of this period, however, it was questionable whether agricultural production would be able to satisfy the demands of an even larger population in subsequent decades. It was likely that Japan would have to divert valuable foreign exchange in order to import larger quantities of food. The government did little to discourage population increase, since it believed that numbers meant strength; and the warnings of demographers and economists seem to have had no important influence.

On the whole there was a worsening of agrarian conditions during this period. The peasantry still bore the heaviest tax burden since the government continued to maintain low tax rates as an incentive for industrial investment. It has been estimated that peasants paid out 28 per cent of their income in taxes, whereas merchants and industrialists gave up only 14 per cent. The uneconomic size of landholdings, the ever-widening gap between prices of agricultural commodities and those of manufactured goods, social obligations, the squeeze of marketing, and the lack of adequate credit facilities also contributed to the continuing decline of the peasantry. By 1910, 45 per cent of Japan's arable land was worked by tenants who not only paid high rents, ranging from 45 to 60 per cent of the main crop, but also supplied their own implements, seed, and fertilizer. About two-fifths of the total number of cultivators were tenants, another two-fifths were peasant proprietors, and the remainder owned part of their land and rented additional plots.

To supplement the meager income derived from agriculture, most farm families still engaged in handicraft production of some type or in subsidiary activities, the most important of which was sericulture, and many of them sent their daughters and second sons to work in factories and textile mills. In the case of the cotton-spinning industry, 80 per cent of its operatives were females recruited from the rural areas, and about one-fourth of this total were under sixteen years of age. Since factory laws were not enforced until 1916, they worked for extemely low wages and lived under miserable conditions.

The Taisho Change

The relative stability of Japanese politics in the years immediately following the Russo-Japanese War was the result of co-operation between the civil and military factions among the genro and the support by the Seiyukai majority

341

in the house of representatives of cabinets headed by Katsura and Saionji. For example, the Seiyukai, under Saionji's leadership, did not join the Kenseihonto in condemning the Treaty of Portsmouth and denouncing Katsura's cabinet. Only when an enraged public opinion led to riots and a declaration of martial law in Tokyo was Katsura replaced as prime minister by Saionji; and when Saionji was in office, Yamagata and the military gave him a certain amount of support. In fact, the cabinet, which was formed in January, 1906, included only two Seiyukai members, the others being followers of Yamagata. The Saionji cabinet essentially followed the lines of its predecessor, adopting the Katsura budget, continuing emergency taxation, and pushing through the railway-nationalization scheme which had long been a goal of the military and nationalist groups.

This relatively calm period gave way to conflict when co-operation between the two factions of the genro broke down and when the Seiyukai withdrew its support from the cabinet. When Saionji tried to implement some provisions of the Seiyukai platform—especially the enactment of a bill to reform the highly centralized local government system which had been perfected earlier by Yamagata—the house of peers, with encouragement from the military, would not give its approval. When Saionji later found that he could not effect a program of financial retrenchment in face of a budget deficit of 150,000,000 yen, he offered his resignation (May, 1908), but the emperor refused to accept it. A year later, however, in July, he resigned "for reasons of health" when the house of representatives tried to impeach the cabinet because of its efforts to get tax increases.

An important characteristic of Japanese politics in this period was the continuing tendency for party politicians to seek favor with the genro as a means of achieving political power. One noteworthy and highly instructive case of this occurred during the tenure of the Katsura cabinet that assumed office in July, 1909. When Katsura established an alliance with the Seiyukai, which held a majority in the house of representatives after its victory in the general election of May, 1909, a faction of the Kenseihonto led by Oishi Masami began to urge that compromise with the Katsura forces was the only way the party could achieve power. This stand taken by the Oishi faction split the Kenseihonto and its slightly larger successor, the Rikken Kokuminto (Constitutional Nationalist Party), which was organized in March, 1910. The Kokuminto continued to demand party cabinets and the "consummation of the constitutional system," but Oishi was still intent on having it replace the Seiyukai in alliance with the genro and the military.

Concurrently, a number of former bureaucrats began to emerge as political party leaders. As parties increased in importance, membership in them became more attractive to ambitious officials, and particularly to the followers of the powerful genro Ito Hirobumi, who had founded the Seiyukai. In fact, many of them came to support the concept of party government and worked to effect it. But on the whole they did not think in terms of democratic principles; on the contrary, because of their training and background, they generally feared democracy. Hara Kei, a leading figure in the Seiyukai, was an excellent example of this type. Like Saionji he had taken an early interest in the party movement, but he deserted it for a post in the bureaucracy. In 1896 he left government service to become editor of the Osaka *Mainichi* but returned to political life in 1900 as a member of Ito's Seiyukai.

After 1910 Katsura was unable to maintain harmony between the military and the party politicians. Once again the army and navy requested an increase in appropriations, and only with great difficulty was Katsura able to persuade them to wait. He simply did not want to antagonize the Seiyukai supporters of the cabinet, but in the end he was unable to stand up to the relentless pressure of the military and turned the problem over to another Saionji cabinet. In the diet session of December, 1911, to March, 1912, the new cabinet pushed through the house of representatives a program of retrenchment which included administrative reforms, tax reductions, and deferment of the army and navy expansion programs. When there was strong opposition by both the minister of the army and the minister of the navy and when retrenchment was blocked by the house of peers, Saionji dissolved the house of representatives and was sustained by the general election victory of the Seiyukai, which won a clear majority of 214 seats. But the army remained determined to press its long-standing demands for two new divisions; and when the army minister died in April, 1912, his post was filled by a Yamagata appointee, who demanded that the cabinet agree to include the funds for the two divisions in the next budget. Since Saionji refused, the military, led by Yamagata, forced the resignation of the army minister in December and refused to provide a replacement. By this tactic, the army used its peculiar constitutional power to cause the resignation of the entire cabinet despite the fact that the Seiyukai held a majority in the house of representatives and its stand had been approved by the Japanese electorate.

Yamagata had successfully overturned the Saionji government, but he had a difficult task in finding a successor. He finally had to turn to Katsura, who had lost favor with his military colleagues because of his proclivity to compromise with the Seiyukai. In forming his cabinet, Katsura found himself faced with the opposition of the navy, which had been aroused by the army's efforts to expand. The navy, which had been developed largely by former samurai from Satsuma, refused to provide a minister; the admirals, e.g., Yamamoto Gombei, were jealous of their Choshu counterparts in the army and, ironically, formed an alliance themselves with the Seiyukai. Thus the general rivalry between the services was reinforced by competition between former samurai of two great han. Katsura, however, forced the hand of the navy by securing an imperial order for the appointment of a navy minister; but in the house of representatives he faced the united opposition of the parties, which had joined to criticize army tyranny.

This action by the parties finally forced the military to enter the political arena directly. Realizing that they could not depend on alliances with political parties which they could not control, they, like Ito earlier, reached the decision to form their own party. By February, 1913, Katsura had organized the Rikken Doshikai (Constitutional Fellow-Thinkers Association), which included the small number of pro-Katsura members of the house of representatives and the power-hungry Oishi faction of the Kokuminto. Despite the use of intimidation and bribery to win more members, the new party was no match for the overwhelming majority of the Seiyukai and Kokuminto.

The political party attack upon Katsura and the military reached its peak in February, 1913. Newspapers and party spokesmen, notably Ozaki Yukio, condemned them for utilizing the prestige and powers of the emperor for their own purposes, and on February 5 the house of representatives passed a motion of nonconfidence in the cabinet with 299 votes. Katsura retaliated immediately by proroguing the diet for five days. When he was unable to persuade the Seiyukai to support him, Katsura had the Taisho emperor, who had succeeded his father in the previous year, summon Saionji to the palace on February 9 and order him to avoid a political crisis.

On the following day Saionji dutifully informed party leaders and members of the emperor's request that they withdraw the nonconfidence motion, but the Seiyukai, with strong support from Admiral Yamamoto and the navy, finally refused. When Katsura prorogued the diet for three more days, a mob of thousands of people, who had been milling around the diet building in support of the parties, burst out of control and repeated the Portsmouth disturbances. The impasse between the cabinet and the parties was broken when Katsura resigned on February 11; however, the outcome of the struggle was not a complete victory for the parties since Admiral Yamamoto, who was willing to accept party support but not the principle of party government, succeeded as prime minister.

But Katsura's fall did have several important results. The emperor, who was mentally incompetent, proved unable to wield the personal power of his father and could not be used effectively by the genro in politics. Another important change concerned the qualifications for appointment to the service ministries. The army and navy had to accept an alteration which permitted the selection of retired officers, and the latter, especially if they had developed political or business affiliations, could not be so effectively controlled by the military establishments. Although in practice the army and navy ministers continued to be drawn from the active-duty list, it is significant that there was no more cabinet-wrecking by forced retirements until the mid-1930's. After the so-called "Taisho change" there were also important shifts in the leadership of the political parties. Katsura, who was still trying to strengthen the Doshikai, died shortly thereafter and was succeeded as leader of that party by a group of influential former bureaucrats, notably Kato Takaaki, Wakatsuki Reijiro, and Hamaguchi Osachi, all of whom had distinguished political careers. The party, moreover, soon included most of the remaining Kokuminto group. Saionji gave up his affiliation with the Seiyukai and thereafter acted only as a genro. He was succeeded as leader of the Seiyukai by Hara Kei. Like their predecessors, these men and their party colleagues were not leaders of popular movements.

The economic transformation of Japan during this period had a significant impact on politics and political parties. For businessmen, intimacy with bureaucrats and legislators was a practical necessity since it was impossible to carry on large enterprises without some government aid and protection. Thus the attitude of Japan's modern political merchants was much the same as those of the Tokugawa period, and their activities contributed to the corruption of bureaucrats and party politicians. High officials as well as their lowly subordinates accepted favors in return for influence. Numerous scandals concerning corrupt practices in the government came to light in this period, and later, when the navy scandal of the Yamamoto ministry involved some of highest-ranking naval officers, there was suspicion that no segment of the government had escaped the taint of corruption.

Relationships were also clearly established between the zaibatsu and the political parties. In the case of the Seiyukai, Mitsui interests were represented directly by Yamamoto Teijiro, formerly president of the Taiwan Sugar Company, a Mitsui subsidiary; Saionji's brother was president of the Sumitomo Company; and Hara Kei became one of the four top directors of the Furukawa Mining Company. The Mitsubishi Company attempted to effect an alliance between Okuma and Matsukata; when its efforts failed, it supported the Kokuminto to counter the alliances between the Seiyukai and its competitors, and sizable amounts of money were alleged to have gone to Kokuminto leaders. The Mitsubishi Company was also active in the Doshikai, and after Katsura's death Kato Takaaki, son-in-law of Iwasaki Yanosuke, who was head of the Mitsubishi interests, became president of the party.

The zaibatsu constantly made gifts to party leaders, wholly apart from the large campaign contributions which were given before each election, and in some cases businessmen resorted to outright bribery to secure the legislation they wanted. In the sugar scandal of 1907–1908 sixteen members of the house of representatives and three ex-members were indicted, along with six company directors. Such practices quite naturally had a devastating effect on the public image of political parties, and on occasion indignation led to violence; for example, Hoshi Toru, who had long been accused of corrupt practices on behalf of himself and the Seiyukai, was assassinated in June, 1901.

There are indications that during this period businessmen were developing a greater degree of self-confidence. Stimulated by the writings of Fukuzawa Yukichi and Shibusawa Eiichi, they began to abandon some of their servility and to fight for their rights. Shibusawa himself helped to lead the newly organized Japanese Chamber of Commerce in its battles to abolish the export tax on cotton thread, the import tax on raw cotton, and, after the Russo-Japanese War, to reduce military expenditures. In fact, the pressure on Saionji to resign in 1908 and 1909 was in part because of business opposition to his fiscal and administrative policies.

The Rise of the Left Wing

The growing political consciousness of Japanese businessmen was paralleled by efforts to establish socialist parties and left-wing schools of thought and to develop a labor movement. Economic and social inequalities provided the potential for mass support of all such undertakings. In the countryside there was the constantly increasing concentration of landownership, and in urban areas technological unemployment, poor working conditions, and low pay were common. As early as the 1890's the labor movement got under way with the organization of the Iron Workers Union and a union among the engineers and firemen of the Nippon Railway Company, and in the same decade small radical political parties began to be established. For example, in 1892 Oi Kentaro and other former samurai organized the Toyo Jiyuto (Oriental Liberal Party), which pledged to assist poor peasants and workers through a policy of stronger government intervention in the economy as a whole. It established the muckraking newspaper, *Azuma Shimbun,* and the first labor magazine, *Shin Toyo (The New Orient),* both of which condemned businessmen and their political allies, and it also founded the Greater Japan Labor Society, the League to Petition for Universal Suffrage, and the Committee of Investigation on Farm Tenancy Regulations. Among laborers it formed Tokyo unions of shoemakers, carpenters, stonemasons, and rickshawmen. Although the Toyo Jiyuto was short-lived, it did help to orient labor toward a kind of primitive socialism.

Labor unionization came to an abrupt halt, however, when the diet in May, 1900, passed the Public Peace Police Law, which revived provisions of the notorious Peace Preservation Law, repealed in 1898 after a long struggle between the parties and the bureaucracy, and added a clause which made it practically impossible to organize and maintain legal labor unions. Later, in 1912, Suzuki Bunji formed the small Yuaikai (Fraternal Association), but it was not so much a labor union as a mutual-aid society for laborers. Since it emphasized the need to maintain harmony between capital and labor, it was almost never subjected to interference and suppression by the government; consequently, it enjoyed rapid growth and provided the basis of Japan's subsequent labor movement after World War I.

In May, 1901, a group of socialist intellectuals, including Kotoku Shusui and Katayama Sen, all of whom had been active in the development of labor unions, founded the Shakai Minshuto (Social Democratic Party), which announced its program as follows: disarmament with a view to the attainment of world peace, abolition of the existing system of class distinctions, establishment of public ownership of land and capital, state ownership of the means of transportation and communication, equitable distribution of wealth, equality of political rights, and the establishment of a system of free education at the expense of the state. The reaction of the Japanese government was immediate. On the very day that the party was publicly organized, Prime Minister Ito summoned Katayama to the home ministry and gave instructions to disband. Later in the year the same group established the Nihon Heiminto (Japan Commoner Party), but it, too, was banned immediately by Prime Minister Katsura.

Deprived of the opportunity to establish an effective labor base and prohibited from engaging in politics, the Japanese socialists turned their attention to the dissemination of ideas. Many of them toured the country, holding meetings and discussions among intellectuals and workers, but their efforts to achieve some kind of unity were handicapped by the fact that they were a heterogeneous collection of utopians, Marxists, anarchists, syndicalists, Christians, humanitarians, liberals, and other discontented elements, bound together only by vague ideals of social justice and international amity rather than by economic theory or political doctrine. Socialist opposition to nationalism and imperialism also caused difficulty; for example, the antiwar stand of the *Heimin Shimbun (Commoner's News)* during the early part of the Russo-Japanese War caused the publication to be banned by the government. A kind of national socialism was also beginning to emerge at this time. In August, 1905, the Kokka Shakaito (National Socialist Party) was organized and attacked commercialism. Its stated purpose was to check the tyranny of the urban rich with the help of the imperial family, which, it claimed, had from ancient times practiced socialism. When the party participated in the anti-Katsura demonstrations following the Treaty of Portsmouth, the government ordered its dissolution.

In February, 1906, a union of socialists established the Nihon Shakaito (Japan Socialist Party), with the objective of effecting socialism within the limits of the law; and although the party actively disseminated socialist ideas, it was not suppressed by the government. But the new party, which had less than two hundred members, was soon rent by factionalism based on differences of opinion regarding political tactics. In February, 1907, a party council debated fundamental policy, and several basic lines of thought emerged. One was expressed by Kotoku Shusui, a disciple of Kropotkin, who opposed reformism and parliamentarianism, as espoused by Katayama Sen and Tazoe Tetsuzo, and advocated sole reliance on direct action; both Kotoku and Katayama thought of themselves as Marxists, but they regarded Marxism as a general principle of their movement and not as a discipline for analyzing existing conditions or determining strategy and tactics. A third point of view was stated most ably by Sakai Toshihiko, whose knowledge of Marxism, much more thorough than that of Kotoku or Katayama, included an understanding of materialist philosophy and its view of history, the theory of surplus value, and the concept of class struggle. He urged that the party combine a parliamentary policy, emphasizing universal suffrage, with direct action. Although he was personally closer to the viewpoint of Kotoku, he was seeking to reach a compromise between reformism and anarchism. Sakai's proposal won twenty-eight votes, Kotoku's twenty-two, and the view of Katayama and Tazoe only two. After this February meeting was reported in *Heimin Shimbun,* the government moved quickly on February 22 to ban the party and in April to force the newspaper to cease publication. The government also blamed the party directly for labor riots at the Ashio copper mines, which caused destruction of equipment valued at over two million dollars. This was the last attempt at political organization by Japan's socialists for more than a decade, since subsequent cabinets maintained a policy of suppression.

Socialists continued privately to condemn capitalists, bureaucrats, and party politicians, but their activities were closely watched by the police. Subversive literature was destroyed, and radical leaders were arrested and jailed. But government suppression tended to encourage anarchistic terrorism. A case in point was the plot of Kotoku's followers to assassinate the Emperor Meiji in 1910. This group was highly irrational, having no clear plan for initiating a revolution or establishing an anarchistic society. The plot was uncovered by government agents in advance, and those involved were quickly convicted of treason, without the right to appeal to a higher court. Eleven of them, including Kotoku, who was not in sympathy with his followers, were executed, and another twelve were sentenced to life imprisonment. The exposure of the plot so shocked the Japanese people and so stimulated government suppression that the entire leftist movement was cast in a shadow from which it did not emerge for more than a decade. Many socialists withdrew from active participation in the movement. Some, like Katayama in 1914, fled to the United States, where they formed the Japanese Socialist Group in America, while others went to Europe or withdrew to their home villages. Several broke under the strain of constant police surveillance and went insane or committed suicide. Some renounced their beliefs, but many died in Japanese prisons for them. Of the important leaders, only Osugi Sakae, Sakai Toshihiko, Arahata Kanson, and Yamakawa Hitoshi remained in Japan and quietly continued to work on behalf of their cause. All four belonged to Kotoku's group; the latter three were later instrumental in founding the Japanese Communist Party (Nihon Kyosanto), while Osugi became the outstanding exponent of syndicalism.

The spread of democratic and socialist ideas stimulated the nationalist intellectuals and societies to greater activity in urging the people to follow "the Japanese way of life." They placed new emphasis upon the old concept of *kokutai,* centering on the peculiar unity of the Japanese people around the imperial institution, as the basic element of the country's moral structure. While many nationalists were willing to admit that there was still much to learn from foreign countries, they proclaimed the spiritual superiority of Japan. For example, in his works Inouye Tetsujiro stressed kokutai, state Shinto, bushido, the family system, and Confucian morality, all of which emphasized loyalty and obedience. And nationalistic societies like the Kokuryukai engaged in a nationwide campaign to stamp out "subversive ideas" of democracy and socialism and on occasion used intimidation and violence against scholars, intellectuals, political leaders, and businessmen who espoused or expressed sympathy with either. While it is clear that the great majority of intellectuals continued to look to the West for principles and standards, there can be no doubt that nationalist thought, especially as channeled through the education and military systems, had a decisive influence among the great mass of people. Even the small minority of Japanese Christians established the Nihon Shukyo Sha (Japan Religions Society) in an effort to integrate Christian principles into the intellectual and social patterns of Japan. In the case of the extremist nationalist societies, it must be remembered that their membership was small, as in the case of the socialist movement; and although it is true that they did at times influence the actions of government leaders, other, more important, factors were usually at work as well.

Political Instability and the China Problem

Admiral Yamamoto Gombei took office as prime minister in February, 1913, and immediately faced demands by his Seiyukai supporters that a party cabinet be established, that the ministers of the army and navy be selected differently, that the civil service be reformed with a view to opening it broadly to party members, and that the army not get its two divisions. He was willing to appoint Seiyukai members to the cabinet, with the exception of the foreign affairs, army, and navy ministries, but at the same time he upheld the doctrine of imperial sovereignty, making it clear that the best that the advocates of party cabinets could hope for was that "importance" would be placed on the views of party members and on public opinion. He did make some minor concessions with regard to the civil service regulations, which would facilitate slightly the practice of party patronage, and he handled the service ministries issue skillfully, as noted above. But the matter of army expansion was not resolved.

Yamamoto fell from office in the aftermath of the naval scandal. On January 21, 1914, a navy replacement appropriations bill, which would provide the sum of 160,000,000 yen for a six-year period, came up before the house of representatives, and two days later a scandal broke when it was disclosed that several high-ranking naval officers had accepted bribes from foreign companies which were bidding on the construction contracts. Immediately the naval appropriations bill was attacked; and although the Seiyukai was able to exercise a moderating influence in the house of representatives, the house of peers, influenced by Yamagata and the army, cut the naval budget by 70,000,000 yen. A conference of the two houses could not reach agreement, and a nonconfidence motion against the cabinet was introduced in the house of representatives. In the background, public opinion mounted against Yamamoto, and finally (January 26) he resigned.

The genro, notably Yamagata and Matsukata, were hard put to find a new prime minister. Since their antiparty attitude still dominated, especially in the case of Yamagata, they would not consider either Hara Kei or Kato Takaaki, the leaders of the two major parties. Saionji was approached but said that he was not interested, and Prince Tokugawa refused to give up his secure position as president of the house of peers. Kiyoura Keigo attempted to form a cabinet, but the parties, the navy, and public opinion branded him as a front man for Yamagata and the military. Since he found it impossible to secure a navy minister and thus could not complete his cabinet, Kiyoura withdrew. His experience made it clear that a cabinet without some party support stood very little chance of survival under normal conditions.

The genro finally turned to Okuma Shigenobu, who had retired from politics in 1907 to serve as chancellor of Waseda University, which he had founded in 1882. As a compromise candidate he appeared to be the man best qualified to stabilize the political situation, and in April, 1914, he formed his cabinet. In the past he had been an advocate of party government, and he still commanded the respect of the diet and the public as a whole. On the other hand, as a cabinet minister on several earlier occasions, he had proved to be tractable to policies dictated by the genro. The army was satisfied that he would support its expansion program, which had been the subject of debate for several years. In the house of representatives Okuma could depend for support on the Doshikai, led by Kato, but he needed Seiyukai votes as well in order to get the army the appropriations for two new divisions. When the Seiyukai balked, he promptly dissolved the house of representatives (December 25, 1914), and in the general election of March, 1915, using every means of corruption and bribery at its disposal, his cabinet was rewarded with a resounding Doshikai majority. Despite a storm of criticism, which included that of the old liberal party politician and minister of justice, Ozaki Yukio, Okuma's position remained strong. He was able to push through the army expansion program and continue the strong China policy, which guided the most important activities of his ministry.

For some time there had been increasing interest in the affairs of China, particularly among the nationalist secret societies. For example, after 1905 the Kokuryukai, whose activities at first were directed primarily toward Korea and then toward Manchuria, began to concentrate its attention upon China as a field for Japanese expansion. Prior to the Russo-Japanese War, Japanese nationalists, in and out of government, had supported Chinese revolutionaries because of the need, they felt, to develop resistance to the advances of the Western powers, especially Russia. The activities of the Kokuryukai in China therefore generally received backing from high-level Japanese government officials, but after the Russo-Japanese War the desirability of helping the Chinese nationalist movement was not so obvious, particularly to government officials who began to feel that Japan had more to gain from a weak and divided China. The Kokuryukai, however, continued to give assistance to the Chinese nationalists, and in 1907 its efforts were rewarded when Sun Yat-sen made it known that he would be willing to give Japan a free hand in Manchuria and Mongolia in return for support of his revolutionary movement. When the Chinese authorities heard of this promise, they put pressure on the Japanese cabinet to expel Sun from Japan. Although the Kokuryukai continued to work on Sun's behalf, it could not win the cabinet over to its position.

The emergence of Yuan Shih-k'ai as the key figure in the Chinese political scene had a significant impact on Japanese policy. When Yuan and Sun Yat-sen came to terms during the 1911 revolution, Japanese ultranationalists condemned the union, claiming that Yuan was no friend of the revolutionary movement and that he would seize the first opportunity to destroy it. According to the Kokuryukai interpretation of Chinese affairs, this would be a serious blow to Japan's interests. However, after the split between Yuan and Sun, contacts were renewed between Japanese and the revolutionary Chinese nationalists. Yet it was Yuan himself who provided the most ammunition for the Japanese expansionists. When he moved against Chinese republican forces at Nanking and that city fell (September, 1913), his soldiers manhandled or killed scores of Japanese consular guards and residents. Spurred by public opinion, Prime Minister Yamamoto was forced to take positive action; and in October, 1913, he sent an ultimatum to Yuan Shih-k'ai demanding financial compensation for the outrages committed against Japanese subjects and apologies by the commanders responsible. Apparently realizing the intensity of feeling in Japan, Yuan complied and agreed to pay an indemnity, execute the "murderers," remove the officers in command, and grant to Japan a concession for the construction of five railway lines.

Thereafter continuous pressure was exerted on Yamamoto by ultranationalists, who favored the adoption of a more "positive" policy toward China. The more aggressive societies demanded the resignation of the cabinet and were therefore elated when Yamamoto fell as a result of the naval scandal. They welcomed the new prime minister, Okuma Shigenobu, because he had long been recognized as a leader alert to Japan's opportunities on the continent, and they expected that under his leadership the government would adopt a strong China policy, especially since this was compatible with the known views of his foreign minister, Kato Takaaki. The Okuma ministry's opportunity came with the outbreak of war in Europe.

21 *World War I and Japan*

Japan became involved in World War I in the summer of 1914 because of its obligations to Great Britain under the Anglo-Japanese Alliance, which had been renewed in July, 1911, under interesting circumstances. The British regarded the alliance as essential for their national security since it bound Japan to what was essentially a four-power treaty arrangement, which included Great Britain, France, Russia, and Japan. But at the same time there was increasing rivalry between the British and the Japanese as a result of Japan's industrial development and commercial expansion, which threatened British interests in China. There was also a strong anti-Japanese sentiment in New Zealand, Australia, and Canada because of immigration problems comparable to those that had embarrassed the United States in her relations with Japan. These elements of the British Empire were also concerned that they might be drawn into a war against the United States in support of the alliance. The 1911 renewal excluded the United States from its scope in the event that either partner concluded an arbitration treaty with her, and on August 3, 1911, Great Britain and the United States signed such a treaty, but it was not approved by the American Senate. Thus the status of the United States under the terms of the alliance was not clear. Despite these difficulties, the alliance was a basic element in British foreign policy, for its dissolution could conceivably bring about a *rapprochement*, if not an alliance, between Germany, Russia, and Japan—a consideration based on improved German-Russian relations following the Potsdam meeting of the kaiser and czar in November, 1910, and the growing co-operation between Japan and Russia in East Asia.

War with Germany

When Great Britain declared war on Germany on August 4, 1914, public demand for entry into the conflict mounted in Japan. The Japanese press assumed a militant tone, recalling Germany's role in the Triple Intervention of 1895 and charging that German naval power in the Pacific Ocean was a threat to all neutral shipping; it insisted also that German military preparations at Kiaochow were a menace to the peace of East Asia.

On August 4 the British ambassador in Tokyo requested Japanese assistance should war spread to East Asia and should Hong Kong or Wei Hai-wei come under German attack. The Japanese government agreed that in either eventuality the alliance would automatically be invoked. Three days later the British ambassador presented a formal memorandum stating that "it is most important that the Japanese fleet should, if possible, hunt out and destroy the armed German merchant cruisers who are now attacking our commerce," but the Japanese response far exceeded British expectations. On August 8 the Japanese cabinet decided to demand that Germany not only should surrender to Japan her armed vessels in Asian waters but should also transfer to Japan the Kiaochow Leasehold and German rights in Shantung Province. It was clear that the Okuma cabinet was ready to embark on a campaign to destroy German influence in China and at the same time enhance Japan's position. Foreign Minister Kato, who strongly urged entry into the war on the British side despite substantial opposition on the part of the genro, promptly notified London of Japan's intentions.

The British government became alarmed, fearing that a Japanese attack on Kiaochow would mean not only a full extension of the war into Chinese territory, thereby adversely affecting British commercial interests, but also gains for Japan at the expense of Germany, which might upset the balance of power among the nations with interests in China. London therefore urged Japan to confine her activities to "protection of the sea trade" and to postpone her declaration of war, but Kato steadfastly maintained that an attack on Kiaochow was part of the over-all campaign to safeguard sea trade. When the British reversed their position completely on August 11, withdrawing the request for assistance under the alliance, Kato stood his ground and insisted that, since Japan had completed her military preparations and was poised for war, she could not back down.

In the end, the Okuma cabinet was extricated from an embarrassing situation when on August 13 London again reversed itself and agreed to the Japanese ultimatum to Germany for the surrender of armed vessels and for the transfer of the Kiaochow Leasehold and rights in Shantung. The British requested, however, that Japan confine hostilities to the leasehold and neighboring waters and that she state this limitation in the ultimatum.

In the meantime the Chinese government was apprehensive about the spread of hostilities to its territory and on August 3 approached the United States to use her good offices to secure pledges from the powers to respect China's neutrality. Although Secretary of State Bryan approached them with an ambitious plan to neutralize the entire Pacific Ocean region as well as China, none favored any scheme that might protect German interests.

In her ultimatum of August 15 Japan demanded that Germany withdraw all armed vessels from Chinese and Japanese waters, disarm those that could not be withdrawn, and deliver by September 15 without condition or compensation the Kiaochow Leasehold with a view to its eventual restoration to China. Japan expected an answer by noon August 23. Shortly thereafter, in response to a British inquiry regarding the sphere of action of Japanese troops,

Kato denied that Japan had any territorial ambitions in China and promised that her military activities would be limited to self-defense. But these fine words did little to alleviate the general suspicion throughout the world regarding Japanese intentions, and Yuan Shih-k'ai hastened to secure an agreement with Germany whereby the Kiaochow Leasehold and special rights in Shantung would be restored to China. When this failed, Peking on August 20 suggested that Germany cede her interests to the United States for their subsequent transfer to China.

This was such an obvious attempt to get the United States to oppose Japan that Washington made it clear to Peking that, while it would gladly exert any influence to further the peaceful development of the Chinese people, "it would be quixotic in the extreme to allow the question of China's territorial integrity to entangle the United States in international difficulties." Despite concern over Japan's intentions, none of the powers was willing to risk complications in East Asia. It seemed that almost any price, including the territorial integrity of China, was worth paying to keep Japan pacified.

When Germany did not reply to the ultimatum, Japan declared war. Ignoring the Chinese declaration of neutrality and attempts to limit the zone of hostilities, Japan on August 27 blockaded Tsingtao and on September 2 landed troops to the north for an attack from the rear and for occupation of the railroad zone extending from Tsingtao to Tsinan, far into the interior of the province. On the last day of October the Japanese forces launched a general offensive; and when German resistance was crushed, the Kiaochow Leasehold fell to Japan (November 10). Japanese forces took over all German interests in Shantung, including the Tsingtao-Tsinan Railroad and its branch lines, mining properties, and other miscellaneous holdings like public works. Although in the process Japan placed all of Shantung Province under military occupation, not until December did Okuma's ministry declare that Japan was not committed to any power on the future of the Kiaochow Leasehold and the German rights in Shantung.

Japan's declaration of war on Germany also extended hostilities to the Pacific Ocean region. Japanese warships joined forces with the British fleet to combat commerce raiders, and Japanese marines occupied German islands north of the equator, which included the Marianas except Guam, the Carolines, and the Marshalls. Their Australian allies seized those south of that line. Japan extended her strategic position to a point that was scarcely more than 2,500 miles from Hawaii, and she also acquired control of Yap Island in the Carolines, which was a key link in the network of German-Dutch submarine telegraph cables between the East Indies and China and in the American trans-Pacific cable running through Guam to Manila.

Japan made other contributions in the struggle against Germany and her allies. The Japanese navy convoyed Australian and New Zealand troopships to the European theater, and during the German submarine campaign of

1917 Japan sent three destroyer divisions into the Mediterranean Sea. After 1917, moreover, the entire ocean region between Australia and South Africa was patrolled by Japanese naval forces. Japan did refuse, however, to send troops to Europe, even though there were constant requests by Great Britain, France, and Russia that she do so; the government adamantly clung to the position that the home islands would be vulnerable should it send troops in sufficient numbers to be of value on the European fronts. Lastly, Japanese industry was an invaluable arsenal for the Russian armies that fought on the eastern front against Germany.

The Twenty-one Demands

Many Japanese were quick to realize that World War I presented an unequaled opportunity to extend their nation's power on the Asian continent. Within and without the government, various individuals and societies developed plans for expansion in China. Three weeks after the surrender of the Kaiochow Leasehold (November 29, 1914), the Kokuryukai presented "a memorandum for the solution of the China problem" which proposed that the government make efforts to induce Chinese republicans and other dissatisfied groups to rise up against Yuan Shih-k'ai, order the Japanese army to move into China to support the revolution and restore order, and conclude a defensive alliance with the new government. The alliance was to include assurances that Japan would have a predominant position in the internal and external affairs of China. The leaders of the Japanese government could scarcely countenance such blatant interventionism, but as early as September, 1914, Foreign Minister Kato persuaded his colleagues to permit him to enter into negotiations with Yuan's government as soon as the Germans at Kiaochow surrendered. Working closely with army and navy officials, Kato formulated a policy under which Japan would acquire greater concessions in Manchuria and Inner Mongolia as well as German rights in Shantung Province.

At Peking on January 18, 1915, the Japanese minister, Hioki Eki, presented to Yuan Shih-k'ai a list of twenty-one demands designed to extend Japan's position in China at a time when Europe was preoccupied with war. Hioki pointed out that there were close relations between Chinese republicans and certain "irresponsible" Japanese and hinted that, unless the demands were accepted, Yuan might have a revolution on his hands. He also informed Yuan that the Peking regime was very unpopular in Japan and advised him to demonstrate his "friendly intentions" by accepting the demands if he wished to secure Japanese support for his own ambitions.

The Twenty-one Demands were broken down into five groups. Under group one China was required to assent to any subsequent German-Japanese agreement disposing of German rights in Shantung; to agree not to cede or

355

lease any part of Shantung to any other power; to agree to Japanese construction of a railway between Chefoo and the Tsingtao-Tsinan line; and to consent to the opening of certain cities in Shantung to "residence and commerce of foreigners."

The demands under group two, which was designed to make permanent Japan's various rights and concessions in Manchuria, included the following: the extension of the Kwantung Leasehold from twenty-five to ninety-nine years; the similar extension of rights concerned with the South Manchurian Railway and the Antung-Mukden Railway; permission for Japanese subjects to "lease or own land" for "commercial and industrial uses or for farming"; the grant to Japanese subjects of the "liberty to enter, reside, and travel in south Manchuria and eastern Inner Mongolia"; the grant of permission to Japanese subjects to engage in mining; the promise from China that she would secure Japan's consent before granting to any third power a concession to construct railroads or to extend industrial credits in those areas; the promise that Japan be consulted first if China required foreign advisers in these areas; and acceptance of Japanese control and management for ninety-nine years of the Kirin-Changchun Railroad, the latter to be eventually connected with Japanese ports in northern Korea.

In group three Japan attempted to secure a source of iron ore by making the Hanyehping Company a Sino-Japanese concern and by giving that company a mining monopoly in certain areas of the Yangtze River Valley. Since the turn of the century Japanese firms had been interested in the iron and coal properties of central China, and they had made extensive purchases of ores. In the case of the Hanyehping Company, Japanese interests had provided loans of 30,000,000 yen to be repaid over a period of forty years in iron ore and crude iron. Many Chinese criticized the steady flow of iron ore from China to Japan and demanded nationalization of the mines; and when Yuan Shih-k'ai began to take such action in November, 1914, he threatened the ore deliveries under the loan arrangement. Thus Japan sought to acquire control of the company and of its mineral resources in the central Yangtze region.

Under group four China was asked to pledge not "to cede or lease to any other power any harbor or any other island along the coast of China." This stipulation was designed to prevent the return of Germany at the close of the war and to preclude China from making territorial grants to other powers, especially the United States.

Group five went beyond rights and interests and was a conscious effort to extend Japan's power throughout China generally. Under this group the following demands were made:

1. China engage influential Japanese as political, financial, and military advisers.

2. China grant the right to own land to Japanese hospitals, temples, and schools situated in the interior.
3. China place her police under joint Sino-Japanese administration in designated regions were Sino-Japanese disputes had occurred.
4. China obtain from Japan a supply of arms, or that she grant to Japan a share in administration of arsenals.
5. China grant to Japan a concession to construct railroads in south China.
6. China grant to Japanese the right to preach.
7. China declare Fukien a Japanese sphere of interest. [There were rumors that the Bethlehem Steel Corporation planned to construct a naval dockyard near Foochow.]

Although Minister Hioki cautioned Yuan Shih-k'ai to keep these demands secret, Yuan let them leak to the foreign legations and to the press. He hoped that the powers would intervene on China's behalf and, if not, that world public opinion might deter the Japanese from their goals. Although there was much sympathy for China abroad, there was no practical assistance. Great Britain indicated that she would not oppose Japan's plans so long as they did not infringe upon British interests in the Yangtze River Valley, while France and Russia were too deeply involved in war to take a stand.

President Woodrow Wilson wanted to protect China out of sympathy and American rights out of interest, but he knew that he had to move cautiously if he was to avoid antagonizing Japan to the detriment of both ends. The Japanese government did modify its policy after objections in March, 1915, by Secretary of State Bryan to the extent that it dropped the demands concerning the purchase of arms and employment of Japanese advisers and police in China. Bryan did concede that although the United States had grounds for objecting to the Japanese demands regarding Shantung, south Manchuria, and Inner Mongolia, she nevertheless frankly recognized that territorial contiguity created special relations between Japan and these areas. This concession was, unfortunately, ambiguous, since "special relations" meant one thing to the United States and another to Japan.

Lacking strong foreign support, Yuan found that the opposition of Chinese public opinion to the Twenty-one Demands—which he did much to create—had become a liability; and he had to suppress anti-Japanese agitation to preclude situations that might give Japan pretexts for expanding her demands or assisting his political rivals.

From February 2 to May 7, 1915, the Japanese and Chinese negotiated on the basis of the Twenty-one Demands, and, all together, twenty-five fruitless meetings were held. The Okuma cabinet realized that the whole affair was dragging on. It had failed to achieve a quick *fait accompli* and was increasingly under attack by the press and the Seiyukai minority in the house of representatives. The genro, moreover, were angered by Kato's independence and were urging a more conciliatory approach in face of the strong reaction of the Chinese people as a whole. Finally, on May 7, Japan presented a modified form of the Twenty-one Demands, omitting group five, in the form of an ultimatum with a two-day time limit.

China gave in on May 9, and two weeks later China and Japan signed a number of agreements and notes embodying the objectives set forth in the ultimatum. The only significant opposition to this action came in the form of identical notes from the United States to both powers, in which Secretary of State Bryan stated that his country would not recognize

any agreement or undertaking which has been entered into or which may be entered into between the governments of Japan and China, impairing the treaty rights of the United States and its citizens in China, the political or territorial integrity of the Republic of China, or the international policy relative to China, commonly known as the Open-Door Policy.

The doctrine of nonrecognition had little effect, however, since Tokyo understood that the United States was not prepared to challenge Japan openly. Bryan's notes, moreover, were weakened by his recognition of Japan's "special and close relations, political as well as economic, with China." It seems clear now that Bryan intended his notes as a reservation, "so that the agreement forced upon China could be properly a subject for discussion in the future when conditions are more propitious."

Domestic Politics and Diplomacy

When Okuma resigned as prime minister on October 8, 1916, under pressure from party politicians for election interference and for antagonizing China, from the genro for his China policy, and from the navy for failing to increase its size, he set the scene for an important political drama. During September and October, in anticipation of Okuma's move, the Doshikai co-operated with several minor factions in the house of representatives to form a new party, the Kenseikai (Constitutional Association), in opposition to the antiparliamentary forces of the genro and the military. In fact, the Kenseikai promulgated its platform on the very day that Okuma resigned in order to create the impression that its leader, Kato Takaaki, was Okuma's choice to form a cabinet.

The genro, however, bypassed Kato, whom they disliked, and appointed as prime minister General Terauchi Masatake, a Choshu militarist and favorite of the Yamagata faction. Actually Yamagata sought Kato's support for the new cabinet, but Kato refused to make the Kenseikai the pawn of the genro and the army. In rejecting Kato the genro stated that in their opinion it was unnecessary for the prime minister to be president of the majority party; to set such a precedent would, they claimed, be contrary to the spirit of the constitution and would have the effect of restricting the imperial prerogative. In a more practical vein, they argued that Kato was not well regarded in China and Russia and that, for the sake of satisfactory relations with both countries and the successful termination of the European war, Terauchi was the better man. In fact, the genro had, under Yamagata's leadership, engineered Kato's resignation as foreign minister in the summer of 1915.

Despite the powerful attack that Kato and his party launched on the new cabinet and the genro, calling upon the public to rise against antiparliamentarianism, Terauchi found strong support in the Seiyukai, which was anxious to regain a majority in the house of representatives. When Terauchi dissolved the house in face of a nonconfidence bill introduced by the Kenseikai on January 24, 1917, the government instructed the prefectural governors to work for the defeat of Kenseikai candidates, who in total had constituted a majority of 200 out of 381 seats in the house.

The elections of April 20 produced the following results: Hara's Seiyukai, 160; Kato's Kenseikai, 119; Inukai Tsuyoshi's Kokuminto, 35; and independents, 67. Terauchi then formed an alliance with the Seiyukai, the Kokuminto, and a new progovernment party, the Ishinkai (Restoration Association), based on one-half of the independents, but these parties were not the unwitting instruments of the cabinet, as was evidenced by their veto of a tax-increase program. In the final analysis, the Terauchi cabinet demonstrated that, despite the genro's disapproval of party government, a cabinet which did not enjoy party support of some kind could not exist for long.

In the field of foreign policy, especially with regard to China, Terauchi tried to achieve greater political unity. He persuaded the heads of the three major parties to remove foreign policy from politics, and he established the foreign policy deliberation committee, composed of representatives of the major parties and influential nonparty figures. Both Hara and Inukai joined the new organization. Kato did not, on the ground that the committee was hardly an answer to the real question of power and responsibility; he felt that if Terauchi wanted the advice of party leaders, he should take them into the cabinet.

For some time the Japanese government had been concerned about the relationship between the general postwar settlement and its own policy toward China. Under the terms of the Declaration of London, announced on October 19, 1915, Great Britain, France, Russia, and Japan agreed not to make a separate peace or to discuss peace terms except in common. This assured Japan of participation in the peace conference, where she could arrange the disposition of Germany's Kiaochow Leasehold and special rights in Shantung Province. When in 1916 there was the possibility that Russia might sue for a separate peace, Japan reached an agreement with Russia on July 3, 1916, which recognized Japan's considerably strengthened position in south Manchuria and Inner Mongolia. Both powers pledged that, in the event that the territorial rights or special interests of either were menaced, they would confer on measures to be taken to safeguard those rights and interests; they also set up a secret defensive alliance for five years. The two powers recognized that it was vital to the interests of both that China should not come under the domination of any third power hostile to either of them. In the event of war in defense of these vital interests, each was bound to come to the aid of the other on demand and to undertake not to make peace without the previous consent of the other. Later, in the winter of 1917, after China had entered World War I against Germany, Japan secured from her European allies a pledge of support regarding her claims to Shantung and the German islands north of the equator by a series of secret commitments.

After the American declaration of war on Germany in April, 1917, Japan was also concerned about American attitudes regarding the peace settlement, and she wanted to secure from the United States an official recognition not only of her "special interests" in Manchuria but also of her "paramount interests" in China. At Washington the Japanese ambassador asked the new secretary of state, Robert Lansing, to confirm the Bryan statement of March, 1915, on "territorial contiguity" and to reassert America's "friendly attitude toward Japan in respect of Chinese problems." This preliminary move was followed in the summer of 1917 by the arrival in Washington of a special diplomatic mission headed by Viscount Ishii Kikujiro, which, under the pretext of bringing unity and co-operation into the combined war efforts of Japan and the United States, sought to reach some basic understanding on China. Ishii hoped to allay American suspicions concerning Japan's motives and to secure from the American government a public admission of Japan's "paramount interests" in China. His conversations with Lansing led to a formal exchange of notes which acknowledged Japan's "special interests" in China but which once again endorsed the principles of territorial integrity and the open door. Specifically the United States recognized that "territorial propinquity creates special relations between countries, and consequently, the government of the United States recognizes that Japan has special interests in China, particularly in the part to which her possessions are contiguous." The announcement of the exchange (Bryan's notes had not been published) was met with great enthusiasm in Japan, where the term "special interests" was defined in the broadest sense, including special political interests. Although the meaning of the exchange was interpreted quite differently in the United States, the Chinese generally regarded the notes "as indicating the withdrawal, in favor of Japan, of the American government's desire to exercise any influence in Chinese affairs." This interpretation is not corroborated by close examination of American policy toward China.

President Wilson had been endeavoring to check Japan's domination of the Peking government, and in this activity he had some support from Great Britain and France. He hoped to encourage American as well as other sources of capital to provide China with loans in order to prevent a financial monopoly by Japan. Peking accepted several loans from American sources, which assumed British and French shares, and granted concessions to American firms for the construction of railroads in Inner Mongolia, Kwangsi, and Chekiang. By November, 1917, Wilson was determined to organize a new four-power consortium representing the United States, Great Britain, France, and Russia. He was convinced at last that no amount of State Department promotion could produce independent loans adequate for his purposes. However, when the American minister to Peking, Paul Reinsch, boldly attacked Japan's exclusive railroad claims in south Manchuria by suggesting to the Japanese minister that the United States and Japan co-operate in railroad construction in that region, he was informed by Lansing that the United States had recognized Japan's special interests in Manchuria and that the United States did not desire to do anything to interfere with them.

Japan had been using financial policy to advance her interests in China ever since Prime Minister Terauchi dispatched his close friend, Nishihara Kamezo, as his personal representative to Peking in June, 1916. For example, between September, 1917, and September, 1918, the Peking warlords contracted Japanese loans in the amount of some 145,000,000 yen from Nishihara, who acted under special instructions from Terauchi and the military without the knowledge of the Japanese foreign ministry. These Nishihara loans were not investments in the usual meaning of the word; instead, they were payments to Tuan Ch'i-jui and the Anfu clique in exchange for certain agreements that would be to Japan's advantage, especially in south Manchuria. They were not secured by anything more substantial than promissory notes; and although the greater part of the funds were never accounted for, Japan achieved substantial gains. For example, on September 24, 1918, the Peking regime gave its consent to the transfer of the Kiaochow Leasehold to Japan with the understanding that Japan would in turn restore it to China but would retain in expanded form Germany's economic rights in Shantung Province.

In 1918 Wilson finally re-established the consortium, but he had to make certain concessions to Japan. Under the terms of the consortium arrangement the four members agreed that all preferences and options held by member banks were to be pooled and that the administrative integrity and independence of China would be respected. Although this provision collided sharply with her China program, Japan complied when the other members excluded from the scope of the consortium's activities the South Manchurian Railroad Zone and a number of other railway projects and their related mining and industrial privileges in Manchuria and Inner Mongolia. But, by the time that all these details had been worked out, the agreement was largely a forgotten affair. China showed no enthusiasm for the consortium and refused to do business with it, which was ironic in view of the fact that it was generally regarded as a means of preserving China's integrity. The Peking government and many Chinese took the view that the consortium threatened international control of Chinese finance and was designed to deprive China of a free world market where she could borrow on the best terms available. Peking was able to negotiate loans from the Banque Industrielle; and when several other important banks remained outside the consortium, it felt that it had succeeded in restoring at least a semblance of free competition in the field of finance. By this time, also, the chief threat to Japan's China policy was not the machinations of international diplomacy but the vigor of a newborn Chinese nationalism.

The Siberian Intervention

The Terauchi ministry also committed Japan to an adventurous policy in Siberia following the outbreak of the Bolshevik Revolution in Russia in 1917. When the Soviet regime came to power in November, it moved quickly to end the war with Germany. By December 15 it had concluded an armistice, and on March 13, 1918, it signed the Treaty of Brest-Litovsk, which officially terminated the war. During these months Great Britain and France worried about the consequences of Soviet policy. They lamented the collapse of the eastern front and feared that a defeated Russia would become a German granary. Thus they considered the possibility of intervention to reactivate the eastern front and of having Japan take possession of the Trans-Siberian Railway in order to insure the continued flow of supplies.

The initial reaction of the Japanese government, including that of the army, was not very enthusiastic, for it wanted to stabilize Japan's position in China. But the spread of Russian communist activity to Siberia altered this view. Japanese had invested heavily in Russian enterprises through government bonds and had developed a sizable trade with Harbin and Vladivostok; in fact, many Japanese companies had established branch offices in northern Manchuria and eastern Siberia. These interests were threatened by the establishment of local soviets, and by December 1, 1917, Vladivostok was in danger of falling into Red hands.

It is clear that by this time Prime Minister Terauchi and the army were beginning to think in terms of establishing an independent anti-Soviet state in Siberia. When Great Britain proposed an expedition to protect Vladivostok, composed largely of Japanese forces but including British, French, and American elements, the Terauchi cabinet was receptive to the idea, but it wanted to be sure that it would have freedom of action despite collaboration with its allies. Learning of the dispatch of a British warship to Vladivostok in January, 1918, to guard Allied supplies valued at one billion dollars and to protect the foreign consular corps, Japanese naval units raced to that port and arrived on the scene two days ahead of the British. But there was no immediate intervention, despite the fact that in the following month the communists took over the city. It seems that Great Britain, by holding back, was endeavoring to persuade the Moscow regime to invite an Allied expedition to re-establish the eastern front against Germany. But early in April, after a robbery of military stores and an attack upon three Japanese, one of whom died, Japanese marines in company with a small British force landed to protect foreign nationals and the Allied equipment. At home the Japanese army decided to use the plight of Japanese subjects in Siberia as a pretext for sending two divisions into the Maritime Province and three into the Trans-Baikal region to crush the soviets.

The actions of Czechoslovakian troops in Siberia complicated the situation. Early in World War I a Czechoslovakian detachment was formed in Russia to fight as part of the Russian army against the Central Powers. These troops, recruited from Czechs and Slovenes resident in Russia and from soldiers who deserted the Austrian army or were captured, amounted to almost 50,000 men, and after the disintegration of the Russian army in the winter of 1917 they remained intact. On January 25, 1918, the Czech national council in Paris declared the corps to be part of the Czech army in France, and it hoped to secure Allied assistance to transport the force to the western front by way of Vladivostok. The new Soviet regime granted the Czechs permission to cross Siberia en route to France; but when they became involved in Russian political struggles, there were clashes between the Czechs and communist forces, beginning in April, 1918. For example, in the region of the Volga there was open warfare between the communists and Czech-supported opponents of the new regime.

The break between the communists and the Czechs was one of the most decisive factors in the final decision of the Allies to intervene in Siberia. Since the Czechs gained control of the Trans-Siberian Railway and held a strong strategic position in the Volga region, there appeared to be a substantial foothold from which a new eastern front might be built. By July, moreover, Czech troops were in possession of Vladivostok, and at the same time other Czech units began to move eastward from central Siberia. These circumstances helped to win Great Britain and France away from flirtations with Moscow and to transform American opposition into support of intervention.

The decision to intervene was finally made in the summer of 1918. On July 2, Great Britain, France, and Japan invited the United States to join a Siberian expedition, and on July 8 Washington proposed to furnish, on an equal basis with its allies, arms and ammunition to the Czechs, to land forces to protect Vladivostok, and to dispatch an expedition, each power contributing 7,000 men, to guard the lines of transportation for the Czechs as they moved east. Despite Wilson's efforts to limit the size of the expeditionary force, Japan sent some 72,000 troops into Siberia from August to November;

the next largest force, 9,000, was from the United States. But in its approval of the expedition on August 2 the Terauchi cabinet had been careful not to agree to any limitation and had in fact reserved the right to send additional troops if, in its view, the circumstances demanded it.

During July a struggle had taken place within the political councils of the Japanese government between the large-scale interventionists, led by the military clique of Yamagata, and the proponents of limited intervention, led by Hara Kei of the Seiyukai, who did not want to antagonize the Western powers, particularly the United States. The army, which had been concentrating on China as a means of making up Japan's economic deficiencies, regarded the Russian revolution as a threat to its China policy and decided to attempt to establish a pro-Japanese regime in the region of the Amur River Basin. The American proposal of July 8 actually broke the deadlock in the Japanese government and permitted agreement between the two groups, but for different reasons.

Political conditions in Siberia tipped the scales in favor of the large-scale interventionists. The collapse of the czarist regime at first caused a revival of the late-nineteenth-century movement for Siberian autonomy, but after the Bolshevik Revolution in November, 1917, local soviets were organized throughout Siberia. However, the communists lacked men and arms and were forced to confine their activities to guerrilla warfare. By November, 1918, there was no effective communist local or regional authority in Siberia, and the most powerful element on the political scene was the czarist regime at Omsk under Admiral Kolchak. Locally, however, conditions were still generally chaotic, and various opportunists seized power.

The Allies had agreed upon the principle of noninterference in Russian politics, but this pledge was quickly forgotten once foreign troops were in Siberia. Since the Japanese, British, and French forces, and even some Americans, concluded that the purpose of the intervention was to fight the communists, they became *de facto* allies of the czarist elements. In fact, they were responsible for bringing Admiral Kolchak to Siberia, where they installed him as head of the government at Omsk. It is clear that national interests dominated the policies of the intervening powers. France was concerned for her investment in Siberian enterprises, Great Britain seemed chiefly apprehensive about the spread of communism to India, and Japan worked to gain a dominant position in eastern Siberia and the Maritime Province. Although the Japanese recognized Kolchak, they assisted anti-Kolchak Cossack leaders like Semenov and Kalmykov. While the United States sought to check the Japanese, Great Britain and France, ignoring the consequences, encouraged Japanese efforts against the communists.

Long after Germany had fallen and the need for an eastern front had disappeared, the struggle in central Siberia continued, but Kolchak's cause was ultimately lost when his armies were defeated in the Ural region in the summer of 1919. Soviet armies reached Omsk by November, and Kolchak was captured at Irkutsk and executed in February, 1920. The communists, however, did not venture to penetrate deep into Siberia because the Moscow regime needed their arms elsewhere; moreover, they had no desire to antagonize Japan at that time. In April, 1920, Siberia was organized as a buffer state separating Soviet Russia and the Japanese forces. In theory it was independent and sovereign, with a purely democratic constitution, but what actually emerged was a communist-dominated one-party regime.

During this period an American-Japanese struggle developed over the Siberian and Manchurian railroads. As early as March, 1917, when the United States severed diplomatic relations with Germany, Washington became concerned over the strategic importance of the Trans-Siberian Railway. On April 2, after the fall of the czarist regime, it approached the Kerensky government with an offer of American technical assistance to rehabilitate the railroad for war purposes; the British went further, suggesting American management of the Siberian system. When Kerensky approved, in June, 1917, an American railroad commission was sent to Russia under John F. Stevens, formerly chief engineer of the Panama Canal, and in November 288 American railway engineers arrived at Valdivostok. When conditions there became too disturbed, the corps retired temporarily to Nagasaki, and at the end of February, 1918, about 100 members moved to Harbin, to the alarm of the Japanese.

After the Bolshevik Revolution, north Manchuria became a political battleground. At Harbin Russian soldiers and workmen, organized by the communists into a soviet, sought to gain control of the Chinese Eastern Railway from its manager, General Horvath. The czar-appointed Russian envoy to China, who was still recognized by the Peking regime, and his diplomatic colleagues protested against the actions of the Harbin Soviet, and in December, 1917, Chinese authorities, with the consent of the powers, sent a regiment into the railway zone to intervene whenever conditions made it necessary. In the meantime, delegates of the soviet at Harbin declared themselves official representatives of the Moscow government, and they were supported in this by a personal telegram from Lenin, who instructed them to take over the Chinese Eastern Railway. The railway workers went on strike to force Horvath's resignation, but the Harbin Soviet was unable to stand up against the Chinese troops that intervened to take possession of Russian property and to replace certain Russian officials with their own countrymen; for example, they reorganized the Chinese Eastern Railway Company with Chinese officers in control. It is significant that most of the Allies did not want China to re-establish her control over north Manchuria since such action would create an unfortunate precedent. Great Britain warned Peking to this effect, and the United States, while recognizing that "China is entirely within her right in employing means to protect her sovereignty and territorial integrity," cautioned Peking against any steps that might lead to armed conflict. Thus, early in January, 1918, most of the Chinese troops were withdrawn from the railway zone, and czarist authority, in the person of General Horvath, was restored.

Japan was anxious to take advantage of the political uncertainties in north Manchuria for her own purposes. In May, 1918, she signed two treaties with the Peking government providing for Sino-Japanese military co-operation if the "general peace and tranquility" of East Asia were menaced, and late in July, 1918, after Semenov's troops had been decisively defeated by communist forces and had retreated into Manchuria, Japan invoked these agreements and dispatched troops into the zone of the Chinese Eastern Railway. The United States opposed Japan's efforts to establish control over north Manchuria by insisting that inter-Allied, not exclusive Japanese, control be established over the Chinese Eastern Railway. After much negotiation, the powers concluded an agreement (January, 1919) by which the operation of the Trans-Siberian and Chinese Eastern railroads was placed in the hands of an inter-Allied commission, to be advised by Stevens, the American engineer, and a technical board. In March the agreement was modified slightly, and the Chinese Eastern Railway came under the protection of Chinese military forces. But Japanese troops remained in the area and continued to support Semenov, who ignored the railroad agreements.

The Economic Boom

World War I, in addition to providing an unprecedented opportunity for Japanese expansion on the Asian continent, also had a tremendous impact on the Japanese economy. The outbreak of hostilities in 1914 caused a temporary dislocation of foreign trade and international exchange for Japan, and this in turn created an industrial and agricultural depression; but by the spring of 1915 the economy had recovered from this initial shock as new markets were thrown open, especially in China and Southeast Asia, where former suppliers, preoccupied with the war, were unable to satisfy local demands. Japan also became an important producer of military equipment for the combatants in Europe. Like the United States, she prospered from a multitude of ammunitions contracts and demands for shipping. An unprecedented industrial boom gave birth to many new enterprises and to expansion of existing ones. The increase in the capital of corporations between 1915 and 1920 was eight times that of the ten-year period from 1905 to 1915, and the new investment of banks and corporations rose from 251 million yen in 1915 to a peak of 2.6 billion yen in 1918. The following figures give some indication of production increases in the period from 1913 to 1920: the number of mechanical spindles in the cotton-spinning industry jumped from 2,415,000 to 3,814,000, finished steel from 255,000 tons to 547,000 tons, pig iron doubled, and coal went from 21,000,000 tons to 31,000,000 tons. Since the import of goods from the belligerent nations stopped completely, Japan was forced to initiate or increase the production of such items as drugs and dye-stuffs, and by 1920 she was in fact exporting these items to China. In the case of steel, which had been supplied in large quantities by Great Britain, the government helped private industry to increase production facilities; and after July, 1917, mills producing a specified minimum tonnage of pig iron were exempted from business and income taxes. By 1921 industrial pro-ductivity was clearly more important than agricultural productivity; more-over, urban capital was making itself felt more and more in land investments. Despite the widening gap between agricultural and industrial prices, the following figures are indicative of Japan's economic transformation:

| | Value of Production (In Yen) | |
	1914	1921
Agriculture	1,401,210,000	3,420,400,000
Industry (plants with 5 or more workers)	1,371,600,000	5,978,400,000

In foreign trade and related activities the expansion was enormous. Be-tween 1914 and 1918 foreign trade increased in volume by 25 per cent and in value by 300 per cent, and by 1919 Japan's favorable trade balance was 1.48 billion yen. The combined foreign specie holdings of the government and the Bank of Japan by 1919 totaled 1.34 billion yen, and the specie holding both at home and abroad by the end of 1920 reached an all-time high of 2.17 billion yen. In this period Japan's shipping tonnage doubled, amounting to a total of 3,000,000 tons; and with net income from ocean freights rising from 40,000,000 yen in 1914 to 450,000,000 yen in 1918, ship-yards paid dividends ranging from 25 to 100 per cent. The favorable trade bal-ance permitted Japan to increase her investments in China and to provide loans to Russia, Great Britain, and France. Almost overnight Japan changed from a debtor to a creditor nation, enjoying undreamed-of prosperity. The structure of her foreign trade also changed. Processed or manufactured goods came to comprise 90 per cent of Japan's exports; and of the imports, raw materials comprised 66 per cent, partly processed goods 14 per cent, and manufactured goods only 20 per cent. In order to stabilize Japan's commercial gains in China, Southeast Asia, and India, the government established more consulates and special business agencies in those areas.

Japan prospered, but this furious economic activity caused inflation. Commodity prices, which had been rising before the war as a result of un-favorable trade balances, increases in currency circulation, and food short-ages, spiraled to new heights as consumer goods became increasingly scarce in the face of high demand. Since commodity prices increased 150 per cent in the period from 1914 to 1919, the standard of living of most Japanese was threatened. By 1918 the situation was dangerous, and in March of that year the government placed an export ban on rice, wheat, and wheat flour in the hope of curbing runaway food prices. It also encouraged the importation of rice, but the gap between food supply and demand for some 54,000,000 people was not closed. In April the government established markets, managed by local administrative agencies, to sell commodities at prices lower than regular market schedules.

Perhaps hardest hit by inflation was the industrial working class, whose wage increments did not keep pace with price increases. Between December, 1917, and September, 1918, prices rose by 80 per cent but wages by only 20 per cent. Under these conditions laborers began to strike. In 1913, before inflation had reached such proportions, there were only 47 labor disputes affecting slightly more than 5,000 workers, but in 1918 there were 417 disputes involving more than 66,000. Some of the increase in capital-labor strife must be explained in terms of the larger number of factory workers; in the period under consideration the number of employees in factories of five or more persons jumped from 948,000 to 1,612,000.

Inflation ultimately toppled the Terauchi cabinet from power. Despite government efforts, from 1917 to 1918 the price of rice doubled, and in August, 1918, the wives of urban workers raided the rice shops in Toyama Prefecture. Rice riots soon spread to all parts of Japan. The government was forced to call out troops to quell riots in forty towns and cities, and in the process more than one hundred demonstrators were killed. Although order was quickly restored, the unrest forced Terauchi's resignation in September, 1918. The genro, now including only Yamagata, Matsukata, and Saionji, could not agree on a successor; and when the emperor finally ordered Saionji to form a cabinet, he declined and recommended Hara Kei, president of the Seiyukai, whose 165 members constituted the largest bloc in the house of representatives.

When Hara assumed office as prime minister on September 29, 1918, it was in many ways the end of an era. Since the inauguration of the cabinet system in 1885 the genro had been the dominant force on the political scene. With the exception of the short-lived Okuma-Itakagi cabinet in 1898, the genro monopolized the office of prime minister, and their subordinates served as ministers of departments. In fact, of the nine men who had been prime minister, only Okuma and Saionji did not come from Satsuma or Choshu. It is important to note also that five of the nine—Kuroda, Yamagata, Katsura, Yamamoto, and Terauchi—were army or navy officers. Hara, on the other hand, was a party man, one who was a generation removed from the restoration struggle, and he personified the new type of political leader that was coming to the front as the influence of the genro began to wane with the depletion of their ranks through death or advanced age. But Hara's accession to power was not the complete innovation that many have claimed it to be, for from his bureaucratic background he brought to office something of the genro's notion of "stewardship." By Western standards, Hara was comparable to a nineteenth-century liberal; he was certainly not a democrat.

22 The Aftermath of World War I in Japan

The Hara cabinet was not the beginning of party government in Japan. It is true that Hara formed a cabinet largely of Seiyukai members, some of whom were also former bureaucrats, but he had to appoint military men to the service ministries and an administrative official to the ministry of foreign affairs. Hara simply could not avoid compromise with the civil and military bureaucracy, which had become entrenched in positions of power during the long period of genro dominance; and he and his ministers were of necessity deferential to the genro, especially Yamagata, who had only reluctantly approved of his appointment. The military, moreover, continued to wield a powerful influence through War Minister Tanaka Giichi and Navy Minister Kato Tomosaburo. Hara was also careful not to offend the conservative Kenkyukai (Study Association), the dominant faction in the house of peers, and he was careful to sidetrack or oppose measures which would incur its disapproval. For example, one of the reasons for Seiyukai opposition to immediate implementation of universal manhood suffrage was the antagonism of the peers, as well as the genro and privy council, toward any major extension of the right to vote.

Hara, an adroit politician, built the Seiyukai into a powerful party, but he treated most of its rank and file with an officiousness which they endured because he brought them the spoils of victory. During the 1918–1919 diet session the Seiyukai was able to put through the house of representatives and the house of peers its own suffrage bill, which lowered the tax qualification to three yen, as well as a small-district electoral bill which increased the size of the house of representatives to 464 members.

When the Kenseikai and the Kokuminto joined together in the following diet session to propose universal manhood suffrage, Hara dissolved the house of representatives on February 26, 1920, since the Seiyukai did not have a majority. In the general election held on May 10, the Seiyukai won a spectacular victory which was tainted by many charges of corruption and official interference. In the new house of representatives, with its new total of 464 seats,

369

the Seiyukai captured 281, the Kenseikai 108, the Kokuminto 29, and the independents 46. With a clear majority, Hara was able to secure legislation in support of his policies.

Debate in the house of representatives was more or less useless, since the important discussions ordinarily took place secretly between party leaders and bureaucrats. When Kato's Kenseikai resorted in desperation to demonstrations in order to get press publicity for its views, the Seiyukai retaliated by employing strong-arm men to intimidate the opposition. Hara kept his own party members pacified by appointing them as prefectural governors, which enabled the party to control the local administrative machinery in its own interests, and as colonial administrators in Korea, Formosa, and south Manchuria.

The Versailles Conference

The Hara cabinet adopted a "positive" foreign policy, which met its first test at Versailles, where, in January, 1919, delegates from twenty-seven countries gathered to begin deliberations on the conditions of peace with the Central Powers. Hara selected the Japanese delegates with utmost care, since participation in the conference as one of the major powers was the realization of a long-standing Japanese desire to attain a position of great prominence in international affairs.

Saionji, the genro and long-time friend of Clemenceau, was chairman; but Makino Shinken and Chinda Sutemi did most of the actual negotiating. Although they took small interest in European questions, which constituted most of the business of the conference, they were active members of all those commissions in which Japan did have particular interests; these included the disposition of German rights in Shantung Province, the disposition of the German islands in the Pacific Ocean, and the discussions regarding the declaration of racial equality which Japan sponsored as a clause in the Covenant of the proposed League of Nations.

The question of the declaration of racial equality was decided first. On January 25, 1919, the conference delegates as a whole officially agreed to create a League of Nations to promote international co-operation, to insure fulfillment of accepted international obligations, and to provide safeguards against war. In discussions that followed the Japanese delegates took an active part in asking that a declaration of racial equality among states be included as a basic principle of the League's Covenant. On February 7 Makino asked that the delegates approve the following declaration: "The equality of nations being a basic principle of the League of Nations, the high contracting parties agree to accord, as soon as possible, to all alien nationals of state members of the League equal and just treatment in every respect, making no distinction, either in law or in fact, on account of their race or nationality."

Makino indicated clearly that the clause was not intended to encroach upon the internal affairs of any nation but rather should serve as a declaration setting forth a guiding principle in the conduct of international relations in the future. President Wilson approved of the declaration as complementary to the whole spirit of the League, and China, Italy, France, Greece, Poland, and Czechoslovakia also supported it. It is clear that Wilson was also anxious to appease the Japanese in order to gain their good will, particularly since he hoped to restore Shantung to China and to entice Japan into joining a new consortium for loans to China.

But Prime Minister Hughes of Australia, with British support, opposed the declaration; he feared that any provision concerning racial equality might imply the right of the League of Nations to interfere in questions regarding immigration and the rights of aliens, which were generally considered matters of purely domestic responsibility. Australia in 1901 and New Zealand in 1908 had established a language dictation test to bar Chinese and Japanese immigrants. Canada, too, had become alarmed by Japanese immigration, despite a gentlemen's agreement with Japan, and in May, 1910, had passed an act empowering the governor-general to exclude whatever national or racial groups he deemed "unsuited to the climate or requirements of Canada, or of immigrants of any specified class, occupation, or character"; however, aliens, including the Japanese, enjoyed the right to acquire, hold, and dispose of real and personal property of every description in the same manner as natural-born British subjects, and Canadian law contained no racial qualification for citizenship.

When Prime Minister Hughes threatened to arouse public opinion against the Japanese declaration, President Wilson was put in a very embarrassing situation since he feared the reaction of the American Pacific Coast states, which were already enforcing discriminatory legislation in regard to land-ownership or rental. Despite the immigration controls of the 1907 agreement, Japanese population in these states had increased from 24,236 in 1900 to 72,157 in 1910 and to 111,010 in 1920. Anti-Japanese agitation remained active, and in 1913 the California legislature passed a law prohibiting land-ownership by aliens ineligible for citizenship and limiting leases of land to three years. While the law did not mention them by name and carefully reserved all rights held by treaty (despite the fact that the 1911 commercial treaty between Japan and the United States did not confer on the Japanese the right to own land), it was obviously aimed at the Japanese.

On April 11, 1919, a vote was taken by the commission on a milder declaration, submitted by Makino, which asked for "endorsement of the principle of equality of nations and just treatment of their nationals." The vote approved the amendment eleven to six, but Wilson, who was chairman of the session, ruled against its adoption since the vote was not unanimous. Wilson evidently was concerned about the treatment the peace treaty and the League of Nations would meet in the American Senate, and he feared the possibility of greater discrimination against Japanese in California should the Covenant include even the suggestion of racial equality.

The Japanese were disappointed, but they had already begun to exploit their anticipated defeat in this area to gain a favorable decision regarding Japan's claims to German rights in Shantung. Thus, when the plenary session of the peace conference met on April 25 to approve the final version of the Covenant, Makino did not press for the adoption of his amendment. He did say, however, that "the Japanese government and people feel poignant regret at the failure of the commission to approve of their just demand . . . ; they will continue to insist on the adoption of this principle by the League of Nations."

The transfer of German rights in Shantung was the second issue to be decided. Japan asked for the confirmation of her claims to them, which were based on the agreement of May, 1915, with China and on the secret treaties concluded with her allies. Great Britain, France, and Italy were not disposed to oppose Japan on this issue; in fact, they had promised to support her claims. Their own plans to strip Germany of her colonies, partition the Turkish empire, and redeem *Italia irredenta* required that they make good on their promises to Japan.

Opposition came from the Chinese delegation, which represented both the Peking and Canton governments and was typical of the new revolutionary nationalism in China. Its leaders, C. T. Wang and Wellington Koo, asked for return to China of all former German rights in Shantung, the liquidation of German and Austro-Hungarian rights in China, and the abnegation of the treaties and notes originating in the Twenty-one Demands. They argued the invalidity of the agreements and notes of 1915, which had been signed under duress; moreover, they held that China's participation in the war released her from any treaty commitments to Japan. The Chinese delegates also planned to submit a list of requests which dealt primarily with the general unequal treaty system; and while they did encounter some sympathy, especially from Wilson and the United States, none of the major powers was willing to undermine in principle the spheres of interest and the unequal treaties.

Makino presented the Japanese case officially on April 22; and on April 24, when the Italian delegation suddenly walked out of the conference, following the break with Wilson over its Adriatic claims, he pressed harder for settlement of the Shantung issue on terms favorable to Japan. He was willing to pledge the return of Shantung and the Kiaochow Leasehold in full sovereignty to China in exchange for retention of German economic privileges in that province. On April 30 Wilson, Clemenceau, and Lloyd George finally reached the decision to uphold Japan's claims. They were under tremendous pressure, since Japan had threatened to bolt the conference if her demand was not met. Wilson refused to call what was possibly a Japanese bluff; and, as he put it, "This was the best that could be done with such a dirty past." He anticipated that a Japanese withdrawal might lead to a Russian-German-Japanese alliance and a return to the old balance of power in the world. He could only hope that the League of Nations would right China's wrongs as a whole. The Treaty of Versailles provided that Japan was to "hand back the Shantung Peninsula in full sovereignty to China, retaining only economic privileges granted to Germany." In the end Wilson had to suffer for his decision; as he had foreseen, the "irreconcilables" in the American Senate used the Shantung award as one of the chief reasons for rejecting the League of Nations and the Versailles Treaty.

Japan's claim to the German islands in the north Pacific violated Wilson's principle of no annexations, but he was faced with pressures on all sides from victors who were insistent upon the cession of German colonies. The best that the American president could do was to fashion the mandate system of the League of Nations. In the case of the German islands, which were given a class-C mandate status, Japan acquired a control which, for all practical purposes, was hardly to be distinguished from annexation.

After agreement was reached among the Allies on the terms of peace, formal negotiations with the German representatives were started in May, 1919. Although at first the Germans balked, the presentation of an ultimatum on June 15 left them no alternative but to accede to Allied demands, and on June 28 they signed the treaty. Influenced by the storm of nationalist feeling which swept China in May, the Chinese delegates refused to sign the treaty. To the end they persisted in their refusal to accept the validity of the 1915 and 1918 treaties with Japan, claiming that China's entrance into the war had canceled German rights in Shantung and that the treaties were invalid on the grounds of equity. China did not make peace with Germany until September, 1919, when a presidential proclamation of peace was issued in Peking. As a result of the Chinese refusal to sign the Treaty of Versailles, the Japanese army continued to maintain its military occupation of Shantung.

The Postwar Issues

For the next few years the indeterminate status of Shantung threatened the peace of East Asia. Despite American efforts to persuade Japan to restore Shantung to China, it was clear that Japan was determined to exact the most extensive rights and privileges possible before relinquishing her hold on the province. Japan repeatedly professed her readiness to enter negotiations with China as soon as the latter would establish a police force to replace the Japanese troops guarding the Tsingtao-Tsinan Railway, but China demanded withdrawal of these troops as a condition precedent to negotiation. Great Britain also became concerned about Japanese activity in China and felt that

373

Japan had far overreached the bounds prescribed by the Anglo-Japanese Alliance. The Japanese were showing no scruples in attacking Great Britain's economic position in China.

The China situation, however, was only one of several problems that involved the three powers. At war's end Great Britain, the United States, and Japan found themselves involved in a gigantic and costly naval race which took on new importance in light of the deteriorating relations between Japan and the other two powers. In the United States the war debt was of such vast dimensions that the thought of adding to costs through a naval race made the leaders of both political parties pause to reflect; many Americans also felt that competition in armaments had been one of the chief causes of World War I and that the United States should take the lead in promoting universal disarmament. By 1920 many Japanese were beginning to feel the impact of economic recession and were concerned about the fact that their government was spending annually a total of 800,000,000 yen in military expenditures. Lastly, Great Britain, in straitened financial circumstances caused by four years of war, could ill afford to maintain a strong position in an Anglo-American-Japanese naval race. The pressure for disarmament mounted in all three nations.

The armament problem was influenced by the existence of the Anglo-Japanese Alliance, against which there was strong opposition in various quarters. The United States regarded it as a political instrument which threatened her traditional policies in East Asia and which might be invoked against her. Washington wanted some modification of it which would include provisions safeguarding the principles of equality of commercial opportunity in China and Chinese administrative and territorial integrity. Great Britain constantly deprecated the idea that the alliance might be invoked in a war between Japan and the United States; in fact, Great Britain and Japan during 1920 and 1921 made it clear that the United States was not subject to its military sanctions.

The strongest pressure to end the alliance came from within the British Empire. Canadian apprehensions caused Prime Minister Meighen to secure an agreement at the London imperial conference of June, 1921, to the effect that Great Britain would terminate the alliance and replace it with a new and broader multipower treaty covering the Pacific Ocean area. Meighen actually succeeded in the face of almost overwhelming odds. The British had wanted to renew the alliance in order to safeguard their position in India as well as their territorial and economic interests in East Asia, if only from the menace of Japan herself; moreover, the British looked upon Japan as a bulwark against the spread of communism to China and to India. The British stand was supported by Prime Minister Hughes of Australia, who was influenced by the realities of Australia's financial and military dependence on London.

The fact that Japanese troops remained in Siberia also constituted a major problem, since by 1919 most of the Allies had decided that maintenance of the intervention was foolhardy. Germany had been defeated, and the efforts to crush communism had ended in dismal failure. When, by the end of 1919, the remnants of Kolchak's armies had been routed, the powers grew tired of the whole business. The United States took the lead by withdrawing her troops early in 1920, and British, French, and Canadian contingents were withdrawn soon afterward. The Czech forces, which continued to fight against the communists, were finally repatriated at Allied expense in the summer of 1920, three years after their advance guard had reached Vladivostok.

The United States pointedly intimated that she would welcome a similar withdrawal on the part of Japan, but Prime Minister Hara, who originally had opposed the expedition except in self-defense, did not wield sufficient power to order the army home. The Japanese military continued to dream of annexing the Maritime Province, and the massacre of Japanese at Nikolaevsk in 1920 seemed to confirm the wisdom of this view. By this time Japanese forces had seized Khabarovsk and were moving toward the Lake Baikal region. On March 31, 1920, Hara attempted to justify Japan's loose control over a great area of eastern Siberia by explaining that chaotic conditions would adversely affect the regions of Manchuria and Korea and endanger the lives and property of Japanese residents. He emphasized that Japan would withdraw her troops as soon as conditions were stabilized, dangers to Japanese life and property were removed, and freedom of movement and transportation was assured. Working through the foreign ministry, Hara had already been able to initiate negotiations between Japan and the new Far Eastern Republic, to which he had extended *de facto* recognition in July, 1920.

Hara faced the pressures of international criticism, the demands of the Japanese army, and national political opposition, especially on the part of Kato and the Kenseikai. The latter pointed out that at a cost of 100,000,000 yen and 3,000 casualties Japan had earned only the distrust and ill-will of the powers as well as the antipathy of the Russians. Kato and others pressed Hara for immediate withdrawal of troops and demanded his resignation. But the army was equally adamant; and even though Hara won Yamagata's support for withdrawal from Siberia, he was unable to persuade the chief of staff. By this time Yamagata had lost his control over the army and could not swing it behind the cabinet. The army was no longer controlled by officers who felt strong bonds of loyalty to the old genro. The unity among high-ranking officers based upon common Choshu background had come to an end.

In negotiations with the Far Eastern Republic, Hara made the following demands: all Russian fortifications on the Pacific Coast to be destroyed, Vladivostok to become a purely commercial port, and the Far Eastern

Republic to remain independent of the Russian communist regime. Japanese subjects, moreover, were to enjoy the same economic rights as Russians even in cases where there was discrimination against other nationals. The Russian delegates refused to accept these demands, and they hoped for diplomatic support, particularly from Washington, which continued to ask for the immediate evacuation of Japanese troops on the ground that there was no longer any reason for Japan to remain in Siberia. In a declaration dated May 31, 1921, the United States held that "neither now or hereafter [could she] recognize as valid any claims or titles arising out of the present occupation and control, and [could not] acquiesce in any action taken by the government of Japan which might impair existing treaty rights or the political or territorial integrity of Russia."

Another problem was the status of the island of Yap. The Versailles Peace Conference had mandated Yap, one of the Carolines, to Japan, and the United States regarded Japan's control of the island as a threat to the security of the Philippines. At Paris Wilson had expressed the hope that this important center for telegraphic cable communication would be internationalized, and this position continued to be presented by the United States in discussions with Japan.

All these issues constituted the basis of the Washington Conference of 1921–1922. The initiative for an international meeting came from both the United States and Great Britain. It was mentioned by President Harding in his inaugural address on March 5, 1921; and after the imperial conference held in June, London on July 5 suggested to the American ambassador that Harding invite the powers directly concerned to take part in discussions to consider all essential matters bearing on East Asia and the Pacific Ocean area with a view to arriving at a common understanding which would insure settlement of disputes by peaceful means, the elimination of naval warfare, and the consequent limitation of excessive armaments in general. The British proposal actually coincided with a cable from Secretary of State Charles Evans Hughes asking whether London would react favorably to an invitation to a disarmament conference called by the United States. Hughes willingly accepted the idea of an enlarged East Asian and Pacific Ocean conference, as had been suggested by London. Finally, on July 11, the press of the world heralded the fact that President Harding planned to invite the powers to an international meeting and that the United States was arranging the time, place, and agenda.

Much depended upon the Japanese reaction. Japan was reluctant to attend a conference which would discuss questions concerning East Asia in general, since it was impossible to disguise the fact that it would be an occasion to check Japanese activities and designs. Many responsible Japanese concluded immediately that the conference was part of a plot on the part of the United States and Great Britain to divest Japan of her special rights in Manchuria and Inner Mongolia, wreck the proposed naval expansion program which was already under way, and deprive Japan of all her new advantages in China that had been won at great expense. They believed that the powers intended to supersede Japan in her role of leadership in East Asia. Despite the fact that the Hara ministry promised to protect Japan's position and extend it, many Japanese militarists and chauvinists were highly critical of foreign policy "deficiencies." Japan, moreover, was not anxious to scrap the Anglo-Japanese Alliance, which she regarded as a bulwark of her foreign policy.

Under all sorts of pressures the Hara government finally took the stand that Japan should seek to maintain her advantageous position in East Asia but should support international co-operation contributing to peace and accept reduction of the heavy burden of armament without endangering national security. On July 13 Tokyo announced that it would agree to take part in an arms-limitation conference but would hesitate to accept an invitation to confer on Pacific Ocean and East Asian problems until informed of the nature and scope of the discussions. Suspecting a trap, Hara wanted a bill of particulars on the agenda concerning these areas, and, when Hughes refused, Hara reluctantly consented to send a delegation. Hughes had talked about the nature and scope of the agenda informally with the Japanese ambassador, and in accepting the invitation the Japanese government gave notice that "problems that are the exclusive concern of certain particular powers and matters that may be regarded as accomplished fact should be scrupulously avoided." What Tokyo meant were references to the Twenty-one Demands and the Siberian expedition.

The Washington Conference

On August 11, 1921, Washington extended formal invitations to the conference to the following eight powers: Great Britain, France, Italy, Japan, Belgium, China, the Netherlands, and Portugal. By the time that the conference convened, it was apparent that the course of negotiations would be determined by three key delegates: Secretary of State Hughes; Arthur Balfour, a former prime minister and foreign secretary in the British government; and Admiral Kato Tomosaburo, navy minister in the Hara cabinet. The Soviet Union, unrecognized at this time by the "respectable society" of nations, asserted her undeniable interests in East Asia and proclaimed her own "nonrecognition" doctrine applicable to "any decision taken" by the proposed conference. Ignoring the opening-day amenities, Hughes on November 12 surprised the delegates with an unexpected and concrete plan for the immediate slashing of naval strength. He suggested the following:

1. A naval holiday for ten years in capital-ship construction.
2. Scrapping of many ships, including some already in commission and others in the process of construction.

3. Application of the scrapping so as to leave navies in the ratio of 5 (Great Britain), 5 (United States), 3 (Japan), 1.75 (France), and 1.75 (Italy).
4. Capital-ship requirements to be limited by treaty to 500,000 tons each to the United States and Great Britain and to 300,000 tons to Japan.
5. Similar ratios to be applied to aircraft carriers, cruisers, destroyers, and submarines.

Implementation of Hughes's proposals would have meant the scrapping by the three leading naval powers of finished or projected battleships having an aggregate total of 1.87 million tons. The total was broken down as follows: the United States, 845,740 tons; Great Britain, 581,375 tons; and Japan, 448,928 tons. With this call to action the delegates began their work, and their negotiations, which extended over the next few months, can be divided essentially into two interrelated parts—disarmament and the problems of the East Asian and Pacific Ocean areas.

The big three concentrated initially upon a satisfactory termination of the Anglo-Japanese Alliance. Balfour had come to Washington hoping to substitute a tripartite agreement with the United States and Japan for the old two-power alliance, and he was convinced that the Japanese would accept this if they could not keep the latter intact. The Japanese government and public opinion regarded abandonment of the alliance as undesirable; for the alliance acted in certain ways to check the growth of anti-Japanese sentiment, and, furthermore, it went a long way toward insuring peace in East Asia. Japan wanted to continue it with exclusion of the United States from its scope, but this line was blocked by Hughes, who feared that the old arrangement would imply American recognition of the special interests of Great Britain and Japan in East Asia. He hoped that the alliance would be replaced by an agreement embodying the principles of the Root-Takahira notes of 1908, which had stressed preservation of the status quo in the Pacific Ocean area. Although at first opposed by Balfour and Kato, Hughes not only won his point but secured inclusion of France in a four-power treaty, to be effective for a ten-year period. Under its terms the powers agreed to the following:

1. To respect one another's rights in the regions of the Pacific in respect to their "insular possessions and insular dominions."
2. To meet in joint conference "for consideration and adjustment" of any controversy arising out of any Pacific question and involving their said rights which is not satisfactorily settled by diplomacy.
3. If the rights of the contracting parties are threatened by the aggressive action of any other power, to communicate with one another fully.

According to American interpretation based on Senate amendments, there was no commitment to use armed force, no alliance, and no obligation to join in any defense. The Four-Power Treaty thus replaced the Anglo-Japanese Alliance, which was formally terminated on August 17, 1923, but as a substitute it was hardly more than a general consultative obligation and a pledge for the integrity of territorial possessions in the Pacific Ocean area. During these negotiations the United States brought up the problem of Yap and concluded a treaty with Japan whereby the United States recognized the Japanese mandate over Yap and other former German islands in the Pacific Ocean, while Japan in return granted to American citizens residential, cable, and radio rights on Yap.

The second major treaty to be signed at Washington was the Five-Power Naval Treaty of February 5, 1922. From the beginning there were strong doubts whether Japan would accept Hughes's plan regarding naval reductions unless she could maintain naval supremacy in East Asian waters. With British approval, Kato proposed Japanese acceptance of reductions and a smaller navy if an agreement could be reached on maintenance of the status quo in Pacific fortifications and if Japan could keep the new battleship "Mutsu," which was nearly ready for launching, and scrap the old "Settsu" instead. Kato's formula became the basis of negotiations, and on December 15, 1921, the big three reached agreement on a fortification principle, which later became Article Nineteen of the Five-Power Naval Treaty. The three powers agreed that "the status quo at the time of the signing of the present treaty, with regard to fortifications and naval bases, shall be maintained in specific possessions," as follows:

1. The United States: the Aleutians, Guam, Pago-Pago, and the Philippine Islands.
2. Great Britain: Hong Kong and British insular possessions in the Pacific east of 110 east longitude, excepting the islands adjacent to Canada, Australia, and New Zealand.
3. Japan: the Kuriles, Bonins, Amami-Oshima, the Ryukyus, Formosa, and the Pescadores.

By this clause, according to the naval technology of that day, the United States ruled out the possibility of conducting offensive naval operations against Japan in her own waters. Thus Japan gained the protection she wanted against a possible Anglo-American attack. In the discussions concerning application of the Hughes ratio, Japan held out for 10–10–7, but in the end she accepted 5–5–3, but only in application to capital ships. As finally concluded, the naval treaty provided for the following:

1. A ten-year holiday in capital-ship construction.
2. A capital-ship ratio of 5 (Great Britain), 5 (United States), 3 (Japan), 1.75 (France), and 1.75 (Italy).

3. The scrapping of specified vessels in commission and in construction in the amounts of 845,000 tons for the United States, 583,000 tons for Great Britain, and 435,000 tons for Japan.
4. Limiting the tonnage of capital ships and aircraft carriers to 35,000 and 27,000 tons, respectively, and the caliber of guns on them to sixteen inches and eight inches, respectively.

The treaty would remain in effect until December 31, 1936, and might be terminated thereafter upon two years' notice by any signatory.

As was expected, with the exception of Italy, all the powers expressed their dissatisfaction, and their naval experts lamented that they had given more than they had received. The Japanese admirals from the beginning had desired "parity" and had advocated policies that were more concerned with national security than with the general proposition of naval disarmament, but certainly the fortification clause enhanced the security of the Japanese homeland. The British, since they were able to maintain fortifications in Australia, New Zealand, and Singapore and to increase them, could feel safe from the threat of a Japanese offensive. Hughes regarded the treaty as a realistic addition to American foreign policy. He felt that the cost of fortification and the naval race would not be borne by the American public; moreover, Hughes knew that the American people would not fight for the principles of the open door and the integrity of China nor would they support an Asian policy based on force. In the final analysis, East Asia, still a relatively unimportant market for American commerce and investment, was an area in which no vital American interests of any kind were at stake.

If the naval treaty is regarded as an American withdrawal from East Asia, this view must be balanced by an analysis of the Nine-Power Treaty, signed on February 6, 1922. Throughout the conference Hughes was anxious to give new vigor and reality to the principles of the open door and the territorial and administrative integrity of China, and he was assisted by Balfour, who suggested a five-power treaty designed to achieve those ends. Hughes secured adherence of all the powers attending the conference, and in the Nine-Power Treaty they pledged the following:

1. To respect the sovereignty, the independence, and the territorial and administrative integrity of China.
2. To provide the fullest and most unembarrassed opportunity to China to develop and maintain for herself an effective and stable government.
3. To use their influence for the purpose of effectively establishing and maintaining the principle of equal commercial opportunity for the commerce and industry of all nations throughout the territory of China.
4. To refrain from taking advantage of conditions in China in order to seek special rights and privileges which would abridge the rights of subjects or citizens of friendly states, and from countenancing action inimical to the security of friendly states.

5. To agree that they would not seek, or support their respective nationals in seeking:

   a) Superior commercial rights or development rights in any designated region of China.

   b) China agreed to be guided by the principles in (a) in dealing with applications for economic rights and privileges from governments and nationals of all foreign countries, whether parties to this treaty or not.

Although the Nine-Power Treaty was totally lacking in effective sanctions, it was a tangible and realistic advance over any previous enunciations of the principles of the open door and the integrity of China. It is true that it did not renounce rights acquired in the past, but it did seek to limit future activities. Its success would depend on the good will of the signatories, who in the past had more often than not disagreed in their definition of these principles.

The Chinese delegates were not happy with the Nine-Power Treaty, since they had demanded a "bill of rights" freeing their country from all the unequal treaties. They wanted abolition not only of Japan's special interests but also of the convention tariff, extraterritoriality, and all spheres of interest. Hughes answered their demands quite realistically, pointing out that the Nine-Power Treaty represented the best that could be achieved, given the time and the conditions. He asserted that the real problem was the weakness of China. Until China put her own house in order and established an efficient government, little consideration could be expected from the powers. In Hughes's mind, China had to demonstrate that she was capable of carrying out the duties as well as having the privileges of nationhood.

In the end some concessions were made to the Chinese delegation. The powers revised the Chinese tariff upward to yield an effective 5 per cent, which meant an increase in rates and higher revenues for China, and they agreed to establish a commission for study and reform of the Chinese tariff administration, thus keeping the door open for further concessions if and when China's government showed itself capable of assuming fuller responsibility. On extraterritoriality the conference passed a resolution setting up a commission which was to study the entire problem and prepare the way for the abolition of extraterritorial jurisdiction in the future. The powers also agreed to abolish foreign post offices in China, except those in leased territories, with the condition that China set up a satisfactory postal service. Before the end of 1922 the British closed their twelve post offices; the Japanese, sixty-four; the French, thirteen; and the Americans, one. But the powers did continue to maintain post offices in leased territories and in other places specifically mentioned in the treaty; for example, the Japanese continued to operate post offices in the zone of the South Manchurian Railway, pending further negotiations with China. Lastly, the powers put restrictions on foreign-owned and operated radio stations on Chinese soil, most of them coming under Chinese regulation.

Settlements with China and the Soviet Union

At Washington the Shantung issue was settled by direct negotiations between the Chinese and Japanese delegations. In January, 1920, Japan had asked for bilateral negotiations, but China refused, largely because of the pressure of public opinion. But a compromise was reached whereby China and Japan agreed to "converse" at the Washington conference about Shantung under the good offices of Great Britain and the United States. Japan was prepared to restore Shantung and the Kiaochow Leasehold but only under the terms of the 1915 and 1918 treaties, while China demanded full and direct restoration of all former German rights. Hughes and Balfour were finally able to break the deadlock, and on February 4, 1922, the Chinese and Japanese delegations concluded a treaty under which Shantung was returned to China but with Japan retaining control of the Tsinan-Tsingtao Railway and its properties for fifteen years, the time period of a Japanese loan through which China would purchase it.

China made no headway in her efforts to abrogate the Manchurian clauses of the 1915 agreements with Japan. Aside from the United States, none of the powers was willing to uphold her contention that the treaties were invalid, for this would lead to questioning of the entire unequal-treaty system. Japan did, however, make two concessions. She opened her new railway options to the joint activities of the consortium, and she denied any intent to impose political, military, or financial advisers upon the Chinese administration in south Manchuria. But Japan made it clear that she was determined to maintain her existing position in that area, and her insistence on the validity of the 1915 treaties in face of the Chinese refusal to regard them in that light was the source of numerous later difficulties. For example, in March 1923, the Peking government sent a note to Japan demanding the abrogation of the Sino-Japanese agreements of 1915 and the return of the Kwantung Peninsula, the lease of which would have expired on March 27 of that year had it not been for the 1915 extension to ninety-nine years. When Japan rejected the demand, the Chinese retaliated with demonstrations and boycotts. The anti-Japanese agitation went far beyond the usual economic measures, for it included a ban on the supply of raw materials to Japan, dismissal of Japanese employees in Chinese firms, withdrawal of Chinese employed by Japanese companies, and refusal to use Japanese currency or to deposit funds in Japanese banks. The movement dealt a severe blow to Japanese trade with China and to Japanese banking activities on the continent.

In the following few years, as nationalist fervor mounted in China, anti-Japanese agitation increased. These conditions, complicated by Japan's postwar recession, inspired the China "friendship" policy, associated with its foremost advocate, Foreign Minister Shidehara Kijuro, who reflected the demands of Japanese business, which did not want to stir up anti-Japanese boycotts in China. As stated by Shidehara: "It is of utmost importance for us to concentrate our attention and energy on the promotion of trade, without unjust infringement upon the interests of any nation. It is not territory, but markets, that we have in view. It is not alliance, but economic solidarity, that we seek in our foreign relations."

Settlement of the Siberian intervention was also part of the agenda of the Washington conference. During one of the sessions Hughes pressed the Japanese for a clear-cut statement regarding their activities in Siberia, and on January 23, 1922, Shidehara declared that Japan respected the territorial integrity of Russia and would observe the principle of noninterference in the internal affairs of that country as well as the principle of equal opportunity for the commerce and industry of all nations in every part of the Russian possessions. He stated also that Japan did not intend to maintain her troops on Russian soil any longer than necessary.

Following the conference, Japan resumed negotiations with the Far Eastern Republic at Dairen; but when the Russians again refused Japan's demands, the conference disbanded (April 15, 1922). The Far Eastern Republic appealed to Washington, and once again Hughes pressed Tokyo. The Japanese government informed Washington that the evacuation of Siberia would be completed by October, 1922, but that the pledge did not apply to Sakhalin. Hughes expressed his satisfaction but at the same time asked that Japan withdraw her forces from that island. Representatives of the Far Eastern Republic and Japan met at Changchun in September, 1922, to discuss the Sakhalin question. When Japan insisted upon permanent far-reaching privileges connected with economic exploitation of the island, discussion again ended without agreement. In the meantime Japanese troops had withdrawn from the mainland, and in November the national assembly of the Far Eastern Republic ordered the dissolution of the government. With the fiction of independence now discarded, Moscow resolved to incorporate the Siberian territories into the Soviet Union.

Not until 1925 was Japan finally able to normalize its relations with Soviet Russia and to settle outstanding difficulties between the two countries. At Peking, in January, 1925, Leo Karakhan and Yoshizawa Kenkichi, minister to China, signed a treaty which provided for the resumption of diplomatic relations and the exchange of diplomatic and consular representatives. The Soviet Union recognized the validity of the Treaty of Portsmouth but secured Japan's consent to the revision or abandonment of all other treaties, agreements, and conventions made in the period 1905–1917 between the two countries. The Japanese were permitted to fish in Siberian coastal waters pending revision of the fisheries convention of 1907, and until the conclusion of a new commercial treaty the nationals of each country would enjoy most-favored-nation treatment. Both pledged to refrain from engaging in propaganda or any activities, overt or covert, liable in any way to endanger the order and security of any part of their respective territories. To satisfy Japan's needs for natural resources, the Soviet Union granted concessions to Japanese for exploitation of the mineral, forest, and other resources of eastern Siberia. In protocols and annexes to the treaty the Soviet Union agreed to adjust its debts to Japan, Japan agreed to complete the withdrawal of her troops from northern Sakhalin by May 15, 1925, and the Soviet Union granted to Japan oil, lumber, and coal concessions in northern Sakhalin for a period of forty to fifty years, subject to stipulations that Soviet labor laws be observed and that half of the technical staffs and three-quarters of the unskilled labor be Soviet citizens. In later years the promise of developing northern Sakhalin was not fully realized by the Japanese, as they encountered increasing opposition from the Russians in the exploitation of the oil and coal reserves. In the end the Japanese were gradually squeezed out of the promising enterprises.

Economic Readjustment and Politics

The Japanese economic boom collapsed in the period following World War I. The signing of the armistice in November, 1918, brought an end to the demand for munitions and a gradual restoration of the productive capacities of Europe. The effects were soon felt by Japanese industry and trade, and by early spring, 1920, prosperity had given way to a general recession. Japan's foreign trade indicated most clearly what was happening; exports dropped by a billion yen from 1919 to 1921, or approximately 25 per cent of the total volume. Even more serious was the disappearance of Japan's favorable trade balance. In 1918 this had amounted to 300,000,000 yen, but as early as 1919 imports began to exceed exports, and in 1921 the unfavorable balance reached a figure of more than 360,000,000 yen. Much of this decline was the result of the Chinese boycotts stimulated by the Shantung controversy and the return of Western merchants and investors into Chinese markets. In 1918 Japan controlled almost 40 per cent of China's foreign trade, but this fell to 35 per cent in 1919 and to 29 per cent in 1920.

The policies of the Hara cabinet, especially those of Finance Minister Takahashi Korekiyo, sought to protect the business community from the recession. Even after the termination of the war in Europe the Japanese government continued to support industrial expansion; but when markets began to vanish, a financial panic swept the country, with prices and stocks falling by one half and thousands of concerns facing bankruptcy. The Hara cabinet quickly initiated large-scale relief measures designed to salvage urban and rural enterprises and to maintain the economy at its fullest productive level. Although many corporations, old and new, collapsed, many others, which faced the same fate, were saved by government financing. Since government support of business tended to keep commodity prices high despite unemployment, a decreased demand for goods, and a general tightening of the money market, there was little relief for the masses of Japanese and little stimulation of foreign trade.

Support of business also facilitated widespread corruption throughout the government and business world, which brought criticism from all sides. In some cases, radical Japanese took direct action. For example, a youth murdered Yasuda Zenjiro, president of the Yasuda Bank, on September 20, 1921. Businessmen often received threatening letters, and a bomb exploded in front of Baron Sumitomo's home. Finally, on November 24, 1921, a railway switchman assassinated Hara himself. His successor, Finance Minister Takahashi, was the choice of the genro when Saionji again refused appointment as prime minister. The new head of the government, who also assumed the presidency of the Seiyukai, continued to assist the business community.

Meanwhile Japan's unfavorable balance of trade was steadily draining the reserves built up during the war, making more precarious the entire financial structure of the nation. The earthquake of 1923, which caused tremendous loss of life and destruction, initiated a reconstruction boom which boosted imports in 1924 to 2.6 billion yen, a record figure, and in the following year to 2.7 billion yen, another all-time record. Although exports rose in volume to 2.37 billion yen in 1924 because of the devaluation of the yen to 0.385 dollars and the rising economic prosperity of the United States, the balance of trade remained unfavorable. By the middle of the decade specie holdings and foreign exchange were practically exhausted.

Urban labor was perhaps hardest hit by the depression, and by 1920 there was a marked increase in the number of labor disputes. Demands for higher wages were replaced by even more determined opposition to wage cuts. Despite the restrictions of the Public Peace Police Law, the first amalgamation of labor unions occurred in 1919 with the establishment of Nihon Rodo Sodomei (Japanese Federation of Labor), comprising seventy-one unions with a total membership of 30,000. In that year labor abandoned the policy of submission in favor of a more militant and aggressive action policy. Strikes became more frequent and more violent. On September 19 more than 16,000 workers in the Kawasaki Shipyards at Kobe demanded a wage increase; on October 1 factory workers in the Osaka-Kobe area walked out in demand for an eight-hour day; and during November strikes were called by the workers at the Asano Shipyards, the Osaka Municipal Railway, the Yokohama Municipal Railway, and the Ashio Copper Mines. The Hara cabinet reacted by arresting labor leaders and thousands of workers. But the strikes continued, and in February, 1920, 24,000 workers at the government-owned iron works at Yawata left the job, damaged the steel furnaces, and clashed with the police. By 1921 the labor movement included 300 unions with a total membership of about 100,000 workers. The number of labor disputes decreased after 1920, however, when the economic recession hit with full force and workers became more anxious to keep their jobs than to challenge management; consequently,

385

there were fewer strikes, and the union movement lost some of its momentum, although its membership increased. In this period the labor movement also took on a political orientation. Under the prodding of leftist intellectuals, workers began to take a more active interest in political issues, particularly the question of universal suffrage. This was reflected in the meeting of the Labor Federation of Universal Suffrage held in Tokyo in December, 1919.

A greater degree of economic and political consciousness also developed among the peasantry, especially tenant farmers. Beginning in 1918, tenancy disputes became increasingly common in various parts of the country, and in the following years there were widespread and concerted efforts on the part of aroused and informed peasants to improve their economic and social status, especially in relation to landlords. By 1921 disputes spread to all sections, and peasant unions began to be organized on a national basis. By 1922 there were over 1,100 peasant unions with more than 130,000 members. Until this time tenant-landlord relationships and disputes had followed, in general, a traditional pattern; they tended to be local and were confined mainly to bad crop years and the desire for temporary relief from rental charges. By 1920, however, there was a greater feeling of class consciousness and an insistence upon more basic measures, such as land redistribution, universal suffrage, revision of the police regulations, and minimum wages for agricultural labor. But, as in the case of urban labor, only a fraction of the total number of peasants entered the union movement, and the unions were often fragmented and un-co-operative.

The Re-emergence of the Left Wing

In the period following World War I the Japanese left wing began to establish a more solid foundation for its activities. The leadership, as earlier, was largely intellectual, but in the new industrial Japan it began to develop roots within the labor movement. For example, the Shakaishugi Domei (Socialist League), established in December, 1920, was largely a group of prewar socialists, younger representatives from student groups, labor leaders, and members of various cultural associations. All shades of ideology were represented: trade unionism, various types of socialism, anarchism, syndicalism, and communism, which was a more distinct school of thought following the Bolshevik Revolution in Russia.

The members of the league supposedly put aside their ideological differences and agreed to co-operate in the creation of an organization which could effectively struggle for democratic freedoms. The avowed purpose of the league was to study socialism and to plan a broad, popular movement for political action. The inauguration meeting held on December 10 was ordered dissolved by the government soon after the opening, and scores of participants were arrested by the police. The second convention was held on May 9, 1921, with about 3,000 in attendance, and was instantly banned; and the league itself was suppressed by the government on May 28.

Short-lived as it was, the Socialist League played an important role in the popularization of socialism, and it helped remove the prejudice against socialism among labor leaders and intellectuals. Even after the dissolution of the league, the members did not quit the movement but continued to be active in small groups. For example, left-wing societies and clubs were founded on university campuses by students who were increasingly unable to find employment and blamed wealth and privilege for their plight. The miserable lot of Japanese workers, disclosures of corruption on the part of government officials and businessmen, and antimilitarism were additional stimulants. In the summer of 1923 various intellectual and labor leaders organized the Seiji Mondai Kenkyukai (Society for the Study of Political Problems) to educate the workers, advance organizational activities, and prepare for a strong labor party. At first a broadly based leftist organization, it was later taken over by the Japanese Communist Party. In this period books on socialism sold by the thousands, and reputedly more than 100,000 copies of Kautsky's analysis of Marx's *Capital* were distributed secretly within a matter of days.

The repressive policies of the Hara cabinet tended to force elements of the left wing into radical channels. Until 1920 the new labor unions had been strongly influenced by democratic principles, and they had placed great confidence in representative government as the best way to advance their cause. But Hara's failure to yield to popular demands for universal suffrage made labor leaders more interested in syndicalism, a movement that was spreading throughout Europe. The syndicalist opposition to parliamentarianism met with a ready response in Japanese labor circles, and many labor leaders also accepted its program of achieving social change by direct-action tactics like the general strike. Syndicalism, like anarchism, however, lacked a realistic approach, and by 1922 it was already retreating before the advances of socialism and communism. For example, a key issue among the various leftists was whether the labor movement should take the form of "centralized unionism," as advocated by the socialists and communists, or of "autonomous organizations," as proposed by the anarchists and syndicalists. Although it ended in a brawl and suppression by the government, the inaugural rally on September 30, 1922, of the Nihon Rodo Kumiai Sorengokai (Japan General Federation of Labor Unions) marked the defeat of the latter group, and the Sodomei resolution of October 3 approved the policy of "centralized unionism." Within this framework socialist and communist influence in Sodomei clearly increased.

Japanese communism began to take form in 1921, when a small group of intellectuals, including Sakai Toshihiko, Yamakawa Hitoshi, and Arahata Kanson, formed a preparatory committee for the establishment of a Japanese

387

branch of the Comintern. They had no idea, however, of organizing a party, since they were well aware of the difficulties associated with such a move. When Kondo Eizo was arrested by the Japanese police after returning from a meeting of the Comintern bureau at Shanghai, the communist group suspended activity. Shortly thereafter, young radicals, mainly Waseda University graduates, who preferred political action to the discussions and study of the "old Bolshevists" like Yamakawa, joined under the leadership of Kondo, who had been released by the authorities, to form the Gyomin Kyosanto (Enlightened People's Communist Party). In the winter of 1921, however, Kondo was arrested along with forty of his colleagues for distributing subversive literature among troops in the Tokyo area.

In the following few years the Japanese communists became closely tied to the Comintern. A small delegation of Japanese left-wing thinkers attended the January, 1922, First Congress of Far Eastern Communist and Revolutionary Organizations at Moscow. These included the old socialist, Katayama Sen; Japanese socialists and communists from the United States; Takase Kiyoshi, who spoke for the Gyomin Kyosanto; and Tokuda Kyuichi, who represented the former communist group. During the congress a committee of Japanese and Comintern leaders urged that a communist party be formed in Japan, and on their return Takase and Tokuda joined secretly with Yamakawa, Arahata, and others in July, 1922, to found a party "under the direction and with the assistance of the Comintern." At the July meeting little was accomplished beyond the selection of a central committee headed by Sakai Toshihiko and including Yamakawa, Arahata, Takase, and Tokuda.

The actual program of the secret Japanese Communist Party was to have been based on the so-called "Bukharin Theses," which Takase brought home from the Fourth Congress of the Comintern in Moscow, held in 1922. This document directed the leaders of the party to aid in the completion of the "bourgeois-democratic revolution" together with other groups, particularly the poor peasantry. According to the theses, although Japanese capitalism and nationalism were well advanced, Japan at the same time had many feudal qualities, especially in rural economic relationships and in the structure of power in the Japanese state. Thus a bourgeois-democratic revolution was a necessary prelude to a proletarian revolution, which would overthrow bourgeois domination and realize the dictatorship of the proletariat.

As for immediate objectives, the theses specifically urged the party to work for the abolition of the imperial system, the house of peers, and the various police agencies and to secure basic freedoms, including universal suffrage, freedom to organize labor unions, groups, and political parties, and freedom to publish, demonstrate, and strike. On economic lines, it urged the party to demand confiscation with compensation of shrine and temple lands, imperial estates, and landlord holdings for redistribution to impoverished peasants and the enactment of a progressive income tax. In the field of foreign affairs, the party was called upon to advocate suspension of interventionist plans, with-drawal of all troops from colonies, and recognition of the Soviet Union.

The Japanese Communist Party made no concrete decisions regarding the Comintern directions; and although there is some evidence that party meet-ings discussed rules, qualifications for membership, and revolutionary formulas consistent with the theses, there is little to indicate that Japanese communists took them very seriously or understood the revolutionary process. Later, in 1925, the Comintern bureau at Shanghai blamed the Japanese Communist Party for having neglected the Comintern's advice.

Communist activities ultimately brought the weight of the government's police power down upon the movement. In June, 1923, the Tokyo police carried out a series of mass arrests which netted most of the active party mem-bers, and during the chaotic days that followed the great earthquake of September, 1923, the police murdered a number of radicals. One attack was directed at the Nankatsu Labor Union, which Watanabe Masanosuke had founded and directed before he was arrested in June. The Kamedo police ap-prehended nine of the more militant members, including the chairman of the Japan Communist Youth League, and had them bayoneted and be-headed by soldiers of the Tokyo garrison. And at military police headquarters a gendarme captain, Amakasu Masahiko, murdered Osugi Sakae, perhaps the most brilliant independent radical, along with his wife and his little nephew. It was clear that the government was determined to destroy any opposition that advocated a basic alteration of Japanese political and economic life. To the government the communists represented the most dangerous of such radical groups.

Bibliographical Notes

The most detailed surveys of this period are Chitoshi Yanaga, *Japan since Perry* (New York: McGraw-Hill, 1949), and Hugh Borton, *Japan's Modern Century* (New York: Ronald Press, 1955); and useful as a shorter, more analytical work is Edwin O. Reischauer, *The United States and Japan* (Cambridge, Mass.: Har-vard University Press, enlarged and revised edition, 1957). G. B. Sansom, *The Western World and Japan* (New York: Alfred A. Knopf, 1950), is an important work concerning the problem of acculturation. Okuma Shigenobu (compiler), *Fifty Years of New Japan* (London: Smith Elders, two volumes, 1910; English version by M. B. Huish), is still useful as a reference work.

E. H. Norman, *Japan's Emergence as a Modern State: Political and Economic Problems of the Meiji Period* (New York: Institute of Pacific Relations, 1940),

389

Robert Scalapino, *Democracy and the Party Movement in Pre-War Japan* (Berkeley: University of California Press, 1953), Delmer Brown, *Nationalism in Japan* (Berkeley: University of California Press, 1955), W. W. McLaren, *A Political History of Japan during the Meiji Era, 1867–1912* (London: Scribner's, 1916), and Fujii Jintaro (editor and compiler), *Outline of Japanese History in the Meiji Era* (Tokyo: Obunsha, 1958; translated by Hattie K. Colton and Kenneth E. Colton), are useful surveys basically concerned with political development. O. Tanin and E. Yohan, *Militarism and Fascism in Japan* (New York: International Publishers, 1934), is a doctrinaire communist interpretation. More specialized works include Marius B. Jansen, *Sakamoto Ryoma and the Meiji Restoration* (Princeton: Princeton University Press, 1961), Albert M. Craig, *Choshu in the Meiji Restoration* (Cambridge, Mass.: Harvard University Press, 1961), and Robert A. Wilson, *Genesis of the Meiji Government in Japan, 1868–1871* (Berkeley: University of California Press, 1957), E. H. Norman, *Soldier and Peasant in Japan: the Origins of Conscription* (New York: Institute of Pacific Relations, 1943), A Mounsey, *The Satsuma Rebellion* (London: Murray, 1879), Nobutaka Ike, *The Beginnings of Political Democracy in Japan* (Baltimore: Johns Hopkins Press, 1950), George M. Beckmann, *The Making of the Meiji Constitution: The Oligarchs and the Constitutional Development of Japan, 1868–1891* (Lawrence, Kans.: University of Kansas Press, 1957), and A. Morgan Young, *Japan in Recent Times, 1912–1926* (New York: Morrow, 1929).

The only important autobiography in English is *The Autobiography of Fukuzawa Yukichi* (Tokyo: Hokuseido Press, third and revised edition, 1947; translated by Kiyooka Eiichi). With the exception of H. van Straelen, *Yoshida Shoin, Forerunner of the Meiji Restoration: A Biographical Study* (Leiden: E. J. Brill, 1952), most of the work in this field has been done by Japanese and is uncritical. Such works include K. Nakamura, *Prince Ito* (New York: Anraku, 1910), K. Hamada, *Prince Ito* (Tokyo: Sanseido, 1936), Ijichi Junsei, *The Life of Marquis Shigenobu Okuma* (Tokyo: Hokuseido Press, 1956), Y. Takekoshi, *Prince Saionji* (Kyoto: Ritsumeikan University, 1933), and Omura Bunji, *The Last Genro, Prince Saionji, the Man Who Westernized Japan* (Philadelphia: Lippincott, 1938).

The best survey of Japanese government is Paul Linebarger, Djuang Chu, and Ardath Burks, *Far Eastern Government and Politics: China and Japan* (Princeton: Van Nostrand, second edition, 1956); and still useful are Harold S. Quigley, *Japanese Government and Politics, An Introductory Survey* (New York: Century, 1932), and Robert K. Reischauer, *Japan, Government and Politics* (New York: Thomas Nelson, 1939). Japanese official attitudes can be studied in Ito Hirobumi, *Commentaries on the Constitution of the Empire of Japan* (Tokyo: Chuo Daigaku, third edition, 1931; translated by Ito Myoji), and in Japan, Ministry of Education, *Kokutai no Hongi* (Cambridge, Mass.: Harvard University Press, 1949; translated by John Owen Gauntlet).

The most comprehensive survey in its field is William W. Lockwood, *The Economic Development of Japan; Growth and Structural Change, 1868–1938* (Princeton: Princeton University Press, 1954), and a more concise work is G. C.

Allen, A Short Economic History of Modern Japan, 1867–1937 (London: Allen & Unwin, 1946). More specialized studies include Thomas C. Smith, Political Change and Industrial Development in Japan: Government Enterprise, 1868–1880 (Stanford: Stanford University Press, 1955), Ohara Keichi (editor and compiler), Japanese Trade and Industry in the Meiji-Taisho Era (Tokyo: Obunsha, 1957; translated and adapted by Okata Tamotsu), and Kobayashi Ushisaburo, The Basic Industries and Social History of Japan, 1914–1918 (New Haven: Yale University Press, 1930). An interesting popular account is O. D. Russell, The House of Mitsui (Boston: Little, Brown, 1939).

Ruth Benedict, Chrysanthemum and the Sword (Boston: Houghton Mifflin, 1946), presents an idealized picture of a static society, but it is well worth reading. More historical is Shibusawa Keizo (editor and compiler), Japanese Society in the Meiji Era (Tokyo: Obunsha, 1958; translated and adapted by Aora H. Culbertson and Kimura Michitaka). Ishimoto Shidzue, Facing Two Ways, The Story of My Life (New York: Farrar & Rinehart, 1935), and Sugimoto Etsu, A Daughter of the Samurai (Garden City: Doubleday, Page, 1925) are interesting personal documents.

Kosaka Masaaki, Japanese Thought in the Meiji Era (Tokyo: Pan-Pacific Press, 1958; translated and adapted by David Abosch), provides an introduction to a field in which there has been little work. Warren Smith, Confucianism in Modern Japan: A Study of Conservatism in Japanese Intellectual History (Tokyo: Hokuseido Press, 1959), is also useful.

Kishimoto Hideo (editor), Japanese Religion in the Meiji Era (Tokyo: Obunsha, 1956; translated and adapted by John Howes), is a rather uneven collection of essays, the best of which are concerned with early Japanese Protestant Christianity. Modern Shinto is ably described and analyzed in Daniel C. Holthom, The National Faith of Japan: A Study in Modern Shintoism (London: Kegan Paul, 1938), and in his Modern Japan and Shinto Nationalism: A Study of Present-Day Trends in Japanese Religions (Chicago: University of Chicago Press, second edition, 1947).

Donald Keene (editor), Modern Japanese Literature, An Anthology (New York: Grove Press, 1956), is the best work of its kind in the Japanese field. Useful also is Okazaki Yoshie and V. H. Vigliemo, Japanese Literature in the Meiji Era (Tokyo: Obunsha, 1955). Some of the works of Japan's novelists in this period have been translated, and two by Natsume Soseki are of particular interest, Kokoro (Tokyo: Hokuseido Press, 1941; translated by Sato Ineko), and Botchan (Master Darling) (Tokyo: Ogawa Seibundo, 1924; translated by Mori Yasotaro).

In the field of foreign policy, Seiji Hishida, Japan among the Great Powers: A Survey of Her International Relations (New York: Longmans, Green & Co., 1940), and Roy H. Akagi, Japan's Foreign Relations, 1542–1936; A Short History (Tokyo: Hokuseido Press, 1936), are surveys written from the Japanese point of view. Tatsuji Takeuchi, War and Diplomacy in the Japanese Empire (New York: Doubleday, Doran, 1935), is more objective and emphasizes decision-making. The best of the textbook accounts is Paul H. Clyde, The Far East (Englewood Cliffs, N.J.: Prentice-Hall, third edition, 1958). E. Hertslet, Treaties and Tariffs Regulating the Trade between Great Britain and Foreign Nations,

Volume Six, Japan (London: Butterworth's, 1879), Carnegie Endowment for International Peace, Division of International Law, *Korea, Treaties and Agreements* (Washington: The Endowment, 1921), E. B. Price, *The Russo-Japanese Treaties of 1907–1916 Concerning Manchuria and Mongolia* (Baltimore: Johns Hopkins Press, 1933), Carnegie Endowment for International Peace, Division of International Law, *The Sino-Japanese Negotiations of 1915* (Washington: The Endowment, 1921), Carnegie Endowment for International Law, Division of International Law, *The Consortium* (Washington: The Endowment, 1921), and Senate Documents, 67th Congress, Second Session, No. 126, *Conference on the Limitation of Armament, Washington, 1921–1922* (Washington: U.S. Government Printing Office, 1922), are all important reference works.

There are a number of excellent studies concerning foreign policy and the Meiji Restoration. For the American "opening of Japan," A. Walworth, *Black Ships off Japan: The Story of Commodore Perry's Expedition* (New York: Alfred A. Knopf, 1946), and Mario E. Cosenza (editor), *The Complete Journal of Townsend Harris* (New York: Doubleday, 1930), provide adequate coverage. The Russian advance is described in George Alexander Lensen, *Russia's Japan Expedition of 1852–1855* (Gainesville, Fla.: University of Florida Press, 1955), his *The Russian Push toward Japan* (Princeton: Princeton University Press, 1959), and John A. Harrison, *Japan's Northern Frontier* (Gainesville, Fla.: University of Florida Press, 1953). British interests are described in W. G. Beasley, *Great Britain and the Opening of Japan* (London: Luzac, 1951); and his *Select Documents on Japanese Policy, 1853–1868* (New York: Oxford University Press, 1955), is indispensable for the study of the foreign policy debate in Japan. Two useful contemporary accounts are Sir Rutherford Alcock, *The Capital of the Tycoon: A Narrative of a Three Years' Residence in Japan* (New York: Harper, two volumes, 1863), and Sir Ernest Satow, *A Diplomat in Japan* (London: Seeley, 1921).

Special studies of foreign policy and international relations in the Meiji period include Hilary Conroy, *The Japanese Seizure of Korea* (Philadelphia: University of Pennsylvania Press, 1961), A. M. Pooley (editor), *The Secret Memoirs of Count Tadasu Hayashi (1850–1913)* (New York: Nash, 1915), C. F. Chang, *The Anglo-Japanese Alliance* (Baltimore: Johns Hopkins Press, 1931), and Andrew Malozemoff, *Russian Far Eastern Policy, 1881–1904, with Special Emphasis on the Russo-Japanese War* (Berkeley: University of California Press, 1958). American-Japanese relations are surveyed by P. J. Treat, *Japan and the United States, 1853–1921* (Stanford: Stanford University Press, revised edition, 1928), and Kamikawa Hikomatsu, *Japan-American Diplomatic Relations in the Meiji-Taisho Era* (Tokyo: Pan-Pacific Press, 1958; translated and adapted by Kimura Michiko). More specialized works include T. Dennett, *Roosevelt and the Russo-Japanese War* (Garden City: Doubleday, 1925), Thomas A. Bailey, *Theodore Roosevelt and the Japanese-American Crisis* (Stanford: Stanford University Press, 1934), Herbert Croly, *Willard Straight* (New York: Macmillan, 1924), and Charles Vevier, *The United States and China, 1906–1913* (New Brunswick, N.J.: Rutgers University Press, 1955).

The diplomacy of the World War I period and its aftermath, culminating in the Washington Conference, are surveyed in A. W. Griswold, *The Far Eastern Policy of the United States* (New York: Harcourt, Brace, 1938). More specialized studies include Thomas E. La Fargue, *China and the World War* (Stanford: Stanford University Press, 1937), Roy Watson Curry, *Woodrow Wilson and Far Eastern Policy, 1913–1921* (New York: Bookman Associates, 1957), Russell Fifield, *Woodrow Wilson and the Far East* (New York, 1953), Li Tienyi, *Woodrow Wilson's China Policy, 1913–1917* (New York: Twayne, 1952), and, for Japanese attitudes, Ishii Kikujiro, *Diplomatic Commentaries* (Baltimore: Johns Hopkins University Press, 1936; translated by William R. Langdon). James W. Morley, *The Japanese Thrust into Siberia* (New York: Columbia University Press, 1957), is an excellent study concerning Japanese attitudes, while Betty Unterberger, *America's Siberian Expedition, 1918–1920* (Durham, N.C.: Duke University Press, 1956), and John A. White, *The Siberian Intervention* (Princeton: Princeton University Press, 1950), are useful for the American side. Y. Ichihashi, *The Washington Conference and After* (Stanford: Stanford University Press, 1928), and R. L. Buell, *The Washington Conference* (New York: Appleton, 1922), are satisfactory studies.

China and Japan
in Transformation

PART

China in Transformation

The history of China since the 1920's centers largely around the growth and development of nationalism and communism. From a narrow viewpoint the major theme is the struggle between the Kuomintang, or Nationalist Party, and the Chinese Communist Party, which began with their marriage of convenience in the 1920's, continued through the period of civil war from 1927 to 1937 and their resistance to Japan from 1937 to 1945, and concluded with the triumph of communism after World War II. Two important subtopics are the factional struggles between Chiang K'ai-shek and Wang Ching-wei and their supporters within the Kuomintang and the similar struggle for power within the Chinese Communist Party, which resulted in the victory of Mao Tse-tung.

From a broader standpoint the recent history of China is a continuation of efforts to achieve a synthesis between modern Western ideas and institutions and, if not the institutions, at least some of the spirit of Chinese tradition. This was particularly true when Chiang K'ai-shek held power and even to some extent characterizes the regime of the revolutionary Mao Tse-tung, especially in the field of foreign relations. But it is abundantly clear that cultural factors rooted deeply in Chinese history have influenced both the Kuomintang–Chinese Communist Party struggle and the eventual triumph of the Chinese Communist Party.

From the international standpoint recent Chinese history must include some discussion of the rise of strong anti-imperialist forces in China and must be related to the international conflict between the Axis powers, the Soviet Union and international communism, and the Western democracies that *culminated in World War II and to the contemporary conflict involving the communist bloc, the anticommunist allies, and the new, underdeveloped nation-states.*

23   *The Nationalist Revolution, 1920–1928*

As the 1920's began, China was still a divided country under the domination of the warlords. The Anfu clique had controlled the Peking government since 1917, but in 1920 it was driven from the capital by the combined forces of the Manchurian warlord, Chang Tso-lin, and Ts'ao K'un, who, after the death of Feng Kuo-chang, headed the Chihli faction (the warlords of Kiangsu, Kiangsi, Hupeh, Hunan, and Chihli). After cementing bonds of friendship by a marriage between their families, these two generals parceled out cabinet posts among their respective nominees and defined the territorial jurisdiction of their military allies; but at Peking Chang Tso-lin came to dominate. At the time of the fall of the dynasty Chang had been a minor officer in a garrison in Manchuria, but during the early years of the republic he emerged as an important local military figure. He allied himself with the movement against Yuan Shih-k'ai's enthronement, but Yuan placated him by making him military and civil governor of south Manchuria and by appointing one of his allies to similar posts in Heilungkiang Province. After Yuan's death Chang made himself master of all Manchuria and one of the foremost warlords in China.

In 1922, however, he was driven from Peking back into Manchuria by a coalition of warlords (Shensi, Kiangsi, Kiangsu, Hupeh, Shantung, Honan, and Anhwei) led by Wu P'ei-fu, who assumed the role of restorer of constitutionalism in the north. He reconvened the parliament that had been dissolved in 1917 but forced the election of his old chief, Ts'ao K'un, as president. Wu declared that he was going to unify China by force and instructed the parliament to return to its duty of drafting a constitution. A permanent constitution, based on the original draft of 1913 and the revision of 1917, was promulgated on October 10, 1923, but by that time it was already a dead letter and of only historical interest. Wu P'ei-fu, like the warlords before him, was paying lip service to republicanism. His ambition was to impose his will on China, but he was weakened by factional strife with his "ally," the ambitious Ts'ao K'un.

In the south, too, republicanism was at the mercy of the warlords. In October, 1920, the Kwangsi military clique withdrew from Kwangtung, and the military government that had been established at Canton disintegrated. A Cantonese army under Ch'en Ch'iung-ming returned from Fukien and controlled the city. In November, Ch'en, who had cast his lot with the revolutionaries in 1911 and with the opposition to Yuan in 1913, invited the cooperation of Sun Yat-sen in the formation of a new government. Supported by a majority of the members of the parliament dissolved by Yuan Shih-k'ai in 1914, Sun proposed the re-establishment of republican government under a newly elected president. Ch'en inclined toward a federation of self-governing provinces but yielded when Sun would not concur. On April 7, 1921, two hundred members of the old parliament convened at Canton and approved an outline for the organization of a government based on the 1912 constitution. On the 10th they elected Sun as president and Ch'en as governor of Kwangtung and commander-in-chief of the army of the republic.

Anxious to destroy this new regime, Peking allied itself with the neighboring Kwangsi warlord clique, but in June and July of 1921 Sun and Ch'en joined forces and defeated their Kwangsi enemies. In the following winter, however, Sun led a foolhardy military expedition north, and, when it ended in complete failure, Sun blamed Ch'en for lack of financial and logistic support. More important to his defeat, however, were developments in the north. Sun was allied with the Manchurian warlord, Chang Tso-lin, and Ch'en with the Chihli clique of Wu P'ei-fu. So when the Manchurian faction was defeated by the Chihli group, Sun's expedition had little chance for success; and the alliance between the Canton warlords and the republicans came to an end in July, 1922, when Ch'en drove Sun from the city. Sun returned to Shanghai, where he ultimately negotiated an alliance with the Soviet Union and the Chinese Communist Party.

The Soviet Union and Revolution in Asia

Until the 1920's the new communist regime in Russia had focused its attention on imminent revolution in Europe on the theory that the triumph of the Bolsheviks heralded the downfall of capitalism throughout the world and the beginning of a new world order based on social ownership of the means of production. Lenin had regarded the civil war in Russia that followed the revolution as a holding operation which would enable the Bolsheviks to cling to power until the workers' revolution in Europe, particularly Germany, took over leadership of the anticapitalist struggle. In accordance with Marx's interpretation of history and the dialectical process culminating in the clash between capital and labor, Lenin believed that communism could achieve victory only in the more advanced industrial West. Yet as early as November, 1919, he advised his Asian disciples to "adapt communist theory and practice to conditions where the bulk of the people are peasants." He called upon them to fight "not against capital but against medieval remnants"; accordingly, they were to ally themselves with the bourgeoisie against their common enemies, the feudal exploiters and the Western imperialists.

When the frontal attack against capitalism in Europe failed, Lenin and his colleagues turned more of their attention to Asia. They reasoned that in this part of the world the capitalists were less capable of defending themselves against movements which would sap their strength and would thus help to bring about their eventual destruction in Europe. In his theory of imperialism as the last phase of capitalism, Lenin explained that surplus profits derived from the exploitation of colonies and backward areas enabled the European capitalists to maintain their industrial wage slaves above the starvation level and to postpone the inevitable revolution. Take away those profits, free the colonies, and then the workers at home would rise in revolt. This shift in strategy was aimed particularly at Great Britain, which had greater interests in Asia than any other power. The Russian communist approach to Asia, and to China especially, was to search for allies who, by fighting imperialism, would advance the proletarian revolution in Europe; moreover, a struggle between Asian nationalism and European imperialism would relieve pressure on the Soviet Union.

The basic strategy for Asia was determined at the Second Congress of the Comintern in August, 1920, when it approved Lenin's "Theses on the National and Colonial Question." According to Lenin:

The Communist International should form temporary understandings, even alliances, with the bourgeois democracy of the colonies and backward countries, but not merge with it, unconditionally preserving the independence of the proletarian movement, even in its most embryonic form. . . . We, as Communists, must and will support bourgeois emancipation in colonial countries only when in those areas these movements are really revolutionary, when their representatives will not hinder us in educating and organizing the peasantry and the large masses of the exploited in the revolutionary spirit.

Lenin was distinguishing between the revolutionary nationalist movements which would fight imperialism to the end and bourgeois nationalist movements which, he warned, would try to compromise with imperialism.

Lenin also emphasized that the anti-imperialist struggle was only part of the process of the ultimate communization of Asia:

The revolution in the colonies is not going to be a Communist revolution in its first stages. But if from the outset the leadership is in the hands of a Communist vanguard, the revolutionary masses will not be led astray, but will go ahead through successive periods of development of revolutionary experience. . . . In the first stages, the revolution in the colonies must be carried on with a program which will include many petty bourgeois reform clauses, such as the division of the land, etc. But from this it does not follow that the leadership of the revolution will have to be surrendered to the bourgeois democrats. On the contrary, the proletarian parties must carry on vigorous and systematic propaganda for the Soviet idea and organize the peasants' and workers' Soviets as soon as possible. These Soviets will work in co-operation with the Soviet Republic in the advanced capitalist countries for the ultimate overthrow of the capitalist order throughout the world.

In the case of Russia, Lenin as early as 1905 had thought that it would be possible to ignore the bourgeoisie and consummate the revolution in alliance with the peasantry.

The Comintern worked to get the support of Asian revolutionaries. At Baku in September, 1920, Russian leaders met with representatives from Asian nations and colonies to stimulate the establishment of communist parties and to shape their ideological and tactical policies in accordance with Moscow orthodoxy. In July, 1921, Comintern agents helped to organize the First Congress of the Chinese Communist Party at Shanghai, and the small group of intellectuals that constituted the party elected Ch'en Tu-hsiu chairman. In the following months branches of the party were organized in various provinces and cities, and communist cells were organized among Chinese students in France, Germany, Russia, and Japan. In January, 1922, at the First Congress of Far Eastern Communist and Revolutionary Organizations, held in Moscow and Petrograd, the Comintern defined the tasks of the Chinese communists, in accordance with Lenin's theses, as follows:

The chief task with which they are confronted is to achieve their emancipation from the foreign yoke. It is the duty not only of Communists, but of all honest Chinese democrats, to criticize most unsparingly the various Chinese politicians who are entering into any kind of understanding with any of the imperialist gangs. . . . It is imperative to conduct an energetic struggle for the overthrow of that regime which is supporting the feudal anarchy. . . . All Chinese democrats must fight for the federative Chinese republic.

At its Second Congress, in May, 1922, the Chinese Communist Party voted to join the Comintern, and it issued a manifesto in accordance with the policy outlined above. In a united front with the poor peasantry and the petty bourgeoisie, the proletariat would support a democratic revolution against imperialism and militarism, and, upon the successful conclusion of the democratic revolution, the proletariat would overcome the bourgeoisie and establish the dictatorship of the proletariat in alliance with the poor peasantry. To prepare for the second stage of the struggle, the party emphasized the need for workers to fight for their own class interests and to organize themselves in the party and in labor unions.

The Soviet Union also assisted in the training of Asian communists. The center for this was the University for the Toilers of the Far East, also known as Stalin University. Divided into two sections, one for Russian citizens and the other for non-Russians, the school had a normal enrollment of fifteen hundred to two thousand students, among them five hundred women, representing more than sixty nationalities. The curriculum, covering a two to three year period, included courses in the Russian language, the history of the world labor movement, interpretation of basic Marxist writings, and the history of the communist party of Russia along with military and other technical training.

There were other Russian efforts to establish a working alliance with any group, including cliques of warlords or politicians, which might be ready to join with them against British imperialism and the Anfu regime at Peking. In August or September, 1921, the Comintern delegate to the Chinese Communist Party, Maring, met with Sun Yat-sen at Kweilin in Kiangsi Province. No specific agreement resulted from their conversation, but Sun came away from the meeting firmly convinced that Russian communism in practice resembled what he himself taught, and Kuomintang party members attended the First Congress of the Toilers of the Far East in January, 1922. Actually the Russians were chiefly attracted by the military strength of Wu P'ei-fu, who was interested in overthrowing and replacing the Anfu clique and its successor at Peking, Chang Tso-lin. But when Wu succeeded in seizing Peking in 1922, he made it clear that he wanted no part of Russian support.

The Soviet Union and the Peking Regime

The Soviet foreign office also sought to establish diplomatic relations—which would mean recognition—with the Peking government; and, to dissociate itself from czarist foreign policy, it announced, as early as January, 1918, a "complete break with the barbarous policies of bourgeois civilization, which builds the welfare of the exploiters and a few select chosen nations upon the enslavement of hundreds of millions of toilers in Asia, in the colonies in general, and in small states." In a multitude of articles, reviews, and speeches, Soviet leaders affirmed their friendly attitude toward China and their readiness to abolish all privileges acquired by czarist Russia at the expense of China. In July, 1919, the Soviet government issued a "Manifesto to the Chinese People," in which it offered to return all territory wrongfully taken from China by the Russian imperial government, to restore to China the control of the Chinese Eastern Railway, to renounce its claims to any share of the Boxer indemnity, to give up rights of extraterritoriality, and to abandon other special privileges inconsistent with the equality of nations. While this manifesto had the desired effect upon Chinese intellectuals, it fell on deaf ears in Peking, which was not ready to recognize the Soviet Union or even to break off relations with the diplomatic representatives of the czarist regime. In September, 1920, the Soviet foreign office restated its offer to terminate the unequal treaties with China, but this time it altered its position with regard to the Chinese Eastern Railway. It did not offer to give up its property rights but would negotiate with regard for the needs of the Soviet Union. Judging that the future of the Soviet regime was uncertain, Peking took a compromise position, suspending recognition of the old Russian representatives and taking all Russian interests, including the railway, under its control until such time as it would recognize the new government. The Soviets unsuccessfully sought to initiate negotiations in 1921, but in 1922 Peking informed Moscow that it would negotiate on the basis of the 1919 and 1920 declarations. Adolphe Joffre, one of the ablest of the Soviet diplomats, arrived in Peking in August, 1922.

The stumbling block in the negotiations was Mongolia, which for a long time had served as a buffer zone between China and Russia. Traditionally part of the Chinese empire, it had largely been left to its own devices; however, in 1907 the Manchus encouraged Chinese farmers to emigrate into Mongolia and enacted a series of administrative reforms designed to make the area an integral part of China. Mongol children were sent to newly constructed Chinese schools, mixed marriages were encouraged, lamaseries received government support, and Mongol princes were given high posts in Peking. Mongol leaders, willing to recognize Chinese suzerainty but resenting integration into China, turned to Russia for help. In July, 1911, the Hutukhtu (the living Buddha) and the princes met at Urga, the capital, and decided to appeal to the czar for assistance against the Chinese. A delegation was sent to St. Petersburg, but it found the Russian government reluctant to act boldly. Japan, fearing international complications, was pressuring the Russians to be careful and to be patient. Shortly thereafter the dynasty reinforced its garrisons at Urga and the other important towns, and in August it refused to renew the 1881 commercial treaty with Russia. Chinese officials also began to levy customs duties on Russian goods entering Mongolia. With the outbreak of the republican revolution in October, however, Chinese forces withdrew, and an independent government under the Hutukhtu was established at Urga. The Mongol princes, declaring that their loyalty to the dynasty was at an end, seceded from China.

After the establishment of the Chinese Republic in 1912, Yuan Shih-k'ai informed the Mongol princes that Mongolia would become an integral part of China and be treated like the home provinces; but despite concessions to local autonomy, Mongol attitudes did not change. In view of European conditions, Russia could take advantage of the situation only by diplomatic activity; in November, 1912, the Russian government recognized the Mongol regime and, in return for commercial concessions, promised to help preserve Mongol autonomy. Finally, in November, 1913, China and Russia concluded an agreement by which China recognized the autonomy but not the independence of Mongolia and promised not to send more troops or colonists into

Mongolia or to interfere in Mongolia's internal politics. Later, by a tripartite treaty of June, 1915, which recognized Chinese sovereignty, China and Russia pledged not to meddle in the internal affairs of Mongolia; but, since both powers were permitted to maintain limited military detachments in the area, the future was uncertain.

The chaos resulting from the extension of the Russian Revolution to Siberia altered the situation in Mongolia. In the autumn of 1919 a Chinese army under the warlord Hsu Shu-cheng entered Urga and forced the Mongol government to renounce its autonomy, and on November 22 Peking proclaimed the reunification of Mongolia with China despite the protests of czarist officials in Urga and Peking. In October, 1920, however, a small White Russian army under General Ungern-Sternberg crossed into Mongolia and in February, 1921, ousted the Chinese garrison at Urga. With Japanese support he proclaimed the complete independence of Mongolia from China and restored the Hutukhtu as ruler. He also sought to use Mongolia as the base for an attack against Russian communist forces, but after re-entering Russian territory in May, 1921, he lost a series of battles and was taken prisoner by the Red army in July. His execution in November, 1921, terminated White Russian activities in Mongolia; moreover, in their pursuit of the White army, Red troops entered the area and on July 6, 1921, captured Urga.

The groundwork for the ultimate Soviet domination of Mongolia had in the meantime been well prepared. In March, 1921, in meetings on the Manchurian border, the Russian communists had helped to form a People's Revolutionary Party, made up of procommunist Mongol refugees, and a Provisional Revolutionary Government, which on April 10 officially asked for Soviet assistance. Once in control of Urga, the People's Revolutionary Party became the Nationalist Party, and the new government, supported by Russian arms, was proclaimed the result of a purely nationalist movement. The Hutukhtu was for the time being the nominal head of state, and in form the government was a constitutional monarchy. Russian officials kept in the background, but Russian domination was being firmly established. On November 5, 1921, a treaty between Mongolia and the Soviet Union provided for mutual recognition of the two governments, establishment of consulates, and a Russian concession for the construction of postal and telephone communications. In Urga offices were opened by Soviet economic agencies such as the Oil Syndicate and the Siberian State Trade and Wool Purchase Company; moreover, the new Mongol Bank was dependent upon the Soviet State Bank. Soviet military instructors remained on after the departure of the main body of Russian troops, and a secret police, modeled on that of Russia, began to be organized in 1922. Mongolia was becoming the first Soviet satellite.

Joffre failed to settle the outstanding differences between China and the

Soviet Union. He had been instructed to establish diplomatic relations, to preserve Russian influence in Mongolia, and to salvage Russian interests in the Chinese Eastern Railway in spite of earlier declarations.* Joffre insisted, however, that Russia had not surrendered all her rights in China, and he made it clear that Russia wanted to maintain her economic rights in the Chinese Eastern Railway. He urged that a new provisional management of the line be organized pending a more permanent settlement of the question. Mongolia, however, remained as a more difficult issue. Peking insisted that Mongolia was Chinese territory and demanded Russian evacuation as a precedent to any general agreement. Since Russia took the position that her hold over Mongolia was more valuable than diplomatic recognition by China, the negotiations failed.

A general settlement was finally reached in the treaty of May 31, 1924. Peking came to the conclusion that it could not alter the situation in Mongolia, and the new Soviet envoy, Leo Karakhan, anxious to secure Peking's recognition of his government and its confirmation of Russian interests in the Chinese Eastern Railway, was willing to concede Chinese sovereignty over Mongolia, at least on paper. The two countries resumed formal diplomatic relations, and Russia renounced all its concessions in China. With regard to the Chinese Eastern Railway, it was agreed that it was a purely commercial enterprise and that administration within the railway zone was to be in Chinese hands. Peking informed Karakhan, however, that the decision would be effective only if Chang Tso-lin acknowledged it. Karakhan therefore met with Chang at Mukden, and after some renegotiation they signed a separate treaty in September. The Chinese Eastern Railway was confirmed as a commercial enterprise under a Russian and Chinese board of directors, with profits to be divided equally between Moscow and Chang. Russia's right to a 50 per cent share was secured for thirty-two years; in 1956 the railroad was to revert to China without payment, and she was accorded the right to redeem the railroad before that date at a price to be determined by a special Chinese-Russian commission. This arrangement was, of course, the death knell for the claims of foreign investors, especially the French. In March, 1925, with Chang Tso-lin once again in control of Peking, the treaty was ratified by the government of China.

Russia followed up these diplomatic gains by consolidating her position in Mongolia. In 1924 the Hutukhtu died, and a Mongolian People's Republic was established on the model of the government of the Soviet Union. As a symbol of the change the city of Urga was renamed Ulan Bator, "City of

---

* In 1920 Chang Tso-lin had entered into a contract with the Russo-Asiatic Bank (which had been reorganized at Paris), by which China assumed the position of trustee of the railroad. A new board of directors was appointed, consisting of five White Russians and five Chinese, with a Chinese as president and a Russian as vice-president. The Technical Board continued to operate the line, but the Chinese policed it.

the Red Hero." Russian army units withdrew, but advisers remained to instruct and train Mongol troops. To hasten the transformation of Mongol life, great emphasis was placed upon the training of youth as leaders to replace the lamas and princes, who still held important positions and who would stand in the way of communism. The important instrument in this connection was the Revolutionary Youth Corps, which took its orders directly from Moscow. Moreover, under Russian domination Mongolia was increasingly cut off from the outside world. When Soviet-Mongol economic relations became even closer after the establishment of the Russian-controlled Mongol Industrial and Commercial Bank, foreign business interests found it impossible to operate and by 1928 had retired from the scene. Foreign advisers and missionaries were expelled, and by 1928 it was necessary to obtain a visa from the Russian government to travel through Mongol territory. C. P. Fitzgerald has noted that "On the great map of Asia which hung on the wall of the Far Eastern Section of the Revolutionary Museum in Moscow, Mongolia was splashed Red like any other Soviet Republic within the orbit of Russia."

The Nationalist-Communist Alliance

While the Soviet Foreign Office was conducting these negotiations with Peking, the Comintern was endeavoring to effect an alliance between the Chinese Communist Party and the Kuomintang. Soviet leaders were developing a strategy based on Lenin's prescription that the first objective of the revolution in colonial and semicolonial countries like China was the elimination of feudalism (landlordism and warlordism) and imperialism. They concluded that this objective could be most easily achieved within the framework of a bourgeois-democratic revolution such as Sun Yat-sen and the Kuomintang were planning. It became Comintern policy, therefore, to persuade the Chinese Communist Party to join with the Kuomintang but to make sure that the identity of the proletarian movement was completely preserved, especially its right to educate and organize the masses in the communist revolutionary spirit. Under Russian prodding, the Chinese Communist Party in June, 1922, approved the alliance with the Kuomintang to effect a revolution against warlordism and imperialism and to establish a democratic republic. Party members agreed that a successful democratic revolution would facilitate the development of capitalism and serve as a necessary prelude to the ultimate struggle between the bourgeoisie and the proletariat.

When Sun Yat-sen arrived in Shanghai in August, 1922, he was met by Dalin, a delegate of the Young Communist International, who proposed the two-party alliance to Sun. Anxious to secure Russian assistance and to make use of Russian revolutionary experience and organizing talent, Sun declared his willingness to accept individual Chinese communists into the Kuomintang as party members, but he would not countenance the formation of separate communist cells within the Kuomintang. Sun had no objections to the communists' keeping their identity as a separate party, but he expected the Russians to keep them under control. Later in August, Maring, who had just arrived from Moscow, met with the central committee of the Chinese Communist Party at Hangchow and proposed that the communists enter the Kuomintang and use it to develop their own propaganda and contacts with the masses. He was forced to invoke Comintern discipline to get the policy adopted because of the opposition led by Ch'en Tu-hsiu, who wanted the party to maintain greater independence. Maring then returned to Moscow, where the Comintern formally approved the Chinese Communist Party–Kuomintang alliance. A January 12, 1923, resolution of the executive committee of the Comintern reads:

Under the present circumstances it is useful to have the members of the Chinese Communist Party remain within the Kuomintang, but the party must maintain its own organization with a strongly centralized machine. . . . On the other hand, the Communist Party of China must influence the Kuomintang with a view to uniting its efforts against European, American, and Japanese imperialism.

Moreover, during the Comintern congress Karl Radek told the dissident Ch'en Tu-hsiu that it was the task of the Chinese Communist Party to bring the workers into "rational relationship with the objective revolutionary elements of the bourgeoisie." Chinese communists, Radek said, simply had to grasp the fact that socialism was not the order of the day. The Third Party Congress of the Chinese Communist Party upheld this decision in June, 1923, when it styled the Kuomintang the "central force in the nationalist revolution," but the communists planned to control it ultimately from within by the occupation of key posts and from without by pressure of mass organizations. Meanwhile, Adolphe Joffre had already established a formal relationship with Sun Yat-sen and the Kuomintang.

Joffre met with Sun, who was living in the French Concession at Shanghai, in January, 1923, and concluded the basis of an alliance between the Soviet Union and the Kuomintang. They agreed that neither communism nor the soviet system could be introduced into China, whose most pressing problem was the attainment of national unity and complete independence. In the solution of this problem China was assured of Soviet assistance. It would have been foolish for Joffre to argue about ultimate ends, for Russian faith in historical inevitability was firm. After all, the immediate need was completion of the nationalist revolution. Joffre also reaffirmed the Soviet declaration of September, 1920, in which Moscow renounced the imperialism of the czars while carefully preserving certain rights in the Chinese Eastern Railway, and he stated in diplomatic double-talk that it was not the policy of the Soviet Union to pursue an imperialist approach to Mongolia or to induce

Mongolia to secede from China. Sun stated that he had no objection to the temporary occupation of Mongolia by Russian forces.

Within a month of his conference with Joffre, Sun was able to make Canton the base for revolution once again. Early in the autumn of 1922, with warlord assistance, Sun had organized an army in Fukien to fight Ch'en Ch'iung-ming, and he had also made allies of the Yunnanese warlord, Yang Hsi-min, the Kwangsi warlord, Liu Chen-huan, and the Kwangtung warlord, Hsu Ch'ung-chih. In December, 1922, these forces began to campaign against Ch'en and in January, 1923, drove him from Canton, where in March Sun established a new military government with himself as grand marshal and the warlords as his subordinate generals.

Russian support of the nationalist revolution was channeled through communist agents, particularly Michael Borodin, who arrived in Canton in September, 1923. Borodin was a man of extraordinary energy and intelligence with a long career of communist service behind him. He had become a Social Democrat in 1903, the year in which the Russian Social Democrats split into Mensheviks and Bolsheviks. Forced to flee his homeland after the revolution of 1905, he settled temporarily in Chicago, where he served for a time as a school principal. He returned to Russia after the 1917 revolution, and because of his proficiency in English and Spanish he served as a communist agent in Great Britain, Mexico, and Turkey. He was not always successful, and in Great Britain he was arrested and sentenced to hard labor for six months for undercover activities. Contemporaries remember him as a man of unusual charm, poise, and force of character.

The Transformation of the Kuomintang

Borodin's first task was to make the Kuomintang, which was hardly more than a collection of factions under Sun Yat-sen's leadership, into a revolutionary political party. He sought to transform it into a highly organized party of disciplined individuals united by belief in a common program of action rather than by the loose tie of personal loyalty to Sun. Acting on Borodin's advice, Sun in October, 1923, created a provisional central executive committee to prepare for the convocation of a party congress in January, 1924, which would pass on the party's reorganization. Half of the party delegates were to be selected by Sun and half chosen by trusted local branches. In the meantime, the central executive committee would draft a party constitution based on that of the Russian Communist Party. The First Congress of the Kuomintang, meeting on schedule with 165 participants, accepted the alliance with the Soviet Union and the Chinese Communist Party. Sun argued for both, maintaining that Russian good will was expressed in the agreement with Joffre and that the Chinese Communists would be merely an auxiliary force in the revolution. It was his understanding that the communists entering the Kuomintang as individuals would observe its discipline and eventually be submerged in its ranks; moreover, he expected the Comintern to reinforce the hold of the Kuomintang over its communist members. When someone suggested that the Kuomintang should not accept as members applicants who still retained membership in another party, a communist delegate, Li Ta-chao, replied that communists would obey the Kuomintang's principles and rules. He stated that the communists would participate in the nationalist revolution, would entertain no intention of converting the Kuomintang members to communism, and would join the Kuomintang as individuals, not as a group bent on infiltrating the party.

The congress also approved the party constitution. Under its provisions, a biannual national congress was designated as the final authority on policy; but in the actual operation of party politics, power passed into the hands of a twenty-four man central executive committee (including three communists) chosen by the congress. This committee would determine the number of delegates to subsequent congresses, their apportionment, and their method of election; moreover, when the session of the congress came to an end, its delegates' term of office would expire. However, between 1924 and 1931 the party congress met only twice; and the central executive committee, convoked in plenary session once every six months, selected a smaller standing committee, which met weekly to determine party policy. Within this framework Sun Yat-sen had tremendous power. As president of the party for life, he had veto power over all party decisions—a right which apparently sprang from the fact that the Kuomintang had for so long been his personal organ. The central executive committee was empowered to create a national government, and for this purpose it appointed a central political council, which included the nine members of the standing committee and six other leading members of the Kuomintang. Government and party were to be organized like an interlocking directorate, for the party was regarded as the trustee of the country. Organization of the party at provincial and district levels was set up on the Leninist principle of "democratic centralism," according to which power descends from the top and it is consequently the first duty of any unit to execute the orders of the body above. For example, a district party might not even summon its own district congress without the approval of a higher authority. On the lower levels, too, power tended to pass to an executive committee and even further to a standing committee.

Under the direction of Borodin and Sun the Kuomintang developed more fully the ideological basis of a propaganda compaign designed to secure mass support for the revolution. The most important documents were the "Party Manifesto" adopted by the First Congress in January, 1924;* Sun's lectures of 1924, printed under the title *The Three Principles of the People (San Min*

---

* See Appendix 2.

Chu I); and his more concise "Fundamentals of National Reconstruction," dated April 12, 1924.

Students, often more radical than Sun Yat-sen, were the group most receptive to party propaganda, since it offered ideas not far removed from their own. Business support was strong, although there was opposition in this quarter to the alliance with communism and the Soviet Union. Sun, who gave special attention to the organization of peasants and workers, established a labor and peasant workers department under the central executive committee and appointed Liao Chung-k'ai, one of his most trusted lieutenants, to be its head. For work among the peasants and urban workers, Borodin also founded an institute to train party members in the techniques of agitation and propaganda, and after 1925 several hundred party members received additional special schooling in Moscow at the new Sun Yat-sen University.

With the vigorous support of the Chinese Communist Youth Corps, the Kuomintang was able to develop extensive labor support. Much of China's labor force was still organized into guilds, but in the larger cities, especially the treaty ports, factory laborers provided the raw material for a labor movement. Toward the close of World War I the treaty-port transport workers were organized, and unions later took hold in the cotton textile mills at Shanghai and Hankow and in the flour mills at Tientsin and Harbin. It was not until 1921, however, that there was a systematic attempt to integrate the labor movement on a national scale. The First Congress of the Chinese Communist Party at Shanghai set up the China Labor Union Secretariat to plan and direct the organization of trade unions. Among the most successful of the new unions was the Chinese Seamen's Union, organized in 1921. Late in that year it demanded wage increases for seamen operating out of Hong Kong, and when the shippers did not comply, the union struck, despite the efforts of the British to declare the union illegal. A series of sympathy strikes followed which tied up business and commerce generally. By February 1, 1922, some 50,000 workers left their jobs, and by March 5 the shipping tie-up was so acute that the foreigners capitulated, granting the seamen a 20 per cent wage increase and recognizing their union. In early May, under the leadership of the triumphant seamen, the First Congress of the All-China Labor Federation met at Canton with 230,000 union members on hand, and under the direct pressure of this convention, Sun Yat-sen's Canton government revised its penal code to legalize trade unions. The path was thus cleared for labor activities, and in the next few years the labor movement expanded, especially through strikes which secured wage increases and the recognition of unions as bargaining agents. There were thirty unions in Shanghai and over ten each in Hankow, Tientsin, Canton, and Changsha. Of their membership, approximately 150,000 workers were under the control of communists.

In the January, 1924, First Congress the Kuomintang decided on a labor platform to protect unions, to improve working conditions, to permit unions to bargain collectively and form arbitration committees, to recognize the right of unions to strike, and to guarantee security of union property and funds. On May Day, 1924, 100,000 workers marched through the streets at Shanghai, and twice that number celebrated at Canton. Meanwhile the Peking government and the local warlord regimes attempted to suppress the labor movement, often brutally breaking up strikes with military power. For example, on February 7, 1923, Wu P'ei-fu's soldiers routed strikers on the Peking-Hankow Railroad, killing sixty of them. This incident restrained the surge of the Chinese labor movement for a time and helped to check Ch'en Tu-hsiu's conviction that the Chinese proletariat was strong enough to act alone. Thereafter he and other communists of like mind were more willing to comply with Comintern policy.

The Kuomintang also sought peasant support, and in this endeavor the communists were again very active. By 1924 vast numbers of peasants were willing to listen to promises of relief, and in Kwangtung Province they were already beginning to organize associations. One of the leaders of this movement was P'eng Pai, a Japanese-educated son of a wealthy landlord and later a schoolteacher, who joined the Chinese Communist Party. According to his own estimate, P'eng had organized only 500 peasants in associations by September, 1922, but by January 1, 1923, the Haifeng District Peasant Association had a membership of approximately 20,000 families, representing 100,000 persons. By the middle of 1923 the framework of a provincial peasant association was already in existence, and demands for rent reduction had evolved into forcible attempts to abolish tenancy.

Russian assistance was decisive in the development of the Kuomintang's revolutionary military power. Before the end of 1923 General Galen (Vassily Blucher), an ex-Austrian army officer, who had experience in training the army of the Soviet Union, arrived at Canton, and during the next six months as many as thirty Soviet officers became advisers to the army of the Kuomintang. Soon shiploads of Russian arms were flowing into Canton harbor, the first arriving on October 7, 1924. The center of this military activity was the Whampoa Military Academy, founded in May, 1924, on the model of the Russian Red Army Officers School. Its commandant was Chiang K'ai-shek.

Chiang was born in Chekiang Province in 1888 and after a normal beginning in traditional education decided upon a military career. He attended Paoting Military Academy and continued his training at the Tokyo Military Academy as a Chinese government scholar. During the 1911 revolution he served briefly under the Shanghai military governor, Ch'en Ch'i-mei, and in 1913, after the failure of the summer insurrection, he accompanied Ch'en to Tokyo, where he was introduced to Sun Yat-sen. When Sun returned to Canton in 1917, Chiang joined him as a staff member. In 1922 he served as chief of staff of Sun's Fukien army, and in 1923 he was sent to Moscow to investigate the Soviet military system, the organization of the Red Army, and the strict discipline of the Russian Communist Party. Chiang's experience in Russia made him particularly attractive to Borodin and the Soviet military advisers.

The new army of the Kuomintang received its baptism under fire in 1924 and 1925, when it helped the party consolidate its position in Canton. The merchants and gentry in and around Canton had organized a military corps to protect themselves against the heavy exactions of the Yunnan and Kwangsi warlords, but by 1924 they were more concerned about the radicalism of the Kuomintang, particularly its support of labor unions and peasant associations. In this concern they had allies in the British commercial community at Hong Kong, which assumed that it would be the first anti-imperialist target of the Kuomintang-Soviet coalition. As a preventative measure the British began to agitate among the Cantonese merchants for support of Ch'en Ch'iung-ming and other warlords in order to overturn the Kuomintang regime. A clash was precipitated in October, 1924, when Sun ordered the confiscation of a consignment of rifles which were being imported for use by the merchants' corps, and in just a few days the Kuomintang army was able to disband the corps. In February, 1925, Ch'en, who still enjoyed military control over most of Kwangtung, threatened the city, but he was beaten off by the Kuomintang army and by peasant attacks upon his rear, which cut his communications and supplies. He fell back and gave up his plan to take the city.

Sun Yat-sen had always clung to the hope that China could be united without recourse to a prolonged civil war. He called upon the northern warlords, principally Chang Tso-lin and Tuan Ch'i-jui, to take simultaneous military action against the Peking government of Wu P'ei-fu. Wu, however, fell from power in 1924 because of the defection of his first lieutenant, Feng Yu-hsiang, one of the most colorful of the warlord personalities. He began life as a coolie but soon turned soldier, seeking a precarious livelihood among the mercenaries of the dynasty. Working his way up in the ranks, he finally entered Peiyang Military Academy at Paoting, where he was famous for his capacity for work. At first a subordinate of Yuan Shih-k'ai, he later served under Wu P'ei-fu, and, with Wu's support at the Tientsin Conference in 1921, he became warlord of Shensi. A seemingly ardent convert to Christianity, this "Christian general" baptized his troops with a fire hose, but like most of his warlord contemporaries Feng was dominated by selfish ambition and had few scruples as far as his own personal loyalty was concerned. In October, 1924, he seized control of Peking while Wu was attempting to meet attacks by Chang Tso-lin and Tuan Ch'i-jui. Wu retired to his base of power in Honan, and Peking fell to the coalition of Feng, Chang, and Tuan. Tuan, the senior warlord, became president of the new regime. Conscious of the rising power of the Kuomintang, the Peking coalition invited Sun to collaborate in an attempt to unite China under one government.

Sun accepted, but Kuomintang opinions concerning the meeting were divided. Radicals and communists objected on the chance that Sun would compromise with the warlords, but conservative members, anxious to secure political power, looked forward to an expedient settlement. Sun explained that the aim of the nationalist revolution still was to eradicate the warlords permanently and to abolish all unequal treaties; moreover, he advocated the convocation of a national people's assembly, preceded by a preparatory conference. However, when he arrived in Peking on December 31, Sun discovered that Chang and his colleagues had already worked out their plans on terms unacceptable to him. Sun had gone to Peking a sick man, so sick that he had to be hospitalized there on January 26, 1925. An exploratory operation revealed that he was suffering from an incurable cancer of the liver and that his days were numbered. He died in Peking on March 12 after undergoing another operation in an effort to prolong his life. One of his last acts was to dispatch a message to the Soviet Union, asking for her continued assistance to the revolution. Stalin reaffirmed the support of the Russian Communist Party in a telegram received after Sun's death, and Zinoviev cabled similar assurance on the part of the Comintern.

Sun Yat-sen was transformed almost overnight into a legendary hero and patron saint of the Kuomintang. As one of his more critical Western biographers, Lyon Sharman, has pointed out, he became a national symbol: a symbol of unity in the Kuomintang, a symbol of disinterested love of country, a symbol of his country's purpose to reconstruct herself along modern lines after the manner of the West, a symbol of the unfinished revolution, and a symbol of the very idea of democracy. His *Three Principles of the People* became the party bible and the promise of a brighter future. Sharman has written: "In spite of all his mistakes and ineptitude, his inconsistencies of thought, his blindness to them, and his shifting of opinions, he was regarded as a fount of wisdom. Perhaps this was because he was the epitome of the groping Chinese intellectual of his day." The dates of his birth and death later became national holidays.

Factional Struggles in the Kuomintang

While Sun Yat-sen was alive, he had been able to maintain a substantial degree of unity among the several factions that made up the Kuomintang—especially the radicals and the conservatives, who differed on the necessity of alliance with the Soviet Union and the Chinese Communist Party and on the general aims of the revolution. The radicals, or the so-called "left wing" of the Kuomintang, largely intellectuals and students, supported the alliance with the communists in order to maximize the strength of the various revolutionary forces, and they believed in the need not only to unite China politically but to carry out drastic economic and social reforms. The conservatives, or the so-called "right wing" of the party, tied closely to business and landed interests, felt that the alliance with the communists was unnecessary and dangerous and regarded the revolution as essentially limited to political goals. Of course, many Kuomintang members did not belong to either faction and constituted a kind of center group; for example, Chiang K'ai-shek, who held the key post of commandant of the Whampoa Military Academy, which was training the officer corps of the new revolutionary army of the Kuomintang, belonged to neither the left nor right wing of the party.

After Sun's death, leadership in the Kuomintang passed to the left wing, which was led by Wang Ching-wei, long a revolutionary associate of the party's founder. This was made clear in the establishment of the provisional national government in July, 1925, when Wang Ching-wei succeeded to most of the important posts in the party and administration. He was elected chairman of the national government, of the standing committee of the national government council, of the Kuomintang political council, and of the military council. Of course, in the actual workings of the party-government relationship, the Kuomintang political council was the all-powerful body since it controlled both the national government council and the military council. Another able leftist, Liao Chung-k'ai, who had also been one of Sun's strongest supporters, was named minister of finance and controlled the distribution of funds; moreover, he also served as party representative to the Whampoa Military Academy and the revolutionary army, chief of the labor department, and governor of Kwangtung Province. And in the army, left-wing party members, appointed to serve as liaison officers, had the power to countersign and even countermand the orders of military commanders. Their duties also included ideological training and the maintenance of party discipline. After Liao Chung-k'ai was assassinated during a party factional struggle in August, 1925, a young communist, Chou En-lai, succeeded to the post of political commissar of the army. Chou had recently returned from France, where he had helped to organize a communist youth corps among his fellow students.

The position of the left wing within the Kuomintang was further strengthened when Canton became the center of an anti-imperialist movement that had been developing for several years. For example, in the early months of 1925 violence attended a series of strikes for wage increases by textile workers in Japanese mills at Shanghai and Tsingtao. Several strikers were shot down in Tsingtao, and at Shanghai a Chinese worker was murdered by a Japanese foreman. The climax came on May 30 when students and workers organized a protest parade in the International Settlement. When several of the marchers were arrested, demonstrators massed before the police station and demanded the release of their comrades. The police, on the orders of a British sergeant, fired on the mob and killed thirteen people. The incident provoked a general strike supported by virtually the entire population, and business at Shanghai came to a standstill. The situation did not return to normal until the end of the summer, when a warlord subordinate of Chang Tso-lin closed down the communist-dominated Shanghai General Labor Union led by the young, dynamic Li Li-san. Meanwhile, however, the anti-imperialist agitation had assumed national proportions as antiforeign outbreaks, resulting in loss of life and property damage, occurred in widely scattered points, even spreading to the interior city of Chungking. In Canton on June 23 approximately forty Chinese were killed and one hundred seventeen were wounded by British and French troops during demonstrations opposite the foreign concessions to protest the Shanghai incident. Among those dead were four university students and twenty-four cadets of the Whampoa Military Academy.

Many of the Kuomintang leaders, particularly the military, threatened a direct attack on the British-held Shameen Island. Chiang K'ai-shek was especially outspoken in a speech to the military council on July 26 in which he accused imperialist countries, particularly Great Britain, of backing Chinese warlords and other enemies of the Kuomintang. "How can we tolerate this? We must resolutely attack them until they are all eliminated!" Borodin, however, warned against any precipitate action, and in September he pressed the Kuomintang leaders to settle the strike that followed the incident in Canton. Borodin and his superiors in Moscow evidently feared that the British might unite with Wu P'ei-fu to crush the fledgling National-ist regime. For the next fifteen months a successful boycott of all British goods and a general strike of Chinese workmen paralyzed business at Hong Kong. British trade losses were tremendous. The new provisional national government demanded that the British retrocede the Canton concessions and withdraw their vessels from Kwangtung waters; and the workers at Hong Kong demanded the right to vote in the selection of Chinese representatives in the government of the colony, improvement of working conditions, pro-hibition of child labor, and enforcement of an eight-hour day. The British, however, refused to negotiate.

Meanwhile, factional differences which continued to divide the Kuomin-tang grew wider and threatened to disrupt its organization. In November, 1925, conservative members of the central executive committee met in Peking before the coffin of Sun Yat-sen in the Western Hills and drew up a program asking for the dismissal of the Russian advisers and the expulsion of the com-munists from the Kuomintang. The dominant left-wing authorities at Canton declared that these resolutions were illegal since the central executive com-mittee did not have a quorum, and they decided to convene a party congress to consider the issues and to decide on punishment for the Western Hills faction, which was already beginning to set up a separate party organization at Shanghai. The Second Party Congress, controlled by a left-wing majority, reconfirmed the alliances, expelled the Western Hills faction, and approved the adoption of communist methods of agitation and propaganda. Wang Ching-wei reasoned that the Kuomintang and its allies were pursuing the same immediate objectives—the overthrow of imperialism and warlordism— and although he admitted that there were basic long-range differences, he emphasized that these did not bear upon the more immediate problems. Borodin and the Chinese Communist Party for their own purposes supported Wang's point of view.

There can be no doubt that the Chinese communists were increasing their power within the Kuomintang. Seven of their number were elected to the central executive committee, the membership of which was expanded from 24 to 36, and, of these, 3 were elected to the 9-man standing committee. Moreover, they controlled two important departments. Lin Tsu-han headed the peasant department, and under the leadership of T'an P'ing-shan 26 of the 29 persons on the staff of the organization department were communists. Communists also served as secretaries of the labor, youth, overseas, merchants, and women's departments. Finally, Liu Fen, another communist, was chief secretary at central party headquarters.

However, co-operation between the Kuomintang and its Soviet and Chinese communist allies was not so evident in the military field. In fact, Chiang K'ai-shek, certainly the most important officer in the revolutionary army, was beginning to have serious disagreements with his Russian advisers. Chiang was anxious to launch the military phase of the revolution, i.e., the so-called "Northern March" from Canton to destroy the warlords and unite China militarily and politically. And when the Russian officers advised him that his plans were premature, he regarded them as obstructionists and began to take steps to restrict their power. Moreover, he came to be alarmed over the activities of the communists within the Kuomintang; and there is no doubt that right-wing elements in the party played upon his fears, emphasizing that Wang Ching-wei and the communists were blocking his plans.

Chiang K'ai-shek took power into his own hands on March 20 when he declared a state of martial law in Canton. Under the pretext of an impending communist *coup d'état*, Chiang used his military power to carry out a sweeping series of arrests, which included members of the left wing, communists, and all political workers attached to his command, most of them communists. Although Borodin was in the north, conferring with the warlord Feng Yu-hsiang regarding military operations against Peking, Chiang dismissed a small group of Russian military advisers and sent them back to Russia. Chiang K'ai-shek was master at Canton, but not all his initial actions were pleasing to the conservatives. On April 3 he issued a manifesto which supported the Russian alliance and promised arrest and court martial to any critic of this policy who appeared at Canton. On the following day he issued a circular telegram condemning a second congress held by the Western Hills faction at Shanghai, and in subsequent speeches he denounced "the alliance between the right wing and the imperialists." When right-wing demonstrations were planned at Canton, he ordered suspected right-wing members dismissed from the Kuomintang. On April 16, in a speech at the Whampoa Military Academy, Chiang expressed the opinion that the Chinese revolution was organically related to the world revolution and that the Kuomintang would accept the assistance of the Comintern. At the end of the month Borodin returned from the north, and Chiang's relations with him were cordial. In fact, Borodin appointed other Russians to the advisory posts vacated by those with whom Chiang had disagreed. Evidently Chiang and the Russians had agreed that the time had come for the Kuomintang armies to drive north.

Wang Ching-wei was the most important casualty of Chiang's coup. On March 20, when he learned of Chiang's actions, he denounced him as a counterrevolutionary, but shortly thereafter he dropped from sight. When he continued to remain in seclusion despite Chiang's offer to resign, the central executive committee of the party proceeded to make appointments to the posts that he held. On April 16, in a meeting with the national government council, it elected T'an Yen-k'ai as chairman of the political council and Chiang as chairman of the military council. After this turn of events, Wang officially retired and left Canton on May 9 with Paris as his ultimate destination.

Later in May the central executive committee redefined the relationship between the Kuomintang and the Chinese communists. The communists were permitted to remain in the party, but they were ineligible for election as heads of departments, and the number of communists who might become members of governing bodies of the Kuomintang or of the provisional government was not to exceed one-third of the total in any case. The Chinese Communist Party, moreover, was to submit to the direction of a joint committee of five Nationalists and three communists, with a representative of the Comintern as political adviser. Finally, it was to hand over a list of its members so that the Kuomintang would know against whom to enforce the adjustment. Borodin retained his position as chief political adviser and went so far as to praise Chiang for his actions against those "too far to the left."

These events created strong pressures among the Chinese communists to regain a position of political independence, and in June the central committee of the Chinese Communist Party proposed to Moscow that it replace the existing relationship with the Kuomintang by a formal two-party alliance. Josef Stalin, who was emerging as the dominant leader in the Kremlin, rejected the request and ordered the Chinese Communist Party to continue its efforts "of directing the entire Kuomintang to the left and guaranteeing it a stable left policy." Stalin was committed to policies based on the two-stage theory of revolution, which implied the hegemony of the bourgeoisie in the first stage. He characterized the Chinese revolution as a fight for independence by the Kuomintang, which, he claimed, was not a bourgeois party but a community of interests. To dissolve this coalition would be a heavy blow to the communist cause in China. Evidently Stalin and Borodin felt that Chiang's recent actions had given no cause to abandon hope that the Kuomintang could still be controlled. Ch'en Tu-hsiu, however, thought that the Kuomintang had been captured by what he called the "new warlords." In this view he was supported in part by Leon Trotsky's theses directed against Stalin's China policy.

Russian policy for China had become involved in the struggle, following Lenin's death, between the new communist bureaucrats and the old revolutionaries, which continued until Trotsky's complete defeat in 1927. Trotsky and his colleagues, Zinoviev and Kamenev, warned that the Chinese Communist Party would be destroyed by the reactionary bourgeoisie, which would compromise with imperialism and turn on the masses. In fact, Trotsky had opposed the original instructions to the Chinese Communist Party to join the Kuomintang. He asked this question: How can we overlook the fact that in Russia the bourgeois and proletarian revolutions were fused in one and then revert in the case of China to the notion of rigidly separated stages in the revolutionary process? He had his own answer. It was because the Soviet regime desperately wanted to convert the Chinese bourgeoisie into an ally against Western imperialism, and thus it unwisely proceeded to endow it with an infinite revolutionary capacity. The clear implication was that Stalin was subordinating the Chinese revolutionary movement to Russian national interests at the expense of the international socialist revolution—a trend which Lenin actually initiated through Russian domination of the Comintern and, through it, of communist parties abroad. Trotsky maintained that, with the world maturing for socialism, it was both possible and necessary in the case of the underdeveloped areas to skip over the stage of capitalism and bourgeois democracy. And it could be done in China, he thought, if the urban working class cast aside the bourgeoisie, who were not capable of leading the country through these changes, and struck out on its own by establishing soviets at Shanghai and Canton and by expanding the agrarian movement against the landlords. Once in power the workers could set out to make over the economy and political institutions of the country on the basis of social ownership of the means of production.

The Northern March

By the late spring of 1926 the Kuomintang, under the leadership of Chiang K'ai-shek, was ready to begin the military campaign to unite China under its banner. An emergency plenum of the central executive committee on June 4 appointed Chiang as commander-in-chief and abolished the military council to give him a firm control. And later, on July 5, the party appointed him chief of the military personnel department with power to select and dismiss party representatives in military units. Finally, on the following day, he was formally elected as chairman of the standing committee of the party's central executive committee. One of his first duties was to direct the negotiations with the British to settle the Hong Kong strike and boycott. Although the talks, which began in July, collapsed when the Kuomintang attempted to hold up the British for a $10,000,000 loan, in October the provisional government at Canton called off the strike and boycott. By this time the armies of the Kuomintang were already driving north, and Chiang was anxious to minimize differences with the foreign powers.

One of the basic goals of the Northern March was to destroy the enemy warlords, and by 1926 their position was as follows. In November, 1925, the Peking coalition headed by Tuan Ch'i-jui collapsed. Chang Tso-lin sought to impose his will upon the city but found himself blocked by his colleague, Feng Yu-hsiang, and a former subordinate in Manchuria, Kuo Sung-ling. The latter had been influenced by the Soviet envoy, Karakhan, and he was assisted by the Russian manager of the Chinese Eastern Railway, Ivanov, who refused to let Chang transport his troops against Kuo on the pretext that Chang had failed to pay for earlier services. Chang had for some time pursued an anti-Russian policy in Manchuria, and there had been one dispute after another over the Chinese Eastern Railway. Japanese troops, in support of Chang, moved against Kuo in December, and Chang arrested Ivanov, who was re-placed temporarily by a Russian of Chang's own choosing. Karakhan urged his government to send in troops, but the realization that this would cause Japanese intervention on a large scale prevented Russian action. Thus Kuo was defeated. Chang Tso-lin also got unexpected support from Wu P'ei-fu, who had reformed his armies with the backing of British commercial interests. Feng Yu-hsiang, who had occupied Tientsin, was caught between Chang and Wu, and he gave up the fight and fled the country, accepting a Russian invitation to visit Moscow. He later returned to the northwest, establishing his headquarters at Kalgan, and with Russian assistance built a peasant army. Thus Chang Tso-lin emerged as the dominant northern warlord, holding sway over four provinces—Chihli and three in Manchuria—and by June, 1926, he repudiated the moribund republic and established a simple military dictatorship at Peking. His major ally, Chang Tsung-ch'ang, controlled Shantung, while Wu P'ei-fu once again retired to the central Yangtze Valley, where he controlled Hupeh and Honan provinces.

Other prominent warlords included Yen Hsi-shan, the so-called model governor, in control of Shansi; Sun Ch'uan-fang, based at Nanking and governing five provinces—Fukien, Kiangsu, Kiangsi, Anhwei, and Chekiang, including control of Shanghai; and T'ang Sheng-chih, professed ally of the Kuomintang, in Hunan and ready to challenge Wu P'ei-fu.

The plan of the Kuomintang military expedition—the Northern March, which got under way in July, 1926—was to drive through Hunan Province toward Hankow and through Kiangsi Province to Shanghai, and, once these objectives were taken, the Kuomintang armies would drive toward Peking along the Peking-Hankow and Tientsin-Pukow railway lines. Chiang, personally commanding the eastern front, met with strong resistance in Kiangsi Province, with Nanchang, the capital city, exchanging hands three times between his forces and those of Sun Ch'uan-fang. In fact, he did not reach the south bank of the Yangtze River until November 5, and then the coming of winter compelled a suspension of hostilities. The armies driving on Hankow, commanded by T'ang Sheng-chih, Chang Fa-kuei, and Li Tsung-jen, had a much easier time of it, partly because advance political workers, largely communists, weakened Wu P'ei-fu's hold on the area. Peasants welcomed the Kuomintang, and large numbers of Wu's soldiers defected. He finally gave up the struggle and retired to study Buddhism and write poetry. Hanyang fell to the revolutionaries on September 6, Hankow on September 7, and Wuchang on October 10. These three cities are known collectively as Wuhan.

The transfer of the Nationalist government from Canton to Hankow began in November. At Hankow the left wing of the Kuomintang sought to re-establish the party's power over the military and particularly over Chiang K'ai-shek. Despite Chiang's opposition, a joint session of the central executive committee and delegates from various provincial organizations passed a resolution inviting Wang Ching-wei to return and resume the chairmanship of the different councils in the party and government. When many of the army commanders accepted this decision and when Borodin and the Chinese communists threw their support behind the left wing, Chiang himself began to see that perhaps the only way to maintain discipline in the revolution was to co-operate with Wang.

In the autumn and winter of 1926–1927 the Kuomintang became increasingly radical. Borodin and the Russian advisers regarded the transfer of the Nationalist government to the Wuhan area as an opportunity to direct the revolution to the left, as Stalin had ordered, and in this regard the Chinese communists were especially active in organizing laborers and peasants. They rapidly organized labor unions in Hunan and Hupeh provinces under the aegis of the All-China Federation of Labor, which claimed 300,000 workers in the Wuhan area alone, and they continually plagued Wuchang and Hankow with strikes. In the rural areas the communists by the end of January, 1927, claimed that ten million peasants had joined peasant associations—with two million in Hunan Province alone—which advocated rent reduction and the abolition of the worst of the miscellaneous excise taxes. In villages where authority fell completely to peasant associations, tenant farmers refused to pay rents and began to seize the land outright.

The Chinese Communist Party exploited these successes to win new

419

members, and by the spring of 1927 it claimed a membership of 50,000. Despite increases in its power, the party was under orders from Moscow to maintain its alliance with the Kuomintang, which was still designated a coalition party of labor, peasantry, petty bourgeoisie, and national bourgeoisie. Stalin continued to insist that any split with the Kuomintang would mean abandoning the masses, but in December, 1926, he did acknowledge through the Comintern that the Chinese communists should make a direct bid for "proletarian hegemony within the Kuomintang." Stalin was directing the Chinese communists to walk a political tightrope. If they continued to question the alliance with the Kuomintang, they could be accused of abandoning the peasantry and the petty bourgeoisie, and, if they did not succeed in capturing leadership of the Kuomintang, they could be accused of having sabotaged the radical strategy of the Comintern.

The Factional Struggle Continued

The increasingly radical bent of the revolution brought factional differences in the Kuomintang into open conflict once again. Chiang K'ai-shek had not opposed the transfer of the Nationalist government to Hankow, which began in November, but in the following month he became alarmed by the excesses of the labor and peasant movements in the Wuhan area and by the increased influence of the communists, who, he was convinced, were a menace to the Chinese revolution. Thus he wanted the seat of the Nationalist government transferred to Nanchang, and on January 7, 1927, a number of party leaders at Nanchang voted to remain there temporarily. And in an effort to overcome the objections of the left wing, Chiang made a trip to Hankow on January 11, but he failed to get its approval of the shift. After his return to Nanchang, Chiang announced openly his intention of crushing the communists, and later, on March 7, he delivered a tirade against Borodin and the other Russian advisers, who supported the left-wing refusal to move to Nanchang.

The left wing at Hankow retaliated quickly by convoking a meeting of the central executive committee, which Chiang and his supporters did not attend, to reorganize the party and the government under the slogan "Return all power—political, military, financial, foreign affairs—to the Party." In order to limit Chiang's power, the left-wing-dominated central executive committee established a seven-man presidium of the political council as the supreme authority in the party, in effect replacing the chairman (Chiang) and the standing committee of the central executive committee; and it re-established the military council in an effort to strengthen party authority over Chiang and the other field commanders. In elections to party and government posts, the left wing won controlling positions in all organs, and there was no doubt as to who was its leader. Wang Ching-wei, who had not yet returned from France, was elected to the presidium of the political council, the standing committee of the central executive committee, the military council, and the national government council. Not wanting to break completely with Chiang K'ai-shek, the left wing elected him to the standing committee, the military council, and the national government council but not to the powerful presidium of the political council. He was also replaced by Wang as head of the important organization department.

The central executive committee meeting also endorsed the labor unions and peasant associations and called for closer co-operation between the Kuomintang and the Chinese Communist Party. T'an P'ing-shan, Chinese representative to the Comintern, was appointed minister of the peasantry, and Su Chao-ching, a former Hong Kong butcher who had become prominent in the labor movement, became minister of labor. Communist penetration of party organs, however, was restricted as before. Only two communists were elected to the nine-man standing committee, no communist was elected to the sixteen-man military council, and, in keeping with the central executive committee resolution of May, 1926, no communist headed a party department.

The left wing at Hankow also renewed the attack against foreign imperialism, again concentrating on the British. In January, 1926, under the threat of mob violence, Great Britain abandoned her concessions at Hankow and Kiukiang, and by March she relinquished these in a formal agreement with the Hankow government. The left wing took no measures against the Japanese and French concessions, and it permitted the Russians and Germans to continue to do business in the concessions areas which they had already given up. But in March revolutionary troops at Nanking carried out a general attack on the foreign community. The American, British, French, Italian and Japanese consulates were besieged, and foreign nationals were killed, wounded, or subjected to various atrocities. British and American gunboats were forced to land marines and to lay a protective barrage around the properties of the Standard Oil Company, where the foreigners had taken refuge. The foreign powers demanded an apology, reparations, and guarantees for the future, and they reinforced their troops in Peking, Tientsin, and Shanghai.

Chiang K'ai-shek, meanwhile, moved his forces north from Nanchang and in March was able to enter Shanghai in the wake of a general labor uprising that weakened the forces of the local warlord, Chang Tsung-ch'ang. Earlier, on February 19, the Shanghai unions under communist influence began a general strike, which was suppressed with great brutality by warlord troops; but on March 21 the General Labor Union called another strike, which was soon transformed into a successful labor insurrection. Once in Shanghai, Chiang was able to force financial support from the business community and the right-wing Kuomintang politicians; furthermore, members of the Hankow government who were disturbed by the growing strength of the communists joined him.

Fearing a complete split among the revolutionary forces, Chiang K'ai-shek did make a last effort at reconciliation with Wang Ching-wei, the favorite of the left-wing group, who returned to China on April 1. Passing through Shanghai on his way to Hankow to take office, he met Chiang, who on April 3 issued a declaration in which he proclaimed his obedience to the central executive committee and submitted to Wang's political leadership but reserved military power for himself. Wang agreed to convene a plenum of the central executive committee at Nanking, considered by both men to be a more neutral site, in order to discuss the demand of Chiang and others for the dismissal of Borodin and the ouster of the communists from the Kuomintang. Yet, before he departed for Hankow to persuade the left-wing central executive committee members to meet with Chiang at Nanking, Wang made clear his own position on the communist issue. Together with the communist leader, Ch'en Tu-hsiu, he issued a statement reaffirming the alliance between the Kuomintang and the Chinese Communist Party. Wang was evidently satisfied that the communists would continue to remain loyal to the Kuomintang and accept Sun Yat-sen's Three Principles of the People as the ideological basis of the revolution.

Disappointed by Wang's stand, Chiang finally broke completely with the left wing at Hankow and set up an alternate revolutionary government at Nanking. On April 12 the uneasy relationship between Chiang and the Shanghai unions ended when his troops turned on the workers and slaughtered them. Among a few communist leaders who escaped was Chiang's former colleague at the Whampoa Military Academy, Chou En-lai, who estimated that 5,000 union members lost their lives. Three days later Chiang informed Wang that he would not accept the orders of the Hankow government until it broke with the communists; moreover, he demanded that labor unions be made subject to the orders of local military commanders. However, Wang stood fast against the expulsion of the communists and joined again with Ch'en Tu-hsiu in issuing a statement of unity of purpose. It is interesting to note that Ch'en later claimed that his actions in this period were determined by Comintern pressure and were contrary to his own thinking. He explained that the politicians and generals of the Hankow regime seemed to him hardly more trustworthy than those supporting Chiang. Finally, the split within the Kuomintang was complete when Chiang, along with Hu Han-min, Chang Ching-chiang, and other conservatives moved upriver to Nanking, where on the 18th they established the new revolutionary government and invited the support of all those who were opposed to communism. At Hankow the central executive committee under Wang's leadership retaliated by formally reading Chiang and other conservatives out of the party.

The Fifth National Congress of the Chinese Communist Party, held from April 27 to early May, officially interpreted these events as follows. Chiang, as representative of the bourgeoisie, had led his class into an alliance with feudalism and imperialism in order to suppress the mass movement of workers and peasants, which was still allied with the petty bourgeoisie and the Hankow government. Chiang's Nanking regime was thus a counterrevolutionary union of the bourgeois-feudal Kuomintang elements and the imperialists, while Hankow stood for a purified Kuomintang of the workers, peasants, and petty bourgeoisie. This interpretation was imposed by Moscow as a means of alibiing Chiang's defection, which was explained as a progressive step, purifying the revolutionary Kuomintang. Ch'en Tu-hsiu, however, wanted to bolt the alliance with the Kuomintang left wing and preserve the gains which the Chinese Communist Party had already made. It is interesting to note that the Hankow government was already beginning to depend on the support of General T'ang Sheng-chih, the warlord owner of many landed estates in Hunan, who had turned against Chiang in order to supplant him.

In the spring of 1927 the Kuomintang left wing at Hankow became increasingly concerned about the rising power of the communist-led labor unions and peasant associations. Left-wing leaders began to realize that the revolution was taking a more radical course than they had expected. Labor agitation and strikes crippled local industry, and the unions pressured the government to take over banks, factories, and shops. In fact, during May the workers at Hanyang confiscated fifteen private factories and then organized workmen's councils to manage them. In a meeting of the political council of the Kuomintang, Wang Ching-wei proposed to take measures for the security of commerce and industry, and, although there was serious disagreement, the proposal carried. Moreover, the majority of Kuomintang left-wing politicians indicated that they were ready to break with the labor movement. In the countryside the peasant movement caused a similar reaction. The ferocity of peasant demands for lower rents and for land redistribution, by force if necessary, went beyond the intentions of the Kuomintang left-wing leaders. In the political council the communist members proposed without success that the Kuomintang experiment in Hunan Province with the policy of land equalization, and when the communists attempted to implement an unauthorized policy of land confiscation through the provincial Kuomintang and the provincial government, Kuomintang troops at the provincial capital, Changsha, on May 21 and 22 attacked the headquarters of the peasant associations and labor unions, massacred their leaders, whom they denounced as communists, and destroyed their organizations. This attack was followed by a general assault on peasant associations throughout the province.

While these events were seriously straining the alliance between the Kuomintang left wing and the communists, Russian influence at Hankow was discredited when it was disclosed that Moscow was using the revolution for its own purposes. Early in 1927 Chang Tso-lin began to crack down on communist activities in Peking, and a group of Chinese, including Li Ta-chao of the National University, sought refuge in the Soviet embassy. On March 1 Chang's agents seized large quantities of communist propaganda from a Russian steamer detained at Pukow on its way to Hankow, and among several Russians arrested was the wife of Borodin, traveling on a diplomatic passport. On March 20 the authorities at Peking conducted a general search of schools and colleges and arrested a number of students. The climax to these efforts came on April 6, when Chang Tso-lin, ignoring diplomatic immunities, raided the Soviet embassy and seized documentary evidence concerning the real purposes of the Soviet Union and the Chinese Communist Party. Li Ta-chao and sixty communists were arrested, and Li was shortly thereafter executed. Within a few months, moreover, Hankow learned more directly of Soviet intentions. Stalin, handicapped by lack of information from China, continued to insist that the workers and peasants co-operate with the Hankow government, but at the same time he also ordered the Chinese communists to form their own army and to permit land confiscations, with only land of the military exempted. He urged the communists to eliminate unreliable generals and to effect a purge of reactionary elements from the central executive committee of the Kuomintang in order to increase communist, labor, and peasant leadership in the party and government organs. Ch'en Tu-hsiu has summed up the dilemma that these orders created for the Chinese Communist Party. "The Comintern asks us to implement our own policies. On the other hand, it will not allow us to withdraw from the Kuomintang. There is thus no way out." To achieve closer collaboration between the Kuomintang and the Chinese Communist Party, the Indian communist, M. N. Roy, indiscreetly showed Stalin's instructions, telegraphed on June 1, to Wang Ching-wei. Roy told Wang that the telegram was the equivalent of an ultimatum. If the Kuomintang co-operated, the Comintern would continue its assistance, but, if not, the Comintern would have nothing to do with the Kuomintang.

Wang Ching-wei and the Hankow regime began to suppress the mass movement and to expel members of the Chinese Communist Party from positions of power. For another month, however, the Chinese Communist Party continued to recognize the Kuomintang left wing as the leader of the revolution, for not until July did Moscow finally order it to "trust to your own forces alone." It withdrew from the Hankow government but at the same time announced that it "had no reason to leave the Kuomintang or to refuse to co-operate with it." Moscow instructed the communists to persuade the mass of the members of the Kuomintang to demand that the party rid itself of its reactionary leaders. Stalin in this way kept the Chinese Communist Party ideologically pure, but he could not prevent its expulsion from the Kuomintang on July 15. The central executive committee, however, was willing to recognize the Chinese Communist Party, with its individual members having full rights of citizenship provided that they did not interfere with Kuomintang activities.

Finally, on July 30, at Nanchang in Kiangsi Province, military forces under Ho Lung and Yeh T'ing declared their independence from Hankow and formed a revolutionary committee under communist control. This uprising was crushed, and Hankow banned the Chinese Communist Party as an illegal organization. Despite these events, the Hankow regime was anxious not to alienate Moscow's support, and in fact for a time Wang Ching-wei planned to send a delegation to Russia to strengthen Chinese-Russian friendship. Borodin, who had wanted to resign for some time, left Hankow with full honors. He was joined by his wife, who was released from captivity by Chang Tsung-ch'ang, and they both returned to the Soviet Union after a brief stay with the warlord Feng Yu-hsiang at Loyang. In the end, however, Hankow found it impracticable to continue close relations with Russia.

The Conclusion of the Northern March

In the weeks that followed there was the beginning of a *rapprochement* between the Hankow and Nanking regimes. Working through Feng Yu-hsiang as mediator, Hankow undertook to unite the revolutionary movement under the authority of the central executive committee of the Kuomintang. Chiang K'ai-shek, however, wanted to settle the matter by a test of arms; but when news came from the north that his troops had been defeated by Chang Tsung-ch'ang and Sun Ch'uan-fang, he had to postpone the conflict. In fact, within a few days he was forced into retirement by his warlord allies, Li Tsung-jen and Pai Chung-hsi, who demanded a reconciliation with Hankow. In a telegram dispatched on August 8, these two Kwangsi generals proposed the convocation of a plenary session of the central executive committee to settle all outstanding questions and invited the Hankow members to meet at Nanking. Wang's reply on August 10 agreed to the meeting, but it suggested Hankow as the site. After this exchange, Chiang's resignation from the Nanking group was made public on April 15, and he left for Shanghai, accompanied by his personal bodyguard of four hundred men and by conservative politicians like Hu Han-min and Chang Ching-chiang.

Wang Ching-wei and his Hankow colleagues finally joined forces with the Nanking government in September, but the new unity of the Kuomintang was short-lived, as quarrels between the left and right wings continued unabated. During the autumn Wang and others, like T. V. Soong, withdrew their support and went to Canton, where they tried in vain to establish another government. At Nanking the Kwangsi militarists and the conservative Western Hills faction dominated the party and revolutionary government. In November, 1927, Chiang K'ai-shek returned to Shanghai from a brief visit to Japan, and Wang began negotiations with him in order to form a common front against the Nanking regime. But when a communist uprising at Canton completely discredited left-wing policies, Wang once again went into exile. Late in 1927 the Nanking leaders opened negotiations with Chiang, having decided that they could not create a satisfactory civil government during the military stage of the revolution. They were willing to restore Chiang to power, but they got his assurance that at the end of military operations he would resign his command and join in inaugurating the second stage of the revolution, the period of political tutelage.

Chiang's power was confirmed by a reorganization of the Kuomintang and of the government at Nanking in February, 1928. A meeting of a new central executive committee—the first since March, 1927, at Hankow—elected Chiang as chairman, and the majority of its members could be trusted to carry out his policies. The central executive committee also rescinded all resolutions relating to the alliance with the Soviet Union and communist participation in the revolution; moreover, it made provision for a new registration of party members. Chiang was also elected chairman of the national government council, commander-in-chief of the armed forces, and chairman of the military council, which was authorized to issue orders directly to provincial and local governments and to enforce them by military means if necessary. There was only one important limitation set upon Chiang's power. The central executive committee marked August 1, 1928, as a tentative time limit on the period of military dictatorship, for it hoped that by that date a party congress would enact the measures necessary to effect the beginnings of political tutelage.

Chiang's power and the stability of the Nanking government were based in large part on compromise with warlordism. By the spring of 1927 both Feng Yu-hsiang and Yen Hsi-shan had thrown in their lot with the Nationalists. In fact, it was the prospect of a united front between Feng, Yen, and Chiang that helped the various Kuomintang politicians to heal their dissensions, at least temporarily, in order to accomplish the military unification of China. Both Feng and Yen had declared war against the warlord coalition headed by Chang Tso-lin, which still controlled northern Anhwei, Chihli, Shantung, and Manchuria. Feng had announced his support of the Kuomintang on his return from Moscow in September, 1926, and he rallied his scattered armies and forced his way down the Yellow River. He drove Chang's allies from Shensi and in the spring of 1927 attacked the flanks of the northern warlords in Honan, while a Kuomintang army coming up from Hankow drove Chang's troops across the Yellow River. Rapidly consolidating his conquests in the northwest, Feng made it clear that he had to be reckoned with in all plans for the further development of the revolution. In June, 1927, he helped to persuade the Hankow left-wing politicians to turn their backs on the workers' and peasants' movements even at the cost of breaking with the Soviet Union and the Chinese Communist Party. At the same time he made an agreement with Chiang K'ai-shek by which he pledged to join in purging the Kuomintang of communists and to follow Sun Yat-sen's program for China. Later, in the summer of 1927, he urged Hankow to capitulate to the Nanking regime. Both Feng and Yen (who had remained neutral until the summer of 1927, when he joined Chiang against the northern warlords) were represented on the national government council and the military council. Although nominally under the control of the Nationalist government, south China was also dominated by local warlords. For example, at Canton, when the provisional government was transferred to Hankow, beginning in November, 1926, the task of maintaining law and order in Kwangsi and Kwangtung provinces fell to the warlord Li Chi-sen. In fact, even with the defeat of T'ang Sheng-chih, the power of the Nanking regime was effective in only five provinces in the Yangtze Valley. In the areas under their control, the warlords nominated themselves and readily accepted appointments from the central political council of the Kuomintang as heads of branch political councils. The members of the branch councils were nominally selected by Nanking, but in reality they were hand-picked by their warlord chairmen. In many ways the revolution and the establishment of the Nationalist regime covered warlordism with a new garment of respectability.

The Northern March was resumed in May, 1928, with parallel movements toward Peking by the armies of Chiang K'ai-shek, Feng Yu-hsiang, and Yen Hsi-shan. The occupation of Tsinan in Shantung Province by the Japanese, however, stopped the advance of Chiang and threw the burden of the fighting upon his two warlord allies. Japanese policy with regard to China was generally conciliatory in this period, but at times Japan did seek to protect her rights, by force if necessary. The Japanese had not participated in the Nanking bombardment, but the new cabinet under General Tanaka decided to send troops into Shantung to guard Japanese interests. In spite of objections from the Peking and Nanking governments, Japanese troops landed at Tsingtao and began to garrison points along the Tsingtao-Tsinan Railway. On May 1, entering Tsinan, Chiang K'ai-shek demanded the withdrawal of Japanese forces. By May 3 fighting broke out between the Chinese and Japanese, but through the mediation of the British and American consuls an agreement was reached under which the Nationalists were to withdraw from the city to a point six miles away. Since on May 7 there were still several thousand Chinese soldiers in the city, General Fukuda, the Japanese commander, issued a twelve-hour ultimatum demanding a formal apology from Chiang for the earlier fighting, punishment of those responsible, and withdrawal of Chinese troops in accordance with the consular mediation. When Chiang did not capitulate, the Japanese army attacked, and by May 11 it was in control of the city. The Nanking government appealed to the League of Nations for arbitration, but the League took no action, since the Kuomintang regime had not yet been given *de jure* recognition by the powers. When Nanking also failed in an attempt to secure mediation by the United States, Chiang acceded to the Japanese demands. The only effective Chinese resistance was the subsequent boycott of Japanese goods.

By the end of May the armies of Feng Yu-hsiang and Yen Hsi-shan began to encircle Tientsin and Peking, and suddenly, without making any attempt at resistance, Chang Tso-lin ordered a general evacuation to the north. He left the city on June 3 on a special train bound for Mukden, but on the following day, at dawn, his car was blown up at the point where the South Manchurian Railway crossed the Peking-Mukden line. This incident remained a mystery until after World War II, when it was disclosed that the assassination was the act of a Japanese colonel in the Kwantung Army who was convinced that Chang Tso-lin was no longer useful to Japan. The Kwantung Army feared that he was leaning toward collaboration with Great Britain and the United States. At any rate, since the summer of 1927 he had become increasingly anti-Japanese, permitting anti-Japanese demonstrations in Mukden and openly opposing new Japanese railroad projects in Manchuria. The bitter feeling between Chang and the Japanese army reached a climax when General Tanaka advised him to withdraw from China, and he accused the Japanese of assisting Chiang K'ai-shek. Colonel Kawamoto simply volunteered to get rid of him. On June 8 the army of Yen Hsi-shan entered Peking, but Japan prevented Chinese forces from moving into Manchuria. In fact, in July Tokyo warned Chang's son and successor, Chang Hsueh-liang, not to join with Nanking. Chang complied for several months, but in December, 1928, he hoisted the Kuomintang flag and voluntarily accepted union with China. Nanking appointed him governor of Manchuria, Jehol, and a portion of Inner Mongolia as well as commander of the Northeast Frontier Defense Forces.

24 *China under Chiang K'ai-shek, 1928–1937*

The military phase of the revolution was completed, and Chiang K'ai-shek resigned his offices as commander-in-chief of the Kuomintang armies and chairman of the military council, thereby returning to the party much of the power which supposedly had been granted him. The capital of the country was shifted to Nanking, and Peking (Northern Capital) was renamed Peiping (Northern Peace). As a symbol of this transfer the body of Sun Yat-sen was later (June, 1929) brought in a splendid procession from Peiping to its last resting-place in the magnificent granite and marble mausoleum on the side of Purple Mountain at Nanking. The era of political tutelage was beginning, and the Kuomintang had to establish a national administration for that purpose.

The Dictatorship of the Kuomintang

Between August and October, 1928, the central executive committee of the Kuomintang met at Nanking to establish the dictatorship of the party. Chiang K'ai-shek was elected as its chairman and as head of its standing committee, which was composed largely of experienced politicians but which lacked any prominent member of the former Hankow regime. On October 3 the standing committee promulgated principles that were to guide the Kuomintang in the period of political tutelage. The party was formally charged to educate the people in the exercise of the four rights—suffrage, initiative, referendum, and recall—assigned to them by Sun Yat-sen. The five powers— executive, legislative, judicial, examination, and control—were to be vested in the central government at once in order to facilitate the establishment of a constitutional regime as soon as the people were sufficiently experienced in local administration. During the period of political tutelage, sovereign power was placed, in theory at least, in the biannual congresses of the Kuomintang, which would constitute a national representative body; between meetings of the party congress, political power was to be delegated to the central executive committee and its standing committee of nine members, which met weekly. To govern the relationship between party and government, the central executive committee had already established a central political council to supervise and direct the national government on behalf of the party. The central political council was nothing more than an extension of the standing committee, which had Chiang K'ai-shek as its chairman and included the nine standing committeemen and six other leading Kuomintang figures.

The Organic Law of October 10 implemented Sun Yat-sen's five-power constitution under the direction of a state council of twelve to sixteen members and a chairman. The chairman served as president of China and commander-in-chief of the armed forces, and the heads of the five branches *(yuan)* of government were chosen from among its members. The executive yuan, composed of ten ministries and five special commissions, conducted the day-to-day administration of the country and submitted bills to the legislative yuan. The duties of the former military council were relegated under the new system to the ministry of war, but the armies remained under the command of the president. The legislative yuan, composed of forty-nine to ninety-nine appointed members, recommended bills to the state council. The judicial yuan was charged not only with the general administration of justice but also with disciplinary action against officials. One of its most important responsibilities was the drafting of codes of law and procedure that would enable China to persuade the foreign powers to relinquish extraterritoriality. The examination yuan was responsible for testing the qualifications of candidates for office, and the control yuan was to supervise such testing and act as watchdog of the government in rooting out inefficiency and corruption.

In operation the government and the Kuomintang were a series of interlocking directorates dominated by a relatively small group of politicians and generals. An analysis of government personnel forces the conclusion that the examination yuan assumed that party membership was *prima facie* evidence of competence; moreover, the same individuals served on the standing committee and the central political council of the party and the state council of the government. Chiang K'ai-shek was chairman of each and president of China, and his colleagues on these councils served as heads of four of the five yuan and filled six ministerial posts. There was no provision for the popular election of any of the members of the national government. The bridge between the party and the government was the party's central political council, the equivalent of the Politburo of the Russian Communist Party. Its powers included jurisdiction over general problems of national reconstruction, legislation, administrative policies, and important military matters; revision or amendment of the Organic Law; and appointment of state councilors, heads of yuan, chairmen of special administrative commissions, and ministers. Had the political council remained small, composed of only the top party leaders, it is conceivable that a collective leadership might have emerged, but it grew large and unwieldy, facilitating Chiang's dominance. His power was further enhanced by the fact that he was careful to maintain personal command of the army. In March, 1929, he established a general headquarters of the commander-in-chief distinct from the national government, and he subordinated the general staff board, the inspectorate-general, and the war council to it. Although the ministries of war and navy were in theory subject to the orders of the executive yuan, they were in fact brought under the direct command of Chiang.

Provincial government, like the organization of the Kuomintang, was based on the principle of democratic centralism, but in actual administration local autonomy was tolerated where warlord strength persisted. The Nanking regime was forced to recognize the existence of regional warlordism, and at Canton, Hankow, Kaifeng, Taiyuan, Peiping, and Mukden it established branch political councils of the Kuomintang under the leadership of the regional warlords, who were in most cases also members of the state council of the central government. Through these branch councils and lower provincial councils of the Kuomintang the warlords and their subordinates were able to dominate local government in much the same way that the Kuomintang dominated the central government. Local autonomy was particularly evident in matters of finance. According to a report of the finance minister in 1929, not more than five provinces made any pretense of remitting revenues to Nanking, apart from those pledged for the repayment of foreign loans, and only two of them furnished the bulk of the revenue that supported the national government.

The district, or *hsien*, was to become the principal area of operation for the political education of the people. The hsien magistrate continued as the local administrative officer, and he was appointed by and responsible to the governor of a province. New legislation, however, required the establishment of political councils elected by the inhabitants of the hsien to advise the magistrate in matters of policy. The hsien budget and proposed by-laws were to be submitted to the political council for discussion and were not to go into effect without its approval. Finally, for administrative purposes the hsien was divided into urban and rural subdistricts, based on the distribution of population between towns and villages.

In March, 1929, the Third Congress of the Kuomintang met to approve these political acts, and the 366 delegates representing 420,000 party members who met at Nanking were a carefully selected group. Less than one-fifth of the representatives were elected; the remainder were appointed by the standing committee or by local party organs in such a way as to guarantee their support of Chiang and the top party leaders. The so-called "left wing" that had followed Wang Ching-wei was not represented; in fact, Wang had recently been censured by the party for breaches of discipline. In retaliation, Wang and thirteen other prominent members of the party issued a manifesto on March 12 declaring the congress illegal.

The congress was actually little more than a rubber stamp of the standing committee. It approved the political changes, and the delegates listened to reports of government ministers and endorsed their projects for national reconstruction. The only important innovation was the dissolution of the regional branch political councils of the party, but there was still no solution to the problem of the distribution of power between the central and provincial governments. Lastly, provision was made for another party congress after two years. The main purpose of the Third Congress was carried out: to proclaim the authority of the party to govern the country during the period of political tutelage. Several months later, in June, the central executive committee issued a manifesto pledging itself to establish local self-government and promising that the period of tutelage would terminate by July, 1935.

In 1929 Chiang K'ai-shek began to take steps to eliminate the military power of the major warlords, who stood in the way of real unification. In February he invited Feng Yu-hsiang, Yen Hsi-shan, Li Tsung-jen, and Li Chi-sen to a Troop Disbandment Conference at Nanking. In July, 1928, these generals had pledged a military reduction before the tomb of Sun Yat-sen at Peking, but at the Nanking meeting they showed little interest in dissolving their armies. Chiang proposed that the combination of forces then totaling over 2,000,000 men be replaced by a modern standing army of 600,000 and a gendarmerie of an additional 200,000. The warlords, however, feared this concentration of military power in the hands of Chiang and his Whampoa officers and would not agree. Chiang proceeded to implement his plan to create a relatively small but well-disciplined national army, and for this end he hired a German military mission. Much of the development of the national government's military training program, which was centered at the new Central Military Academy at Nanking under Chiang's control, was dominated by German concepts and owed much to General Hans von Seeckt and his principal assistants, Wetzel and von Falkenhausen.

When persuasion failed, Chiang K'ai-shek turned to the use of force to diminish the power of the warlords. In March, 1929, he arrested Li Chi-sen, who attended the party congress, and with the assistance of Feng Yu-hsiang and other warlords, who thought that they might add to their own territories, he drove Li's allies from the Hankow area. The Kwangsi generals thereafter confined their activities to the province of their origin. Chiang finally had it out with Feng Yu-hsiang in 1930, when Feng, with the support of Yen Hsi-shan and Wang Ching-wei, who was trying to make capital for himself out of the rift between the central government and the warlords, established a rival government at Peking.

Wang Ching-wei's action was consistent with the attitude of the Kuomintang left wing, which had denounced Chiang's packing of the Third Congress of the Kuomintang and had demanded a radical reorganization of the party because of the concentration of power in Chiang's hands. In December, 1929, at Canton, using the troops of Chang Fa-kuei, Wang and his followers went so far as to attempt to seize control of the city but failed. They then began negotiations with Feng and Yen, with the result that Wang Ching-wei and Ch'en Kung-po joined the short-lived Peking regime. When the rupture finally came, Chiang faced a coalition of warlords and left-wing politicians, but he was aided by the neutrality, and later the active support, of Chang Hsueh-liang, the warlord of Manchuria. After a brief period of hostilities, Yen fled to Manchuria, returning later to Shansi Province, and Wang fled to Europe. Feng was driven into northwest Shansi, where for a time he set up a government at Kalgan, but he later went into retirement, spending most of his last years writing poetry and perfecting his calligraphy. In 1935, when the menace of Japan was great, Feng and Yen, once again governor of Shansi, made up with Chiang and accepted posts as deputy chairmen of the military commission. In the post–World War II years Feng renewed his feud with Chiang, and in 1947 in the United States he publicly attacked Chiang for the first time in many years. He left New York intending to return to China, seemingly to work with the Chinese Communists, but while crossing the Black Sea by Russian ship in September, 1948, he perished in a mysterious fire.

When Feng and Yen were defeated in 1930, Chang Hsueh-liang took over most of their territories, but he was careful to reaffirm his allegiance to the Nanking government. In the south the Kwangsi generals continued to dominate Kwangsi and Kwangtung provinces, asserting that they remained the true heirs of the revolution, and in the summer of 1931 they went so far as to launch, without success, an expedition against Chiang K'ai-shek.

The Communist Revolutionary Strategy

The Chinese Communist Party came under the direction of new leaders and new policies in the summer of 1927, following the expulsion of the party from the Kuomintang. At a meeting of party leaders at Hankow Ch'en Tu-hsiu was attacked for having adopted a conciliatory line toward the left wing of the Kuomintang—in other words for following Stalin's instructions by holding in check the workers' and peasants' movement. Along with eighty of his close followers, he was condemned as a rightist deviationist. Ch'en remained a communist but an opponent of the new orthodoxy of the party, and in 1930, when the Comintern invited him to Moscow to "talk things over," he refused to go. In 1932 he was arrested by the Kuomintang government, tried, and sentenced to thirteen years in prison. In ill health, he was released in 1937 and lived in west China under house arrest until his death in 1942. It is interesting in the light of later history that one of Ch'en's last suggestions while he was in a position of power was that the communist movement be transferred to the northwest provinces, in closer proximity to the Soviet Union.

On instructions from the Comintern, Ch'u Ch'iu-pai, who led the attack against Ch'en, was elected secretary-general of the party, and through the Comintern agent, Lominadze, Stalin forced on the party a policy of armed insurrection based on his evaluation of the revolutionary potential of the Shanghai and Canton workers and the peasantry of Kwangtung, Kwangsi, Hunan, and Hupeh provinces. In Marxist terms, the Chinese Communists, basing their strength on the proletariat and allying themselves with the peasantry and petty bourgeoisie, were to rise against the Kuomintang reactionary alliance of the feudal classes and the national bourgeoisie. It was the task of the Chinese Communist Party to overthrow the Kuomintang regime and consummate the bourgeois-democratic revolution. Trotsky, Stalin's most important critic until his expulsion from the party and exile in December, 1927, proclaimed that the bourgeois revolution had already reached its consummation and implied that Stalin's insistence upon co-operation with the Hankow regime had destroyed the revolutionary opportunity of the communists.

If Stalin had counted on strong labor support for the new policy, he was quickly disillusioned. The Chinese communists were routed in a series

of urban uprisings that they instigated in the autumn of 1927 in central and
south China. The bloodiest failure was in Canton in early December, when
the communists, goaded on by Stalin, attempted to take advantage of local
fighting between the forces of Wang Ching-wei and the warlord, Li Chi-sen,
to seize the city. Defeat piled upon defeat, but the political bureau of the
Chinese Communist Party blamed the failures on mistakes in local leadership. It prophesied that the party would go on to organize successful uprisings
"on the crest of the new revolutionary upsurge of which Canton had been
the harbinger." In Moscow the executive committee of the Comintern took
the same line a month later and rebuked Ch'u Ch'iu-pai, who remained
there as Chinese delegate to the Comintern. In the Chinese Communist
Party, power passed to Li Li-san and Hsiang Chung-fa.

The communists, Russian and Chinese, did some revolutionary soul-
searching during the simultaneous meetings of the Comintern Sixth Congress
and the Sixth Congress of the Chinese Communist Party between July and
September, 1928, at Moscow. These bodies decided that after the failure of the
Canton insurrection it was no longer possible to speak of a "rising wave of
revolution"; on the other hand, they could not accept Trotsky's view that
the wave had definitely receded and that the communists had missed their
opportunity. The new dogma was that in China the revolution was in a
"trough between two waves." During this interval, the length of which was
impossible to predict, the Chinese Communist Party was to prepare for a
bourgeois-democratic revolution aimed at eliminating imperialism and feudalism. The formula for revolution was Lenin's "Democratic Dictatorship of
Workers and Peasants" through councils (soviets) of workers, peasants, and
soldiers. Lenin had stated, in the case of the Russian Revolution, that its leadership could not be entrusted to the bourgeoisie because that class would seek
an opportunity to make a deal with the autocracy. But the proletariat in alliance with the peasantry could effect a genuine bourgeois-democratic revolution, and, once this objective had been achieved, the proletariat would break
its alliance and pursue its own goal—the socialist revolution. The Comintern
and the Chinese Communist Party condemned Ch'u Ch'iu-pai for leftist
deviation and putschism ("wishing to attack an obviously far superior enemy
by continual military actions" and "blind and impetuous measures which
forsake and ignore the masses") and confirmed Li Li-san and Hsiang Chung-
fa in power.

Actually, the political bureau of the Chinese Communist Party had already begun to establish soviets during the abortive uprisings of 1927. On
September 19 it declared that "the uprisings can under no circumstances
take place under the Kuomintang banner." It substituted the red banner of
the soviets, and shortly thereafter the central committee proclaimed: "All
power to the delegates' councils of workers, peasants, soldiers, and city poor—

the soviets." In practice the new slogan merely gave doctrinal sanction and recognition to the attempts of Chinese communist guerrillas to establish bases in the countryside. For example, the young Mao Tse-tung had been ordered to foment peasant disturbances in Hunan Province. Mao came from a peasant background, had studied under Ch'en Tu-hsiu and Li Ta-chao at Peking, joined the party in 1921, and had for some time been working among the peasantry in Hunan. He managed to create a patchwork army of peasants, some Hanyang miners, and deserters from the Kuomintang forces, but when one uprising after another ended in failure, he was dismissed from his post in the political bureau. Much more successful was P'eng P'ai, who in November, 1927, organized a peasant militia and formed the first Chinese soviet in the Haifeng and Lufeng area of Kwangtung Province, where he had formerly been active in the peasant associations. Despite this necessary emphasis on the agrarian content of the revolution, the communists would not concede that the peasantry was its central class; on the contrary, they insisted that the main emphasis was on directing labor in the cities. They constantly reiterated that the peasantry must be under proletarian leadership and that the soviets would begin the process of transformation to the dictatorship of the proletariat. The party was committed to recapturing its hold on the urban working population.

The successes of the Chinese communists in the next few years were not in the cities, however, but in the countryside. In May, 1928, a communist military officer named Chu Teh, together with survivors of the "autumn harvest" uprisings, arrived at Chingkangshan, a mountain area on the Hunan-Kiangsi border; here they were joined by peasant detachments from Hunan under the command of Mao Tse-tung. Chu Teh, the older of the two men, came from a Szechwanese peasant background, was educated to the level of the hsien examinations under the dynasty, joined the T'ung Meng Hui, served Ts'ai Ao in the Yunnan army which opposed Yuan Shih-k'ai, renounced his military career and licentious life in 1921, went abroad, and in Germany became a communist. He and Mao, who had come to realize that the peasantry represented the most important revolutionary force in Chinese society, merged their troops in the Fourth Red Army and by 1929 succeeded in establishing a soviet covering a six-hsien area on the Hunan-Kwangtung border. By 1930 they claimed to have an army of 10,000 men and 2,000 rifles.

Meanwhile, other communist forces, all smaller, formed soviets in Hupeh Province, in northeastern Kiangsi, and along the Honan-Anhwei and Kiangsi-Fukien borders. In May, 1930, delegates from the various soviet areas met near Shanghai and passed a resolution proposing the establishment of a central soviet government and the implementation of an Organic Law, a Draft Land Law, which contemplated the founding of collective farms, and a Labor Law of the Soviets. At the meeting, party leaders made it clear that they still accepted the dogma that, "unless we have the industrial cities and industrial

435

zones, we shall never gain a victory in one or several provinces. All of this talk of 'encircling the city with the country' or of relying on the Red Army to take the cities is sheer nonsense."

Moscow became quite concerned about the successes in the soviet areas, which were beginning to emerge as a powerful independent force, and wanted to use their power to recoup the lagging fortunes of the party in the cities. In June, 1930, it pressured Li Li-san into using rural-based troops, including those of Mao and Chu, to attack Changsha and the Wuhan cities in conjunction with labor uprisings which, it reasoned, would turn the tide in favor of the communists. They seized and held Changsha from July 27 to August 5 but were quickly routed once Kuomintang reinforcements were brought up. It was clear that party forces were not strong enough to capture and hold even modest-sized towns and cities, particularly when, as in the case of Changsha, labor did not rise. Li's subsequent demand for an attack on the Wuhan area was simply ignored by the soviets.

The failure of this strategy precipitated a struggle for power among various factions in the central committee of the Chinese Communist Party. The most important factions were the one headed by Li Li-san and another formed by a group of ambitious students who had returned from a period of study at Sun Yat-sen University in Moscow. The first salvo was Wang Ming's (Ch'en Shao-yu) criticism of Li as a putschist, and although for a time Li's leadership and policies were upheld, the factions working against him gained strength. Moreover, Pavel Mif, the Comintern representative and former director of Sun Yat-sen University, was anxious to oust Li and advance the fortunes of his protégés, the returned students. Finally, in November, in its perennial search for a scapegoat, Moscow forced Li's resignation, and later, in the Russian capital, he formally admitted errors, not of strategy but of tactics and timing. He confessed to being a putschist and a "semi-Trotskyite" because he had been convinced that success in the Chinese revolution and the world revolution were mutually dependent and that a separate victory in China was thus impossible.

In January, 1931, after Li's departure for Moscow, leadership in the party fell to the returned students, who had the advantage of Mif's support; and the party decided, on orders from Moscow, to abandon the idea of seizing urban areas with peasant troops. Neither Moscow nor the Chinese Communist Party renounced the recapture of the urban proletariat as the party's basic aim, but it is significant that a group of members with important labor connections resigned when the party rejected their proposal that it seek to regain its proletarian base by associating itself with the *economic* struggles of the workers; it has been said that by this act the party lost its last concrete link of any consequence with the urban proletariat. Most of the defectors were soon arrested by the British and were later executed by the Kuomintang. Meanwhile, on November 7, 1931, in the small village of Juichin in southern

Kiangsi, Mao Tse-tung, Chu Teh, and others, who had remained aloof from the party's factional struggles, inaugurated the Chinese Soviet Republic, and a year later the central committee of the party was finally compelled to move its headquarters from Shanghai to the soviet area. Thus by 1931 the communist shift to the countryside was complete.

The Nationalist Government and Foreign Rights

The Kuomintang regime at Nanking, basing its foreign policy on Sun Yat-sen's principle of nationalism, continued the attack on the unequal treaty system that had been waged by the warlord regimes at Peking as well as by the Kuomintang–Chinese Communist Party alliance.

One of the basic problems between China and the Western powers was the tariff. As early as 1925 Peking had been able to arrange a tariff conference, as had been suggested at the Washington Conference, when the powers pledged to consider the question of tariff autonomy and to adjust the tariff upward as high as $12\frac{1}{2}$ per cent ad valorem through surtaxes. The tariff conference convened in Peking in October, 1925, but a renewal of civil war among the northern warlords prevented effective discussions. The Nationalist regime at Canton, however, did manage to collect the new surtaxes. In 1926 the British, having felt the impact of the Chinese boycott and strike since the summer of 1925, circularized the treaty powers for the consideration of a more conciliatory policy toward China. And in December the British chargé at Peking proposed to his colleagues that the powers approve Canton's collections, that they recognize and deal with regional governments, that they seek to develop better relations with China even though no national government existed, and that they implement tariff autonomy immediately upon China's promulgation of a national tariff. Unfortunately, British policy, which was designed to placate the revolutionaries, spurred them to new outbursts of fury, e.g., the seizure of the concession areas in the Yangtze Valley. The Kuomintang described British policy as a design to weaken China by creating regional governments and by encouraging warlords to dominate the ports and to profit from the collection of surtaxes. In June, 1928, the new Nationalist government at Nanking issued a declaration calling for new treaties negotiated with full regard to the sovereignty and equality of states. The powers were disposed to negotiate, but the one great obstacle to treaty revision was the fact that the Nanking incident of 1927 had not been settled.

The foreign representatives were unwilling to enter into relations with Chiang's Nationalist government until reparations had been made for the attack on foreigners and their property at Nanking. Chiang's regime, established in April, 1927, had indicated its readiness to a reach a settlement, but not until April, 1928, did the Nationalist government accept responsibility, blaming the incident on communist activity. Separate reparations agreements were made with the United States in April, Great Britain in August, France in October, and finally with Japan in April, 1929—the latter being the last to extend formal recognition to the Nanking government (June, 1929).

After the Nanking regime accepted responsibility for the antiforeign outbreak, the tariff problem was quickly solved. In July, 1928, the United States and China signed a treaty conceding the principle of tariff antonomy, subject to most-favored-nation treatment. The treaty was to become effective on January 1, 1929, by which date the Nationalist government had expected to apply a national tariff law to all trade. Similar treaties were negotiated by China in 1928 with ten other states, including Great Britain and France. The Japanese agreed to the application of the Chinese tariff on February 1, 1929, although a treaty to that effect was not signed until May, 1929, by which time Japanese troops had retired from Shantung Province and China had agreed to revenue allotments for the security of certain Japanese loans. Success in these negotiations did much to increase the prestige of the Nanking government; moreover, it could look forward to higher revenues and protection for China's industrialization. In return, China had agreed to abolish likin.

Extraterritoriality was another issue between China and the Western powers. The liquidation of German, Austrian, and Hungarian rights in China during World War I, the subsequent Russian renunciation of extraterritoriality, and the recent successes of Turkey and Siam in eliminating it gave added impetus to the Chinese campaign for its abolition. At the Washington Conference the powers resolved to establish a commission to investigate judicial practices in China and to recommend reforms which would lead to the termination of extraterritoriality. The Peking government prepared to host a meeting of the commission in November, 1923; but a number of the powers objected to the unsettled political conditions, and the first meeting did not take place until January, 1926. The commission reported in September and politely praised Chinese reforms; however, it criticized the military and magistrates courts, which drew no distinctions between judicial and administrative functions. The commissioners recommended that China protect its judicial system against military and administrative interferences and that China complete the revision of her legal codes, modernize her prisons, and make adequate financial provision for the judicial system. The commission did agree to certain modifications of the consular courts and indicated that the powers would consider abolition of extraterritoriality when China had made substantial progress on the principal reforms suggested.

Despite continued efforts, the Nationalist government was not successful in negotiating the termination of extraterritoriality. The powers refused to consider anything but a gradual abolition of the system; so with a view to forcing the issue the Kuomintang central political council passed a resolution on December 26, 1929, instructing the state council simply to issue an order terminating extraterritorial rights after January 1, 1930. Great Britain, seconded by the United States and Japan, replied that she was willing to consider this date only as the commencement of the process of bringing the system to an end. Negotiations were continued throughout 1930, but no agreement was reached. The Nationalist government, however, did promulgate regulations, to go into effect on January 1, 1932, for the control of foreigners and for the assumption of jurisdiction over them, but the opposition of the powers and the unsettled conditions caused by Japan's occupation of Manchuria in 1931 forced Nanking to suspend the regulations in December, 1931. The Nationalist government was unable to complete this phase of treaty revision, but in the decade of the 1920's significant progress had been made. Ten nations had definitely lost or had given up extraterritoriality, and the rest were committed to the gradual elimination of it.

The Nationalist government also had some success in securing the return of concessions. Great Britain, which had already given up concessions at Hankow and Kiukiang during the course of the revolution, relinquished others at Chinkiang and Amoy as well as the naval base at Wei Hai-wei, and Belgium restored her Tientsin concession to China. Despite these gains, the Nationalist government still had to recognize the existence of thirteen concessions and the International Settlement at Shanghai. In the case of the latter area, which by 1930 had a population of over one million Chinese and forty thousand foreigners, Nanking's only success was in getting representation for the Chinese on the municipal council, which was normally elected by the foreign ratepayers; in March, 1928, the foreigners agreed to admit three Chinese members to the council (this was expanded to five in 1930) and to appoint six Chinese to administrative committees.

The Manchurian Issue

A special focus of the Kuomintang's so-called "Rights Recovery Movement" was Manchuria, which had been divided since 1905 into Russian and Japanese spheres of interest. Nanking felt that complete national unity would not be attained so long as Russia and Japan maintained their special positions in Manchuria. Politically Manchuria was Chinese, with a long tradition of warlord control, and in December, 1928, Chang Hsueh-liang had recognized the authority of Nanking in the face of strong contrary advice from Japan. In practice, Chang retained administrative autonomy over Manchuria, but the direction of foreign affairs and matters of "national interest" were turned over to Nanking. While previously Russia and Japan had been able to negotiate directly with the Mukden government concerning Manchuria, Chang now insisted that all questions of foreign relations must be discussed with the foreign office at Nanking. The Nationalist government was less amenable to direct pressure than Mukden was; it was also more inclined to settle questions

439

only on its own terms. Even more important, the Nationalist government, with Chang's co-operation, began to undermine Russian and Japanese interests. Kuomintang propagandists, teachers, organizers, and administrators poured into Manchuria to incite popular patriotism and loyalty to the Chinese republic.

In December, 1928, China began a frontal assault on the Russian position in north Manchuria. Chinese-Russian relations had never been good when it came to Manchurian matters, and after the establishment of the Nanking regime they went from bad to worse. Chinese authorities seized the telephone network operated by the Chinese Eastern Railway as the first move in a drive to pressure the Russians into accepting a considerable reduction of the prerogatives of the railway administration in Harbin and the liquidation of all enterprises not connected with the operation of the railway. For example, in Harbin the municipal council and the police force were entirely under the control of the railway company. In March of the following year, when the Soviet consul-general, Melnikovat, sought to make a new agreement regarding the Chinese Eastern Railway with Chang Hsueh-liang, the latter declined to negotiate without the participation of the Nanking government. A few months later, on May 27, 1929, Manchurian police arrested Chinese and Russians meeting at the Soviet consulate in Harbin on the charge that it was a meeting of the Comintern. Finally, the decision to use force to seize the Chinese Eastern Railway was made in July at a special conference attended by Chang, Chiang K'ai-shek, and a number of Chinese generals and diplomats. On July 10 Manchurian authorities seized the railroad, and the Russian manager was replaced by a Chinese. The trade union of the railroad workers was declared illegal, and various offices of the Soviet Union were closed down.

The Russians reacted quickly. On July 13 the Soviet Union sent a three-day ultimatum to both Nanking and Mukden demanding reinstatement of the Soviet employees of the Chinese Eastern Railway but offering to negotiate immediately on all outstanding questions affecting the railroad. When the time period elapsed and China did not comply, the Soviet Union broke off relations. China retaliated by expelling from Manchuria the Russian manager and 142 other Russian employees of the railroad. By the end of the month an informal sort of border warfare was under way, and both China and Russia began massing troops in preparation for general hostilities. Interestingly, in August, 1929, the Comintern explained that Russia insisted upon joint administration of the railroad with the Nanking regime, which represented the bourgeoisie and landowners, to prevent the transfer of the railroad to the imperialists subjugating China. Thus, according to this interpretation, the Soviet Union was acting as a trustee for the Chinese people, who would ultimately experience their democratic revolution under the leadership of the Chinese Communist Party; and Russian participation in the administration of the railway helped to defend the Soviet Union against the threat of invasion on the part of hostile capitalist powers.

The fact that both China and Russia had only recently (August, 1928) signed the Treaty of Paris (Kellogg-Briand Pact), which renounced war as an instrument of national policy, made possible mediation efforts by the American secretary of state, Henry Stimson. Under the terms of the Paris pact an overwhelming majority of the nations of the world had agreed to use only pacific means in the settlement of disputes. Stimson proposed to Great Britain, France, Italy, Japan, and Germany that a commission of conciliation be appointed and that a neutral figure, acceptable to China and Russia, be made president and general manager of the Chinese Eastern Railway. The first three agreed with this plan, but Germany and Japan suggested that the Soviet Union negotiate directly with Chiang K'ai-shek. In the meantime, China and Russia both gave assurances that they would not resort to force, save in self-defense. Negotiations between Soviet and local Manchurian officials and between the Russian ambassador and the Chinese minister at Berlin produced no settlement, and by November there was open though undeclared warfare on the Manchurian border. Stimson made another attempt at mediation when he proposed that the powers act collectively to prevent war. Japan and Germany again refused, and the Russian press denounced the United States, Great Britain, and France for their diplomatic intervention.

Russian military power finally decided the issue. In November the Russian army invaded Manchuria, and Chang's forces retreated in confusion. At Hailar 10,000 Chinese troops surrendered. On December 3 Chang agreed to Russian terms, which were given legal form in the Khabarovsk Protocol, signed at Nanking on December 22. The settlement provided for the reopening of Russian consulates and commercial enterprises, the release of prisoners and internees, the disarming of White Russians in Chinese employ, the restoration of Soviet executives and employees of the Chinese Eastern Railway, and convocation of a conference in Moscow for discussion of all outstanding problems as well as resumption of diplomatic relations. This fiasco in applied nationalism made it clear, particularly to Japan, that the Nationalist government was unable to back up its policies with force and that the Kellogg-Briand Pact was not an effective sanction for international peace and collective security.

Japan, like Russia, was determined to protect her interests in south Manchuria against Chinese claims; she stressed that her rights were based on legal commitments and that Japanese capital was principally responsible for the development of the area. Japan's fixed policy was to protect her position, to expand it when and where possible, and to foster the idea that Manchuria and eastern Inner Mongolia (Jehol) were special areas, distinct from China, in which it was Japan's obligation to maintain peace and order. She governed the Kwantung Leasehold "with practically full rights of sovereignty"; she owned and operated the South Manchurian Railway Company and all its associated enterprises and administered all areas contiguous to the railroad, including towns and large sections of the cities of Mukden and Changchun, controlling within these areas police, taxation, education, and public utilities; and she maintained railroad guards along the South Manchurian Railway, a large standing army in the Leasehold, and the consular police scattered throughout the entire region.

The Chinese view was that justice, not the law, was on her side and that she would live up to her treaty obligations no more than expediency required. The Chinese denied the legality of railroad guards and consular police, annulled mining rights of the Japanese, impeded negotiation of leases to Japanese citizens, restricted their rights of residence and travel, evaded tax engagements, and limited the rights of Koreans while imposing discriminatory taxes upon them. One of the fundamental differences between China and Japan was the latter's interpretation of the Russo-Chinese Railroad Agreement of 1896 and of her treaty of 1915 with Yuan Shih-k'ai. The political rights of the South Manchurian Railway Company were based on the Russo-Chinese treaty, which became the basis of Japan's position after the Treaty of Portsmouth and the Treaty of Peking in 1905. The 1896 treaty conferred on the Chinese Eastern Railway the absolute and exclusive administration of its railroad lands, but Nanking denied on legal grounds that this conferred political control in the railroad zone and pointed to other clauses of the agreement which suggested that it was never intended that Russia, or later Japan, should exercise broad administrative rights such as police, education, taxation, and public utilities. As for the 1915 treaty, which had extended Japanese rights as part of the Twenty-one Demands settlement with Yuan, Nanking claimed that it was illegal since it had been signed under duress.

Railroad competition was another important aspect of the Sino-Japanese dispute. Since 1924 the Chinese had been busy constructing railroads to compete with the South Manchurian Railway Company. The Japanese financed some of the Chinese lines, and the South Manchurian Railway Company even carried out contracts for their construction. By 1931 there were about 3,600 miles of railway in Manchuria, divided into three competitive systems: the Chinese Eastern Railway, with over a thousand miles; the South Manchurian Railway, with seven hundred; and the Chinese State Railways, with almost two thousand. The latter had its own port facilities at Yinkow (Newchang) and Hulatao, which was being developed by a Dutch company. Competition between the Chinese and Japanese systems resulted in rate wars, with each side accusing the other of rate discrimination and secret rebates; and although there were discussions to adjust the difficulties in the first six months of 1931, neither side displayed much desire to compromise.

Problems concerning the leasing of land to Koreans, who were Japanese subjects, added to the friction. The 1915 treaty with Yuan Shih-k'ai had provided that Japanese subjects could lease land, but in the following years Chinese authorities did little to protect their rights, especially in the case of Koreans. Chinese-Korean tension reached a climax in an unfortunate incident in the village of Wanpaoshan near Changchun in the summer of 1931. Korean peasants had leased land from a Chinese company, and since the success of the venture depended on irrigation, they immediately undertook the construction of the necessary ditches and dam. This aroused the hostility of neighboring Chinese landowners, since the main irrigation ditch, several miles long, crossed their land. When Chinese farmers drove the Koreans off, Japanese consular police came to the aid of the Koreans and took control of the area, enabling the Koreans to complete their work. In Seoul and Tokyo there were anti-Chinese riots, and Nanking blamed the Japanese government for permitting inaccurate and inflammatory press reports and for taking no steps to suppress riots until after Chinese had suffered loss of life and property destruction. These events took on enormous importance in the press of Korea, Japan, and China, and the reporting was sensational, the Chinese newspapers claiming that 127 of their countrymen were killed, 339 injured, and property of enormous value damaged. The Japanese government offered compensation to the bereaved families; but before a settlement could be reached, the Kwantung Army had moved to seize Manchuria by force, and China had already instituted a boycott of Japanese goods.

The mysterious activities and death of one Captain Nakamura also added fuel to the fire. Nakamura was a Japanese army officer on active duty who represented himself as an agricultural expert to Chinese authorities at Harbin. He was killed by Chinese soldiers near Taonan in north Manchuria in June, 1931. Tokyo, insisting that this was not only an unjustified act but a demonstration of arrogant disrespect for the Japanese army and nation, demanded an apology, an indemnity, and punishment of Nakamura's "murderers." China delayed investigating at first but soon replied that Nakamura had been detained pending an examination of his passport; that he was shot by a sentry while trying to escape; and that documents found on him proved that he was either a military spy or an officer on a special military mission. Regardless of the facts of Nakamura's death, the incident had a tremendous effect in inflaming Japanese public opinion, and it strengthened the feeling, long held in Japanese army circles, that a strong policy had to be followed toward China if Japan was to maintain her position. The Chinese Nationalists were equally determined to regain the area for China. Negotiations became increasingly difficult because of the extremists on both sides.

Japanese Aggression in Manchuria

Japan's Kwantung Army finally used force to solve the Manchurian problem. The pretext for armed action came on the night of September 18, 1931, when a portion of one of the rails of the South Manchurian Railway near Mukden was destroyed by bombing, although the damage did not delay the night express. The Japanese claimed that the bombing was the act of Chinese soldiers, who were caught in the act and fired upon by Japanese railway guards, but this charge was denied by the Chinese, who accused the Kwantung Army of staging the incident for its own purposes. Japanese troops, claiming self-defense, attacked the Chinese barracks nearby and moved upon Mukden before dawn. It became evident that the Kwantung Army was operating according to a carefully prepared plan. Mukden was quickly seized, Chang-chun fell to Japanese troops on September 19, and Kirin on September 21; and from these vantage points the Kwantung Army began the conquest of all Manchuria.

Unable to stem the tide of the Japanese advance, China appealed to the outside world for help. On September 21 Nanking formally requested assistance from the League of Nations under the provisions of Article XI of the Covenant, and when Chiang's government also requested the United States to aid in preserving the peace, there was immediate consultation between the secretary-general of the League, the American State Department, and the major powers of the League. The United States urged caution to avoid action which might excite nationalistic feeling in Japan in support of the Japanese military. The American State Department held the view that the aggression was an affair engineered by the army, very likely without the previous knowledge of the Japanese civil authorities, who had not acquiesced but were unable to oppose it effectively. Secretary of State Henry Stimson hoped that a cautious approach to the problem would help the civil government of Japan, particularly Foreign Minister Shidehara. On September 22 the League of Nations sent identical telegrams to China and Japan, appealing to them to refrain from any further acts of hostility that would be prejudicial to a peaceful settlement and urging them to withdraw their troops at once without endangering the safety of their nationals and property. In support of the League stand, the United States sent similar notes two days later which expressed the hope that the two nations would settle their differences without further hostilities.

On the same day, September 24, the Japanese government, caught between its own generals, who supported the actions of the Kwantung Army, and the Western powers, issued a long public statement, asserting that Japan had already taken steps toward the withdrawal of troops and a solution of the controversy, that she harbored no territorial designs on Manchuria, and that her desire was only to protect her nationals engaged in peaceful economic pursuits. Tokyo also pledged to co-operate with the Chinese authorities in removing once and for all the causes of the friction over Manchuria. Although this was a sincere statement of purpose by the civil government of Japan, the Kwantung Army continued its advance in Manchuria. China's reply to the League of Nations disclaimed any responsibility for the outbreak and blamed it on Japanese aggression; moreover, China stated that she would not engage in bilateral negotiations so long as Japan occupied territory outside the railway zone in Manchuria.

"If anyone had planned the outbreak with a view to freedom from interference from the rest of the world, his time was well chosen." These are the words of Secretary Stimson, and they were indeed an accurate appraisal of the situation. Great Britain and France were in no position to take resolute action, and it was clear that the United States wanted to avoid active entanglement. When the League of Nations did sound out Stimson on the possibility of an embargo, he rebuffed its overtures. By the autumn of 1931 the full force of a great world-wide depression was being felt by every major power; in fact, depression in Japan was a basic condition to popular Japanese support of the action of the Kwantung Army. In Europe economic chaos, resulting from the collapse of the Credit Anstalt in Germany and Great Britain's desertion of the gold standard, had forced President Hoover's moratorium on foreign-debt payments. Moreover, as John V. A. MacMurray, former American minister to China, astutely observed,

The policy of co-operation among the powers, which might well have averted the catastrophe of subjugation by Japan, was no longer available. It was wounded in the house of its friends—scorned by the Chinese and ignored by the British and the United States, until it became a hissing and a byword with a Japanese nation persuaded in the belief that it could depend only on its own strong arm to vindicate its rightful position in eastern Asia.

In the autumn it was clear that the Kwantung Army planned to conquer Manchuria with little concern for the objections of the Japanese government and the world community. In fact, in October it announced that it no longer recognized the administration of Chang Hsueh-liang. Meanwhile, the council of the League of Nations, strengthened by the participation in its meetings of Prentice Gilbert, the American consul at Geneva, decided to send a commission of inquiry to Asia, and both China and Japan approved, although the Japanese representative on the League council asked that assurances be given that the commission "would not be empowered to intervene in the negotiations that may be initiated between the two parties or to supervise the movements of the military forces of either." In December the council appointed the Earl of Lytton to head the commission, which included representatives from the United States, France, Italy, and Germany. In Tokyo the Japanese government worked against overwhelming odds to check the military and finally resigned in defeat on December 11.

On January 3 Chinchow, the last Chinese stronghold, fell to the Kwantung Army, and all Manchuria passed under Japanese control. On January 7 Stimson announced that it was the policy of the United States not to recognize gains or changes accomplished as a result of the use of methods proscribed under such international instruments as the Kellogg-Briand Pact. In identical notes to China and Japan he stated that the United States would not recognize "any situation, treaty, or agreement entered into by those governments in violation of the covenants of those treaties which affect the rights of our Government or its citizens in China." But, like Bryan before him in 1915, Stimson was unable to go beyond diplomatic coercion. He invited Great Britain and France to take similar action, and he was disappointed when they did not. He continued, however, to put constant pressure on Geneva and London to bring judgment against Japan.

The only effective opposition to Japan was the Chinese boycott that followed the Wanpaoshan affair. Japanese exports to China fell from the September, 1931, figure of 12,700,000 yen to the December, 1931, total of 4,299,000 yen; moreover, as anti-Japanese feeling in China grew more intense, Chinese often violently attacked Japanese merchants. The boycott was harmful to Japan economically, and it was a great embarrassment to the Japanese army. The Tokyo government finally declared the boycott an act of aggression by China, and in January, 1932, it dispatched warships and troops to Shanghai, where anti-Japanese demonstrations were strongest. Fighting broke out at Shanghai in mid-January; but in the face of stubborn resistance by the Chinese army, the Japanese troops made little progress until the arrival of heavy reinforcements in March.

On January 29 China again appealed to the League of Nations, invoking Articles X and XV of the Covenant, under which the League would be required to assess responsibility and eventually, perhaps, to apply sanctions. Concerned that the fighting might spread to the Yangtze Valley, the British took the lead in organizing a League committee at Shanghai, consisting of local consular officials, to report directly to Geneva. On January 31, when Japan requested the good offices of the neutral powers to re-establish peace at Shanghai, Stimson was also inspired to act. He drew up peace terms that met with the approval of Great Britain, France, and Italy and presented them to China and Japan on February 2. Stimson called for an immediate armistice, no further mobilization, mutual troop withdrawals, the establishment of a neutral zone policed by neutrals, and negotiations with the assistance of neutrals to settle all outstanding controversies between the two nations in the spirit of the Kellogg-Briand Pact. China accepted Stimson's proposals, but Japan would not agree either to suspend war preparations until her immediate demands on China were met or to make a comprehensive settlement with the aid of third parties.

Stimson began to consider more drastic measures, including a joint British-American invocation of the Nine-Power Treaty of the Washington Conference as a step toward the imposition of sanctions, which he hoped would be implemented by the American Congress and the League of Nations; however, Great Britain was not certain of American action and preferred to act within the League. In March the League adopted the nonrecognition doctrine through a resolution proposed by the British, but it would go no further until the Lytton Commission had reported. In May peace was finally arranged at Shanghai on terms worked out by the consular committee. Japan had decided to withdraw because of the stubborn resistance of the Chinese and the danger of serious diplomatic involvement with the other powers while the Manchurian situation was still unstable.

Manchukuo and the League of Nations

On February 18, 1932, Japan established the puppet state of Manchukuo. During the course of its military occupation of Manchuria, the Kwantung Army had reorganized local governments and finally consolidated these into a new state, whose territories included the three northeastern provinces of China. The climax to these political efforts came on March 4 when the deposed Manchu emperor of China, Henry P'u Yi, became the chief of state. This unfortunate man, who had been living quietly in a concession at Tientsin, was literally abducted and brought to Manchukuo by agents of the Kwantung Army. On March 9 the Japanese promulgated an organic law centralizing executive, legislative, and judicial authority under the new head of state. In form the government was a republic in order to make more plausible the Japanese claim that it had been created in response to the "spontaneous wish" of the thirty million people of Manchuria; but in actuality the government, with Japanese nationals in most of the key positions, was the creature of the Kwantung Army and took orders from its generals. On September 15, 1932, Japan extended recognition to the new state, serving notice to the world that she would accept no solution of the Manchurian question that involved even a partial restoration of the status quo ante. Although many Japanese civil leaders understood that these developments might well force Japan out of the League of Nations, they were unable to stand against the united front of the Kwantung Army and the war ministry in Tokyo; moreover, by September, 1932, party government had begun to give way to military domination.

Japanese recognition of Manchukuo coincided with the publication of the Lytton Commission report, which was completed at Peking on September 4 and released on October 2. The report found that, on the basis of Manchuria's unique historical development, neither the status quo (Manchukuo) nor a restoration of the status quo ante was a satisfactory solution, but on all major points it found against Japan. It denied the Japanese claims that China was not an organized state, that Manchuria was not Chinese and that therefore China was not entitled to sovereignty over it, that her occupation of Mukden and south Manchuria had been an act of self-defense, and that Manchukuo's origin was autonomous. Its verdict was that, "without a declaration of war, a large area of what was indisputably Chinese territory has been

447

forcibly seized and occupied by the armed forces of Japan, and has, in consequence of this operation, been separated from and declared independent from the rest of China." The report concluded that Japan had violated the following international obligations: under Article X of the League of Nations Covenant to respect and preserve against external aggression the territorial integrity and existing political independence of her fellow-members of the League; under Article II of the Kellogg-Briand Pact not to seek the settlement or solution of disputes except by pacific means; and under Article I of the Nine-Power Treaty of the Washington Conference to respect the sovereignty, the independence, and the territorial and administrative integrity of China and to provide the fullest and most unembarrassed opportunity to China to develop and maintain for herself an effective and stable government. The commission's recommendations for settlement insisted upon Chinese sovereignty in Manchuria but would have strengthened rather than weakened the position Japan held in Manchuria as of 1931; moreover, the commission sought to encourage an economic *rapprochement* between China and Japan in place of the economic warfare that had helped to bring about the aggression. Finally, the commission recommended extensive international assistance for the national reconstruction of China.

When the council of the League of Nations convened on November 21, 1932, the Japanese delegate, Matsuoka Yosuke, spoke against the conclusions of the Lytton Commission. He insisted that Japan alone was the judge as to whether her military action was justifiable self-defense; that the creation of Manchukuo resulted from the spontaneous character of the independence movement among the people of Manchuria; that there had been no violation of the Nine-Power Treaty, the Covenant of the League of Nations, or the Kellogg-Briand Pact; and, finally, that the solutions proposed by the commission were "too refined and intricate" to meet conditions as they existed. Later, in the December meeting of the League of Nations assembly, Matsuoka again repudiated the commission's findings on all the important issues in the controversy, insisting that no settlement was possible which did not include recognition of Manchukuo by the powers. In view of the Japanese characterization of the "spontaneous independence movement" in Manchuria, the following population figures are interesting. By 1931, after a decade of extensive emigration from north China, the total population of Manchuria included 29,000,000 Chinese, 250,000 Japanese, 800,000 Koreans, and 150,000 Russians. There were some Manchus and Mongols, but they were very small minorities.

When the League of Nations adopted the recommendations of the Lytton Commission, Japan withdrew from the League. In February, 1933, a special committee of the League recommended nonrecognition of Manchukuo, the establishment of a Manchurian government compatible with Chinese sovereignty, and the extension of invitations to China and Japan to undertake direct negotiations under the good offices of a League commission. The report was adopted by an almost unanimous vote in the League assembly, with only Japan dissenting, and on February 24 Matsuoka walked out. Actually he had been instructed to express Japan's views fully but to avoid the drastic step of withdrawal, although the army had felt that a break with the League was inevitable. On March 27 Japan formally resigned from the League of Nations. The world condemned Japanese aggression and imposed diplomatic sanctions, but the success of the aggression was an accomplished fact.

One significant by-product of the Manchurian incident was the new Far Eastern emphasis in Russian policy. The Japanese military action in northern Manchuria had posed a threat to the Soviet position in the area; but since both powers were anxious to avoid hostilities, Japan promised to protect Russian interests and Russia was careful to remain neutral. Soviet leaders discerned the Japanese threat in Asia, and they began to prepare for the defense of Siberian territory by stationing more troops in border areas and by focusing the second five-year plan on the development of Siberia. As a correlate policy the Soviet Union resumed diplomatic relations with China. Chiang's government, failing to get support from the Western powers, was willing to turn to Russia for help, but Moscow, though it finally declared Japan an aggressor, was unable to give positive assistance to the Chinese.

In January, 1933, the Kwantung Army embarked on a second act of aggression by attacking Jehol. The Japanese quickly overran the province and occupied the capital, Chengteh, on March 3; but when the attack was carried into north China, the Chinese troops held fast at the passes into Hopei (formerly Chihli) Province. Evidently it was not the intention of the Kwantung Army to push into China but to negotiate for a buffer zone between China and the new state of Manchukuo. Both sides, in order to terminate the hostilities, signed the Tangku Truce on May 25, 1933. Under its terms the Chinese army was immediately withdrawn to the west and south, making the Peiping-Tientsin area a demilitarized zone as far as China was concerned, while Japan, on the other hand, under the Boxer Protocol had the right to station troops along the railway lines from Peiping and Tientsin to the sea. Moreover, the main part of the Japanese army was permitted to remain in Jehol, which for all practical purposes was annexed to Manchukuo. In the demilitarized zone between the Great Wall and the line south of Peiping and Tientsin, Chinese police were to maintain peace and order. Hopei Province, however, was the scene of continuous political conflict. The Japanese endeavored to establish a regime of officials acceptable and amenable to them, while Nanking did its best to maintain some measure of control. Friction often marked the relations between Japanese and Chinese residents, and propaganda campaigns by both sides increased the tension. In most cases it was difficult for local officials not to bend to Japanese pressure; for example, in July, 1933, they agreed to reorganize their police forces in accordance with Japanese demands.

Japanese Policy and North China

Events soon proved that Japan's ultimate plan was to establish a special position for herself in China. In 1934 the council of the League of Nations adopted a report recommending lines of future technical assistance to China; and the United States, through the agency of the Curtiss-Wright Corporation, began to help China develop an air force. Curtiss-Wright built an assembly plant in China for military aircraft, American aviation officers established training schools for Chinese pilots and crews at Hangchow and Canton, and sales of aircraft and accessories to China rose from $150,000 in 1932 to $1,750,000 in 1933. In 1934 the Japanese government made its attitude toward China and foreign aid very clear. On April 18 Eiji Amau of the Japanese foreign office stated to a group of foreign representatives in Tokyo that the policy of the Western powers, in the interest of peace, order, and stability, must be satisfactory to Japan as the guardian of peace in the Far East and the defender of the integrity of China against the assaults of Europe. Japan declared herself to be in favor of strengthening China but only through China's own efforts or through Japanese aid. According to Amau, Japan would oppose any joint efforts by the powers to assist China, since these would acquire political significance; however, individual countries might assist her economically so long as their aid was not detrimental to the maintenance of the peace in the Far East. Japan would oppose military and political aid. Amau's views were reiterated by the Japanese foreign minister, Hirota Koki, later that year; by the Japanese ambassadors to Berlin and Washington; and, in more qualified terms, by notes to the governments of the United States, Great Britain, and France.

China and the Western powers quickly answered Amau. On April 19 the Nanking government asserted that "no state has a right to claim exclusive responsibility for maintaining the peace in any part of the world" and reaffirmed its trust in the collective security system of the League of Nations. Nanking also made it clear that it would permit no one, whether individual states or the League of Nations, to infringe upon Chinese sovereignty. Although they were careful not to antagonize Japan, the powers reaffirmed their treaty rights in China; moreover, they continued aid to China in the form of loans for railroad construction by Great Britain, France, and Belgium and the dispatch of military advisers and the sale of war equipment by Germany and Italy. It is interesting to note that the American ambassador to Tokyo, Joseph C. Grew, advised his government to rearm if it wished to deter the ambitions of the Japanese nationalists and militarists. Similar warnings to Washington came from Germany.

By 1935 the Japanese government was seeking to work out a co-operative policy with China. The service chiefs and the foreign ministry drafted a series of proposals that were presented to the Chinese ambassador in Tokyo on October 28, 1935, and discussed by the Japanese ambassador and Chiang K'ai-shek at Nanking. In January, 1936, Foreign Minister Hirota gave a full exposition of his government's China policy to the Japanese diet. He stated that Japan had three objectives.

First, it was seeking to conclude a treaty of friendship which would bring about the cessation by China of all unfriendly acts and measures, e.g., the murder of two pro-Japanese journalists at Tientsin in May, 1935.

Second, it hoped to regularize the relations between Manchukuo and China "because the interests of these two countries and Japan are directly and closely bound up." Japan was particularly interested in north China. Its cotton would free her from dependence on the United States and India, and its iron and coal reserves, along with those of Inner Mongolia, would be more valuable than those of Manchuria. Japan was also interested in the market potentialities of north China as a controlled outlet for her industrial production. Smuggling, including a large-scale trade in narcotics, was already profitable, as goods were brought in from Manchukuo by sea to Hopei Province or through the northern passes into Hopei and Chahar provinces. The north, as far south as the Yangtze River, was flooded with Japanese goods on which no tariff had been paid; this caused a loss of revenue for Nanking and ruinous competition for Western commerce. The smuggling continued despite protests from Nanking, the United States, and Great Britain. The Kwantung Army was also encouraging the zaibatsu to increase their investments in north China, and enterprises such as the Oriental Development Company, the Bank of Korea, and the Kanegafuchi Spinning Mills were already active and expanding their operations.

Third, the Hirota policy included co-operation between Japan and the Nanking government for the eradication of communism. Subsequent negotiations between the two governments revealed that Tokyo wanted to develop a joint Chinese-Japanese military force in equal numbers to fight the Chinese communists. In his diet address, Hirota reported that Chiang K'ai-shek had agreed to work with Japan in accordance with the three principles, but this claim was promptly denied by Nanking. There were pro-Japanese elements in the Kuomintang, including Wang Ching-wei, but their influence declined quickly after an attempt on Wang's life and his temporary retirement from politics. Throughout 1936 Hirota tried in vain to secure acceptance of his policy.

Meanwhile, the Kwantung Army was exerting strong pressure on local officials in north China in order to persuade the provinces of Hopei, Chahar, Suiyuan, Shantung, and Shansi to declare their independence from Nanking and make themselves subservient to Japan; and by the fall of 1935, after

451

Nanking's commander-in-chief, Ho Ying-chin, had agreed (Ho-Umezu Agreement, May, 1935) to withdraw his troops from Hopei, reports began to circulate of local desires to create an autonomous regime in the north. These reports were clearly of Japanese inspiration, and the Japanese went so far as to threaten the use of force, if necessary, to prevent Nanking from interfering with the "essentially Chinese" movement. On November 18 it was announced that an autonomous regime of the five provinces would be established within a week, but the deadline was not met since the Kwantung Army could not mobilize sufficient popular support to intimidate local officials, Moreover, Nanking took the initiative out of Japan's hands by sending new officials to the north to organize semiautonomous regimes that would remain loyal.

The only success that the Kwantung Army had was the creation of the East Hopei autonomous council in December, 1935, which was completely dominated by the Japanese military authorities at Tientsin and Peiping. The Hopei-Chahar political council, created under Japanese pressure in the same month, had as its leader General Sung Cheh-yung, who proved to be no puppet. In 1936 the Japanese government in Tokyo disavowed responsibility for the autonomy movement, placing the onus upon the Kwantung Army, in the hope that Nanking might accept the milder Hirota policy. Tokyo was apparently not prepared to push its demands for control of north China to the point where they would have to be backed up with military action; conversely, however, its disavowal of the autonomy movement made less effective the Japanese military pressure which could be brought to bear locally in the north.

In 1936 the Kwantung Army concentrated its attention on Inner Mongolia—the provinces of Chahar, Suiyuan, and Ninghsia—which since the decline of the Manchus had been a semiautonomous region under the control of Mongol princes. This was a situation that Japan had tried to exploit ever since the treaties of 1915 with China, but not until after the seizure of Manchuria was she able to penetrate the region. The Japanese tried to operate through the Mongol princes, while the latter astutely used the Japanese menace to secure from Nanking autonomy and limits to Chinese colonization. In January, 1935, the Kwantung Army incorporated part of eastern Chahar into Manchukuo, and in June, 1935, it established a demilitarized zone along the Chahar-Hopei border; within a year's time it had helped a group of secessionist Mongol princes set up an independent Mongolian government in northern Chahar which claimed sovereignty over Chahar, Suiyuan, and Ninghsia. In November, 1936, the princes invaded Suiyuan with Japanese support, but they were met by Chinese forces under General Fu Tso-yi and were routed. Chiang K'ai-shek flew to Taiyuan to encourage its defenders and to make certain that the fighting would not lead to a general war, since he was planning an all-out attack against the Chinese communists. The defeat was a severe blow to Japanese prestige among the Mongols, and at the same time it stimulated popular feeling in China for resistance, which, paradoxically, Chiang felt forced to suppress.

The Politics of the Nationalist Regime

The history of Chinese society in the period 1931–1937 was in large part the history of the development of Chinese unity in resistance to Japan. Unity, however, was based on temporary compromises; fundamental differences continued to exist between various factions within the Kuomintang and between these factions and the Chinse communists. Even a temporary compromise between these groups was not achieved until the Japanese threat to all China was imminent, and by that time valuable energy and strength had been dissipated in factional struggles and in Chiang's determined drive to destroy communism. To him the Chinese Communist Party was the fundamental enemy, and only under great pressure did he accept even a limited agreement with it to achieve military unity against Japan.

It would be a mistake to regard the Nanking government as the administrative center of a united China in the period 1931–1937, for outside of the Yangtze River Valley Nanking's control was slight. The central government made compromises with some warlords, though it destroyed others, and it was forced to increase local autonomy under the threat of Japan's advance. The communists had successfully established soviets in the southeast, especially in Kiangsi Province, and in the northwest in remote Shensi Province. In other words, the Nanking regime under Chiang and the Kuomintang was hardly able to inaugurate the period of political tutelage and begin the transformation of China according to the three principles of Sun Yat-sen; this lack of unity was also a convenient excuse for postponing efforts along these lines.

The relationship between the central and local governments in Kwangtung Province was typical of the distribution of political power. By 1931 at Canton former Kuomintang left-wingers, including Wang Ching-wei, had allied themselves with the Kwangsi generals—warlords like Chen Chi-tang, Li Tsung-jen, and Pai Chung-hsi. This Canton government rejected the authority of Nanking and claimed to be the legitimate repository of power. Its prestige was increased when it was joined by Kuomintang rightists who split with Chiang K'ai-shek on the issue of the provisional constitution, which had its genesis in the following series of events.

When the short-lived separatist regime formed by Feng Yu-hsiang, Yen Hsi-shan, and Wang Ching-wei at Peking had adopted a provisional constitution in 1930, Chiang wanted one for his own regime. With that end in mind he transferred consideration of important matters of state from the jurisdiction of the state council to the executive yuan, of which he was chairman, in order to exclude certain high officials, particularly Hu Han-min,

453

from the discussion of a "Tutelage Constitution." Since 1928 Chiang had been allied with the rightists, and both he and Hu had agreed that there was no need for a constitution during the period of tutelage. Thus, when Chiang changed his mind, he had Hu taken into protective custody (March, 1931) in order to "conserve his revolutionary reputation." Later, Hu was able to leave Nanking for Canton, but he and Chiang never again worked together.

In May, 1931, a Kuomintang-controlled National People's Convention approved a provisional constitution which superseded the Organic Law of 1928. This was regarded as a concession to the principle of transition to democratic constitutional government; but the organization of the central administration remained substantially the same as before, with the executive agencies of the Kuomintang holding the reins of dictatorship. The constitution, which was implemented by the Organic Law of December, 1931, was to remain in force until the termination of the period of tutelage—supposedly in 1935. In practice, it remained in effect until 1947.

Under the pressure of the Japanese menace, however, Chiang K'ai-shek was forced to broaden the basis of power in the central government in December, 1931. Although he kept close control over military power, he accepted the formation of a new coalition, which included representatives of the Wang and Hu factions in the Kuomintang; and after the Japanese attack on Shanghai he bent further to maintain his position and worked out a division of power with Wang Ching-wei. Chiang assumed the chairmanship of the new military commission, while Wang became president of the powerful executive yuan. Li Sen, who was appointed president of the national government in 1931 when the provisional constitution stripped the position of its power, continued in office. Within this framework Chiang's position as military leader gave him the upper hand in view of the Japanese threat and the anticommunist campaigns of the period. Moreover, his civil powers were once again extensive after the establishment of the General Headquarters for Bandit Suppression in 1932, for within the communist-infested areas he had full power over administration and even over party authorities; and since the communists were spread widely over much of China in the 1930's, the General Headquarters covered one area after another. In the central government Chiang undermined Wang's power by gaining control over the Central Political Institute, which was responsible for the training of local magistrates and other administrative personnel. With Chiang in practical control of the military and civil branches of government, Wang was virtually powerless. When the Fifth Congress of the Kuomintang met in November, 1935, Wang was recovering from a gunshot wound inflicted by an assassin, and Chiang easily replaced him as president of the executive yuan. However, there was no break between the two men, and later, in 1937, Wang accepted the post of deputy leader of the Kuomintang. Hu Han-min never rejoined the Nanking government, and until his death at Canton in May, 1936, he cooperated with the Kwangsi generals in the southwestern political council;

later in 1936 these militarist opponents of Chiang staged a revolt against Nanking, and, when it failed, Chiang extended his power over Canton.

The military power of the Nanking regime and Chiang K'ai-shek rested on the expansion of the original Whampoa force after 1928, and its German-trained divisions were, with the navy and air force, the most dependable and efficient units. By 1937 the central army numbered about 300,000 effectives, of which approximately 80,000 were equipped and trained according to German standards. This latter force had most of China's artillery, armor, and other specialized units and was commanded directly by Chiang or his minister of war, Ho Ying-ch'in, a close friend from Whampoa days. But the majority of military units in the central army were commanded by officers who did not undergo modern training. In fact, up to 1937 less than 2,000 officers were graduates of higher military schools. On the whole, field commanders still drew their staffs from relatives and schoolmates, and they generally regarded loyalty as more important than training; they also had control over unit finances, and some could not resist the opportunity to enrich themselves at the expense of their troops and their military efficiency.

Throughout this period the Nanking regime had to pay at least lip service to the principle of political tutelage and popular representation in government. Late in 1932 the central executive committee of the Kuomintang accepted the suggestion of Sun Fo, son of Sun Yat-sen, that a permanent constitution be drafted and that the period of tutelage be terminated by its adoption. A draft was completed in 1934 and submitted for study to a special committee preliminary to its consideration by a constituent assembly, which was scheduled for convocation in March, 1935. The assembly meeting was ultimately postponed and then suspended, but the constitution was approved by the central executive committee in April, 1936. After the outbreak of hostilities between Japan and China in 1937, however, the project was given up and the period of tutelage was extended. Although the constitution was never put into operation, an analysis of it is revealing of the political attitudes within the Kuomintang at that time. The draft constitution was designed to perpetuate the dictatorship of the Kuomintang under Chiang K'ai-shek. The national congress, the body to be most directly representative of the people, was to meet for only one month every three years, and legislative power was invested in the easily manipulated legislative yuan. Fundamental human rights were not unconditionally guaranteed, for they could be limited by laws passed by the legislative yuan. It was abundantly clear that the Kuomintang was unwilling to part with political power.

Economic Problems and Progress

On the economic front the Nanking regime had to face two difficult problems simultaneously: the improvement of the conditions of the people in fulfillment of its revolutionary heritage and the development of an economic foundation for national security against the Japanese threat. These two problems were not mutually exclusive, and under certain circumstances the government might have made progress in both. The conditions of the times, however, caused the second problem to be given priority. The increasingly dangerous menace of Japan, the struggle against the communists, the shortage of capital, the lack of effective administration throughout China, the conservative nature of Kuomintang support—all these factors tended to emphasize stability and security over and above reform. Chiang's own views, set forth in his *China's Destiny*, make it clear that this was a well-calculated choice. Because of the failure of international collective security, Nanking realistically fell back on a program expressed in the slogan "Reliance upon China's Own Resources," and the subsequent history of China has often made us forget that China made some economic progress under the Nationalist regime.

The budgetary problems of the central government were, of course, exceedingly difficult. Funds for economic development were limited because of the lack of effective centralized government, the loss of revenues from north China and Manchuria, and the need to divert monies for the relief of flood and drought. Nanking was also heavily burdened by expenditures for military campaigns against the communists and for preparedness against Japan, and it had to assume the obligations of previous governments to pay the public debt, particularly its foreign commitments. It was to the credit of Finance Minister T. V. Soong, Chiang's brother-in-law, that the budget was balanced, although it must be conceded that the feat was based upon rigid economy at the expense of reform.

In November, 1935, Nanking was compelled to abandon the silver standard and set up a managed currency. A rise in the international price of silver, in part the result of American financial policy, caused a drain on Chinese silver, which was the basis of the currency system; and the general trade level declined rapidly instead of increasing, as had been expected. To counter these developments, Nanking nationalized silver and controlled the issue of paper money through the banking system. The new managed currency proved to be more of a success than expected, but there remained serious problems. First, the government was unable to control the activities of foreign banks in China; it could neither take over their stocks of silver nor prevent issue of their banknotes. Second, the Chinese public did not have complete confidence in the new currency, and this added to difficulties in securing control over stocks of silver in private hands. Third, local autonomy in parts of China limited the effectiveness of the government's financial policies, and in the north the Japanese opposed Nanking's efforts and worked to develop a currency tie-in between north China and Manchukuo. To provide adequate foreign exchange and to stabilize the currency, Nanking was able to conclude a loan agreement with the United States and to arrange for American purchases of Chinese silver with gold.

The banking system of China, which had over 140 modern institutions, made modest progress in the 1930's. The Central Bank of China, established in 1928, was the capstone of the system, although it engaged only in government business. The Bank of China was probably the largest bank and was chartered for foreign-exchange transactions. It competed successfully with foreign banks in that field, and it also became important for its commercial undertakings. The Bank of Communications, founded in 1908 to hold revenues of the railways and post offices, was by the 1930's supposed to act as an industrial bank, furnishing industry with long-term loans, but its activities in this field were not extensive. There were some provincial government banks that served the basic needs of local governments, but most of them were simple commercial institutions, some of which had a substantial business.

While Nanking felt that industrialization was the key to the "people's livelihood" and to the defense of China against Japan, the problems that industrialization implied were enormous. During World War I Chinese had begun to invest in modern industry, but as early as 1922 retrenchment set in with the advent of the world depression. In 1932 the Nanking regime was determined to end the depression, which had prevailed for a decade; the national economic council announced a four-year program to convert the Yangtze Valley into a highly industrialized area. The state planned to construct communication systems, open up mines, and establish all kinds of industries. State enterprises were to operate for the benefit of the people, with profits reinvested in badly needed public works. On the whole, however, the emphasis was military; and to facilitate the construction of plants, the national defense planning commission, formed in 1933, began to survey mineral resources and raw materials. By 1936 an expansion program for heavy industry was formulated under the direction of the national resources commission. This program involved the exploitation of mines and construction of factories in Kiangsi, Hunan, and Hupeh provinces; and as a preliminary step toward state control of essential raw materials and production of finished goods, the commission recommended nationalization of tungsten-, iron-, and antimony-mining and government construction of two steel plants, exploitation of two coal seams, construction of two copper refineries, establishment of machine shops for the production of precision tools, and development of electric power and chemical industries. It is important to note that civilian industries which had war-production potentialities were generally ignored; and when war came in 1937, Nanking did not know how to harness much of the existing industrial power to the tasks of the military.

By 1937, although there had been much planning, China had scarcely achieved even a modest industrialization. Coal production was hardly more than 20,000,000 tons, approximately half the Japanese output, and blast-furnace capacity for the production of pig iron was only 870,000 tons a year, much of which represented small furnaces which were often idle. Nanking had planned to erect four new steel mills, but only one small plant—the privately owned Hoshing Steel Works at Shanghai—was operating; and, with the exception of the metallurgical laboratory of the Academia Sinica, no alloy steel was being produced in China. There were approximately 200 electrical-equipment factories in China, but over two-thirds of these were located in the vulnerable Shanghai area. Petroleum supply was an even more glaring deficiency, and only with the greatest effort was the Kansu Petroleum Administration able to maintain an annual production of more than 400,000 pounds of crude oil and more than 100,000 barrels of gasoline. As for direct military production, Chinese arsenals were able to manufacture light arms of good quality, and by 1937 they were able to equip practically all of the infantry divisions of the central government. Materials for heavier armaments came largely from Germany.

Success in the field of transportation was closely related to the government's extension of its power by military means. The ministry of communications worked out extensive plans for railway construction, to be undertaken as rapidly as circumstances permitted. Some old projects, dating back as far as the days of the consortium, were completed with the assistance of foreign financing, but as late as 1940 the total railway mileage was less than 15,000 miles; half of this total was concentrated in north China and Manchuria, and at least nine provinces were without railroads. The ministry of communications also emphasized highway development, and by 1937 there were 68,000 miles in operation, although only one-fourth of this mileage was surfaced.

After the break with the communists in 1927, the Kuomintang effectively controlled the labor movement. Chiang K'ai-shek ordered the suppression of communist-led unions, and in 1929 Nanking promulgated the provisional regulations for the settlement of disputes between capital and labor, which became law in 1930. Trade unions, such as those of the railway workers, seamen, postal workers, and miners, were legal, but the law was carefully designed to prevent any union from receiving official recognition if the government disapproved of its policy or suspected it of affiliation with the communists. Legislation was also enacted for the arbitration of labor disputes and for the improvement of working conditions, such as the eight-hour day. By 1933 Nanking had created a bureau of social affairs to supervise all labor unions, and in that year it organized a central factory inspection bureau to check on standards of management, working conditions, hours, and wages. In 1936 there were 872 registered unions, with over 700,000 members.

Despite the emphasis on industrialization and transportation, the basic economic problems that faced China were agricultural. Peasant cultivators were in an extremely difficult position: rents were high, taxes were oppressive, and purchasing power was low; moreover, they suffered from a lack of cheap credit and adequate marketing facilities. Their farming methods were primitive; ancient tools were used, and fertilizing methods were inadequate and unscientific. Of equal importance was the fact that agricultural production continued to decline, and even staples like rice and wheat were scarce. Unrelieved famine and constant local warfare depopulated huge areas. For example, in the period from 1927 to 1937 the cultivated area of Kansu Province declined by 32 per cent according to Nanking government statistics. The Kuomintang drafted an agricultural development program, but funds for its implementation were limited. These plans included projects for flood control, irrigation, and land reclamation, the establishment of farm credit agencies, colonization schemes, stimulation of home and village industries, development of transportation facilities, afforestation, and the introduction of agricultural experiment and educational stations.

Much of the stimulus for agricultural improvement came from the co-operative movement. In 1934 the Nanking regime promulgated the Co-operative Societies Act, which legalized co-operatives, and by the end of that year there were already in existence over 14,000 units with more than a half-million members. Co-operatives were not confined to agriculture but included other economic activities, such as fishing, transportation, and public utilities. In 1935 a division of co-operatives was established in the ministry of industries to encourage the spirit of mutual aid, better co-ordination between co-operatives and economic activities of the government, and the establishment of a banking system within the co-operative network; in connection with the banking system, Nanking formed an agricultural-capital organization to provide short- or long-term credit at low rates of interest to farm co-operatives through local agencies in key agricultural centers. By 1938 there were more than 60,000 co-operatives with over 3,000,000 members; however, the movement, organized on a provincial basis under government legislation, was a virtual appendage of the government instead of a popular movement. Co-operatives received financial assistance from the government and its credit agencies, and they were under a strong measure of government control through provincial co-operative institutes.

The co-operative movement made significant progress, but it was handicapped by a lack of trained personnel, particularly experts in processing and marketing products and commodities, engineers for utility projects, and other specialists. The government was aware of these deficiencies and sought, without much success, to direct university graduates into these fields. It gave special attention to the problem of marketing facilities since traditionally the merchant middleman reduced the farmer's share of the consumer's expenditures and lack of storage space often forced peasants to dispose of crops at low prices after the harvest. To rectify this situation, the government constructed various kinds of storage facilities and supplied the farmers with new marketing channels. Some warehouses were located at terminal markets and others near primary markets or centers of railroad, highway, and water transportation. But the great majority were located near production centers and smaller marketing towns. The system was well planned; and where sufficient warehousing existed, the storage and marketing demands were met. Unfortunately there were not enough installations to serve more than limited areas. The government also established a national agricultural research bureau, which had some success in popularizing scientific techniques. Its activities included the introduction of new types of rice and other staples, chemical fertilizers, and chemical sprays to check insect infestation of granaries.

Nanking had little success in the field of land reform. The Land Law of 1930 was intended to alleviate some of the evils of tenancy, but the law was not well enforced. According to its provisions, rents were not to exceed 37½ per cent of the main crop, and the land tax was reduced to 1 per cent of the assessed value of the land. Tenancy contracts were to be extended automatically unless landlords needed the land for their own use; moreover, the tenant could not be evicted unless he was two years in arrears on the rent or had not worked the land for a year without proper reason. The tenant was also free to make improvements at the expense of the landlord.

The politico-economic structure of Chinese society prevented the implementation of this law. The Chinese ruling classes—rural landlords and urban businessmen—did not liberate the peasantry because they were organically dependent upon its continued exploitation. The peasantry, on the whole, remained subject to the depradations of the landlord, usurer, merchant, banker, and officials. In the Hangchow district of Chekiang Province, where 70 per cent of the peasants were tenants or semitenants, rents averaged about 50 per cent of the main crop, and in Hupeh Province they ranged all the way from 45 to 80 per cent. Throughout the country the average was between 50 and 70 per cent. Kuomintang statistics show that approximately 10 per cent of the population in rural areas owned 65 per cent of the land, while the remaining 90 per cent owned the other 35 per cent of the land. The figures of the Chinese communists indicate an even higher rate of land concentration. Usury continued, despite the creation of new credit facilities, and it has been estimated that over 90 per cent of rural credit needs were still provided in the traditional manner. In fact, there is evidence that in some areas Kuomintang banks extended low-interest loans to landlords and rich peasants who in turn passed them on to poor peasants at high interest rates. The *pao chia* system was a particularly effective instrument of landlord domination. Designed as a system of rural development and control with ascending units of ten, one hundred, and a thousand families, its headmen were invariably landlords who used it as a means to collect rents, debts, and taxes.

Kuomintang leaders failed to realize sufficiently that their power, both political and economic, rested at least in part upon the good will of the masses of peasants. They faced a dilemma, for they could not hope to satisfy the masses of people without upsetting all existing property relations and destroying the economic foundations of the ruling classes in town and countryside alike.

Education and Ideology

Success of much of the Kuomintang's planning depended on improvement of the educational system. Between the end of World War I and the establishment of the Nanking regime, the Chinese educational system was threatened with collapse, chiefly because of lack of funds. Teachers were poorly trained, and their low salaries were often months in arrears. Schools were meagerly equipped and in miserable condition. Morale was particularly low in the universities, where there was a general lack of discipline and much insecurity. College students made extravagant demands on educational authorities, insisting on the right to elect and dismiss their instructors, determine school hours and classroom schedules, fix fees, and dictate policy on school publication. On the slightest provocation the student body called strikes that sometimes ended in destructive riots.

In 1928 Nanking established a system of education, based on the French model, under the control of a national academy of education, which had branches in each province and representatives in each hsien. One of the founding principles of this system was provincial autonomy in education, and Nanking hoped that ultimately there would be a university in each province which would control all the schools in its sphere. In 1929, however, this philosophy gave way to a centralized system under a ministry of education, but not until 1932 were the details of the new approach worked out. Under the control of the minister of education, each province had its own commissioner, who headed a department of education, and each hsien had a bureau of education under a director appointed by the provincial commissioner. Nanking gave priority to the higher levels of education and founded many new universities, colleges, and teacher-training schools, hoping thus to increase the supply of trained personnel in such fields as agriculture, engineering, medicine, and law. On the lower levels, particularly in middle schools, there was also an increasing emphasis on vocational education. The basic problems that remained in the way of expanding local elementary education were lack of teachers and shortage of funds for school construction, and by 1937 only a small percentage of China's children of school age received any kind of instruction.

In order to counter communism, Nanking also developed a program of ideological training based on Chiang K'ai-shek's New Life Movement. In launching it in February, 1934, Chiang told the people that the weakness of China was related directly to the fact that her ancient virtues were being completely disregarded, and he therefore asked them to cultivate the four cardinal Confucian virtues: sincerity and courtesy in dealing with others, a

461

spirit of mutual helpfulness, respect for the rights of others, and self-respect for upholding one's honor. A month later he told a mass meeting of 100,000 persons to pursue an industrious and Spartan existence and to cultivate personal neatness and cleanliness. He constantly denied the validity of class warfare and emphasized self-sacrifice and loyalty to the state as two indispensable virtues for all Chinese, and he called upon the people to "move forward in a grand co-operative effort to reform the distorted, disorderly, and degenerate social conditions which are endangering the very existence of the country."

Cults of Confucius and mid-nineteenth-century Confucian statesmen like Tseng Kuo-fan were an important ingredient of the New Life Movement. In 1928 the Nanking government had abolished official Confucian rites on the ground that the principles of Confucius were despotic and superstitious, but by 1934 the old master had been recanonized. His birthday became a national holiday, and traditional rites were reinstituted under the direction of government officials. Chiang K'ai-shek was compared to Tseng Kuo-fan, since he was taking the lead in restoring the stable relationships of the Confucian order. The government sponsored a read-the-Classics movement and printed the works of Tseng Kuo-fan for assignment in the schools, and it discouraged education in the Western humanities and social sciences. Chiang resurrected the old argument that, with Chinese studies as the basis, only science and technology had to be borrowed from the West. But, whereas Tseng Kuo-fan had known his Mencius, Chiang K'ai-shek seemed to have forgotten the greatest of the Confucian disciples. He instructed party workers that it was an error to assume the need to provide for the people's welfare before teaching virtues; instead he insisted that through virtue the people would obtain the moral strength to obtain food and clothing. It is difficult to refute the conclusion that Chiang's Confucianism was little more than a romantic nationalism designed to secure a maximum amount of social stability; it is equally difficult to be certain whether this was an end in itself or an expedient dictated by circumstances.

The Communists and the Long March

Throughout this period Chiang K'ai-shek and most of the members of the Kuomintang continued to regard the Chinese Communist Party as their fundamental enemy. By 1931 the communists had formed a territorial base in Kiangsi Province, and in November at Juichin they convened the First All-China Congress of Soviets. The 290 delegates approved the Constitution of the Chinese Soviet Republic, a land law, and a labor law and elected a central committee of 61 members with Mao Tse-tung as chairman. The Chinese Soviet Republic was officially designated a "democratic dictatorship of the proletariat and peasantry," according to the Leninist formula of 1905. The party stated:

It shall be the mission of the Constitution of the Chinese Soviet Republic to guarantee the democratic dictatorship of the proletariat and peasantry in the soviet districts, and to secure the triumph of the dictatorship thoughout the whole of China. It shall be the aim of this dictatorship to destroy all feudal remnants, eliminate the influence of materialist powers in China, to unite China, to limit systematically the development of capitalism, to carry out economic reconstruction of the state, to promote the class-consciousness and solidarity of the proletariat, and to rally to its banner the broad masses of poor peasants in order to effect a transition to the dictatorship of the proletariat.

The party stated explicitly that its ultimate aim was a communist state of the Marxist-Leninist conception.

Like the relationship between the Nanking regime and the Kuomintang, that of the Chinese Soviet Republic and the Chinese Communist Party was a series of interlocking directorates. Political power rested in a council of people's commissars, which was appointed by the central committee of the party. The relationship of local to central government was, again like the Kuomintang government, based on the principle of democratic centralism. The Chinese Communist Party itself was divided into factions, and its stability depended on an uneasy balance of power between Mao Tse-tung and Chu Teh, on the one hand, and the returned students and Chou En-lai, on the other. In 1932–1933 the area under its control consisted of six widely separated regions, of which the largest, the so-called Kiangsi "Central Soviet District," covered about seventeen hsien along the Kiangsi-Fukien border and had a total population of about 3,000,000 people.

The Chinese communist movement was of necessity based on peasant support, and in this respect Mao Tse-tung's experience was particularly valuable. As early as 1925, and especially in the year 1927, Mao, who worked closely with peasant associations, saw the poor peasantry as the vanguard of the revolution. He distinguished between rich, middle, and poor peasants, and he concluded that "to reject the poor peasants is to obstruct the revolution. Without the poor peasants there will be no revolution." In that period, however, the Chinese Communist Party hierarchy under Ch'en Tu-hsiu had never considered that the peasantry would be a decisive factor in the Chinese revolution.

Mao's successes in organizing the peasantry in Hunan Province provided the basis of the agrarian policy of the Kiangsi Soviet. The land law of November, 1931, implemented class warfare in the villages by ordering the confiscation without compensation of all lands belonging to "feudal lords and landlords, militarists and village bosses, gentry, and other big private landowners."

The confiscated lands were to be distributed among the poor and middle peasantry, the latter being defined as those peasants who received 15 per cent or more of their total income from hired labor or tenant farming. According to the law, the rich peasants, who were both landowners and usurers by definition, would have their land seized; however, if a rich peasant, after his land was seized, did not participate in any counterrevolutionary activities and was willing to work land with his own labor power, he might be assigned land but not that of the best quality.

In practice, however, land reform did not always work out, since landlords and rich peasants in many areas managed to retain political authority by declaring themselves for the soviets; and, being thus in a position to control the implementation of land reform, they would either escape expropriation entirely or allot themselves the best land in the process of distribution. In many cases the land hunger of rural paupers remained unsatisfied, and their continuing demand for land caused repeated redistributions, which finally had to be halted by decree in order to insure production. Constant attack by Kuomintang forces, moreover, forced the communists to modify their land-reform program because they simply could not alienate too many people. Often they fell back on the Kuomintang land law of 1930, which had set the maximum rent at $37\frac{1}{2}$ per cent of the main crop.

Despite a blockade enforced by the Nanking regime, the Chinese communists built up several prosperous industries. They operated tungsten mines, selling the ore secretly to the Kwangtung tungsten monopoly, and they owned and managed weaving plants, textile mills, and machine shops. In fact, the Chinese Soviet Republic claimed a "foreign export trade" of over $12,000,000 in value in 1933, most of which was transacted through merchants who risked the Kuomintang blockade to make large profits. The bulk of the nonagricultural production, however, was by handicrafts and home industry, and distribution of goods was largely through co-operatives. The communists also operated their own printing plant at Kian and published many books, magazines, and a "national" newspaper, the *Red China Daily News*.

The Kiangsi Soviet felt the constant pressure of Chiang Kai-shek's extermination campaigns. Between December, 1930, and April, 1933, Chiang's troops failed in four attempts to destroy the communist movement in southeast China, but in November, 1930, some 900,000 men, about one-third of whom were used in a direct attack upon the Kiangsi Soviet army of 100,000 effectives, began a fifth offensive combined with an economic blockade. In earlier campaigns Chiang's troops had made rapid and deep thrusts into communist territory but were unable to hold their positions; however, this time Chiang was careful to consolidate his gains before extending the lines of his soldiers. Superiority in numbers and equipment finally told, and, according to Chou En-lai, the communists suffered over 60,000 casualties. Kuomintang sources claimed that about 1,000,000 people were killed or starved to death as a result of the fighting and the blockade. The success of the fifth campaign also had an important effect on the struggle for power within the Chinese Communist Party. Mao Tse-tung was forced to assume much of the responsibility for the disaster, especially since he had prevented co-operation with a Kuomintang left-wing revolt in Fukien in November, 1933; and evidently in June, 1934, at the Second All-China Congress of Soviets or shortly thereafter, he was stripped of his powers.

Beginning in October, 1934, the communists were forced to evacuate their strongholds in Kiangsi Province. The First Army, built by Mao and Chu Teh but under the control of the returned students and their military adviser, the German communist known as Li Teh, and some 30,000 civilians broke through the blockading forces in the west and began the famous "long march" to the borders of Tibet and north to Shensi Province. When the inadequate leadership of the returned students brought the venture near to disaster, Mao took advantage of the discontent of the military commanders and was able to seize control of the party and military machinery at a conference held at Tsunyi in Kweichow Province from December, 1934, to January, 1935. Despite constant harassment by the troops of Chiang K'ai-shek and the warlords, between August and November, 1935, an advance force of 20,000 men led by Mao Tse-tung and Chou En-lai reached their objective in the northwest and joined with local communist guerrilla units under Liu Tse-tang and Kao Kang. And in 1936 another 40,000 men, out of the total of 200,000 which had finally departed from the southeast, made their way into northern Shensi. In December, 1936, the communists occupied the city of Yenan, which became their new capital early in 1937. In their "new home," an area well known for its maladministration and oppressive taxation by local warlords, the communists began to duplicate their Kiangsi successes through agrarian class warfare.

During the period of the "long march" the fortunes of the Chinese communists were often at their lowest ebb, and this condition caused another important split in the party leadership over the future of the movement. Despite Mao Tse-tung's optimism regarding the drive to the northwest and the re-establishment of the Soviet Republic, Chang Kuo-t'ao proposed that the party seek an effective compromise with the Kuomintang. Although Mao's view was upheld in a party conference at Maoerhkai in Szechwan Province, Chang endeavored to persuade Chu Teh, whose military support was essential in a party power struggle, to make a bargain with the Kuomintang whereby he and his troops would be integrated into a national army. Chu Teh, however, remained loyal to Mao and joined him in Shensi in 1936. Tried a year later for his attempted defection, Chang was removed from his posts and ordered to undergo a period of "self-criticism and study of his errors." In April, 1938,

465

he was permitted to leave Yenan for Hankow; and when he joined the Kuomintang, he was finally dismissed from membership in the Chinese Communist Party.

The United-Front Issue

The long march of the Chinese communists coincided with mounting pressures on Nanking to resist Japanese aggression. There was a growing anti-Japanese sentiment among the Chinese populace; a Japanese druggist was killed by a mob at Pakhoi in Kwangtung, a Japanese consular policeman was killed at Hankow, the Japanese consul at Swatow reported the discovery of a bomb in a Japanese restaurant, a Japanese army officer and his orderly were assaulted at Fengtai near Peiping, and three Japanese sailors were shot by a Chinese gunman at Shanghai's International Settlement. The Cantonese political leaders strongly criticized Chiang K'ai-shek for his failure to resist Japan. In September, 1934, a number of them joined to sign a circular telegram demanding changes in national policies at the party congress which was scheduled for November, 1934, and they accused Chiang of having refused to put into effect decisions made at the 1931 party congress with reference to Japan.

The will to resist Japan culminated in the "National Salvation" movement, begun in 1935 by professors and students in north China. Great student demonstrations in favor of ending the strife with the communists in order to strengthen the country against Japan spread in a chain reaction from Peking to other cities; but Chiang K'ai-shek, refusing to bend to popular outbursts, arrested and imprisoned the leaders of the National Salvation group. In Canton the Kwangsi generals, Pai Chung-hsi and Li Tsung-jen, encouraged student agitation and in May, 1936, reiterated their demand for action against Japan. They even threatened to rebel against Nanking if Chiang and his generals refused to join with them in an attack on Japan in the north. In a few weeks it appeared that widespread civil war might result, but the southern revolt collapsed without any serious fighting. In the end Chiang was able to extend his control over Canton and develop a closer working relationship with the southern warlords.

In 1935 the Chinese communists joined the demand for resistance against Japan and called upon Nanking to form with them an anti-Japanese united front. Prior to this time the communists had issued manifestoes to that effect, but there was no unity of opinion among the Chinese communist leaders. For example, Mao Tse-tung steadfastly opposed the united front with the Kuomintang until 1935, when the Seventh Congress of the Comintern, meeting in Moscow, ordered communist parties throughout the world to seek allies against fascist parties within a state and to co-operate with the bourgeois democracies against Germany, Italy, and Japan. The Soviet Union, in the vanguard of this shift, had joined the League of Nations, which it had hitherto branded as "the international organization of capitalists for the systematic exploitation of the working peoples of the earth." It had also re-established normal relations with the United States, and it had signed mutual-assistance pacts with France and Czechoslovakia. The Comintern congress, moreover, criticized the Chinese Communist Party for failing to carry out the united-front policy to date, and it passed a resolution proclaiming the united front in China against Japan. In December, 1935, the Chinese Communist Party accepted this reprimand and resolved to implement Comintern policy. Finally, in January, 1936, it proposed an eight-point program to Nanking as the basis for unity:

1. Continued resistance to Japan until all lost territory has been recovered.
2. Confiscation of property belonging to traitors for use by refugees.
3. Removal of onerous taxes, reorganization of national finances, and development of industry, agriculture, and trade.
4. Increases in wages and salaries, and improvement in the living conditions of workers and peasants.
5. Provision for free compulsory education and jobs for the unemployed.
6. Equality of all races living in China and defense of the Chinese people living abroad.
7. Union of all anti-imperialistic elements to fight against aggression.
8. Co-operation with all sympathetic nations and establishment of friendly relations with neutral powers.

Refusing to negotiate, Chiang K'ai-shek moved troops into the northwest to destroy the Chinese communists. He placed Chang Hsueh-liang in command of the government forces, including the Manchurian army, which had been driven from its homeland by the Japanese. But this was a "new" commander and a "new" army. Chang had shaken off his addiction to narcotics and devoted himself to transforming his troops, 140,000 strong, into an effective fighting force. He vowed to devote his life to the task of recovering Manchuria. The communists, however, continued their efforts to establish a united front with Nanking, and in May, August, and September they issued manifestoes calling on the Nationalists to halt the civil war and co-operate with them in fighting Japan. These efforts were in vain since Chiang did not relent.

The issue of the united front came to a head in the famous Sian mutiny. By the summer of 1936 Chang Hsueh-liang began to side with the communist point of view. He and his entire army were affected by communist slogans, such as "Chinese Must Not Fight Chinese" and "Unite with Us and Fight back to Manchuria." In fact, in June Chang met with Chou En-lai and became convinced of the communists' sincerity. The two men arranged a cessation of hostilities and began to work out a union of their forces against Japan.

Sian, the so-called "bandit-extermination headquarters," became a refuge for anti-Japanese agitators and students. Meanwhile, Chiang K'ai-shek was preparing for a sixth general offensive against the communists. In October he sent his crack First Army to attack them in Kansu Province, and he visited Sian to complete over-all war plans. In November, however, his attention was temporarily diverted from the communists by the Japanese-Mongol attack in Suiyuan and by his own suppression of the National Salvation movement. Chiang's determination to crush the communists was perhaps best borne out by his refusal to dispatch Chang's Manchurian army to Taiyuan against the Japanese.

Despite reversals suffered by the First Army, Chiang in December flew to Sian to put an end to the fraternization between Chang and the communists and to put new vigor into the extermination campaign. But on December 12, Chang and his officers arrested their commander-in-chief and presented him with a list of demands similar to those issued by the National Salvation group in May, 1936, and by the Chinese Communist Party in a circular telegram on December 1, 1936.

1. Reorganization of the Nationalist government and admission of political parties other than the Kuomintang to share the joint responsibility of national salvation.
2. Termination of the civil war and unity in armed resistance to Japan.
3. Release of political prisoners in Shanghai. [Seven leaders of the National Salvation movement were detained there in November.]
4. Pardon for all political prisoners.
5. Guarantee of the liberty of assembly and safeguard of the people's rights and political liberty.
6. Convening of a National Salvation conference.
7. Implementation of the will of Sun Yat-sen.

Chiang K'ai-shek refused to negotiate with his subordinates, and he ordered them to release him and accept the consequences of their mutiny. Several weeks later Chiang was freed, and he returned to Nanking with Chang Hsueh-liang as his prisoner. What occurred at Sian has remained under a cloud. In fact, the central figure in the incident, Chang Hsueh-liang, was still being held incommunicado under house arrest on Taiwan in 1961. We know that Madame Chiang flew to Sian and persuaded her husband to talk with Chang and Chou En-lai, who had been consulted immediately after Chiang's arrest. On the basis of recently disclosed evidence, it seems probable that the communists had encouraged Chang to detain his superior as the first step in setting up a national anti-Japanese government at Sian. They planned to give Chiang a public trial and discredit him, but at this point an order came from Moscow for his release. Evidently Stalin feared that without Chiang the Kuomintang might join with Japan in an anticommunist, anti-Russian pact.

After a week of discussion, described by Chou En-lai as "the most difficult decision of our whole lives," the Chinese communists complied with Moscow's order. When the communist support faltered, Chang Hsueh-liang made his decision to free Chiang.

In the months that followed the Sian mutiny the Chinese communists continued their efforts to create a united front against Japan, and in February, 1937, the Kuomintang issued a resolution which stated that it would give the Chinese communists a chance to reform on four conditions:

1. Abolition of the separate army and its incorporation into the united command of the nation's armed forces.
2. Dissolution of the so-called "Chinese Soviet Republic" and similar organizations, and unification of government power in the hands of the national government.
3. Absolute cessation of communist propaganda and acceptance of "The Three Principles of the People."
4. Termination of the class struggle.

In the spring Chou En-lai held discussions with Chiang K'ai-shek and other Kuomintang officials at Kuling, the summer capital of China, and other meetings were held within communist territory. On its part the Chinese Communist Party ordered the termination of land confiscations and moderated its propaganda, while the Kuomintang prepared for the convocation of a people's national congress in November, 1937, to inaugurate a new constitution. But it would be a mistake to conclude that the united front was already in the making. Chiang continued to develop new strength against the communists, and by June, 1937, he had scattered the Manchurian army and moved his own forces into Shensi to blockade them.

25 *China at War, 1937–1945*

The basic cause of the undeclared war between China and Japan in 1937–1941 was control of north China. The initiative in the use of force was taken by the Japanese north-China garrison, but, according to the American ambassador in Tokyo, Joseph C. Grew, there was complete unanimity of opinion among the cabinet, the military, the foreign office, the press, and businessmen to resist any efforts to weaken Japan's position in north China. The Japanese garrison, which had been active in the earlier autonomous movements, planned to seize north China in case of war and establish a state which would be independent of Nanking. On July 7, while engaging in maneuvers at Marco Polo Bridge near Peiping, some of its units demanded permission to enter the nearby town of Wanping to search for a missing soldier. The Japanese claimed that troops of the Twenty-ninth Army of the Chinese central government refused to admit them and that this made it necessary to send a battalion to force entrance into the town, which the Chinese tried in vain to defend. However, the Chinese claimed that they suggested a joint-committee search for the missing soldier and that, while negotiations were being conducted, Japanese troops opened fire and forced the Chinese to retaliate.

The Undeclared War with Japan

On instructions from the general staff in Tokyo, the Japanese North China Army did not extend the hostilities but was ordered to negotiate with local Chinese authorities and to secure an apology, a promise to punish those responsible for the firing on Japanese troops, withdrawal of Chinese soldiers from the area, their replacement by peace-preservation militia, and guarantees of strict control over anti-Japanese elements. Japan sent reinforcements to China, but on July 11 Nanking accepted the Japanese demands and began implementing them. However, the Japanese North China Army, swelled with reinforcements, was anxious to provoke hostilities, and on July 25 units of it engaged the Chinese at Langfang and Wanping. In Tokyo the government decided to attempt to establish Japanese dominance in the Peiping-Tientsin area; and when the Nanking regime opposed this move, the local engagement was quickly transformed into an undeclared war. On July 29 large-scale fighting began as the Japanese marched on Tientsin, and on August 1 the city fell to them. Chinese troops evacuated Peiping to avoid its bombardment, and on August 8 Japan established its control over the city and set up a military government. Thereafter the entire province of Hopei was quickly occupied.

On August 13 fighting broke out between Chinese and Japanese at Shanghai, where tension had mounted following the eruption of hostilities in the north. Fighting began after a Japanese naval officer and a seaman were shot near a Chinese airport on the outskirts of the city. Two days later Japan began to move regular army units to Shanghai to reinforce the normal complement of 2,000 men stationed there for the protection of Japanese nationals and interests, and the Tokyo government issued a public statement to the effect that "drastic measures" were necessary to chastise the Chinese army and to impress upon the Nanking government the necessity to reconsider its attitude toward Japan. The Japanese prime minister, Prince Konoye, attempted to dispatch a personal envoy to China to discuss with Chiang K'ai-shek the possibility of settling the dispute peaceably, but the Japanese army intercepted and detained him. Once their swords were unsheathed, the Japanese militarists wanted to fight.

The Japanese aggression created a Chinese resistance that was national. Important provincial military leaders went to Nanking to offer their services and to reassure Chiang K'ai-shek of their loyalty, but, more important, the negotiations between the Kuomintang and the Chinese Communist Party for the creation of a united front were rapidly completed. In a manifesto drafted on July 4, handed to the Kuomintang on July 15, and published by the Central News Agency on September 22, 1937, the central committee of the Chinese Communist Party declared:

1. The Three Principles of the People enunciated by Dr. Sun Yat-sen are the paramount need of China today. This party is ready to strive for their enforcement.
2. This party abandons its policy of overthrowing the Kuomintang of China by force and the movement of Sovietization and discontinues its policies of forcible confiscation of land from landowners.
3. This party abolishes the present Soviet government and will enforce democracy based on the people's rights in order to unify the national political machinery.
4. The party abolishes the Red Army, reorganizes it into the National Revolutionary Army, places it under the direct control of the military affairs commission of the national government, and awaits orders for mobilization to share the responsibility of resisting foreign invasion at the front.

On the following day Chiang K'ai-shek officially answered the communist declaration thus:

The Chinese Communist Party, by surrendering its prejudices, has clearly recognized the vital importance of our national independence and welfare. I sincerely hope that all members of the communist party will faithfully and unitedly put into practice the various decisions reached, and under the unified military command that is directing our resistance, will offer their services to the state, fighting shoulder to shoulder with the rest of the nation for the successful completion of the nationalist revolution. In our revolution we are struggling not for personal ambition or opinions, but for the realization of The Three Principles of the People. Especially during this period of national crisis, when the fate of China lies in the balance, we ought not to argue over the past, but to try as a nation to make a new start. We should earnestly strive to unite, so that as a united nation we may safeguard the continued existence of the republic.

The hostilities never legally became a war since neither party formally declared that a state of war existed. Japan referred to the "China incident" and later to the "China affair." For internal as well as international reasons the Japanese government felt it desirable to minimize the scope and significance of the fighting in China. For example, the American Neutrality Act of 1935 gave President Roosevelt full discretion to find or not to find a state of war in existence and thus to invoke or not invoke embargoes on loans and munitions. The Nanking government also preferred not to declare war since it shared the widely held view that the Japanese army was acting on its own in China without the approval of its government. The Chinese also hoped that the League of Nations would declare Japan an aggressor, thus preventing nations from proclaiming their neutrality and withholding shipments of strategic materials to both belligerents, a circumstance which would hit China harder than Japan.

The superior Japanese army was pinned down at Shanghai until November, but, once Chinese resistance was cracked, the Japanese moved inland quickly. The Chinese fought stubbornly and heroically at Shanghai, but they lacked equipment and fought without an air force. The Japanese were able to bomb bases, lines of communications, and troop concentrations at will; moreover, they also struck at nonmilitary objectives to break the Chinese will to resist. The Chinese defenders were finally compelled to evacuate the city when a Japanese force landed at Hangchow on November 5. The flank of the Chinese armies was exposed, forcing them to withdraw up the Yangtze River to Nanking, where preparations were made for a prolonged defense. In mid-November the Japanese launched their drive toward Nanking, moving along the Yangtze River and via the Shanghai-Nanking Railway. In December they drove the Chinese out of the capital, and in the process they shattered the best armies of Chiang K'ai-shek. Nanking itself was the scene of a week-long orgy of plunder and rape by undisciplined and unrestrained Japanese soldiers. After this defeat, the Chinese government was forced to move its headquarters further up-river to Hankow.

Meanwhile, in north China, Japanese armies were engaged in extensive operations. Moving westward into Shansi Province, they captured the capital city, Taiyuan. Further north, in Inner Mongolia, the Kwantung Army gained control of Chahar and Suiyuan provinces, and on October 29, 1937, it established a Federated Autonomous Government of Mongolia. Other armies moved southward down the Tientsin-Pukow and Peking-Hankow railways (Peiping became Peking again), and, although they met with stubborn resistance, they drove Chinese forces south of the Yellow River and began negotiating a surrender with General Han Fu-chu, governor of Shantung Province.

The Japanese government believed that China would sue for peace once Nanking and the key cities of north China fell. It then hoped to create in China an obedient government which would assume administrative responsibilities but take orders from Tokyo, permitting the resources of northern and central China to be exploited by Japanese capital. Thus, shortly after the fall of Nanking, Prime Minister Konoye attempted to open peace negotiations with Chiang K'ai-shek through the good offices of the German ambassador to China, Dr. Oscar Trautmann, and Konoye indicated his willingness to go to

Hankow to sign a treaty. However, the Japanese war minister, General Sugiyama, and other extremists were opposed to such a move. They believed that with the loss of Nanking there would be military defections from Chiang K'ai-shek and that his administration would collapse. Japan would then establish a new government more amenable to her direction. On December 12 Konoye, still anxious to negotiate directly with Chiang, threatened to resign, but he was persuaded by officials of the imperial court to remain in office. On December 20 a special conference of top Japanese civil and military officials outlined peace terms that Japan would submit to Chiang, as follows: China was to recognize Manchukuo and collaborate with Japan against communism; establish demilitarized areas and specify independent administrative organs in such areas; co-operate closely with Japan and Manchukuo in economic matters; and pay necessary reparations to Japan. At Hankow, Chiang K'ai-shek turned down the Japanese terms, and Chinese troops massed to defend the Wuhan cities. Finally, on January 14, 1938, Konoye was compelled by army pressure to state that his government would no longer negotiate with Chiang K'ai-shek.

Japan had won the battles but not the war, and her dreams of a short campaign and a profitable peace were unfulfilled. Her government began to emphasize the need for protracted war. In China, Japanese control was limited to towns and arteries of transportation, but the countryside did not readily accept Japanese political direction. When organized, the peasants gave support to guerrilla forces which began to operate in areas reported conquered by Japanese arms.

After the failure of the negotiations with Chiang K'ai-shek, Japan proceeded to establish a series of governments in China. On December 14, 1937, the Provisional Government of the Chinese Republic, with jurisdiction over Shantung, Hopei, and portions of Shansi and Honan, was formed at Peking under the control of the North China Army. The Chinese who participated in the regime were men with records of co-operation with Japan, and through them the Japanese set out to eradicate resistance activities. The North China Army commander of special services, Major General Kita, expected this regime to develop into a new national government for all China. In central China Japanese strategists worked to organize a Chinese puppet government at Nanking, and on March 28, 1938, they set up a Reformed Government of the Chinese Republic. In September, 1938, the Japanese army attempted to consolidate the northern and central regimes under the direction of a China Affairs Board, formed in Tokyo under the chairmanship of the prime minister. The only result of negotiations, however, was the establishment of a "United Council of China," which was essentially a liaison committee of members of the rival governments. The political problem was complicated by the fact that in Tokyo there was still a strong body of military and civil officials who wanted to negotiate a direct settlement with Chiang K'ai-shek, while the

473

Japanese high command refused to deal with Chiang and preferred to wait until the outcome of the drive on Hankow.

In the autumn of 1938 Japan scored another series of spectacular military victories. Japanese troops moved on the Wuhan cities from three directions: down the Peking-Hankow Railway; westward from Shantung, where General Han Fu-chu did not oppose them with any vigor; and up the Yangtze River from Nanking. On October 25, 1938, Hankow fell despite stubborn Chinese resistance, which included even changing the course of the Yellow River by cutting dikes and thus flooding the Japanese troops in a vast area south of Shantung. The national government of China fled to Chungking, far to the west in Szechwan Province. Canton was another primary target of the Japanese army, for this city and the Hankow-Canton Railway were vital to the transit of British and American aid to China. The Chinese defenses at Canton were not particularly strong because China felt that Japan would not dare make a move in an area so close to Hong Kong. However, the British position in East Asia had deteriorated; and when Great Britain helped deliver Czechoslovakia to Hitler in the Munich Settlement of September 29, 1938, Japan felt that there was little need to worry about British reactions. The city of Canton fell to the Japanese on October 21, 1938.

Despite these successes, there was no peace in China, and the war settled down to a stalemate. Occupied China constituted the territory east of a line from Peking to Hankow to Canton; and although there were some occasional limited offensives to the west, Japanese actions were generally confined to bombing principal railways and cities, especially Chungking. Since the Chinese did not have adequate power to take the offensive on any large scale, Nationalist armies concentrated on conducting holding operations along the broad north-south front, which helped to tie down large numbers of Japanese troops; and in the north, communist guerrillas harassed the Japanese and prevented any further incursion into northwest China.

Military Stalemate and Occupied China

Following the fall of Hankow and Canton, the Japanese government proclaimed that it would establish a New Order in East Asia, which would embrace Japan, Manchukuo, and China and consolidate the political, economic, and cultural forces of the three countries. The New Order was proclaimed by Prime Minister Konoye on November 3, 1938, and reaffirmed in another speech by him on December 22, 1938. A detailed explanation of the New Order was made to the privy council by Foreign Minister Arita on November 29. Konoye had Arita redefine the relationship of China to Japan to explain the shift in his policy since his statement of January, 1938, in which he had refused to negotiate with the Nationalist government. Arita disclaimed any Japanese intention of annihilating China as a nation, and he offered the Kuomintang a role in the New Order, providing it repudiated its anti-

Japanese policies, reformed its system of government, and eliminated its offensive personnel. According to Arita, this meant replacement of the Chiang K'ai-shek regime with one which would act under the direction of Tokyo. The alternative for China was continued Japanese military operations until Chiang and his government, labeled "a local regime," had been completely destroyed. In a speech on December 26, 1938, Chiang denounced the New Order, calling it a term "for the overthrow of international order in East Asia and the enslavement of China." He urged his countrymen to continue the struggle and hinted that foreign assistance would eventually turn the tide against Japan.

The Japanese army took the offensive once again in the spring of 1939. The central army began a campaign to strengthen its Yangtze River communications system by a series of attacks in Kiangsi Province, which resulted in the capture of Nanchang; but in September, 1939, Japanese forces were defeated when they attacked Changsha in neighboring Hunan Province. In the south a Japanese campaign in Kwangtung and Kwangsi provinces was generally unsuccessful. In June, 1940, the Japanese army reached the limits of its success when it moved up the Yangtze River to Ichang, which put it only 240 air miles from Chungking; thereafter the Chinese capital began to suffer almost daily air attacks. During the remainder of 1940, Japanese units carried out mopping-up operations, with varying degrees of success, against guerrilla attacks upon their lines of communication.

There were a number of reasons why Japan did not pursue the fighting in China more vigorously after 1939. The Japanese war effort was beginning to run into difficulty at home. There were shortages of skilled labor and bottlenecks in production, especially of machine tools. The Japanese people were becoming somewhat weary of the struggle in China and were irritated by shortages of consumer goods, particularly clothing and footwear. Increased taxation and savings, however, were holding inflationary tendencies in check, and there was no serious unrest. International considerations also complicated Japan's over-all view of expansion after the outbreak of hostilities in Europe in September, 1939. For some time she had been preparing for the possibility of war with the Soviet Union, but in the autumn of 1939 and thereafter she had the increasingly attractive opportunity of moving against the British and French colonies in Southeast Asia. Japan's China policy was to continue efforts at terminating hostilities by a favorable peace settlement, which was unlikely, and to consolidate her conquests. Japan was certainly not ready to extend the war, and in fact Japanese military men were nervous about possible Russian intervention in China, especially if Japan drove further west.

The major focus of the consolidation policy was to establish a Chinese regime amenable to Japanese direction. During the first two years of the war Japan was unable to persuade any prominent Chinese to join such a government, but she did continue to court Wang Ching-wei, who was known to have urged Chiang K'ai-shek to capitulate at the time of the siege of Hankow.

Although he was overruled, Wang remained in the Chungking regime, but he became more of a defeatist as time wore on. The differences between Chiang and Wang increased and reached a climax in December, 1939, when Wang deserted the Kuomintang and went to Hanoi, where he indicated his willingness to negotiate with Japan. Wang felt that he could establish a satisfactory relationship with Japan and thereby avert what he regarded as national suicide. In April, 1939, he left Hanoi for Shanghai and in June proceeded to Tokyo, where he began discussions with the new prime minister, Baron Hiranuma, concerning the establishment of a new Chinese central government with himself as president.

Wang negotiated for more than a year before he accepted the presidency of the Japanese-sponsored Nanking government in March, 1940. The slowness of the negotiations resulted not so much from differences between Wang and the Japanese but from Tokyo's continuing peace overtures to Chungking. The Japanese, moreover, were endeavoring to get the old warlord, Wu P'ei-fu, to join them in the hope that he might cause a major military defection from Chiang K'ai-shek—something that Wang had been unable to accomplish. Wu did not take the bait, and his death in February, 1940, put an end to Japanese efforts along these lines. Wang's life at Nanking was not a happy one, for he lived in fear of assassination and was a virtual prisoner of the Japanese. Although Japan extended formal recognition to the new Chinese regime in November, 1940, political and military power remained in the hands of the Japanese ambassador, General Abe Nobuyuki. To complete the farce, Japan compelled Wang to recognize the government of Manchukuo.

Chiang K'ai-shek and the Western powers reacted to the new regime as expected. Chiang reaffirmed China's intention to resist until Japan was driven from Chinese territory, and he stated emphatically that his government would regard de jure or de facto recognition of the Nanking government as an unfriendly act and a violation of international law and treaties. On March 30, 1940, the American secretary of state, Cordell Hull, remarked that the new regime at Nanking had the "appearance of a further step in a program of one country by armed force to impose its will upon a neighboring country and to block off a large area of the world from normal political and economic relationship with the rest of the world." He noted that the puppet regime would "especially favor the interests of Japan and deny to the nationals of the United States and other third countries long-established rights of equal and fair treatment to which they are legally and justly entitled." Great Britain, in a much more difficult position in China and under terrific pressure from Japan, also maintained its recognition of the government of Chiang K'ai-shek.

Japan sought to exploit occupied China economically. In the autumn of 1938 the China Affairs Board at Tokyo established the North China Development Company, which was given a virtual monopoly over economic enterprises in the northern provinces of China. In the provinces of the Yangtze River Valley the Central China Promotion Company monopolized basic economic enterprises, and a smaller company was planned but never formally authorized for south China. Through these agencies Japan took control of the industries, transportation systems, telegraph and telephone systems, dockyards, shipping companies, banks, and many other business enterprises; moreover, Japanese also increased their own capital investment in China.

Japan also revised the tariff in her favor, and there was a considerable expansion of imports from Japan, rising from a valuation of 190,000,000 yen in 1937 to 343,000,000 yen in 1938. The increase of exports from China was less marked, rising from a valuation of 160,000,000 yen in 1937 to 179,000,000 yen in 1938. Although the trade achieved better balance in the following years, Japan continued to have to import cotton, iron and steel, machines, machine tools, and petroleum products from outside the area of her political control, notably from the United States, in order to maintain her industries and to sustain her war effort.

Japanese economic planning was often sabotaged by the Chinese; for example, in north China peasants substituted food crops for the cotton which Japan needed to relieve her of the necessity of making extensive foreign purchases of cotton. Japan was anxious to conserve foreign exchange in order to pay for imports essential for military purposes. The Chinese also destroyed food crops, when possible, to prevent their falling into Japanese hands. Japan discovered that effective economic exploitation of Chinese resources could hardly be expected under wartime conditions, and this was another reason for endeavoring to bring Chiang K'ai-shek to accept peace on Japan's terms.

As late as September, 1941, Japan transmitted the following peace terms to the Chungking government:

1. Co-operative defense between Japan and China for the purposes of preventing communist and other subversive activities which may constitute a menace to the security of both countries and of maintaining public order in China. Stationing of troops and naval forces by Japan in certain areas in the Chinese territory for a necessary period for the purposes referred to above and in accordance with the existing agreements and usages.

2. Withdrawal of Japanese armed forces upon settlement of the China affair, excepting those troops which come under No. 1, above.

3. Economic co-operation, with the development and utilization of essential raw materials for national defense in China as its principal objective. This would not restrict any economic activities by third powers in China so long as they are pursued on an equitable basis.

4. Fusion of the Chiang K'ai-shek and Wang Ching-wei regimes.

5. No annexation of territory.

6. No indemnities.

7. Recognition of Manchukuo.

Chiang K'ai-shek remained adamant in his refusal to negotiate on Japanese terms, and thus Japan continued to be involved in a war of attrition. The

Chinese will to fight was not broken, and Japan was prevented from gaining victory.

The Impact of War on Nationalist China

The struggle against Japan gave great impetus to Chinese nationalism. At first anti-Japanese in form, it was soon closer to a positive loyalty to China. Both the Kuomintang and the Chinese Communist Party declared that the conflict was a "war for the very existence of our nation and the completion of our national revolution," and for many Chinese the new outpouring of nationalism revived the hopes and aspirations which had inspired the revolution of the 1920's. Chiang K'ai-shek became more of a symbol of national unity for most patriotic groups and for the mass of the Chinese people. Chinese hoped that in the west, beyond the reach of Japanese forces, an entirely new political, social, and economic structure would be built. At the same time, the guerrilla tactics of armed peasants would continue to harass the Japanese in occupied territory. These bands operated almost entirely behind Japanese lines and were self-governing and generally self-sufficient. The communists were more adept at the use of guerrilla tactics, particularly in making the necessary social and political adjustments essential for the maintenance of popular support. They instructed the people in "communist democracy," and they established in each village a mobilization committee, self-defense corps, and partisan detachments.

Administrative changes in the Nationalist government reflected the impact of war. Chiang K'ai-shek and the Kuomintang continued to exercise sovereign power but acted through a party supreme defense council which replaced the unwieldy central political council. The new organ issued decrees to the state council, which became a supervisory administrative committee, passing orders on to the five yuan and the military affairs commission. The latter body was of special importance. Chiang K'ai-shek was its chairman—considered his most serious wartime responsibility—and its membership was appointed by the state council upon the nomination of the supreme defense council. The military affairs commission was responsible for the direction of the war and the co-ordination of political functions with those of the military, but it also engaged in propaganda and secret-police activities.

Chiang's military subordinates fell into two groups, the military bureaucrats, led by General Ho Ying-ch'in, minister of war for fourteen years and chief of staff since 1927, and the young officer graduates of Whampoa Military Academy, whose key spokesmen were Ch'en Ch'eng and Hu Tsungnan. Both groups were clearly authoritarian, but the latter group, largely divisional commanders, wanted a more efficient administration even if it meant demotion of their bureaucratic superiors. Chiang K'ai-shek generally stood behind Ho but was ultimately forced to replace him with Ch'en Ch'eng as minister of war because of Ho's military corruption and inefficiency.

China remained under the tutelage of the Kuomintang, but there were some important shifts in the influence of party factions. The most potent force in the party and the government was the reactionary and antiforeign clique led by Ch'en Li-fu, who had built a strong following in the previous decade. Enjoying Chiang's favor and patronage, it controlled the schools and the press and administered an independent secret-police force responsible to the party alone. In his zeal to combat communism and defend Chinese customs, Ch'en Li-fu, as minister of education, "established an intellectual reign of terror" at Chinese universities. Moreover, progressive-minded groups like the businessmen and intellectuals of the coastal cities became subordinate to the relatively unenlightened landlords and merchants of the interior provinces. The former provided the backbone of the so-called "political-science clique," whose members were largely trained in Japan and the United States and respected rule by law and efficient administration. Although they were used increasingly by Chiang as his relations with Americans expanded, their power was never very real. In the final analysis, of course, power and responsibility rested with Chiang K'ai-shek, and after 1938 he assumed the post of party leader with an absolute veto over decisions of the most important party councils and a veto—by suspension—over party congresses.

Censorship, which had been a normal function of Kuomintang power, became harsher after the outbreak of hostilities with Japan. For example, in 1937 the military affairs commission established a wartime press censorship bureau which forbade any publication from carrying critical items dealing with political, military, or foreign affairs. This was justified as an emergency measure. Foreign press dispatches were also carefully censored by the international department of the ministry of information, which deleted news items regarded as derogatory to the best interests of the Chinese government and its handling of domestic and foreign affairs. This resulted in a virtual blackout of accurate news from China as far as the rest of the world was concerned. Similar restrictions were placed on radio broadcasting, which became essentially a propaganda arm of the government. Unfortunately for China such vigorous censorship prevented effective criticism of public policy or of the activities and behavior of the higher public officials or of individuals protected by them. Public opinion was unable to prevent the exploitation of power for individual aggrandizement.

The establishment of the people's political council was the only concession the Kuomintang made to multipartisan participation in government. With the outbreak of hostilities in July, 1937, the Kuomintang set up a national defense advisory council, which included leaders of opposition parties as well as independents. Although this body did serve for a time as a symbol of national unity, its members soon demanded the convocation of an assembly with a large membership. In March, 1938, at Hankow an emergency session of the Kuomintang party congress decided to establish the people's political council. This was explained as a first step toward representative government; more realistically, it was a compromise between an elective united-front government and a continuation of the Kuomintang dictatorship. The first people's political council was composed of 200 members, all selected by the central executive committee of the Kuomintang, and by 1941 the membership was extended to 240, 90 of whom were to be elected by various provisional provincial and municipal assemblies. The membership of the council remained overwhelmingly Kuomintang, but the Chinese Communist Party and the smaller political parties were also represented. The council had no actual power but was an influential advisory body that reflected various shades of Chinese opinion. It was able to discuss important measures regarding domestic and foreign affairs, submit proposals to the supreme defense council, hear reports from various ministries, and interpellate officers of state on demand The council held its initial meeting at Hankow in July, 1938, and two sessions were held later in the year at Chungking. Two more meetings were held in 1939, and thereafter only one a year.

During the September, 1939, meeting the council recommended that the government convene the national assembly to consider the adoption of the draft constitution of 1936, and in November, 1939, the central executive committee of the Kuomintang set November, 1940, as the date for convoking such a constituent body. The people's political council appointed a 25-man committee known as the "Association for the Promotion of Constitutionalism," the main function of which was to examine and suggest modifications of the 1936 draft. On March 30, 1940, the committee finished its work and submitted to the government a revised draft which placed legislative power in the national assembly and a standing committee of it. That the committee had gone too far in broadening the basis of the government was clear when in September, 1940, the standing committee of the central executive committee voted to postpone indefinitely the convening of the national assembly. In 1943, under American pressure, Chiang K'ai-shek spoke to the people's political council of the desirability of forming another committee to prepare for constitutional government, and the central executive committee of the Kuomintang passed a resolution which promised the convocation of a national assembly to adopt and promulgate a constitution within a year after the defeat of Japan. Chiang ultimately appointed a constitutional committee, but it was controlled by Kuomintang politicians who feared to take any initiative.

The people's political council was also active in demanding greater political freedom for the Chinese people. The "Program of Armed Resistance and National Reconstruction," approved by both the Kuomintang and the people's political council in 1938, pledged the government to guarantee the freedoms of speech, press, assembly, and association within the limits of the Three Principles of the People and of law. During the first session of the people's political council, the members requested the government to protect the freedoms of the people and to amend or repeal laws which contravened them. However, when specific proposals were passed by the council and submitted to the supreme defense council, they were generally disallowed on the claim that the government was already permitting maximum freedom under wartime conditions. In some cases the government passed "freedom decrees" which it had no intention of enforcing.

Local government in Nationalist China remained under the domination of the Kuomintang and the military. Provincial governors were usually generals who were assisted by party hacks and their subordinates. Local military establishments were powerful, and they often resorted to forced conscription to obtain recruits and to requisitioning for their food requirements. For hsien administration, which according to Sun Yat-sen was to be the training-ground in self-government, Chungking promulgated new regulations in 1939. These provided for the establishment of hsien assemblies that might well have served Sun's purpose had they been constituted differently, but almost all of them were packed and tightly controlled by either the hsien magistrate or the hsien organization of the Kuomintang.

Nationalist China faced tremendous economic problems. It had to develop an economy capable of both sustaining the war effort and supplying the needs of an increased population resulting from the migration of thousands of Chinese from the coastal areas into the interior provinces. Fortunately, however, the refugees had been able to move large amounts of essential machinery from some of the eastern urban areas. They salvaged less than 10 per cent of textile machinery, but they saved more than 80 per cent of the capacity of eleven arsenals and about 40 per cent of the machine shops and heavy industry. In January, 1939, the minister of economic affairs announced that 300 factories had been transplanted from the coast and approximately 210 from the Wuhan area.

In Szechwan, Yunnan, Kweichow, Kwangsi, and Sinkiang new industrial centers with arsenals, factories, and mills sprang up. Szechwan, where a dozen small iron and steel plants were set up, became the center of China's mechanized industry, and Chiang K'ai-shek assumed the post of chairman of the provincial government in order to keep a tight rein on war production. All available factories, private and state, were converted to the production of essential military goods, but because of a shortage of raw materials, they were unable to fill production quotas. And there continued to be serious shortages of industrial labor, technicians, and skilled managers.

The government tightened regulations covering laborers and trade unions in order to keep a continuous flow of goods moving to the fighting front. By 1940 the bureau of social affairs, which was elevated to the status of a ministry, began to issue regulations designed to force both unions and employers to freeze wages and hours, and by August, 1941, control of labor and unions was almost complete when the government issued regulations providing for compulsory participation in unions by qualified workers, appointment of government officials to direct and supervise the work of unions, and the shifting of union administrative personnel. The government expected the unions to stabilize wages, give accurate information to supervisors on the workers' cost of living, assume responsibility for welfare projects, and assist the government in the requisition of labor for war production. Practically all workers were subject to the labor draft but at the same time were virtually frozen in their jobs.

The Chinese industial co-operative movement made the village a new and important center of production. Indusco, sponsored and supported by the government, was organized at the start of the war to mobilize China's vast labor supply for production in numerous small workshops scattered throughout the country. The central headquarters was at Chungking, and by the end of 1939 there were over 1,300 individual co-operatives in the western and southwestern provinces. Many of them formed federations to co-ordinate procurement of materials, processing, and marketing and to assume responsibility for educational and welfare work within a given area. Some were managed efficiently under strict regulations, but a large number were makeshift enterprises, lacking adequate tools and machinery. Despite difficulties of operation, the co-operatives did help produce essential goods for the civilian population and the army. From the point of view of the government, they were merely a supplement to its own enterprises, and in the latter stages of the war it took less interest in their development.

Problems in agricultural production were equally as great as those in industry. China needed greater quantities of food to sustain her armies and the refugee population that had fled into the interior. Under government orders, some 200,000 acres previously used for poppy cultivation were planted in wheat; and cotton production increased, although the coveted self-sufficiency was not achieved. A basic problem was lack of adequate credit for peasant cultivators. The government attempted to establish a centralized credit system, but it lacked the resources for this purpose. Usury was still general.

Because of the pressing need to increase production, little was accomplished in the way of agricultural reform. The government tended to rely politically upon gentry support in the villages, and there was little desire to disturb the status quo in property relations. Rents remained high, and in fact they were driven higher by population pressure.

Production difficulties resulted in incipient inflation and ultimately in runaway inflation. It was impossible to increase industrial and agricultural output to the point where all the requirements of the people and the armies could be met. Nationalist China starved for consumer goods. The government could not prevent hoarding and speculation in staple commodities; consequently, prices constantly increased, causing great hardships for the masses of people and dissatisfaction in society as a whole. Some goods trickled into China via the Burma Road, but they were largely war matériel.

Government policy actually increased the pressures of inflation. Confronted by mounting costs of war and industrial development, it resorted to the printing press to issue more paper money. Taxes which might have checked inflation were unfortunately circumvented by corrupt practices through which the potentially big taxpayers often escaped payment altogether. In fact, inflation tended to accelerate a breakdown in private and official standards of behavior. Government officials and army officers, whose fixed salaries shrank in buying power day by day, resorted to unethical practices to maintain their level of living. Hoarders and speculators, who made new fortunes, put their profits into commerce and land, while industry, which was so sorely needed, went begging for investment capital. On the bottom of the economic and social pyramid, the peasantry was hardest hit. Peasants had little to sell for cash; on the other hand, the basic wartime tax—the land tax in kind—bore very heavily upon them.

The United Front

The Chinese communists mobilized the areas under their control for the war effort against Japan. Under the united-front policy the Eighth Route Army of the communists was reorganized under the command of Chu Teh and was designated by the Nationalist government as the garrison for the border region of the three provinces Shensi, Kansu, and Ninghsia. By July, 1938, this was a force of only 120,000 regulars and 100,000 poorly equipped partisans. However, it made a significant contribution through its guerrilla tactics, which tied down large numbers of Japanese troops. In southeast China, in Fukien and Kiangsi provinces, communist units were included in the New Fourth Army of 12,000 men organized by the Nationalist government with Yeh T'ing and Hsiang Ying as commander and deputy commander. This force was ordered into Kiangsu and Anhwei provinces to harass the Japanese rear. The Nationalist government also formally recognized local governments which had been organized and dominated by the Chinese communists in the northern border region; moreover, Chungking for a brief period gave monetary subsidies and allotments of ammunition to these regimes. Lastly, the Chinese Communist Party, whose area of control was expanding as a result of its guerrilla operations behind Japanese lines, received the approval of the Nationalist government in January, 1938, for the establishment of the Shansi-Chahar-Hopei border-region government.

There was also more direct co-operation between the Chinese communists and the Kuomintang, first at Hankow and subsequently at Chungking. Chou En-lai, the official communist representative to the Nationalist government, was a participant in the extraordinary national congress of the Kuomintang which met in March, 1938, and was appointed vice-minister of the political training board of the military affairs commission, a position he held until 1940. And in July, 1938, seven Chinese communist delegates including Chou attended the first session of the people's political council at Hankow. Perhaps the high point of the united-front relationship was the acceptance by both parties of the "Program of Armed Resistance and National Reconstruction." On close analysis, however, it is clear that, politically, united-front co-operation hardly extended beyond acceptance of generalized policies—intensification of military activity, political reforms, and economic growth. The fundamental antagonism between the communists and the Nationalists never disappeared.

The Nationalist government was greatly concerned about the expansion of communist influence as a result of communist military operations. Beyond the territories of the border government communist forces infiltrated Honan, Shantung, Suiyuan, Chekiang, and eastern Hopei; and the New Fourth Army, formed basically from remnants of the communists who had not made the long march, was active between Shanghai and Nanking. The dominant elements in the Kuomintang were suspicious of these activities and were increasingly antagonistic to the communists. As early as August, 1938, for example, the Hankow-Wuchang defense headquarters outlawed three communist-sponsored mass organizations because it feared the Chinese Communist Party would use them to gain influence in Nationalist territory.

After the fall of Hankow in October, 1938, relations between the two parties worsened steadily. More Chinese Communist Party organizations were suppressed, although the communist newspaper, the *New China Daily News*, continued to be published; and the communists were severely criticized for failing to yield control over their area in Shensi Province to the Nationalist government and for not allowing the government to exercise direct command over the Chinese Communist Party armies in the field or to direct their training. Armed clashes between the Nationalists and communists began in the summer of 1938, and from then on isolated units fought with increasing frequency. By the autumn of 1939 there was fighting on the divisional scale in Shansi Province, but it was halted by a negotiated truce in the spring of 1940. During 1939, moreover, Chungking began to enforce a rigid military blockade of the communist areas to prevent communist infiltration into Nationalist China.

After the New Fourth Army incident there was a revival of hostilities between the communists and the Nationalists. In November, 1940, as the New Fourth Army, on orders from Chungking, was endeavoring to join with communist forces in northwest China, Kuomintang troops under General Ku Chu-t'ung attacked its rear guard, still south of the Yangtze River, and during the course of the fighting captured its commander, Yeh T'ing, and killed his assistant, Hsiang Ying. Some units of the army escaped into northern Kiangsu and Shantung. Thereafter the Nationalist government was successful in preventing the infiltration of Chinese communist guerrilla forces into southeast China and was able to regain control of the rural areas in the

Japanese-occupied provinces south of the Yangtze River. By early 1941 it was clear that the united front against Japan was only nominal. The Chinese communists refused to attend the March, 1941, session of the people's political council unless Chungking complied with a series of demands, including cessation of anticommunist activity, reparations for the New Fourth Army incident, and punishment of the persons responsible, including Ho Ying-ch'in. Chiang K'ai-shek rejected these demands and explained to the people's political council that he had been forced to "suppress disobedient and rebellious troops."

The united-front policy had been merely a temporary expedient for both the communists and the Nationalists. Although it had adopted a more moderate wartime policy, particularly toward the rural class struggle, the Chinese Communist Party after 1937 continued to insist on retaining control of its own territorial bases and maintaining its own armed forces. The Chinese communists had learned valuable lessons from their experiences in the 1920's, and Mao Tse-tung had only reluctantly agreed to the united-front policy. The Chinese Communist Party continued to state in no uncertain terms that it was "the Marxist-Leninist Party of the Chinese working class" and that "only a communist society will completely realize the final liberation of the Chinese nation and the Chinese people." The party "must steadfastly maintain its political and organizational independence, expand and reinforce the party forces . . . and retain as well as develop our traditional spirit of relentless struggle." The party, with more than 200,000 members in July, 1938, did take advantage of the united front consistently to champion basic freedoms in Kuomintang areas in face of increasing Kuomintang disregard or suppression of them, and it made special pleas to the "petty bourgeoisie"—the white-collar workers and students in the cities. Under the united front the communists tended to emphasize the need to complete the bourgeois-democratic revolution as the goal of Sun Yat-sen's Three Principles of the People, but at the same time they made clear their ultimate objectives. In a speech on March 3, 1937, to the congress of delegates from Soviet areas, Mao Tse-tung stated:

There are several stages of development in the democratic revolution. The United Front with the bourgeoisie, though desirable and even necessary, is only transitional. The democratic revolution will transform itself in the direction of socialism. The final goal is socialism and communism. During this transitional stage, the Kuomintang is regarded as a competitor in the struggle for leadership of the masses and of the revolution.

Communism and "New Democracy"

During the years of struggle with Japan, Chinese communist policy was based on Mao's *On New Democracy*, which was published as a pamphlet in

January, 1940. This ideological summing-up more closely defined the transition to communism as a two-stage process of revolution, comparable to the theory Bukharin advanced in the 1920's. Mao explained that democracy in the ordinary sense meant a system of government equivalent to bourgeois dictatorship but that the "new democracy" represented the interests of the revolutionary classes. According to Mao, the new democratic revolution still had to clear away the obstacles which stood in the way of capitalist development, but it could not permit this effort to be led by the bourgeoisie for the building of a capitalist society and a bourgeois dictatorship. The Chinese bourgeoisie, moreover, was not a true bourgeoisie but a "colonial bourgeoisie which served foreign finance and monopoly capitalism." The new democratic revolution would be led wholly or in part by the proletariat; its first stage aimed at the establishment of the joint dictatorship of all revolutionary classes—the proletariat, peasantry, intelligentsia, and petty bourgeoisie. The fundamental character of this revolution would not change until the arrival of the stage of communist revolution. According to Mao, it was inevitable that the new democracy would be transitional to proletarian, communist world revolution.

In *On New Democracy* Mao Tse-tung gave particular attention to the economic situation. He wrote of the Chinese Communist Party carrying out the Three Principles of Sun Yat-sen and even used the expression "the new Three Principles of the People." According to Mao, big banks, big industries, and big business would be owned by the new democratic republic. In order that private capital might not manipulate the livelihood of the people, all native or foreign-owned enterprises, either monopolistic or of a dimension too large for private efforts to manage, such as banks, railroads, and airlines, would be managed and controlled by the state. Other capitalist private property would not be confiscated, and development of capitalist production that would not manipulate the people's livelihood would be permitted.

Explicit in new democracy was the mass support of the peasantry; consequently, Mao touched on problems of land reform. The new democratic republic would adopt measures to confiscate big landlord holdings for distribution among peasants who had no land or very little in order to realize Dr. Sun's slogan "The Tiller Should Own His Own Land" and to liquidate the feudal social relations in rural areas. This would not build up communist agriculture, but it would at least turn the land into the private property of the peasants. Mao distinguished between landlords and rich peasants, and he would permit the latter to continue as they were. He acknowledged that the peasant question was the fundamental question of the Chinese revolution and that the force of the peasantry was its main force. Yet he insisted that the revolution could not succeed without the workers, for they were the leaders of the revolution and had the highest revolutionary spirit.

The publication of *On New Democracy* began a movement that continued in the early 1940's to rally and consolidate the forces of the Chinese Communist Party, to restore the party to its true revolutionary role, and to make articulate the party's doctrinal position in terms of its minimum and maximum aims. Ideologically speaking, there was not much that was original in *On New Democracy*. Mao's important innovation appeared to lie in the realm of practical political action rather than in the field of Marxist theory. For a long time he had realized that in China the party derived its dynamism not from any organic tie with the industrial proletariat but from the fact that it was a tightly organized, highly disciplined elite which had achieved power through manipulation of peasant discontent. Thus Mao was concerned to maintain the discipline and loyalty of party members, especially in view of the fact that the party had undergone a tremendous growth after 1937.

The party organization continued to be based on the Leninist principle of democratic centralism, with power centered in the central committee and its smaller co-ordinate, the central political bureau, which acted as the directing organ of the party between plenary sessions of the central committee, which were held every three months. After 1938 Mao was chairman of both bodies. He and his colleagues gave particular attention to the expansion of party cells in factories, mines, public organizations, units of the army, schools, streets, and villages. Cells of three or four party members had various functions: they spread propaganda among the masses to strengthen party programs and the decisions of the higher party organs; absorbed new members; collected membership fees; enforced party discipline among members; and educated party members.

The success of the Chinese Communist Party in the war years was based on its ability to win popular support; for though it concentrated on the problems of the peasantry, it was careful not to alienate other groups. It encouraged the peasants to participate actively in local administration through popular elections; improved their material welfare by reductions of rent, interest, and taxes; and educated, indoctrinated, and stimulated them through popular organizations, cultural movements, and social reforms. Land policy, however, was generally moderate and was intended to attract support for the war effort from all rural classes. Only the estates of absentee and collaborationist landlords were confiscated and rented by the government to peasants, and in most cases the civil, political, and property rights of the resident landlords were guaranteed. After the implementation of rent and interest reductions, landlords were entitled to their rents and interest receipts. The Chinese communists generally enforced the Nationalist government's land law of 1930, which set a rent ceiling of $37\frac{1}{2}$ per cent and which reduced interest rates. A new law protected the rights of tenants to use the land, but it provided that, "if a tenant gives up cultivating the land for two years without reason or deliberately refuses to pay rentals even though capable of doing so, the owner of the land has the right to take the land back." With regard to interest, new regulations stipulated that "it can be freely decided in accordance with local customs and conditions"; and the communists stated that "the government should not stipulate too low an interest rate, for it may result in a slowdown of credit and harm the people's welfare." (Ten per cent seems to have been the party's ideal.) The new law also declared that,

If the debtor cannot pay either interest or capital on debts newly contracted since the war, the creditor has the right to dispose of collateral according to contract. However, in case of natural disasters, war, etc., the government may mediate for a certain reduction of interest and for the payment of capital without interest.

These moderate reforms were implemented by peasant associations and popularly elected local administrations in the villages, and communist party members were instructed not to side with peasants or landlords but to mediate between the two. Taxation was progressive, on the principle that "expenses for fighting the Japanese are to be borne by all classes except paupers." The commissioner of finance admitted, however, that taxation was essentially confined to the landlords, usurers, and big merchants and in some cases amounted to virtual confiscation.

The policy of moderation also extended to politics. The areas under Chinese communist control had no central government since they were in many cases holdings in what was nominally Japanese territory. Government was regional, and each region had a congress, elected by all adults, which in turn selected executive and standing committees to which it delegated power and responsibility. For example, in the spring of 1939 the First Congress of the border region's (Shensi-Kansu-Ninghsia) people's political council convened for this purpose. On the hsien level magistrates were elected and worked with elected councils, and each village selected its own chairman and administrative committee. In July, 1940, the Chinese Communist Party introduced the so-called "three-thirds system," by which governmental bodies were to be one-third communist, one-third Kuomintang, and one-third nonparty. Of the eighteen members of the border region's people's political council only six were communists. This division proved to be an effective communist device for enlisting noncommunist support, and behind the façade of self-denial they used mass organizations like the Poor People's Society and the Peasant Guards to indoctrinate and activate the rural population so that the nonparty majority supported the communists under the illusion of self-government.

The Chinese communists, like the Kuomintang, faced problems in their efforts to increase production. Their economy was a mixture of private ownership, co-operatives, and state ownership. Private investment to increase production was encouraged, but at the same time the government operated enterprises such as coal mines, salt wells, and oil wells, and carried on trade in cattle, hides, salt, wool, cotton, paper, and other items. It did not have a monopoly over these commodities, and in all of them private enterprises competed to some extent. The communists encouraged the formation of all sorts of co-operatives and particularly those in agriculture, which emphasized collective use of labor, implements, and farm animals. Agricultural co-operatives were most common on public lands assigned to peasants or to the army. The communists used mass organizations of farmers, workers, women, and young people to spur production drives, and they emphasized the role of labor-exchange groups and labor heroes. They also required armies, schools, and administrative organs to be economically self-supporting. By vigorous efforts the Chinese Communist Party achieved considerable success in solving its economic problems. By the latter stages of the war the communist areas had become more nearly self-sufficient in such essential commodities as grain and cloth, and they generally kept the prices of staple commodities under control.

China and World War II

When the Japanese attacked Pearl Harbor on December 7, 1941, the United States and China became allies in the Pacific War; and following the German and Italian declarations of war upon the United States, the Pacific War became part of World War II. Before December, 1941, however, the United States, officially and unofficially, had already been extending some assistance to China's war effort. She sent Lend-Lease aid through India and Burma, dispatched American engineers to improve the transport of goods into China, assisted an American volunteer air force, the Flying Tigers, under Claire Chennault, and organized an American military mission at Chungking. After December China was one of the Allies in the struggle against the Axis powers, but, in spite of Chiang K'ai-shek's hopes, Chungking never became a major war center. The important military decisions were generally made by Winston Churchill and Franklin Roosevelt in their emergency meetings between 1941 and 1945.

At Washington in December and January, 1941–1942, Churchill and Roosevelt determined the basic global strategy for the world-wide conflict: Europe first, the Pacific Ocean area second, and the China-Burma-India theater last in terms of priorities. From the beginning they disagreed on China's role in the war. Roosevelt felt that Chinese armies, if they were given adequate equipment and leadership, could make a major contribution to the ultimate defeat of Japan. Although he disagreed, Churchill deferred to his colleague, and they proposed to establish the China-Burma-India theater under the command of Chiang K'ai-shek.

Meanwhile, Chiang had asked Roosevelt to send an American officer to be his chief of a joint general staff. After consulting with General George Marshall, chief of staff of the American army, Roosevelt appointed General Joseph Stilwell to serve under Chiang. In January, 1942, Stilwell received his

489

orders: to save Burma from Japanese conquest if possible, increase the effectiveness of American aid to China, and improve the combat efficiency of the Chinese army. It was already clear that it would be difficult if not impossible to hold Burma, and as early as February, 1942, the United States conceived the idea of flying supplies into China over "the Hump," the air-force designation for the mountains between China and India. The United States was convinced that Chiang K'ai-shek needed support to prevent the complete collapse of Chinese resistance against Japan. Chungking was already talking of tremendous "morale problems."

Stilwell was unable to hold the line against Japan in Burma. He took over command of Chinese and British forces in February, 1942, but the Japanese continued to advance and in April, 1942, cut the Burma Road, thus depriving China of military supplies. Stilwell, having retreated into India, was bitter over the loss of Burma and blamed it essentially upon the defeatist attitude of the British and on Chiang K'ai-shek's interference with his orders to Chinese generals under his command. From the beginning he was unable to establish cordial relations with the Chinese and the British. When Burma fell, a deep gloom settled over Chungking. Chiang was particularly bitter about the loss of American aid, and Stilwell became his scapegoat. Chiang accused him of sacrificing Chinese armies and denied Stilwell's charges of corruption in Chinese politics and military affairs.

For the rest of 1942 the China-Burma-India theater was of little significance in terms of the global war. Even after the inauguration of the Hump supply route by the American Air Transport Command, very little aid reached China. Priorities elsewhere took precedence: the Russian front, the projected invasion of North Africa, the defense of Australia, and the first counter-offensive in the southwest Pacific. Stilwell, however, was planning the reconquest of Burma in order to bring larger amounts of matériel into China, and to accomplish this purpose he concentrated on improving the combat efficiency of the Chinese army. He hoped to train and equip thirty Chinese divisions—fifteen in Yunnan Province and fifteen in northern India—but his efforts were obstructed by the opposition of Chiang K'ai-shek and General Claire Chennault. Chiang was far from enthusiastic about the Burma campaign, being unwilling to risk the sacrifice of a large number of Chinese troops. Chennault, who had transformed his Flying Tigers into a regular American Air Force unit, provided moral and practical support for Chiang by concluding that a Burma campaign was unnecessary in the over-all strategy against Japan. Stilwell, an infantry man, and Chennault, an air-power enthusiast, differed with regard to tactics. Stilwell saw the Burma Road as the only way to provide large-scale assistance for the rebuilding of Chinese armies needed for the ultimate defeat of Japanese forces on the mainland of Asia, but Chennault felt that air power could defeat Japan by driving the Japanese air force from China, bombing Japanese sea routes, and, finally, attacking the homeland. According to Chennault, the limited American aid carried over the Hump should therefore be used in building air power in China. Chiang K'ai-shek strongly seconded Chennault's opinion and generally obstructed Stilwell's Burma planning through most of 1942.

Problems concerning the China front were discussed by Roosevelt and Churchill in their January, 1943, conference. Once again global priorities were determined as follows: the air offensive against Germany; the Mediterranean campaign, including the conquest of Italy; military assistance to the Soviet Union; development of the European invasion force; and the central and southwest Pacific thrusts. Roosevelt settled the military dispute in China by promising assistance to both sides. Chiang and Chennault would get their air support, but they had to agree to the Burma campaign, which was to get under way in November, 1943. During the course of the discussion of the military situation in China, General George Marshall pointed out that air power in China would require sufficient infantry protection if it was going to resist possible Japanese retaliation. He emphasized that, once air power hurt Japan, the Japanese would make every effort to destroy it. In April, 1943, Stilwell and Chennault were recalled to Washington for brief conferences to work out the details for stepping up the air offensive and implementing the Burma campaign. Despite Marshall's warnings with regard to infantry support, Chennault insisted that air power would be effectively used within a six-month period, and he informed Stilwell that Chiang K'ai-shek would agree to the Burma assault only in conjunction with a British amphibious operation against Rangoon.

In August, 1943, at Quebec Roosevelt and Churchill once again considered global strategy. Italy had surrendered, the Soviets were pushing back the Germans on the eastern front, and there was a good possibility that Germany would be defeated by the end of 1944. The Allied leaders set May, 1944, as the target date for the Normandy invasion and decided to step up the attacks on Japanese holdings in the Pacific Ocean area, but they split on the importance of Burma and China. Churchill held that the Burma campaign, designed to open the land route to China, would make no important contribution to the war against Japan; instead he emphasized a direct assault through the Pacific. But Roosevelt refused to give up his estimate of China's contribution to the war effort. General Arnold of the American air force comforted him with the news that B-29's would soon be able to operate out of Chinese bases against Japan. Finally, to smooth over their differences, Roosevelt and Churchill agreed to separate the China theater from the Southeast Asia Command of Louis Mountbatten.

The differences between Stilwell and Chiang K'ai-shek in the first few years of the war pointed up important implications of the split between the Nationalists and the communists in China. Driven by the idea that China should try to make an all-out effort against Japan, Stilwell criticized the

491

corruption in the Kuomintang regime and urged co-operation between it and the Chinese communists. Chiang replied with complaints about shortages of American aid and the failure to get the B-29's in operation as quickly as expected. But by the autumn of 1943 Washington had new reasons besides military considerations for its determination to effect political unity in China. It was beginning to think that China would have to fill the power vacuum that would be created in East Asia by the ultimate defeat of Japan, and it hoped that a strong, united, and democratic China, friendly to the United States, would be a force for stability and provide a bulwark against the spread of communism in East Asia. Moreover, Roosevelt and his aides were already looking forward to some form of postwar international body which could maintain international collective security. Within such an organization they would place special responsibility on a smaller group that Roosevelt called "the four policemen"—Great Britain, the United States, Russia, and China.

The Moscow conference of foreign ministers, held in October, 1943, made the United States even more concerned about Chinese lack of unity. Secretary of State Cordell Hull was able to secure Russian recognition of China as a great power and a Russian promise to respect Chinese sovereignty and territorial integrity. Russian leaders also made clear their concern about the lack of political unity in China and suggested that the Chinese create a coalition government of all major political forces. Through Marxist publication outlets they had for some time been popularizing the view that the Chinese communists were not Marxist revolutionaries but simple agrarian reformers. At Moscow Stalin told Hull something that gave the United States an additional reason for wishing to hasten the settlement of Chinese political differences. He asked Hull to tell Roosevelt that Russia planned to enter the Pacific War. This meant that Russian armies would move into Manchuria and possibly into north China and Korea.

In December, 1943, Roosevelt and Churchill met with their allies, Chiang K'ai-shek at Cairo and Stalin at Teheran. The Pacific allies—the United States, Great Britain, and China—issued the Cairo Declaration, which listed as war aims the unconditional surrender of Japan, the restoration to China of all territory seized by Japan, and the establishment of Korean independence in due course. At Teheran Stalin agreed to the Cairo pronouncement but insisted that China would have to make some substantial contribution to the war effort to deserve consideration as a great power. He reaffirmed his promise to enter the war in the Pacific against Japan but presented the following stipulations to Roosevelt for discussion: Korea to be placed under a forty-year period of tutelage; Dairen to be made a free port, with free transit of Russian goods through Manchuria; the Kuriles and southern Sakhalin to be turned over to Russia; and Manchurian railways to become the property of China. At Cairo and Teheran the Allied leaders also made several important military decisions. Chiang approved the Burma campaign, and Great Britain promised an amphibious attack on Rangoon. Chiang left Cairo thinking that the matter was settled; but when Stalin insisted that the Normandy invasion be speeded up, the Rangoon assault had to be postponed until the autumn of 1944. After his return to China, however, Chiang agreed to begin the campaign in north Burma.

In the spring of 1944 the China theater erupted with military action. Stilwell attacked in north Burma with the Chinese troops that he had trained and equipped in India, and by May he was able to persuade Chiang K'ai-shek to permit the Yunnan force to cross the Salween River into Burma. Later in the spring, however, the Burma campaign bogged down with the coming of the rainy season, and Stilwell's troops concentrated on constructing a link with the Burma Road. In April the Japanese began an infantry attack, employing over half a million men, against the B-29 bases in southwest China. Chiang and Chennault claimed that the air force and the Chinese ground armies were strong enough to repel the attack if they got sufficient supplies, but in the spring of 1944 there was simply not enough material and equipment for operations in Burma and China. Chiang began to panic. He summoned Stilwell to Chungking and demanded more aid, which Stilwell refused.

American Diplomacy and the China Problem

While the military situation was worsening in China, the United States was embarking on a diplomatic effort to improve Chungking's relations with the Soviet Union and the Chinese communists. Convinced that there was no fundamental difference between China and Russia that could not be decided peacefully, Roosevelt dispatched his vice-president, Henry Wallace, on a mission to China to confer with Chiang and at the same time ordered the American ambassador to Moscow, W. Averell Harriman, to consult with Stalin and Foreign Minister Molotov.

Harriman began his talks with the Russian leaders on June 10, 1944, just four days after the Allied landings in Normandy. Stalin again declared his support of Chiang K'ai-shek, but he criticized Chiang for the inadequacy of his resistance against Japan and for the corruption that was increasingly common in the Kuomintang regime. He also criticized Chiang for not reaching a political accord with the Chinese communists, who he insisted were not real communists but "margarine communists," i.e., not the real thing. Finally, he suggested that the United States use her influence to "clean out corruption" in the Chungking government and to broaden its foundations by inclusion of other political forces.

Wallace's visit to Chungking was preceded by the transmission of the following special instructions to the American ambassador to Chungking, Ambassador Gauss, on June 15, 1944: encourage Chinese military efforts; work for the termination of the blockade of the Chinese communists to effect

493

the release of Kuomintang troops for the Japanese front; encourage co-operation between the Kuomintang and the Chinese communists; and take steps
to get a closer understanding between China and the Soviet Union. Wallace
spent three days, from June 21 to June 24, at Chungking, trying to convince
Chiang K'ai-shek of the need to end the division in China and to improve
Sino-Soviet relations, and he listened to Chiang's views on these subjects.
Chiang tried to convince Wallace that the Chinese Communist Party was
bent on his destruction and that the Chinese communists were Marxist
revolutionaries and Russian puppets. He stated that he would grant the
Chinese Communist Party status as an independent political organization
with freedom of assembly and discussion if it gave up its separate army and
turned over to him its control over northwest China. Wallace saw little chance
of effecting a settlement between the two groups on Chiang's conditions.
Concerning Sino-Soviet relations, Chiang asked that the United States act
as his broker in concluding an agreement which would preserve China's
political and territorial integrity. With regard to the military situation,
Wallace made it clear that the United States was disappointed in China's
fight, but Chiang claimed that the situation was not so bad as Roosevelt
feared. The generalissimo condemned Stilwell's unco-operative attitude,
particularly in the matter of supply allocations, and he asked that Roosevelt
send a special representative to China to act as a direct line of communication
between the President and himself. Wallace left China with the feeling that
the military situation was desperate as far as the air bases were concerned,
and he was convinced that American pressure would have to be exerted on
Chiang through an American officer who was more tactful than Stilwell.
Wallace had Chennault in mind. In July Roosevelt appointed Patrick Hurley
as the representative Chiang requested, and he suggested to the generalissimo
that Stilwell be given the power to co-ordinate all defense activities on the
China front.

In the summer of 1944 the friction between Chiang and Stilwell grew
more intense. Hurley had arrived and had begun to discuss with Chiang the
appointment of Stilwell as co-ordinator of Chinese defenses, but in the meantime the military situation had grown critical. Stilwell needed reinforcements in Burma, and the Japanese were closing in on the B-29 base at Kweilin.
Stilwell wanted Chiang to commit those forces which he was using to blockade the Chinese communists in the northwest, but Chiang preferred to pull
out of Burma completely. On September 14 Stilwell flew to Kweilin and
ordered the destruction of the American base.

These circumstances were analyzed by Roosevelt, who was then with
Churchill determining the grand strategy for the defeat of Japan. Since their
plans, at American insistence, included the opening of the Burma Road,
Roosevelt was angered by Chiang's intention to give up in Burma. On September 19 he sent a forceful message to Chiang, delivered with great pleasure

by Stilwell. The American president told Chiang that, if he withdrew the Chinese troops from Burma, he would have to assume the responsibility for the act and its consequences, and he suggested that Chiang place Stilwell in unrestricted command of China's armies. Chiang proved willing to accept this ultimatum on one condition. He demanded that Roosevelt recall Stilwell to the United States. Roosevelt complied and appointed as Chiang's chief of staff General Albert Wedemeyer, an officer more diplomatic than Stilwell, who had served on George Marshall's planning staff and with Mountbatten in India. Washington directed Wedemeyer to advise and assist Chiang K'ai-shek in military operations against Japan, to control allocation of Lend-Lease aid according to instructions of the joint chiefs of staff, and not to use American resources to suppress civil strife except where necessary to protect American lives and property. When Wedemeyer arrived in Chungking on October 31, 1944, Chiang welcomed him and promised to keep the Burma campaign going; but when he offered Wedemeyer complete command of his armies, the American general refused. According to his orders, he was only to "advise and assist." In the months that followed, the military situation in China improved, largely because the Japanese halted their attack in order to transfer troops to other theaters, where the Allies were advancing.

Patrick Hurley was responsible for American political policy in China which, according to his instructions, was to prevent the collapse of the Nationalist government and to sustain Chiang K'ai-shek as president of China and general of her armies. Many Americans in China disagreed with this policy. Some felt that the United States should support the Kuomintang regime only if it made reforms and co-operated with other parties, and others thought that Chiang was finished and that the United States should be getting ready to deal with the Chinese Communist Party. In the autumn of 1944 Hurley began to attack the problem of disunity in China. In November he flew to Yenan, where in discussion with Mao Tse-tung he formulated the following five-point program:

1. The Kuomintang and the Chinese Communist Party to work for military unification against Japan and for the reconstruction of China.
2. The Nationalist government to be reorganized as a coalition. Policies for political, military, and economic reforms to be announced.
3. The coalition government to support the principles of Sun Yat-sen.
4. A united military council to control all troops and distribute supplies equally.
5. The coalition government to recognize the legality of the Chinese Communist Party and all anti-Japanese parties.

When Hurley returned to Chungking, accompanied by Chou En-lai, to negotiate with the Kuomintang, Chiang K'ai-shek rejected the five-point plan and substituted three points of his own:

1. The Chinese Communist Party military forces to be integrated into the national army.
2. The Chinese communists to give up control over local government.
3. The national government of China to become more democratic, and the Chinese Communist Party to be legalized.

Despite these obvious differences, Hurley remained optimistic and arranged a conference at Chungking of representatives of the Kuomintang, Communist, and other parties. At the outset Chiang K'ai-shek announced that he would call a meeting for May 4, 1945, for the purpose of taking steps to draft a constitution, to transfer control of the national government to the people, and to terminate one-party rule. The conferees agreed to form a political consultative conference to establish constitutional government, to devise a common political program, and to unify the armed forces of China. They further agreed that unanimous decisions of the political consultative conference would be referred to the national government for its consideration and execution. Chou En-lai was enthusiastic, since he felt that a coalition government was in sight and that "democratic government" was inevitable, but Chiang, who was not ready to surrender his authority at that time, envisaged only the establishment of a limited coalition in which the Kuomintang would still dominate.

Hurley departed for Washington in mid-February, 1945, and on March 1 Chiang issued a statement in which he promised to form a war cabinet representing the various parties but not a coalition government. He did not intend to extend legal status to the Chinese Communist Party unless it adhered to the military and administrative demands of the Kuomintang. He did pledge, however, that he would convene a people's congress in November, 1945, as a step toward the inauguration of constitutional government, but this measure was subject to the approval of the Sixth Congress of the Kuomintang, to be held in May. The reaction of the Chinese communists was made clear in a letter written by Chou En-lai to Hurley on March 9, 1945. Chou stated that, since it was obvious that the Kuomintang wanted to dominate the writing of the constitution, there was no need to continue negotiations. He did ask, however, that a Chinese communist be made a member of the Chinese delegation to the initial meeting of the United Nations, and Chiang agreed to include one communist and two other non-Kuomintang delegates among the ten that he was going to send to San Francisco. Despite the failure of the negotiations, the United States continued to support Chiang and the Kuomintang. There was opposition to this policy within the American government, but Roosevelt was convinced that Chiang was the only alternative to the communists.

The Yalta Conference and Its Aftermath

President Roosevelt thought that he had accomplished much in support of Chiang's regime by his meeting with Churchill and Stalin at Yalta in February, 1945. Problems connected with the impending defeat of Germany were first on the Yalta agenda, but the conferees also discussed problems that were vital to the war in the Pacific and to China. Of greatest importance were the Russian demands that constituted the price for her entry into the war against Japan and the impact of that entry upon the military and political situation in China. It was the judgment of most Allied military leaders that Russian participation in the Pacific War was essential to achieve a rapid victory which would minimize the loss of lives. The Soviet Union would be able to defeat the Japanese in Manchuria, assist in the invasion of Japan, (projected for November, 1945, at an estimated initial casualty loss of 500,000 men), and provide air bases in eastern Siberia for shuttle bombing of Japan by American B-29's. The Yalta Agreement, signed on February 11, 1945, by the United States, Great Britain, and the Soviet Union, is a short document and worth quoting in full:

The leaders of the three great powers have agreed that two or three months after Germany has surrendered and the war in Europe has terminated the Soviet Union shall enter the war against Japan on the side of the Allies on condition that:

1. The status quo in Outer Mongolia (the Mongolian People's Republic) shall be preserved.

2. The former rights of Russia violated by the treacherous attack of Japan in 1904 shall be restored, viz.:
   (a) The southern part of Sakhalin as well as all the islands adjacent to it shall be returned to the Soviet Union.
   (b) The commercial port of Dairen shall be internationalized, the pre-eminent interests of the Soviet Union in this port being safeguarded and the lease of Port Arthur as a naval base of the U.S.S.R. restored.
   (c) The Chinese Eastern Railroad and the South Manchurian Railroad, which provides an outlet to Dairen, shall be jointly operated by the establishment of a joint Soviet-Chinese Company, it being understood that the pre-eminent interests of the Soviet Union shall be safeguarded and that China shall retain full sovereignty in Manchuria.

3. The Kurile islands shall be handed over to the Soviet Union.
   It is understood that the agreement concerning Outer Mongolia and the ports and railroads referred to above will require concurrence of Generalissimo Chiang K'ai-shek. The President will take measures in order to obtain this concurrence on advice from Marshal Stalin.

The heads of the three great powers have agreed that these claims of the Soviet Union shall be unquestionably fulfilled after Japan has been defeated.

For its part the Soviet Union expresses its readiness to conclude with the National Government of China a pact of friendship and alliance between the U.S.S.R. and China in order to render assistance to China with its armed forces for the purpose of liberating China from the Japanese yoke.

Roosevelt thought that he had made minimum concessions to Stalin, but much depended on interpretation of the words "pre-eminent interests." To the American President the most important part of the agreement was the last sentence, which he regarded as a pledge by the Soviet Union not to take advantage of Chinese difficulties to advance her own interests or the interests of the Chinese communists at the expense of the Nationalist government. The Yalta Agreement was a secret pact; Chiang was not informed of it until months later, and the American people did not learn of it until after the war.

Within a few months following Yalta, the military situation in Asia improved dramatically. The Pacific onslaught of the American army and navy liberated the Philippines, and the attack on Okinawa was in the offing. By spring the battle for Burma was won, and land communication to China was reopened (ironically, by the end of the war it was easier to fly supplies in over the Hump). And by the summer of 1945 the coastal ports of south China were opened when Chinese forces overcame the Japanese garrisons. Wedemeyer, meanwhile, was having success in the reorganization and outfitting of the Chinese armies, although the war ended before he could complete the job.

With the end of the war in sight, President Truman, who assumed office after the death of Roosevelt in April, was anxious to discover whether Stalin would adhere to the Yalta Agreement. Reports from the American embassy in Moscow indicated that Russia would probably attempt to expand her power in Asia. On April 15, 1945, Stalin had assured Hurley in Moscow that the Soviet Union would continue to support Chiang K'ai-shek and co-operate with the United States, but Hurley had been cautioned by Secretary of State Stettinius to curb his optimism and to emphasize to Chiang, when he returned to Chungking, the need to effect military and political unification. American policy continued to be based on supporting Chiang K'ai-shek, since he offered the best hope of unification; but it was thought to be flexible enough to work with others should Chiang's regime collapse. In late May, Truman dispatched a sick Harry Hopkins to Moscow to get Stalin to reindorse the Yalta Agreement. Stalin told Hopkins that the Soviet Union would be ready to enter the war on August 8 but that the final decision would depend on China's acceptance of the Yalta concessions. He stated that, even if China was not united by then, the Soviet Union would support the Nationalist government. When Russian armies entered Manchuria, Stalin promised to ask Chiang to organize the civil administration within the areas of Soviet occupation.

In the spring of 1945 both the Kuomintang and the Chinese Communist Party issued manifestoes to the Chinese people. On May 21, 1945, the Sixth Congress of the Kuomintang, after reiterating the need to defeat Japan and establish China's true independence, reaffirmed the party's obligation of political tutelage and improvement of the people's livelihood. The party promised to convene a national assembly on November 12, 1945, to adopt and promulgate a constitution, stating: "Before the congress meets, we shall with absolute sincerity seek the collaboration of all the truly patriotic leaders of the nation toward the early inauguration of constitutionalism in China." Much depended, of course, upon the definition of the words. The manifesto also stated:

In national reconstruction the question of the people's livelihood should receive first attention. . . . All measures, including the prevention of monopoly by capitalists, the elimination of hindrances to production, the prevention of land aggrandizement, the promotion of the policy of farmers owning the land they till, the improvement of living standards of the front line of soldiers, the safeguarding of the livelihood of the farmers and the laborers and of the government and school employees, and affording youths chances of receiving education and securing jobs, shall be faithfully carried out.

The communist position was summarized in Mao Tse-tung's statement, "On Coalition Government," issued on April 24, 1945. Mao declared that the minimum goal of the Chinese communists was the establishment of the "new democratic state":

The carrying out of this program will push China one step forward from her present national and social character, that is to say, from her colonial, semicolonial, and semifeudal character to the national and social character of a new bourgeois democracy.

He went on to say:

The carrying out of this program will not advance China to socialism. This is not a question of the subjective willingness or unwillingness of certain individuals to do the advancing; it is due to the fact that the objective political and social conditions in China do not permit the advance.

He once again defined "new democracy":

A new democracy of a union of democratic classes is different in principle from a socialist state with the dictatorship of the proletariat. China, throughout the period of her new democratic system, cannot and should not have a system of government of the character of one-class dictatorship or one-party monopoly of government. We have no reason not to co-operate with noncommunist political parties, social groups, or individuals who are willing to co-operate with the communist party and are not hostile to it.

In an appeal to Chinese national feeling, he stated: "Chinese history will determine the Chinese system. A unique form—a new democratic state and regime of a union of the democratic classes—will be produced, which will be entirely necessary and rational to us and different from the Russian system." He admitted, however, that "our future or ultimate program is to advance China into the realm of socialism and communism. This has been settled and cannot be doubted." He concluded:

Under the present conditions in China, a government that excludes the communist party excludes the overwhelming majority of the people. No one can entertain the idea that the communists demand to be admitted into the government because they covet official positions; communist participation in the government means the carrying out of the new democratic reforms. Even when China has a democratic election system, there should be a coalition government working under a commonly accepted new democratic program, for better accomplishing the constructive work of the new democracy, no matter whether the communist party is the majority party in the national assembly or not.

After learning of the Yalta Agreement, Chiang K'ai-shek sent T. V. Soong to Moscow in July, 1945, to negotiate a treaty with the Soviet Union. These negotiations were interrupted for a time by the Potsdam meeting between Truman, Stalin, and Attlee but were resumed when Stalin returned to the Russian capital. A treaty was not forthcoming until August 14, a few days after the conclusion of the war with Japan. Its terms included mutual respect for the sovereignty of China and Russia; Russian assistance and support for the Nationalist government of Chiang K'ai-shek; Chinese agreement to recognize the independence of Outer Mongolia if a plebiscite indicated that result; recognition of Dairen as a free port, with Chinese administration and lease by Russia of half of the port facilities; establishment of Port Arthur as a joint Russian-Chinese naval base; and joint ownership and operation by the two powers of the Chinese Eastern and South Manchurian railways. The last three points were to be guaranteed for a thirty-year period.

By this settlement Russia forced on China a broad interpretation of the "pre-eminent interest" clauses of the Yalta Agreement, but, despite these added concessions, the Chinese reaction to the treaty was generally favorable. Chiang was still suspicious of the Soviet Union, but he did have a pledge from Stalin. Washington was optimistic despite counsels of caution by the

American embassy in Moscow, which pointed out that the Chinese Communist Party had ordered its forces into Manchuria and would make contact with the Russian army. The Soviet Union could have no better opportunity to support the communists against Chiang.

26 *China after World War II*

The suddenness of Japan's surrender on August 12 created a number of serious problems in China. Overnight a tremendous political-military vacuum was created in Japanese-occupied China, and, since both the Nationalists and communists wanted to fill it, what amounted to a race for control began. Legally Chiang K'ai-shek had the advantage because both Russian and American military forces were committed to facilitating the surrender of Japanese troops and the transfer of sovereignty to China. On August 15, moreover, the Japanese emperor ordered his troops in China to surrender to Chiang's forces, while in Manchuria they were to surrender to the Russians. In the meantime, however, the Chinese Communist Party radio ordered Japanese and Chinese puppet troops to surrender to the communists. Civil war seemed very likely in China unless the Nationalists and communists could be persuaded to reach some settlement to effect unity.

The Nationalist-Communist Problem

Immediately after the signing of the Sino-Soviet agreements, Hurley urged Chiang K'ai-shek to invite Mao Tse-tung to Chungking; and when Mao refused Chiang's invitation of the 16th, Hurley flew to Yenan and persuaded the communist leader to return with him to Chungking. Mao arrived on August 28 and stayed a month, arguing the Chinese communist cause. Chances for the realization of political unity seemed better than ever before. Chiang seemed to have realized that the United States would not continue unqualified and unlimited aid, while the communists had to face the implication of the Sino-Soviet accord that Moscow would not provide them with assistance. Hurley urged both sides to agree on essential principles and to avoid quarrels over minor points. With little difficulty they agreed to collaborate in the establishment of democratic government in China, the reconstruction of China and prevention of civil war, support of the leadership of Chiang K'ai-shek and the doctrines of Sun Yat-sen, recognition of the Kuomintang as the dominant party in control of the government during the period of transition from the present form of administration to a democratic regime, and establishment of basic freedoms.

The Kuomintang and the Chinese communists did not, however, agree on terms of co-operation with regard to the adjustment of political and military power. Local government was one specific issue that divided the two parties. The Chinese communists claimed the right to appoint, select, or elect governors and mayors in certain provinces, while the Kuomintang maintained that until a constitution was adopted and a democratic form of government inaugurated, the prerogative of appointing governors and local officials was vested in the president of the republic. Chou En-lai explained that the Chinese Communist Party wanted governors appointed by a council which would be elected from districts and villages in the disputed provinces, particularly Hopei, Shantung, and Chahar. Military matters were another point of division. The Chinese communists contended that they should have 48 communist divisions in the new army of China, but the Kuomintang answered that China's peacetime army, projected at 80–100 divisions, could not be half-communist. The Nationalist government offered the Chinese communists 20 divisions, or what would constitute approximately one-fifth of the planned peacetime military strength. After considering the matter more carefully, the Chinese communists accepted this arrangement.

In early October the Kuomintang and the Chinese Communist Party agreed to the organization of a political consultative conference made up as follows: eight Kuomintang, seven Chinese communists, thirteen third-party representatives, and nine nonpartisans. The conference, to meet early in November, would consider a draft constitution for submission to a people's congress and a policy for peaceful national reconstruction. Discussions were to be open to the public, and decisions reached were to be final and conclusive. On October 11 Mao Tse-tung and Chiang K'ai-shek issued a statement pledging their desire for peace and unity, and they stated that agreement had been reached on two of the three most difficult problems. The lack of accord on the third disputed issue—political control of communist areas claimed by right of liberation—was minimized to induce the belief that the two sides were not far apart. On the surface, at any rate, there seemed to be genuine progress toward a peaceful settlement. After Mao left Chungking on October 11, talks between the Kuomintang and the communists continued in preparation for the meeting of the political consultative conference.

While these discussions were progressing, Chiang K'ai-shek was trying to establish effective control over China. The precipitous termination of the war had thrown off balance existing plans for the gradual return of the Nationalist government into liberated areas. The situation in China was as follows. Neither the Chinese nor the American military organizations were ready and in position to take over the areas held by the Japanese. The United

States simply did not have adequate forces to take care of Japan, Korea, and China; moreover, it must not be forgotten how eager the American people were to bring home their troops. As George Marshall said, shortly before he was sent to China, "For the moment, in a widespread emotional crisis of the American people, demobilization has become, in effect, disintegration, not only of the armed forces but apparently of all conception of world responsibility and its demands of us." Not only was the task a military one, involving the movement of armies and the establishment of supply routes, but there were civil governments to be formed in scores of localities and cities to prevent their loss to warlords or to the communists. Many Americans questioned whether the Kuomintang had the vitality to meet this challenge.

The United States devised emergency measures to assist Chiang's regime. While Mao Tse-tung was still in Chungking, American planes and ships began moving Nationalist troops and officials into the vital ports and cities of east and central China. During September and October American transport planes moved three large armies: the Ninety-fourth, numbering some 35,000, from Liuchow to Shanghai, 900 miles; 40,000 veterans of the Burma campaign, from Chichang to Nanking, 800 miles; and other forces from Hankow and Shanghai to Peiping. American marines, 50,000 strong, landed to secure ports and airfields at Tsingtao, Tientsin, Peiping, and Chingwangtao for the purpose of evacuating Japanese. In addition, small detachments of American marines protected the railroad between Tangku and Chingwangtao and the coal mines and bridges at Tanshan.

On the whole, American assistance was directed toward the re-establishment of Chiang's government in China, but General Wedemeyer was careful not to get involved in operations which could be construed as having the direct purpose of striking against the Chinese communists. Communist forces were careful to avoid fights with Americans as they expanded the territory under their control, but the communist party did complain that the United States was enabling Chiang to spread his authority. At Chungking, Wang Ping-nan, a communist representative at the unity negotiations, informed the American embassy that Chiang had no interest in a political settlement but was only playing for time while securing a superior military position. He voiced communist resentment against "American intervention" in landing troops at many points in north China for the purpose of holding them for Chiang. He expressed the view that the Soviet Union was careful not to intervene in the internal conflicts of China, preferring to let the Chinese work out their own problems, but he intimated that, should the United States continue to assist the Kuomintang, the Soviet Union might find some action necessary.

Chiang K'ai-shek was putting pressure on the United States to help increase his military power. He fell back on a promise made by President Roosevelt at Cairo that the United States would continue to equip Chinese troops to the total of 90 divisions. He wanted the United States to honor this pledge, and he also wanted the United States to maintain a permanent military mission in China under General Wedemeyer. Washington, however, would promise no more than equipment and training for 39 divisions, a small air force, and a small navy, suitable for coastal and river operations. The Truman administration still clung to the idea that China's internal difficulties should be settled by peaceful means and that military assistance furnished by the United States should not be diverted for use in civil war or to support undemocratic government.

After Japan's surrender, Chinese communist forces moved far and wide in north China. The countryside around Tientsin and Peiping and the coastal areas in Shantung north up to the Great Wall were alive with them. They might well have gained control over some large cities and railways had these not been guarded by the Japanese until Kuomintang or American troops arrived. Although Japanese generally evaded or resisted their demands for surrender, the Chinese communist forces managed to capture substantial amounts of arms, ammunition, and supplies. While they avoided direct clashes and usually gave way or scattered before strong government forces, they maintained their control over rural areas and by attacks on railroads effectively prevented the movement of Nationalist troops. They did offer to refrain from attacking lines of communication while the negotiations were proceeding at Chungking if the Nationalist government would promise to stop movement of troops in north China; this Chiang refused to do, and the communist attacks continued. At times the communists were strengthened by defections of Kuomintang troops. For example, in November in northern Honan two Nationalist armies went over to the other side. In many cases, also, puppet troops joined the communists. An American observer, Colonel R. B. Rigg, estimated the number of such converts in Manchuria during 1945–1946 at 75,000.

On October 30, 1945, Chiang K'ai-shek made the following proposals to the Chinese communists:

1. Both sides to give orders to their troops to remain where they are and not to attack the other side.
2. The Chinese Communist Party to withdraw its troops from places along railroads which they have been raiding, and the government will not undertake to send troops to those places. These sections to be guarded entirely by railroad police.
3. The government, in case it finds it necessary to send troops into north China along the main railroad lines, to consult the Chinese Communist Party first in order to reach agreement.
4. Both sides to endeavor earnestly within one month to reach a fundamental agreement about the reorganization of the Chinese communist army and the allotment of places where they will be stationed.
5. The proposed political consultative conference to be convened at once.

When the Chinese communists rejected these proposals on November 8 and the communist counterproposals were unsatisfactory to Chungking, there seemed to be little chance to avoid war.

Both sides endeavored to strengthen themselves militarily. Chiang realized that his forces in north China were insufficient to combat the communists, and he asked the United States to transport more of his troops by air and sea and not to withdraw her marines. Wedemeyer felt compelled to refuse Chiang's request; such assistance was not within the scope of his mission as defined by Washington. By November Chinese communist forces had made contact with Russian armies in Hopei and Chahar, and shortly thereafter Soviet missions flew into Yenan to co-ordinate military activities. In fact, Soviet representatives attended meetings of the politburo of the Chinese Communist Party. Meanwhile, Lin Piao, one of the ablest Chinese communist generals, entered Manchuria with some 100,000 unarmed soldiers from Shantung and other northern areas. There they armed themselves with quantities of captured Japanese equipment, including rifles, machine guns, and field artillery.

Russian actions made it impossible for Chiang K'ai-shek to gain control over Manchuria. In the closing days of the war Soviet forces had occupied the entire area, including the cities of Harbin, Kirin, Changchun, Mukden, Dairen, and Port Arthur. Russian policy, while often legally correct, worked against the interests of the Nationalists and to the advantage of the Chinese communists. For example, Manchurian local government fell under the domination of "democratic unions," and it was Chiang's fear that these groups would combine with Chinese communist elements then on the move toward Manchuria. In August, Stalin had assured T. V. Soong in Moscow that Soviet forces would begin to withdraw from Manchuria three weeks after Japan's surrender and would complete the process in three months. Chiang naturally wanted to return to Manchuria as quickly as possible, but it took some weeks to arrange the passage of troops. He appointed General Hsiung Shih-hui to co-operate with General Malinovsky to prepare for the transfer of control from the Russians to representatives of the Nationalist government, but Hsiung was forced to arrange a postponement of Russia's withdrawal because Nationalist troops were delayed. In October, when Chiang's troops reached Dairen in American transports, the Russians refused to let them land, on the pretext that Dairen was only a commercial port, and suggested that they land at Hulatao, Yingkow, or Antung. Chiang and the Americans deferred to the Russians; but when the transports entered the harbor at Hulatao, they found Chinese communist forces in control there. The same thing happened at Yingkow. In the end, the troops were disembarked at Chingwangtao, and during the second week of November they began their march north toward the Great Wall to be on hand when the Russians withdrew. When they arrived at Shanhaikwan Pass, they found that the Russians had permitted the Chinese communists to block the route from that point into the interior of Manchuria.

The Nationalist forces overcame the communists at the pass, but they were harassed constantly by communist raids on their rail communications. By the end of November they had taken Hulatao and were approaching Mukden. In the meantime the Soviet Union agreed to permit the Kuomintang to bring its troops into Manchurian cities by air. Such operations were to begin five days after the withdrawal of Russian troops, regarding which the Russians promised to give Chiang ten days' notice. Chiang asked the United States to transport his troops to Mukden and Changchun in American planes piloted by Americans. Wedemeyer had no enthusiasm for this plan, for he thought that Chiang had better consolidate his control over the area south of the Great Wall and north of the Yangtze River, making the over-land lines of communication secure before sending his troops into Manchuria. When Wedemeyer refused to provide air transport, Chiang went ahead on his own. He ordered a mission of about 500 men flown into Manchuria to establish organs of civil administration. At first the Russian forces were cordial, and the "democratic unions" co-operated with the Kuomintang officials. But when communist strength increased, Chiang was forced to withdraw the mission for fear it would be captured, and he had to arrange with the Russians to postpone their scheduled evacuation until January.

The Marshall Mission

The United States continued to work for a political settlement in China. On November 26 Hurley, who had returned to the United States, resigned, charging that a number of his subordinates were sabotaging American policy by privately advising the Chinese communists that his efforts to prevent the collapse of the Nationalist government did not represent the policy of the United States. President Truman thereupon appointed General George Marshall as his special representative in China with the rank of ambassador. (The official post of ambassador remained vacant until the appointment of Leighton Stuart on July 11, 1946.) In his instructions to Marshall, dated December 15, 1945, Truman pledged that there would be no American military intervention in China, and he urged the convocation of a national conference of the major Chinese political elements, not only to end the internal strife but also to bring about unification of the country on terms which would give those elements fair and effective representation in the Chinese government. The main weapon at Marshall's disposal was a promise of American loans, economic-technical assistance, and military aid. All Chinese leaders, including Chiang K'ai-shek, were to be told frankly "that a China disunited and torn by civil strife could not be considered realistically as a proper place for American assistance along these lines." Marshall acted as an intermediary between the Kuomintang and the Chinese Communist Party and often as an adviser or member of certain bodies set up to reach agreement on specific problems. He exercised initiative in giving to both sides his impartial views of their differences and in drafting various statements and agreements which he thought would facilitate progress in the negotiations, but he was usually unable to bring the two parties into complete agreement on a set of terms before circumstances changed, frequently as a result of what he considered bad faith on one side or the other.

While Marshall was beginning his task, the American secretary of state, James Byrnes, was trying to fit Washington's China policy into a general world peace settlement. At the meeting of the council of foreign ministers at Moscow in mid-December, he explained the purpose of the Marshall mission, and, despite Molotov's criticisms of American troops in China, he got the impression that the Soviet Union would live up to her treaty with Chiang K'ai-shek and would co-operate with American policy. Chiang's troops were moving closer toward Mukden, and by December 7 they were just twenty miles from the city and expected to enter it very soon. The Chinese communists avoided battle. At Chungking the Soviet ambassador told Chiang that his government was prepared to guarantee a safe landing for Chinese troops at air fields at Mukden and Changchun. Chiang was able to persuade Russian forces to postpone their withdrawal until February 3, 1946, but in return the Soviet Union demanded that the Chinese government concede to her control over former Japanese industrial interests. When China refused, Soviet forces began to remove the machinery and equipment of plants into Siberia, and they continued to allow the Chinese communists to move about Manchuria freely and to establish local regimes wherever they could. The United States supported Chiang in his refusal to make concessions to the Soviet Union with regard to Japanese enterprises. Byrnes emphasized that this would be contrary to the principle of the open door and would constitute a clear discrimination against Americans who might wish to participate in the development of Manchurian industry.

Marshall got off to a good start in China with the convening of the political consultative conference in January, 1946. The communists and Nationalists agreed to establish a military truce which for all practical purposes would freeze the status quo. Violations of the truce were to be investigated by three-man teams, composed of representatives of the Kuomintang, the Chinese Communist Party, and the United States. The conferees also accepted a short-range political settlement. They divided territorial holdings on the basis of the status quo and agreed to negotiate regarding areas in dispute. They concurred on the need to establish within the national government a new state council as the key policy-making body. Its membership, totaling forty, was to include twenty representatives of the Kuomintang and twenty delegates from all other parties. With regard to the long-range political settlement, the members of the conference thought that all the troubles arising out of party dictatorship and civil war would be cleared up by the adoption of a constitution, to be approved by a national assembly in May, 1946. In the matter of the integration of Chinese communist and Nationalist military forces, they worked out a plan whereby one-fifth of the army of China would be constituted of communist troops. The two parties pledged a gradual reduction and amalgamation of their armies so that after eighteen months there would remain only sixty divisions under a unified command; moreover, the parties accepted the principle of civil control of the military through the creation of a new ministry of national defense in the executive yuan. It is interesting to note that, when this ministry was established by Chiang K'ai-shek in July, 1946, to supersede the powerful military commission, there were still no effective checks upon his military power.

The unity of the political consultative conference broke down, however, when attempts were made to implement some of the basic agreements. The communists and Nationalists remained divided on the matter of provincial authority. They were unable to achieve any formula by which stable provincial administrations satisfactory to both sides could be established. This was an especially thorny problem in the case of Manchuria. The state council also presented problems. A Chinese Communist Party–Democratic League coalition demanded fourteen seats, or the equivalent of veto power, since all decisions would require a two-thirds majority for passage. In the end, the Kuomintang central executive committee, dominated by the uncompromising right wing, refused to approve any of the agreements reached by the political consultative conference.

Negotiations continued throughout 1946, with Marshall making every effort to achieve a compromise. When the differences between the two parties could not be reconciled, fighting, at first sporadic, became increasingly general, particularly in north China and in Manchuria. At the end of July, Marshall imposed an embargo on the sale of arms and ammunition to China, and in August President Truman issued an executive order which prevented China from acquiring surplus American weapons "which could be used in fighting a civil war." Although the embargo, which was observed by Great Britain as well, was effective for almost a year, it did not have the desired effect of forcing a settlement. After his return to the United States in 1947, Marshall blamed the extremists among both the communists and the Nationalists for the failure of his mission. He explained that the right wing of the Kuomintang counted on the continuance of American support and would not reach a compromise with the communists:

There is a dominant group of reactionaries who have been opposed, in my opinion, to almost every effort I have made to influence the formation of genuine coalition government. . . . They were quite frank in publicly stating their belief that co-operation by the Chinese Communist Party in the government was inconceivable and that only a policy of force could settle the issue.

On the other hand, he made the point that the communists counted on economic collapse to topple Chiang's regime:

The dyed-in-the-wool communists do not hesitate at the most drastic measures to gain their ends as, for instance, the destruction of communications in order to wreck the economy of China and produce a situation that would facilitate the overthrow or collapse of the Government, without any regard to the immediate suffering of the people involved.

The denouement came when the communist delegation to the political consultative conference was expelled from Nanking. In February, 1947, China entered a period of open civil war.

The Civil War

Although the decision was ultimately decided on the battlefield, the war was fought against a background of deteriorating morale in Nationalist China. The story behind this is complicated, but certain factors can be delineated clearly. The basic deficiency in Nationalist China was the lack of a vigorous, stable administration to fill the power vacuum created by the defeat of Japan. The Kuomintang no longer had vitality. It was not a body of men willing to put national interests above personal gain; consequently, selfishness, nepotism, and corruption in their worst forms progressively weakened the administration.

Economic instability was perhaps the most serious problem. Shortages of consumer goods, restrictions on legitimate business, speculation, hoarding, and corruption all tended to increase the spiral of inflation. Furthermore, the government lacked an adequate tax base, and it pursued foolish fiscal policies, often using the printing press to finance its operations. A few figures give some indication of the severity of the inflation. By the beginning of 1947 the Chinese dollar was rated at 7,000 to one American dollar; by the end of February, 1947, this figure was 18,000 to one; and by August, 1947, it reached the astounding peak of 45,000 to one. Prices multiplied forty-five times in the first seven months of 1948 and were then three million times higher than 1937 prices. The urban population, not sustained, as the peasants were, by subsistence farming, was hardest hit by inflation. As urban morale deteriorated, Chiang lost the support of thousands of Chinese, especially the intellectuals and salaried class. Even Chinese businessmen, hampered by the activities of government agencies, became disillusioned with the regime.

Political reform, regarded as a panacea for maintaining popular support, was a failure. A Kuomintang-controlled national assembly, boycotted by the

509

Chinese Communist Party and the Democratic League, met in November, 1946, and declared that political tutelage was at an end. It promised that a constitution would go into effect in December, 1947. This document embodied responsible cabinet government—responsibility of the executive yuan to an elected legislative yuan—but this concession was emasculated by the grant of national emergency powers to a president elected by the national assembly, which would meet once every three years. A packed assembly of several thousand delegates met in April, 1948, and elected Chiang K'ai-shek president. There was a struggle over the vice-presidency in which Li Tsung-jen, the former Kwangsi warlord, defeated the government-supported candidate, Sun Fo. Li's victory angered Chiang, widened the gulf between the central army and the Kwangsi forces, and led to Chiang's dismissal of the able defense minister, Pai Chung-hsi. The failure of genuine constitutional reform disappointed most Chinese liberals, and many of them, particularly those organized in the Democratic League, went over to the Chinese Communist Party. In October, 1947, the League was outlawed by the Nationalist government.

The first phase of the military struggle took place in Manchuria. Chiang had been able to airlift troops into the large cities, but they made little effort to seek out Chinese communist troops and destroy them. Chiang seemed content to conserve his strength rather than engage in aggressive operations against the enemy. Despite constant American warnings that he would be unable to supply these northern garrisons, he was determined to hold Manchuria because of its economic potential. The Americans reasoned that the communists were strong enough in the north to cut Chiang's line of communications and isolate his garrisons. This is precisely what happened. From the spring of 1947 on, the Manchurian cities depended increasingly upon airlift operations. A communist offensive launched in the autumn of 1947 cut the rail lines into Mukden, and the Nationalists were barely able to fly in a third of the supply requirements of their forces in that city. That the airlift was extremely costly was borne out by a report of Minister of Defense General Ho Ying-ch'in to a secret session of the legislative yuan that the entire military budget for the latter half of 1948 had been completely expended on air-supplying the single city of Changchun for two months and four days. Moreover, the southern troops, which constituted the main body of the Nationalists' Manchurian force, were not prepared for the extremes of the northern winter, and the winter of 1947–1948 was one of the worst on record.

By November, 1948, the Manchurian situation was a complete disaster for Chiang K'ai-shek. The loss of the area and some 300,000 of their best troops, along with tremendous amounts of American equipment, was the beginning of the end for the Nationalists. Nearly 360,000 communist troops were freed to move into China proper, and in a well-co-ordinated action 550,-

000 men of the communist Second and Third field armies, commanded by Ch'en Yi and Liu Po-ch'eng, marched on Hsuchow, where Chiang maintained twenty divisions, shortly thereafter increased to seven army groups.

An analysis of the subsequent loss of north China makes clear most of the weaknesses of the Kuomintang armies. Field commanders often lacked adequate economic and military support, in many cases because Chiang was concerned about their personal loyalty; moreover, the efforts of the Whampoa clique to concentrate power in its hands caused it to ignore the talents of generals like Li Tsung-jen and Pai Chung-hsi. Often Kuomintang generals made decisive blunders. For example, troops stationed around Paoting and Shihchiachuang, a rail center, actually marched right into communist hands, losing American equipment sufficient to equip three communist armies.

The key battle in north China took place at Hsuchow in December, 1948. A million men fought on each side, and the Kuomintang troops still had a superiority in equipment and were supported by an air force. The communists, however, proved to be the superior strategists, largely because Chiang refused to accept the advice of Li and Pai to retreat to a more favorable position along the Huai River but chose instead to stand at Hsuchow, where his flank was exposed on three sides. The communists launched flank attacks against the stationary position of the Kuomintang troops and smashed them. Chiang lost close to a half-million men, including most of his mechanized forces. After Hsuchow the Kuomintang position in north China was hopeless; consequently, the northern commander, General Fu Tso-yi, surrendered the city of Peking and an additional 100,000 soldiers. By the beginning of 1949 the approaches to the Yangtze River lay open and undefended.

Political repercussions followed immediately. The criticism of Chiang and the demand for negotiations with the communists were so widespread that Chiang retired from the presidency in January, 1949, being succeeded by Li Tsung-jen. The acting president sought to improve the defenses of south China, but at the same time he entered into negotiations with the Chinese communists on terms offered by Mao Tse-tung in January and reaffirmed by the party's central committee in March. These terms amounted to a demand for unconditional surrender by the Kuomintang and went so far as to list war criminals for punishment. The communists, moreover, promised to establish a "democratic" government based on a coalition of democratic parties, groups, political organizations, and personages. This commitment served as part of the communist propaganda offensive aimed at attracting as many followers as possible, and in this context it is interesting to note that, although Li and the Kuomintang rejected these terms, the negotiators themselves went over to the communists.

On April 21, 1949, the communist military offensive was resumed with the crossing of the Yangtze River. This operation, one of the most gigantic in military history, was made easier by Kuomintang failures. Chiang interfered and prevented troops from being moved upriver to those sections where the communists would be most likely to attempt a crossing. Kuomintang naval and air forces failed to provide effective support for the defending forces, and one bribed commander protected the communist crossing by shelling Nationalist naval units. The communists occupied Nanking on April 24 and began their drive toward Shanghai, where the defensive efforts of the Kuomintang often took on a comic-opera appearance. For example, the Nationalist forces erected a wooden fence, which extended for some twenty-five miles along the outer perimeter of Shanghai, with gates only at the main road-crossings. When Chinese merchants tried to bribe the commanding general not to defend the city, Chiang intervened and ordered the troops to defend Shanghai. The residents were informed shortly thereafter that the Nationalists had inflicted a series of defeats on the communists in the outskirts of the city, and they were ordered to prepare for a tremendous victory celebration. Flags were raised, and crowds gathered to cheer the victorious troops who paraded through the city. One truck carried a brass band which played popular tunes such as "Marching through Georgia" and "Britannia Rules the Waves." Unfortunately the purpose of the parade was the embarkation of these troops to safety on Taiwan (Formosa). On May 27, 1949, the city that had the most Western orientation of any city in China fell to the communists. Fighting continued in south and west China through 1949, but by December the mainland was in communist hands. On December 7 Li Tsung-jen gave up at Chengtu in Szechwan Province and flew to the United States, planning to return ultimately to Taiwan.

The Kuomintang Collapse in Retrospect

In March, 1950, Chiang K'ai-shek once again assumed the presidency of China in spite of the opposition of Li Tsung-jen. Nationalist China was now limited to the island of Taiwan and the few offshore islands like Quemoy and Matsu in the harbors of Amoy and Foochow. Chiang's return to power was accompanied by a series of ruthless acts, including the execution of opposition officials and officers. Li Tsung-jen chose to remain in the United States. On Taiwan, Chiang began the long, agonizing process of analyzing the reasons for the Kuomintang's defeat and of establishing a program that would reinvigorate the party as the revolutionary leader of the Chinese people. Chiang's conclusions, as explained in an address he made in July, 1950, make interesting reading today. He stated:

All corrupt, reactionary, selfish, and unstable elements will be strictly eliminated in order to revive the party's revolutionary spirit. Positively, we must strengthen ourselves by uniting all the patriotic youths and loyal citizens both at home and abroad in the revolution, and direct all antiaggressive, antitotalitarian, and freedom-loving people to the road of The Three People's Principles. Factionalism must be eradicated. New members must be enlisted from the anticommunist and National Salvation movement, while good workers must be trained through political and economic reforms. We must emphasize group action in order to influence individual activities. Every member of the party must be organized into a basic unit which lives in the masses. We must take the people's needs as the basis in formulating the political program of the party and take the current social thought as the guide of our revolution.

Second, he emphasized the party's failures in effecting the principle of the people's livelihood, stating:

It is the consensus that our party has failed during the past four years because we have failed to enforce the principle of the people's livelihood. Everyone has now realized that we must enforce the principle of the people's livelihood to defeat the communists. May I ask: During the past four years, has any village party organ made a land survey? Has any municipal party organ compiled labor statistics? Has any provincial party organ submitted to the central party headquarters any systematic social survey or economic research? The practice of the principle of the people's livelihood does not depend on theories or experiments alone; it must be based on facts. It does not provoke class struggle but promotes co-operation in order to improve social and economic relationships of the people. We must, therefore, abandon subjectivism and formulism and cultivate the scientific spirit in dealing with actual conditions. Only thus can we effect social reform based upon the principle of the people's livelihood.

Chiang K'ai-shek must accept his share of the responsibility for defeat. Ch'ien Tuan-sheng has summarized the case against Chiang:

Chiang K'ai-shek is a man of strong will, fortified by an unusual amount of shrewdness and tenacity. Yet he is totally devoid of that quality of progressivism which saved Sun Yat-sen from prizing power for power's sake. A conservative by instinct, Chiang K'ai-shek has no feeling of the spirit of the times. His lack of intimate contact with people of enlightenment, not to say the common people, further deprives him of an opportunity to grow. The Actonian axiom, "Power corrupts and absolute power corrupts absolutely," is illustrated with devastating effect in his relationship with other men. In his anxiety to cling to power, more and more he distrusts people who criticize him or even dare to differ with him. The men who work with him have to be first and last loyal to him personally. In the end he became the leader of a party of servile men but not a party of men and ideas, which were once the glory of the reorganized Kuomintang.

Much soul-searching with regard to Chiang's defeat occurred elsewhere, particularly in the United States by politicians and China specialists. Soul-searching soon turned into a great debate, acrimonious in tone and characterized generally by political considerations rather than mature judgment. Although it is probably not conclusive, the following explanation includes most of the decisive factors emphasized by those individuals who were closest to the situation.

The Kuomintang was not an effective instrument of political, economic, and social revolution. It was not organized and disciplined to carry out reform programs, and its constant failures resulted in the loss of popular support. It was not that the Chinese people embraced communism; they simply became disillusioned with the Kuomintang-dominated regime. Many of them were neutralized politically by communist propaganda which appealed to their ideals of reform and security. A people tired of war, high taxes, and corruption accepted communist leadership. In the final analysis, however, much consideration must be given to military decisions. The communists proved to be the superior tacticians and strategists. Furthermore, their armies maintained high morale and fought effectively; from top to bottom the communist forces were well indoctrinated with the party's political and military objectives. The communist party was quick to follow up military victory with political consolidation. Thousands of cadres moved into villages and mobilized the peasantry in the pattern of class struggle. In brief, the communist party was able to move into the vacuum created by the defeat of Japan and the ineptitude and inefficiency of the Kuomintang.

One last question remains to be considered. Was the triumph of communism the result of the failure of the United States to provide the Nationalist government with adequate military assistance? In its explanation of Chiang's defeat, the American State Department quoted American military experts to the effect that Chiang never lost a battle for lack of equipment; however, there was some evidence in 1947 and 1948, reported by responsible observers, that some Nationalist armies were desperately in need of ammunition. Generals like Pai Chung-hsi and Fu Tso-yi did lack supplies, but this was generally due to inequalities in the dispersal of American aid by the Kuomintang. Li Tsung-jen wrote to President Truman on May 5, 1949: "It is regrettable that, owing to the failure of our government to make judicious use of this aid and to bring about appropriate political, economic, and military reforms, your assistance has not produced the desired effect. To this failure is attributable the present predicament in which our country finds itself." Much discussion has also turned on the question of whether the United States should have intervened in China. The wisdom of such a move may be debated for generations, but in the historical context of the years 1945–1949 such intervention was unlikely. It is difficult to get away from the conclusion that the decision in China was determined basically by factors in the Chinese scene.

It is instructive to analyze the problem from the Russian point of view. Stalin stated in February, 1948:

It is true, we also have made mistakes. For instance, after the war we invited the Chinese comrades to come to Moscow and we discussed the situation in China. We told them bluntly that we considered the development of the uprising in China had no prospects, and the Chinese comrades should seek a *modus vivendi* with Chiang K'ai-shek, and that they should join the Chiang K'ai-shek government and disband their army. The Chinese comrades . . . acted quite otherwise. They mustered their forces, organized their armies, and now, as we see, they are beating Chiang K'ai-shek's armies. Now in the case of China, we admit we were wrong. It has proved that the Chinese communist comrades and not the Soviet comrades were right.

In July, 1948, at a Chinese communist strategy conference in southern Hopei, Soviet agents tried to persuade the Chinese communists to continue guerrilla warfare and not to undertake an all-out offensive. This, they claimed, would weaken the United States, which was "pouring aid into the Chiang regime." The Chinese communists, however, rejected the Russian proposal. Even in November, 1948, the Soviet Union seems to have desired a Chinese communist settlement with Chiang K'ai-shek. Only in April, 1949, when the Chinese communist armies crossed the Yangtze River, did the Soviet Union change her views.

The Communist Political System

At Peking in September, 1949, the Chinese communists convened a people's consultative conference of 662 delegates representing the various "democratic parties," occupational groups, and minorities, and this communist-dominated body approved a "Common Program"* and an Organic Law of the Central Government of the People's Republic of China. The Common Program, based on Mao Tse-tung's *On the People's Democratic Dictatorship*, emphasized that the continuing process of revolution would be led by the communist party "as the vanguard of the working class, the leading member of the joint revolutionary alliance which includes the peasants, the petty bourgeoisie, and the national capitalists." As a formula for China's development, it stressed such short-term objectives as economic rehabilitation and land reform and held up "socialism" as the future goal. According to the Organic Law, the supreme executive body of the government was the central people's government council (whose 63 members were elected by the people's political consultative conference) and, under its direction, the state administrative council of 20 members, which acted as a kind of functional cabinet. The people's revolutionary military council managed the military affairs of the state and was responsible for stabilizing local government under six regional administrations: Manchuria, North China, Eastern China, Northwest China,

---

* See Appendix 3.

Southwest China, and Central and Southern China. Military control and discipline were essential since, initially, many of the local officials of the Kuomintang regime were left in office and few changes were made in the existing local governments. At the end of 1951, however, the communists replaced these functionaries with their own trainees.

The coalition nature of the central government was maintained in form by the appointment of a few noncommunists to positions of prestige, as in the cases of the widow of Sun Yat-sen, Li Chi-sen, a former Kuomintang general, and Chan Lan, chairman of the Democratic League, all of whom became vice-chairmen of the central people's government council. Actual power was in the hands of the communists, especially the trusted friends of Mao Tse-tung. Mao himself was the chairman of the government council and the military council; Chou En-lai served as chairman of the state administrative council and as foreign minister; Chu Teh was a vice-chairman of the government council and commander of the armies; and Liu Shao-ch'i, who with Mao was a leading party theoretician, served as a member of the government council and the military council. All these men also held key positions in the communist party; for example, Mao was party chairman and Liu vice-chairman.

The present political structure of China was determined by the constitution of September, 1954, which was the result of two years of careful preparation. In fact, the regime went to great lengths to create the impression of popular participation in the drafting process. According to Peking's estimates, 8,000 persons discussed the preliminary draft prepared by a committee under the chairmanship of Mao Tse-tung, and 500,000 persons in one province alone were organized to publicize and explain it to the masses. The same source claimed that 400,000 copies of the draft were sold within a two-week period in Peking. Meanwhile preparations were under way for nation-wide elections for the national people's congress. On the basis of a census, which disclosed a total population of 583,000,000 in mainland China, the regime declared that 323,000,000 Chinese, eighteen years or older, were eligible to vote. According to communist records, 80 per cent of those eligible voted for 5,500,000 delegates to people's congresses at the lowest levels of government, and in turn the successful candidates voted for delegates to hsien congresses, and so on through the provincial to the national level. Finally, in September, 1954, 1,197 deputies of the national people's congress convened and approved the constitution unanimously.

The constitution, which attributed the success of the Chinese revolution to the leadership of the communist party, defined the nature of the political system as a "people's democracy led by the working class and based upon the foundation of a worker-peasant alliance." In theory the national people's congress is the supreme organ of state power and meets yearly to enact legislation, and its members are elected indirectly by provincial congresses and by organizations representing large cities, minorities, the army, and the overseas

Chinese. In practice, however, the national congress is hardly more than a rubber stamp for the leadership of the bureaucracy, and, when it is not in session, its functions are managed by a standing committee under the chairmanship of Liu Shao-ch'i. Political power rests in the various executive offices, councils, and committees which control and supervise the vast bureaucratic network of government. The most important of these are the chairmanship of the People's Republic of China, a position held by Mao Tse-tung until 1959, when he resigned in favor of Liu Shao-ch'i; the supreme state conference, an *ad hoc* body comprising the chairman and vice-chairman of the republic, chairman of the standing committee of the national people's congress, chairman, or premier, of the state council, and any other persons that the head of state wishes to invite to the conference, which serves primarily as a forum for his views; the state council of some forty ministries, commissions, and affiliated agencies, which conducts the ordinary business of government and is responsible, although only nominally, to the national people's congress or its standing committee; the council of national defense, also headed by Mao Tse-tung; the commander of the armies, a post held by Chu Teh, who also serves as vice-chairman of the republic; the supreme people's court, which supervises a hierarchy of lower courts corresponding to the various levels of administration; and the supreme people's procurator's office, which controls a similar chain of subordinate offices and acts as public prosecutor in criminal cases.

Local government is based on the Leninist principle of democratic centralism and has the following levels: 21 provinces, municipalities, urban districts, towns; 2,000 rural counties (hsien); and 26,000 rural communes, which in 1958 replaced the *hsiang*, or group of villages. The political structure of these units, similar to that of the central system, is based on a people's congress and a people's council, the chairman of the latter being the head of government at a specific level. Elections are carefully controlled by the communist party, which draws up the lists of candidates; the only rights that the voters may exercise are to reject a few candidates as unacceptable and perhaps to nominate others by petition. While the council is elected by the congress at each level and is nominally responsible to it, in practice the congress does not change the essentials of policies submitted by the council for its discussion. In the government chain of command, power runs downward from the state council to the people's councils at the various levels; and Peking, Shanghai, and Tientsin are under the direct administration of the central government.

Each of the five "autonomous" regions—Inner Mongolia, Sinkiang Uighur, Ninghsia Hui, Kwangsi Ch'ung, and Tibet—has its own government, which is controlled by Peking. Tibet was invaded in October, 1950, and "liberated" from "Anglo-American imperialism" on May 23, 1951, but the arbitrary behavior of the Chinese occupation forces, the steady influx of Chinese settlers into the eastern regions, and the initiation of "democratic

517

reforms," such as land redistribution, including the estates of the numerous monasteries, precipitated revolt as early as 1956. Although the Chinese communists first sought to appease the Tibetans by withdrawing sizable forces and promising not to introduce reforms until after 1962, local discontent mounted and erupted in the revolution of March, 1959, which the Chinese brutally crushed. Thereafter, Peking abandoned any pretense of recognizing Tibetan autonomy, increased Chinese controls, and accelerated the process of social revolution.

As in all communist states, the government and the communist party are for all practical purposes one and the same. The party determines policy and monopolizes almost all of the key posts in the administration. Although in theory the party congress and the central committee are the supreme bodies, they are rarely convoked, and power rests in the political bureau of twenty members and its standing committee of seven, headed by Mao Tse-tung and including Chu Teh, Chou En-lai, and Liu Shao-ch'i. Like the system of local government, party organization is based on the principle of democratic centralism, and below the central organs on the next level are the provinces, the special municipalities, and the autonomous regions, each with its own party congress and party committee. The county and municipal party organizations have a similar structure. The lowest official organ of the party is the branch or cell of approximately twenty persons working in the same activity. Every party member must belong to one of the cells, which meet regularly for the discussion of various topics.

Although the Chinese Communist Party has over 15,000,000 members, its leadership has been able to maintain loyalty and discipline, chiefly, perhaps, because the party controls all channels through which the individual can gain high station in society. The party also engages in a constant process of self-criticism, and it systematically purges unreliable and inefficient members in order to tighten discipline. On the highest levels the party has demonstrated an amazing degree of unity, largely because of the personality and strong leadership of Mao Tse-tung; and although there have been important differences of opinion among the the top leaders on specific policies, these have been carefully hidden from public view. In fact, during the past decade the only serious break in party solidarity was the alleged attempt in 1954 and 1955 by Kao Kang and Jao Shu-shih to establish their own regional power at the expense of the central government. After their execution there was a nation-wide campaign to tighten party organization.

The communist party has also been careful to maintain its control over military power. In 1953 and 1954 it abolished the various regional field armies and centered control over the military establishment in its own military committee, composed of the party's most powerful members, which operates through various governmental executive agencies such as the national defense council, the army general staff, and the ministry of defense in the state council. The party also monopolizes important command and staff positions, and each commander down through the company level has a political officer who is a party member and whose approval of all orders is required except in times of military emergency. The political officer is also responsible for the continuing process of indoctrination of the men, especially the several thousands of youths who are conscripted each year.

There are other political parties in China, such as the Revolutionary Committee of the Kuomintang, the Chinese Peasants and Workers Democratic Party, and the China Democratic League, but each has pledged the following:

We, the democratic parties of China, are unconditionally united under the leadership of the great Communist Party and Chairman Mao Tse-tung for the building of an independent, free, democratic, united, and prosperous China. To achieve this, we pledge ourselves to carry out fully the Chinese Communist Party's slogans.

These parties are useful as members of the "united front," and on the occasion of the Eighth Chinese Communist Party Congress in September, 1956, the *People's Daily*, the official organ of the party's central committee, promised that "the Communist Party will carry out the policy of long-term coexistence and mutual supervision with other democratic parties; so long as the Communist Party exists, the other democratic parties will also exist." Evidently the value of these organizations is so great that the regime will not permit their members to join the communist party.

The party also works through the following mass organizations: the All-China Federation of Trade Unions, the Communist Youth League (before 1956 the New Democratic Youth League), the All-China Federation of Democratic Youth, the Young Pioneers, the All-China Federation of Democratic Women, peasant associations, and the Sino-Soviet Friendship Association. Each of these, also organized on the basis of democratic centralism, has a national body, which holds periodic congresses; regional and branch units; and local cells, through which the party orders are transmitted and which conduct meetings and discussions serving the purposes of the regime.

Communist Social and Thought Control

Although the 1954 constitution pledged the state "to protect the safety and rights of the citizens," in practice the regime interprets this to mean benevolent control. Through the agency of the mass organizations, rural communes, street committees in urban areas, trade unions, and numerous other bodies, the government informs the people regarding correct thought and promotes their "welfare." A large part of the population, especially in urban areas, has been organized into small study groups in which they learn communist orthodoxy and are put under pressure to confess and denounce past errors. Should persuasion fail, the communists can fall back on the use of terror by the agencies and forces of the ministry of public safety. During recent years as many as a half-million public security troops have been stationed at key centers throughout the country, as many or more people's armed police in the counties, and a million militiamen in the communes.

The communists have constantly suppressed enemies of the state. Under a law promulgated in July, 1950, and applied hastily after the beginning of 1951, all "war criminals, traitors, bureaucratic capitalists, and counterrevolutionaries" lost their property and were subject to punishment ranging from three years' imprisonment to death. The implementation of this law became linked with a campaign against American "imperialism" and led to mass arrests, including the imprisonment of many foreigners, and public trials, which were carefully staged in cities like Shanghai and were carried over the radio for their propaganda effect on larger audiences. According to an official estimate by the American government, in this campaign and others, such as the persecution of landlords, 15,000,000 people were killed and more than 20,000,000 were sent to forced-labor camps. The constitution empowers the state to suppress and punish all "treasonable and counterrevolutionary activities," and such power has continued to be directed not only against subversives but against anyone who has "impeded progress."

The communist regime has also systematically discredited the old Confucian social principles and Western values, especially among the youth of the country. The pages of *Young China*, the organ of the Communist Youth League, are replete with examples of "progressive" advice. For example, in answer to an inquiry from a boy regarding his duty to denounce his father, a former landlord, who was hiding with his family, the editor stated:

Yes! Liquidate blood relations in the cause of justice. But wait, liquidation is only a figure of speech. The regime kills only the worst criminals. It reforms the rest by hard labor. Once his thoughts are reformed, your father will be returned. Your father will be grateful, and you will be the instrument of his salvation. If he has not reformed, you can denounce him again.

In defining the nature of love, *Young China* commented:

In old China there was love for love's sake. Now there is no love without a political foundation.

If some of our youth take too much interest in love and devote too much time and energy to this problem, it would be detrimental to the national interests.

To consider marriage and family problems merely as individual problems of private life is unilateral and incorrect.

The regime has suppressed traditional religions that have no foreign affiliations, especially Religious Taoism, but both Islam and Buddhism have been treated with some deference for almost a decade. Despite the harsh treatment of foreign missionaries, Christianity survives, although as an organization it is completely subordinate to the state and is isolated from foreign relationships.

Intellectual and artistic life has come under close control and supervision, and on occasion the regime has made examples of figures in these fields. "To direct authors in their work and in their lives, that is one of the goals of the Federation of Writers and Artists," i.e., a committee of writers under the direction of the Federation examines a manuscript before publication, discusses its merit, decides how to improve it in content and style, and helps the author to raise its artistic level and to have it ideologically correct. The case of Yu Ping-po makes the emphasis upon ideology clear.

Yu, an old and well-known professor, had written a monumental critical work on the famous traditional love story, *Dream of the Red Chamber*, and it was published in 1952 with no adverse criticism. But in 1954 two students launched a savage attack upon him in several publications, and before long the *People's Daily* made its own accusations, blaming Yu for failing to show that *Dream of the Red Chamber* was a manifestation of the class struggle of the Chinese people in the seventeenth century. Yu appeared before a tribunal of his peers, composed of fifty professors and leaders of the academic world, and his case became part of a national campaign of Marxist-Leninist *vs.* idealist thought when Peking ordered local discussions of the case by intellectuals. Yu finally confessed his errors, and locally there was much self-criticism. When Hu Feng, a member of the Chinese Communist Party for eighteen years, deputy for Shanghai in the national people's congress, and a member of the steering committees of two important literary federations, criticized the denunciation of Yu and attacked the "warlords of literature," he, too, was denounced in February, 1955, and this became the pretext for another national campaign. Although Hu confessed his mistakes in May, 1956, he was called insincere and treacherous. The *People's Daily* branded him a counterrevolutionary and accused him of heading an organized network of writers and intellectuals. When a meeting of seven hundred intellectuals in Peking demanded that Hu be tried by the state, he was arrested, and the authorities began a hunt for Hu Fengists. The search in Shanghai netted one traitor for each ten intellectuals.

Shortly thereafter, however, taking its cue from a speech by Mao Tse-tung, the communist party began to advocate freedom of thought and debate so long as it was "in accordance with the consolidation of the people's regime." "Let all flowers bloom together, let diverse schools of thought contend," was the slogan. Most intellectuals were skeptical, but there were some worker and student strikes as well as expressions of discontent among minorities. And, after the Soviet military repression in Hungary, the Chinese communists decided to permit freer expression—perhaps designed to uncover critics and sup-

521

press them. When some courageous individuals attacked the severity of the party dictatorship, the regime struck back with a campaign of counter-criticism in 1957, denouncing rightist critics and hinting that they would be treated as counterrevolutionaries. In the wake of retractions and public confessions, three prominent members of noncommunist parties were expelled from ministerial posts and more than fifty lost their seats in the national people's congress. As the "rectification" movement continued into late 1957 and 1958, there was a general purge of the party on the local level, and well over a million bureaucrats were transferred to working jobs in the villages. Finally, in 1959, the communist party insisted that, as a necessary condition of the "socialist leap forward," intellectuals must become "Red as well as expert."

The Chinese communists have expanded and reformed education in order to develop the skills that the country requires and to inculcate ideological orthodoxy among the masses. By 1960 primary-school enrollments reached the total of approximately 70,000,000, about three times that of 1949, and the total of 6,000,000 secondary-school students constituted a similar increase. The quality of education is not very high, except in technical schools and institutes, and, despite a great emphasis upon evening classes and adult education, 70 per cent of the population is still illiterate. The colleges, universities, and technical institutes, with enrollments of about 500,000 in 1960, are under great pressure to train the various kinds of specialists that the country needs so desperately. There is a great deal of ideological content in education at all levels, and teachers are constantly engaged in self-criticism in order "to truly improve and raise their own ideology." Language reform has accompanied the expansion of educational facilities, and in 1956 the government simplified several hundred of the most complicated characters and advocated a common spoken language based upon the Peking dialect. It also announced a plan to introduce a slightly augmented Latin alphabet as the standard means of writing within ten years, but to date the new script has been used only as an aid to the study of characters.

Communist Industrialization

Among their economic goals the Chinese Communist Party has given industrialization the highest priority. "Modern industry is the symbol of complete independence, national power, and economic improvement." The initial emphasis was upon rehabilitation of the country's productive capacity, and by 1952 the regime claimed that, on the average, production levels had reached their pre-1949 peaks. In 1953 the government announced the inauguration of the first five-year plan, which signaled the beginning of "the transition to socialism," with production goals set for the first year. These were revised drastically several times, and not until 1955 were the final over-all production goals made public. The Chinese communists planned to invest in capital construction at the rate of approximately $3–$4 billion per year, or about 20 per cent of the national income. The preponderance of investment in heavy industry, centering in Manchuria and to a lesser extent in Lanchow, was apparent; and in fact, considering depreciation, there was hardly any net investment in light industry. At the same time, the state was spending about $2.3 billion, or 16 per cent of national income, for military purposes, especially the maintenance of a conscript army of about 3,000,000 men, a substantial reduction from the 4,900,000 under arms in 1949. The percentage of national income applied to military purposes was about the same as that of the United States, but it contrasted vividly with the mere 2 per cent of national income devoted to this purpose by the government of India. The government also conducted numerous geological surveys, which discovered or confirmed the existence of large coal and iron reserves in north and northwest China.

According to communist claims, 800 large industrial projects were completed, the value of gross industrial output had increased by approximately 120 per cent, and China's total national income had increased by over one-half. Specifically, the communists raised steel production threefold, to 5,350,000 metric tons; pig iron threefold, to 5,940,000 tons; coal twofold, to 130,000,000 tons; electricity twofold, to 19.3 billion kilowatts; cement over twofold, to 6,860,000 tons; and machine tools twofold, to 28,000 sets. But the output of consumer goods lagged and did not satisfy domestic demands. While the communists were evidently successful in achieving most of their basic goals, it must not be forgotten that at the end of the first five-year plan in 1957 the level of industrial production remained below that of the Soviet Union in 1928, when she commenced her first five-year plan; and despite the construction of 2,500 miles of railway, it will be some time before China reaches the position of India in this field. In fact, in 1955, Chinese communist leaders estimated that it would take some forty to fifty years before their nation became "a powerful country with a high degree of socialist industrialization"; however, in 1957, as the second five-year plan got under way, they called for an "upsurge" and "a great leap forward." Evidently the communist party hopes to make China a major industrial power comparable to the United Kingdom by about 1973, after four five-year plans. It intends to continue to invest about 20 per cent of national income for that purpose, and the ratio of investment in heavy industry to that in light industry will remain at approximately seven to one.

The bulk of China's capital for investment has been provided from national sources, especially from taxes, the profits of state monopolies and other enterprises, and increases in national indebtedness, and there has been some assistance from the Soviet Union. In 1950 the Russians provided a loan of $300,000,000, and in a series of commitments in 1953, 1954, and 1956 they promised to help construct 211 major industrial projects by selling necessary equipment and supplies in the value of $2 billion and by providing several thousand technical advisers. Actually, Russian capital resources have been limited; moreover, Moscow has been aware that the investment of capital in China will mature much more slowly than in the Soviet Union or in eastern Europe. The desire to keep China dependent upon the Soviet Union has probably also influenced investment considerations. The greater part of Russian assistance, both capital and technical, has been paid for by the export of Chinese agricultural products and raw materials, and 80 per cent of China's trade has been with the Soviet Union and her European satellites.

One of the most significant aspects of the first five-year plan was the consummation of state ownership and management of the means of industrial production and of business in general. This process was facilitated by the fact that the Kuomintang had already expropriated Japanese capital, which controlled a majority of China's modern industrial plants in 1945; moreover, other foreign capital was forced out by increased restrictions on its activity. By 1952, according to communist statistics, 67 per cent of all industrial production was state-owned, 90 per cent of bank loans and deposits were managed by the people's bank, and 90 per cent of foreign trade was handled by state companies.

Chinese capitalists were made subservient to the state from the very beginning of the communist regime because of heavy taxes, which absorbed 75 per cent of profits, wage and price controls, raw-material allocations, priority of government purchase, and state credit controls. And from October, 1951, until June, 1952, class warfare was carried on against some 450,000 businessmen, who were charged with bribery, tax evasion, theft of state assets, and cheating in labor and materials, all of which the state claimed was taking $2½ billion out of the economy each year. Special courts were established to try businessmen and firms for their alleged criminal acts, and, according to communist sources, over $2 billion was recovered through fines paid by those guilty of such practices, which was of great help to the financial position of the government. Many businessmen were imprisoned or executed, and a larger number committed suicide.

Later, in 1955, Mao Tse-tung launched a program to "transform" private business into "joint state-private enterprises" which would be state-controlled and from which former owners would receive a low rate of interest on their "investments" instead of profits. In 1958 these investors were promised that they would continue to receive interest payments at least through the second five-year plan and that the minimum rate would be 5 per cent instead of the original 1 per cent. By the end of the first five-year plan in 1957, the state controlled 70 per cent of all industry, 100 per cent of banking and insurance, 95 per cent of the wholesale trade, 85 per cent of retail trade, and 100 per cent of foreign trade. But most state enterprises suffered from the traditional bureaucratic weaknesses. They were overstaffed with administrative personnel, were inadequately integrated, and paid more attention to production goals than to quality.

Labor is closely controlled by the All-China Federation of Trade Unions, which is dominated by the Chinese Communist Party. In 1956 the chairman, two-thirds of the vice-chairmen, and all eight members of the federation's secretariat were party members. The basic functions of unions are to boost production and to supervise and propagandize labor. Unions do not have the right to strike, and grievances must be submitted to compulsory arbitration. When a worker changes jobs, he must have a certificate of satisfactory performance from his former employer and his "labor book," in which all his previous employment since 1949 has been entered; and violators of union discipline have been branded as anarchists "with a bourgeois predilection for indolence, pleasure, selfishness, individualism, and liberal laxity."

Although the living standards of workers are somewhat higher than those of peasants, they work harder under the pressure of a piece-work system in which the norms are constantly changing on the basis of the output achieved by the most productive workers. In 1956 the regime made various promises, including the reduction of the working day to eight hours, but it is doubtful whether they were ever carried out. In addition, there are millions of forced laborers who are employed on heavy construction projects, such as water conservation, railroads, and highways.

Communist Agricultural Development and Reform

The communist government has also placed great emphasis upon increasing agricultural production, especially to provide food for the growing urban population, to supply larger quantities of raw materials like cotton for industry, and to provide export commodities to finance required imports. In the period from 1949 to 1952 agriculture made great progress, largely because of the restoration of peace and order and because of favorable weather conditions; but during the period of the first five-year plan, when the regime sought to raise the production of grains by 30 per cent, agriculture was handicapped by serious floods and peasant resistance to collectivization. Thus in 1955 Peking reduced the grain target to a figure which represented a five-year increase of 17 per cent. Significant advances were made in reforestation and in water conservation and flood control. The regime completed the Huai River project, which involved an area of 83,500 square miles with a population of 60,000,000 persons, and improved the dikes of the Yellow and Yangtze rivers. In the Yellow River area the regime hopes to add some 5,000,000 irrigated acres over a fifteen-year period.

From 1950 to 1952 the Chinese communists carried out an extensive land-reform program directed at the expropriation of landlord holdings. According to statistics compiled by Peking, ownership of Chinese farm land in 1949 broke down as follows:

	Percentage of Total Number of Families	Percentage of Total Acreage Owned
Landlords	3	26
Rich peasants	7	27
Middle peasants	22	25
Poor peasants	68	22

Under the June, 1950, Land Reform Law, the state was empowered to confiscate the land, tools, and surplus houses of landlords, the land of religious bodies, and the land of industrialists and merchants in the countryside. But it would protect the land of rich peasants cultivated by themselves or by hired labor and the land rented by them unless it exceeded their own worked holdings. At first the program was implemented by the communists in an orderly manner; but when the Chinese entered the Korean War, the class-struggle attack against "feudal" landlords became increasingly violent, and there was much loss of life as well as property. It became clear that in addition to its economic aspects the measure was used to destroy the power of anti-communist elements in the rural areas and bring them under firm control.

The amount of land that was redistributed among the poor peasants and agricultural laborers varied from province to province depending upon population pressure and productivity, but on a national average it came to one-third of an acre, and in the heavily populated eastern areas of China it was only one-sixth of an acre. The regime also levied a progressive land tax, which averaged about 25 per cent of the main crop, with provision for reductions in case of bad harvests; and it imposed excise taxes on almost every commodity.

There is no doubt that the reform benefited many peasants, but they were still faced with many problems, the most important of which probably was the lack of adequate credit facilities. The regime was forced to sanction private credit provided by rich and middle peasants at interest rates amounting to as much as 100 per cent per year. Before long the traditional process of class differentiation was under way, and poverty-stricken peasants began to move into towns and cities, where they were unable to find employment.

A basic problem for the state was to find a way to increase the marketable portion of agricultural production; under the old system this was accomplished by the landlord class through the sale of surplus grain. Destruction of the landlord system caused a marked decline in the commercial supply of grain because the peasantry tended to increase its own consumption, and the price differential between urban and rural products encouraged them to do so. Rice and other grains that did enter commercial channels were generally sold on the black market.

In reaction to these developments, the state established a monopoly system under which the peasants were required to sell a fixed quantity of grain at official prices, but this proved to be difficult to administer because of the great number of farm units involved. In order to increase its control over the countryside, to improve agricultural efficiency, and to secure a larger share of agricultural production, the state began to plan the collectivization of agriculture. At first it encouraged the formation of mutual labor teams and then of co-operatives; but after it had established its centralized administration over the provinces according to the terms of the constitution, it moved quickly to complete the process of collectivization as part of the first five-year plan. In July, 1955, in a speech which was published only after the harvests in October, Mao Tse-tung proposed that by the end of the year 50 per cent of the peasants should be organized into "semisocialized co-operatives" of about one hundred families, and in October the Sixth Plenary Session of the Central Committee of the Chinese Communist Party raised the total to approximately 75 per cent. In a "semisocialized co-operative" the peasant would be paid partly on the basis of land contributed and partly for his labor. Finally, at a supreme state conference held in January, 1956, it was decided to attain "socialism" by the beginning of 1959 and, more particularly, to complete the collectivization of agriculture in 1957, bringing all peasants into "fully socialized co-operatives"—actually collective farms in which peasants' income would largely be based on labor. It appears that, by the end of 1956, 83 per cent of the peasants, or 125,000,000 rural households, had formed 750,000 collectives under pressure from the state.

The most decisive change in rural organization came with the "communization" program in 1958. After the formation in April of a model commune, called "Sputnik," the central committee of the communist party in August ordered nation-wide communization of the rural areas, and by the end of the year almost all of the 750,000 collective farms were merged, at least on paper, into approximately 26,000 large communes of about 5,000 families. Almost every activity—farming, commerce, local industry, education, and military affairs—is administered by the commune, while the members are organized into production brigades and teams for all work and other functions. Although the regime has been forced to concede, at least for the time being, the existence of some private property for family units, the goal of the new system is to pay members on a "wage-plus-supply" basis, by which the commune administration will ration and distribute some commodities "free" to members and pay certain wages in kind or in money. The communes also have revolutionary social goals, which are designed to destroy the family as an institution. For example, cooking, child care, sewing, and weaving will be subject to the new division of labor, with the result that great numbers of women will be free to join the general labor force as equals of men. Meals will be eaten in mess halls; children will be put in nurseries and eventually completely separated from their parents; and old people will be placed in special homes. In some cases the rural population has already been rehoused in new villages or in special dormitories. In urban and industrial areas, where the communists had only begun to experiment with communes, they postponed the whole program.

While the present rural communes are still in a transitional stage because of the regime's reluctance to push the people too hard in face of discontent, it seems clear that the ultimate goals are still supported by the communist leadership. The August, 1958, resolution of the party's central committee called the commune "the best form of organization for the attainment of socialism and gradual transition to communism" and claimed that it "will develop into the basic social unit of communist society." And, despite two successive years of low agricultural production, in January, 1961, the central committee of the party declared its faith in the communes. It blamed China's agricultural difficulties on severe floods and droughts and on "an extremely small number of landlord and bourgeois elements [who] take advantage of difficulties brought about by natural calamities and some shortcomings in work at lower levels to carry out sabotaging activities."

Many of China's difficulties are still due to the population problem. The 1953 census ascertained that the total population was 583,000,000 and that the annual increase was 2 per cent, or 13,000,000 people. According to statistics compiled by Peking, the population increased by 65,000,000 people between 1952 and 1957, bringing the total to 634,000,000 in mid-1957. If the present trend continues, China will have about one billion people in the 1980's. This circumstance puts tremendous pressure on existing resources and minimizes the results of economic development programs. Since the rural areas cannot absorb the surplus population, there is constant migration to the cities, which increases urban unemployment. Despite their denials of overpopulation under a socialist system, the state and party endorsed and promoted birth-control measures; and although in 1957 and 1958 there was much talk about the desirability of a large and growing population, the government has continued to support measures which will check population growth.

Communist Foreign Policies

The Chinese communist regime, which is determined that China shall play the role of a great power, with a special and leading position in Asian affairs, bases its foreign policy upon alliance with the Soviet Union and international communism. The Chinese Communist Party regards itself as a member of a "free federation of communist parties, on an equal and voluntary footing, united in a common ideology and common allegiance to the Soviet Union." On the occasion of his first trip outside China, to Moscow to attend the celebration of Stalin's seventieth birthday on December 21, 1949, Mao Tse-tung was joined by Chou En-lai, premier and foreign minister, and the two Chinese leaders negotiated a series of agreements to replace the Sino-Soviet accord of August, 1945, as the basis of Chinese-Russian relations. They provided for a thirty-year alliance directed against Japan or "any state allied with Japan," meaning the United States; Russian utilization of the principal Manchurian railways and the naval base at Port Arthur until conclusion of a peace treaty with Japan or the end of 1952, depending upon which came earlier; restoration by the Soviet Union to China of all property in the commercial port of Dairen; a Russian loan of $300,000,000 to enable China to buy industrial equipment from the Soviet Union, this loan to be repaid in raw materials and in currency beginning no later than 1954; and acceptance by China of the status quo, i.e., Soviet-dominated "independence," in Mongolia. Another agreement in March, 1950, provided for the dispatch of Russian military and economic advisers to China and for the creation of Sino-Soviet "joint-stock companies" to develop civil airlines between the two countries, extract nonferrous and rare minerals in Sinkiang, extract and refine petroleum in Sinkiang, and build and repair ships at Dairen.

The Russian misadventure in Korea was the first important test for the alliance. It is not clear to what extent, if any, China participated in the planning of the attack by the North Korean forces, but it seems likely that before June, 1950, Peking had not itself been preparing to wage war in Korea. After that date, however, when the Chinese communists gave up their invasion plans following the movement of the United States Seventh Fleet into the straits between Taiwan and the mainland, they began to concentrate troops in Manchuria, many of them withdrawn from Fukien Province. Peking was ready to intervene in Korea if necessary, and in October Chou En-lai announced that China would not tolerate a northward crossing of the thirty-eighth parallel by the United Nations forces in Korea. When the North Korean troops began falling back as the result of Soviet miscalculations, Peking rescued them. The Chinese People's Volunteers (so called to avoid formal entanglement in war) scored initial successes in North Korea, but in 1951 their two drives toward Seoul were disastrous failures. China, upon whom the fighting imposed a terrific strain, welcomed the truce talks; but not until after Stalin's death in March, 1953, did the negotiations make much progress. The truce was finally signed on July 27, 1953, and thereafter, with a large Chinese force remaining in North Korea, there was an increase in Chinese influence on the North Korean communist regime.

During this period China's new position of power was given practical recognition by the Soviet Union. In September, 1952, while Premier Chou En-lai was in Moscow, the two governments announced that the Manchurian rail-roads would be returned to sole Chinese management by the end of that year but that the Russians would remain in Port Arthur in joint control, allegedly at Peking's request—probably because of the Korean conflict and China's lack of a strong navy. Later, in October, 1954, a Soviet delegation to Peking, headed by Khrushchev and Bulganin, agreed to evacuate Port Arthur, dissolve the four joint-stock companies, co-operate in the construction of a Sino-Soviet railroad through Sinkiang, and to extend $130,000,000 in economic aid. Khrushchev paid his respects to Mao Tse-tung, lauded the accomplishments of the Chinese comrades, and declared that "after the Great October Socialist Revolution, the victory of the Chinese People's Revolution is the most out-standing event in world history."

Following the death of Stalin, there was a basic shift in international com-munist foreign policy and a relaxation of Soviet domination within the com-munist bloc of nations. With the failure of their militant policies and the subsequent reinforcement of the defensive strength of the "imperialists" in Europe and Asia, the communist powers moved toward a policy of "peaceful coexistence." This trend was strongly endorsed by China because of the strains of the Korean fighting and her desire to launch the first five-year plan, and as a principle it was incorporated into the October, 1954, Sino-Soviet agreements. It is important to note that China supported the aspirations of the Poles for greater autonomy, but in the case of Hungary, which rejected communism and wished to secede from the bloc, Peking gave its prompt and full endorse-ment to the Soviet military suppression.

The shift from a "hard" to a "soft" policy was best reflected in China's relations with the new states of Southeast Asia. In 1949 Peking supported communist-led revolutions in Burma, Viet-Nam, Malaya, the Philippines, and Indonesia; and Liu Shao-ch'i advocated that their leaders utilize the Chinese experience by developing the armed struggle of the proletariat and the peasantry with the communist party as its center and the rural areas as its base. In the case of the Viet Minh movement against the French in Viet-Nam, the Chinese communists gave direct assistance and contributed greatly to its partial success. In fact, Communist China participated in her first major international conference at Geneva in 1954 and was instrumental in achiev-ing the truce settlement and the division of the area at the seventeenth paral-lel.

After 1951, on the whole, the communist regime shifted to a policy of persuasion and friendship in its dealings with the new nations "freed from the camp of imperialism" and uncommitted to either of the major world power blocs. For example, the April, 1954, Sino-Indian Treaty of Tibet, by which India indirectly recognized the legitimacy of the communist govern-ment in that area, included the Five Principles of Peaceful Coexistence, which were incorporated in the Sino-Soviet agreements of October, 1954: mutual respect for each other's territorial integrity and sovereignty; nonaggression; noninterference in each other's internal affairs; equality and mutual benefit; and peaceful coexistence. At the Asian-African Conference at Bandung in April, 1955, in which twenty-nine nations participated, Chou En-lai impressively stressed peaceful coexistence in China's relations with noncommunist states. And China's Asian neighbors, weak and anxious to concentrate upon urgent domestic problems, welcomed his assurances and found the need to make some sort of accommodation with Peking more desirable.

The policy of Communist China and the Soviet Union was to align the neutralist states with them against the "Western imperialists" and their military alliances—the Southeast Asia Treaty Organization was then under consideration—but they did not give up their long-range goal of encouraging communist-led revolutions. And the Chinese communists have been active in facilitating this process through propaganda campaigns, trade and assistance, cultural exchanges, co-operation with local communist parties and front organizations, and pressure on overseas Chinese communities. It is clear, however, that conflicts in policies have arisen and created numerous difficulties for them. For example, the move against Tibet in 1959, which involved strong pressures on the Indian border in order to seal off "Chinese territory," was hardly in keeping with the principle of peaceful coexistence. The same can be said with regard to the border skirmishes between China and Burma. The increasing use of pressure, especially since 1957, has made the neutralist nations and their peoples quite wary of the avowals of Peking and has destroyed the effectiveness of the Five Principles and the Bandung spirit.

Communist China regards the United States as her most important enemy, who blocks her foreign policies and intervenes in her domestic affairs. The United States is the strongest prop of the Taiwan regime, thus preventing "liberation" of that island and completion of the territorial unification of China; has refused diplomatic recognition; has opposed China's entry into the United Nations; and, since the Korean conflict, has imposed a total embargo on all trade with China and has been the strongest force in the maintenance of the United Nations embargo on the shipment of strategic goods. The United States seeks also to prevent the spread of communism and communist influence by encouraging the political and economic development of the noncommunist Asian states, and to this end she has concluded mutual security pacts with Japan, the Republic of Korea, the Philippines, Taiwan, Pakistan, and Thailand; she was also the driving force in the organization of SEATO and maintains military bases and forces throughout East Asia, all of which are directed against the threat of communist aggression. Peking, however, insists that the United States is the champion of imperialism. Although the British have extended recognition to the communist regime and maintain a diplomatic mission in Peking, it is clear that the communists regard the United Kingdom as on the "imperialist" side. China has squeezed out most

British trade and has virtually confiscated British investments; however, she has left Hong Kong alone because of its practical value as a contact point with the outside world.

Peking is hostile toward Pakistan, Thailand, South Viet-Nam, the Philippines, and the Republic of Korea because of their diplomatic and military alignment with the United States, but it works to persuade them to become neutral, "a step closer to socialism." Although the Chinese communists have had little success in influencing governments, they have caused a segment of the educated public to question the need to take an active stand against Peking. In the case of Japan, with whom she has been as yet unable to "normalize" relations, China appeals to pacifism, neutralism, and the desire to trade, and she has strong support in the Japanese Socialist Party, labor unions, and among many intellectuals. But direct interference in Japanese politics has boomeranged, as in the case of the attempt in May, 1958, to influence the Japanese electorate to reject Prime Minister Kishi and the Liberal-Democratic Party.

In recent years, while Khrushchev has continued to maintain a fairly conciliatory approach toward the West, climaxed by the "summitry" of 1959 and 1960, the Chinese communists have tended to adopt a more militant attitude in their foreign policies. In fact, by 1960 there were three principal matters in dispute between Moscow and Peking: the inevitability of war, the suicidal effects of nuclear war, and the necessity of bloody revolution in order to overthrow capitalism. The Soviet position is that war is no longer inevitable, that nuclear war would devastate the entire earth, and that evolutionary methods of social change are possible. The Chinese insist that war will be inevitable so long as imperialism exists, that communism can survive nuclear war, and that only violent revolution can produce social change. On November 8, 1960, the English-language *Peking Review* made the Chinese communist position clear to the whole world:

No dictatorship can be realized or maintained unless it rests directly on violence. Marxism-Leninism has repeatedly pointed out the indisputable truth that the reactionaries will not step down from the stage of history of their own accord. . . . It is muddleheaded to confuse these two things—the seizure of political power by the working class and the carrying out by the working class of socialist transformation by peaceful means after it seizes power.

The Nationalist Regime on Taiwan

After the defeat of Japan in 1945, Taiwan, a rich, tropical island slightly larger than Massachusetts and Connecticut combined, was restored to Chinese control on the basis of the pledge made by the United States, the United Kingdom, and China at the Cairo Conference in 1943, later adhered to by the

Soviet Union, that "Formosa and the Pescadores shall be restored to the Republic of China." The Nationalist government appointed Ch'en Yi, a former warlord who went over to Chiang K'ai-shek in 1927, as governor of the island, and Ch'en and his cohorts administered the area as their own private domain with little concern for the interests of the 8,000,000 Taiwanese, descendants of South Chinese who had emigrated between the seventeenth and late nineteenth centuries. Discontent caused by economic decline and oppression mounted among the islanders, and in February, 1947, it erupted in a popular revolt, in which at least 10,000 Taiwanese lost their lives. Ch'en Yi was transferred to the mainland, where he ultimately became governor of Chekiang Province, and in January, 1948, he was arrested on the charge of conspiring with communist agents to surrender the province. In June, 1950, he was executed on Taiwan.

In January, 1949, when it became clear that Taiwan would have to serve as a haven for the Nationalists, Chiang K'ai-shek and his followers led a migration of some 2,000,000 Chinese, including 500,000 troops, from the mainland; and on December 8, 1949, Taipeh was proclaimed the capital of the Nationalist government. However, with the completion of the communist triumph on the mainland, it appeared doubtful whether Taiwan could hold out against an invasion. And in January, 1950, President Truman stated that the United States did not have "any intention of utilizing its armed forces to interfere in the present situation" and would "not provide military aid or advice to the Chinese forces on Formosa."

The outbreak of the Korean conflict, however, caused a basic shift in American policy. On June 27, 1950, President Truman declared that "in these circumstances the occupation of Formosa by communist forces would be a direct threat to the security of the Pacific area" and announced a policy designed to "neutralize" Taiwan. "I have ordered the Seventh Fleet to prevent any attack on Formosa," said the President; and "I am calling upon the Chinese Government on Formosa to cease all air and sea operations against the mainland." After the Chinese communists intervened in the Korean conflict, the American government embarked on a program of large-scale military and economic assistance to the Nationalist regime. Since that time, moreover, the United States has made a firm commitment, by the Mutual Defense Treaty of December, 1954, to defend Taiwan and the Pescadores against communist attack, but she has not openly supported Chiang K'ai-shek's goal of returning to the mainland. In the case of the offshore islands, Quemoy and Matsu, off the coast of Fukien Province, which are held by Nationalist forces, Washington's position has been ambiguous. In January, 1955, the American Congress passed a resolution at the request of President Eisenhower which empowered the chief executive to decide whether or not American forces would be used to defend the offshore islands.

Despite her support of the Taiwan regime, the United States has been reluctant to define Taiwan's legal status. By the terms of the treaty of peace, Japan renounced all "right, title, and claim" to Taiwan and the Pescadores, but the treaty did not state that sovereignty over them had actually been transferred to China. Chiang's government was not designated as the successor state, and, according to the American delegate at San Francisco, John Foster Dulles, the United States was "leaving the future to resolve doubts by invoking international solvents other than this treaty."

The political life of Taiwan is dominated by the personality of President Chiang K'ai-shek—who in 1960 assumed a third term despite constitutional limitation—and by his dedication to the reconquest of the mainland. There is no doubt that his powerful control of the Kuomintang, the government, and the army has given Taiwan a certain degree of stability, but at the same time it has stifled the development of new leadership, especially at the higher levels. And while the tightening of discipline in the Kuomintang in accordance with Chiang's interpretation of the communist success on the mainland has eliminated much inefficiency and corruption in the government, it has hardly been a stimulus to the advancement of democracy. This is true despite the recruitment of large numbers of Taiwanese into the party in recent years. Only in rare instances have non-Kuomintang candidates won elections in open fights against Kuomintang-sponsored persons. The Kuomintang is still based on the Leninist principle of democratic centralism, but it includes factions which have been characterized as "totalitarian" and "genuinely liberal." Intrigue is common, but any argument, however petty, can be resolved by Chiang K'ai-shek. Party loyalty and political realities for the most part prevent open clashes with the party leader and president. The ideological basis of the regime is still rooted in Sun Yat-sen's Three Principles of the People, which, although it provides some sort of justification for the domination of the Kuomintang, has become an almost meaningless dogma. Efforts by Chinese intellectuals to reform and rejuvenate the party have all been frustrated; and although there are other parties, like the Young China Party and the Social Democratic Party, they lack power or influence. Schools and universities pursue "safe" studies and avoid critical discussion of post-1920 politics.

The administration of Taiwan is complicated by the fact that the central government and local government coexist and operate within such a limited area. The former, still based on the undemocratic constitution of 1947 and the five-yuan system, is a cumbersome bureaucracy composed largely of mainlanders, while the latter has been increasingly turned over to the Taiwanese. At the county and municipal levels the councils and executive officials are elected; and at the provincial level, although the governor is appointed and is a mainlander, the appointed council is composed of Taiwanese and the assembly is elected. It is important to note that the overwhelming majority of Taiwanese who serve in government at these levels are members of the Kuomintang.

Police control and supervision, managed in large part by Chiang K'ai-shek's elder son, Chiang Ching-kuo, although not actively felt by the bulk of the people, impose serious limitations on basic democratic rights and prevent the development of legitimate political opposition. Although police power is justified on the basis of the danger of subversion, which is certainly real, in practice it has been used quite arbitrarily. In fact, in 1954 Governor K. C. Wu broke with the Kuomintang on the ground that the government was nothing more than a police state and took up residence in the United States; and in 1955 the regime disgraced and retired the able field commander, Sun Li-jen, who had criticized Chiang K'ai-shek and objected to the actions of Chiang Ching-kuo's political departments in his units.

In the past decade Taiwan has made remarkable economic progress, and its standard of living, one of the highest in Asia during the period of Japanese control, has risen even higher. Food production has increased by approximately 5 per cent annually during the past few years, largely as the result of the many successful projects of the Sino-American organization, the Joint Commission on Rural Reconstruction, in such fields as irrigation, forestry, soil conservation, and crop improvement. In 1957 rice production exceeded the peak figure for the Japanese period by some 400,000 tons. This improvement has significantly been accompanied by a land-reform program. At first rents were set at a maximum of $37\frac{1}{2}$ per cent and tenures were made reasonably secure. Thereafter government land and landlord holdings were sold to tenants. Some 75 per cent of Taiwan's farm families benefited from the reform, and rented land was reduced from 41 per cent to 16 per cent of the total farm acreage. Despite difficulties in capital accumulation, industrial progress has been just as great, and, when the first four-year plan ended in 1957, industrial output had been increased by 132 per cent over 1950. The following figures indicate the change:

	1949	1957
Fertilizers	45,800 tons	215,000 tons
Paper	3,000 tons	60,000 tons
Cloth	29,000,000 sq. meters	155,000,000 sq. meters
Cotton yarn	2,000 tons	28,000 tons
Coal	1,600,000 tons	2,900,000 tons
Cement	291,000 tons	604,000 tons
Electricity	854,000,000 kw.	2,500,000,000 kw.

Much of this progress has been the result of American aid in the amount of $1 billion in the economic field alone; and although the Taiwan regime hopes to become self-supporting, it is doubtful whether it can achieve this goal. For one thing, population growth is putting tremendous pressure on resources; for example, although rice production exceeds prewar figures by 30 per cent, population has almost doubled. The basic problem is that the growing population consumes more domestic production, leaving less for export; and it consumes more imports, requiring larger exports to earn the necessary foreign exchange. Moreover, the amazing growth rate of $3\frac{1}{2}$ per cent a year guarantees that the population will double in the next generation. The large military establishment, based on a standing army of approximately 600,000 men, is of course a costly burden. And despite the fact that it is essentially a defensive force, particularly in view of the recruitment of large numbers of Taiwanese, the regime continues to expend large amounts of revenue in preparation for the return to the mainland. The burden of military expenditures would have been substantially greater had not the United States during the past decade provided armed assistance in the amount of approximately $1 billion.

Some Problems and Prospects

During the past decade the communist regime at Peking has carried out an unprecedented series of reforms designed both to transform Chinese society along Marxist-Leninist lines and to make China a major world power. There can be no doubt that it has achieved conspicuous successes in both endeavors.

It is difficult, however, to make a comprehensive assessment of current conditions in communist China because of a lack of adequate information; nevertheless, there is sufficient evidence to conclude that the so-called "great leap forward" has not been a success. This is particularly true in the case of the attempt to impose the commune system upon the peasantry. A combination of factors—insufficient experienced administrative personnel, peasant intractability, and weather difficulties causing flood and drought—have handicapped efforts to bring about the much-needed increases in agricultural production which are so vital to the nation's over-all economic development. In fact, in some areas there have been serious production failures, and widespread starvation has been prevented only because of the ability of the government to maintain some efficiency in the distribution of existing grain supplies. It is probable that several tens of millions of Chinese would have died had this not been the case. But, even so, the Chinese people are suffering in increasing numbers from malnutrition, the effect of which is presently impossible to estimate. In the face of this condition, the communist regime has been forced to modify the commune system by recognizing the existence of some private property and the maintaining of family life, although it has not yet abandoned the project in principle. No doubt peasant discontent has increased, but it is hardly likely that it will have sufficient political direction and organization to challenge the power of the regime. At best it will probably cause the government to find scapegoats to pay for failures and to reconsider the whole crucial problem of the organization of agricultural production.

On Taiwan the political foundation of the Nationalist regime has become increasingly stable, but it continues to suffer from two serious deficiencies, namely, the lack of a broad popular base and the preponderant power of Chiang K'ai-shek. It is easy to speculate about, but impossible to predict accurately, what will happen to the government after Chiang's death. At present the consensus is that there will be no drastic change but only a broadening of executive power and responsibility, with group leadership replacing the one indispensable individual. Much will depend upon the relationship of Taiwan to communist China. Economic development continues to be orderly; but despite substantial progress, the island is still basically dependent on American aid programs.

The existence of two Chinas is of course one of the most unsettling factors in East Asia and in the general international situation. While the China policy of the United States is widely criticized because it supposedly prevents a satisfactory adjustment of the division, many of the critics actually overlook or minimize the one condition that is fundamental to the problem. The crucial point is that neither Chinese government will accept in principle the existence of the other. Both are adamant in their conviction that there is but one China. Peking insists that it will use military power if necessary to complete the unification of China, and Chiang, hardly realistic, refuses to relinquish the goal of returning to the mainland. Even a complete change in American policy to include diplomatic recognition of communist China and the seating of Chinese communists in United Nations bodies will not resolve the conflict of views. The best that can probably be hoped for is the mobilization of world public opinion to put pressure on the two Chinese governments to give legal recognition to the existing reality of division.

Bibliographical Notes

Ch'ien Tuan-sheng, *The Government and Politics of China* (Cambridge, Mass.: Harvard University Press, 1950), surveys the period in great detail, but John K. Fairbank, *The United States and China* (Cambridge, Mass.: Harvard University Press, revised edition, 1958), is a more stimulating approach. A good popular account is Kenneth Scott Latourette, *A History of Modern China* (London: Penguin Books, 1954). Conrad Brandt, Benjamin Schwartz, and John K.

Fairbank, A *Documentary History of Chinese Communism* (Cambridge, Mass.: Harvard University Press, 1952), is an indispensable work.

There are a number of good works concerning the period of the Nationalist revolution. Despite its interesting left-wing slant, Harold Isaacs, *The Tragedy of the Chinese Revolution* (Stanford: Stanford University Press, revised edition, 1951), is the best over-all account. Hollington K. Tong, *Chiang K'ai-shek, Soldier and Statesman: Authorized Biography* (Shanghai: China Publishing Company, two volumes, 1937), presents the official Kuomintang line. Arthur N. Holcombe, *The Chinese Revolution* (Cambridge, Mass.: Harvard University Press, 1930), is an objective study with emphasis upon the Kuomintang and government. Sun Yat-sen, *San Min Chu I: The Three Principles of the People* (Shanghai: Institute of Pacific Relations, 1927; translated by F. W. Price), provides the ideological content of the revolution. T'ang Leang-li, *The Inner History of the Chinese Revolution* (London: G. Routledge, 1930), is an interpretation by a noncommunist radical. The development of the Chinese Communist Party in this period is ably described by Benjamin Schwartz, *Chinese Communism and the Rise of Mao* (Cambridge, Mass.: Harvard University Press, 1951); Schwartz has corrected an important mistake regarding the establishment of Mao Tse-tung's dominance within the Chinese Communist Party in "On the Originality of Mao Tse-tung," *Foreign Affairs*, Vol. 34 (October, 1955), pp. 67–76. Conrad Brandt, *Stalin's Failure in China, 1924–1927* (Cambridge, Mass.: Harvard University Press, 1958), analyzes the development of Russian policy regarding the revolution, and M. N. Roy, *Revolution and Counter-Revolution in China* (Calcutta: Renaissance Publishers, 1946), is an eyewitness account by an Indian communist. There is much important historical material in *Documents on Communism, Nationalism, and Soviet Advisers in China, 1918–1927: Papers Seized in the 1927 Peking Raid* (New York: Columbia University Press, 1956; edited by C. Martin Wilbur and Julie Lien-ying How). George M. Beckmann, *Imperialism and Revolution in Modern China, 1840–1950* (Lawrence, Kans.: Student Union Bookstore, 1955), is a useful general compilation of source materials.

Paul Linebarger, *Government in Republican China* (New York: McGraw-Hill, 1938), and his *The China of Chiang K'ai-shek: A Political Study* (Boston: World Peace Foundation, 1941), are standard works concerning the decade of the 1930's. Emily Hahn, *Chiang K'ai-shek: An Unauthorized Biography* (Garden City: Doubleday, 1955), and Hsiung Shih-i, *The Life of Chiang K'ai-shek* (London: P. Davies, 1948), are adequate popular accounts. Chiang K'ai-shek, *China's Destiny* (New York: Macmillan, 1947; translated by Wang Chung-hui), is the best introduction to the thought of the Kuomintang leader. Edgar Snow's journalistic account, *Red Star over China* (New York: Modern Library, 1944), is one of the few works on the Chinese communists in this period and is supplemented by his *Random Notes on Red China, 1936–1945* (Cambridge, Mass.: Harvard University Press, 1957). *Selected Works of Mao Tse-tung* (New York: International Publishers, four volumes, 1954–1956), is valuable but must be used with care.

L. K. Rosinger, *China's Wartime Politics, 1937–1944* (Princeton: Princeton

University Press, 1945), is a straightforward brief survey based largely upon newspaper materials. *United States Relations with China* (Washington: Government Printing Office, 1949) provides substantial documentation relating to relations between the Kuomintang and the Chinese Communist Party. Theodore White and Annalee Jacoby, *Thunder out of China* (New York: William Sloan Associates, 1946), is a journalistic attack on both Chiang K'ai-shek and American policy, and Jack Belden, *China Shakes the World* (New York: Harper & Bros., 1949), is one of a number of popular accounts by American newspapermen that are sympathetic to the Chinese communists. Chiang K'ai-shek defends himself in *Soviet Russia in China: A Summing-Up at Seventy* (New York: Farrar, Straus, & Cudahy, 1957). Carsun Chang, *The Third Force in China* (New York: Bookman Associates, 1952), presents the views of a leader of the Democratic League. Liao Kai-lung, *From Yenan to Peking* (Peking: Foreign Languages Press, 1954), is a communist account. Two valuable scholarly studies are Robert North and Ithiel De Sola Pool, *Kuomintang and Chinese Communist Elites* (Stanford: Stanford University Press, 1952), and Liu Chin-pu, *A Military History of Modern China, 1924–1949* (Princeton: Princeton University Press, 1956).

R. H. Tawney, *Land and Labour in China* (New York: Harcourt, Brace, 1932), is the best introduction to economic problems in pre-Communist China, and J. B. Condliffe, *China Tody: Economic* (Boston: World Peace Foundation, 1932), is a good general survey of the economy. Gerald F. Winfield, *China: The Land and the People* (New York: William Sloane Associates, 1948), is an excellent postwar account. Useful specialized studies include Cheng Yu-k'uei, *Foreign Trade and Industrial Development of China* (Seattle: University of Washington Press, 1956), John Lossing Buck, *Land Utilization in China* (Shanghai: Commercial Press, three volumes, 1937), D. K. Lieu, *China's Economic Stabilization and Reconstruction* (New Brunswick, N.J.: Rutgers University Press, 1948), Chang Chia-ao, *China's Struggle for Railroad Development* (New York: John Day, 1943), Frank Tamagna, *Banking and Finance in China* (New York: Institute of Pacific Relations, 1942), Nym Wales (Helen Snow), *Chinese Labor Movement* (New York: John Day, 1945), and K. H. Shih, *China Enters the Machine Age* (Cambridge, Mass.: Harvard University Press, 1944; edited and translated by Fei Hsiao-tung and Francis L. K. Hsu).

There are several good village studies, including Fei Hsiao-tung, *Peasant Life in China: A Field Study of Country Life in the Yangtze Valley* (New York: Dutton, 1939), Fei Hsiao-tung, *Earthbound China: A Study of Rural Economy in Yunnan* (Chicago: University of Chicago Press, 1945), and Martin Yang, *A Chinese Village: Taitou, Shantung Province* (New York: Columbia University Press, 1945). Another interesting work is Morton Fried, *Fabric of Chinese Society: A Study of the Social Life of a Chinese County Seat* (New York: Praeger, 1953). Pearl Buck's novel, *The Good Earth* (New York: John Day, 1931; reissued many times), is an excellent introduction to peasant life. Y. H. Lin, *The Golden Wing: A Sociological Study of Chinese Familism* (London: Kegan Paul, 1948), is a useful novelized work. Lin Yutang, *My Country and My People* (New York: Reynal & Hitchcock, 1935), presents an idealized picture of Chinese society and its culture.

The following works are penetrating studies of Chinese social life by competent scholars: Olga Lang, *Chinese Family and Society* (New Haven: Yale University Press, 1946), Marion Levy, *The Family Revolution in Modern China* (Cambridge, Mass.: Harvard University Press, 1949), Francis L. K. Hsu, *Under the Ancestor's Shadow: Chinese Culture and Personality* (New York: Columbia University Press, 1948), and Francis L. K. Hsu, *Americans and Chinese: Two Ways of Life* (New York: H. Schuman, 1953).

The only general work in the foreign relations field that attempts to present the Chinese view is Werner Levi, *Modern China's Foreign Policy* (Minneapolis: University of Minnesota Press, 1953). Useful for basic reference are *Treaties and Agreements with and concerning China, 1919–1929* (Washington: Carnegie Endowment for International Peace, Division of International Law, 1929), and *Treaties and Agreements between the Republic of China and Other Powers, 1929–1954* (Washington: Sino-American Publications Service, 1957; edited by Ch'en Yin-ching). There are a number of surveys reflecting a particular national point of view. A. W. Griswold, *The Far Eastern Policy of the United States* (New York: Harcourt, Brace, 1938), and *United States Relations with China* (Washington: Government Printing Office, 1949), which contains useful documentary material, present the American position. Seiji Hishida, *Japan among the Great Powers: A Survey of Her International Relations* (New York: Longmans, Green & Co. 1940), and Tatsuji Takeuchi, *War and Diplomacy in the Japanese Empire* (New York: Doubleday, Doran, 1935), can be used for Japan. Russian policies are described in Aitchen Wu, *China and the Soviet Union* (New York: John Day, 1950), David Dallin, *Soviet Russia and the Far East* (New Haven: Yale University Press, 1948), and Cheng Tien-fang, *A History of Sino-Russian Relations* (Washington: Public Affairs Press, 1957). More specialized is Robert North, *Moscow and the Chinese Communists* (Stanford: Stanford University Press, 1953).

R. T. Pollard, *China's Foreign Relations, 1917–1931* (New York: Macmillan, 1933), is a competent, detailed work on the period of the Nationalist revolution. More specialized studies include Allen Whiting, *Soviet Policies in China, 1917–1924* (New York: Columbia University Press, 1954), X. J. Eudin and Robert North, *Soviet Russia and the East, 1920–1927: A Documentary Survey* (Stanford: Stanford University Press, 1957), and Dorothy Borg, *American Policy and the Chinese Revolution* (New York: Macmillan, 1947).

J. W. Christopher, *Conflict in the Far East: American Diplomacy in China from 1928–33* (Leiden: E. J. Brill, 1950), is a good introduction to the Manchurian crisis. *Report of the Commission of Inquiry* (Geneva: League of Nations, 1932), and Henry L. Stimson, *The Far Eastern Crisis: Recollections and Observations* (New York: Harper & Bros., 1936), are essential works. Other useful works for this period are T. A. Bisson, *Japan in China* (New York: Macmillan, 1938), I. S. Friedman, *The Relations of Great Britain with China, 1933–1939* (New York: Institute of Pacific Relations, 1939), and Charles McLane, *Soviet Policy and the Chinese Communists, 1931–1946* (New York: Columbia University Press, 1958).

Herbert Feis, *The China Tangle* (Princeton: Princeton University Press,

1953), is an excellent work on the diplomacy of the World War II period. Much can be learned about key personalities from *The Stilwell Papers* (New York: William Sloane Associates, 1948; edited by Theodore White), Don Lohbeck, *Patrick J. Hurley* (Chicago: Henry Regnery, 1956), and Albert Wedemeyer, *Wedemeyer Reports!* (New York: Henry Holt, 1958). *The Meaning of Yalta* (Baton Rouge: Louisiana State University Press, 1956; edited by John L. Snell) is a valuable contribution. For Russian policy consult Max Beloff, *Soviet Policy in the Far East, 1944–1951* (London and New York: Oxford University Press, 1953), and *Soviet Source Materials on USSR Relations with East Asia, 1945–1950* (New York: Institute of Pacific Relations, 1950; compiled by William Mandel).

A. Doak Barnett, *Communist China and Asia: Challenge to American Policy* (New York: Harper & Bros., 1960), which has excellent bibliographical notes, and Peter S. H. Tang, *Communist China Today: Domestic and Foreign Policies* (New York: Praeger, two volumes, 1957–1958), are good surveys. Useful also are Ygael Gluckstein, *Mao's China: Economic and Political Survey* (Boston: Beacon Press, 1957), and Chang-tu Hu and others, *China: Its People, Its Society, Its Culture* (New Haven: Human Relations Area Files, 1946; edited by Hsiao Hsia). Two works by competent journalists are Robert Guillain, *600 Million Chinese* (New York: Criterion Books, 1957), and Frank Moraes, *Report on Mao's China* (New York: Macmillan, 1953). An interesting historical interpretation is C. P. Fitzgerald, *Revolution in China* (New York: Praeger, 1952).

Robert S. Elegant, *China's Red Masters: Political Biographies of the Chinese Communist Leaders* (New York: Twayne Publishers, 1951), and Nym Wales (Helen Snow), *Red Dust: Autobiographies of Chinese Communists* (Stanford: Stanford University Press, 1952), provide excellent background information.

The economic development of communist China is surveyed by T. J. Hughes and D. E. T. Luard, *The Economic Development of Communist China, 1949–1958* (London, New York, and Toronto: Oxford University Press, 1959), Li Choh-ming, *Economic Development of Communist China: An Appraisal of the First Five Years of Industrialization* (Berkeley and Los Angeles: University of California Press, 1959), and Wu Yuan-li, *An Economic Survey of Communist China* (New York: Bookman Associates, 1956).

Two useful works in the foreign policy field are Michael Lindsay, *China and the Cold War* (Melbourne: University of Melbourne Press, 1955), and Howard L. Boorman and others, *Moscow-Peking Axis Strengths and Strains* (New York: Harper & Bros., 1957).

Developments on Taiwan are best described in periodical literature, but the following works are still useful for the early years: Joseph Ballantine, *Formosa, A Problem for United States Foreign Policy* (Washington: Brookings Institution, 1952), Fred W. Riggs, *Formosa under Nationalist Rule* (New York: Macmillan, 1952), and H. Maclear Bate, *Report from Formosa* (New York: Dutton, 1952).

Japan in Transformation

The history of Japan since the 1920's has much greater continuity than is generally realized. In the decade that followed the conclusion of World War I, Japanese society, feeling the full impact of industrialization, witnessed the beginnings of a political struggle between the self-appointed leftist leaders of the masses of peasants and workers and the dominant conservative political and economic interest groups. But what was probably an important stage in the evolutionary development of Japanese political democracy did not reach fulfillment for two important reasons. First, the masses were not yet really participants in the struggle, and second, during the 1930's the conservatives—especially the political parties and the zaibatsu—compromised their power with the militarists and ultranationalists.

Perhaps the most decisive factor influencing the political scene in these two decades was the circumstance that Japanese nationalism did not develop as part of any democratic, socialist, or communist movement but was closely related to traditional values. And when overindulgence in ultranationalism, already something of an anachronism, led the country on a program of foreign conquest, Japan moved inexorably to national disaster, losing an empire she had been developing for almost a century.

In this context, the attempt by the United States during her occupation of Japan to reconstruct Japanese society was really only a forced acceleration of a process that had been blocked by the force of tradition, so well utilized by the conservatives in general, and the irrational adventurism of the military. The American occupation authorities, moreover, going well beyond the goal of establishing the forms of political democracy, sought through a series of

542

*basic reforms to create an economic and social environment in which demo-
cratic attitudes and actions would prosper and reach fulfillment.*

*In contemporary Japan, a sovereign nation since 1952, the process of
transformation continues as the true meanings of many of the recent reforms
are realized by leadership groups and by the population as a whole. But traditional values are still strong in many quarters, and, as a result, Japan is still a
democracy in form but not in substance.*

27 Party Government in Japan

Despite the Seiyukai majority in the house of representatives, party factionalism and criticism by the militarists caused the downfall of the Takahashi
cabinet in June, 1922, and the Hara-Takahashi cabinets, regarded by many
as a giant stride toward party government, were followed by a series of
ministries headed by high-ranking civilian and military bureaucrats. The most
important reason behind this development lay not in the power of the genro,
who were no longer really significant, nor in the influence of the bureaucracy,
but in the fact that the parties themselves were by no means united on the
principle of party government. The Seiyukai, for instance, was only interested in the perpetuation of its own power; thus, when a resurgence of
Kenseikai strength seemed likely, it was willing to transfer control of the
cabinet to the bureaucracy. Kato Tomosaburo, minister of the navy under
Takahashi, became prime minister with Seiyukai support, and it was his
cabinet that carried out the arms limitations imposed by the Five-Power Naval
Treaty of the Washington Conference and effected an initial slashing of army
expenditures to secure economy in government budgeting.

The death of Kato in July, 1923, paved the way for a second "bureaucratic"
cabinet, formed in September under Admiral Yamamoto Gombei, who was
largely the selection of Saionji, by then the only active genro. Saionji seems to
have concluded that neither major political party was in a position to hold
power. The Seiyukai was plagued by internal friction, and the Kenseikai
lacked sufficient strength in the house of representatives and influence in the
bureaucracy. Yamamoto, however, had been unable to live down his unsavory
reputation, dating from the naval scandals of his previous cabinet, and press,
public, and party reactions to his appointment were generally unfavorable.
His tenure in office, which was only slightly more than three months, was
characterized by a lack of party support and by general cabinet disunity. The
high-handed methods with which he handled the socialists and communists

after the great earthquake increased his disfavor in public eyes, and he finally submitted his resignation after the Toranomon Affair of December 27, when Naniwa Daisuke attempted to assassinate the regent crown prince and the emperor. Although his resignation was rejected by the emperor, Yamamoto left office before the end of the year.

During the so-called "peers cabinet," headed by Viscount Kiyoura Keigo, president of the privy council, and composed of conservative members of the house of peers, the parties carried out a political reorganization that ultimately returned them to power. The willingness of some elements within the Seiyukai to co-operate with Kiyoura in return for political spoils split that party into two almost equal groups: the Seiyuhonto (True Seiyu Party), with 149 members in the house of representatives, favoring co-operation with the bureaucratic ministry; and the Seiyukai, with 129 members, who joined in an antigovernment alliance with the Kenseikai and the Kakushin Club, which had been formed out of the old Kokuminto.

The three opposition party leaders, Kato Takaaki of the Kenseikai, Takahashi Korekiyo of the Seiyukai, and Inukai Tsuyoshi of the Kakushin Club, jointly declared: "We pledge the establishment of a political party cabinet system in accordance with the basic principles of constitutional government." This powerful demonstration of political unity forced Kiyoura to dissolve the house of representatives; but despite government assistance to the Seiyuhonto, the combined opposition was victorious in the election of May 10, 1924. The results were as follows: Kenseikai, 153, a 50 per cent gain, which made it the leading party after nine difficult years; Seiyukai, 101; and Kakushin Club, 30—a total of 284 seats for the coalition. The Seiyuhonto fell to 114, and the independents numbered 66. Kiyoura was unable to face the next diet session and resigned on June 7, 1924. Kato Takaaki was then appointed as prime minister, and he formed a party cabinet based on the coalition.

The Kato Cabinet

Kato's selection was almost inevitable since three successive failures seemed to indicate that the bureaucracy could no longer control the state. Moreover, the genro, who had been the most important antiparty element on the political scene, had died off. Yamagata succumbed in 1922 at the age of eighty-one, and Matsukata in 1924 at the age of eighty-four. Only Saionji, aged seventy, remained, and he was in sympathy with the principle of party government.

The parties were still the most effective focus for what might loosely be described as "the popular movement." In this decade Japanese universities were centers of liberalism as well as the more radical socialism and communism. Professors like Yoshino Sakuzo of Tokyo Imperial University championed the cause of representative government, advocating universal suffrage and the restriction of the power of the house of peers and the privy council. Attacking imperialism and militarism in particular, they emphasized that the goal of politics should be the realization of the popular will. Kato's coalition utilized the rising tide of democratic thought and theories of representative government to criticize the bureaucracy, and it supported the demand for universal manhood suffrage.

Kato's ministry reflected the ever-increasing power of the commercial and industrial interests of the country. Kato had the backing of the powerful Mitsubishi Company, and like his foreign minister, Shidehara Kijuro, was related to the Iwasaki family through marriage. His cabinet was popularly referred to as the "Mitsubishi cabinet," while previously the Hara and Takahashi governments had been called "Mitsui cabinets." Although businessmen generally supported the practice of party government, their views were hardly democratic. Business, on the whole, tended to accept the primacy of state power and authority; and as Robert Scalapino has pointed out, the concurrent development of nationalism and industrialization caused primary stress to be placed upon the responsibility of capitalism to the state, with obligations to the individual considered a matter of secondary importance. In the absence of a theory which would legitimize private interests, there was a compulsion on the part of the business class to protect and advance its interests secretly, with minimal resort to open political action or democratic procedures.

The political attitudes of the majority of party politicians and businessmen had their intellectual foundations in the scholarship of Minobe Tatsukichi, professor of law at Tokyo Imperial University. In an attempt to reconcile representative government with the institution of the emperor, he advanced the thesis that the diet was an independent organ, reflecting the opinion of the people and giving consent to legislation. According to Minobe, the emperor was one of the organs of the state, possessing no authority over and above it. This theory directly challenged the claims of the divine-right theorists, who in turn criticized Minobe for violating the doctrine of imperial sovereignty and tending to make sovereignty jointly held by the emperor and the people. The official interpretation was that the emperor was in no way an organ of the state but *was* the state; according to this view, even though the Meiji Constitution recognized the existence of various separate powers, such as the executive and legislative, and of such organs as the cabinet and diet, all the organs exercising these powers were subordinate to the emperor.

The Kato cabinet proved to be a disappointment to those Japanese who had hoped for an attack on the bureaucratic institutions, especially the house of peers, which time and again had blocked legislation passed by the lower house. The party coalition had made reform of the peers an immediate issue; but Kato, faced with the necessity of getting other legislation through the diet, had no intention of creating a political crisis. He ultimately did sponsor a bill which was accepted by the peers without much outcry because it did not make a single change of major significance; all it did was limit the number of hereditary members and establish a new category of representatives of the imperial academy. Kato did not attempt to interfere with the powers of either the administrative bureaucracy or the military elements.

The Kato cabinet did keep its promise to pass a universal manhood suffrage bill. While the party coalition deserves much credit, in the final analysis the press, the intellectuals, and the radical political organizations were the most effective forces in the struggle for suffrage expansion. The bill was introduced in February, 1925, and quickly passed the house of representatives. Strong opposition in the house of peers failed to materialize in the face of overwhelming public support of the bill. After a series of conferences between the two houses of the diet, the Universal Manhood Suffrage Law was promulgated on May 5, 1925. By removal of all tax qualifications for the right to vote, the electorate was quadrupled from 3.3 million to 14 million people.

This great stride in the direction of democratic government was checked in part by the passage in April, 1925, of the Peace Preservation Law, which was directed at any group which sought to radically alter Japanese government or the economic and social systems. The first article of the new law read as follows: "Anyone who has formed a society with the object of altering the national polity or the form of government or denying the system of private ownership, or anyone who has joined such a society with full knowledge of its objects, shall be liable to imprisonment with or without hard labor for a term not exceeding ten years." It is interesting to note that a similar law had been introduced in the diet in 1922 but had failed to pass and that in 1923 the government had promulgated a temporary Peace Preservation Ordinance. The new law, passed largely to control communist and other radical activities, was used for much broader purposes. Its vagaries placed in jeopardy persons holding any of a great range of opinions and permitted suppression of the press, academic institutions, or any activity critical of the status quo and dedicated to basic change. As the director of the criminal affairs bureau explained to the house of representatives, it could be used against someone advocating amendment of the constitution. Thus, in the face of critical attacks by radicals, political parties in the period after 1924 showed conclusively that they could be quite as repressive as bureaucratic administrations when the fundamental character of Japanese society was threatened.

While the Peace Preservation Law was generally condemned by public opinion, some of Kato's policies were extremely popular and even won for him the support of the moderate social democrats. For example, Finance Minister Hamaguchi Osachi was able to effect substantial economies in the operations of the government despite the opposition of various segments of the bureaucracy. Budget estimates were slashed in unprecedented fashion, and among the sharpest reductions were those in army and navy appropriations. In March, 1925, the government did away with four army divisions, and Army Minister Ugaki Kazushige carried out a reduction of army manpower which involved the release of more than 2,000 commissioned officers of career status as well as the shortening of the period of compulsory service. At the same time financial provision for the modernization of the army—by the addition of an air corps, tank units, and motor transport—was postponed. The government did, however, make concessions to the army by enlarging the system of military training within the regular school framework. The lower echelons of the bureaucracy also suffered under the policy of financial retrenchment. Estimates range all the way from 20,000 to 40,000 in the case of personnel cuts that were effected.

The cabinet's foreign policy, too, was more appealing to liberals and social democrats. Foreign Minister Shidehara believed that a stable and prosperous China, organized to produce and able to buy, would be a blessing for Japan and that "equal commercial opportunity in China meant the actual salvation of Japan"; but he could not avoid criticism from the Japanese military for his refusal to deal with Chinese warlords to obtain special privileges for Japan. It was Shidehara, also, who effected the 1925 recognition of the Soviet Union and the termination of the Siberian intervention.

The Kato cabinet also sponsored social legislation that was attractive to elements of the left, especially to labor unions, which had continued to increase their membership. For example, under its leadership the diet abolished Article Seventeen of the Public Peace Police Law, which had been used in the past to prevent the formation of labor unions, and it passed the National Health Insurance Law, the Factory Law, and the Labor Disputes Mediation Law. There can be no doubt that the policies of the Kato ministry were in large part responsible for the fact that Sodomei, the leading labor federation, assumed a more co-operative attitude toward the government; moreover, most socialists had their eyes set on the 1928 general election, the first in which all adult males would have a voice.

The Left-Wing Parties

The Japanese Communist Party found itself increasingly isolated by these developments, and the party suffered by the constant arrest and detention of its leaders. By March, 1924, under the leadership of Yamakawa Hitoshi, who argued that neither the times nor the stage of Japanese development were propitious for a communist party, the remaining members decided to disband their formal organization. Yamakawa favored additional work in building up the labor movement and expanding propaganda activities without jeopardizing these efforts by the existence of an illegal party. Only Arahata Kanson, recently returned from Moscow, opposed dissolution. Yamakawa and his followers thereafter advocated a plan of co-operation "with all progressive groups in an effort to develop the masses," and they joined with other groups to support such popular causes as universal manhood suffrage.

The initiative in reactivating the Japanese Communist Party came from the Comintern. In January, 1925, at Shanghai Japanese communists, including Tokuda Kyuichi, Arahata Kanson, and Sano Manabu, listened to a stinging attack on their past leadership and received orders to establish a new party with a broader basis in the Japanese proletariat and to develop new propaganda organs for the working masses. After their return to Japan they formed a preparatory communist group in August, 1925, with three major objectives: to establish a new communist party; to support "truly left-wing organizations" and proletarian parties whose emphasis was solely on the interests and participation of the masses themselves and to build communist factions within them; and to drive the social democrats out of the proletarian movement. They decided that the core of the new communist party was to be the factory cell, with the familiar principle of "democratic centralism" binding the cells and the intermediate units to policy and technical decisions of the party high command.

The Japanese communists came under socialist as well as government attack. As more and more communists were arrested, the social democrats discovered that communist participation in such organizations as Sodomei had been far more extensive than they had imagined. When the social democrats gained firmer control of Sodomei, they forced the communist-led elements to secede. The split began in December, 1924, and by May, 1925, it was complete. Communists formed the Nihon Rodo Kumiai Hyogikai (Japan Council of Labor Unions) with thirty-two unions and 12,500 members, while Sodomei retained some thirty-five unions with a membership of 13,500. The Seiji Mondai Kenkyukai (Society for the Study of Political Problems) also reflected this division, and by 1925 the moderates had either been ousted or had resigned, leaving it as an auxiliary of the Hyogikai.

Meanwhile the government continued its suppression of the communists. On December 1, 1925, the police raided the homes of more than a score of students and the headquarters of the Students' Federation for the Study of Social Science at Kyoto University. Between mid-January and late April of the following year the police took more than thirty-five students into custody on the grounds that they had violated the Peace Preservation Law and the Publications Law and that they were guilty of *lèse majesté*. The police accused them of spreading the social revolutionary ideas of Marx and Lenin in an attempt to overthrow the government and abolish private property. Later, in April, 1928, the government ordered all student organizations for the study of social science to disband.

After the passage of the Universal Manhood Suffrage Law, various leftist elements attempted to form a legal political party, but their efforts were hampered by their own factionalism and government policy. The difficulties in achieving unification were clear in the case of the Nomin Rodoto (Farmer-Labor Party), the organizing force of which was the Nihon Nomin Kumiai (Japan Farmers' Union). In July, 1925, the latter, which had been formed in 1922 and which had enjoyed success in electing members to rural local assemblies, proposed the formation of a proletarian party in co-operation with the working class, especially Sodomei and Hyogikai. But Sodomei's refusal to join with communist elements doomed the attempt to failure; therefore, when the Nomin Rodoto was formally established on December 1, 1925, it was largely a rural party. Even the Hyogikai, under the influence of Yamakawaism, had withdrawn on the grounds that without the participation of Sodomei it was impossible to form a party. Finally, within thirty minutes of its formal establishment, the party was banned by the Kato cabinet as a communist organization.

The noncommunist Left still sought to achieve party unity. On March 5, 1926, the Nihon Nomin Kumiai, Sodomei leaders, and other labor moderates formed the Rodo Nominto (Labor-Farmer Party), which disavowed the communist line and pledged through legal means to enact democratic political reforms and to remove inequalities in landownership and distribution of production. But party unity soon broke over the matter of forming a "popular front." Some of the leaders held that there should be no co-operation with the communists or with communist-dominated organizations, while others, particularly in the Nihon Nomin Kumiai, believed that the radical Left, for example Hyogikai, should be admitted into the party. The issue came to a head when certain district branches, which had been quickly organized by extremist elements, demanded admission. In reaction, the more conservative peasant groups and Sodomei withdrew, and the Rodo Nominto became the popular-front party through which the communists channeled their legal political activities. The conservative peasant elements subsequently formed their own party, Nihon Nominto (Japan Farmer Party), which temporarily discarded the policy of peasant collaboration with urban workers.

On December 5, 1926, the social democrats once again combined to establish a political party, the Shakai Minshuto (Social Democratic Party), under the leadership of intellectuals like Abe Iso, Yoshino Sakuzo, and Horie Kiichi, as well as the major Sodomei figures. Fundamental to the party platform was the principle of change through legal, parliamentary action; it emphasized modification of the diet, reorganization of the bureaucracy and the military services, and enactment of necessary economic and social legislation pertaining to tenancy relief, social security, nationalization of the major industries, basic freedoms, and women's rights. Despite this auspicious beginning, the Shakai Minshuto split, largely because of personality differences. On December 9 centrist elements of Sodomei under the leadership of Aso Hisashi, who had formed his own labor federation, Nihon Rodo Kumiai

Domei (Japan Labor Union League), established a separate party, the Nihon Ronoto (Japan Labor-Farmer Party), which, though professedly anticommunist, favored efforts to build a more broadly based popular front composed of the discontented elements in society. It opposed what it called the "radical left wing" (the communists and the Rodo Nominto) and the "reactionary right wing" (Shakai Minshuto) and attempted to steer a middle course in the proletarian movement.

Meanwhile, in early December, 1926, the Japanese Communist Party was finally re-established in secret. Although many of the communist leaders like Tokuda Kyuichi, Ichikawa Shoichi, and Nosaka Sanzo were in jail, the party, with a nucleus of about one hundred fifty members, set up a central committee to direct its various activities, organized regional committees, and formed cells in factories, trade unions, and the newly founded political parties. The organizational meeting of the party was dominated by Fukumoto Kazuo, a young teacher, whose power in the communist movement had grown steadily during the past year. Fukumoto directed the party members to concentrate on attaining a complete understanding of Marxist essentials. He held that the party should be composed exclusively of Marxist intelligentsia, separate from the labor and mass movements, and this view was contrary to the opinion of Tokuda, Nozaka, and Arahata, who had endeavored to secure a mass basis for the party. Fukumoto also concluded that Japanese capitalism had already entered the advanced stage which characterized the "declining and disintegrating capitalist societies of the West," a judgment which contradicted the Comintern analysis of Japanese society. When Tokuda, Arahata, and others were released from prison a few weeks later, Fukumotoism became an issue. Arahata, advocate of a proletarian mass party, flatly refused to participate in a party that would be composed solely of indoctrinated professional revolutionaries isolated from the masses. When reports of factionalism reached Russia, the Comintern summoned Japanese party leaders to Moscow, where a special committee to deal with Japanese problems had been established.

In July, 1927, this committee, headed by Bukharin, met with Fukumoto, Tokuda, Watanabe Masanosuke, and others "to help the Japanese comrades overcome ideological and political problems." Under pressure, Fukumoto recanted, and the Japanese delegation unanimously adopted the views expressed by Bukharin, who labeled Yamakawa's dissolution of the party in 1924 as "right-wing opportunism" on the ground that the Japanese Communist Party had already demonstrated its effectiveness, and who branded Fukumotoism as "left-wing extremism" because it had exposed the party to the danger of isolation from the masses, thus enabling the social democrats to capture control of the proletariat. In his analysis of Japanese society, which was intended to correct past errors, Bukharin stressed the development of Japanese imperialism, which he declared to be a threat to the Chinese revolution and the Soviet Union. He admitted that Japanese capitalism had made extraordinary advances and that in many respects the situation matched Lenin's objective conditions for a proletarian revolution, but he made note of the political apathy and ignorance of the masses and the absence of what Lenin called the subjective conditions for revolution. With other Russians he criticized the Japanese Communist Party for splitting such organizations as Sodomei and the Nihon Nomin Kumiai, although his suggestion that it should have seized leadership in them while denouncing all other elements was hardly realistic.

Thus, while these so-called "1927 theses" carried forward the former line by continuing to discuss the importance of a bourgeois-democratic revolution, they differed in emphasizing a worker–poor-peasant alliance to carry out a socialist revolution against the "reactionary capitalist–landlord league." Comparisons with China for tactical purposes were called foolish. The basic line was that the bourgeois-democratic revolution would be quickly transformed into a socialist revolution. The former would eliminate the remnants of feudalism, such as the emperor system and landlordism, and, once this stage was attained, the successful and rapid completion of a socialist revolution would be assured. The party, under the leadership of Ichikawa, Sano, Arahata, and Watanabe, was urged to unite labor, farmers, and the petty bourgeoisie into a single bloc. According to the theses, "the petty bourgeoisie are rapidly falling into the proletarian class" and "the bourgeoisie are not only unfit for a common front but must be fought vigorously." For the immediate future the Japanese Communist Party was ordered to carry on through the Rodo Nominto.

The Wakatsuki and Tanaka Cabinets

While the left wing was preparing for the 1928 general election, the coalition on which Kato's ministry was based collapsed. Despite its participation in the cabinet, the Seiyukai desired the restoration of its complete supremacy, but it lacked a leader who had the aggressiveness and influence to advance the interests of the party. It finally rejected Takahashi, the antimilitarist and financial genius, and turned to General Tanaka Giichi, who had worked closely with the Seiyukai during the tenure of the Hara cabinet. Tanaka, although he was an army man, was not in sympathy with the military extremists and in fact had won their enmity for his collaboration with political parties; he also had access to financial resources and was influential with many bureaucratic elements whose support was crucial to the Seiyukai. The party's position was further strengthened when the Kakushin Club disbanded and Inukai brought his followers into the party. The Kato coalition formally came to an end in July, 1925, when the Seiyukai cabinet members resigned after a clash over tax policy. In August Kato formed a Kenseikai cabinet, but his party held only 165 seats in the house of representatives; he was thus forced to fall back on an alliance with the conservative Kenkyukai of the house of peers and, ironically, with the Seiyuhonto. By various means he maintained an absolute majority of 252 members in the house of representatives.

After a serious illness, Kato died in January, 1926, and his position as prime minister and president of the Kenseikai was assumed by Wakatsuki Reijiro, an old friend with similar views. Continuing the alliance with the Seiyuhonto, the Wakatsuki cabinet was able to reduce the land tax by 1 per cent, increase the national treasury grant for compulsory education by 10,000,-000 yen, and raise import duties on grains in order to protect agricultural producers. Wakatsuki also inherited the military's antagonism to Foreign Minister Shidehara's conciliatory policy toward China and faced mounting criticism of Japan's inability to combat the antiforeign attacks of Chinese Nationalist forces and their supporters. But Shidehara continued to insist that respect for China's sovereignty and territorial integrity entailed strict noninterference in her domestic politics, economic co-operation, an attitude of sympathy and good will toward China's legitimate aspirations, a desire to aid in their realization, and protection by legitimate means of Japan's rights in China.

The financial crisis of 1927 toppled the Wakatsuki ministry. Overexpansion of credit and a steady increase in national indebtedness to over five billion yen, reflecting a reluctance on the part of government and business to liquidate World War I values, placed many Japanese banks in difficulties, and several failed. For example, the Mitsui and Mitsubishi interests were attempting to force their competitor, the Suzuki Company of Kobe, out of business by calling in their loans to the Bank of Taiwan and to other banks affiliated with the Suzuki Company. By April the general financial situation was so desperate that Wakatsuki called an emergency meeting of the cabinet, which decided to issue an emergency ordinance to save the Bank of Taiwan by making good its losses to the amount of 200,000,000 yen in the hope of clearing the atmosphere and dispelling economic uncertainty. When the cabinet submitted a draft of the ordinance to the privy council, its policies, especially those of Shidehara, came under blistering attack. When the privy council rejected the ordinance, it was unmistakably clear that it was determined to force the resignation of the cabinet. Since public opinion seemed to back up the privy council, Wakatsuki resigned on April 17. On the following day the Bank of Taiwan and all its branches closed, touching off a nationwide run on banks, which brought on a financial panic of unprecedented proportions. Many unsound industrial and commercial companies were bankrupted, and the number of banking institutions was reduced from 1,359 to 1,031.

Within several days General Tanaka formed a Seiyukai cabinet, with the exception of the two service posts and the ministry of justice. To combat the financial crisis, Tanaka appointed Takahashi as finance minister and Inouye Junnosuke, a Mitsui man, as governor of the Bank of Japan, and on their advice he proclaimed a three-week moratorium on banking, to begin on April 22. On May 4 Tanaka called an extraordinary session of the diet, which voted 200,000,000 yen for the Bank of Taiwan and a special fund of 500,000,000 yen for the Bank of Japan. Much of these funds was used for the relief of zaibatsu interests, while small-scale bank depositors, numbering several hundred thousand, who had suffered losses through bank failures, were not indemnified. In fact, many banks which were unable to get relief were finally absorbed by the Showa Bank, a joint operation of zaibatsu banking interests, which by the end of 1928 held 26 per cent of all deposits and 34 per cent of the deposits of ordinary banks.

Tanaka's policies thus assisted the large and politically influential companies but did little to alleviate the nation's economic problems, many of which were closely related to international trends and foreign policy. The Tanaka cabinet had as one of its objectives the stabilization and expansion of Japan's markets in Asia, but its "positive policy" in Manchuria and Shantung actually had the effect of reducing the China market substantially by provoking open hostility and boycotts against Japan. Its policy of keeping prices comparatively high had a detrimental effect on foreign markets which were already contracting. The cabinet's economic and foreign policies thus created a situation in which capital overexpansion in terms of marketing potential continued, relatively high prices underwritten by the government remained, and urban unemployment and agrarian indebtedness mounted.

The position of the Tanaka cabinet was precarious, since the Seiyukai was a minority party. When the Kenseikai and the Seiyuhonto merged to form a new party, the Rikken Minseito (Constitutional Democratic Party), which did have a majority in the house of representatives, Tanaka moved quickly to dissolve the diet and submit the fate of his ministry to the enlarged electorate in a national election. The Japanese people voted on February 20, 1928, with the cabinet exerting tremendous pressure; but the results were inconclusive, as the Seiyukai won only 219 seats out of a total of 466 and the Minseito only 217. Thus there was no majority party, and the independents and representatives of the new left-wing parties were in a stronger position.

Suppression of the Left Wing

The first election under universal manhood suffrage found not one proletarian party in the field but four, with a fifth, the Japanese Communist Party, working underground. According to 1928 statistics of the ministry of home affairs, the membership of the parties was as follows: Nihon Nominto, 92,792; Shakai Minshuto, 47,267; Nihon Ronoto, 23,520; and Rodo Nominto, 15,374 (1927 figure). This fragmentation handicapped left-wing candidates, since they were unable to conduct a unified campaign and engaged in heated arguments among themselves, which was harmful to their public image;

moreover, it was easier for the government to restrict their activities. The communists, while not constituting a legal party, were able to infiltrate the Rodo Nominto to the extent that they placed ten of their own members on the ballot as Rodo Nominto candidates. Of the 88 candidates who ran under various proletarian party labels, only 8 were elected to the house of representatives: 4 from the Shakai Minshuto, 2 from the Rodo Nominto, 1 from the Nihon Ronoto, and 1 from a district labor party. The total vote for the left-wing candidates was nearly 500,000, but this was small compared to the 4,274,898 cast for the Seiyukai and the 4,201,219 cast for the Minseito candidates. Although the Rodo Nominto received 193,000 votes, none of the communist candidates was successful.

These election results, indicating lack of mass support, were extremely disappointing to the left wing. For one thing, Japanese labor was not sufficiently organized and lacked power. By this time the labor movement could claim no more than 6 per cent of the industrial working force, and its 330,000 union members were divided into numerous small factions. The average membership in individual unions was only 524. Conditions of labor surplus gravely handicapped the development of strong unionism, and throughout most of the 1920's unions found their effectiveness minimized by the fact that workers had to fight to maintain their jobs against the great numbers of unemployed. Moreover, the political class consciousness of Japanese labor was checked by the paternalism which characterized employer-employee relationships in Japanese business and industry, particularly in small units. Despite generally bad working conditions, employers were for the most part able to maintain the appeal of the classical virtues of harmony, loyalty, and obedience. They based the amount of wages on the number of dependents, retained superfluous labor to the extent of causing underemployment, and granted wage bonuses according to service. In the rural areas landlordism was still powerful politically as well as in economic and social relations, and the conservatives retained the support of the bulk of the peasantry.

The election results and the policies of the Tanaka cabinet, which threatened the whole leftist movement, made the unification of the left-wing parties desirable, and efforts were made to bring the various factions together. Ideological and personal differences, however, were too great to permit amalgamation of the parties for any long period of time. The center group, largely the Nihon Nomin Kumiai faction within the Nihon Ronoto, conducted a popular-front campaign, which gave birth to the Nihon Taishuto (Japan Mass Party) on December 20, 1928. This party was essentially a coalition which included the Nihon Ronoto, the Nominto, district labor parties, and a number of representatives from the Rodo Nominto, which had been ordered by the government to disband in April, 1928. It did not include the communists or the Shakai Minshuto, whose leaders had come to the conclusion that union with more radical parties was not in their own interests. The platform of the Taishuto opposed militarism, demanded reform of Japanese politics and parties, and urged the enactment of progressive legislation, such as universal suffrage for all Japanese above twenty years of age, land reform, and nationalization of basic industries. Despite initial successes in local elections, the coalition did not endure for long and was reduced to little more than the faction from the Nihon Ronoto and some Nominto elements. In November, 1929, the large faction of the banned Rodo Nominto which had objected to amalgamation with the Taishuto formed the Shin Ronoto (New Labor-Farmer Party) and took upon itself the duty of "protecting the everyday interests of the oppressed classes, carrying on a vigorous struggle to secure political liberties, and expanding labor and peasants' unions."

The communists were also active in this period, but they found it increasingly difficult to operate because of police interference. In the 1928 general election they campaigned on behalf of Rodo Nominto candidates, especially their own party members, and they distributed party propaganda widely. All these activities gave the police and their political spies an excellent opportunity to collect an abundance of data which led to the arrest of over a thousand radicals shortly after the election. Since very few communists escaped the police dragnet, the party's leadership was once again decimated. In a subsequent nation-wide crackdown the police rounded up approximately 65,000 persons, including 2,500 students, and on April 10 the government banned the Rodo Nominto, the Hyogikai, and the Musan Seinen Domei (Proletarian Youth League), another large communist-front organization. Those few communists who escaped the arrests went underground or fled the country.

The government continued to react against the communist menace. The Tanaka cabinet felt a definite need for a more efficient police system and for more stringent legislation to control political agitation. On June 29, 1928, by an emergency imperial ordinance it amended the Peace Preservation Law to include the death penalty, and in the following month it created the special higher police for the control of social movements throughout the country. This new organ employed several thousand agents to work with local police in investigation of subversive organizations, and it maintained branches at Shanghai, Vladivostok, and even as far away as London. In August, 1928, the cabinet prohibited all outdoor assemblies and mass demonstrations and required promoters of indoor meetings to file in advance programs, proclamations, and resolutions. Universities, regarded as incubators of radical thought, came under closer control. Student organizations under suspicion were ordered to disband, and a number of professors suspected of leftist leanings were forced to resign. By the summer of 1928 "student supervisors" were added to the staffs of imperial universities and other state-supported schools in order to prevent the revival of radical organizations and to guide student thinking.

Despite these steps taken by the government, communist activity continued. Ichikawa Shoichi, who participated with Sano Manabu, Watanabe Masanosuke, and others in the Sixth Congress of the Comintern at Moscow in the summer of 1928, returned to Japan in November of that year, and under his direction the underground party sought to increase its influence in mass organizations. For example, in December, 1928, it helped to establish the Nihon Rodo Kumiai Zenkoku Hyogikai, or Zenkyo (National Conference of Japanese Trade Unions), with headquarters in Tokyo. Although government pressure was not relaxed and arrest followed arrest, by March, 1929, active party membership equaled the previous high, set in March, 1928; but a second wave of nation-wide arrests began on April 16, 1929, which jailed more than one thousand suspected communists. Although most of the leading party members avoided the initial wave, they were picked up in the following months. For example, Sano Manabu was arrested at Shanghai and extradited to Japan in June. The arrests were blows from which the communist movement did not recover, and by the summer of 1929 nothing remained of the party but a small group of undisciplined adventurers who advocated the use of violence. A third series of arrests was carried out in February, 1930, and some four hundred intellectuals and labor leaders, many of them communists, were imprisoned.

The Nationalist Reaction

During the 1920's there was a nationalist reaction against the democratic, socialist, and communist movements, which were challenging the "very foundations of Japanese society." Nativist societies arose to criticize Western thought, and among many of the new nationalist organizations there was a dedication to the "Japanese spirit" against Western radicalism. These societies acted as magnets, drawing together many conservatives from among businessmen, landlords, bureaucrats, party politicians, and the military. Perhaps the most important of them was the Kokuhonsha (National Foundation Society), which was founded in 1924 under the leadership of Hiranuma Kiichiro, a former minister of justice, and included many of Japan's outstanding leaders, e.g., bureaucrats like Suzuki Kisaburo, soon to become president of the Seiyukai, representatives of the Mitsui and Yasuda companies, and high-ranking military officers like Generals Ugaki Kazushige, Araki Sadao, and Mazaki Jinzaburo and Admirals Saito Makoto and Arima Ryokitsu. Like similar societies, its program emphasized preservation of the status quo and was characterized by abstractions, with a kind of Confucianist state nationalism the predominant theme. But there were some nationalists, including a faction of the Kokuhonsha, who realized that any attempt to eradicate subversive tendencies had to be based on a plan of political, economic, and social reform. Despite ideological and personal differences among the nationalists, there was a basic unity among them. All made national self-sufficiency their ultimate goal, and all sought to strengthen the pattern of Japanese life and culture. Basically the movement was an emotional one, which appealed to the people's absolute, incorruptible veneration of the emperor; and in its extreme forms it became an irrational and chauvinistic patriotism, which called freely for the sacrifice of life whenever necessary.

Some of the radical nationalist societies based their programs on the thought of Kita Ikki, a former intelligence agent of the army in China, who was the foremost proponent of national socialist reform. Influenced by the Confucian Classics, early Japanese socialism, and the nationalist revolution in China, he sought to develop his own system of socialism compatible with the national polity of Japan. His writings, particularly *Nihon Kaizo Hoan Taiko (An Outline for the Reconstruction of Japan)*, which became the bible of many of Japan's young army officers, reveal two very significant tendencies. Kita had no faith in class revolutions or in the democratic process, and in emulation of the Meiji Restoration he desired a *coup d'état* by an enlightened few which would free the state from the corrupt and selfish cliques composed of the older army officers, bureaucrats, party politicians, and representatives of economic vested-interest groups. Kita's view of history was heroic; that is to say, he believed that a nation's destiny, or the world's destiny, could be altered by a dedicated group or a dedicated man. Rejecting determinism and democracy, he was the embodiment of irrationalism and romanticism. Kita hoped to mold his young officer converts into a tightly knit leadership corps which would act in the name of the emperor to suspend the constitution, declare martial law, dissolve the diet, abolish the peerage, and form a national reconstruction cabinet to direct the reform of Japanese society.

Kita envisaged the use of political power by an army junta to pave the way for a planned economy. His thinking along this line was clearly a reaction against the continuing concentration of economic power in Japanese society. During the decade of the 1920's landlordism increased, and in industrial, commercial, and financial enterprises the zaibatsu improved their position at the expense of smaller firms. The Mitsui Company, for example, comprised 120 corporations and controlled 15 per cent of Japan's entire corporate wealth. Adverse economic conditions had also caused many of the larger companies in the major industrial fields to form cartels through which they could regulate supplies and prices for the protection of their mutual interests. According to Kita, the nationalist cabinet would expropriate all assets of a single household in excess of 1,000,000 yen and landholdings in excess of 100,000 yen at market price. In the case of land, the state would redistribute it to the landless on easy-payment terms. Industrial, commercial, and financial enterprises exceeding 10,000,000 yen in evaluation of total assets would be subject to state ownership and management. Prominent also in Kita's plans was the strengthening of the military for purposes of national expansion,

557

which he regarded as a partial solution to Japan's shortages of natural resources and need for markets.

In contrast to Kita Ikki, Gondo Seikyo was the nationalist spokesman for a return to an agrarian economy based solidly on independent small and middle-class farmers. Central to his reform program was the prohibition of absentee ownership of land. In a more general way he invoked the prestige of the emperor, traditionalism, and doctrines of racial supremacy to criticize the forces of urbanism, capitalism, and Westernization; and in attacks on Prussian-style centralization and bureaucratic controls, he extolled the values of rural self-government and a completely decentralized society. More than any other nationalist, Gondo reflected the mounting agrarian discontent resulting from the total impact of urban capitalism on the rural areas of Japan, and with greater success than his leftist contemporaries he was able to channel this source of discontent toward the acceptance of nationalist solutions that seemed to promise emancipation from capitalist domination and possibly the restoration of agrarian supremacy.

The radical nationalists derived their most powerful support from the young army officers of middle-class background. By the decade of the 1920's a larger segment of the officer corps came from families of small landowners, small industrialists, shopkeepers, and petty bureaucrats. Year by year the percentage of officer recruits from these groups increased, and by 1927 it was approximately 30 per cent. Their background made them highly critical of the effects of monopoly capitalism and of political parties which seemed to represent capitalist interests; and their military indoctrination, which included a heavy emphasis on familiar nationalist themes, made them supporters of expansionist schemes. The conclusion reached by many young army and navy officers was that Japan would be better off if the army came to power and administered the state in the interests of the people as a whole. In some cases, moreover, they were critical of many of the older, conservative generals, who, they felt, were allied with the parties and the zaibatsu.

While the army nationalists tended to be divided on the issue of national reconstruction, they were united on the need for a more forceful foreign policy, especially regarding China, backed if necessary by military power and action. In the case of the Tanaka cabinet, it hoped to facilitate Japan's peaceful economic penetration of China, and it was quick to utilize military power whenever Japan's rights and the life and property of her nationals were threatened. Tanaka readily intervened in Shantung both in 1927 and again in the spring of 1928, and he also pursued an aggressive policy with regard to Manchuria.

Manchuria had always been of special concern to Japan, since it was regarded as having a crucial strategic as well as economic importance; and when Chang Tso-lin proved not to be a pliable puppet, a group of extreme nationalists within the Kwantung Army murdered him in anticipation of a Japanese drive into Manchuria. The army chief-of-staff prevented such a move; but when Tanaka sought to establish greater controls over the army, he was resisted by headquarters generals who insisted that the army would take care of its own discipline and problems. When the assassins remained unpunished, Tanaka resigned (June, 1929). Thereafter the army and nationalist societies exerted strong pressure on the government to act positively in defense of Japanese interests that were being threatened by the policies of the Nanking regime; and the radicals insisted that if the army—the only disinterested, uncorrupted force in Japanese life—were in control of the government, Manchuria might be exploited in the interests of the whole nation and not of a few capitalists.

28 The Triumph of Japanese Militarism

The Tanaka ministry was succeeded by a Minseito cabinet, formed by Prime Minister Hamaguchi Osachi in July, 1929; and Shidehara, lacking party affiliation, returned to the office of minister of foreign affairs. In the hope of strengthening the basis of his power, Hamaguchi dissolved the house of representatives, in which the Seiyukai held a majority, and campaigning on a platform of economy, with emphasis on disarmament, purification of politics, and reform of the China policy, the Minseito won an election victory in 1930, returning 273 members to the lower house. Meanwhile, after General Tanaka's sudden death in October, 1929, the presidency of the Seiyukai fell to Inukai Tsuyoshi.

The Hamaguchi Cabinet and the Military

The Hamaguchi cabinet tried desperately to bring greater stability to the Japanese economy, which had suffered from the spreading world depression. It sought to achieve a balanced budget, a sharp reduction in administrative expenses, and a return to the gold standard, with the free movement of gold. Its first major move was to lift the gold embargo, which had been in effect since the Terauchi ministry; this action caused a sharp reduction in prices, providing some relief to consumers. But the merits of the Hamaguchi program were lost with the collapse of the American economy in 1929. For example, the American demand for raw silk, Japan's largest single export, fell rapidly and in 1930 was only 53 per cent of the 1929 value. The heavy impact of this can be measured by the fact that by 1929 two-fifths of Japanese farm families were engaged in sericulture as a subsidiary occupation. As the situation worsened, the average export price of raw silk plummeted from 1,420 yen per 100 *kin* (132 lbs.) to a low of 390 yen in June, 1932. In urban areas unemployment increased, and many more small business firms were forced into bankruptcy. A general decline in agricultural prices, particularly the price of rice, which because of a series of good harvests fell from 29 yen a *koku* (4.96 lbs.) in 1929 to 17 yen in November, 1930, afforded some relief to the urban population but created desperate conditions in the rural areas, especially among the tenant farmers. Between 1926 and 1931 the gross income of Japanese farmers was cut almost in half, and there was a corresponding increase in rural indebtedness.

Under these circumstances the cabinet was forced to revise its economic planning in the spring of 1930, when it inaugurated a silk subsidization program—which proved completely inadequate—instituted some public works, and made large loans to private business. But nothing could rehabilitate the lost markets of the world during this period, and the financial structure of the country was weakened as gold was exported in large quantities, with speculators buying dollars in anticipation of a fall in the value of the yen. When Great Britain left the gold standard, Japan's fiscal condition grew even worse, and by the end of 1931 the gold reserves of the Bank of Japan were only 470,000,000 yen as compared to 1,072,000,000 yen two years earlier.

While the economic policies of the Hamaguchi cabinet earned for it the contempt of Japanese radicals, socialist and nationalist alike, its clashes with the military lost the support of the more conservative generals and admirals. In the course of the London Naval Conference in the spring of 1930 the Japanese delegation had been instructed by the navy to insist on a 10–7 ratio vis-à-vis the United States and Great Britain in heavy cruisers and all auxiliary craft, but in face of American and British opposition the chief delegate, Wakatsuki Reijiro, on instructions from the cabinet, accepted the compromise of a 10–6 ratio in heavy cruisers, slightly higher ratios in light cruisers and destroyers, and equality in submarines. The conferees also agreed not to construct new battleships for a six-year period. But in Japan the navy strenuously opposed ratification of the London Naval Treaty, and in the negotiations between the cabinet and the supreme command no compromise was reached. The Seiyukai, anxious to make political capital out of the controversy, sided with the navy; but Hamaguchi, though agreeing in theory to the independence of the supreme command, insisted that such matters as national armed strength fell within the jurisdiction of the cabinet. The navy, on the other hand, claimed that any retrenchment not approved by the supreme command was unconstitutional. When the treaty was submitted to the privy council as part of the ratification process, the councilors, who were hostile to the cabinet, supported the navy's view; but when Hamaguchi refused to yield and was applauded by public opinion, the privy council reluctantly approved the treaty. Hamaguchi had won his point, but his success made more apparent the gulf between the moderate party politicians and the military.

The controversy was the occasion for numerous discussions concerning the theory and operation of Japanese government. Liberal Japanese scholars were quick to support Hamaguchi, especially Professor Minobe, who wrote in the public press that matters concerning the determination of the strength of the armed forces were the responsibility of the cabinet and that the advice of the military authorities was not binding upon it. Minobe went on to state that the emperor was head of the state as a whole but also, as commander-in-chief, exercised supreme command over the armed forces; he implied that the military authorities were thus subordinate to the civil government. These views, which certainly had not been in the minds of the framers of the Meiji Constitution, were extremely disturbing to the army and navy. The radical officers regarded them as a clever argument by a defender of those business interests which prospered at the expense of soldiers and farmers, and they began to organize to develop their own strength.

In September, 1930, a group of senior staff officers, including Lieutenant General Koiso Kuniaki, head of the bureau of military affairs, Major General Tatekawa Yoshitsugu, director of the second section of the general-staff office, and senior staff officers like Lieutenant Colonel Hashimoto Kingoro, formed a society—known as the Sakurakai (Cherry Society) after 1931—to discuss the possibility of a *coup d'état* and the establishment of a military government. Later, in January, 1931, War Minister Ugaki presided over a meeting of army officers, including representatives of the Sakurakai and others like Lieutenant General Sugiyama Hajime, vice-minister of the army, which plotted a coup to set up a military regime under Ugaki. In co-operation with civilian rightists under the leadership of Okawa Shumei, who had been trying to stir the army into action for some time, they planned to stage demonstrations against the government, blow up the headquarters of the Minseito and Seiyukai as well as the residence of the prime minister, surround the diet and dissolve it, force the cabinet to resign, and form a new government of high-ranking officers. However, shortly before March 20, 1931, the day which had been selected for the uprising, Ugaki, Koiso, and Sugiyama withdrew their support, and the plot was abandoned. Evidently the conservative generals felt that similar results should and could be achieved through orderly and legal means.

In the spring of 1931, however, the army did begin a campaign to strengthen its position and to win popular support for its views. In May its big three—the war minister, the chief of the general staff, and the inspector-general of military education—declared that no further reductions of military expenditures were possible and stressed the need to modernize the army's equipment. This constituted a warning by the army that it would not submit to cabinet dictation as had the navy in the previous year. The army also hired professional newspapermen to write sympathetic accounts of its views and intimidated others who wrote unfavorably about them. The main emphasis in the press campaign was on behalf of increased armaments, and, aware of the attitude of a large segment of the population that had welcomed relief from the heavy burden of military expenditures, the army played on popular patriotism, foreign policy crises, and the interests of the state as a whole.

While the radicals were held in check at home, their colleagues in the Kwantung Army were busy planning to implement a strong foreign policy by perpetrating an incident in Manchuria. By summer the Chinese Nationalist drive against Japanese rights and interests had caused a reaction in Japanese public sentiment, and rumors of an impending crisis in Manchuria flooded Japan. Time and again the opinion was expressed publicly that the policy of leaving so many issues in Manchuria unsettled had caused the Chinese authorities to make light of Japan. "Settlement of all issues, by force if necessary," became a popular slogan, and reference was freely made in the press to discussions between the army minister, the general staff, and other officers regarding a resort to force. Although the Minseito government opposed this solution, Prime Minister Wakatsuki (who had assumed office after Hamaguchi's resignation in March, 1931, following the attempt on his life by a young fanatic in November of the previous year) and Shidehara could advise no countermeasures. They did consult with Army Minister General Minami Jiro, but his last-minute efforts to restrain the Kwantung Army radicals, including the dispatch of Major General Tatekawa to Manchuria, failed.

The Aftermath of the Manchurian Incident

Although the news of the September 18 incident came as no surprise to top civilian officials of the Japanese government, they were unable to control the situation and prevent the subsequent aggression. The majority of key military figures were in sympathy with the direct-action tactics, and even those with some misgivings were under strong pressure from subordinates and were unwilling to voice any opposition. The cabinet was split, with several Minseito members defending the Kwantung Army, and only Shidehara and Inouye Junnosuke, minister of finance, openly condemned the aggression. From a constitutional standpoint, the action of the Kwantung Army was defended on the ground that the emperor had "accepted" the military's advice rather than the cabinet's; and the latter had to accept what was already done, although it sought to prevent further unauthorized action. But the cabinet itself was under constant attack by nationalist societies and could do little to hold the army in check. The Kwantung Army went so far as to threaten that if the cabinet would not support its campaign but adopted an obstructive attitude, it would declare its independence and rule Manchuria itself. The Manchurian incident demonstrated dramatically the weakness of party government and the schismatic character of the administration as a whole. The cabinet proved to be helpless to prevent the initiation of an independent foreign policy by a small overseas clique supported by radical and conservative elements at home.

When the Manchurian incident gave way to general aggression, the plotting against the Minseito government was revived by the radical officers; and one group, composed largely of Sakurakai members, conspired to occupy the metropolitan police headquarters and to isolate the war ministry and offices of the chief of staff until it could establish a military government under the leadership of General Araki Sadao. The minister of war, General Minami, learned of the plot when several of the conspirators defected, and on October 16 the military police arrested the leaders at their meeting place in Tokyo. The army, however, hushed up the incident and by way of disciplinary action broke up the group by reassignments. While the army generals would not condone revolutionary action against the government, they were quick to realize that the threat of terrorism strengthened their hand in many respects. They were able to argue persuasively that only the military could control the increasingly explosive situation. At the same time, other conservatives—party politicians, bureaucrats, and businessmen—realized that compromise with the older military leaders was necessary to foreclose more radical alternatives. In fact, many of them now joined nationalist societies committed to direct-action tactics and positive programs.

In the autumn of 1931 the Minseito government found itself in an impossible political situation. In Japan it was compelled to assume responsibility for the actions of the military, whom it could not effectively control, and for its efforts it earned the animosity of the public as a whole; at the same time, the cabinet sought to reconcile the actions of the Kwantung Army with Japan's obligations under the Covenant of the League of Nations and under treaty provisions. But the specific issue which finally forced the resignation of the Minseito government was the demand by some members of the party that it form a coalition with the Seiyukai. This split the Minseito, and Wakatsuki resigned in December, 1931. On the advice of Saionji, the veteran Seiyukai leader, Inukai Tsuyoshi, formed a cabinet which included Araki, the favorite of the radical officers, as minister of the army.

Party government was thus maintained; but since the Seiyukai had always been an advocate of a stronger foreign policy, it could be expected to give more vigorous support to the army's Manchurian venture. Saionji, however, hoped that Inukai would find some solution to the Manchurian incident and restore normal relations between China and Japan. One of Inukai's first actions was to dissolve the house of representatives, and in the ensuing election in February, 1932, the Seiyukai won an amazing total of 304 seats. The party, however, far from being united, was split into several factions, based upon the personal ambitions of various leaders, and was thus unable to take a strong stand against the army.

Nationalism also had a significant impact on the left wing in Japan. After the 1930 general election, in which the leftist parties won only 5 seats in the house of representatives (Shakai Minshuto, 2; Nihon Taishuto, 2; and Ronoto, 1), new parties were formed and dissolved with great rapidity. But the only step in the direction of unity was the establishment of the Zenkoku Rono Taishuto (National Labor-Farmer Mass Party) in July, 1931, through the amalgamation of the Zenkoku Taishuto (National Mass Party)—until July, 1930, called the Nihon Taishuto—and the Ronoto. In the general election of February, 1932, left-wing parties polled only 287,000 votes, but they managed to maintain their five seats in the house of representatives by concentrating upon fewer candidates. After the election the Shakai Minshuto and the Zenkoku Rono Taishuto merged to form the Shakai Taishuto (Social Mass Party), with a vague program of anticapitalism, antifascism, and anticommunism that it maintained in some fashion until its dissolution in 1940; however, during this period there was constant dissension within its ranks, and it suffered from numerous withdrawals. For example, in April, 1932, a group led by Akamatsu Katsumaro founded the Japan National Socialist Party, whose platform defended the Manchurian incident by insisting that it was an inevitable step in the realization of national socialism, and a month later this party split into two separate parties; although both were anticapitalist, they replaced Marxist universalism and internationalism with an intense nationalism and statism.

In this period the Japanese Communist Party redefined its policy on two occasions. In 1931, after Bukharin's fall from power in the Soviet Union, the Comintern dispatched Kazama Jokichi, who had been studying in Moscow, to Japan to assume leadership of the weakened party and to draft new theses. Kazama and his small group of colleagues reached the conclusion that "Japanese capitalism has attained the final stage of monopoly capitalism," and they attached little importance to the role of "feudalistic remnants" in society. Viewing the basic struggle in Japan as one between the bourgeoisie and the proletariat, they advocated an immediate proletarian revolution.

However, the Comintern condemned these 1931 theses for lacking "a clear and correct understanding of the character and tasks of revolution in Japan," and it had Nosaka Sanzo, who had arrived in Moscow after two years of confinement in Japanese jails, plan a new strategy. His 1932 theses emphasized the need to overthrow the emperor system and to struggle against Japanese imperialism "under the banner of a bourgeois-democratic revolution." As in the case of the 1927 theses, Nosaka stressed the importance of feudalistic remnants (the imperial system and landlordism) within the political, economic, and social structure of Japan, and he branded the program of an immediate proletarian revolution as a "Trotskyist scheme."

This policy shift was added evidence of the Japanese Communist Party's dependence on Moscow, and the disgust of some party members with Russian direction, as well as continued repression by the police, tended to reduce the party to insignificance. From June, 1931, to October, 1932, arrests and public trials resulted in long jail sentences for the following: Sano Manabu, Ichikawa Shoichi, and Nabeyama Sadachika, life; Kokuryo Goichiro and Takahashi Sadaki, fifteen years; and Tokuda Kyuichi, Shiga Yoshio, and Fukumoto Kazuo, ten years. In 1933 Sano, Nabeyama, and Takahashi among many others (and later including Kazama) defected from the party, partly on the ground that it was nothing more than "a society of friends of the Soviet Union." Most of them took the position that Japanese socialism had to develop along national lines. Although communist activity continued throughout the decade of the 1930's, by the end of 1933 the national party was broken, and all attempts at reorganization were stymied by the police.

The Downfall of Party Government

The fall of the Minseito government did not have the result anticipated by the army extremists, who had hoped that General Araki or General Mazaki Jinzaburo would get the nod as prime minister. The radicals wanted national reconstruction as well as overseas expansion, and they were not satisfied with the Inukai cabinet. Unfortunately, economic scandals gave added weight to their demand for the elimination of party government. During the Wakatsuki ministry large financial and business firms bought large quantities of American dollars, gambling on the prospect that the gold embargo might be reimposed. Wakatsuki had stubbornly resisted this move; but when Inukai came to power, he finally returned Japan to the gold standard. Overnight, speculators profited in the amount of millions of yen; and since one of the firms reaping the largest profits was Mitsui, there were loud cries that Mitsui, in concert with the Seiyukai, had sabotaged the nation to enrich itself.

On February 9, 1932, Inouye Junnosuke, former finance minister in the Wakatsuki cabinet, was assassinated by an agrarian nationalist, and about a month later, on March 5, Baron Dan Takuma, head of the Mitsui interests, fell victim to another agrarian assassin. Both of these terroristic acts were carried out by the Ketsumeidan (Blood Brotherhood League), which had been founded in 1930 by six young fanatics from Ibaragi Prefecture. By 1931 the Ketsumeidan had come under the leadership of young army radicals and Nissho Inouye, a Buddhist priest of the Nichiren Sect, who had served as an army spy in China and Manchuria, and it plotted to kill a great number of politicians, bureaucrats, and businessmen, whom it held responsible for agrarian misery. According to police records, the marked men included Inukai and other Seiyukai politicians; Wakatsuki and Shidehara from the previous Minseito cabinet; Saionji, Makino Shinken, Prince Tokugawa, and Ito Myoji, all of whom were court advisers; and numerous zaibatsu officers.

Most of the Ketsumeidan leaders were arrested, but they constituted the nucleus of only one group among many similar organizations.

The terror came to a climax on May 15, 1932, when a number of army radicals attacked the metropolitan police headquarters in Tokyo, the Mitsubishi Bank, Seiyukai headquarters, and electric transformer stations in various parts of the city and issued a manifesto calling attention to the dangers confronting the nation and urging the people to take up arms to save Japan. Specifically, the radicals demanded liquidation of the political parties and the zaibatsu and called for punishment of arbitrary bureaucrats and advisers to the throne. There was no popular uprising, but the army officers assassinated Prime Minister Inukai and made an attempt on the life of Count Makino, lord keeper of the privy seal, who was himself a nationalist but not among the radicals. The attempted coup forced the resignation of the cabinet, the last party government until after World War II.

In the subsequent trials of the assassins the army was careful to avoid outright condemnation of the actions of military personnel, regardless of the factions to which they belonged. The defendants were treated as "misguided patriots" rather than as murderers, and the courtroom became the equivalent of a public platform from which the patriots, one after another, could condemn political parties, economic interest groups, and even those foreign powers which opposed Japanese expansion. There can be no doubt that the trials were useful to those army leaders who were determined to destroy party government and win the support of Japanese conservatives for army-dominated cabinets within the framework of the Meiji Constitution. By the judgment of the court, most of the accused were found guilty of the assassination, but they were given such light sentences that their terms were substantially covered by the time spent in jail during the period from the commission of the offense to the conclusion of the trial. The single severe punishment was fifteen years in jail.

After the May 15 incident, party government gave way to a series of military-dominated cabinets. When called upon to recommend a successor to Inukai, Saionji found a compromise candidate in Admiral Saito Makoto. In Saionji's view, it was necessary to suspend party government, since the army warned that another party cabinet would infallibly produce fresh acts of violence; but he hoped that this was only a temporary measure and that the parties would be restored to power when conditions proved more favorable. Saito, moreover, was regarded by the inner court circle, leading businessmen, and some party leaders as an able man who might be capable of balancing the conflicting political élites and thus preventing revolution or complete army control. But from the outset, even though his cabinet contained four Seiyukai and three Minseito members, it was clear that the voice of the military, especially that of the militant army minister, General Araki, was decisive. As the new American ambassador, Joseph Grew, wrote in his diary on June

13, 1932, "Whatever way it fall out, one thing is certain and that is that the military are distinctly running the government and that no step can be taken without their approval." In fact, the army appointed a member of the imperial family, Prince Kanin, as chief of its general staff in order to use the emperor's prestige to intimidate the government and the public, and, not to be outdone, the navy appointed Prince Fushimi as chief of the naval general staff.

The power of the military was revealed when the Saito ministry upheld the actions of the Kwantung Army in Manchuria and adopted the long-desired program of modernization of the army's equipment. The Saito cabinet also withdrew Japan from the League of Nations, in which she had been an active and co-operative member since its inception. This isolationist move represented a fundamental defeat for moderate political elements but was of advantage to the army, which exploited the international condemnation of Japanese action in Manchuria in order to create the impression that the Western nations, as well as China, were resisting Japan's "righteous mission" in Asia.

There was once more a general stirring of the type of nationalist sentiment that had prevailed during the period of the Russo-Japanese War, and, according to Ambassador Grew, a considerable section of the public and the army believed that an eventual war between Japan and the United States or the Soviet Union, or both, was inevitable. It was at this time, too, that Japanese businessmen began to show great concern about economic barriers that were being thrown up against Japanese goods throughout the world, which many of them regarded as convincing evidence that the Western nations were determined to put roadblocks in the way of Japan's continuing economic recovery. After the low point of the depression had been reached, between 1930 and 1932, the Japanese economy had begun to make a comeback; and gradually its foreign-trade volume expanded until, by 1936, it was double that of the year 1930.

The Isolation of Japan

The decade of the 1930's proved to be a period of strong economic nationalism. The United States restricted access to its markets by the passage of the Smoot-Hawley Tariff in 1931, and even the Netherlands Indies, the outpost of a colonial power that had been a staunch advocate of free trade, turned protectionist in 1933. More important, however, was the fact that the British sought to restrict Japanese competition, which was causing a marked reduction in Great Britain's export of cotton textiles and other fabrics. The Ottawa agreements of 1932, allowing British products to enjoy special preferences in the dominions and colonies, marked the start of an economic offensive against Japanese goods, and in May, 1934, the British government imposed quotas, based on average imports during the period 1927–1931, on all foreign cotton and silk goods imported into its colonies and protectorates. The order had the effect of reducing Japanese trade in these areas by approximately 50 per cent of its total during the two preceding years. On the other hand, Japan began to insist, without much success, that Australia, from whom she purchased large quantities of wool, should import more Japanese products. By 1935 American businessmen also began to protest that Japanese goods were flooding the home market as well as those of the Philippines and other areas of interest to them. Japan found new markets in Europe, Africa, Latin America, and Oceania, and she regarded China all the more as potentially the most profitable market for her manufactures and the cheapest source of raw materials for her industries. Japan concentrated on increasing her sales, especially in north China, and on securing an abundant supply of Chinese iron, coal, cotton, and salt. Her aggressive policy was bound to clash, sooner or later, with British and American interests. Certainly the statement of Mr. Amau regarding China on April 17, 1934, and other similar pronouncements by the Tokyo government did not serve to relieve Anglo-Japanese and American-Japanese tensions.

The Saito ministry did not prove capable of reconciling the wide range of views in the Japanese political scene. For example, in the budget discussions of October and November, 1933, Finance Minister Takahashi, an obstinate opponent of expansion, with some support from the minister of foreign affairs, Hirota Koki, opposed the demands for increased military appropriations. Takahashi felt that Japan was in no present danger and would only create further ill-will abroad, which would cost Japan more than the margin of safety was worth; while the army and navy ministers, caring little about foreign opinion and having little grasp of financial affairs, were ready to go to almost any length to insure what they conceived to be the country's needs. In the end, something of a compromise was reached; the army and navy got their funds, but only on the ground that new equipment was needed in order to keep pace with general technical advances in modern armaments; in return, the military promised that it would not embarrass the foreign ministry by measures and utterances tending to nullify efforts to improve Japan's foreign relations. The compromise was regarded as a victory for the military, and, as a result, the Saito cabinet lost much prestige and was weakened by a series of resignations. The blow that finally toppled it from power was an indiscretion by the vice-minister of finance, Kuroda Hideo, and other officials of that ministry who were arrested on charges of accepting bribes from the Teikoku Rayon Company. Since Saito had taken office as a supra-party man with the avowed purpose of eliminating corruption from the government, he could hardly remain as prime minister.

A new cabinet, formed in July, 1934, under Admiral Okada Keisuke, announced that it would follow a policy of moderation, but it was clear that the new prime minister was an ardent champion of a strong navy. For some time Japanese naval experts had been contending that the increased cruising radius of battleships and aircraft carriers had offset the advantages that Japan had gained in the fortification clause of the Five-Power Naval Treaty at the Washington Conference, and in discussions held at London in the autumn of 1934 the Japanese delegates demanded a common upper limit in tonnage, within which each country could build the type of war vessels that it felt were necessary for its security. When the demand was rejected by the British and American governments, the Japanese ambassador in Washington formally notified Secretary of State Cordell Hull of his government's abrogation of the naval agreements of the Washington and London conferences. As a high-ranking Japanese naval officer told Ambassador Grew, "No Japanese government which agreed to the present 5–5–3 ratio could survive, and no Japanese delegates who signed such a treaty could return to Japan and live."

Although the notification meant that naval limitations would expire in December, 1936, Japan continued to seek parity through negotiations. For example, in December, 1935, in accordance with the provisions of the Naval Treaty of 1930, additional discussions were held at the British capital; but when the Japanese delegation's demand for parity was once again refused, it walked out. After December, 1936, a new naval race began as Great Britain, the United States, and Japan sought to increase their naval power. With the greatest peacetime naval appropriations in American history, the Roosevelt administration aimed at increasing its margin of superiority over Japan, especially in capital ships; and Great Britain committed herself to unprecedented naval expenditures, which included funds for the rapid modernization of the base at Singapore.

The psychological impact of foreign policy problems on Japanese politics can hardly be exaggerated. Japan's "isolation" began at mid-decade, when her resignation from the League of Nations became effective and naval limitations expired. The Japanese military hammered away on the theme of "the coming international crisis" and insisted that there be complete unity so that the country could cope with its "life-and-death problems." The army, particularly, did not rest content with exerting pressure from behind the scenes but entered politics directly in a number of ways. It encouraged the formation of nationalist societies, and it began to organize political groups for officers and enlisted men, to acquaint them with "correct policy." Beginning in 1934, it also published large quantities of pamphlets intended for civilian as well as military consumption and devoted to a justification of armament expenditures, defenses of expansionist policy, and appeals for a "rebirth of the Japanese martial spirit."

The threat of an international crisis was actually an illusion. In the period following the aggression in Manchuria there was no serious challenge from the outside world to Japan's conquest. Whatever world public opinion might have been, it was never transformed into practical sanctions, either economic or military. The policies of the United States, most important to Japan, easily bear out this contention. The Roosevelt administration maintained the position of "watchful waiting," not surrendering on principles but doing nothing to defend them. The American government was preoccupied with combating economic depression by a program of economic and social reform, and the American people were in no mood for war. With regard to foreign policy, pacificism and isolationism dominated the American mood, and the American Congress, reflecting this sentiment, passed the Neutrality Act of 1935 to make it impossible for the country to be "dragged into another war." Among other things, the Act forbade the export of arms, ammunition, and other implements of war to any belligerent country. In the same period the Tydings-McDuffie Act, granting the Philippines their independence, was regarded by many astute political observers as an American withdrawal from East Asia. Prime Minister Neville Chamberlain of Great Britain noted prophetically in 1934 that the United States would make no agreement with his country to resist by force any action by Japan, short of an attack upon Hawaii. Later, in the spring of 1937, Chamberlain approached Hull on the possibility of an Anglo-American-Japanese agreement to preserve the peace of East Asia and to avert the danger of a two-front war, but Hull rejected the idea and added a scarcely veiled warning against any Anglo-Japanese accord that deviated from the principles of the Nine-Power Treaty of the Washington Conference. At the same time, however, he declined to state in advance what the United States would do in the event of further Japanese aggression.

Factionalism in the Army

While the army generals were strengthening their power within the government, they were unable to put an end to the division within their own establishment. In fact, there continued to be a basic polarization into two main groups, the radicals and the conservatives, which was based in part upon personal rivalries and ambitions but more importantly upon differences in outlook.

The radicals, often called the Kodoha (Imperial Way Faction), were for the most part officers of company grade, although included in their ranks were Generals Araki, Mazaki, Yanagawa, Hata, and Obata. Despite some differences of opinion reflecting the relative influence of Kita Ikki or the agrarian Gondo Seikyo, they wanted the army to use its power directly to destroy the political parties and the zaibatsu as initial steps in a thorough reconstruction of Japanese society. The conservative officers, or Toseiha (Control Faction), whose number included Generals Nagata, Minami, Matsui, Tatekawa, Watanabe, and Tojo, preferred to employ legal, nonterroristic methods to bring the political system and the capitalists under their direction. They hoped to preserve and control the existing bureaucracy, to unite political parties into a single-party system which they would dominate, and to render the imperial court officials subordinate to their will; and, once their political supremacy was assured, they felt that they would have little difficulty in winning over the zaibatsu by holding out the prospect of profitable contracts.

The two factions also had differences regarding foreign policy. The Kodoha thought that the army should concentrate all its energies on building up Manchukuo as a continental war base, in the likelihood of a conflict with the Soviet Union, and on establishing there the kind of political and economic order which they held up as an ideal at home. The Toseiha was equally intent on the exploitation of Manchukuo by the army, but it wanted also to establish an "autonomous regime" in north China and to penetrate Inner Mongolia. The conservative officers also planned to undermine Russian influence in Outer Mongolia and thus prevent any effective collaboration between China and the Soviet Union.

Army radicals continued to conspire against the government during 1933 and in the following few years. In July, 1933, while the trials of the Ketsumei-dan assassins were still in progress, a plot by the Shimpeitai (God-Sent Troops) to liquidate the entire Saito cabinet was uncovered on the very eve of its execution. Evidently the members of this society hoped to force martial law on Japan by creating such disorder and confusion that an army cabinet would be formed to carry out a Showa Reform (the reign name of the present emperor, who assumed the throne in 1926), involving basic changes in the constitution, laws, and political and economic institutions. The plotters were not put on trial until after the outbreak of hostilities in China in 1937, and not until March, 1941, were their sentences pronounced. The penalties asked by the prosecution ranged from one to five years, but all forty-four defendants were acquitted on the ground that they were attempting to uphold the emperor's sovereignty.

Another group of army radicals issued a pamphlet through the army press section in October, 1934, entitled "The Essence of National Defense and Proposals to Strengthen It," which advocated the abandonment of individualistic economic concepts and the establishment of a rigidly controlled, collective economy. The authors advanced the thesis that the existing economic system tended to serve individual interests rather than the general interests of the state; they claimed that the concentration of wealth in the hands of a small minority was responsible for the failure of small businesses and industries, strife between capital and labor, and general distress among the people, all of which upset the equilibrium of national life.

This army pamphlet rudely shocked conservative forces in Japanese society, especially the political parties and the zaibatsu, because they had begun to feel somewhat complacent when General Hayashi Senjuro replaced the outspoken Araki as army minister in January, 1934. Hayashi had at first been a neutral in the factional struggle that divided the army, but he was finally won over to the Toseiha point of view. After assuming office, he had striven to create the impression that order and discipline had been restored within the army and that the radical elements had been effectively checked; and although it appeared that an alliance of various conservative elements was in the making, it did not become firm in this period because of the many differences that still divided them. Despite the efforts of politicians like Matsuoka Yosuke to create a single political party to support the military, party leaders and the interests they represented continued to oppose such policies as expansion and increases in armaments. In fact, some of the attacks on the army and navy through interpellations in the house of representatives were the most direct and forceful that had occurred since the Manchurian incident. It was clear that there was still no unity in Japanese government and that political irresponsibility was at an all-time high. Saionji attempted to find a solution to this problem by the establishment of a special council of inner court officials and former prime ministers, but this body had no defined responsibility or legal status.

The conservative sentiment of the time can be gauged by the notorious attack upon Professor Minobe, an honored member of the house of peers and one of the officials on the civil service examination board. The attack began in February, 1935, with a speech in the house of representatives branding Minobe a traitor because his theories rejected the doctrine of the emperor's independent power and stressed the rights of the elected representatives of the people. On February 25 Minobe defended himself, arguing that the emperor was an organ of the state and that his sovereignty was limited. The matter might have ended at that point had not the army openly joined the controversy. On April 4 the inspector-general of military education, General Mazaki, issued directives to all army personnel calling attention to the duty of Japanese subjects to be loyal to the throne and emphasizing that the "organ theory" was incompatible with Japan's national polity.

The Minseito avoided taking a stand on the issue, but the Seiyukai officially branded the Minobe theory a danger to the Japanese state. Prime Minister Okada sought to ignore the controversy, but under pressure from the army and the Seiyukai he issued a statement in October announcing his cabinet's decision to stamp out the "organ theory." To this end it planned to investigate the views of professors as well as the content of university courses on the constitution, place a ban on the use of textbooks and other materials that were deemed undesirable, and rigidly enforce penalties against the publication and sale of proscribed books. By this time Minobe had been forced to resign his peerage, his emeritus professorship, and all other honors, and he barely survived an attempt on his life.

The Army Mutiny

When the Kodoha continued to be active in 1934 and 1935, General Hayashi, the apparent leader of the Toseiha, put much of the blame on General Mazaki, the inspector-general of military education; for example, he held Mazaki responsible for the controversial October, 1934, pamphlet. Thus in July, 1935, Hayashi forced the removal of Mazaki and the appointment of the conservative General Watanabe Jotaro. There was, in addition, a sweeping personnel shift by which the Toseiha sought to destroy the influence of the radicals.

The army radicals had been useful to the conservative generals, but the Toseiha realized that it had to regain prestige and inspire confidence in the army. It was generally known that the officer behind the reorganization was General Nagata Tetsuzan, director of the military affairs bureau of the army. Nagata and his colleagues wanted to impress the palace advisers, political leaders, and business circles with the fact that they had purged the army of undesirable elements and averted a complete collapse of discipline and morale. These efforts to placate civilian critics, while securing a greater degree of co-operation between the army and other political groups, were, nevertheless, dangerous, because the radicals now discharged their animosity not only against their former "enemies" but also against the conservative generals. Tokyo newspapers warned the public of the highly charged, if not explosive, atmosphere within the army, caused by the indignation of the pro-Mazaki elements.

The warnings proved true on August 12, 1935, when Lieutenant Colonel Aizawa Saburo, who had just received orders for transfer to Formosa, cut down Nagata with his sword in the war ministry building. Aizawa, a close friend of Mazaki, had previously urged Nagata to resign and had received his transfer order for the suggestion. The murder created a tremendous sensation. Army Minister Hayashi resigned in embarrassment, and other changes were quickly made in the military establishment in a desperate attempt to quiet the radicals. Aizawa's trial brought out once again the fact that the extremists were bent on national reconstruction. According to his testimony, Aizawa felt that the conservative generals were allied with politicians, bureaucrats, and businessmen in an effort to block reform of Japanese society. On May 7, 1936, the court sentenced Aizawa to death, and he was executed on July 3 of the same year. Although he was regarded as a patriot in many quarters, his fate was determined when subsequent extremist actions, especially the February, 1936, army mutiny, influenced the court.

In the winter of 1935–1936 the political parties made one last effort to strengthen their position within the framework of constitutional government. The leaders of the Seiyukai majority laid aside their factional quarrels long enough to propose a vote of nonconfidence in the Okada cabinet. The

573

government reacted immediately, dissolving the house of representatives and calling for general elections, which had not been held since 1932. The Japanese public went to the polls on February 20, 1936, and, as a result of their vote, the Minseito, winning 78 new seats, became the leading party in the house of representatives with a total of 205 members, while the Seiyukai, losing 68 seats, had its total cut to 174. Perhaps the most striking election result was the gain of the Shakai Taishuto from 3 seats to 18.

Since there were no really clear-cut issues before the Japanese people, it is difficult to interpret the election results. The Seiyukai had expected an easy victory, especially since most of its members had kept abreast of nationalist currents far more than the Minseito had; but it would be a mistake to interpret the election as a victory for parliamentary government as against military dictatorship, since support of "nationalism" was the dominant theme in all camps. Even the Shakai Taishuto, which had doubled its popular vote to a total of 518,000, attempted to exploit nationalist sentiments and reflected the tendency of many of its members to deny internationalist sentiments. The Minseito's success was largely a vote of confidence for the Okada cabinet and against the Seiyukai. Most of the Minseito candidates had been non-committal on fundamental matters and had campaigned mainly on their support of Okada, a nonparty man. Thus it can be said that the voters of Japan tended to support the more moderate elements within a nationalist framework. Perhaps more importantly the election indicated widespread political apathy, particularly in the urban areas; many people apparently felt that parties and elections were unimportant, and absenteeism from the polls was extremely high.

The election victory of the moderates precipitated an army mutiny in Tokyo. On February 26, units of the First Division, already under orders for transfer to Manchuria, attempted a *coup d'état* to establish a military government under the leadership of General Mazaki. In a statement left by groups of soldiers at each of the principal newspaper offices, the rebels alleged that the government had been drifting away from the true spirit of Japan and that it had usurped the prerogatives of the emperor. The leadership group behind the mutiny was composed largely of young officers below the rank of major, many of whom had been closely associated with Kita Ikki and his militant follower, Nishida Zei. Both Kita and Nishida opposed the hasty action, but, once it was under way, they did participate in minor capacities. Other civilian rightists joined in, not a few of whom were militant Nichiren Buddhists, and strong financial support came from the ambitious Seiyukai leader, Kuhara Fusano-suke, an ultranationalist of long standing.

The mutineers, with more than 1,400 soldiers under their command, carried out a series of assassinations directed against the conservatives who stood in the way of the national reconstruction of Japan. Among those killed were Saito Makoto, lord keeper of the privy seal and former prime minister,

Takahashi Korekiyo, who had only just returned to the cabinet as finance minister, and General Watanabe, inspector-general of military education. Admiral Suzuki Kantaro, grand chamberlain, was seriously wounded. The rebels had planned also to kill Okada, Saionji, and Makino Shinken, but all three escaped quite miraculously. In Okada's case, the assassins killed his brother-in-law by mistake. Following these blows, the insurgents seized the war ministry building, metropolitan police headquarters, the new diet building, the Peers Club, and the Sanno Hotel. For a period of three days the army authorities tried to find a solution that would avoid bloodshed, but finally, after the declaration of martial law, loyal troops, reinforced by tanks, took up positions to attack the insurgents should they not heed an imperial ultimatum to surrender. The rebels, having failed in their mission and in the face of the emperor's personal command, surrendered on terms arranged by General Mazaki, whom they trusted.

The radicals were this time not treated with the same forebearance and leniency as their predecessors. After their surrender they were given two hours to commit ceremonial suicide; this they refused, anticipating civil trials in which they hoped to stir up popular resentment against the government. The army, however, court-martialed the leaders of the mutiny, and on July 7 death sentences without appeal were handed down for thirteen officers and four civilians, including Kita and Nishida. The executions were carried out five days later. Five officers got life imprisonment, and many of lesser culpability got shorter prison terms. The army also transferred to the reserves those officers who had connections with the radicals, and both Araki and Mazaki retired.

In the end, the February 26 incident resulted in the destruction of the Kodoha as an organized group and firmly established Toseiha control over army policy. That the dominant conservative generals were determined to prevent any repetition of the incident was made clear by the unprecedented death sentences against army officers. Although the army had suffered a severe setback in public opinion after the outbreak of the mutiny, its prestige was quickly regained by the efficient and peaceful manner in which it restored order.

The Hirota Cabinet and the Quest for National Unity

Okada resigned as prime minister early in March, and Hirota Koki, a former nonparty foreign minister, was invited to form a cabinet. Hirota announced his determination to bring about national unity in fact as well as name, to form a strong cabinet, to respect parliamentary government by inviting party members to join his cabinet, and to select cabinet members who would inject new life and spirit into the government. But the army, regarding his cabinet choices as too liberal, refused to furnish a minister except on its own terms, which included the reduction of the number of party posts in the cabinet to two. Although Hirota was able to get the army to accept two posts for each of the major political parties, he capitulated to all other army demands, including the expansion of armaments—the cost of which had already increased from 442.8 million yen in 1930–1931 to approximately 1 billion yen in 1935–1936; the restoration of the active-service qualification for the army and navy ministries; the augmentation of economic controls; and additional supervision over public information. Finally, on March 9, Hirota, in a statement to the press outlining his basic policies, emphasized that, in view of the existing domestic and foreign situations, there should be a thorough reform of government and that diplomacy should be placed on a "positive, self-assertive, and self-reliant" basis if the nation was to weather the crisis. He promised sweeping national reforms and national policies to be planned and executed by a united government without any distinction as to political parties, the bureaucracy, or the military.

In August these generalities were defined more specifically when the cabinet approved the following "basic principles of national policy," originally drafted by the two service ministries:

1. Japan must strive to correct the aggressive policies of the great powers and to realize the spirit of the imperial way by a consistent policy of overseas expansion.
2. Japan must complete her defensive armament to secure the position of her empire as the stabilizing power in East Asia.
3. Japan should strive to eradicate the menace of the Soviet Union in the north in order to stabilize Japan-Manchukuo national defense and to promote sound economic development. Japan should also be prepared against Great Britain and the United States and attempt to bring about economic development by close co-operation between Japan, Manchukuo, and China. In achieving these objectives, Japan should pay due attention to friendly relations with other powers.
4. To further her plan to promote social and economic development in the South Seas and without arousing other powers, Japan should attempt to extend her strength by moderate and peaceful means.

Articles 3 and 4 reflected important differences between the army and navy. The former tended to regard the Soviet Union as its greatest enemy and looked northward on the continent of Asia for the protection of Japan's interests, while the navy inclined to expansion southward, even against the opposition of Great Britain and the United States. Although civil leaders tried to play off one service against the other, they ended by capitulating to both. The cabinet agreed that the army should endeavor to match Russian forces on the mainland and that the navy should develop strength equal to that of the American fleet in the Pacific Ocean.

Within the framework of the Hirota program there was much greater co-operation between the army and the zaibatsu. While still nervous about the ultimate plans of the army for control of industry, Japanese big business became increasingly reconciled to expansionist policies, in part because of the obstacles to peaceful penetration of foreign markets in the 1930's but more importantly because of the opportunities for profit in the industrialization programs sponsored by the military. On its part the army realized that it could not build up Japan's war potential without utilizing the skill and experience of the large companies. For example, the army's efforts to build up Manchukuo caused capital exports to rise from a total of 97,200,000 yen in 1932 to 431,000,000 yen in 1938. But Manchukuo's economic development created certain fundamental problems.

While the Japanese army strengthened its base in northeast Asia and the zaibatsu profited, Japan as a whole hardly benefited. A major portion of capital available for investment was diverted to Manchukuo with no prospect of any substantial immediate return; moreover, since Manchukuo's industrial development was based in large part on the desire of the Kwantung Army to make the area self-sustaining in case of war, it was not supplementary to, but was instead competitive with, the industries of Japan. It was clear that the economic development of Manchukuo would ultimately produce competition with Japanese industry in the home market or at least reduce the market for Japanese goods in the puppet state. Thus, when the zaibatsu hesitated to co-operate, the army had to turn to other sources of capital and technical competence. This was especially true in the case of competitive industries like metallurgy and chemicals, which the army was most anxious to develop in Manchukuo.

Perhaps the most important accomplishment of the Hirota cabinet was the inauguration of close co-operation with Germany. The army, fearful of the prospect of isolation, looked toward Germany for some sort of *rapprochement*, and one of the leading figures in this effort was General Oshima Hiroshi, military attaché at Berlin. In the autumn of 1935 Oshima informed his superiors by telegraph that Foreign Minister Ribbentrop had asked him to ascertain the views of the Japanese army with regard to the conclusion of a German-Japanese pact by which neither power would afford assistance to the Soviet Union should the other be involved in a war with her. With approval from Tokyo, Oshima conducted negotiations at Berlin during November and December which established the basic principles of the German-Japanese Anti-Comintern Pact. From the standpoint of the Japanese army the agreement was invaluable; it would provide Japan with allies in the struggle against communism and the Soviet Union, and it might also cause the Chinese government to be more receptive to Japan's offer of help against the Chinese communists in return for important economic concessions throughout China.

By the end of July, 1936, the army prevailed upon the cabinet to accede to the conclusion of the Anti-Comintern Pact, and the formal agreement, which was to be effective for five years with provision for renewal, was signed at Berlin on November 25, 1936. The published parts were merely a pledge by the two powers to aid each other in resisting international communism by the exchange of information regarding the activities of the Comintern and collaboration in preventive measures. They agreed, moreover, to invite other states to adopt defensive measures in the spirit of the pact or to take part in it. Although it was denied by both powers, a secret commitment provided that if either country were threatened or attacked by the Soviet Union without provocation, the other would not give relief to the Soviet Union and that the two would consult about measures to preserve their common interests. Furthermore, neither would conclude a political accord with the Soviet Union which did not conform to the spirit of the agreement, except with the consent of the other.

Although the anti-Comintern treaty was ratified by both powers, there was much opposition to it in both countries. In Japan it was denounced by political parties, financial circles, and others as a concrete example of secret diplomacy carried on with complete disregard for public opinion; and although opposition was not strong enough to prevent ratification, it was a factor in Hirota's subsequent downfall. In Germany the regular foreign ministry officials disapproved of the pact and refused to consider that it in any way committed Germany to support Japanese policy in China.

The German-Japanese *rapprochement* had important repercussions throughout the world, especially in the Soviet Union. Russian-Japanese relations had deteriorated rapidly after the establishment of Manchukuo, and hostilities had been avoided largely because of the Soviet Union's refusal to be drawn into war. Despite the sale of the Chinese Eastern Railway to Japan in March, 1935, the new common frontier between Russian and Japanese forces was the scene of numerous clashes. In fact, during the period of negotiations between Germany and Japan, the Soviet Union and Outer Mongolia signed a mutual security pact (March, 1936) under which, according to a statement by Stalin, an attack on the latter by Manchukuo, supported by Japan, would be considered an act of war on the Soviet Union itself. As for the Anti-Comintern Pact, the Russians denounced it as having the potential effect of fostering aggressive war on two continents and underscored the impossibility of achieving Soviet-Japanese amity in face of it. The Russians gave concrete evidence of this judgment by refusing to extend fishing privileges in Siberian waters on any long-term basis. In 1928 the two powers had signed a fisheries convention which only modified certain details of the 1907 agreement whereby Japanese fishermen had the right to operate in Russian Siberian waters and could rent canning sites on the Siberian coast. Negotiations for a new agreement had long been in progress, but news of the German-Japanese accord caused them to be terminated with Soviet approval of a mere one-year extension of the 1928 treaty. Japanese fishing interests were in a precarious position as a result.

Great Britain, France, and the United States regarded the Anti-Comintern Pact as a threat to the peace of the whole world, and all three suspected that there was more to it than had been announced. Nanking reacted by deciding to work more closely with the Soviet Union, although it continued to hope that Great Britain and the United States would check Japan's attempts to achieve her aims in China. As for the Chinese communists, it had the effect of accelerating their efforts to realize a united front against Japan.

Although the Japanese army worked quite successfully through Hirota's cabinet, there was still strong opposition to the idea of military dominance; moreover, by the beginning of 1937 there was much popular criticism of government policies, especially in the field of foreign affairs, and there was dissatisfaction with the rising cost of living, budget increases, and the pressure of taxes. Some of this sentiment was reflected in the dispute between Army Minister Terauchi Hisaichi and Hamada Kunimatsu, a Seiyukai member of the house of representatives. When the diet convened in December, 1936, General Terauchi demanded the establishment of a "controlled, unified state," and his contempt for the parties was so obvious and his browbeating tactics so ruthless that some of the more courageous members of the house of representatives could not remain silent. Hamada denounced the army for attempting to force a dictatorship upon the country, and in an emotion-laden exchange with Terauchi the aging member held his ground. Thereupon Terauchi accused Hamada of holding the army in contempt and demanded an apology. Hamada retorted that if his denunciation could be construed as contempt, he would apologize by committing ceremonial suicide, but he demanded that Terauchi promise to do the same should his accusations prove groundless. Terauchi pressed Hirota to dissolve the lower house; and when the prime minister would not comply, he resigned. The army thereupon refused to appoint an officer to succeed him as army minister, and the cabinet fell on February 23, 1937.

On February 25 the civilian advisers to the emperor, a small, informal group called *jushin* (chief retainers), composed of imperial court officials and former prime ministers and headed by the aged Saionji, nominated General Ugaki Kazushige, who represented the most conservative elements within the army, for the prime ministership. They felt that he would have the support of political parties and business, but Ugaki found that he could not form a cabinet since the army would not nominate an officer to take the post of army minister. Most of the generals thought that Ugaki was too close to the Minseito and could not be trusted to carry out their program for the establishment of a "total national defense structure." They remembered that he had consented to the reduction of the army's size in 1925 and that he had been most responsible for the cancellation of the March, 1931, *coup d'état*. Finally, on February 29, Ugaki had to admit his inability to complete a cabinet in the face of the army's determination to block the formation of any cabinet it deemed inimical to its interests. This stand by the army proved that its power could not be successfully challenged by civilians. And the jushin, without any defined constitutional status and preferring a course of compromise rather than opposition, capitulated to the army's wishes.

The jushin were forced to appoint General Hayashi Senjuro as prime minister, and in his first public statement he asked for the abandonment of the principle of party government, although he promised to admit party members to his cabinet provided they would renounce their party allegiance. When both the Minseito and the Seiyukai protested Hayashi's stand, he dissolved the house of representatives, and, whenever possible, he deliberately struck blows at the parties, hoping to weaken their will to resist. His goal was the creation of a single party that would not have the power to oppose or censure the government but would merely give it unquestioned support. He was willing to maintain the Meiji Constitution, but, within its framework, he wanted authoritarian government under the control of the military. Like many militarists and their allies within the higher echelons of the bureaucracy, he thought that if the house of representatives were dissolved several times in succession the parties would soon lose their will to fight and would give way before the one-party movement.

In Japan's last prewar competitive election, which was held at the end of April, 1937, the Minseito maintained its position as the strongest party in the lower house despite a reduction in total number of seats to 179. The Seiyukai won 174 seats, and the Shakai Taishuto, which branded Hayashi as a fascist, doubled its representation to a total of 36. It is true that the army, without its own party in the field, could hardly win an election, but the results were considered a strong rebuke to Hayashi. He remained in power, however, until June 3, by which time it was clear that another leader was needed in order to maintain in some fashion the balance of power between the army, the bureaucracy, and the political parties.

29   *The Road to War*

A so-called "national" government was formed on June 4, 1937, by Prime Minister Konoye Fumimaro, who a year earlier had declined the post on grounds of ill health but now accepted in the hope of effecting political unity. The various political forces found him acceptable, and although his cabinet was dominated by the army minister, General Sugiyama Hajime, and the navy minister, Admiral Yonai Mitsumasa, the public received it with enthusiasm. Konoye appointed several party members to cabinet posts as individuals, but he did not ask the parties for their official support.

The most important problem that he faced immediately after assuming office concerned the designs of the Kwantung Army against China. Although Konoye agreed that there was a need to expand Japan's interests on the Asian mainland, he did not want the Kwantung Army to force the hand of the cabinet as it had often done since 1931. The army general staff concluded, moreover, that in view of the increasing power of the Soviet Union in East Asia and of the growing national feeling in China, the Japanese forces stationed on the continent should do their best to avoid trouble. On the other hand, General Tojo Hideki, who succeeded to the post of chief of staff of the Kwantung Army in March, 1937, warned of the danger of a Sino-Soviet coalition and suggested that Japan strike the first blow against China. Although Tojo's advice did not find favor with the army minister or the chief of the general staff, the Kwantung Army went ahead and precipitated the crisis that followed the Marco Polo Bridge incident of July.

The Konoye Cabinet and the New National Structure

When the Konoye cabinet announced its program on July 24, 1937, which included promises to create "a new nationalist structure of totalitarian government" and to establish "an East Asian economic bloc comprising Japan, Manchukuo, and China," it was clear that the army was still the dominant force in government. Although Konoye sought to reinforce the cabinet with councilors representing various important civilian factions and parties in an effort to balance the role of the army, his attempt had the opposite effect. In October, 1937, he created the cabinet advisory council, composed of outstanding representatives of the army (including even moderates like General Ugaki), the political parties, the bureaucracy, and the business world, to deliberate upon important national problems; but the council, which drew much of its personnel from virtually every ministry, proved to be a medium for collaboration between the military and the bureaucracy and ultimately for army-bureaucratic contol of the national administration. The power of the military was increased further in the following month when the wartime imperial headquarters was established to co-ordinate military and naval activities with other government operations. Lastly, a large measure of control in Japan as well as on the continent came to be vested in the China Development Board, which the army also dominated.

For the most part the members of the diet faithfully voted for government bills based on the national defense plan which the general staff had compiled in 1936; this consisted of a five-year program for the expansion of the armaments industry, a six-year program for the expansion and modernization of the armed forces, and a five-year plan for the economic and military development of Manchukuo. The tremendous increase in government expenditures which these projects necessitated was paid for by higher taxes and by domestic loans. The people of Japan simply were forced to provide the government with an ever-mounting share of the nation's income at the expense of their standard of living.

Imports were limited more and more to materials essential for war purposes. Under the Foreign Exchange Control Law of March, 1933, the finance ministry had the power to control all foreign-exchange transactions involving imports in excess of 30,000 yen per month, and in July, 1937, a revision of the law reduced the limit to 1,000 yen per month and extended the licensing provisions to include the remittance of dividends and payments for foreign service. In autumn, 1937, the government published the first list of prohibited imports and enforced it strictly. Within a year Japan's adverse trade balance was converted into a surplus; but despite this significant gain, Japan was faced with a serious economic dilemma. She needed exports beyond the so-called "yen bloc," comprising Japan, Manchukuo, and occupied China, to help finance essential imports because of her deficiencies in natural resources; but to maintain and extend exports, a substantial portion of imports had to be allocated to the export industries. Thus, the more that Japan emphasized imports for war purposes, the more difficult it became to finance them. It was possible to finance necessary war materials to some extent through large gold shipments, but this practice steadily reduced the gold reserve toward the danger point. In August, 1938, the Japanese government began imposing the "link system," under which foreign exchange was made available for the importation of raw materials to manufacture goods for export; however, the manufacture of goods for domestic consumption was limited to the use of domestic materials. The imposition of this system necessitated considerable internal readjustment and a constant enlargement of the area of government control over the economy.

New economic control legislation, like the Temporary Capital Adjustment Law and the Revised Manufacturers Association Act of 1937, culminated in the National Mobilization Law enacted on March 24, 1938, the very last day of the diet session. There had been much opposition to the bill, but it was overcome when Prime Minister Konoye promised that it would be applicable only in time of extreme emergency and that the cabinet would appoint a majority of diet members to the national mobilization council, which would be responsible for drafting imperial ordinances to adapt the law to changing conditions.

The National Mobilization Law was a *carte blanche* delegation of wartime legislative powers to the cabinet, enabling it to legislate by ordinance even in areas of individual rights and freedoms. The passage of the act was a virtual death sentence for parliamentary government, since for all practical purposes the legislative body was superseded by the bureaucracy; moreover, it was a triumph for the military, who regarded the law as the instrumentality by which they could legally create a totalitarian structure. The only attraction for Japanese businessmen was that the law did provide for profits at certain rates as well as compensation for losses. Two months later, in May, 1938, the cabinet found it necessary to invoke parts of the law to secure greater control over industry in general, and subsequently it issued ordinances prohibiting labor and agricultural disputes and providing for compulsory mediation in both cases. As the hostilities in China continued, the cabinet invoked the law again and again, despite substantial criticism by the public.

Government controls went far beyond the economic sphere. In autumn, 1937, the cabinet sponsored a movement for "total national spiritual mobilization to whip public opinion into shape for the holy war in China." The army, education, and home ministries co-operated to establish the headquarters of the movement, and they persuaded nearly one hundred civilian organizations to carry on a propaganda program throughout the entire country. In September, 1938, the army expanded its own press section into a general public information bureau.

Also of grave concern to the army was the deplorably poor physical condition of the nation's youth, revealed in the annual physical examinations of military conscripts; so in January, 1938, the government established a welfare ministry, responsible for protecting and advancing the health of the people and thus strengthening the nation's military potential, and in March, 1938, it made military training compulsory in all schools. One of the first achievements of the new ministry was the National Health Insurance Law, which was passed by the diet and became effective on July 1, 1938, despite the organized opposition of the Japan Medical Association.

The China Incident and the Western Powers

The basic diplomatic problems of the Konoye ministry were related to the China incident. In July, 1937, the United States was asked by China to mediate her differences with Japan; but Washington, though it did urge restraint upon Tokyo and Nanking, refused the request on the ground that an American offer to mediate would only anger the Japanese government and assist it in its bid for greater support at home. Great Britain offered her good offices on July 15, but Japan replied that she had not given up hope for a local settlement. On July 20 Great Britain approached the United States regarding a joint recommendation to China and Japan to suspend all further troop movements and a joint proposal for a final settlement of their differences, but Secretary of State Cordell Hull refused on the ground that such an action would enrage the Japanese militarists and American isolationists. In May, 1937, the American Congress had passed a revised and strengthened Neutrality Act, which empowered the president to apply an arms embargo whenever he found that a state of war existed between foreign nations or whenever civil strife was likely to endanger the peace of the United States.

President Roosevelt chose not to invoke the neutrality legislation, for he felt that an embargo would hurt China more than Japan; moreover if the United States declared that China and Japan were at war, a step from which both nations were holding back, the action might later be regretted, since wars are harder to end than incidents. Roosevelt merely issued a statement on September 14 to the effect that merchant vessels owned by the American government would not be permitted to transport arms, ammunition, or implements of war to China or Japan and that any merchant vessel under the American flag which attempted to transport such articles would do so at its own risk.

In September China appealed to the League of Nations as she had done in 1931. The Far East advisory committee, on which the United States had been represented by a nonvoting member since 1931, considered the appeal, found Japan guilty of violating the Nine-Power Treaty of the Washington Conference and the Kellogg-Briand Pact, and recommended that the signatory powers of the Nine-Power Treaty be requested to consult together and find a solution that would bring the hostilities to a conclusion. The report and recommendation were adopted by the Assembly on October 6, but what action the League of Nations might take against Japan depended to a large extent on the attitude of the United States. Great Britain and France, faced with the growing power and ambitions of Germany and Italy, could not risk involvement in East Asia against Japan without assurances of American cooperation. On October 5 President Roosevelt had publicly suggested a "quarantine" of aggressor nations and implied that the United States should join a concerted plan of opposition to Japan and Germany. The adverse reaction to his speech in the United States led the powers at Geneva to rule out any form of pressure against Japan.

The representatives of nineteen powers finally convened at Brussels on November 3, 1937, to discuss the China incident. Japan refused to attend, but her view that the matter was outside the scope of the Nine-Power Treaty and was something for China and her to settle directly was adequately presented by Italy. Without the direct representation of Japan, the exercise of mediatory or conciliatory functions proved impossible. Germany would not appoint a delegate, which increased the alarm of Great Britain and France; and the Soviet Union, while not in attendance, stated that she would join in any action that Great Britain and the United States were prepared to take, although she was careful not to propose any concrete measures against Japan. When the Chinese delegate raised the question of aid to his country and economic sanctions against Japan, he received no support. The conference adjourned on November 24 with the delegates branding Japan as a treaty-breaker and an aggressor and expressing the belief that, although satisfactory agreement could not be achieved by direct negotiations between China and Japan, it was advisable to suspend the conference until deliberations could be resumed advantageously.

While the powers avoided intervention in the political issues of the China incident, they did seek to defend their established national interests in China when Japan brought pressure upon them. For example, they sought reparations for damage to property or injury to persons, which were inevitable as a result of Japan's war operations. The Japanese disclaimed responsibility for much of the damage on the plea of military necessity; but when representations were made vigorously and claims substantiated after investigation, Tokyo usually gave assurances against the repetition of such actions and on occasion paid reparations. For example, on December 12, 1937, the U.S.S. "Panay," a river gunboat carrying members of the American embassy staff, was moving up the Yangtze from Nanking together with Standard Oil Company boats carrying American refugees; Japanese shore batteries were apparently under orders to fire indiscriminately on all vessels, and in an unexpected barrage the "Panay" was sunk and its survivors were strafed by Japanese machine-gun fire. The Japanese ambassador at Washington apologized immediately, promised full indemnities for all the losses and appropriate measures against those responsible for the incident, and stated that strict orders had been issued to prevent similar occurrences. The Japanese apology was accepted by the United States, and what was potentially an explosive situation was settled amicably in less than a month. It later became known that the whole affair was precipitated by the local Japanese military commander, General Hashimoto Kingoro, who apparently had hoped to provoke war between Japan and the Western powers in order to facilitate a "Showa Reform." During the course of the attack on the "Panay" the British gunboat "Ladybird" had also been damaged, and the Japanese made a similar apology and pledge.

In 1938 the United States began to take a stronger stand against Japan. The widespread and indiscriminate bombing of Chinese civilians by the Japanese army incensed American public opinion, and on June 11, 1938, Secretary Hull condemned the practice and "the indirect military encouragement that was given by American manufacturers." On July 1 the State Department notified manufacturers and exporters of aircraft that the government was strongly opposed to the sale of airplanes and aeronautical equipment to countries whose armed forces were using airplanes for attacks on civilian populations. Thereafter American businessmen observed a "moral embargo," which was extended in December, 1939, to include materials essential to aircraft manufacture and also plans, plants, and technical information for the production of high-octane gasoline. Beginning in 1938, the American government also adopted a policy of informally discouraging the extension of credit by American nationals to Japan.

In its diplomacy regarding China the United States objected to specific Japanese practices, such as the institution of exchange controls and the modification of the tariff in areas under Japanese occupation, which she held were violations of the principle of equal commercial opportunity. On October 6 a note from Ambassador Grew to the Japanese government hinted that the continuance of these practices might affect the status of the Treaty of Commerce of 1911 between the United States and Japan. Since it feared that failure to renew the treaty might ultimately lead to the imposition of economic sanctions, the Konoye cabinet replied that Japan would respect the open door. However, after the fall of Canton and Hankow, on November 3, 1938, Konoye boldly listed Japanese aims as follows:

1. The liquidation of Western imperialism in China and ultimately in Southeastern Asia, and its replacement by Japan's economic domination.
2. The economic co-ordination of Japan, Manchukuo, and China with a closed-door policy to non-Japanese trade and investment except through the medium of Japan.
3. Sino-Japanese co-operation to eliminate communism in East Asia, to freeze the Russian position in the north, and bring about the elimination of Russia from the area east of Lake Baikal.

The Western powers replied to Konoye's proclamation of Japan's "New Order in East Asia." An American note of December 31, 1938, defended the Washington Conference agreements and stated that Japan had no right to prescribe the terms and conditions of a new order in areas not under its sovereignty. Shortly thereafter Great Britain supported the American contention in a similar note to Japan on January 14, 1939, and France did the same on January 17, 1939.

This stand in opposition to the new order was reinforced by economic assistance to China. The United States, through the Export-Import Bank, established a credit for China of $25,000,000, much of which was used for vehicles and fuel on the Burma Road. Later the United States increased this credit to $50,000,000, and in total, down to November 30, 1940, she provided Export-Import Bank loans amounting to $120,000,000. In addition, she made available to China a sum of $68,000,000 for stabilization of the dollar-yuan rate of exchange. In December, 1938, Great Britain granted credits to China in the amount of £450,000 for the purchase of motor trucks essential for the movement of war supplies over the Burma Road, and she also extended a currency stabilization fund of £5,000,000. Hoping to influence American and British public opinion, Japan retaliated by threatening that economic warfare might lead to actual war.

Relations with the Soviet Union and Germany

One of the most important influences on Japanese foreign policy in this period was the successful effort of the Soviet Union to improve her relations with China. Negotiations undertaken in the spring of 1937 led to the conclusion of a pact on August 21, 1937, by which the two nations agreed to refrain from aggression against each other and pledged that if either nation were subjected to attack, the other would refrain from extending aid to the aggressor and would refuse to enter into any agreement which might be used by the aggressor to the disadvantage of the nation under attack.

Thereafter Japan was quite concerned about possible armed intervention in China by the Soviet Union, especially in 1938, when the Japanese army was operating in central China and was suffering from ammunition shortages. Although the Soviet Union did not intervene on the Chinese side, she did provide China with economic and military assistance. She arranged three loans, amounting in total to $250,000,000; moreover, she sent tanks, trucks, planes, arms, and ammunition in exchange for partial payments in tungsten, tin, antimony, and tea. The Russian government also dispatched instructors and pilots with their planes, established aviation schools at Urumchi and Chengtu, and built a sizable air base at Anchow, and it attached Russian officers to Chinese field headquarters as tactical advisers. The Russian personnel —who were constantly rotated to give experience to as many as possible— remained in China until the summer of 1938, when they were withdrawn because of the menace of war in Europe.

These Russian actions were an important factor in the Japanese decision to undertake no further advance in China after the autumn of 1938 and to endeavor to achieve their ends by political and diplomatic rather than military means. The army, moreover, was anxious to limit its expenditure of men and materials in China, since it was planning to attain a position of readiness for war with the Soviet Union by about 1940, several years before the Russians should complete their economic and military expansion program in Siberia.

For some time there had been border clashes between Russian and Japanese troops. As early as the winter of 1935–1936 there was a skirmish along the frontier between Manchukuo and Outer Mongolia, and in July, 1937, there was another on the Amur River between Blagoveshchensk and Khabarovsk. In the latter incident the Japanese forces sank two Russian gunboats and occupied two small islands which the Soviet Union had claimed. But perhaps the most serious clash occurred in July, 1938, when Japanese troops attempted to force the Russians to withdraw from a disputed area near the Korean port of Wonsan. Superior Russian strength forced the Japanese to accept a truce, and in August the two powers agreed to establish a bilaterial commission to define the border more closely.

The China incident also had important repercussions on Japan's relations with the Axis powers. Germany, because of her own commercial ambitions, wanted to avoid antagonizing China, but she agreed with Italy—which had joined the Anti-Comintern Pact in November, 1937—not to assist China and recalled the military mission that had been advising Chiang K'ai-shek. But until the outbreak of war in Europe in 1939, Germany did continue to sell military equipment to the Chinese government in order to gain much-needed foreign exchange and valuable strategic materials like tin and wolfram. Germany, moreover, sought to use her good offices to arrange a peace settlement in China; and when Japan terminated her own initial efforts to negotiate peace in January, 1938, Germany pointed out to Japan that the continuation of hostilities was draining strength that might be needed against the Soviet Union. Italian-Japanese relations were based generally on mutual recognition of each other's interests. For example, in November, 1936, Japan closed her legation in Ethiopia, thus according *de facto* recognition to the new "Roman Empire," and at the same time Italy stationed a consul-general in Mukden, which was the equivalent of *de facto* recognition of Manchukuo.

Despite their differences over China, Germany, Italy, and Japan began in the summer of 1938 to consider seriously the idea of converting the Anti-Comintern Pact into a political and military alliance. Negotiating through General Oshima, the military attaché at Berlin, and Ambassador Shiratori Toshio in Rome, the Konoye cabinet made known its willingness to discuss a pact directed against the Soviet Union; but Germany and Italy wanted a pact that would apply to either the Soviet Union or the Western powers, or both. When the Japanese army generals put pressure on the Konoye cabinet to go along with Germany and Italy, and when a number of admirals, still insistent upon an advance south, joined them, Konoye simply avoided making a decision; but it was already apparent that his days in office were numbered.

Toward the end of 1938 Konoye had made up his mind to resign because he had been unable to settle the China incident through negotiations and because he had failed to resolve the issues of the Axis pact and the totalitarian single-party system, both of which divided Japanese political forces. There was a great deal of opposition to the single-party idea, and in fact Admiral Suetsugu Nobumasa, the home minister, had made himself extremely unpopular in the house of representatives because of his vigorous advocacy of it. Konoye himself opposed totalitarian methods and the Axis alignment, but he preferred to take the line of least resistance, to procrastinate as long as possible, and to lay down the burden of office when evasion was no longer practicable. After the fall of Canton and Hankow, he felt that his resignation would not have serious repercussions, and toward the end of 1938 he reached an understanding with Hiranuma Kiichiro, president of the privy council, to succeed him as prime minister.

Hiranuma, who completed the formation of his cabinet on January 5, 1939, was an ardent nationalist whose earlier activities indicated that he might be expected to strengthen the position of the army at home even though he was not a military man. But, contrary to expectations, the prime minister preferred government by an oligarchy which would formulate policy on the basis of discussion and compromise between the various ruling groups.

The Hiranuma and Abe Cabinets and War in Europe

When the Japanese continued to put pressure on Western interests in China, especially on the British concession at Tientsin, and began to expand south with the occupation of Hainan Island in February and the Spratley Islands in March, 1939, the American government took a stronger line in its diplomacy. On July 10 Secretary of State Hull called in the Japanese ambassador to tell him that while the protection of specific rights and interests was important to the United States, a more decisive consideration was that the whole of China and the South Pacific should not be "Manchukuo-ized" by a process of lawless violence, treaty-breaking, and military conquest. And on July 26 the United States notified Japan that she did not plan to renew the Treaty of Commerce of 1911, the most-favored-nation clause of which had legally stood in the way of economic discrimination against Japan. Since termination required six months' notice, all legal obstacles to American economic sanctions against Japan would be removed by January, 1940.

Tokyo made excited efforts to find out what would happen when the treaty expired, but Hull would give no enlightenment. He wanted to keep the Japanese guessing in order to secure some relaxation of the pressure on the British; moreover, he did not want to take a stand until Washington had a clearer view of the European situation. Within the Japanese government Hull's attitude strengthened the desire to secure access to raw materials in China or elsewhere, which would free Japan from her dependence upon American supplies; and disputes regarding the military alliance with Germany and Italy were intensified.

Pressures for the transformation of the Anti-Comintern Pact into a military alliance were becoming stronger. The Japanese army endorsed the idea, and both Germany and Italy were anxious to make the change before they embarked on fresh moves in Europe which would arouse Anglo-French hostility. But within the Japanese government the opponents of a full alliance held their ground, and throughout the spring and summer of 1939 the Hiranuma cabinet engaged in constant wrangling over drafts of an alliance. Even hints of a possible German-Russian nonaggression pact or a possible Anglo-Russian accord had no effect. The basic points at issue were, first, was the pact to apply only in case of war with the Soviet Union or also with others, and, second, was the pact to be an unconditional military alliance. Foreign Minister Arita and other civilian leaders stood firm against any obligation that might bring Japan into war with the United States or Great Britain, while the army and their civilian nationalist allies worked to stir up popular feeling against both powers. Hiranuma himself preferred to avoid a final and irretrievable commitment to the Axis powers, although he was willing to use the threat of it to secure United States and British acceptance of Japan's policy in China. The final decision, made on June 5, in which the

589

navy reluctantly concurred and which the emperor approved in fear of an army revolt, was that Japan would promise to enter a war at once if the Soviet Union were the enemy, but in other cases Japan wanted the right to determine her own course.

The Japanese army continued its probing of the Russian defense network in Siberia in the summer of 1939, and in the Nomohan district east of the Khalka River and Lake Buir the Japanese fought with Russian troops from May through August. The hostilities involved the use of aircraft, artillery, and tanks; and, according to Russian figures, Japanese-Manchukuoan casualties exceeded 50,000 while Russian-Mongolian losses were hardly more than 9,000. The Japanese acknowledged at least 18,000 casualties within the Kwantung Army. After the announcement of the German-Russian Nonaggression Pact in Europe, a cease-fire was arranged on September 16, which provided that the frontier, the ostensible cause of the fighting, was to be determined by a boundary commission; and the incident was finally settled in August, 1940, in accordance with the Russian claims.

The German-Russian accord, concluded on August 23, 1939, was a tremendous shock to Japan. Hitler wanted to attack Poland at the end of August, and in preparation he decided to come to terms with Stalin. He hoped that the pact would deter Great Britain and France from coming to the aid of Poland; even if it did not, it would free Germany from the threat of a two-front war, since Hitler counted on crushing Poland quickly. Japanese hesitations regarding a military alliance strengthened Hitler's determination to throw Japan over and reach an agreement with the Russians, who made it very clear that they would expect Germany to cease siding with Japan and to influence Tokyo to improve its relations with the Soviet Union. Hitler complied, and throughout the remainder of the year and into 1940 he tried to persuade Japan to conclude a nonaggression pact with the Soviet Union.

The German-Russian pact was a severe blow to the Japanese army and other pro-Axis elements; and since it destroyed the whole basis of Japanese policy toward Europe and made Japan look foolish, it forced the resignation of the Hiranuma cabinet on August 28. In a statement clarifying the reasons for his decision, Hiranuma explained that the pact had made it necessary to abandon all existing foreign policies and formulate new ones to cope with the extremely complex, if not baffling, situation that had arisen in Europe. He concluded that this could best be achieved by effecting a change in government. General Abe Nobuyuki, a politically inexperienced retired general, succeeded as prime minister, largely because he was the only candidate acceptable to the army and civilian leaders; and in a matter of days he had to develop Japan's foreign policy in consideration of the outbreak of war in Europe. On September 1, 1938, German troops began pouring into Poland, and on September 3 Great Britain and France declared war on Germany.

Although the war in Europe made Great Britain and France more susceptible to Japanese pressure in China, the United States remained firmly opposed to any settlement that would violate the open door or China's integrity. In November, 1939, Great Britain and France approached the United States with the suggestion of a compromise peace between China and Japan "on a basis which would be fair and equitable to both sides, but with the realization on the part of China and Japan that each side would have to make concessions"; but Hull refused to consider such a policy. He continued to hope that the Japanese people would grow weary of the struggle in China and that resistance to army domination would spread, causing a return to power of the leaders of the 1920's.

Within the American government, however, there was much discussion concerning the question of whether or not to impose economic sanctions on Japan. Although in September, 1939, Roosevelt had asked businessmen to cease exporting eleven raw materials which the United States was stockpiling in the event of war, there had been no decision at that time to use sanctions against Japan. Washington continued to maintain a wait-and-see attitude, but it intimated that, after the termination of the 1911 trade treaty, anything might happen. In December Ambassador Grew informed Washington that economic sanctions would not cause Japan to give up her program in China but would arouse her people to fight harder than before. Meanwhile, the Abe government did everything possible to maintain friendly relations with the United States and went so far as to give categorical assurance that Japan had no intention of expelling Americans from China and that the incidents giving rise to this suspicion had been unavoidable accidents. It emphasized that Japanese soldiers had been ordered to try, in every way possible, to protect American property and citizens in China.

The Abe ministry fell, however, in January, 1940, because of its inability to improve Japan's relations with the United States, especially with regard to the commercial treaty. Since this circumstance was certain to cause critical discussion or attacks when the diet convened, the army precipitated the fall of the cabinet by forcing the resignation of the army minister. Abe was succeeded on January 15, 1940, by Admiral Yonai Mitsumasa, who was regarded as a moderate, friendly to the United States. Yonai was also known to be a staunch opponent of the alliance with Germany, as was his foreign minister, Arita. However, through General Oshima at Berlin, Ribbentrop was endeavoring to convince Japan that Germany's pact with Russia would be advantageous; he argued that it would make possible a quick German victory over Great Britain and that this, in turn, would open the South Pacific to Japan. Ribbentrop also promised to mediate between Japan and the Soviet Union.

The Yonai Cabinet and Southeast Asia

In February, 1940, Japan began to put pressure on the Netherlands East Indies government for repeal or modification of restrictions on Japanese im-

591

ports and exports and for an expansion of Japanese enterprises there. Later, in April, in anticipation of the German invasion of the Netherlands, Foreign Minister Arita expressed his deep concern over any development, political or economic, that might affect the status quo of the Netherlands East Indies from the standpoint of the maintenance of the peace and stability of East Asia. What he meant was that Japan did not want Great Britain to take over the Indies. The Dutch authorities, who had delayed answering Japan's February requests, now gave assurances that, no matter what happened in Europe, the economic relationship between the Indies and Japan would be continued. Nor would they seek any nation's protection or intervention.

Arita's diplomacy caused the United States to declare that Japanese intervention in the Netherlands East Indies or any alteration of the status quo by other than peaceful means would be prejudicial to the cause of stability, peace, and security in the entire Pacific Ocean area. But when France suggested that Great Britain and the United States join her in reminding the Japanese that at the time of the 1921 Four-Power Treaty the signatories had promised to respect Dutch rights in the Pacific, Hull refused on the ground that he preferred to take separate action. It was clear that the United States was unwilling to make any gesture that might have to be supported by force. For example, President Roosevelt did not respond to Prime Minister Churchill's request in May that he send naval forces to Singapore; nor would Roosevelt state what he would do if Japan moved against the European colonies in Southeast Asia and the Pacific.

Although Arita denied that Japan had territorial designs in the south, Japan increased her pressure on the Indies government; and in fact, on May 18, she asked for a written promise that no measures be taken to hamper the export to Japan of a specified amount of thirteen raw materials, including bauxite and oil in far larger amounts than she had previously obtained. The Japanese requests amounted to about one-seventh of the total production of the Indies, but this was only about one-fifth of what Japan needed. More ominous, however, was the demand that the Indies accept a general economic agreement. On June 6 the Dutch promised to provide more essential raw materials, but they refused to let the Japanese obtain a larger place in the economic life of the islands or control a larger part of their resources.

The successive conquests by Germany of Denmark, Norway, Belgium, the Netherlands, and France by June, 1940, and the German threat to invade the British Isles inevitably directed Japan's attention to the possibility of obtaining immediately what had been an ultimate objective, namely, the seizure of empire in Southeast Asia. The Japanese army became convinced that the golden opportunity for securing the rich natural resources of that area had arrived. France was neutralized by German power, the Netherlands could put up only a token defense of the Indies, Great Britain's hands were tied by the European war, and the United States, in the opinion of the extremists, dared not challenge Japan while Hitler talked of conquering the Western Hemisphere. Beyond these considerations there was the fear that Germany might attempt to include within her spoils of victory the Asian colonies of the defeated European nations.

The Japanese generals felt that Japan should lose no time in staking out her claims in Southeast Asia against all comers, including Germany, if need be; and thereafter Japan's diplomacy was more active in that area. On June 12 she concluded an agreement with Thailand which provided for mutual respect of territory, exchange of information, and consultation on questions of mutual interest; and on June 20, three days after France had asked Germany for an armistice in Europe, she forced France to accept demands that the border between Tonking and China be closed and that Japan have the right to keep military observers in Indochina to guarantee that war materials would not be sent into China.

In a radio broadcast on June 29 Foreign Minister Arita attempted to clarify Japan's position with regard to an "East Asian Co-Prosperity Sphere." He declared: "The countries of East Asia and the region of the South Seas are geographically, historically, racially, and economically very closely related to each other. They are destined to co-operate and minister to one another's needs for the common well-being and prosperity and to promote the peace and progress of their regions." He called attention to the need "to establish a righteous peace in each of the various regions and then establish collectively a just peace for the whole world." He emphasized that "the destiny of these regions is a matter of grave concern to Japan in view of her mission and responsibility as the stabilizing force in East Asia." Arita concluded by stating that the extension of the Japanese sphere was to be achieved by peaceful means. His attempt to find a middle course actually earned for him the criticism of both the American government, which was surprised by the boldness of his concept, and the Japanese army, which thought that Arita's bold talk lacked real vigor.

The opposition of the Japanese army ultimately forced the collapse of the Yonai ministry. In an important series of conferences, beginning on July 12, between officials of the foreign, army, navy, and finance ministries, Yonai objected to the plans of the army to effect radical political and economic reforms in order to create a "national defense state," and he emphasized that it was the function of the government as a whole to determine national policies in consideration of domestic and international conditions, about which the military services were not always well informed. He did agree with the conferees, however, to speed up mobilization preparations for a south China campaign, which would involve an advance into northern Indochina and the occupation of Hong Kong should Great Britain collapse. Circumstances made more acceptable the idea of a complete alliance with Germany and a *rapprochement* with the Soviet Union, but, despite the army's prodding, the conferees would not go that far. They decided that Japan's policy was to secure German recognition of the fact that Southeast Asia was within Japan's sphere of interest, while in return Japan was to support German policy in Europe and West Asia, take steps as far as possible to harass Great Britain in East Asia, and work more closely with Germany to deter the United States from interfering in Europe. But, for the time being, Japan was to resist proposals that she enter the war. The army generals were dissatisfied with Yonai's refusal to support the establishment of a national defense structure and to develop a firmer military alliance with Germany, and they became convinced that they must get rid of him. When Yonai refused to capitulate under pressure, they forced the resignation of the army minister; and since they refused to appoint a successor, the prime minister tendered the resignation of the entire cabinet on July 16.

The Second Konoye Cabinet and the National Defense State

An alliance of militarists and high-ranking officials in the bureaucracy secured the appointment of Konoye as prime minister in another attempt to establish a truly national government. Although the emperor had not wanted to see Yonai overthrown and showed some resentment, he dared not take an open stand against the army; and the aged Saionji, who was consulted as a matter of form, appears to have washed his hands of the whole matter. At the insistence of the army, Konoye appointed General Tojo Hideki as minister of the army, but he selected Matsuoka Yosuke as foreign minister under the mistaken idea that he would not be too subservient to military direction.

Ambassador Grew analyzed the cabinet as follows: "At first sight the Konoye government gives every indication of going hell-bent toward the Axis and the establishment of a new order in East Asia, and of riding roughshod over the rights and interests, and the principles and policies of the United States and of Great Britain." But, Grew added, "In all probability, Prince Konoye, reflecting the presumable attitude of the emperor and the elder statesmen, will exert responsible control over the 'wild men' and will endeavor to move slowly and with some degree of caution at least until it becomes clear whether Great Britain is going to win or lose the war."

The Konoye ministry worked for the establishment of a unified political structure to be based on a single-party system. For some time the army and civilian nationalists had been demanding the formation of a single political party that would replace the "weak, selfish, and corrupt" political parties, but their views on the matter varied greatly. Some were interested in a new party as a means of increasing military control over all governmental affairs; others thought of it as another Nazi Party; and still others, including some of the high-ranking civilian advisers of the emperor, considered it as a promising instrument for checking military domination. Strangely enough, each group ultimately considered Konoye the logical and acceptable leader of a single party.

On March 25, 1940, over one hundred members of the house of representatives, embracing all parties, formed the Federation for the Prosecution of the Holy War, which pledged the following: support for an alliance between Konoye and the army, collaboration with third powers that approved Japan's establishment of a new order in East Asia, reform of the economic structure which had been based too long on *laissez faire,* and eradication of non-Japanese ideologies such as communism, liberalism, and utilitarianism. This action was followed in April by the formation of the National Federation for the Construction of East Asia by other party members and political cliques. When Konoye resigned the presidency of the privy council on June 24 in order to work for the establishment of a unified national political structure, more and more party politicians joined the cause. Between July 6 and August 15, one after the other the political parties dissolved their organizations and began consultations for the formation of a single-party system.

In October the movement culminated in the establishment of the Imperial Rule Assistance Association, dedicated to preserving national unity, assisting the emperor by formulating public opinion, and acting as a general propaganda outlet for the government; but instead of being a political party in either the Western democratic or the fascist sense, it actually proved to be a government-controlled propaganda agency which absorbed all political parties and mass organizations. Its chief purpose was to create the illusion that the Japanese people were actually participating in the governing process and to avoid the danger of opposition by political organizations. The Imperial Rule Assistance Association was organized like a department of the government, with various bureaus and a centralized national administration. From central headquarters in Tokyo it worked through local branches at the prefectural, district, city, town, and village levels. Although the overwhelming majority of the old party members joined the association, pledging to work for its objectives, in practice "the one great party" was not a spectacular success, since it was characterized by the same old factionalism, lack of mass appeal, and problems of responsibility and leadership. If elements in the army intended to use the party for totalitarian ends, they were unable to overcome the opposition of businessmen and bureaucrats, who branded the movement as communistic; on the other hand, if Konoye sought to use a single-party system to control the army, he, too, failed.

The Konoye ministry was committed to greater planning in the national economy and particularly to the establishment of controls over production, distribution, and consumption as a means of achieving greater self-sufficiency. Despite the application of the National Mobilization Law and other legislation, the empire's economy was not operating as a cohesive unit, and the army continued to insist that government controls be increased and that they be based on some comprehensive economic plan. The army contended that existing controls were ineffective, raw materials were wasted on unessential industries, and tax and profit restrictions were inadequate. Business interests, especially the zaibatsu, insisted that they be permitted to organize industries into stronger cartels which they could control independently of the government. The cabinet finally decided on a compromise solution. It would reorganize and strengthen various cartels but would control them through directors responsible to a supreme economic council. The zaibatsu stubbornly remained unconciliatory, and not until September, 1941, did they accept a greater degree of state control. Until the outbreak of the Pacific War the competition for raw materials and the unwillingness by business to abide by government regulations resulted in much economic confusion. Even in the strategically important iron and steel industry there was no fixed pattern of control until November, 1941.

Government supervision of public information and education became more centralized in these years. By November, 1940, the cabinet information bureau was expanded in scope and took over the information-gathering and dissemination processes, educational and publicity work, and the censorship of the press, radio, motion pictures, and plays, all of which activities had previously been supervised by the army, navy, foreign, home, and communications ministries, with a considerable degree of duplication. For the first time Japan had a single control agency in the mass-communications field. The government also changed all elementary schools into "national schools," which had as their basic objective the training of youth as citizens of a "nation which destiny has made the leader of the East Asia Co-Prosperity Sphere." Almost all educational activities emphasized the glorification of the principles of the imperial way, and approximately one-third of the elementary school curriculum was given over to moral and physical training. New textbooks were written to help destroy "the self-centered and utilitarian ideas that had seeped into Japan from the West" and to extol service to the state.

The "New Order" and the Tripartite Pact

The basic foreign policies of the second Konoye ministry were determined in an unprecedented series of conferences between civil and military officials from July 19 to July 27, 1940. The conferees agreed on two main aims of Japanese policy, namely, settlement of the China conflict and expansion of Japan's power toward the south in such a manner as to avoid war. Specific policies to achieve these ends included the following: maintenance of a firm attitude toward the United States; a sweeping readjustment of relations with the Soviet Union by conclusion of a five- to ten-year nonaggression pact, during which time outstanding questions were to be negotiated and an invincible force built up; conclusion of a military alliance with Germany and Italy; stronger measures against Indochina and Hong Kong to prevent aid to Chiang K'ai-shek; and a more vigorous diplomacy toward the Netherlands East Indies in order to acquire vital materials.

Despite German victories in Europe, the Russian and American governments were not reacting as Japan had hoped. When Ambassador Togo Shigenori opened negotiations with Foreign Minister Molotov at Moscow in July, he found that the Russians wanted to buy out Japan's concessions in northern Sakhalin and that they were not anxious to conclude a pact with Japan. Hoping to benefit from German pressure on the Russians, Matsuoka ordered Togo to suspend negotiations. On July 26 Washington embargoed high-grade heavy melting iron and steel scrap, and the Japanese government protested but to no avail. The new embargo was not completely effective because of loopholes in American control regulations; moreover, Japan continued to obtain from the United States great quantities of high-grade gasoline and crude oil which, with little trouble, she converted into aviation fuel.

In August, 1940, Japan made clear its intentions with regard to Indochina and the Netherlands East Indies. On August 1 Konoye redefined Japan's "new order" to include Indochina and the Indies, and the Japanese increased their pressure in both areas. In negotiations with the French authorities, Japan maintained that Indochina was acting in an unfriendly manner because huge consignments of supplies were reaching Chiang K'ai-shek from Hanoi via the Yunnan Railway. On August 30 Matsuoka and the French ambassador at Tokyo reached an agreement which provided for the use of airports and the movement of Japanese troops through Indochina for the purpose of more effectively carrying on the conflict with China. Moreover, in return for a Japanese promise to respect French sovereignty over Indochina, the Vichy government recognized "the preponderant interests of Japan in East Asia in the economic as well as the political domain." When Japan subsequently stepped up its demands, the French authorities in Indochina tried to resist but were forced to yield when the Japanese army presented an ultimatum for the occupation of Hanoi, Haiphong, and five airports by its forces. On September 22, by the Hanoi Convention, Japan got the right to station troops in northern Indochina, to build air bases, and to control the movement of supplies over the railway from Hanoi to Yunnan. The Japanese were also able to force the French administration to guarantee minimum exports to Japan of rubber, rice, manganese, zinc, industrial salt, tin, and antimony.

As for the Indies, the Japanese government on July 16 notified the Dutch authorities that it wished to dispatch a mission to discuss a comprehensive settlement. The Dutch replied that the mission would be welcome but that on no account would they discuss political questions. The mission, headed by Kobayashi Ichizo, minister of commerce and industry, arrived in September and demanded three million tons of oil annually for five years, about five times the normal amount sent to Japan and about 40 per cent of the Indies' production.

Although the Dutch negotiators refused to make general concessions or to act as a broker between the Japanese and the oil companies, Japan was not prepared to resort to force, especially when her navy estimated that at least eight months more of preparation were necessary. Another important consideration was the fact that an attack on the Indies might involve Japan in a war not only with Great Britain, with whom the Netherlands government in London was allied, but also with the United States, which had large economic interests in the Indies. In fact, both powers had urged the oil companies to stand firm against the Japanese demands, since the sale of large quantities of aviation gasoline and other petroleum products would nullify the effect of the American ban and would also reduce British supplies, which the United States would have to replace. Washington felt, moreover, that Japan would not attack the Indies if the Dutch bargained firmly. Finally, there was the likelihood that Dutch forces in the Indies would be able to destroy the oil stocks and oil equipment before Japan could overrun the area.

Tokyo therefore decided that direct action against the Indies was to be deferred until the defeat of Great Britain; and in a statement issued on October 16 Kobayashi declared that Japan had no hostile intentions toward the Indies and did not claim any hegemony over them. After his departure on October 22 his subordinates continued to negotiate, and on November 12 they reached an agreement by which the oil companies promised to supply half of what Japan wanted under a six-month contract and with virtually no aviation gasoline included.

In the summer of 1940 the Roosevelt administration increasingly committed the United States to opposing Germany in Europe and Japan in Asia. In August Washington urged Americans, about 16,000 in all, to leave Asia and began to send reinforcements to Hawaii and the Philippines. On August 28 the American Congress passed the Selective Service Act, which gave the United States her first peacetime conscript army. Washington also countered Japan's move into Indochina with new economic sanctions. On September 12 Ambassador Grew, who had previously advised against coercive measures, suggested that the time had come for a policy of firmness as the only way to restrain Japan until such time as Germany should have been defeated, after which the whole problem of the Pacific could be readjusted "to the permanent benefit of both the United States and Japan on a just basis"; and on September 26 Roosevelt ordered that the export of all grades of iron and steel scrap be placed under government control. But he was unwilling to do anything more about oil exports since he did not want to push Japan too hard. Although the president's action was also based on Grew's information that a Japanese-German pact was in the making, the show of American force did not change Japanese policy but actually made the Japanese more receptive to the idea of an alliance with the Axis powers. In the summer of 1940 the American government's desire to contain Germany was even more evident, and on September 3, after receiving what amounted to assent from his election opponent, Wendell Willkie, Roosevelt announced an agreement with Great Britain under which the United States turned over fifty old destroyers to reinforce the British navy in its struggle against German submarines in the Atlantic in return for long-term leases of British island and coastal sites in the Western Hemisphere for the construction of American bases against possible German attack.

In August the Japanese government, confident that it could make use of the Germans and Italians while not committing itself too fully to their side, moved to conclude an alliance with the Axis powers. According to Matsuoka, Japan wanted to take advantage of Axis victories in Europe to descend on the overseas territories of France, the Netherlands, and Portugal in Southeast Asia with the minimum risk of involvement in war; and when Great Britain was crushed by Germany, Japan could also seize her possessions. Her leaders reasoned that the United States could be prevented from coming to the aid of Great Britain by the threat of Japan's intervention on the Axis side.

In the negotiations, which began in Tokyo on September 9, the German representative stated that Hitler did not want Japan at that juncture to join the war against Great Britain since he felt that a Japanese attack might make the British all the more determined to resist the Axis. All that Germany wanted was Japan's help in keeping the United States from entering and prolonging the war. Matsuoka and Tojo, the strongest advocates of an alliance, won over Konoye and the emperor by the claim that Japan would reserve her freedom to decide her obligations in the remote chance that the United States did enter the war. It was easy for Japanese to conclude that, with Great Britain in hopeless shape and with American public opinion divided, the United States would have to accept German and Japanese gains, especially after the conclusion of the alliance and its implied threat of a two-front war.

The Tripartite Pact, signed by Japan, Germany, and Italy on September 27, 1940, transformed the Anti-Comintern Pact into a ten-year military alliance, the main points of which were as follows:

1. Japan recognizes and respects the leadership of Germany and Italy in the establishment of a new order in Europe.
2. Germany and Italy recognize and respect the leadership of Japan in the establishment of a new order in Asia.
3. Japan, Germany, and Italy agree to co-operate in their efforts on the above points. They further undertake to assist one another with all political, economic, and military means when one of the three contracting parties is attacked by a power at present not involved in the European War or in the Sino-Japanese conflict.

4. Japan, Germany, and Italy affirm that the above terms do not in any way affect the political status which exists at present as between each of the three contracting parties and Soviet Russia.

The pact was directed at the United States, and the signatories were free to determine what action by the United States would constitute an act of war which would bring into operation its obligations under the alliance. The Japanese continued to insist that they would make their own decisions regarding war with Great Britain or the United States. Finally, Germany promised to promote a friendly understanding between Japan and the Soviet Union, while Konoye hoped to conclude a nonaggression pact with Russia, with Germany's assistance. The Japanese prime minister and the army hoped that such an agreement would help them to secure a peace settlement with Chiang K'ai-shek and thus cut "the chain on Japan's feet."

The American Reaction

The American government's reaction to the Tripartite Pact was contrary to what its signatories had expected. Washington felt that war with Japan was more likely than before. It might be caused not only by Japan's advances into Southeast Asia but also by American assistance to Great Britain. Japan had tied herself to Germany and was thus against the United States in a cause far closer to American hearts than the fate of China. Washington not only planned additional measures to restrict trade with Japan, but it also began to consider for the first time the possible use of armed forces in the Southwest Pacific. Roosevelt agreed with the British that some kind of talks for the purpose of mutual instruction should be started as soon as possible, but he thought that such talks had better take place after the November presidential election. Roosevelt was promising in his campaign speeches that he would take no measures which would lead to the engagement of American forces in fighting abroad. Yet, even before the election, American and British staff officers in London and Singapore had begun to exchange information and ideas on strategic co-operation. The American reaction caused Matsuoka to claim that the Tripartite Pact was defensive and not directed against the United States and that the new order was only a plan for economic expansion in which other nations would share equally. But, at the same time, Matsuoka warned that if Washington imposed additional embargoes on trade, future relations between Japan and the United States would be unpredictable.

In less than a month after Roosevelt's election victory the American government co-ordinated its various efforts against Japan. On November 30 Roosevelt made another $100,000,000 available to Chiang K'ai-shek and promised him fifty new pursuit planes, with more to come as they became available. In December the United States terminated the flow of iron ore, pig iron, steel, and many kinds of tools to Japan, and shortly thereafter she also imposed controls on important raw materials, such as copper, brass, bronze, zinc, nickel, and potash. Washington also began to ponder the question of whether or not to freeze foreign assets in the United States. Despite these steps, Roosevelt continued to refuse to say what his government would or would not do if Japan moved south. What complicated the situation was the crisis in the Atlantic, where the British were having difficulties in keeping the sea lanes open; and when the American president moved a major naval force, including battleships and carriers, from the Pacific to the Atlantic early in 1941, he used this action as an excuse for not committing the United States to the defense of Singapore and the Indies.

Meanwhile, Matsuoka took the lead in efforts to include the Soviet Union in the Tripartite Pact and thus enlarge the combination against the United States. At the end of October the newly appointed Japanese ambassador, General Tatekawa, presented the following terms to Foreign Minister Molotov: that the Soviet Union agree to recognize Manchukuo, to stop aiding Chiang K'ai-shek, to restrain the anti-Japanese activities of the Chinese communists, to refrain from subversive activity in China and Manchukuo, to recognize Japan's traditional interests in the provinces of north China and Inner Mongolia, to safeguard Japan's oil and coal concessions in northern Sakhalin and her fishing rights in the north Pacific by a new agreement, and to acquiesce in Japan's advance into Indochina; in return, Japan would recognize Russia's pre-eminent interests in Sinkiang and Outer Mongolia, recognize a Chinese communist base in the three northwestern provinces of China, and acquiesce in Russia's expansion into Iran and Afghanistan.

Molotov refused to talk along these lines with Tatekawa but did state his desire for improved relations based on a nonaggression pact. In November, at Berlin, Ribbentrop put pressure on Molotov to reach some kind of understanding with Japan; but when Molotov met again with Tatekawa, later in the month, he proposed a five-year nonaggression pact, co-operation between the two powers for an honorable settlement in China, and restoration by Japan of her concessions in northern Sakhalin. The negotiations were suspended again, but Matsuoka still hoped that German pressure would soften the Russians.

In the winter of 1940–1941 Japan was still looking for a way to move south without provoking war. On January 21, in his address to the diet, Foreign Minister Matsuoka emphasized that there was no other course open to Japan but to secure "economic self-sufficiency" in East Asia, and he reiterated that the Netherlands East Indies lay within the Greater East Asia Co-Prosperity Sphere. Speaking before the budget committee of the house of representatives a month later, he declared that "ultimately diplomacy is force, and it goes without saying that diplomacy not backed by strength can accomplish nothing." These statements coincided with a renewal of Japanese pressure on the Indies. At the end of December, 1940, a special envoy, Yoshizawa Kenkichi, arrived at Batavia, and on January 16 he presented new demands by which Japan hoped to control the economic life of the Indies. The Dutch authorities again refused to comply, and Japan, not yet willing to use force, reduced her demands. Negotiations continued, but the Japanese finally departed in June without securing important economic advantages.

Japan also intervened in Thai-French difficulties to advance her position in Indochina. Tokyo supported Thai claims to the three Cambodian provinces west of the Mekong River in return for a Thai promise to co-operate both politically and economically in the establishment of Greater East Asia. As a result of a mediation conference in Tokyo, the French ceded to Thailand a portion of Laos and Cambodia, and as a reward for her services Japan secured commercial privileges and access to Thai rice surpluses and to raw materials like tin and rubber. Indochina, moreover, promised Japan that she would not enter into any agreement with another country which provided for political, economic, or military co-operation directly or indirectly against Japan.

The Japanese actions with regard to Indochina and Thailand were preparatory to a push south; however, the idea of a possible attack on Singapore had to be deferred until advance points could be secured in Indochina or Thailand. The Japanese navy had in mind particularly the use of Camranh Bay and air bases near Saigon; but Thailand and Indochina were both unwilling as yet to make such concessions to Japan.

In Tokyo the Konoye cabinet still sought answers to many questions. How far could diplomacy go, and at what point would Japan have to rely on the use of force? Could Japan risk a southward advance with a firm guarantee from the Soviet Union to secure her rear? Could Japan risk an attack on British possessions before Hitler had made good his promise to invade Great Britain? And could Japan attack British colonies without simultaneously attacking the United States in the Philippines? Ambassador Grew ably assessed the situation. He thought that sooner or later, unless the United States was prepared to withdraw completely from East Asia and the South Seas, she was bound to fight Japan. Grew realized that there was little likelihood that the Japanese militarists would abandon their determination to dominate eastern Asia and the western Pacific.

In Washington, Roosevelt and his subordinates were seeking to devise ways by which, without actual American entry into the war, essential sea lanes to Great Britain could be kept open; and they hoped at the same time to prevent a Japanese attack on British and Dutch possessions in East Asia. Because of his interest in both Europe and Asia, Roosevelt took the initiative in instituting British-American joint-staff conferences, lasting from January until late March, 1941, which settled on the following tentative principles:

1. The principal American military effort was to be exercised in the Atlantic Ocean and Europe, since Germany was the predominant member of the Axis and these were the decisive spheres of combat.

2. The United States would increase its forces in the Atlantic and Mediterranean areas so that the British Commonwealth would be in a position to release the necessary forces to defend British territories in East Asia.
3. The tasks assigned to the American Pacific Fleet were in the main defensive: protection of Hawaii, the Philippines, Guam, and Wake. But the fleet would also relieve pressure on Singapore by a diversion toward the Marshall and Caroline Islands and by an attack on Japanese communications and shipping.

Despite these preliminary arrangements, Washington refused to obligate itself to enter the war or even to specify the circumstances in which it might do so, but the United States did continue discussions after April 1 at Singapore which determined the line at which military resistance against Japan was necessary. When in December, 1941, Japanese warships and troop movements were reported on their way south to an unknown destination, Admiral Stark and General Marshall urged Roosevelt to declare these limits and to warn Japan that the United States would join the fight if they were passed. Had the Japanese not struck at Pearl Harbor and the Philippine Islands, the attack on Malaya would have become the boundary between war and peace. The Japanese government followed the American-British talks very closely, and it felt quite certain that a definite military understanding had been reached between the United States, Great Britain, and the Indies authorities.

By the spring of 1941 the United States was taking a more active role in support of the British and the Chinese. Her navy patrolled the western Atlantic and escorted convoys, reporting the movements of enemy warships to the British. If German submarines or raiders attacked merchant vessels en route to Great Britain, they risked a fight with American warships. On April 10 the United States also began taking over the defense of Greenland and Iceland from the British. And Washington stepped up assistance to her potential allies under the terms of the Lend-Lease Act, passed on March 11, 1941, by which Roosevelt could supply war materials to the British without money payment. Lend-lease was based on the idea of lending weapons, which were to be returned after the war if they were still usable or were to be written off if they had been expended in a struggle which was as much to America's interest as to the British. Lend-lease was also applied to China, particularly for improved transportation over the Burma Road; and by November, 1941, freight moving over this route increased from 4,000 to 15,000 tons monthly. Funds were also allocated to begin construction of a railroad from northern Burma into southwest China, but the subsequent Japanese invasion of Burma halted the plan.

Negotiations with the Soviet Union and the United States

In this same period Japan and Germany began working at cross-purposes. On March 5 at Moscow Matsuoka offered to conclude a nonaggression pact with the Soviet Union; but when Molotov proposed, instead, a neutrality agreement, Matsuoka said that he must defer his answer until he had returned from Berlin. The Japanese foreign minister was unaware of Hitler's plan to attack the Soviet Union while Japan moved against Great Britain in Southeast Asia. In Hitler's mind these moves spelled decisive success for the Tripartite powers, and he was putting pressure on Ambassador Oshima for an attack on Singapore. But the Japanese government remained uncommitted and preferred to wait and see how the war in Europe went, hoping to achieve its ends without a general war.

Tokyo also had doubts that the United States would remain neutral, as Hitler expected. At Berlin, Ribbentrop put additional pressure on Matsuoka for an immediate attack on Singapore, suggesting that Japan would never have such an opportunity again. Matsuoka assured him that it was only a question of time before Japan attacked, even if it meant war with the United States; and he inferred from a conversation with Hitler that if Japan fought the United States, Germany would join her.

Both Hitler and Ribbentrop also made it clear to Matsuoka that the Soviet Union could no longer be regarded as a friend and hinted that a storm was brewing. In fact, Ribbentrop pointed out that a conflict was within the realm of possibility and expressed opposition to a Japanese-Russian *rapprochement*. However, Matsuoka felt that a pact with Russia was all the more necessary to prevent a two-front war, even though Ribbentrop indicated that Germany would strike if the Soviet Union attacked Japan. (In the actual event, the German attack on the Soviet Union precluded a German invasion of Great Britain, thus complicating the Japanese move south.)

On his return to Moscow, Matsuoka signed a neutrality pact on April 13 with the Soviet Union, whose leaders were already informed of the German war plans. The pact provided that each state would respect the territorial integrity and hold inviolable the territories of the other, including Manchukuo and Outer Mongolia, and that each power would maintain its neutrality in case the other was involved in war. Stalin dropped his demand for the surrender of the Japanese concessions in northern Sakhalin, although Matsuoka agreed to do his best to get his government to surrender them in a few months. Despite the fact that the Soviet Union did not promise to renounce her support of China, Matsuoka hoped that Chiang K'ai-shek would now come to terms and that the way south would be safer. Perhaps even Washington might become less belligerent. Hitler, however, was very angry but explained to his generals that Japan would now be ready to move south and put pressure on the British empire.

Tokyo still looked for a diplomatic settlement with the United States and indicated to Roosevelt that the Japanese government would welcome an opportunity to alter its political alignments and to modify its attitude toward China. Although the United States had no great hope of success, she indicated a willingness to explore the possibility of defining a basis upon which formal negotiations might be instituted. Ambassador Nomura Kichisaburo began a series of conversations with Secretary of State Hull on March 8, and from the outset there was a wide divergence between the positions of the two powers. Hull lectured Nomura on the way that Japan was abandoning the principles of peace, law, and order and was wooing "false gods," and he threatened additional sanctions if Japan did not renounce aggression. In rebuttal, Nomura pointed out that Japan's desire to expand was caused not by a wish to conquer other countries but by the need to offset foreign unfairness and pressure. He assured Hull that he did not believe there would be any further military movements unless the United States increased its embargoes. On April 16 Hull stated the following four principles as the basis for agreement:

1. Respect of the territorial integrity and sovereignty of each and all nations.
2. Support of the principle of noninterference in the internal affairs of other countries.
3. Support of the principle of equality, including equality of commercial opportunity.
4. Nondisturbance of the status quo in the Pacific, except as the status quo may be altered by peaceful means.

Hull also suggested that Japan offer specific counterproposals; or, if the Japanese government accepted the first four points, the following proposals might serve for discussion:

1. Japan would declare that she was bound to go to war only if one of her partners was aggressively attacked.
2. The United States would agree to avoid aggressive alliances.
3. Both powers would guarantee the independence of the Philippines.
4. The United States would request China to make peace on the basis of recognition of Manchukuo; no territorial annexations or indemnities; the coalition of the Chungking and Nanking regimes; withdrawal of Japanese troops, with a subsequent Sino-Japanese agreement; and recognition of the open-door principle. Should Chiang K'ai-shek refuse, the United States would end her aid of his regime.
5. The United States would resume normal trade relations with Japan, provide a gold loan to Japan, and promise to co-operate with Japan in securing vital raw materials.
6. The leaders of the two governments, Konoye and Roosevelt, would confer at Honolulu.

In a liaison conference of high civilian and military leaders in Tokyo on April 18 it was agreed that discussions with the United States should continue, for several reasons: the depletion of Japan's national strength made it desirable to terminate hostilities in China as soon as possible; Japan needed essential materials from the United States; and the Japanese military was neither prepared for nor confident of success in a southward advance. The conferees did decide, however, that nothing should be done to affect Japan's obligations under the Tripartite Pact, by which the Axis powers hoped to keep the United States neutral by threatening a two-front war; and they agreed that the United States should be kept in a state of worry over Japan's intentions since, should she be relieved of keeping guard in the Pacific and able to increase her aid to Great Britain, Japan would be breaking faith with Germany and hurting herself. The Japanese leaders thus decided to accept Hull's proposals as the basis of negotiations but with revisions which stressed Japan's determination to adhere to the Tripartite Pact and to build the new order in East Asia. But they agreed that no answer would be given to Hull until Matsuoka returned from Europe.

The Japanese foreign minister arrived in Tokyo on April 22 and insisted that Hull be told that Japan could take no action that would in any way prove injurious to her allies in Europe and that the United States should sign a treaty which would obligate her to remain neutral even in the event of war between Japan and Great Britain. Matsuoka won over his colleagues, and on May 7 Nomura presented the idea of a neutrality pact to Hull. Hull rejected it, and the Japanese cabinet was faced with the problem of deciding whether to negotiate with the United States on issues or to follow Matsuoka's lead into the war on the side of Germany. Against Matsuoka's wishes, Konoye decided that Nomura should present the following comments on Hull's proposals, which he did on May 12:

1. Each government to acknowledge the other as an equally sovereign state and to pledge itself to lasting peace and to noninterference with the other's rights, interests, and social order.
2. Japan to declare the Tripartite Pact to be purely defensive and designed to prevent the nations which are not at present directly affected by the European War from engaging in it. The United States to declare that her attitude toward the war would continue to be directed by no such aggressive measures as to assist any one nation against another but would be determined solely by the interests of her own defense.
3. The United States to request Chiang K'ai-shek to negotiate peace with Japan along lines already enunciated by Konoye and accepted by Wang Ching-wei; and, should Chiang refuse, the United States to give assurance that she would halt her aid to China.
4. The United States to withdraw restrictions on trade. The two countries to agree to supply each other with whatever commodities are respectively available or required by either and to establish normal trade relations.
5. Japan to declare that her expansion in the Southwest Pacific is of a peaceful nature and the United States to co-operate in Japan's procurement of those raw materials such as oil, rubber, tin, and nickel, which she needed.
6. The two governments to jointly guarantee the independence of the Philippines on condition that the Philippines be permanently neutralized and that Japanese nationals not be subject to any discriminatory treatment.

The Japanese position disappointed Hull, who felt that Tokyo offered nothing substantial regarding China, nothing convincing in regard to its plans for Southeast Asia, and nothing specific with regard to its alliance with Germany and Italy. It seemed clear to him that the Japanese government was asking the United States to accept the formation of the Japan-Manchukuo-China bloc and of Greater East Asia and to abandon Great Britain, implying that, if she did not, Japan would have to declare war on her. On the other hand, Washington wanted Japan entirely out of China and probably out of Manchukuo as well. Therefore, by early May there was little likelihood of agreement between Nomura and Hull. On May 31 Hull did reply by asking Japan to withdraw her forces from China in accordance with an agreement with Chiang K'ai-shek, to refrain from acts of force in Southeast Asia, to concur in the view that the United States in aiding Great Britain was acting only in self-defense, and to promise that, if the United States became involved in war with Germany, Japan would not enter the conflict.

Meanwhile Hitler was pressing Matsuoka to inform the American government that its operations in the Atlantic Ocean would provoke a war with Germany which Japan would be forced to enter. He also insisted that any agreement between Japan and the United States should contain a pledge of non-interference in the war against Great Britain and recognition of Japan's conclusive obligations to the Axis. Paradoxically, Germany's victories in Europe provided Japan with her opportunity to strike in Southeast Asia, but it was the alliance with Germany that prevented Japan from paying the one price which might have influenced the United States, namely, a guarantee of neutrality in the Pacific in the event of American entanglement in Europe. For a time Japan played a double game, assuring Washington that the Tripartite Pact in no way obligated Japan to enter an American-German conflict and at the same time trying to convince Berlin that the talks in Washington were simply a shrewd diplomatic maneuver in no way contravening Japan's fidelity to the Axis.

On June 21 Hull gave Nomura a comprehensive oral statement of the American attitude, together with a draft proposal which included the following points:

1. Affirmation by both governments that their national policies were directed toward the establishment of lasting peace and the inauguration of an era of reciprocal confidence and co-operation between the two nations.
2. Affirmation by Japan that the Tripartite Pact was defensive and designed to prevent an extension of the European war, and assurance by the United States that its attitude toward the European war was and would continue to be determined solely by considerations of protection and self-defense.
3. Suggestion by the United States to China for negotiations with Japan.
4. Resumption of normal American-Japanese trade relations.

5. American-Japanese co-operation toward obtaining through peaceful means nondiscriminatory access to the supplies and natural resources needed by each.
6. Mutual affirmation of peace throughout the Pacific area as the basic national policy and a mutual disclaimer of territorial designs in the area.
7. Declaration by Japan of her willingness to negotiate with the United States with a view to concluding a treaty for the neutralization of the Philippine Islands after independence is achieved.

Hull also sought to put Nomura on the spot when he said that the recent public utterances of certain influential members of the Japanese government, especially Matsuoka, stressed Japan's obligations to Germany and caused doubt whether any agreement with Japan was worth pursuing. Generally speaking, Hull's proposals closely followed the Japanese note of May 12 in general form, but his changes in wording transformed the Japanese viewpoint into one that was acceptable to the United States.

In this same period Japan suffered several important economic setbacks which probably accelerated the outbreak of war. On May 28 the American Congress imposed export-control regulations on all American territories and dependencies; and when Roosevelt applied them immediately to the Philippine Islands, Japan was no longer able to get much-needed iron, chrome, manganese, copra, copper, and Manila hemp from that source. In June, when the American east coast faced an oil scarcity because of a transportation shortage, Washington announced that no oil could be exported from eastern ports, including the Gulf of Mexico, except to the British Empire and Western Hemisphere destinations. In the Indies Japan was still confronted by a Dutch administration which stubbornly resisted requests for oil concessions and larger supplies, and on June 17 the Japanese delegation broke off talks and departed for home. From Tokyo Ambassador Grew reported that both German and Japanese extremists were pressing for action against the Indies.

Japanese Pressure on Southeast Asia

On June 22 Germany invaded the Soviet Union, and Hitler asked Japan to violate the Neutrality Pact and join his cause. But at that very moment Japan was becoming increasingly involved in Southeast Asia; in fact, at the time of the attack she was seeking to put pressure on the Vichy government through Germany for bases in southern Indochina. Urged on by Matsuoka, the cabinet for a moment considered the possibility that if Germany won a decisive victory over the Soviet Union, Japan, with a minimum of effort, could carve for herself a new empire in the north without handicapping the drive into Southeast Asia. The army, however, was not anxious to enter the war against Russia, and the navy saw no chance for oil or glory in the north and feared that the United States and Great Britain would use the interval to strengthen their defenses in the south. Although it still hoped to benefit from a German victory, the Japanese cabinet rejected the German pleas, and it assured Moscow that the Neutrality Pact would be observed. When Matsuoka attempted to persuade the emperor that Japan should join the attack on the Soviet Union, he challenged Konoye's leadership, and the relations between the two men became increasingly strained. Konoye, moreover, was aware that Matsuoka was a stumbling block in the negotiations with the United States. In the liaison conferences held between June 25 and July 2 it was apparent that the weight of opinion, including that of the two services, was against Matsuoka.

On July 2 the Japanese cabinet concluded that if Germany defeated the Soviet Union, the United States and Great Britain would give way and allow Japan to establish her new order in East Asia. Hitler informed Tokyo that his campaign in Russia would end in victory in August and that a complete Germany victory would terminate the war before winter. Willing to continue to gamble on German successes against both the Soviet Union and Great Britain, Japan decided to mobilize its resources for war, extend its position south into Indochina, develop operational plans against Malaya, the Indies, and the Philippines, perfect a naval attack on Pearl Harbor to immobilize the American Pacific Fleet, increase the size of the Kwantung Army from 300,000 to 600,000 men, and to call into service 2,000,000 additional reservists.

Most of the Konoye cabinet still eagerly wished to avoid war with the United States; they were hoping that international pressures would force the United States to acquiesce in Japan's plans. The Japanese military, on the other hand, were convinced that the United States would have to be attacked, and, ironically, every American gesture for the purpose of deterring Japan, every indication of Anglo-American solidarity in East Asia, and every reinforcement of the Philippine Islands only tended to confirm them in their judgment. From July to the fateful day of the Pearl Harbor attack, Washington knew much about Japan's plans. American experts had broken Japanese diplomatic codes, and the highest American officials were constantly informed as to Japanese moves. They learned of most of the July 2 decisions, although the version which they obtained did not contain specific mention of war with Great Britain and the United States.

Tokyo still had to decide how to answer Hull's proposals of June 21. On July 10 and 12 Matsuoka insisted that Japanese honor required rejection of the oral statement and termination of the talks, but this appealed to none of his colleagues, civil or military, who wished to throw away no chance of convincing the United States and Great Britain that Japan really wanted peace and order in the Pacific, once her leadership in the area was recognized. Even the army wanted the talks to continue, at least until after Japan had completed the occupation of Indochina and the outcome of the fighting in the Soviet Union was clearer. When on July 14 Matsuoka ordered Nomura to demand the retraction of Hull's oral explanation of amendments to the Japanese draft, his unilateral action precipitated a cabinet crisis which caused its resignation on July 16. The resignation of the entire cabinet, instead of the replacement of Matsuoka, was a device to prevent the foreign minister from posing as a victim of American pressure and arousing public feeling. Konoye simply reorganized his cabinet with Admiral Toyoda, thought to be trusted by the United States, as foreign minister. This incident, however, had no significant impact upon Japanese policy, since the new cabinet was determined to maintain the Tripartite Pact and to move into Indochina.

On July 19 Tokyo once again asked Berlin to persuade the Vichy government to grant Japan concessions in Indochina, and the Japanese ambassador asked Marshall Pétain for the right to occupy eight airfields and to use Saigon and Camranh Bay as naval bases; if consent was not forthcoming, Japanese forces, he said, would determine the issue in their own way. On July 29 the Japanese government concluded a mutual defense agreement with the Vichy government, and Japanese military units began landing at Saigon on the same day. Japan explained the action as necessary to insure an uninterrupted flow of rice, other foodstuffs, and raw materials, the supply of which might be obstructed by Chinese forces or by the Free French, supported by Great Britain. But the broken codes disclosed to Washington the ultimate purpose of the move, namely, preparation for an attack on Singapore and the Indies. On July 24 Roosevelt stated emphatically to Nomura that the Japanese move into Indochina created an exceedingly serious problem for the United States and proposed that, if the Japanese government would refrain from occupying Indochina, he would do everything in his power to obtain a binding neutralization of the area. On the following day the British government declared the Japanese action an obvious threat to its territory and indicated that it was taking defensive measures in Malaya and was consulting with the dominion governments, as well as the United States, about methods of retaliation.

On July 26 President Roosevelt froze all Japanese assets in the United States, bringing all financial, import, and export transactions under the control of the American government. On the same day he recalled General Douglas MacArthur to active duty and placed him in command of American and Filipino units in the Philippines; he also established a military mission in Chungking. Great Britain, the dominions, and the Dutch also froze Japanese assets, and Japan retaliated in kind on July 28. Roosevelt also told Nomura that if Japan attempted to seize oil supplies in the Indies, she would be met with Dutch and British resistance, and that, in view of the American policy of assisting Great Britain, an exceedingly serious situation would immediately result. While the freezing orders were resented by the Japanese cabinet, they did not alter its course. If anything, these sanctions increased the Japanese desire to get access to petroleum, and this factor became the key to the timing of hostilities.

Prime Minister Konoye was still anxious to avoid war with the United States; and because of the impasse in Nomura-Hull negotiations, he made up his mind to meet personally with President Roosevelt. On August 4

Konoye presented the idea to the army and navy ministers, explaining that he did not intend to take a submissive attitude and would firmly insist upon the establishment of the Greater East Asia Co-Prosperity Sphere. The prime minister felt that Japan's position of strength, dependent in large part on a German victory against the Soviet Union, was vanishing rapidly, since it appeared that the German-Russian conflict might reach the point of stalemate. He reasoned that the American attitude would stiffen and that Japan would no longer have an opportunity to attain her goals through diplomacy. Konoye, therefore, was willing to scrap the Tripartite Pact in return for American concessions to Japan in East Asia. The navy had no serious objection to Konoye's views, but the army was reluctant to support him, fearing the impact on relations with Germany. However, Army Minister Tojo informed Konoye that if he firmly intended to support basic Japanese principles and resort to war should the United States not give in, then the army would suspend its objections. Tojo insisted, moreover, that, should he fail, Konoye would have to lead the nation into war.

On August 6, prior to initiating discussion of the Konoye plan, Nomura informed Hull of Japan's willingness to send her troops no further south into Southeast Asia than Indochina and to evacuate the latter area after settlement of the hostilities in China; but in return the United States would have to undertake to suspend her military measures in the South Pacific, restore normal trade relations, co-operate with Japan in securing for her whatever specific raw materials she might require, persuade Chiang K'ai-shek to accept Japanese peace terms, and recognize the special status of Japan in Indochina after the withdrawal of her troops. When on August 8 Hull stated that the proposals were unsatisfactory, Nomura suggested a meeting between Konoye and Roosevelt at Honolulu. Hull cut him short with the remark that, before the United States would consider such a meeting, the Japanese government would have to demonstrate that it wanted agreement.

Roosevelt at this very moment was talking with Churchill at Argentia, Newfoundland. Their discussions were largely concerned with the European war, but the British prime minister did make it clear that, since a Japanese drive south was imminent, the United States should join Great Britain, the dominions, and the Indies government in warning Japan against such a step. Churchill, moreover, wanted a definite understanding that if Malaya or the Indies were attacked, the United States, Congress willing, would fight. Within two days, on August 12, the two leaders learned that the American House of Representatives had extended the Selective Service Act by a majority of only one vote.

After returning to Washington, Roosevelt on August 17 told Nomura that the United States

now finds it necessary to say to the government of Japan that if the Japanese government takes any further steps in pursuance of a policy or program of military domination by force or threat of force of neighboring countries, the government of the United States will be compelled to take immediately any and all steps which it might deem necessary toward safeguarding the legitimate rights and interests of the United States and American nationals and toward insuring the safety and security of the United States.

Churchill had wanted a stronger warning; but Roosevelt felt that, if he went too far, he might precipitate war. It is clear that the president wanted time to prepare his country materially and psychologically for war. Most important, he was still anxious to avoid war in the Pacific if possible because it would impede the war effort in Europe.

In the meeting with the president on August 17, Nomura explained Konoye's desire for a conference, and Roosevelt asked the Japanese government to submit a clearer statement of its attitude and intentions. The president did agree in principle to the meeting with Konoye and suggested that it be held at Juneau, Alaska, around October 15. In Tokyo Foreign Minister Toyoda suggested to Ambassador Grew the desirability of a meeting in Honolulu, and the latter strongly urged Hull to give the proposal careful consideration, for not only was it "unprecedented in Japanese history, but it is an indication that Japanese intransigence is not crystallized completely, owing to the fact that the proposal has the approval of the emperor and the highest authorities in the land." Grew emphasized Konoye's hope that the meeting would produce a *fait accompli* of so dramatic a nature that the Japanese people, directed by the emperor, would be swept into new channels of thought and accept Konoye's program.

In Washington, however, Hull and Secretary of War Stimson had little faith in Konoye's ability to settle basic issues. On August 28 Nomura delivered to Roosevelt a personal invitation from Konoye for an immediate meeting; and, although the president was tempted, he told Nomura on September 3 that he first had to have a clear idea of what Konoye had in mind on disputed points, especially the Tripartite Pact and China. Since Roosevelt supported Hull's insistence upon prior agreement on principles, there was little that Konoye could do.

The Fall of the Konoye Cabinet

In Tokyo Konoye faced renewed pressure from the Japanese military. The supreme command was increasingly concerned about the American and British buildup in the Pacific; although the increases in military and naval power were small and unbalanced, the Japanese army and navy were determined that they should not continue. In their view, the United States was just playing for time. Since Konoye could show nothing for his diplomatic efforts, the army began to call for a policy of force. Minister of the Army Tojo and General Sugiyama, chief of the general staff, demanded that the negotiations be terminated and that war be commenced as soon as Japanese forces could be placed in position. Konoye met with the military every day and insisted on talking with the United States while war preparations were under way; but the army argued that if Japan did not fight soon, her chances of victory would be less.

In an imperial conference on September 6 the government's policy was determined. Unless there was a satisfactory conclusion of the negotiations with the United States by the early part of October, Japan would go to war. The conference set Japan's minimum demands as follows:

1. That Great Britain and the United States not obstruct a peaceful settle- ment in China along Japanese lines. That they end their aid to Chiang K'ai-shek.
2. That the United States and Great Britain were not to establish new bases or increase their forces in East Asia.
3. That Japan retain a special position in Indochina as stated in agreements with the Vichy government.
4. That Great Britain and the United States restore trade relations with Japan and help her to get South Asian materials.
5. That Japan would not use Indochinese bases for military operations to the south and that Japan would observe the Neutrality Pact with the Soviet Union.
6. Should the United States enter the European war, Japan was to decide independently on the meaning and applicability of the Tripartite Pact.

The Japanese army sharpened up its war plans, and the navy went ahead with war games, including simulated attacks on Pearl Harbor. By September 13 the navy ministry completed the preliminary draft of "combined fleet top secret operation #1," the detailed plan for the surprise attack on Hawaii and simultaneous strikes at Malaya and the Philippines. The navy reasoned that if Japan attacked Singapore or the Indies, the United States would sooner or later enter the war. Thus, as early as January, 1941, Admiral Yamamoto Isoroku, commander of the combined fleeets, began planning the attack on Pearl Harbor. In his view, war with the United States was a great gamble, but he felt that "if we have war with the United States, we will have no hope of winning unless the American fleet in Hawaiian waters can be destroyed." In the same month, Ambassador Grew sent his first warning of such a possibility. Washington, though it realized that hostilities would probably begin with a surprise attack, did not consider Pearl Harbor a likely target.

The negotiations in Washington made little progress in September. Japan submitted its minimum demands, but the basic conflict remained. Grew continued to plead from Tokyo that Roosevelt meet with Konoye, stating his view that Konoye would otherwise fall from power and a military dictatorship bent upon war would be formed. He lamented the inflexibility of American diplomacy, which insisted on immediate black-and-white con-formance to every American requirement because, in his mind, this made Konoye's task impossible. Washington, however, continued to feel that the Japanese prime minister was a prisoner of Japan's minimum demands, as decided on September 6, and was hardly able to lead a retreat in Japanese policy. On October 2 Hull stated that Japan's minimum demands would not provide a basis for settlement and that a meeting between Roosevelt and Konoye would have to be postponed until there was a real acceptance of Hull's four principles.

By October it was increasingly apparent that Nazi pressure was being brought to bear on Japanese military leaders with telling effect. Hitler was anxious to throw every obstacle in the way of an American-Japanese agree-ment, and he was pressing for an official statement that Japan would declare war on the United States in the event of hostilities between Germany and the United States. The German ruler wanted Japanese help to keep Washing-ton from intervening to break the stranglehold which the German navy and air force were trying to clamp on Great Britain and her empire. In September a series of sinkings of American ships by German submarines forced the United States to consider defensive measures, and on September 26 the American navy ordered its units to protect all ships engaged in commerce in American defensive waters by destroying German and Italian raiders if necessary. In October the Neutrality Act was amended to permit American merchant ships to enter combat areas and belligerent ports.

When the deadline for agreement with Washington arrived on October 12, Konoye met with the army, navy, and foreign ministers to discuss the next step in American-Japanese relations. Supported by Foreign Minister Toyoda, Konoye wanted to continue negotiations and give way to the United States if necessary, since he felt that success in war was unlikely. Tojo, how-ever, adamantly maintained that there was no hope for agreement and insisted that the army would not yield on China and that any accord must provide for a limited Japanese occupation in order to maintain stability in China, to pre-serve Japan's position in Manchukuo and Korea, to prevent the spread of communism, and to assure orderly economic progress. He argued that the United States wanted to dominate East Asia and that, the more Japan gave way to her demands, the more overbearing would she become. Thus Japan should fight.

Tojo was able to prevent a decision to yield, but because of the attitude of the navy, which at the last moment deferred to Konoye, he could not get a definite decision for war. The navy preferred to have the prime minister bear the responsibility of a final decision. But when the cabinet met on October 14, Tojo virtually monopolized the floor, pressing the necessity of breaking off the negotiations and of deciding on war. Konoye found it im-possible to veer him from this course. That evening Tojo sent a message to the prime minister, urging that if the cabinet was not able to carry out the September 6 plans, it ought to resign and permit a new and unobligated cabinet to decide whether or not to go forward with those plans.

Konoye and his cabinet resigned on October 16, and on the following day a conference of the senior statesmen, or jushin, including Kiyoura Keigo, Wakatsuki Reijiro, Hirota Koki, Kido Koichi, Admirals Okada and Yonai, and Generals Abe and Hayashi, approved Tojo's appointment as prime minister. Interestingly, Kido, leader of the imperial palace advisers, supported Tojo in the mistaken belief that he could avert war with the United States by controlling the war faction within the army, and Konoye strangely went along in the hope that Tojo would not plunge the nation into war in view of the wavering of the navy, especially if the emperor enjoined him to be prudent. Probably the most important reason behind Tojo's appointment was the desire on the part of the jushin to review the decision of the September 6 imperial conference. Kido informed both Tojo and Navy Minister Oikawa that the emperor wished them to study internal and external circumstances more broadly and deeply than before and in so doing not to feel bound by the decisions which had been made in his presence on September 6.

Tojo served as his own army minister and home minister, and he replaced Toyoda as foreign minister with Togo Shigenori, a senior member of the diplomatic service, who extracted the promise from the prime minister that he would make a sincere effort to adjust relations with the United States. Since Togo was a former ambassador to Moscow and had always worked for the improvement of Japanese-Russian relations, his appointment was also regarded as a gesture of appeasement to the Soviet Union and proof that Japan was not intending to attack Siberia. Nomura, who had little idea of what his government was planning, desperately wanted to resign, but Tojo would not let him go. He was urged to remain and to make a greater effort than before.

The Tojo Cabinet and the Decision for War

Early in November the Japanese government once again decided on a course of action. The army still wanted war, and the navy began to reach the same conclusion because its oil stockpiles were declining rapidly in face of economic blockade. Admiral Nagano Osami, chief of the naval staff, who at one time had said that war was out of the question, was converted to the view that if an initial victory led to the capture of oil and other resources, then Japan had no reason to fear a long war. According to Togo, only after a hard struggle and a threat to resign did he get agreement on the submission of new proposals to Washington.

An imperial conference on November 5 decided to place two last proposals, known as "A" and "B," before Washington, and, if these were not accepted by November 25, war would be the only alternative. The German

615

and Italian governments were to be notified of Japan's intention at that date in the hope that they would follow Japan's course, but the conferees agreed that the country should remain at peace with the Soviet Union even if Germany was thereby alienated. In fact, they advocated a mediated peace between Germany and the Soviet Union in order to conserve German resources for the assault on Great Britain. Nomura was informed that some settlement had to be made by November 25 and that Kurusu Saburo, an experienced diplomat with the rank of ambassador, would be sent to help him; but, like Nomura, the new emissary was not informed about the Pearl Harbor attack plans.

On the evening of November 7 Nomura presented Proposal A to Hull and asked for a quick answer. It was a restatement of Japanese terms on the most disputed points:

1. Japanese acceptance of the principle of economic equality in China and throughout the Pacific, provided it was adopted in other parts of the world.
2. Retention of Japanese army units of unspecified size in certain areas of north China, Inner Mongolia, and Hainan Island for a "necessary period." Withdrawal of other troops within two years after the firm establishment of peace and order. The United States to persuade Chiang K'ai-shek to make peace with Japan under the threat of no more aid.
3. Withdrawal of Japanese forces in Indochina when the hostilities in China were settled or a just peace was established in East Asia.
4. Japan's maintenance of her obligations under the Tripartite Pact, although Japan had no desire to see the European war spread through the Pacific.

Hull and Roosevelt knew that this was the beginning of final negotiations, and from Tokyo Ambassador Grew warned that "action by Japan which might render unavoidable an armed conflict with the United States may come with dangerous and dramatic suddenness." Roosevelt received Nomura on November 10 and told him that Japan should prove her peaceful intentions by actions, suggesting a movement of Japanese troops out of Indochina and China, and Hull's formal answer to Proposal A followed the old pattern of American inquiries about the Tripartite Pact and China. Proposal A was rejected, and, although Nomura pleaded with his government against war, Tokyo paid no heed.

On November 10 Vice-Admiral Nagumo ordered all ships that were to participate in the Pearl Harbor attack to complete their preparations by November 20 and to assemble in the Kuriles. A few days earlier Yamamoto had selected December 7 (Washington time) as the tentative attack date. On November 11 some ten or more long-range Japanese submarines left Yokosuka for Hawaii. Their mission was to destroy any American vessels which might escape from Pearl Harbor during the planned assault.

On November 20 Nomura and Kurusu placed Proposal B before Hull. It read as follows:

1. The governments of both Japan and the United States shall undertake not to make any armed advance into any of the regions in Southeastern Asia and the South Pacific area excepting the part of French Indochina where Japanese troops are stationed at present.
2. The Japanese government shall undertake to withdraw its troops now stationed in French Indochina upon either the restoration of peace between Japan and China or the establishment of an equitable peace in the Pacific area.

   In the meantime the government of Japan declares that it is prepared to remove its troops now stationed in the southern part of French Indochina to the northern part of the said territory upon the conclusion of the present arrangement, which shall later be embodied in the final agreement.
3. The governments of Japan and the United States shall co-operate with a view to securing the acquisition of those goods and commodities which the two countries need in the Netherlands East Indies.
4. The governments of Japan and the United States shall mutually undertake to restore commercial relations to those prevailing prior to the freezing of assets. The government of the United States shall supply Japan the required quantity of oil.
5. The government of the United States shall undertake to refrain from such measures and actions as will be prejudicial to the endeavors for the restoration of the general peace between Japan and China.

On the same day General Homma on Formosa received his final orders for the invasion of the Philippines.

Proposal B was unacceptable to the American government, as Hull made clear in his reply on November 26. The United States put no trust in Japanese promises, although Togo hoped that Proposal B would eliminate American suspicions by demonstrating in deed that Japan had no designs on Southeast Asia. To Washington, however, withdrawal from southern Indochina was meaningless, since Japanese troops could easily be dispatched there once again. Hull also knew that Japan had set a deadline and that the Japanese proposals were in the nature of an ultimatum, and he regarded his answer as a counterproposal to keep the negotiations going. It can be broken down into the following three main parts:

1. Japan and the United States were mutually to promise to abide by the principles for inviolability of territorial integrity and sovereignty of nations, noninterference in the internal affairs of other countries, equality that included equality of commercial opportunity and treatment, and reliance on international co-operation and conciliation for the prevention and pacific settlement of disputes and for the improvement of international conditions by peaceful methods and processes.

617

2. Japan and the United States were to sponsor a nonaggression pact among all the countries in East Asia.
3. Japan was to withdraw all military, naval, air, and police forces from China and Indochina.

In Tokyo Hull's reply was taken as a definite rejection of the Japanese position. Foreign Minister Togo suggested that the note had been "studiously prepared, judging from the timing, with a view to forcing Japan to commit the first overt act." Although Nomura and Kurusu pleaded that the talks continue, Prime Minister Tojo used the November 26 reply as a pretext for war. Hull knew that war was coming and remarked to Secretary of War Stimson on November 27, "I have washed my hands of it, and it is now in the hands of you and Knox, the army and the navy." Washington's decipherment of Japanese messages disclosed that large Japanese forces were moving into bases in southern Indochina and that Japanese transports were gathering at the point in the Japanese mandated islands nearest to the Indies.

Tokyo had also cabled Nomura on November 21 that Japan could not wait beyond the 28th for agreement. After that date, the cable read, "Things are automatically going to happen." On November 21 Yamamoto, commander in chief of the combined fleet, sent an order to the Kurile task force, which was not intercepted, to move out on November 25 and proceed without being detected to a rendezvous set for December 2. "X day will be December 7." On November 22 the Japanese Second Fleet sailed from the Inland Sea, setting its course southward for Formosa in order to support the invasion of the Philippine Islands. On the following day Washington sent the first alert to Manila and to Pearl Harbor, and on November 27 warnings were again sent to MacArthur and to the army and navy commanders in Hawaii. "This dispatch is to be considered as a war warning." For a time Hull and Roosevelt considered offering Japan a *modus vivendi* which would provide her with raw materials in exchange for certain concessions and guarantees, but this course was protested by China and Great Britain. According to Churchill, Hull's November 26 note went far beyond anything the British expected.

Last-minute preparations for war were being made in Tokyo. On November 28 Nomura and Kurusu were told that the report of the cabinet's views, which would be sent within two or three days, would terminate the talks, although they were urged not to give the impression that the negotiations were broken off. "From now on do the best you can." On December 1 an imperial conference decided that war was the only means of achieving Japan's aims, and on the next day the supreme command issued orders to army and navy units to commence hostilities on December 7. According to Foreign Minister Togo, the Japanese view was that

unless Japan would wholly withdraw, war with the United States and Great Britain must come sooner or later. Since the military estimate is that the United

States will intensify its pressure upon us after having defeated Germany and Italy—by which time Japan, having been gradually exhausted, would have no strength to resist—Japan should, accepting the American challenge, fight now while she still has the resources and while the outlook is not entirely unpropitious. . . . It is recognized that Japan cannot utterly abandon her continental policy, and the consensus is that since the United States has, despite Japan's utmost efforts to succeed with Japanese-American negotiations, challenged Japan by delivery of such an ultimatum as the Hull note and by application of military pressure, there is for Japan no alternative to fighting in her self-defense.

Thereafter Tokyo concentrated on keeping the United States and Great Britain lulled and in sealing a war pact with Germany and Italy. On December 3 Mussolini gave general assurances but reserved the right to confer with Berlin, while Ribbentrop expressed some doubts. Although no agreement was reached before the Pearl Harbor attack, Germany and Italy declared war on December 11, and the three powers pledged not to conclude a separate peace or armistice with the enemy until the war had been successfully brought to a close.

Washington seemed content to let Japan strike the first blow, and the American people were not warned of the danger of Japanese attack. Throughout the whole year Roosevelt evidently thought it unwise to inform the American public, which, he felt, was essentially determined to keep out of war. At the last minute, on December 6, he did send a personal note to the emperor, but by this time it was too late. From East Asia came reports that two large fleets of Japanese ships were moving around the southern point of Indochina, and on the same day the final Japanese reply was being transmitted to Nomura and Kurusu. It was clear that war was imminent. The last section of the message was not relayed until the following morning, and it stated that negotiations were at an end. Nomura and Kurusu were ordered to present it at one o'clock in the afternoon on Sunday, December 7, but because of the delay in transmission they arrived at Hull's hotel an hour late, about two and a half hours after the Japanese had landed on the Malayan coast at Kota Bahru and an hour after the first bomb had fallen on Pearl Harbor. In Tokyo Ambassador Grew was summoned to see Togo, who handed him a copy of the reply to Hull's note. This constituted the emperor's answer to President Roosevelt. Not a word was said about Pearl Harbor.

War and Defeat

The Japanese attack on Pearl Harbor began at dawn on Sunday, December 7, and the primary target of the waves of airplanes was the warships of the American fleet. Eight battleships were hit, of which two, the "Pennsylvania" and the "Maryland," were restored to service very quickly, and a third, the "Tennessee," after a slightly longer period. Two of the remaining five were total losses, the "Oklahoma" and the "Arizona," but three others were ultimately salvaged and restored to service, the "California," the "West Virginia," and the "Nevada." Three cruisers were seriously damaged and three destroyers wrecked. Two thousand eight-six naval officers and men were lost, and the total number of casualties, including the missing, was finally placed at 3,435.

The Japanese attack knocked out the heart of the American Pacific Fleet and paralyzed it for a period of many weeks. The Japanese losses were trifling: twenty-nine aircraft, five midget submarines, and one fleet submarine. Despite this disaster for the United States, there was something of a bright side. Since a task force of aircraft carriers, crusiers, and destroyers had been sent on a mission to ferry planes to Wake and Midway islands, the Japanese missed some of the most important elements of the Pacific Fleet. In the subsequent naval warfare in the Pacific, battleships proved to be of less critical importance than was supposed at the time, while carriers and heavy cruisers bore the brunt of the fighting. American aircraft losses were trivial considering the immense air fleets that the United States eventually produced. The Japanese attack force also overlooked the base and dockyard facilities as well as the exposed oil storage.

The Japanese tide quickly swept over Southeast Asia. Landings at Kota Bahru were effected easily, and the drive toward Singapore began. The one serious threat to Japanese progress, the British battleships "Prince of Wales" and "Repulse," were destroyed by air attack. Japan also struck at the Philippines, although the initial attack was delayed by fog over Formosa; despite some warning, the American forces on Luzon lost most of their air support, the B-17's or Flying Fortresses, upon which the United States was relying for air power in East Asia. Thus, in the early moments of the war, the main obstacles to Japan's advance were destroyed.

Singapore fell to the Japanese army on February 15, 1942, Rangoon on March 8, Java on March 9, and the Andaman Islands on March 23. The conquest of the Philippines took longer than expected because of the stubborn Filipino and American resistance. Manila fell on January 3, but Corregidor held out until April 4. Meanwhile the unopposed Japanese navy operated freely in the Indian Ocean, shelled naval bases on Ceylon and Madagascar, and even made a surprise attack on Sydney. Japan did not suffer a defeat until the two naval battles of the Coral Sea in May, 1942, which halted the push south, and of Midway in June, 1942, in which the Japanese navy incurred substantial losses.

By 1943, however, the war began to turn against Japan as the Allies broke her outer defense perimeter in the central and southwest Pacific; moreover, air and naval attacks drastically reduced her shipping. At home there was a decline in war production because of labor shortages and dwindling stocks of raw materials, while consumer goods were increasingly in short supply. The Tojo cabinet was unable to withstand the double shock of defeats and economic collapse; and when the fall of Saipan in July exposed the homeland to air attack, it was forced to resign under pressure from the senior civilian statesmen. The new cabinet was headed by General Koiso Kuniaki, who was pledged to carry on the war with renewed energy but who was on watch for an opportunity to obtain a compromise peace settlement. In August a supreme council for the direction of the war was created under the chairmanship of the emperor, who was empowered to break a deadlock or to veto any decisions; this council included the prime minister, the ministers of the army, navy, and foreign affairs, and the army and navy chiefs of staff.

That Japan had lost the war was clear by the spring of 1945. On March 10 Tokyo suffered its first saturation bombing, and on April 1 the Battle of Okinawa began. On April 5 Koiso fell from power, and this precipitated a general discussion concerning the continuation of the war. Although the army insisted on fighting, the senior statesmen and the navy, wanting to avoid complete disaster, favored the selection of a prime minister who would work for peace. The strength of the latter view made possible the appointment of Admiral Suzuki Kantaro, who had escaped assassination in February, 1936, and who was serving as president of the privy council.

The Suzuki cabinet, however, was committed not to accept "unconditional surrender," as demanded by the Allies. In the following months the situation worsened. Okinawa fell, and air attacks on Japan increased in number and intensity. Germany capitulated, and the Soviet Union refused to extend the Neutrality Pact. On June 22, with the approval of the emperor, the supreme council decided to initiate peace negotiations through the good offices of the Soviet Union, but talks with the Soviet ambassador, Jacob Malik, got nowhere. The emperor then ordered Suzuki to dispatch a special envoy to Moscow, and on July 10 the supreme council asked Konoye to serve in that capacity and instructed the Japanese ambassador in Moscow to request the Soviet Union to intercede with the Allies on Japan's behalf. It was to be made clear, however, that so long as the Allies insisted on unconditional surrender, Japan had no alternative but to fight.

By this time the Allies were moving faster than Japan, and on July 26 they issued the Potsdam Declaration, which warned Japan to surrender or face "utter destruction." When Japan did not answer the ultimatum, the United States decided to use the atom bomb. The war then came to a speedy and dramatic conclusion. On August 6 the bomb destroyed Hiroshima, and Foreign Minister Togo conferred immediately with the emperor, urging him to accept the Potsdam ultimatum. On August 8 the Soviet Union announced that she would enter the war on the following day, and this was a staggering blow since Japan had no defense plans for Manchukuo and Korea.

On the morning of August 9 Suzuki met with the emperor, and the two men agreed on the need to end the war even if it meant acceptance of the Allies' terms. But when the supreme council considered the matter, its members were deadlocked. The prime minister, foreign minister, and navy minister voted for acceptance on the understanding that there would be no alteration of the emperor's legal position, but the army minister and the two chiefs of staff posed four conditions: no Allied occupation of Japan, demobilization of the army and navy under Japanese supervision, prosecution of war criminals by the Japanese government, and no impairment of the emperor's status.

Even when news came of the destruction of Nagasaki by the second atomic bombing, the two sides would not alter their position, but at three o'clock in the morning the emperor finally broke the deadlock by throwing his support to Suzuki. The allies were informed of the Japanese decision on the same day, and on August 11 they agreed to preserve the emperor's status so long as he and the government would be subject to the authority of the supreme commander for the allied powers (SCAP), who would be empowered to take whatever steps were necessary to effect the surrender terms. The Japanese government consented, but only after the emperor had again used his influence on the military.

On August 14 the war came to an end, and the Allies began making arrangements for the surrender ceremony. Basic policy for SCAP, which General Douglas MacArthur received by radio from Washington on August 29, emphasized three goals for the occupation: demilitarization of Japanese power, reform and democratization of Japanese institutions, and development of economic stability in Japan. Finally, on September 2, aboard the battleship "Missouri" in Tokyo Bay, the supreme commander, General MacArthur, accepted Japan's surrender on behalf of the Allied powers, and on the same day the emperor issued an edict ordering his people to comply with the terms of the surrender and the directives of the occupation authorities.

30   Japan after World War II

The policy-directing agency of the occupation forces was the general headquarters of SCAP, with appropriate sections to supervise the various operations of the Japanese government, which was made responsible for the execution of basic policy. Most of these sections—political, education, natural resources, and others—were headed by military officers and staffed by civilians, and with only a few exceptions the personnel was American. The administrative side of the occupation was largely controlled by the civil-affairs section of the Eighth Army and its forty-five prefectural civil-affairs teams, which supervised rice and tax collections, schools, religious activities, elections, courts, and local government in general. Later, in 1949, administrative control was transferred from the Eighth Army to the small civil-affairs section in SCAP, and supervision of Japanese local government was the responsibility of eight regional civil-affairs teams, each having jurisdiction over an average of six prefectures.

Before the surrender, the United States had taken steps to meet the desires of the Allies to participate in the occupation of Japan. Washington had submitted a proposal to the United Kingdom, the Soviet Union, and China for the creation of a Far Eastern advisory commission to inform the various governments about the policies adopted to insure Japanese compliance with the surrender terms; but at the council of foreign ministers in London in September, 1945, Molotov offered a counterproposal, recommending the establishment of a control council for Japan similar to the four-power control council in Germany. Despite British support of the Russian suggestion, the United States was unwilling to forfeit her favored position in the occupation, and not until the council of foreign ministers meeting in Moscow in December were the differences finally reconciled. It was agreed to form an eleven-nation Far Eastern Commission in Washington with power to formulate policy and a four-nation advisory Allied Council for Japan in Tokyo. Although four countries—the United Kingdom, the Soviet Union, China, and the United States—had veto power in the formulation of policies, the power proved meaningless in practice. The United States was authorized to deal with "urgent matters" by issuing interim directives, which were to be referred to the Far Eastern Commission for review but were to remain in effect unless the Commission voted otherwise. Thus the United States could use her veto against any attempt to change one of her own directives. The Allied Council for Japan, which included representatives from the United States, the United Kingdom, the Soviet Union, and China, was not a control body on the German model since it could only advise SCAP when General MacArthur wished to consult with it. Its meetings, held every other week, proved largely perfunctory as MacArthur was sensitive to adverse criticism and would not permit the Soviet delegate to use the meetings for propaganda purposes.

The Japanese population proved to be docile and co-operative for the most part. There was some initial fear of foreign soldiers, but that quickly disappeared before the tact and benevolence of MacArthur and the American troops. The psychological background quite naturally played a major part in the attitude of many Japanese. The population as a whole was physically exhausted and disillusioned by war, and what military opposition to surrender that did exist vanished by the end of August, when the first advance units of the occupation forces arrived. The emperor had asked his people to obey SCAP, and the Japanese government made constant appeals to the national feeling of the people to accept the complete and supreme authority of the occupation forces.

Demilitarization

Demilitarization was the first objective of SCAP and certainly the easiest to accomplish. The demobilization of the imperial army, navy, and air force was completed by December under Allied supervision with over 2,000,000 officers and men on the main islands of Japan returned to civilian life. Shortly thereafter the army and navy ministries were abolished. By the end of January, 1946, demobilization had proceeded so well that one of the two American armies of occupation was withdrawn. During the same period some 3,000,000 overseas troops and 3,000,000 civilians began to be repatriated and helped ultimately to swell the Japanese population. The entire process of repatriation was completed by 1948 with the exception of prisoners of war still held in Siberia; and although the Soviet Union finally returned approximately 95,000, another 375,000 military personnel and civilians were never accounted for. Many of these died, in all likelihood, from disease, malnutrition, physical abuse, and lack of housing facilities. Demilitarization was applied to production, and arsenals and other plants engaged in war production were permitted to convert to the manufacture of nonmilitary goods only under license. Existing military stores were destroyed or were divided among the Allies.

Like the Germans, the Japanese were tried as war criminals in the belief that militarism and aggression could be discredited by the punishment of irresponsible militarists and ultranationalists. Throughout East Asia military courts, composed of representatives of the states whose nationals had been victimized by Japanese personnel, held trials in the territory where the "crimes" had been committed. The select group of leaders who had planned the war in violation of international law were tried in Tokyo by an international tribunal, composed of the representatives of eleven nations, which began its deliberations on May 3, 1946. The twenty-eight major war criminals, tried for crimes against the peace, conventional war crimes, and crimes against humanity, included such prominent figures as Kido, Tojo, Koiso, Hirota, Araki, and Matsuoka. In November, 1948, the tribunal found all guilty of planning to secure Japan's domination over Asia by waging a war of aggression. Seven were condemned to die, including Tojo, Hirota, and Matsui Iwane, who was held responsible for the "rape of Nanking"; sixteen were sentenced to life imprisonment; one received a twenty-year term; and Shigemitsu Mamoru, a diplomat, was sentenced to prison for seven years. During the course of the trial, two of the defendants died, and one was committed to an institution for the insane.

If the trial was designed to provide a basic moral lesson for the Japanese people as a whole, it is doubtful that this objective was accomplished. Actually, the opposite was the more general result, because the average Japanese found it convenient to condemn the military for waging a war when it was not certain of victory. The war itself—not the spectacle of the trials—provided the important lesson for the Japanese people. Misery was more effective than justice. In all, approximately 4,200 Japanese were convicted of war crimes in some 2,000 separate or group trials in Japan and elsewhere. Of these, over 700 were executed, and about 2,500 were sentenced to life imprisonment. The remainder generally have been released after serving light sentences.

The demilitarization process also included the purge, which began in January, 1946. Militaristic and ultranationalistic leaders were removed from public office and forbidden to run for election in the hope of facilitating the emergence of fresh national leadership. And despite resistance by Japanese conservatives, in 1947 the purge was extended to officials in local government, leaders of the largest industrial and financial combines, and influential persons in the various media of public information. When the process of screening came to an end in May, 1948, approximately 220,000 persons had been purged, of whom about 180,000 were former military officers; some 1,300 organizations were also dissolved. The purge was decidedly the most unpopular of the occupation reforms since there was a good deal of abuse and confusion in its administration; and when the occupation ended, the purge was the first reform to be rescinded. Because of their age and the six years of enforced inactivity, very few of the purged leaders have succeeded in returning to positions of political prominence, although they have had substantial success in other fields of activity.

The disestablishment of Shinto deserves special mention. A SCAP directive of December, 1945, ordered the abolition of all government connection with State Shinto, and after that date Shinto institutions and priests received no official public support, all government agencies for the control and support of Shinto were abolished, teaching of Shinto doctrines in schools ceased, and shrines were prohibited from propagating militaristic and ultranationalistic doctrines. Much of the foundation of State Shinto was destroyed when SCAP required Emperor Hirohito himself to make a public statement on January 1, 1946, denying his divinity. Thereafter the occupation authorities did as much to humanize the throne as the emperor's co-operation would permit. One technique was to insist that he be more accessible to the people through numerous public appearances, but for the introvert Hirohito this was indeed difficult, and later much of this sort of activity was delegated to his princely brothers.

Constitutional Revision and Politics

The political reorientation of Japan dates from the October 4, 1945, SCAP directive, popularly known as the "Japanese bill of rights," which guaranteed the people fundamental freedoms, abrogated legislation restricting human rights, and freed political prisoners, largely socialists and communists, from jail. The home ministry, the focus of centralized police control, was deprived of most of its powers, and the police were forbidden to interfere with individual liberties. A new civil code established female equality with regard to marriage, divorce, family matters, and inheritance; individual freedom from parental domination after the attainment of legal age; and equality of inheritance instead of primogeniture. Despite the new code, tradition continues to maintain many social inequalities, and economic necessity usually causes younger children to forego their inheritance in favor of the eldest son and go elsewhere to seek employment so that the family farm or enterprise can be passed down intact, as in the past.

The new freedom of the Japanese people was a general stimulus to political activity. The Liberal Party (Jiyuto) was formed by prewar politicians like Hatoyama Iichiro and Yoshida Shigeru, but the party proved to be more conservative than liberal in its platform, which advocated a *laissez-faire* economy, female suffrage, a lower voting age, and reorganization of the house of peers and the privy council but no major changes in the Meiji Constitution. The Progressive Party (Shimpoto), founded by party elders like Machida Chuji, was just as conservative and supported a minimum of government interference in business and private life. More than 270 members of the wartime house of representatives rapidly joined the Progressive Party, in large part because of the Minseito background of its leaders and the hope that it might be favored by the American authorities. The new party immediately threw its support behind Prime Minister Shidehara Kijuro, who assumed office in October.

Two left-wing parties emerged. The Socialists (Nihon Shakaito), with a membership drawn from the labor movement and urban intellectuals, advocated constitutional revision along more democratic lines, higher wages and improved working conditions, and the gradual nationalization of banking and key industries. The Japanese Communist Party (Nihon Kyosanto) was formed by leaders who had been released from prison and others, like Nosaka Sanzo, who had returned from exile. Seeking to broaden their popular support, the communists supported such causes as stricter price controls, higher wages, and alleviation of food shortages. The party's over-all platform concentrated on peaceful evolutionary change toward democracy and socialism rather than immediate proletarian revolution. Elements of the communist program like collectivization of land and abolition of the emperor system, though brought forward from time to time, were subordinated to the need to establish a broad popular front. The Socialist Party, however, refused to form an alliance with the communists.

As the process of democratization gained momentum, constitutional revision became the crucial problem. SCAP informed the Japanese that they should undertake a revision of the Meiji Constitution, and Konoye, now vice-premier, was one of the first to take the initiative in this matter. With the co-operation of SCAP, he headed a constitutional drafting commission; but before the Japanese government could act on his proposals, Konoye took his own life in December for fear of being branded a war criminal. Prime Minister Shidehara then formed a cabinet committee to study revision, but there seemed to be little inclination on the part of Japanese conservatives to make fundamental changes.

When the draft, submitted to SCAP on February 1, 1956, maintained the emperor as the source of political power, failed to provide for cabinet responsibility to the house of representatives, and did not guarantee basic rights and freedoms, SCAP took over direction of constitutional revision. Its draft constitution,* which was published on March 6, 1946, and was endorsed by MacArthur and the emperor, relegated the imperial institution to the position of symbol of the state and made the people sovereign, with their power to be exercised by the executive, legislative, and judicial branches of the government. The prime minister would be elected by the 467 members of the house of representatives and would thus represent the majority party or coalition of parties, and he and his entire cabinet, the majority of which must be diet members, would be collectively responsible to the diet. Members of both houses of the diet, councilors and representatives, would be elected according to the provisions of a new law, passed on April 6 by the diet at the suggestion of SCAP, which provided for suffrage for all Japanese at the age of twenty. In the case of the representatives, who serve four-year terms, each of the 118 electoral districts is represented by from three to five members, although each voter casts his ballot for only one candidate. In the case of the councilors, one half of whom are elected every three years for six-year terms, 150 are elected from prefectures and 100 from the country at large, and each voter casts two ballots, one for the prefectural candidate and another for the national candidate. Within the diet, the house of representatives is the more powerful body; all money bills must originate with it, and any bill passed by it but rejected by the house of councilors can become law if repassed by the house of representatives with a majority of two-thirds or more of the members present. The court system, headed by a supreme court modeled on the American institution, would be independent of the executive and legislative branches of the government but would have the power of judicial review of the constitutionality of "any law, order, regulation, or official act." A bill of rights, the largest section of the constitution, went beyond its American counterpart in the enumeration of specific rights and included many provisions of an economic, social, and cultural nature, such as the guarantee of free, compulsory, and equal education as well as academic freedom, the right to "maintain the minimum standards of wholesome and cultural living," and the right of workers to organize and bargain collectively. These rights are

---

* See Appendix 4.

carefully guarded by the Japan Civil Liberties Union, the various bar associations, and the organs of public opinion. Perhaps the outstanding feature of the constitution was Article Nine, which renounced war and the right to maintain an army, navy, and air force. Amendments to the constitution are to be initiated by the diet and require an affirmative vote of two-thirds or more of the members of each house, and the proposed amendment must then be ratified by majority of votes in a popular referendum.

The draft constitution was submitted for approval to the Japanese government that was formed after the first postwar elections in April, 1946. The fact that both conservative parties were crippled by the purge, especially the Progressives, who discovered that only twenty-seven of their several hundred members in the lower house were eligible for re-election, explains in large part the failure of any party to win a majority. The election results were as follows: Liberals, 139; Progressives, 94; Socialists, 93; and Communists, 5. In view of the outcome, Shidehara resigned; and since the Liberal Party leader, Hatoyama Iichiro, had been purged, his lieutenant, Yoshida Shigeru, who had been arrested in 1944 for opposing continuation of the war, became prime minister.

The Yoshida cabinet, essentially an alliance of the two conservative parties, approved the draft constitution, as did the diet and the privy council in turn, and the government promulgated it on November 3, 1946. The constitution was not to become effective until May 3, 1947, in order to give the diet time to pass the laws needed to implement it. The Imperial House Law subjected the members of the imperial family to the laws of Japan in their status of private citizens, and the Imperial House Economy Law provided that all property of the imperial family belonged to the state and that all expenses of the imperial family would be appropriated in the annual budget.

Before the constitution went into effect, Yoshida fell from power after the election of April, 1947, in which the Socialists won 143 seats in the house of representatives compared to the Liberals' 133. These election returns reflected labor's discontent with economic conditions; in fact, a general strike scheduled for February 1, 1947, was averted only by General MacArthur's direct intervention. With the support of other political parties, including the Democrats—an offshoot of the Progressives—and the Co-operatives, the Socialist Party leader, Katayama Tetsu, formed a coalition cabinet, but it was clear that he had no mandate for the implementation of a socialist program.

Local-Autonomy, Police, and Education Reforms

The occupation authorities also sought to strengthen democracy through the extension of local autonomy. The home ministry was abolished, and most of its functions were dispersed among local government units. The Local

Autonomy Law provided for the election of prefectural governors and made them responsible to popularly elected assemblies, and lesser administrative offices came under the aegis of prefectural civil services. In the cities the former indirect election of mayors and other executive officials by the popularly elected municipal assemblies has been replaced by direct election. Referendum, initiative, and recall have also been provided for at both prefectural and municipal levels.

Although the purpose of these measures was to provide training in democratic government on the local level, the first elections in April, 1947, largely returned to office the officials previously appointed by Tokyo; moreover, there was no clear definition of the respective powers of the national and local units of government. There was much duplication and overlapping of functions between the two, and local governments remained financially dependent on the national treasury, which had pre-empted the most lucrative sources of tax revenue. As a consequence, in the actual operation of the administration, local government units have remained subject to close supervision by Tokyo even in those areas where they have been assigned direct responsibility. But despite defects and abuses, there is much greater opportunity for popular participation in government and greater awareness of the need for responsible administration.

As part of the reform of local government, the police system of Japan was decentralized. In December, 1947, the home ministry was abolished, and under a new law the police were divided into two basic groups—independent local units, with a total strength of 95,000 men, which were under the control of public safety commissions appointed, with the approval of local assemblies, by mayors in all municipalities of 5,000 or more people; and national rural police, with a total strength of 30,000 men, who were under police commissions appointed by the prefectural governors and approved by the assemblies. Both forces were free from central government supervision except in times of national emergency, and their duties were confined to those normally exercised by a police force in a democratic society.

The educational system was revised, by a series of laws passed in 1947–1948, to accord with the American pattern; the new educational philosophy sought to inculcate democracy, responsibility, and individualism. The first nine years of schooling, comprising six years of elementary and three years of junior high school, are compulsory and tuition-free, and they can be followed by three years of senior high school and four years of college, where there is a strong emphasis on general education. Beyond that, specialization can be achieved at professional or academic graduate schools. A general purge of teachers, the elimination of military education and courses in ethics from the curriculum, and the rewriting of textbooks supplemented these changes. Finally, as in the case of the police, educational administration was decentralized. The activities of the ministry of education were confined to

629

technical assistance, and administrative control of elementary and secondary schools was vested in local school boards, elected in the forty-six prefectures and five largest cities and subsequently in town and village committees. These local boards were to decide upon educational policy, budgets, curriculum, textbooks, and teachers. To provide greater educational opportunities, SCAP ordered that all institutions of higher learning be made over into four-year colleges or universities on the American model; and, with usually unfortunate results as far as academic standards were concerned, the three-year higher schools *(kotogakko)*, technical institutions, and normal schools hurriedly complied. SCAP also decreed that there should be a university in each prefecture. These measures brought the total number of colleges and universities to more than two hundred, which was far too many for a nation the size of Japan. Later, when SCAP encouraged the development of junior colleges, there was a further debasement of educational standards.

Economic Reforms

Democratic reform extended also to the economic realm, and one of the first objectives of the occupation authorities was the dissolution of the zaibatsu. Under the direction of SCAP, the government in July, 1946, established the holding-company liquidation commission, which gradually took into its custody the securities held by zaibatsu families and by the holding companies listed for dissolution. The Law for the Elimination of Excessive Concentration of Economic Power, passed in December, 1947, provided for the dissolution of companies considered large enough to restrain competition, and the holding-company liquidation commission was ordered to designate such companies by September, 1948, and plan their reorganization. The actual process of dissolution was carried out by the fair-trade commission, which was established by the April, 1947, Law Relating to Prohibition of Private Monopoly and Methods of Preserving Fair Trade to prevent such practices as intercorporate stockholding, unfair pricing, and interlocking directorates. By the end of 1949, after the application of these measures, 83 zaibatsu holding companies were dissolved, with their securities being offered for public sale, and 53 zaibatsu members were purged from business. The Mitsui and Mitsubishi interests were replaced by 240 smaller companies. The five great banks, with some eight hundred branches, were not broken up, although zaibatsu control was removed; and under law they were forbidden to hold securities in other companies in excess of 5 per cent of the company's assets. Some 5,000 corporations were forced to go through financial reorganization; but of the 1,200 corporations subject to dissolution according to the recommendation of the holding-company liquidation commission, only 9 were actually disbanded. American policy was shifting from reform toward stabilization. In the judgment of the deconcentration review board of American experts, the reform was going too far and might actually impair economic recovery. In the past decade the number of business mergers has constantly increased, and a new concentration of economic power has arisen. Moreover, with capital in short supply, the role of the large banks is as great as ever.

The occupation authorities encouraged the development of an independent and responsible labor movement, not only for purposes of democratization but also to secure a better distribution of income and an improvement of the home market for Japanese products. The Trade Union Law of December, 1945, established the rights of labor to organize, to engage in collective bargaining, and to strike and created labor relations committees at the national and prefectural levels to mediate disputes. The Labor Relations Adjustment Law of September, 1946, improved the means of settling labor disputes, denied public-safety and administrative employees the right to strike, and made it mandatory for public-utility workers to wait thirty days after appealing for government mediation before striking. The Labor Standards Law of 1947 formulated minimum standards for wages, hours, working conditions, unemployment compensation, and old-age insurance.

By the end of 1946 two large labor federations, the All-Japan Federation of Labor (Sodomei), with 900,000 members, and the National Congress of Industrial Unions (Sanbetsu), with 1,600,000 members, had been organized; and by 1949, out of the total industrial labor force of 15,000,000, there were approximately 6,600,000 workers in some 35,000 unions, about half of which were affiliated with some national body. However, the overwhelming majority of unions were small, about half having less than fifty members; and no less than 90 per cent of all unions were so-called "enterprise," or company, unions, including unions of manual and white-collar workers, which accounted for some 85 per cent of total union membership.

While there were many labor disputes for basic economic purposes, such as wage increases, there was also a strong trend toward political strikes, particularly in those unions where communists and radical socialists had strong footholds. For example, the so-called "October, 1946, offensive," launched by Sanbetsu, developed into a political movement which reached its peak in the general strike planned for February 1, 1947, by the Communications Workers Union, the National Railway Workers Union, and the Teachers Union. They hoped that the pressure of a strike by 2,000,000 government workers would achieve the following goals: establishment of a basic minimum wage, conclusion of a labor agreement, elimination of job discrimination, abrogation of the Labor Disputes Mediation Law, abolition of income tax on labor, and elimination of unfair discharges. On this occasion, and again in 1948, SCAP had to intervene to prevent general strikes.

Radical political activity by labor also caused the government in July, 1948, on the advice of SCAP, to deny to regular public-service employees the rights of collective bargaining and striking and to forbid strikes or other tactics

631

from impairing normal operations by public-corporation employees of the railways and the tobacco, liquor, and salt monopolies, although they could still bargain collectively. The Trade Union Law was also amended in 1949 to guarantee democratic processes within unions and specifically to prevent the arbitrary exercise of power by leaders not supported by the majority of the membership and to prevent domination or interference by employers (for example, many union officials received salaries from employers).

Sanbetsu lost most of its membership because its policies had invited this strong reaction, and the labor movement sought to return to policies designed to attain economic objectives. So-called "democratization leagues" in unions affiliated with Sanbetsu and elements of Sodomei joined to form the General Council of Trade Unions (Sohyo) as an anticommunist union federation. By 1954 Sanbetsu membership had dropped to 13,000, largely contained in two small national unions. Sohyo, however, was not a stable body and was subjected to numerous ideological and personality clashes; in fact, the right wing of Sodomei objected to efforts to centralize the power of Sohyo leadership and withdrew, forming a new, independent Sodomei. Moreover, Sohyo's activities became increasingly political, reaching a peak in the prolonged strikes of 1952–1953 in the coal-mining and electric-power industries. Elements that objected to this course formed the National Liaison Council for Trade Union Democracy (Minroren) for the purpose of returning to nonpolitical action; this group ultimately (1953) joined with Sodomei to form Japan's second-largest federation, the Japan Trade Union Congress (Zenro), composed largely of private-industry unions in contrast to Sohyo, which derives some 50 per cent of its membership from government-worker unions.

Land reform, another major accomplishment of the occupation, also had both political and economic objectives. Under a law passed in October, 1946, absentee owners had to sell their land to the government, noncultivators who lived on their land could retain two and a half acres, and cultivators were limited to seven and a half acres. The designation and appraisal of the land to be sold and its transfer to tenants were administered by some 13,000 elected village land commissions, whose activities were co-ordinated by prefectural and national bodies. Some 70 per cent of Japan's agricultural land was claimed outright, purchased with inflated currency, and sold to tenant farmers on a thirty-year payment plan at moderate interest rates. Since peasants made huge profits by diverting part of their produce into the black market, none was so poor as to be unable to buy as much land as was available. Where tenancy remained, rents were limited to cash payments equal to 25 per cent of the main crop, and written leases were required.

By 1950, as a result of this program, 3,000,000 cultivators got 5,000,000 acres of land, and the total amount of land worked by tenants was reduced from 46 to 12 per cent of the cultivated area. The government also acquired an additional 2,800,000 acres for reclamation; by the end of 1949 about 300,-

000 new acres had been brought under cultivation, and by 1955 the figure had risen to 1,250,000 acres.

Agricultural co-operatives, which have long been widespread in Japan, have been made more democratic so that they work in the interests of the majority rather than of the larger operators. By 1949 there were over 32,000 co-operatives, one in virtually every village, with a total membership of about 8,000,000 men and women. Almost every farm family is in some form of co-operative, the most extensive of which perform wholesale and retail functions, extend credit, bank deposits, and operate warehouses.

Despite these changes, the rural areas are still overcrowded and the farm units are still too small. Since about two-thirds of Japan's farming population is surplus and cannot be absorbed in the urban economy, Japanese peasants, although they are much better off than before, remain at a low standard of living. Traditional attitudes still persist to a great extent, but Japanese peasants are slowly becoming aware of their new social status and political power.

Economic Rehabilitation

The Japanese economy, suffering from the damages of war, severe materials shortages, and inflation, and faced with the demands of a population that had increased from 72,000,000 in 1945 to over 80,000,000 in 1948, found economic recovery difficult to achieve. As a result of defeat in the war, Japan lost approximately 45 per cent of her territory and had almost half of her manufacturing facilities destroyed in air raids. Over all, Japan lost 40 per cent of her national wealth. Practically all consumer and producer goods had disappeared from the market, and production remained at a standstill. Under the impact of inflation, wholesale prices of commodities had advanced continually; in September, 1945, they were three times higher than prewar levels, and in the following year they increased many times more. SCAP maintained that the Japanese should solve their own economic problems and that American aid should be kept at a minimum; but when industry and foreign trade did not revive as expected, SCAP intervened and American assistance was increased. But despite aid in the amount of $300,000,000 per year, industrial production by the end of 1947 was only 44 per cent of the 1930–1934 average, when the population had been fifteen million less. In fact, economic difficulties, highlighted by a trade deficit of almost $300,000,000 and an export trade of only 13 per cent of the 1930–1934 levels, caused the socialist Katayama to give way as prime minister to Ashida Hitoshi of the Democratic Party; and these same problems ultimately returned Yoshida and the Liberals to power in October, 1948.

The Yoshida cabinet, on American advice, implemented an economic reform program in December, 1948, that was designed to create stability and to increase production for export. The main features of this program were austerity in government expenditures, reduction of income taxes but improvement in their collection, limitation of the extension of credit to useful projects, wage controls, improvement of rationing, elimination of excess-profits taxes, and establishment of a stable rate of exchange at 360 yen to 1 dollar.

The economy was also strengthened by American willingness to curtail its program of breaking up the cartels and by an awareness on the part of the noncommunist world that Japanese trade should be encouraged, e.g., in October, 1949, the Economic Commission for Asia and the Far East (ECAFE) approved a resolution stating that an expansion of trade between Japan and the countries on the commission would be beneficial to the region as a whole, and a special study recommended that Japan export capital goods to these nations. Popular confidence in Yoshida and the economic program was evidenced by the victory of the Liberal Party in the January, 1949, elections, when it won a majority of 264 seats in the house of representatives. The Democrats, hurt by the corruption scandals of the Ashida cabinet, declined from 90 to 68, and the Socialists went from 111 to 49.

The outbreak of hostilities in Korea in 1950 helped the Japanese economy, which was beginning to make a slow recovery, to make substantial gains. With the national budget balanced for two years, more efficient allocation of raw materials, and tighter credit controls, the industrial index, based on 1930–1934 as 100, rose from approximately 44 in 1947 to slightly over 73 in 1950; moreover, real wages were stabilized and inflation was halted. But price and distribution controls had to remain in effect so long as food, clothing, and other necessities continued in short supply. The unfavorable trade balance was reduced from a peak of $510,000,000 to $220,000,000, but Japan needed to increase her exports markedly since the United States was reducing her direct aid by 50 per cent in 1950–1951. However, during the period of hostilities in Korea the United States purchased Japanese goods in the amount of $800,000,000 annually, which more than matched the unfavorable trade balance, and American servicemen spent several hundred millions of dollars in Japan. Military orders for United Nations forces and other service spending totaled $4,042,000,000 by the end of 1956. The Japanese industrial index rose to 86 in 1951, to 154 in 1953, and to 174 in 1954. With 1934–1936 as a base, per capita real income was 105 per cent by 1954.

The Peace Treaty

By the time of the Korean conflict, the occupation authorities had completed their reform program, and the United States was already planning to conclude a peace treaty with Japan. General MacArthur wanted an early peace, and in fact the State Department had been working on a draft treaty since 1947. But when the United States could not get her allies to agree on the termination of the occupation, she gave up the project temporarily. MacArthur, however, prepared for withdrawal and dissolved the prefectural civil-affairs teams in November, 1949.

By 1950 the United States had won over most of the noncommunist world to her point of view, and in July, 1951, she and the United Kingdom extended invitations to fifty-five of the Allied powers at war with Japan to attend a peace conference, to be held at San Francisco in September. Each power received a copy of a draft treaty and was informed that August 31 was the terminal date for suggested alterations. It was made clear that the purpose of the conference was to sign the treaty. Only Burma, India, and Yugoslavia refused the invitation, and neither of the two Chinas was invited. With the exception of the Soviet bloc, which objected to the fact that the conference did not include Communist China and which disapproved of the forthcoming American-Japanese security pact, forty-eight nations signed the treaty, which provided for the termination of the occupation within ninety days of April 1, 1952.

Japan was once again a sovereign nation, although she had to accept the loss of her empire, part of which—the Ryukyus and the Bonin Islands—was placed under the trusteeship of the United States. With regard to reparations, Japan promised to negotiate with the claimants individually, and by 1958 she had reached settlements with the Philippines, Burma, and Indonesia. Under the security pact signed with the United States, American troops would remain in Japan for an indefinite period, and by an agreement concluded in February, 1952, the United States leased a number of military bases in Japan.

Despite Article Nine of the constitution, Japan had already begun to organize the nucleus of an army. In July, 1950, General MacArthur had ordered the formation of a 75,000-man national police reserve, and during the treaty negotiations the United States emphasized that Japan should develop a security force to deal with internal and external aggression. When such action was upheld by a decision of the Japanese supreme court, the Yoshida cabinet began to transform the national police reserve into the national safety force of 110,000 men.

Japan announced her intention to conform to the Charter of the United Nations and to apply for membership in that body, but in June, 1952, the Soviet Union, still "at war" with Japan, vetoed her application despite its approval by the General Assembly. The Japanese government, however, sent a permanent observer to the United Nations and did affiliate with such bodies as the International Bank for Reconstruction and Development, the Food and Agricultural Organization, and the World Health Organization, and Japan finally became a full-fledged member of the United Nations in 1957, after "normalization" of her relations with the Soviet Union.

Prime Minister Yoshida and the Liberal Party remained in power after the termination of the occupation, although their strength began to deteriorate. In the elections of October, 1952, the Liberal Party won 240 seats, a decline of 24; the Progressives (Kaishinto)—a coalition of members of the Co-operative Party and one wing of the Democrats—won 88; and the socialists, split into the Left-Wing Socialist Party and the Right-Wing Socialist Party, won 56 and 60, respectively. The 1952 election saw the return to political life of Hatoyama Iichiro, who was depurged in 1951. He won a seat in the house of representatives and headed an anti-Yoshida faction of 35 of his Liberal Party colleagues. After the April, 1953, election Yoshida lost his majority and faced the opposition of the Progressives, the two socialist parties, and the Hatoyama faction, all of whom objected to what they called "one-man rule."

Party Politics and Issues

Because of the increasing power and activity of the left wing in Japanese society, Yoshida's Liberal Party in April, 1954, suggested a merger with the Progressives, but the latter, as well as the Hatoyama faction of the Liberal Party, would no longer accept Yoshida's leadership. Instead, the Progressives, headed by Shigemitsu Mamoru, who was paroled in 1950, joined with the Hatoyama faction to form the Democratic Party (Minshuto) in November, 1954. Much of the political negotiating that attended this merger was conducted by Kishi Nobusuke, a former civilian adviser of General Tojo, who had joined the Liberal Party but had been expelled by Yoshida in 1954. With Hatoyama as president and Shigemitsu as vice-president, the new party pledged to clean up politics, alter some of the occupation reforms that had gone too far (especially in order to check radical activities), foster nationalism, conclude peace with the Soviet Union, and normalize relations with Communist China.

The formation of the Democratic Party, with its 121 seats in the house of representatives, reduced the total number of seats held by the Liberals to 185 and forced Yoshida's resignation on December 7, 1954. The house of representatives proceeded to elect Hatoyama as prime minister, but he first had to promise the socialist parties that he would hold a general election in the spring of 1955. In this election, held in February, the Democrats won 185 seats; the Liberals, 112; the Left-Wing Socialists, 89; and the Right-Wing Socialists, 67; and in the lower-house vote for prime minister Hatoyama was elected over Suzuki Mosaburo, the Left-Wing Socialist leader.

In 1955 the two wings of the socialists merged to form the Socialist Party (Shakaito). After the brief tenure of the Katayama cabinet the Social Democrats had gradually split into two parties, the Right- and Left-Wing Socialists. In the January, 1951, party convention the division became firm after a basic difference of opinion regarding the peace treaty. The Right Wing favored signing the treaty, even if it excluded the Soviet Union, while the Left Wing wanted a treaty that included the communist nations.

Underlying the break was the long-standing dispute as to whether the party should be centered in the working class or should seek to be a popular political party without any special class orientation. The Right Wing, led by Kawakami Jotaro and including a larger number of older politicians with experience in the prewar movement, pledged the peaceful development of the state ownership of large industries, refusal to accept rearmament in principle although it tolerated the national safety force, and a foreign policy of neutralism in the cold war, with emphasis on greater independence from the United States. Its largest support came from intellectuals, white-collar workers, and the 680,000 members of the All-Japan Trade Union Congress (Zenro), which sought the gradual achievement of socialism by working through the existing economic framework. The Left-Wing Socialists, led by Suzuki Mosaburo, were more militant Marxists with less political experience. With the exception of its pledge to uphold parliamentary government, its platform was hardly distinguishable from that of the Japanese Communist Party. Its support came from a large number of intellectuals who were influential in education, journalism, and general cultural activities and from the 3,000,000-member General Council of Trade Unions (Sohyo), which was strongly Marxist in orientation and laid great stress on the class struggle.

In January, 1955, the two wings agreed in principle to unite, and in October they formulated a platform and resolved on a distribution of power. The platform emphasized the attainment of socialism through "peaceful revolution," the maintenance of parliamentary government, and opposition to rearmament and to alteration of the occupation reforms. With regard to foreign policy, the socialists contended that Japan was only nominally independent because of the presence of United States bases and troops and because Japanese capitalism and its instrument, the Japanese government, were controlled by the United States. In 1957 the Socialist Party leadership, in a special foreign policy report, advocated "full economic co-operation with the Soviet Union," "recognition of Communist China and establishment of diplomatic relations with Peking," and conclusion of a nonaggression pact between Japan, the United States, Communist China, and the Soviet Union. Suzuki Mosaburo became chairman of the party's central committee and Asanuma Inejiro vice-chairman, and each wing divided the number of seats on the committee. As a united party the socialists held 150 seats in the house of representatives.

The unification of the socialists accelerated efforts by the conservatives to form a united party. They reached agreement in principle in the summer of 1955, and in November they established the Liberal Democratic Party (Jiyu Minshuto). Its platform pledged to preserve parliamentary government; to keep economic activity free from government control; to improve the people's livelihood through governmental measures such as public health insurance, low-cost housing for workers, and care of the aged; to alter certain occupation reforms, especially in regard to the police and education; to maintain a self-defense force appropriate to Japanese national strength; to continue the alli-

637

ance with the United States; and to work for closer political and trade relations with the Soviet Union and Communist China.

Under the leadership of Hatoyama the party held a majority, totaling 299 seats, in the house of representatives. This majority held up amazingly well, and the Liberal Democrats remained in power, although the post of prime minister underwent numerous changes. Hatoyama resigned in December, 1956, after achieving a normalization of diplomatic relations with the Soviet Union that terminated the state of war; and when the party election of a successor became deadlocked between Kishi Nobusuke and Kono Ichiro, the compromise victor was Ishibashi Tanzan, minister of international trade and industry. He, however, was forced to resign in January, 1957, because of ill health, and Kishi succeeded to the post. In the elections of May, 1959, the Liberal Democrats maintained their majority in the house of representatives by winning 287 seats to the Socialists' 122, and Kishi was confirmed in power. Following Kishi's resignation in the wake of the June, 1960, demonstrations against the security pact with the United States, Ikeda Hayato became prime minister, and in the general election of November, 1960, the Liberal Democrats won 301 seats to the Socialists' 144.

The continued success of the Liberal Democratic Party has been the result of several factors. Its political leadership is experienced and has powerful financial backing from the business community. Moreover, conservative bodies like the Federation of Economic Organizations (Keidanren), the Chamber of Commerce and Industry, and the Japan Federation of Employers Associations (Nikkeiren) have been more active politically in the past few years. The Liberal Democrats also derive much popular support from the rural areas, where traditional values are strong; moreover, they take credit for the land reform and are careful to maintain price supports for staple crops. And in small businesses there is still a high degree of paternalism, including political influence in employer-employee relationships. At least 13,000,000 wage earners work in enterprises employing fewer than one hundred workers, and over half of this total are in shops employing fewer than ten workers.

The Socialist Party, on the other hand, has done little to dispel the idea that it is a class party representing the interests of organized labor rather than the interests of the population as a whole. Yet paradoxically, since the enterprise, or company, union is the overwhelmingly dominant type of labor organization, labor is not as politically conscious as one might expect. The national unions, which support the Socialist Party, do not yet wield decisive influence locally in the labor movement. There is, moreover, a general lack of confidence in the ability of the Socialist Party to implement the sweeping changes that it advocates, especially in the field of foreign relations. For example, the Socialists are unable to satisfy many Japanese that their country will not suffer economically if it breaks its close ties with the United States.

The success of the conservatives in maintaining themselves in power must also be explained in part by Japan's ability to continue its economic expansion at an amazing rate. The average annual rate of growth during the past fifteen years has risen to approximately 10 per cent, and in 1959 it was 17 per cent, a figure achieved by no other country in the world. By 1959 the gross national product was three times that of 1946, and individual consumption was 30 per cent higher than prewar levels. Japan's foreign trade has also increased tremendously, with exports in 1959 totaling $3,400,000,000 and imports $3,600,000,000. These figures represent increases of 17 and 48 per cent, respectively, over the prewar period. The pattern of trade has of course changed a great deal in the postwar era, as the following table indicates:

Percentages of Total Trade (Imports and Exports), by Countries

1934–1936		1956	
United States	20.2	United States	28.1
Southeast Asia	17.6	Southeast Asia	28.1
China	14.9	China	3.0
Korea and Taiwan	24.0	Korea and Taiwan	3.5
Other	23.3	Other	37.3

The Ikeda cabinet, which came to power in 1960, maintained that Japan could double her national income in ten years through the accumulation of more capital, modernization of basic industries, expansion of trade, and cooperation with other countries.

Though Japan has, essentially, a two-party system, both parties have continued to be plagued by factionalism based on personal rivalries among the leaders. In fact, personal alliances based on the traditional concepts of obligation, loyalty, and responsibility and on sectionalism and mutual gain have been more important than loyalty to party principles. The successful party leader is the man who has many connections and access to funds, has a capacity for intricate behind-the-scenes negotiations, and is able to build a workable coalition within the party. After the election victory of Prime Minister Ikeda in November, 1960, the Liberal Democrats included some eight or nine factions, the most important of which were headed by Ikeda, Kishi, and Sato Eisaku, while the Socialists were split into four basic groups.

The Japanese Communist Party

The Japanese Communist Party has operated as a legal political organization since 1945. Founded in December of that year by Moscow-trained veterans like Nosaka Sanzo and Tokuda Kyuichi, it supported the occupation reforms as part of the completion of the bourgeois-democratic revolution and sought

639

to win broader support among laborers, peasants, small businessmen, and intellectuals. In the April, 1946, elections the party won 5 seats in the house of representatives; in the 1947 elections it won 4 seats; and in the January, 1949, elections it won its highest total, 35 seats, reflecting a popular-vote total of 3,000,000, or approximately 10 per cent of the total. This success reflected the strength of the party in the labor movement, where probably half of all union workers were communist supporters or members of unions under communist control. Thereafter the party began to attack Yoshida's economic stabilization program by means of demonstrations and strikes in the hope of gaining additional popular support; but this tactic boomeranged, since it caused a SCAP ban on strikes and the beginning of anticommunist activity within the labor movement. The activities of the communists, moreover, were one of the most important reasons for the conservatives' advocacy of the modification of the police and education reforms of the occupation.

When communist-inspired violence reached a peak in the spring of 1950, the Yoshida cabinet considered declaring a national emergency and outlawing the Japanese Communist Party. It did not go that far, but it did raid the headquarters of the party's leading public opinion organ, *Akahata*, and charged it with the illegal sale of rationed newsprint, prosecuted a number of communists arrested for railroad sabotage, dissolved the 400,000-member communist-dominated League of Korean Residents in Japan, and dismissed several thousand school teachers by application of the 1947 Educational Standards Law, which stipulated that teachers could not influence students in politics in or out of the classroom.

General MacArthur meanwhile was considering whether or not to ban the Japanese Communist Party. At the end of May the communists ordered a general strike and turned to violence again, including an assault upon five members of the occupation forces, the first such instance. MacArthur did not declare the party illegal, but on June 6 he ordered the Japanese government to ban twenty-four members of the party's central committee and seventeen employees of *Akahata* from engaging in political activity, writing, or speaking. Most of those who were purged went underground, and the party suffered a tremendous decline.

From March, 1950, to June, 1952, party membership fell from 108,000 to 48,000, and in the October, 1952, general election none of its candidates was elected to the house of representatives. Its continued emphasis upon violence, which reached a peak in May Day riots in 1952, and its obvious domination by Moscow damaged the party's political appeal to the Japanese electorate. For example, in January, 1950, Moscow charged that Nosaka's view that Japan could achieve socialism peacefully and that such a peaceful transition might occur even under the occupation "misleads the Japanese people and helps the foreign imperialists to turn Japan into a colonial appendage." The Japanese Communist Party issued a statement admitting that Nosaka's theory had been deficient, although it insisted that unusual conditions in Japan compelled the party to employ unusual tactics; and Nosaka, in a declaration of self-criticism, admitted that his theory had been basically incorrect. Thereafter, the Japanese Communist Party stepped up its attacks on the occupation and on American policy in general. Seeking to utilize nationalist feeling, it demanded the "liberation of the Japanese race from American slavery" and called for alignment of the Japanese people with "the peace-loving people of the world," led by "the great Soviet Union and our Asian brothers, the Chinese." With the relaxation of the purge in 1956, party leaders once again became active, but in general elections since that date the party has won no more than three seats at one time in the house of representatives. By 1959 party membership was approximately 60,000, but another 150,000 Japanese were regarded by the government as fellow-travelers who participate in communist projects or give financial aid to the party.

The Revision of Occupation Reforms

One of the outstanding features of conservative government in Japan has been the modification of occupation reforms. In the case of police power, the conservatives have argued that it has been difficult to co-ordinate the operations of local urban forces and the national rural police because of ill-defined jurisdiction, that local governments have been unable to finance their police adequately, and that the concept of local responsibility is not yet sufficiently strong to maintain decentralization.

What has been left unsaid publicly is that the conservatives wish to use police power more effectively against the direct-action tactics of the left wing, especially the communists. After the May Day disturbances of 1952, Yoshida persuaded the diet to pass the Anti-Subversive Activity Law, which empowered the cabinet to ban activities that might cause violence, and in January, 1953, he proposed to the diet that it abolish all local police and place police power in a national public safety commission under the prime minister. After much discussion, the issue came to a head in June, 1954, and, despite such Socialist tactics as a filibuster, an attempt to prevent the speaker of the house of representatives from extending the session, and a boycott of the lower house, the conservative majority passed a bill which nationalized the police. Although independent forces would continue to exist in Tokyo, Yokohama, Nagoya, Osaka, Kyoto, and Kobe for one year, thereafter all Japanese police would be organized on a prefectural basis under the national public safety commission, the head of which would hold cabinet rank as minister without portfolio.

In a further move in October, 1958, in reaction to the continued disruption of public order by demonstrations, Prime Minister Kishi proposed a bill that would empower the police to prevent sit-down strikers and others from blocking entrances to public buildings, to halt obstructive parades and demonstrations, to broaden the police right of search, and to establish authority for preventive arrests. The Socialists regarded the measure as an attempt to deprive labor unions of powerful weapons, tried to block its passage by boycotting diet sessions, and organized work stoppages, rallies, and parades by laborers. When popular opposition increased and became linked with the rearmament and foreign policy issues, prominent leaders in the Liberal Democratic Party finally persuaded Kishi in November to withdraw the bill.

Liberal Party cabinets have attempted to curb the influence of the militant leftist Japan Teachers Union (Nikkyoso), which has a total of 500,000 members. Yoshida sought to limit the political activities of teachers, and the diet passed a law in the spring of 1954, over the opposition of the Socialists, which barred teachers from acts committed for a political purpose under penalties of "admonition, salary reduction, suspension, or dismissal." In order to weaken the influence of Nikkyoso and its parent organization, Sohyo, Yoshida also secured passage of a law to regulate teachers' associations. According to its terms, no person may utilize an association made up of teachers in compulsory-education schools, or a federation of such associations, to give teachers or pupils advice concerning, or to agitate for their support of or opposition to, a particular political party. The penalty for violating the law is imprisonment for a period not to exceed a year or a fine not to exceed 30,000 yen.

Hatoyama persuaded the diet to replace the locally elected school boards with boards appointed by prefectural governors and mayors, but he was unable to secure passage of a law to empower a national school board to approve textbooks. Since the end of the occupation there had been increasing talk by conservatives of the need to revise the curriculum for the purpose of reintroducing courses in traditional morals, and in 1957 moral education was established in junior high schools to provide instruction regarding human relationships, behavior between the sexes, and conduct with respect to the community in order to check the alarming growth of juvenile delinquency; but there was no reference to patriotism and filial piety.

Perhaps the most important issue remaining as a legacy from the occupation period concerns rearmament and security. By 1953 the national security force was a small army equipped with modern American weapons; and in March, 1954, by a Mutual Defense Assistance Agreement with the United States, Japan promised to maintain an army of 275,000 men, supplemented by a small navy and air force, to which the United States would provide assistance in the form of goods, equipment, and services. And in July, 1956, the Hatoyama cabinet established the national defense council, headed by a director-general with the status of minister of state without portfolio.

The Socialist Party has maintained that the military establishment is unconstitutional, and it has sufficient votes in the diet to block any amendment of the constitution. In May, 1956, the conservative majority approved the creation of the constitutional revision council, "a research organ to carry out a complete examination of the present constitution from a new national viewpoint," but the Hatoyama cabinet was unable to get passage of an electoral-district law which, through gerrymandering, would probably reduce Socialist representation in the lower house by 50 per cent.

The armament issue came to the fore again in the spring of 1960, when Prime Minister Kishi, who had successfully negotiated a reduction in the size of American forces in Japan, sought to get approval of the diet for a revision of the security pact with the United States, limiting it to ten years and, according to an exchange of letters with President Eisenhower, requiring Japanese approval for the use of bases by the United States in case of war. The Socialists raised objections, but Kishi used his Liberal Democratic majority to force ratification of the pact. Mass demonstrations followed his action; and although the issue was confused by the subversive tactics of the communists and other left-wing radicals and by general distrust of Kishi because of his antidemocratic attitudes and past affiliations, it was clear that there was strong popular antagonism to rearmament and to any alliance that might threaten Japan with involvement in war. On the other hand, the Liberal Democratic Party's victory in the November, 1960, general election indicated that the majority of Japanese, fearful perhaps of the economic consequences, preferred to maintain the existing ties with the United States.

Some Problems and Prospects

During the period of the American occupation, Japanese society experienced a series of almost revolutionary changes, and since that time the Japanese people have been engaged in modifying, consolidating, and extending them. Although the pace has slackened, the process of transformation has continued. In fact, the process of acculturation is the underlying current in the struggles between the various political, economic, and social forces in contemporary Japan. For the present the conservatives dominate, but their position is not so strong that they can resurrect the old institutions and value system, nor is there unity among them as to the wisdom of such an idea. Conversely, under present circumstances there is little likelihood that the Left can achieve power and implement the wide-sweeping changes that it advocates. The great numbers of independent, ideologically uncommitted Japanese provide the basis for a kind of political equilibrium that safeguards the basic reforms achieved in the occupation period.

The establishment of the forms of political democracy, both the guarantees of basic rights and the institutional framework of a government responsible to the people, was one of the major accomplishments of the occupation authorities. But there is more to political democracy than forms. It must also have a substantive content as evidenced by the acceptance of a democratic value system. From this standpoint, Japanese conservatives and leftists alike are woefully deficient. On numerous occasions the leadership of the Liberal Democratic Party has demonstrated its impatience with democratic debate by its steamroller use of parliamentary majorities. The Socialists and others have criticized what they call the "tyranny of the majority" because they insist that the political power of the Liberal Democrats as expressed in the house of representatives does not reflect the true sentiments of the Japanese people. They argue that, although the people have the right to vote, actual freedom of political choice is circumscribed by traditional attitudes and obligations, especially in the rural areas and in small business and industrial enterprises. On the other hand, Socialist leaders, whether politicians, labor unionists, or intellectuals, often have little understanding of or sympathy for political democracy. Those among them who are Marxist-Leninists regard parliamentary government as merely a means to an end in the dialectical process of history, and even their more moderate colleagues ignore the contradiction of the use of extraparliamentary political means, such as demonstrations, obstructionist parliamentary tactics, and even the threat of violent revolution, to achieve their ends. And although there is much talk of political democracy in intellectual and labor circles, there is often wide divergence between words and deeds. However, it would be misleading to end on this pessimistic note, because it is in the very arena of political conflict that basic differences are often compromised. This kind of interaction is an essential element in the effective working of political democracy. In Japanese political parties and among individuals, there must be greater understanding of the relationship of political democracy and responsibility.

Japan's basic economic problem remains unchanged. How can the nation maintain and improve the standard of living of a huge and still-growing population? Lacking adequate land and raw materials, Japan must continue to increase her agricultural competence and to expand her foreign trade. To protect and improve her competitive capabilities, in the pattern of the past decade, she must improve technology, amass more capital, increase the supply of skilled labor, and minimize raw-material costs. There is no doubt that Japan will continue to make substantial economic progress, but there is some question whether she can double the national income in ten years, as Prime Minister Ikeda contemplates. Economic estimates are necessarily complex because of the many international political and economic factors involved. Most important of these, perhaps, will be Japan's position vis-à-vis the European Common Market and Communist China.

Continued economic progress will have important implications for Japanese society as a whole. In fact, a number of important questions come to mind immediately. Will economic gains be shared by the people as a whole? To what extent will the reconcentration of business and industrial power continue? Will the labor movement place greater emphasis upon the attainment of economic objectives? Will the adoption of American legal forms provide a basis for stable labor-management relations? What of the many small businesses and the existing uneconomic small-farm system? Will they be able to survive? To what extent will there be greater economic and social mobility?

While many of the occupation-period reforms implied the establishment of a new set of social values, that end has not been achieved. Traditional social attitudes, reinforced by economic conditions, are still strong in Japan. It is true that most of the prewar social ideology has been officially discredited, but in practice there is still a substantial degree of conflict between the concepts of individualism and equality, on the one hand, and group (e.g., family) responsibility, on the other. Certainly, social frustrations often influence thinking about political and economic problems, and this is particularly true among the young people; it has, indeed, helped to make some young Japanese into revolutionaries of the Left and Right. Conversely, the social and political irresponsibility of the minority of Japan's youth has provoked a conservative reaction, which seeks to reintroduce traditional moral training in education.

Japan's future will of course depend in large part on the international situation, and especially on the tension between the communist bloc and the Western alliance. At present, despite strong neutralist and pacifist sentiments, it is clear that the majority of Japanese consider it to be of value for their country, particularly for economic reasons, to remain allied with the United States. But it is apparent that even the conservatives realize that for successful long-range economic and political planning it may be necessary to make some sort of accommodation with the communist bloc, especially Red China. In fact, political and economic pressures may ultimately force Japan to join the neutralist camp.

Bibliographical Notes

The most detailed surveys of this period are Yanaga, *Japan since Perry*, and Borton, *Japan's Modern Century*, both of which have already been cited.

There are a number of studies concerning the political development of Japan in the period prior to World War II. Hugh Borton, *Japan since 1931* (New York: Institute of Pacific Relations, 1940), provides a general picture; A. Morgan Young, *Imperial Japan, 1926–1938* (New York: Morrow, 1938), is a collection of controversial articles by a newspaperman; Richard Storry, *The Double Patriots:*

A *Study of Japanese Nationalism* (London: Chatto & Windus, 1957), describes the development of nationalist societies and factionalism in the Japanese army; Hugh Byas, *Government by Assassination* (New York: Alfred A. Knopf, 1942), is a vivid account of terrorism in the 1930's by a competent newspaperman; and Yale C. Maxon, *Control of Japanese Foreign Policy: Study of Civil-Military Rivalry, 1930–1945* (Berkeley: University of California Press, 1957), is a careful study of the most crucial aspect of Japanese politics. Still useful on the army and its political activities are K. W. Colegrove, *Militarism in Japan* (Boston: World Peace Foundation, 1936), and Hillis Lory, *Japan's Military Masters* (London: Viking Press, 1947). Two indispensable primary sources are the *Transcript and Exhibits of the International Tribunal for the Far East* and the *Saionji-Harada Memoirs;* the latter work was translated and reproduced by the Civil Intelligence Section of General Headquarters, Far East Command (Tokyo, 1949).

In the field of economics, the following are useful works for the prewar period: E. B. Schumpeter, G. C. Allen, and others, *The Industrialization of Japan and Manchoukuo, 1930–1940* (New York: Macmillan, 1940), C. D. Carus and C. L. McNichols, *Japan: Its Resources and Industries* (New York: Harper, 1944), John E. Orchard, *Japan's Economic Position, The Progress of Industrialization* (New York: Whittlesey, 1930), G. C. Allen, *Japanese Industry: Its Recent Development and Present Condition* (New York: Institute of Pacific Relations, 1939), Uyeda Teijiro and associates, *The Small Industries of Japan* (New York: Institute of Pacific Relations, 1938), Nasu Shiroshi, *Aspects of Japanese Agriculture: Preliminary Survey* (New York: Institute of Pacific Relations, 1941), Nasu Shiroshi, *Land Utilization in Japan* (Tokyo: Institute of Pacific Relations, 1929), Uyehara Shigeru, *The Industry and Trade of Japan* (London: King, second revised edition, 1936), Ernest Penrose, *Population Theories and Their Application, with Special Reference to Japan* (Stanford: Stanford University Press, 1934), and Ishii Ryoichi, *Population Pressure and Economic Life in Japan* (London: King, 1937). John F. Embree, *Suye Mura, A Japanese Village* (Chicago: University of Chicago Press, 1939), is the only study of its kind for the prewar period.

The best commentary on the period of the American occupation is Kazuo Kawai, *Japan's American Interlude* (Chicago: Chicago University Press, 1960). Quasi-official accounts are Edwin M. Martin, *Allied Occupation of Japan* (Stanford: Stanford University Press, 1948), and Robert A. Feary, *The Occupation of Japan, Second Phase, 1948–1950* (New York: Macmillan, 1950). Baron E. J. Lewe van Aduard, *Japan from Surrender to Peace* (The Hague: Martinus Nijhoff, 1953), is excellent for the background of the peace treaty. Works that are critical of the American occupation include W. M. Ball, *Japan, Enemy or Ally?* (New York: John Day, revised and enlarged edition, 1949), T. A. Bisson, *Prospects for Democracy in Japan* (New York: Macmillan, 1949), and Harry E. Wildes, *Typhoon in Tokyo: The Occupation and Its Aftermath* (New York: Macmillan, 1954). Indispensable for the study of the occupation period are the many publications of SCAP, such as *Political Reorientation of Japan, September, 1945—September, 1948* (Washington: U.S. Government Printing Office, two volumes, 1949).

Economic developments during the occupation period are the subject of a number of excellent studies, including J. B. Cohen, *Japan's Economy in War and Reconstruction* (Minneapolis: University of Minnesota Press, 1949), T. A. Bisson, *Zaibatsu Dissolution in Japan* (Berkeley: University of California Press, 1954), Miriam Farley, *Aspects of Japan's Labor Problems* (New York: John Day, 1950), Ayusawa Iwao, *Postwar Developments in Organized Labor* (Tokyo, 1953), Laurence I. Hewes, Jr., *Japan—Land and Men: An Account of the Japanese Land Reform Program, 1945–1951* (Ames, Ia.: Iowa State University Press, 1955), and Ronald P. Dore, *Land Reform in Japan* (London and New York: Oxford University Press, 1959).

There are a number of good studies on Japanese government and politics. The general works include Chitoshi Yanaga, *Japanese People and Politics* (New York: Wiley, 1956), Nobutaka Ike, *Japanese Politics, An Introductory Survey* (New York: Alfred A. Knopf, 1957), and Harold S. Quigley and John E. Turner, *New Japan: Government and Politics* (Minneapolis: University of Minnesota Press, 1956). More specialized are Robert E. Ward (editor), *Five Studies in Japanese Politics* (Ann Arbor: University of Michigan Press, 1957), Allen B. Cole, *Japanese Society and Politics: The Impact of Social Stratification and Mobility on Politics* (Boston: Boston University, 1956), and Allen B. Cole, *Political Tendencies of Japanese in Small Enterprises, with Special Reference to the Social Democratic Party* (New York: Institute of Pacific Relations, 1959). The right and left wings are analyzed in Ivan Morris, *Nationalism and the Right Wing in Japan: A Study of Post-War Trends* (London, New York, and Toronto: Oxford University Press, 1960), Evelyn Colbert, *The Left Wing in Japanese Politics* (New York: Institute of Pacific Relations, 1952), and R. Swearingen and P. Langer, *Red Flag in Japan* (Cambridge, Mass.: Harvard University Press, 1952).

G. C. Allen, *Japan's Economic Recovery* (London: Oxford University Press, 1958), and Solomon Levine, *Industrial Relations in Post-War Japan* (Urbana, Illinois: University of Illinois Press, 1958), are two recent studies by competent specialists.

Frank B. Gibney, *Five Gentlemen of Japan* (Tokyo: Charles Tuttle, 1954), is a popular attempt to explain the impact of defeat and occupation upon the Japanese people. Interesting in this same context is Jean Stoetzel, *Without the Chrysanthemum and the Sword* (New York: Columbia University Press, 1955). Edward Norbeck, *Takashima, A Japanese Fishing Community* (Salt Lake City: University of Utah Press, 1953), Richard K. Beardsley and others, *Village Japan* (Chicago: University of Chicago Press, 1958), and Ronald P. Dore, *City Life in Japan* (Berkeley: University of California Press, 1958), are excellent social studies. The population problem is ably analyzed in Irene Taeuber, *The Population of Japan* (Princeton: Princeton University Press, 1958).

Through literature, particularly novels, we can get a fuller picture of Japanese life and attitudes. Some that are particularly helpful in this respect are John Hersey, *Hiroshima* (New York: Alfred A. Knopf, 1946), Osamu Dazai, *The Setting Sun* (Norfolk, Conn.: New Directions, 1956; translated by Donald Keene), Yasunari Kawabata, *Snow Country* (New York: Alfred A. Knopf, 1956; translated by Edward Seidenstecker), Yukio Mishima, *The Sound of Waves* (New

647

York: Alfred A. Knopf, 1956; translated by Meredith Weatherby), Jiro Osaragi, *Homecoming* (New York: Alfred A. Knopf, 1955; translated by Brewster Horwitz), Junichiro Tanizaki, *Some Prefer Nettles* (New York: Alfred A. Knopf, 1955; translated by Edward Seidenstecker), and Junichiro Tanizaki, *The Makioka Sisters* (New York: Alfred A. Knopf, 1957; translated by Edward Seidenstecker).

In the field of foreign policy and international relations, H. Saito, *Japan's Policies and Purposes* (Boston, 1935), is a useful Japanese analysis, while T. A. Bisson, *American Policy in the Far East, 1931–1940* (New York: Institute of Pacific Relations, revised edition, 1941), describes the American position. Indispensable for its source materials is *Foreign Relations of the United States: Japan, 1931–1941* (Washington: U.S. Government Printing Office, two volumes, 1943). There are a number of useful works concerning the background of the attack on Pearl Harbor, including Herbert Feis, *The Road to Pearl Harbor* (Princeton: Princeton University Press, 1950), perhaps the best account; W. H. Chamberlin, *Japan over Asia* (Boston: Little, Brown, 1941); F. C. Jones, *Japan's New Order in East Asia: Its Rise and Fall, 1937–1945* (London: Oxford University Press, 1954), which is particularly good on Japanese-German relations; Walter Millis, *This Is Pearl! The United States and Japan—1941* (New York: William Morrow, 1947), a good popular account of American attitudes and conditions; Paul W. Schroeder, *The Axis Alliance and Japanese-American Relations, 1941* (Ithaca, New York: Cornell University Press, 1958); and H. L. Trefousse, *What Happened at Pearl Harbor* (New York: Bookman Associates, 1958). Two excellent recent studies of German-Japanese relations are Frank W. Iklé, *German-Japanese Relations, 1936–1940* (New York: Bookman Associates, 1956), and Ernst L. Pressiesen, *Germany and Japan: A Study in Totalitarian Diplomacy, 1933–1941* (The Hague: Martinus Nijhoff, 1958). Robert Butow's two works, *Japan's Decision to Surrender* (Stanford: Stanford University Press, 1954), and *Tojo and the Coming of the War* (Princeton: Princeton University Press, 1961), are excellent studies of Japanese policy before and during the war.

Joseph Grew, *Ten Years in Japan* (New York: Simon & Schuster, 1944), Cordell Hull, *The Memoirs of Cordell Hull* (New York: Macmillan, two volumes, 1948), and Togo Shigenori, *The Cause of Japan* (New York: Simon & Schuster, 1956; translated and edited by T. Fumihiko and B. B. Blakeney), are useful memoir materials, but Kase Toshikazu, *Journey to the Missouri* (New Haven: Yale University Press, 1950), and Shigemitsu Mamoru, *Japan and Her Destiny* (New York: E. P. Dutton, 1958; translated by Oswald White), must be used with great caution because of their civilian biases.

There is some material on contemporary foreign policy problems in Hugh Borton and others, *Japan between East and West* (New York: Harper & Bros., 1957). The most detailed study is Douglas H. Mendel, Jr., *Japanese People and Foreign Policy* (Berkeley: University of California Press, 1961).

APPENDIX 1

Constitution of the Empire of Japan (1889)

CHAPTER I / THE EMPEROR

ARTICLE I. The Empire of Japan shall be reigned over and governed by a line of Emperors unbroken for ages eternal.

ART. II. The Imperial Throne shall be succeeded to by Imperial male descendants, according to the provisions of the Imperial House Law.

ART. III. The Emperor is sacred and inviolable.

ART. IV. The Emperor is the head of the Empire, combining in Himself the rights of sovereignty, and exercises them, according to the provisions of the present Constitutions.

ART. V. The Emperor exercises the legislative power with the consent of the Imperial Diet.

ART. VI. The Emperor gives sanction to laws and orders them to be promulgated and executed.

ART. VII. The Emperor convokes the Imperial Diet, opens, closes, and prorogues it, and dissolves the House of Representatives.

ART. VIII. The Emperor, in consequence of an urgent necessity to maintain public safety or to avert public calamities, issues, when the Imperial Diet is not sitting, Imperial Ordinances in the place of law.

Such Imperial Ordinances are to be laid before the Imperial Diet at its next session, and when the Diet does not approve the said Ordinances, the Government shall declare them to be invalid for the future.

ART. IX. The Emperor issues or causes to be issued, the Ordinances necessary for the carrying out of the laws, or for the maintenance of the public peace and order, and for the promotion of the welfare of the subjects. But no Ordinance shall in any way alter any of the existing laws.

ART. X. The Emperor determines the organization of the different branches of the administration, and salaries of all civil and military officers, and appoints and dismisses the same. Exceptions especially provided for in the present Constitution or in other laws, shall be in accordance with the respecting provisions (bearing thereupon).

ART. XI. The Emperor has the supreme command of the Army and Navy.

ART. XII. The Emperor determines the organization and peace standing of the Army and Navy.

ART. XIII. The Emperor declares war, makes peace, and concludes treaties.

ART. XIV. The Emperor declares a state of siege. The conditions and effects of a state of siege shall be determined by law.

ART. XV. The Emperor confers titles of nobility, rank, orders, and other marks of honor.

Art. XVI. The Emperor orders amnesty, pardon, commutation of punishments, and rehabilitation.

Art. XVII. A Regency shall be instituted in conformity with the provisions of the Imperial House Law.

The Regent shall exercise the powers appertaining to the Emperor in His name.

Chapter II / Rights and Duties of Subjects

Article XVIII. The conditions necessary for being a Japanese subject shall be determined by law.

Art. XIX. Japanese subjects may, according to qualifications determined in laws or Ordinances, be appointed to civil or military or any other public offices equally.

Art. XX. Japanese subjects are amenable to service in the Army or Navy, according to the provisions of law.

Art. XXI. Japanese subjects are amenable to the duty of paying taxes, according to the provisions of law.

Art. XXII. Japanese subjects shall have the liberty of abode and of changing the same within the limits of the law.

Art. XXIII. No Japanese subject shall be arrested, detained, tried or punished, unless according to law.

Art. XXIV. No Japanese subject shall be deprived of his right of being tried by the judges determined by law.

Art. XXV. Except in the cases provided for in the law, the house of no Japanese subject shall be entered or searched without his consent.

Art. XXVI. Except in the cases mentioned in the law, the secrecy of the letters of every Japanese subject shall remain inviolate.

Art. XXVII. The right of property of every Japanese subject shall remain inviolate.

Measures necessary to be taken for the public benefit shall be provided for by law.

Art. XXVIII. Japanese subjects shall, within limits not prejudicial to peace and order, and not antagonistic to their duties as subjects, enjoy freedom of religious belief.

Art. XXIX. Japan subjects shall, within the limits of law, enjoy the liberty of speech, writing, publication, public meetings, and associations.

Art. XXX. Japanese subjects may present petitions, by observing the proper forms of respect, and by complying with the rules specially provided for the same.

Art. XXXI. The provisions contained in the present Chapter shall not affect the exercise of the powers appertaining to the Emperor, in times of war or in cases of a national emergency.

Art. XXXII. Each and every one of the provisions contained in the preceding Articles of the present Chapter, that are not in conflict with the laws or the rules and discipline of the Army and Navy, shall apply to the officers and men of the Army and Navy.

ARTICLE XXXIII. The Imperial Diet shall consist of two Houses, a House of Peers and a House of Representatives.

ART. XXXIV. The House of Peers shall, in accordance with the Ordinance concerning the House of Peers, be composed of the members of the Imperial Family, of the orders of nobility, and those who have been nominated thereto by the Emperor.

ART. XXXV. The House of Representatives shall be composed of Members elected by the people, according to the provisions of the Law of Election.

ART. XXXVI. No one can at one and the same time be a Member of both Houses.

ART. XXXVII. Every law requires the consent of the Imperial Diet.

ART. XXXVIII. Both Houses shall vote upon projects of law submitted to it by the Government, and may respectively initiate projects of law.

ART. XXXIX. A Bill, which has been rejected by either the one or the other of the two Houses, shall not be brought in again during the same session.

ART. XL. Both Houses can make representations to the Government, as to laws or upon any other subject. When, however, such representations are not accepted, they cannot be made a second time during the same session.

ART. XLI. The Imperial Diet shall be convoked every year.

ART. XLII. A session of the Imperial Diet shall last during three months. In case of necessity, the duration of a session may be prolonged by the Imperial Order.

ART. XLIII. When urgent necessity arises, an extraordinary session may be convoked in addition to the ordinary one. The duration of an extraordinary session shall be determined by Imperial Order.

ART. XLIV. The opening, closing, prolongation of session, and prorogation of the Imperial Diet, shall be effected simultaneously for both Houses.

In case the House of Representatives has been ordered to dissolve, the House of Peers shall at the same time be prorogued.

ART. XLV. When the House of Representatives has been ordered to dissolve, Members shall be caused by Imperial Order to be newly elected, and the new House shall be convoked within five months from the day of dissolution.

ART. XLVI. No debate can be opened and no vote can be taken in either House of the Imperial Diet, unless not less than one-third of the whole number of Members thereof is present.

ART. XLVII. Votes shall be taken in both Houses by absolute majority. In the case of a tie vote, the President shall have the casting vote.

ART. XLVIII. The deliberations of both Houses shall be held in public. The deliberations may, however, upon demand of the Government or by resolution of the House, be held in secret sitting.

ART. XLIX. Both Houses of the Imperial Diet may respectively present addresses to the Emperor.

ART. L. Both Houses may receive petitions presented by subjects.

ART. LI. Both Houses may enact, besides what is provided for in the present

Constitution and in the Law of the Houses, rules necessary for the management of their internal affairs.

ART. LII. No Member of either House shall be held responsible outside the respective Houses, for any opinion uttered or for any vote given in the House. When, however, a Member himself has given publicity to his opinions by public speech, by documents in print or in writing, or by any other similar means, he shall, in the matter, be amenable to the general law.

ART. LIII. The Members of both Houses shall, during the session, be free from arrest, unless with the consent of the House, except in cases of flagrant delicts, or of offenses connected with a state of internal commotion or with a foreign trouble.

ART. LIV. The Minister of State and the Delegates of the Government may, at any time, take seats and speak in either House.

CHAPTER IV / THE MINISTERS OF STATE AND THE PRIVY COUNCIL

ARTICLE LV. The respective Ministers of State shall give their advice to the Emperor, and be responsible for it.

All Laws, Imperial Ordinances, and Imperial Rescripts of whatever kind, that relate to the affairs of the State, require the countersignature of a Minister of State.

ART. LVI. The Privy Councillors shall, in accordance with the provisions for the organization of the Privy Council, deliberate upon important matters of State, when they have been consulted by the Emperor.

CHAPTER V / THE JUDICATURE

ARTICLE LVII. The Judicature shall be exercised by the Courts of Law, according to law, in the name of the Emperor.

ART. LVIII. The judges shall be appointed from among those who possess proper qualifications according to law.

No judge shall be deprived of his position, unless by way of criminal sentence or disciplinary punishment.

Rules for disciplinary punishment shall be determined by law.

ART. LIX. Trials and judgments of a Court shall be conducted publicly. When, however, there exists any fear that such publicity may be prejudicial to peace and order, or to the maintenance of public morality, the public trial may be suspended by provisions of law or by the decision of the Court of Law.

ART. LX. All matters that fall within the competency of a special Court shall be specially provided for by law.

ART. LXI. No suit at law, which relates to rights alleged to have been infringed by the illegal measures of the administrative authorities, and which shall come within the competency of the Court of Administrative Litigation specially established by law, shall be taken cognizance of by a Court of Law.

ARTICLE LXII. The imposition of a new tax or the modification of the rates (of an existing one) shall be determined by law.

However, all such administrative fees or other revenue having the nature of compensation shall not fall within the category of the above clause.

The raising of national loans and the contracting of other liabilities to the charge of the National Treasury, except those that are provided in the Budget, shall require the consent of the Imperial Diet.

ART. LXIII. The taxes levied at present shall, in so far as they are not re-modelled by a new law, be collected according to the old system.

ART. LXIV. The expenditure and revenue of the State require the consent of the Imperial Diet by means of an annual budget.

Any and all expenditures overpassing the appropriations set forth in the Titles and Paragraphs of the Budget, or that are not provided for in the Budget, shall subsequently require the approbation of the Imperial Diet.

ART. LXV. The Budget shall be first laid before the House of Representatives.

ART. LXVI. The expenditures of the Imperial House shall be defrayed every year out of the National Treasury, according to the present fixed amount for the same, and shall not require the consent thereto of the Imperial Diet, except in case an increase thereof is found necessary.

ART. LXVII. Those already fixed expenditures based by the Constitution upon the powers appertaining to the Emperor, and such expenditures as may have arisen by the effect of law, or that appertain to the legal obligations of the Government, shall be neither rejected nor reduced by the Imperial Diet, without the concurrence of the Government.

ART. LXVIII. In order to meet special requirements, the Government may ask the consent of the Imperial Diet to a certain amount as a Continuing Expenditure Fund, for a previously fixed number of years.

ART. LXIX. In order to supply deficiencies, which are unavoidable, in the Budget, and to meet requirements unprovided for in the same, a Reserve Fund shall be provided in the Budget.

ART. LXX. When the Imperial Diet cannot be convoked, owing to the external or internal conditions of the country, in case of urgent need for the maintenance of public safety, the Government may take all necessary financial measures, by means of an Imperial Ordinance.

In the case mentioned in the preceding clause, the matter shall be submitted to the Imperial Diet at its next session, and its approbation shall be obtained thereto.

ART. LXXI. When the Imperial Diet has not voted on the Budget, or when the Budget has not been brought into actual existence, the Government shall carry out the Budget of the preceding year.

ART. LXXII. The final account of the expenditures and revenues of the State shall be verified and confirmed by the Board of Audit, and it shall be submitted by the Government to the Imperial Diet, together with the report of verification of the said Board.

The organization and competency of the Board of Audit shall be determined by law separately.

CHAPTER VII / SUPPLEMENTARY RULES

ARTICLE LXXIII. When it has become necessary in the future to amend the provisions of the present Constitution, a project to the effect shall be submitted to the Imperial Diet by Imperial Order.

In the above case, neither House can open the debate, unless not less than two-thirds of the whole number of Members are present; and no amendment can be passed, unless a majority of not less than two-thirds of the Members present is obtained.

ART. LXXIV. No modification of the Imperial House Law shall be required to be submitted to the deliberation of the Imperial Diet.

No provision of the present Constitution can be modified by the Imperial House Law.

ART. LXXV. No modification can be introduced into the Constitution, or into the Imperial House Law, during the time of a Regency.

ART. LXXVI. Existing legal enactments, such as laws, regulations, Ordinances, or by whatever names they may be called, shall, so far as they do not conflict with the present Constitution, continue in force.

All existing contracts or orders, that entail obligations upon the Government, and that are connected with expenditure, shall come within the scope of Article LXVII.

APPENDIX **2**

Manifesto of the First National Kuomintang Congress
(January 30, 1924)

A. ON THE PRESENT SITUATION IN CHINA

The Chinese Revolutionary Movement began in 1894, and was already highly developed before 1900. It finally achieved its initial success in 1911 when the monarchical regime was overthrown. The Revolution was not, however, something of accidental growth. From the time when the Manchus conquered China, a spirit of political unrest had been prevalent throughout the length and breadth of the country.

As soon as the country was opened for foreign trade, the imperialists rushed into China. Like hungry wolves they robbed her of independence by using both military force and economic pressure, and reduced her to the status of a subcolony. When the Manchu government was too weak to resist the external pressure, it tried to please the Powers by adopting a policy of absolute repression within. The members of our Party, knowing that the Manchu House stood in the way of China's political reform and that its downfall was necessary to save China from foreign devastation, resolved to follow our Chairman, Dr. Sun, in the important struggle for national salvation.

When we overthrew the Manchu government in the year 1911, we knew that the more important task of the Revolution, namely, the task of reconstructing China in conformity with modern ideas was ahead of us. We saw what must be done. In interracial relations, the autocracy of one race must be replaced by equality and co-operation among the different races in China. In politics, the absolute form of government must be replaced by a democratic system. In the sphere of economic activities, the old handicraft system must give way to the capitalistic system of production. We resolved not to stop our work until China was changed from a subcolony into an independent and powerful nation.

But the turn of affairs in 1911–1912 was against our original intention. The Revolutionary Government failed at that time to achieve anything beyond liberating the Chinese from alien rule. The first mistake was the compromise with the counterrevolutionary monarchists whereby Yuan Shih-k'ai, their representative, was chosen to be head of the government. This compromise was more or less forced on us, not because Yuan was a strong man, but because, first, we were anxious to avoid the prolongation of the civil war, and second, we had not the backing of a powerful and well-organized political party prepared to undertake the task of reconstruction. If such a party had been in existence, Yuan would have been overcome by the revolutionary forces and the attainment of the true object of the Revolution would not have been delayed.

In another respect, also, the surrender of the reins of the government to Yuan Shih-k'ai was a great mistake, since Yuan, who was the leader of the northern military clique, represented the interests of the surviving officialdom of the Manchu regime, whose only object in life was to procure lucrative jobs for themselves. The reins of the government have never been put into the hands of the men with new ideas.

After the death of Yuan Shih-k'ai, other militarists gradually worked themselves into power, and this meant a further setback from our ideal of political revolution for China. As these militarists represented purely personal interests and had nothing to do with the desires or needs of the people, it was natural for them to play into the hands of the foreign imperialists.

On the one hand, the different militarists depended upon foreign financial assistance and foreign supplies of ammunition and arms to strengthen their positions; on the other hand, the foreign imperialists utilized these militarists to

655

instigate internal strife and thereby to safeguard their special privileges and spheres of influence in China. It is evident then, that our civil strife has been instigated by the imperialists through the militarists.

Civil war has checked the progress of Chinese industry and has put our manufacturers in an unfavorable position in competing with foreign capitalists in our own markets. China has been suffering from economic exploitation by foreign imperialists, as well as from political servitude. This has brought disastrous consequences to the life of the Chinese people. Every day we see with our own eyes the bankruptcy of small entrepreneurs, the unemployment of our handicraft workers, the loss of land by our farmers, the rising cost of living, and the increase of taxation. Honest workers and farmers have been forced to become bandits or highway robbers; and poverty and misery have spread throughout the entire country....

B. THE PRINCIPLES OF KUOMINTANG

The principles of the Kuomintang are really the "San Min" Doctrine, or the Three Principles of the People as outlined by Dr. Sun. As the faithful execution of these principles is the only way to national salvation, the political platform of the Party is based upon these principles and the entire program of the People's Revolution has been determined in accordance with them.

The purpose of the present reorganization of the Party is to maintain better discipline of Party members, so that the Party can have an early realization of the "San Min" Doctrine. Dr. Sun's speech, delivered on November 25, 1923, and his speech on "The Present Condition in China and the Reorganization of the Kuomintang" have explained in detail the meaning and contents of the "San Min" Doctrine. We give here, however, a brief summary of the Doctrine to serve as an introduction to our political program for remedying the present Chinese situation.

The Doctrine of Nationalism

The Kuomintang's Doctrine of Nationalism has two implications: the first is the emancipation of the Chinese people, and the second is the equality of all the races within China.

First of all, the purpose of the Kuomintang's Doctrine of Nationalism is to restore liberty and independence to the Chinese people. Before 1911, the Chinese people were governed by the Manchus who, in turn, were not free, but were under the dominant influence of the imperialistic Powers. At that time, the function of the Nationalist movement was, on the one hand, to free the Chinese people from the Manchu rule, and on the other hand, to prevent the partition of China by the Powers. The first object, namely, the overthrowing of the Manchu rule, was accomplished by the revolution of 1911. But the imperialistic Powers have still kept a dominant influence in China.

Although the danger of political partition seems to be averted, the danger of international control is imminent. In other words, the Powers have substituted for their policy of military conquest a policy of economic exploitation; and the result of imperialistic economic exploitation is the same as the result of military conquest, namely, the loss of independence and liberty on the part of the Chinese people. Not only are the militarists in the country allying themselves with the imperialists, but the capitalist class is also trying to get as much as possible from the common people. Thus, the Chinese people are prevented from making progress in economic activities as well as in political activities.

Seeing the present status of affairs, the members of the Kuomintang feel in duty bound to work for the liberation of the Chinese people from economic and political exploitation. In this struggle, we must have the support of the mass of the people, including support from the intellectual class, from the farmers, from the workers, as well as from the merchants.

Since Nationalism aims to stop the imperialistic invasion of China, it is a doctrine by which all classes will be equally benefited. Without the realization of the Doctrine of Nationalism, the manufacturers will be forever hindered from achieving economic prosperity and development by the foreign domination of business in China. At the same time, the workers will have to depend for their living upon either foreign capitalists or Chinese militarists and so will have to keep on living in a status of slavery.

The motto in the present struggle for national liberation is "Anti-imperialism," because the downfall of imperialism in China will enable the mass of people to organize, to consolidate, and to continue the Nationalist struggle. We pray, therefore, for close co-operation between the Kuomintang and the mass of the people in order to enable the Chinese people to regain their real liberty and their independence.

The second aspect of the Doctrine of Nationalism is racial equality. Before 1911 the Manchus alone were rulers of China. This autocratic position of the Manchus was brought to an end by the Revolution, and it was replaced by a policy of co-operation among all races in China on the basis of equality.

Unfortunately, the present government of China is controlled by the surviving elements of old officialdom who know nothing of racial equality and freedom; and consequently the other races in China are discontented with the present status of affairs. These discontented people have even questioned the sincerity of the Kuomintang's policy of racial equality and racial co-operation. The Kuomintang must convince these people as to the sincerity of its efforts and the honesty of its motives if the party is to carry out the Doctrine of Nationalism. We have over and over insisted upon the common interest of all peoples within China and the necessity of their consolidation in the People's Revolution and in solving all interracial problems. We hereby repeat solemnly that we recognize the right of self-determination for all peoples in China, and that a free, united Republic of China based upon the principles of free alliance of the different peoples will be established after the downfall of imperialism and militarism.

The Doctrine of Democracy

The Kuomintang's Doctrine of Democracy includes direct democracy and indirect democracy. This means that the people will not only have the right of

657

suffrage, but also the rights of initiative, referendum, and recall. Through what channels, and in what ways these rights of the people are to be exercised, will be stated in the constitution based upon the principle of five independent departments (*yuan*) as initiated by Dr. Sun: namely, the legislative, the judicial, the executive, the examining, and the impeachment. All these provisions are meant to remedy the defects in the system of representative democracy and in the existing systems of election.

It has been found that so-called "representative" governments often have not been truly representative of the people, and that they have been only tools used by capitalists to exploit the common people. According to the Kuomintang's Doctrine of Democracy, the people's rights should be enjoyed by all people, not by a few privileged individuals only.

It should also be pointed out that the Kuomintang's Doctrine of Democracy is different entirely from the doctrine of natural rights. Our doctrine is based on the actual needs of the present revolutionary cause in China; for the safety of the nation can be maintained only when all the political power is enjoyed by all the people of the republic, not by those individuals who are opposed to the republic and who may use the power to work indirectly against the interest of the nation. In other words, all individuals or organizations sincerely opposed to militarism may enjoy all the direct rights of the people, and all the individuals or organizations who are betraying the nation's interest by working in the interest of the imperialists or militarists will forfeit their rights.

The Doctrine of Livelihood

The Kuomintang's Doctrine of Livelihood includes two essential points: first, the equalization of landownership; and second, the regulation of capital. The greatest cause of economic inequality in society is the private ownership of land. It is necessary, therefore, for the state to enact laws to regulate the ownership of land and the collection of the land tax. Land owned by private individuals should be assessed and reported to the government, which will levy the tax according to the value of the land and, if necessary, buy it from private owners at the assessed rate. This is the essence of the principle of equalization of landownership.

As to the regulation of capital: big industries such as banks, railways, and steamship lines which can be favorably operated by a monopoly, or are of such dimensions as to exceed the power of individual investment, should be managed by the state. In this way, the private capitalists can have no power to interfere with the normal economic life of the people.

We believe that if these two principles are successfully carried out, a sound foundation will have been laid for the solution of the problem of the people's livelihood. We should like to say this to the farmers: China has been and still is an agricultural nation, and of all the classes of people, the agricultural class has suffered the most from economic exploitation.

According to our Doctrine of Livelihood, the state will provide land for cultivation to those farmers who have been deprived of their land or to those who have suffered from their landlords. Irrigation systems will be provided, and colonization schemes will be devised to help those farmers who are without land of their own. Farmers' banks will be established to facilitate rural credits. It is the earnest hope of the Party that everything be done to restore normal happiness to the farmers.

To the workers, the Kuomintang has also a special message. For centuries, the Chinese government has not done anything to insure the livelihood of the working class. According to our principles, the state should help the unemployed and pass laws to improve the conditions of the laborers. Systems for the relief of the aged, for the care of children, for providing pensions for the disabled, and for providing education for the mass of the people will also be attended to by the Party in order to better the conditions of the less fortunate classes.

Throughout the length and breadth of China, there is no place where we cannot find destitute farmers and exploited workers. Because their conditions are so difficult, their desire for emancipation is correspondingly great. So the laborers and farmers may be counted among those who will most strongly oppose imperialism, and who will help in our work toward a national revolution. On the one hand, the People's Revolution can achieve victory only when the farmers and laborers of the country give it their wholehearted support. On the other hand, the Kuomintang will do its best to help peasant and labor movements in order to strengthen the People's Revolution.

Both the farmers and the workers are asked to join the Kuomintang and to give their continuous devotion and efforts to promoting the People's Revolution. Inasmuch as the Kuomintang is opposed to the imperialists and the militarists, who are the most dangerous enemies of the workers and farmers, participation in the struggle of the Party is to struggle also for their own interests.

Chinese soldiery has been composed largely of farmers; yet the soldiers themselves are unaware of their duty to serve and to protect the people, the majority of whom are farmers. Although imperialists are dangerous enemies of the people, our soldiers do not know the importance of fighting against imperialism and militarism; they have, on the contrary, been utilized by the militarists to fight against the welfare of the people. The Kuomintang regards these facts as a great anomaly, and perceives that the cause for this state of affairs is that poverty has compelled the soldiers to serve anything or any organization which can provide for them a subsistence or a living.

In view of the fact that the Kuomintang is trying its best to educate its own soldiers and to transform them into armies which exist really for the good of the people, the soldiers of the nations should all offer themselves to fight for the cause of the People's Revolution. Those soldiers who have served in the revolutionary army will have the option of returning to agriculture with a grant of a large tract of land, so that they can maintain themselves and their families.

The above is an exposition of the content of the "San Min" Doctrine. After the reorganization of the Party, strong discipline will be enforced in order to strengthen the Party. Every means will be used to strengthen the role of the party in popular movements. At the same time, the Party will try its best to spread its influence and to get new adherents throughout the country, in the hope that the people of the entire nation will arise to struggle against their enemies and to demand the supreme political power.

In this way we shall be able to prevent further counterrevolutionary activities, to discover any new intrigues of the imperialists against our people, and to remove all hindrance to the realization of our Party principles. At that time, the central executive power of the nation will be in the hands of the Party itself, for we believe that only with a strong Party organization based upon popular support will the Party be able to serve the country.

C. THE KUOMINTANG PLATFORM

In order to secure unified action among the members of the Party and in order to define clearly our objectives in the important task of national salvation and political reconstruction, we present the following platform. As China is facing a crisis in which she is in danger of national extinction, we wish patriotic citizens who put the national interest above personal or factional interest to give their utmost co-operation in carrying out the following provisions:

General Introduction

1. The People's Government will reconstruct the Republic of China in accordance with the "San Min" Doctrine and the Five-Power Constitution.

2. The first step in reconstruction is to promote the economic well-being of the people by providing for their four greatest necessities of life, namely, food, clothing, shelter, and transportation. For this purpose, the government will, with the people's co-operation, develop agriculture to give the people an adequate food supply, promote textile industries to solve their clothing problem, institute gigantic housing schemes to provide decent living quarters for them, and build roads and canals so that they may have convenient means of travel.

3. Next is the promotion of democracy. The government will educate the people and give them the necessary political training for the exercise of their rights of suffrage, initiative, referendum, and recall.

4. The third step is the development of nationalism. The government will give assistance to the weaker classes of people and make them capable of self-government and self-determination. At the same time, the government will resist foreign aggression and revise our treaties with foreign powers so as to re-establish our national independence and international equality.

Foreign Policies

1. All unequal treaties, such as those prevailing for the extraterritorial rights of foreign nationals, the foreign control of the Maritime Customs, and those that imply an infringement of China's sovereignty by allowing foreign nationals political rights on Chinese territory, should be abolished, and in their place treaties should be concluded which are based on equality and a mutual respect for sovereign rights.

2. All countries which voluntarily abandon their special rights in this country

and are ready to abolish the unequal treaties they have made with China should be recognized as the nations most friendly to China.

3. Other existing treaties between China and the foreign powers which are in any way detrimental to China's interests should also be revised on the principle of mutual respect for sovereign rights.

4. Within the limit of not injuring China's political and economic interests, foreign loans made to China should be properly secured and repaid.

5. Foreign loans which, although negotiated by the Chinese government, were put through by bribery or by any other illegal process and such loans as were obtained solely for the purpose of financing the militarists in their purely personal campaigns or to enable them to fill their own pockets, and were thus not made for the benefit of the people—all such loans the Chinese people cannot be responsible for repaying.

6. A conference, consisting of delegates from social and commercial organizations, such as banks, Chambers of Commerce, and educational institutions, is to be called for the purpose of discussing plans and measures for the repayment of foreign loans. The carrying-out of such measures would mean the freeing of China from a state of economic bondage arising from her financial complications with foreign powers.

Internal Policies

1. The powers of the central government and those of the provincial governments are to be equally distributed. All affairs concerning the whole nation will be entrusted to the charge of the central government, while those conditioned by local circumstances will be taken care of by the local governments. An inclination toward greater centralization or decentralization will be avoided.

2. The people of each province may draw up their own constitutions and elect their own governors. The provincial constitutions must not conflict with the national constitution. The provincial governors will be at the head of provincial self-government, while at the same time receiving orders from the central government regarding the execution of national governmental affairs.

3. The *hsien*, or district, is to be the unit of the people's self-government. The people of every self-governing hsien will have the right of electing and recalling their own officials and the rights of initiative and referendum in making the laws.

Land revenues, increment of land values, the products of public lands, and all profits accruing from forests, rivers, and mines are to be placed at the disposal of the local governments, which will use them for the development of local enterprises and for relieving the poor and the aged, supporting orphans, carrying out famine relief, and the maintenance of public health and similar public enterprises.

The opening-up of natural resources and the running of big industries which might go beyond the power of local capital will be equally divided between the state and the local governments.

Each hsien must contribute a percentage of its income to the national treasury to help in maintaining the expenses of the state. This contribution should be not less than 10 per cent or more than 50 per cent of its total receipts.

4. Universal suffrage is to be carried out. The regulation limiting the right of election to the propertied class only will be abolished.

5. A civil examination system will be established to remedy the evils of popular election.

6. The people's rights to freedom of belief, freedom of residence, freedom of publication, and freedom of public speech will be established by law.

7. A system of conscription will be put in force instead of the present system of hiring soldiers. At the same time, special attention will be given to the economic welfare of the soldiers and the lower officers and to the advancement of their legal status. In the armies, industrial and agricultural education will be given. The qualifications for officers will be sharply defined and observed, and the method of promoting and dismissing officers will be reformed.

8. The government is to find means of providing for the bandits and the unemployed and of engaging them in useful work for the country. One of the ways of carrying this out is to appropriate the receipts from foreign concessions after they have been returned to the people of China. By concessions, we mean those places which lie under foreign consular jurisdiction and which create the singular phenomenon of "a country within a country." Such a singular state of affairs should be done away with. The rights of foreign subjects residing or doing business in the concessions will be determined by the People's Government in accordance with the special treaties entered into between the Chinese and the foreign governments.

9. The legal tariff for land tax and agrarian tax should be definitely determined. All extra taxes, such as *likin*, and so forth, are to be abolished.

10. A census of the people should be taken; cultivated land should be properly examined; and the production of food supply should be regulated, so that the people may not be in want of food.

11. A reorganization of the farming communities will be effected so as to improve the life of the agricultural population.

12. Labor laws will be enacted, labor conditions will be ameliorated, labor organizations will be protected, and the general advancement of the laboring class will be promoted.

13. Legal, social, educational, and economic equality between the sexes will be recognized, and the general development of women's rights will be encouraged.

14. Universal education will be effectively carried out. Education for the development of children's individuality will be specially attended to, school systems will be revised, education budgets will be increased, and the independence of educational institutions will be guaranteed.

15. The state is to regulate the laws pertaining to the appropriation of land, the collection of the land tax, and the registration of land property. Land owned by private individuals will be assessed and reported to the government by the owners. The state will levy taxes according to the registered value and, when necessary, may also buy it from the owner at the registered price.

16. Enterprises which partake of the nature of monopolies, or which could

not be well undertaken by private individuals, like railways and steamship lines, will be owned and managed by the state.

The above items contain what we believe to be the minimum measures of our Party platform and they are the first steps to be immediately undertaken for reform of our country.

Methods of Carrying Out the Program

1. The reconstruction program will be divided into three periods: (1) the period of military dictatorship; (2) the period of political tutelage; and (3) the period of constitutional government.

2. During the period of military dictatorship, all political machinery will be placed under the direct control of the military government. The government, in order to bring about national unification, will, on the one hand, overcome internal discord by military force and, on the other hand, endeavor to wake up the people through propaganda.

3. When a province has been completely brought within military control, the period of political tutelage begins and the period of military dictatorship ends. During the period of political tutelage, the government will send to different hsien qualified experts who have passed satisfactorily the required civil service examinations to assist the people of the different hsien in organizing local self-government. The work will begin with a survey of population of the hsien and its land areas and boundary lines. Then the police organization of the hsien will be perfected and public roads will be built. When the people in the hsien have been trained to exercise their four rights of self-government, are capable of performing their duties of citizenship, and are willing to carry out the revolutionary principles, they will be permitted to elect their own magistrate and legislators. The hsien will then have become completely self-governed.

4. When all the hsien in a province have evolved a working self-government, then the provinces are to pass into the period of constitutional government. The Representatives' Assembly will elect a provincial governor to supervise the provincial self-government. In matters within the sphere of the national administration, the governor will receive orders from the central government.

5. At the outset of constitutional government, the central government will establish five separate departments (*yuan*) to administer the five political functions: namely, the Executive Department, the Legislative Department, the Judicial Department, the Examining Department, and the Board of Control. The drafting of the constitution will be based on the National Reconstruction Program and the actual experience during the period of political tutelage and the period of constitutional government. The constitution will be drafted by the Legislative Department and will from time to time be made known to the people so as to prepare them for its final adoption.

6. When the majority of the provinces in the country have reached the period of constitutional government, that is, when these provinces have secured effective local self-government, a People's Conference will be held to consider, promulgate, and adopt the constitution. After the constitution has been promulgated, the highest political power of the central government will be vested in

the People's Conference. This conference will have the right of electing and recalling officers of the central government. With respect to national legislation, the conference possesses the right of initiative and referendum.

7. The promulgation of the national constitution will end the third period, that is, the period of constitutional government. A national general election will be held in accordance with the provisions of the constitution. This will be the successful completion of the program of national reconstruction.

APPENDIX **3**

Common Program of the Chinese People's Political Consultative Conference (September 29, 1949)

The great victories of the Chinese people's war of liberation and people's revolution have ended the era of the rule of imperialism, feudalism, and bureaucratic capitalism in China. From the status of the oppressed, the Chinese people have become the master of a new society and a new state and have replaced the feudal, comprador, fascist, dictatorial Kuomintang reactionary rule with a republic of the people's democratic dictatorship. The Chinese people's democratic dictatorship is the state power of the people's democratic united front of the Chinese working class, peasantry, petty bourgeoisie, and patriotic democratic elements based on the alliance of workers and peasants and led by the working class. The Chinese People's Political Consultative Conference (PCC), composed of the representatives of the Communist Party of China, all democratic parties and groups, people's organizations, all areas, the People's Liberation Army, all national minorities, overseas Chinese, and patriotic democratic elements, is the form of organization of the Chinese people's democratic united front. The Chinese People's PCC, representing the will of the people throughout the country, proclaims the establishment of the People's Republic of China and organizes the people's own central government. The Chinese People's PCC unanimously agrees that the New Democracy, namely the people's democracy, shall be the political foundation for national construction of the People's Republic of China. The Chinese People's PCC has also worked out the following common program, which should be observed in common by all units participating in the Chinese People's PCC, all levels of the People's Government, and the people throughout the country.

ARTICLE 1. The People's Republic of China is a state of new democracy, that is, people's democracy. This Republic carries out the people's democratic dictatorship led by the working class, based on the alliance of workers and peasants, and rallying all democratic classes and all nationalities in China. This Republic opposes imperialism, feudalism, and bureaucratic capitalism and strives for the independence, democracy, peace, unification, prosperity, and strength of China.

ART. 2. The Central People's Government of the People's Republic of China must undertake to wage the people's war of liberation to the very end, liberate all the territory of China, and accomplish the cause of unifying China.

ART. 3. The People's Republic of China must abolish all prerogatives of imperialist countries in China; confiscate bureaucratic capital for ownership by the people's state; systematically transform the feudal and semifeudal land-ownership system into the system of peasant landownership; protect the economic interests and private property of workers, peasants, petty bourgeoisie, and national bourgeoisie; develop the people's economy of new democracy; and steadily transform the country from an agricultural into an industrial country.

ART. 4. The right of the people of the People's Republic of China to elect and be elected is prescribed by law.

ART. 5. The people of the People's Republic of China shall have freedom of thought, speech, publication, assembly, association, correspondence, person, domicile, moving from one place to another, religious belief, and the freedom of holding processions and demonstrations.

ART. 6. The People's Republic of China abolishes the feudal system which holds women in bondage. Women shall enjoy equal rights with men in political, economic, cultural, educational, and social life. Freedom of marriage for men and women shall be enforced.

ART. 7. The People's Republic of China must suppress all counterrevolutionary activities and severely punish all Kuomintang counterrevolutionary war criminals and other obdurate arch-counterrevolutionary elements who collude with imperialism, commit treason to the fatherland, and oppose the cause of people's democracy. Reactionary elements, feudal landlords, and bureaucratic capitalists in general must, according to law, also be deprived of their political rights within a necessary period after they have been disarmed and their special power abolished, but they shall at the same time be given means of living and compelled to reform themselves through labor to become new men. If they continue their counterrevolutionary activities, they shall be severely punished.

ART. 8. It is the duty of every national of the People's Republic of China to defend the fatherland, observe the laws, maintain labor discipline, protect public property, perform public service and military service, and pay taxes.

ART. 9. All nationalities in the People's Republic of China have equal rights and duties.

ART. 10. The armed forces of the People's Republic of China, that is, the

People's Liberation Army, the people's public security forces, and the people's police, are armed forces belonging to the people. Their tasks are to defend the independence, integrity of territory, and sovereignty of China and the revolutionary fruits and all legitimate rights and interests of the Chinese people. The Central People's Government of the People's Republic of China shall endeavor to consolidate and strengthen the people's armed forces to enable them to accomplish their tasks effectively.

ART. 11. The People's Republic of China unites with all peace- and freedom-loving countries and people's democracies throughout the world, first of all the Soviet Union, all people's democracies, and all oppressed nations, and stands in the camp of international peace and democracy to oppose jointly imperialist aggression and defend lasting world peace.

CHAPTER II / ORGANS OF STATE POWER

ARTICLE 12. The state power of the People's Republic of China belongs to the people. All levels of the People's Congress and all levels of the People's Government are organs for exercising state power by the people. All levels of the People's Congress shall be elected through universal suffrage by the people. All levels of the People's Congress shall elect the respective levels of the People's Government. The various levels of the People's Government shall be the organs for exercising state power at their respective levels when their respective People's Congresses are not in session. The All-China People's Congress is the supreme organ of state power. The Central People's Government shall be the supreme organ for exercising state power when the All-China People's Congress in not in session.

ART. 13. The Chinese People's PCC is the form of organization of the people's democratic united front. It shall be composed of the representatives of the working class, the peasantry, revolutionary servicemen, intellectuals, the petty bourgeoisie, the national bourgeoisie, national minorities, overseas Chinese, and patriotic democratic elements.

Pending the convocation of the All-China People's Congress, elected through universal suffrage, the plenary session of the Chinese People's PCC shall exercise the functions and powers of the All-China People's Congress, enact the statutes of the Central People's Government of the People's Republic of China, elect the Central People's Government Council of the People's Republic of China, and vest it with the authority of exercising state power.

After the convocation of the All-China People's Congress, elected through universal suffrage, the Chinese People's PCC shall submit proposals on fundamental policies, relating to the construction work of the country and other important measures, to the All-China People's Congress or to the Central People's Congresses.

ART. 14. The duration of military control shall be determined by the Central People's Government in accordance with military and political conditions in the locality.

In all places where military operations have ended, agrarian reform has been thoroughly carried out, and people of all circles have been fully organized, elections through universal suffrage shall be held immediately to convene local People's Congresses.

ART. 15. All levels of organs of state power shall put into practice democratic centralism. Its main principles are: The People's Council is responsible and accountable to the People's Congress. Within the People's Congress and the People's Government Council, the minority shall abide by the decisions of the majority. The appointment of the People's Governments of various levels shall be confirmed by the People's Government of the higher level. The People's Government of the lower level shall obey the People's Government of the higher level, and all local People's Governments throughout the country shall obey the Central People's Government.

ART. 16. The jurisdiction of the Central People's Government and the local People's Governments shall be defined in accordance with the nature of their functions and shall be prescribed by decrees of the Central People's Government Council so as to be beneficial to both national unification and local expediency.

ART. 17. All laws, decrees, and judicial systems of the Kuomintang reactionary government oppressing the people are abolished, and laws and decrees protecting the people shall be enacted and the people's judicial system shall be set up.

ART. 18. All state organs must enforce a revolutionary working style of honesty, simplicity, and service to the people, must severely punish graft, forbid extravagance, and oppose the bureaucratic working style of estrangement from the masses of the people.

ART. 19. People's supervisory organs shall be set up in the People's Governments of county and municipal levels and above to supervise the exercise of functions and performance of duties by the various levels of state organs and public functionaries and to indict organs and functionaries who violate the law or are derelict in the performance of their duties. People or people's organizations have the right to indict before the people's supervisory organs or people's judicial organs any state organ or any public functionary violating the law or derelict in performing their duties.

CHAPTER III / MILITARY SYSTEM

ARTICLE 20. The People's Republic of China shall build up a unified army, that is, the People's Liberation Army and the people's public security forces, which shall be under the command of the People's Revolutionary Military Council of the Central People's Government and which shall institute a unified command, unified system, unified formation, and unified discipline.

ART. 21. The People's Liberation Army and the people's public security forces shall, in accordance with the principle of unity between the officers and rank and file and unity between the army and the people, set up a political work system and educate the commanders and fighters of these troops in the revolutionary and patriotic spirit.

ART. 22. The People's Republic of China shall strengthen the modernized land force and establish an air force and a navy to consolidate national defense.

ART. 23 . The People's Republic of China shall enforce the system of people's militia to maintain local order, lay the foundation for national mobilization, and prepare for the enforcement of an obligatory military service system at the appropriate moment.

ART. 24. The armed forces of the People's Republic of China shall, during peacetime, systematically take part in agricultural and industrial production to assist in national construction work on the condition of not hindering military tasks.

ART. 25. Dependents of revolutionary martyrs and revolutionary servicemen who suffer from privation shall receive preferential treatment from the state and from society. The People's Government shall appropriately provide the means of livelihood and settling-down for disabled servicemen and retired servicemen who have participated in the revolutionary war.

CHAPTER IV / ECONOMIC POLICY

ARTICLE 26. The basic principle for economic construction of the People's Republic of China is to attain the goal of developing production and bringing about a prosperous economy through the policies of taking into account both public and private interests, benefits to both labor and capital, mutual aid between the city and countryside, and interflow of goods both at home and abroad. The state shall co-ordinate and regulate the state-owned economy, the co-operative economy, the individual economy of peasants and handicraftsmen, and the private-capitalist and state-capitalist economies in the spheres of operation, supply of raw materials, markets, labor conditions, technical equipment, policies of public finance, etc., so that all components of the social economy can play their part and effect division of work and co-operation under the leadership of the state-owned economy to promote the development of the entire social economy.

ART. 27 . Agrarian reform is the essential condition for the development of the productive power and the industrialization of the country. In all areas where the agrarian reform has been carried out, the right of ownership over the land obtained by peasants shall be protected. In areas where the agrarian reform has not yet been carried out, the peasant masses must be set in motion to organize peasant organizations and realize "land to the tiller" through such measures as the elimination of local bandits and despots, reduction of rents and interest, and distribution of land.

ART. 28. State-owned economy is of a socialist nature. All enterprises vital to the economic life of the country and to the people's livelihood shall come under unified operation by the state. All state-owned resources and enterprises are the common property of all the people. They are the main material basis of the People's Republic for developing production and bringing about a prosperous economy and are the leading force of the entire social economy.

ART. 29. Co-operative economy is of a semisocialist nature and is an important component of the entire people's economy; the People's Government shall foster its development and accord it preferential treatment.

ART. 30. The People's Government shall encourage the operation of all private economic enterprises beneficial to the national welfare and the people's livelihood and foster their development.

ART. 31. The economy of co-operation between state and private capital is of a state-capitalist nature. Whenever necessary and possible, private capital shall be encouraged to develop along the direction of state capitalism, for example, processing for state-owned enterprises, operating jointly with the state-owned enterprises, and exploiting the state-owned resources through the form of concessions.

ART. 32. The system of workers taking part in the administration of production shall, at present, be put into practice in state-owned enterprises, that is, factory administrative committees shall be set up under the leadership of the factory. In privately operated enterprises, collective contracts should be signed by the trade union—representing the workers and employees—and the employer in order to carry out the principle of benefits to both labor and capital. At present, an eight-to-ten-hour day shall in general be enforced in publicly and privately operated enterprises, but this may be dealt with at discretion under special circumstances. The People's Government shall fix the minimum wage according to the conditions in various places and trades. Labor insurance shall be gradually carried out. The special interests of juvenile and women workers shall be protected. Inspection of industries and mines shall be carried out to improve safety devices and sanitary facilities of the industries and mines.

ART. 33. The Central People's Government shall as early as possible draw up a general plan for rehabilitating and developing the main branches of the public and private economy of the entire country, determine the division of work and co-operation between the central and local governments in economic construction, and carry out unified co-ordination of the mutual relations between the economic departments of the central and local governments. Under the unified leadership of the Central People's Government, the various economic departments of the central and local governments should give full play to their creativeness and initiative.

ART. 34. Concerning agriculture, forestry, fishery, and stock-raising in all areas where the agrarian reform has been thoroughly carried out, the People's Government shall take as its central task the organization of peasants, and all labor power which should be employed in agriculture to develop agricultural production and side occupations; and it shall guide the peasants step by step to organize various forms of labor mutual aid and production co-operation according to the principle of voluntariness and mutual benefits. In newly liberated areas, every step of the agrarian reform should be linked up with reviving and developing agricultural production. The People's Government should, in accordance with the plan of the state and the needs of the people's livelihood, restore the output of grain, industrial raw materials, and export goods to prewar production levels and surpass it within the shortest possible time. Attention should be paid to projects of building and repairing irrigation works, taking preventive measures against floods and droughts, restoring and developing livestock-raising, increasing fertilizers, improving farm tools and seeds, taking preventive measures against pests and plant diseases, relieving the victims of natural calamities, and systematically carrying out migration for land reclamation. Forests shall be protected and reforestation shall be developed according to plan. Fishing grounds along the seacoast shall be protected, and the aquatic-products industry shall be developed. Livestock-raising shall be protected, and preventive measures taken against plague.

Art. 35. Concerning industry, to lay down the foundation for the industrialization of the country, work shall be centered on the planned, systematic rehabilitation and development of heavy industry, such as mining industry, steel and iron industry, power industry, machine-building industry, electrical industry, and the main chemical industries. At the same time, the production of the textile industry and other light industries beneficial to the national welfare and the people's livelihood shall be restored and increased so as to meet with the daily consumption needs of the people.

Art. 36. Concerning communications, railways and highways must be swiftly restored and gradually increased; rivers must be dredged and waterway transportation expanded; postal and telegraphic services must be improved and developed; various communication facilities must be built up and civil aviation inaugurated step by step, according to plan.

Art. 37. Concerning commerce, all legitimate public and private trading shall be protected. Control of foreign trade shall be enforced, and the policy of protecting trade shall be adopted. Domestic free trade shall be adopted under a unified economic plan of the state, but commercial speculation disturbing the market is strictly prohibited. The state-owned trading organs shall undertake to adjust supply and demand, stabilize commodity prices, and foster the people's co-operatives. The People's Government shall adopt measures to encourage the people to deposit their savings, to facilitate overseas remittance, and channelize into industry and other productive undertakings the commercial capital not beneficial to the national welfare and the people's livelihood.

Art. 38. Concerning co-operatives, the broad masses of the working people shall be encouraged and assisted to develop co-operatives according to the principle of voluntariness. Supply and marketing co-operatives, consumers' co-operatives, credit co-operatives, producers' co-operatives, and transport co-operatives shall be organized in towns and villages; and consumers' co-operatives shall first be organized in factories, institutions, and schools.

Art. 39. Concerning finance, financial enterprises shall be strictly controlled by the state. The right of issuing currency belongs to the state. The circulation of foreign currencies within the country is forbidden. Buying and selling of foreign exchange, foreign currencies, and gold and silver shall be handled by the state banks. Private financial enterprises operating within the law shall be subjected to state supervision and direction. Severe punishment shall be meted out to all who engage in financial speculation and undermining of the financial enterprises of the state.

ART. 40. Concerning public finance, the system of budget and final account shall be instituted. The financial spheres of the central and local governments shall be defined. Retrenchment and economy shall be enforced. The balancing of the budget shall be gradually attained, and capital shall be accumulated for the country's production.

The taxation policy of the state shall be based on the principle of insuring supplies for the revolutionary war and taking into account the rehabilitation and development of production and the needs of national construction. The taxation system shall be simplified and a just distribution of the burden effected.

CHAPTER V / CULTURAL AND EDUCATIONAL POLICY

ARTICLE 41. The culture and education of the People's Republic of China are new-democratic, that is, national, scientific, and popular. The main tasks for raising the cultural level of the people are training of personnel for national construction work; liquidation of feudal, comprador, and fascist ideology; and development of the ideology of serving the people.

ART. 42. Love for the fatherland and the people, love of labor, love of science, and the taking care of public property shall be promoted as the public spirit of all nationals of the People's Republic of China.

ART. 43. Efforts shall be made to develop the natural sciences to place them at the service of industrial, agricultural, and national-defense construction. Scientific discoveries and inventions shall be encouraged and rewarded, and scientific knowledge shall be popularized.

ART. 44. The application of a scientific-historical viewpoint to the study and interpretation of history, economics, politics, culture, and international affairs shall be promoted. Outstanding works of social science shall be encouraged and rewarded.

ART. 45. Literature and the arts shall be promoted to serve the people, to enlighten the political consciousness of the people, and to encourage the labor enthusiasm of the people. Outstanding works of literature and the arts shall be encouraged and rewarded. The people's drama and cinema shall be developed.

ART. 46. The method of education of the People's Republic of China is the unity of theory and practice. The People's Government shall reform the old educational system, subject matter, and teaching method systematically, according to plan.

ART. 47. In order to meet the widespread needs of revolutionary work and national-construction work, universal education shall be carried out; middle and higher education shall be strengthened, technical education shall be stressed, the education of workers during their spare time, and education of cadres who are at their posts shall be strengthened, and revolutionary political education shall be accorded to young intellectuals and old-style intellectuals in a planned and systematic manner.

ART. 48. National sports shall be promoted. Public health and medical work shall be extended, and attention shall be paid to safeguarding the health of mothers, infants, and children.

ART. 49. Freedom of reporting true news shall be safeguarded. The utilization of the press to slander, to undermine the interests of the state and the people, and to provoke world war is prohibited. The people's broadcasting work and the people's publication work shall be developed, and attention shall be paid to publishing popular books and newspapers beneficial to the people.

CHAPTER VI / POLICY TOWARD NATIONALITIES

ARTICLE 50. All nationalities within the boundary of the People's Republic of China are equal. Unity and mutual help shall be effected among them to oppose imperialism and the public enemies within these nationalities so that the People's Republic of China will become a big family of fraternity and co-operation of all nationalities. Nationalism and chauvinism shall be opposed and acts of discrimination, oppression, and splitting the unity of the various nationalities shall be prohibited.

ART. 51. Regional autonomy shall be carried out in areas where national minorities are aggregated, and autonomous organs of the various nationalities shall be set up according to their respective population and the size of the region. The various nationalities shall have an appropriate number of representatives in the local organs of state power in places where various nationalities live together and in the autonomous areas of national minorities.

ART. 52. The nationalities within the boundary of the People's Republic of China have the right to join the People's Liberation Army and to organize local people's public security forces in accordance with the unified military system of the state.

ART. 53. All national minorities have the freedom of developing their dialects and languages and preserving or reforming their customs, habits, and religious beliefs. The People's Government shall help the masses of the people of all national minorities to develop their political, economic, cultural, and educational construction work.

CHAPTER VII / FOREIGN POLICY

ARTICLE 54. The principle of the foreign policy of the People's Republic of China is to safeguard the independence, freedom, and integrity of territory and sovereignty of the country; to support international lasting peace and friendly cooperation between the peoples of all countries; and to oppose the imperialist policy of aggression and war.

ART. 55. The Central People's Government of the People's Republic of China shall examine the treaties and agreements concluded between the Kuomintang and foreign governments and recognize or abrogate, or revise or renew them, according to their respective contents.

Art. 56. The Central People's Government of the People's Republic of China may negotiate and establish diplomatic relations on the basis of equality, mutual respect for territory, and sovereignty with foreign governments which sever relations with the Kuomintang reactionaries and adopt a friendly attitude toward the People's Republic of China.

Art. 57. The People's Republic of China may restore and develop trading and commercial relations with foreign governments and people on the basis of equality and mutual benefit.

Art. 58. The Central People's Government of the People's Republic of China shall do its utmost to protect the legitimate rights and interests of Chinese residing abroad.

Art. 59. The People's Government of the People's Republic of China shall protect law-abiding foreign nationals in China.

Art. 60. The People's Republic of China shall accord the right of asylum to foreign nationals who seek refuge in China because they are oppressed by their own governments for supporting the people's interests and taking part in the struggle for peace and democracy.

APPENDIX 4

The Constitution of Japan (1946)

We, the Japanese people, acting through our duly elected representatives in the National Diet, determined that we shall secure for ourselves and our posterity the fruits of peaceful cooperation with all nations and the blessings of liberty throughout this land, and resolved that never again shall we be visited with the horrors of war through the action of government, do proclaim that sovereign power resides with the people and do firmly establish this Constitution. Government is a sacred trust of the people, the authority for which is derived from the people, the powers of which are exercised by the representatives of the people, and the benefits of which are enjoyed by the people. This is a universal principle of mankind upon which this Constitution is founded. We reject and revoke all constitutions, laws, ordinances, and rescripts in conflict herewith.

We, the Japanese people, desire peace for all time and are deeply conscious of the high ideals controlling human relationship; and we have determined to preserve our security and existence, trusting in the justice and faith of the peace-loving peoples of the world. We desire to occupy an honored place in an international society striving for the preservation of peace, and the banishment of tyranny and slavery, oppression and intolerance, for all time from the earth. We recognize that all peoples of the world have the right to live in peace, free from fear and want.

We believe that no nation is responsible to itself alone, but that laws of political morality are universal; and that obedience to such laws is incumbent upon all nations who would sustain their own sovereignty and justify their sovereign relationship with other nations.

We, the Japanese people, pledge our national honor to accomplish these high ideals and purposes with all our resources.

CHAPTER I / THE EMPEROR

ARTICLE 1. The Emperor shall be the symbol of the State and of the unity of the people, deriving his position from the will of the people, with whom resides sovereign power.

ART. 2. The Imperial Throne shall be dynastic and succeeded to in accordance with the Imperial House Law passed by the Diet.

ART. 3. The advice and approval of the Cabinet shall be required for all acts of the Emperor in matters of state, and the Cabinet shall be responsible therefor.

ART. 4. The Emperor shall perform only such acts in matters of state as are provided for in this Constitution, and he shall not have powers related to government.

The Emperor may delegate the performance of his acts in matters of state as may be provided for by law.

ART. 5. When, in accordance with the Imperial House Law, a Regency is established, the Regent shall perform his acts in matters of state in the Emperor's name. In this case, paragraph one of the preceding article will be applicable.

ART. 6. The Emperor shall appoint the Prime Minister as designated by the Diet.

The Emperor shall appoint the Chief Justice of the Supreme Court as designated by the Cabinet.

ART. 7. The Emperor, with the advice and approval of the Cabinet, shall perform the following acts in matters of state on behalf of the people:

Promulgation of amendments of the constitution, laws, cabinet orders and treaties.

Convocation of the Diet.

Dissolution of the House of Representatives.

Proclamation of general election of members of the Diet.

Attestation of the appointment and dismissal of Ministers of State and other officials as provided for by law, and of full powers and credentials of Ambassadors and Ministers.

Attestation of general and special amnesty, commutation of punishment, reprieve, and restoration of rights.

Awarding of honors.

Attestation of instruments of ratification and other diplomatic documents as provided for by the law.

Receiving foreign ambassadors and ministers.

Performance of ceremonial functions.

ART. 8. No property can be given to, or received by, the Imperial House, nor can any gifts be made therefrom, without the authorization of the Diet.

CHAPTER II / RENUNCIATION OF WAR

ARTICLE 9. Aspiring sincerely to an international peace based on justice and order, the Japanese people forever renounce war as a sovereign right of the nation and the threat or use of force as a means of settling international disputes.

In order to accomplish the aim of the preceding paragraph, land, sea, and air forces, as well as other war potential, will never be maintained. The right of belligerency of the state will not be recognized.

CHAPTER III / RIGHTS AND DUTIES OF THE PEOPLE

ARTICLE 10. The conditions necessary for being a Japanese national shall be determined by law.

ART. 11. The people shall not be prevented from enjoying any of the fundamental human rights. These fundamental human rights, guaranteed to the people by this Constitution, shall be conferred upon the people of this and future generations as eternal and inviolate rights.

ART. 12. The freedoms and rights guaranteed to the people by this Constitution shall be maintained by the constant endeavor of the people, who shall refrain from any abuse of these freedoms and rights and shall always be responsible for utilizing them for the public welfare.

ART. 13. All of the people shall be respected as individuals. Their right to life, liberty, and the pursuit of happiness shall, to the extent that it does not interfere with the public welfare, be the supreme consideration in legislation and in other governmental affairs.

ART. 14. All of the people are equal under the law, and there shall be no discrimination in political, economic, or social relations because of race, creed, sex, social status, or family origin.

Peers and peerage shall not be recognized.

No privilege shall accompany any award of honor, decoration, or any distinction, nor shall any such award be valid beyond the lifetime of the individual who now holds or hereafter may receive it.

ART. 15. The people have the inalienable right to choose their public officials and to dismiss them.

All public officials are servants of the whole community and not any group thereof.

Universal adult suffrage is guaranteed with regard to the election of public officials.

In all elections, secrecy of the ballot shall not be violated. A voter shall not be answerable, publicly or privately, for the choice he has made.

Art. 16. Every person shall have the right of peaceful petition for the redress of damage, for the removal of public officials, for the enactment, repeal, or amendment of laws, ordinances, or regulations and for other matters; nor shall any person be in any way discriminated against for sponsoring such a petition.

Art. 17. Every person may sue for redress as provided by law from the State or a public entity, in case he has suffered damage through illegal act of any public official.

Art. 18. No person shall be held in bondage of any kind. Involuntary servitude, except as punishment for crime, is prohibited.

Art. 19. Freedom of thought and conscience shall not be violated.

Art. 20. Freedom of religion is guaranteed to all. No religious organization shall receive any privileges from the State, nor exercise any political authority.

No person shall be compelled to take part in any religious act, celebration, rite, or practice.

The State and its organs shall refrain from religious education or any other religious activity.

Art. 21. Freedom of assembly and association as well as speech, press, and all other forms of expression are guaranteed.

No censorship shall be maintained, nor shall the secrecy of any means of communication be violated.

Art. 22. Every person shall have freedom to choose and change his residence and to choose his occupation to the extent that it does not interfere with the public welfare.

Freedom of all persons to move to a foreign country and to divest themselves of their nationality shall be inviolate.

Art. 23. Academic freedom is guaranteed.

Art. 24. Marriage shall be based upon the mutual consent of both sexes, and it shall be maintained through mutual cooperation, with the equal rights of husband and wife as a basis.

With regard to the choice of spouse, property rights, inheritance, choice of domicile, divorce, and other matters pertaining to marriage and the family, laws shall be enacted from the standpoint of individual dignity and the essential equality of the sexes.

Art. 25. All people shall have the right to maintain the minimum standards of wholesome and cultural living.

In all spheres of life, the State shall use its endeavors for the promotion and extension of social welfare and security, and of public health.

Art. 26. All people shall have the right to receive an equal education correspondent to their ability, as provided by law.

All people shall be obligated to have all boys and girls under their protection receive ordinary education as provided for by law. Such compulsory education shall be free.

Art. 27. All people shall have the right and obligation to work.

Standards for wages, hours, rest, and other working conditions shall be fixed by law.

Children shall not be exploited.

ART. 28. The right of workers to organize and to bargain and act collectively is guaranteed.

ART. 29. The right to own or to hold property is inviolable.

Property rights shall be defined by law, in conformity with the public welfare.

Private property may be taken for public use upon just compensation therefor.

ART. 30. The people shall be liable to taxation as provided by law.

ART. 31. No person shall be deprived of life or liberty, nor shall any other criminal penalty be imposed, except according to procedure established by law.

ART. 32. No person shall be denied the right of access to the courts.

ART. 33. No person shall be apprehended except upon warrant issued by a competent judicial officer which specifies the offense with which the person is charged, unless he is apprehended, the offense being committed.

ART. 34. No person shall be arrested or detained without being at once informed of the charges against him or without the immediate privilege of counsel; nor shall he be detained without adequate cause; and upon demand of any person such cause must be immediately shown in open court in his presence and the presence of his counsel.

ART. 35. The right of all persons to be secure in their homes, papers, and effects against entries, searches, and seizures shall not be impaired except upon warrant issued for adequate cause and particularly describing the place to be searched and things to be seized, or except as provided by Article 33.

Each search and seizure shall be made upon separate warrant issued by a competent judicial officer.

ART. 36. The infliction of torture by any public officer and cruel punishments are absolutely forbidden.

ART. 37. In all criminal cases the accused shall enjoy the right to a speedy and public trial by an impartial tribunal.

He shall be permitted full opportunity to examine all witnesses, and he shall have the right of compulsory process for obtaining witnesses on his behalf at public expense.

At all times the accused shall have the assistance of competent counsel, who shall, if the accused is unable to secure the same by his own efforts, be assigned to his use by the State.

ART. 38. No person shall be compelled to testify against himself.

Confession made under compulsion, torture, or threat, or after prolonged arrest or detention, shall not be admitted in evidence.

No person shall be convicted or punished in cases where the only proof against him is his own confession.

ART. 39. No person shall be held criminally liable for an act which was lawful at the time it was committed, or of which he has been acquitted, nor shall he be placed in double jeopardy.

ART. 40. Any person, in case he is acquitted after he has been arrested or detained, may sue the State for redress as provided by law.

ARTICLE 41. The Diet shall be the highest organ of state power, and shall be the sole law-making organ of the State.

ART. 42. The Diet shall consist of two Houses, namely, the House of Representatives and the House of Councillors.

ART. 43. Both Houses shall consist of elected members, representative of all the people.

The number of the members of each House shall be fixed by law.

ART. 44. The qualifications of members of both Houses and their electors shall be fixed by law. However, there shall be no discrimination because of race, creed, sex, social status, family origin, education, property, or income.

ART. 45. The term of office of members of the House of Representatives shall be four years. However, the term shall be terminated before the full term is up in case the House of Representatives is dissolved.

ART. 46. The term of office of members of the House of Councillors shall be six years, and election for half the members shall take place every three years.

ART. 47. Electoral districts, method of voting, and other matters pertaining to the method of election of members of both Houses shall be fixed by law.

ART. 48. No person shall be permitted to be a member of both Houses simultaneously.

ART. 49. Members of both Houses shall receive appropriate annual payment from the national treasury in accordance with law.

ART. 50. Except in cases provided by law, members of both Houses shall be exempt from apprehension while the Diet is in session, and any members apprehended before the opening of the session shall be freed during the term of the session upon demand of the House.

ART. 51. Members of both Houses shall not be held liable outside the House for speeches, debates, or votes cast inside the House.

ART. 52. An ordinary session of the Diet shall be convoked once per year.

ART. 53. The Cabinet may determine to convoke extraordinary sessions of the Diet. When a quarter or more of the total members of either House makes the demand, the Cabinet must determine on such convocation.

ART. 54. When the House of Representatives is dissolved, there must be a general election of members of the House of Representatives within forty (40) days from the date of dissolution, and the Diet must be convoked within thirty (30) days from the date of the election.

When the House of Representatives is dissolved, the House of Councillors is closed at the same time. However, the Cabinet may in time of national emergency convoke the House of Councillors in emergency session.

Measures taken at such session as mentioned in the proviso of the preceding paragraph shall be provisional and shall become null and void unless agreed to by the House of Representatives within a period of ten (10) days after the opening of the next session of the Diet.

ART. 55. Each House shall judge disputes related to qualifications of its members. However, in order to deny a seat to any member, it is necessary to pass a resolution by a majority of two-thirds or more of the members present.

ART. 56. Business cannot be transacted in either House unless one-third or more of total membership is present.

All matters shall be decided, in each House, by a majority of those present, except as elsewhere provided in the Constitution, and, in case of a tie, the presiding officer shall decide the issue.

ART. 57. Deliberation in each House shall be public. However, a secret meeting may be held where a majority of two-thirds or more of those present passes a resolution therefor.

Each House shall keep a record of proceedings. This record shall be published and given general circulation, excepting such parts of proceedings of secret sessions as may be deemed to require secrecy.

Upon demand of one-fifth or more of the members present, votes of the members on any matter shall be recorded in the minutes.

ART. 58. Each House shall select its own president and other officials.

Each House shall establish its rules pertaining to meetings, proceedings, and internal discipline, and may punish members for disorderly conduct. However, in order to expel a member, a majority of two-thirds or more of those members present must pass a resolution thereon.

ART. 59. A bill becomes law on passage by both Houses, except as otherwise provided by the Constitution.

A bill which is passed by the House of Representatives, and upon which the House of Councillors makes a decision different from that of the House of Representatives, becomes a law when passed a second time by the House of Representatives by a majority of two-thirds or more of the members present.

The provision of the preceding paragraph does not preclude the House of Representatives from calling for the meeting of a joint committee of both Houses, provided for by law.

Failure by the House of Councillors to take final action within sixty (60) days after receipt of a bill passed by the House of Representatives, time in recess excepted, may be determined by the House of Representatives to constitute a rejection of the said bill by the House of Councillors.

ART. 60. The budget must first be submitted to the House of Representatives.

Upon consideration of the budget, when the House of Councillors makes a decision different from that of the House of Representatives, and when no agreement can be reached even through a joint committee of both Houses, provided for by law, or in the case of failure by the House of Councillors to take final action within thirty (30) days, the period of recess excluded, after the receipt of the budget passed by the House of Representatives, the decision of the House of Representatives shall be the decision of the Diet.

ART. 61. The second paragraph of the preceding article applies also to the Diet approval required for the conclusion of treaties.

ART. 62. Each House may conduct investigations in relation to government, and may demand the presence and testimony of witnesses, and the production of records.

ART. 63. The Prime Minister and other Ministers of State may, at any time, appear in either House for the purpose of speaking on bills, regardless of whether they are members of the House or not. They must appear when their presence is required in order to give answers or explanations.

ART. 64. The Diet shall set up an impeachment court from among the members of both Houses for the purpose of trying those judges against whom removal proceedings have been instituted.

Matters relating to impeachment shall be provided by law.

CHAPTER V / THE CABINET

ARTICLE 65. Executive power shall be vested in the Cabinet.

ART. 66. The Cabinet shall consist of the Prime Minister, who shall be its head, and other Ministers of State, as provided for by law.

The Prime Minister and other Ministers of State must be civilians.

The Cabinet, in the exercise of executive power, shall be collectively responsible to the Diet.

ART. 67. The Prime Minister shall be designated from among the members of the Diet by a resolution of the Diet. This designation shall precede all other business.

If the House of Representatives and the House of Councillors disagree, and if no agreement can be reached even through a joint committee of both Houses, provided by law, or the House of Councillors fails to make designation within ten (10) days, exclusive of the period of recess, after the House of Representatives has made designation, the decision of the House of Representatives shall be the decision of the Diet.

ART. 68. The Prime Minister shall appoint the Ministers of State. However, a majority of their number must be chosen from among the members of the Diet.

The Prime Minister may remove the Ministers of State as he chooses.

ART. 69. If the House of Representatives passes a non-confidence resolution, or rejects a confidence resolution, the Cabinet shall resign en masse, unless the House of Representatives is dissolved within ten (10) days.

ART. 70. When there is a vacancy in the post of Prime Minister, or upon the first convocation of the Diet after a general election of members of the House of Representatives, the Cabinet shall resign en masse.

ART. 71. In the cases mentioned in the two preceding articles, the Cabinet shall continue its functions until the time when a new Prime Minister is appointed.

ART. 72. The Prime Minister, representing the Cabinet, submits bills, reports on general national affairs and foreign relations to the Diet, and exercises control and supervision over various administrative branches.

ART. 73. The Cabinet, in addition to other general administrative functions, shall perform the following functions:

Administer the law faithfully; conduct affairs of state.

Manage foreign affairs.

Conclude treaties. However, it shall obtain prior or, depending on circumstances, subsequent approval of the Diet.

Administer the civil service, in accordance with standards established by law.

Prepare the budget, and present it to the Diet.

Enact cabinet orders in order to execute the provisions of this Constitution and of the law. However, it cannot include penal provisions in such Cabinet orders unless authorized by such law.

Decide on general amnesty, special amnesty, commutation of punishment, reprieve, and restoration of rights.

Art. 74. All laws and cabinet orders shall be signed by the competent Minister of State and countersigned by the Prime Minister.

Art. 75. The Ministers of State, during their tenure of office, shall not be subject to legal action without the consent of the Prime Minister. However, the right to take that action is not impaired thereby.

Chapter VI / Judiciary

Article 76. The whole judicial power is vested in a Supreme Court and in such inferior courts as are established by law.

No extraordinary tribunal shall be established, nor shall any organ or agency of the Executive be given final judicial power.

All judges shall be independent in the exercise of their conscience and shall be bound only by this Constitution and the laws.

Art. 77. The Supreme Court is vested with the rule-making power under which it determines the rules of procedure and of practice, and of matters relating to attorneys, the internal discipline of the courts, and the administration of judicial affairs.

Public procurators shall be subject to the rule-making power of the Supreme Court.

The Supreme Court may delegate the power to make rules for inferior courts to such courts.

Art. 78. Judges shall not be removed except by public impeachment unless judically declared mentally or physically incompetent to perform official duties. No disciplinary action against judges shall be administered by any executive organ or agency.

Art. 79. The Supreme Court shall consist of a Chief Judge and such number of judges as may be determined by law; all such judges excepting the Chief Judge shall be appointed by the Cabinet.

The appointment of the judges of the Supreme Court shall be reviewed by the people at the first general election of members of the House of Representatives following their appointment and shall be reviewed again at the first general election of members of the House of Representatives after a lapse of ten (10) years, and in the same manner thereafter.

In cases mentioned in the foregoing paragraph, when the majority of the voters favors the dismissal of a judge, he shall be dismissed.

Matters pertaining to review shall be prescribed by law.

The judges of the Supreme Court shall be retired upon the attainment of the age as fixed by law.

All such judges shall receive, at regular stated intervals, adequate compensation, which shall not be decreased during their terms of office.

ART. 80. The judges of the inferior courts shall be appointed by the Cabinet from a list of persons nominated by the Supreme Court. All such judges shall hold office for a term of ten (10) years, with privilege of reappointment, provided that they shall be retired upon the attainment of the age as fixed by law.

The judges of the inferior courts shall receive, at regular stated intervals, adequate compensation, which shall not be decreased during their terms of office.

ART. 81. The Supreme Court is the court of last resort, with power to determine the constitutionality of any law, order, regulation, or official act.

ART. 82. Trials shall be conducted and judgment declared publicly.

Where a court unanimously determines publicity to be dangerous to public order or morals, a trial may be conducted privately; but trials of political offenses, offenses involving the press, or cases wherein the rights of people as guaranteed in Chapter III of this Constitution are in question shall always be conducted publicly.

CHAPTER VII / FINANCE

ARTICLE 83. The power to administer national finances shall be exercised as the Diet shall determine.

ART. 84. No new taxes shall be imposed or existing ones modified except by law or under such conditions as law may prescribe.

ART. 85. No money shall be expended, nor shall the State obligate itself, except as authorized by the Diet.

ART. 86. The Cabinet shall prepare and submit to the Diet for its consideration and decision a budget for each fiscal year.

ART. 87. In order to provide for unforeseen deficiencies in the budget, a reserve fund may be authorized by the Diet to be expended upon the responsibility of the Cabinet.

The Cabinet must get subsequent approval of the Diet for all payments, from the reserve fund.

ART. 88. All property of the Imperial Household shall belong to the State. All expenses of the Imperial Household shall be appropriated by the Diet in the budget.

ART. 89. No public money or other property shall be expended or appropriated for the use, benefit, or maintenance of any religious institution or association, or for any charitable, educational, or benevolent enterprises not under the control of public authority.

ART. 90. Final accounts of the expenditures and revenues of the State shall be audited annually by a Board of Audit and submitted by the Cabinet to the

Diet, together with the statement of audit, during the fiscal year immediately following the period covered.

The organization and competency of the Board of Audit shall be determined by law.

ART. 91. At regular intervals and at least annually the Cabinet shall report to the Diet and the people on the state of national finances.

CHAPTER VIII / LOCAL SELF-GOVERNMENT

ARTICLE 92. Regulations concerning organization and operations of local public entities shall be fixed by law in accordance with the principle of local autonomy.

ART. 93. The local public entities shall establish assemblies as their deliberative organs, in accordance with law.

The chief executive officers of all local public entities, the members of their assemblies, and such other local officials as may be determined by law shall be elected by direct popular vote within their several communities.

ART. 94. Local public entities shall have the right to manage their property, affairs, and administration and to enact their own regulations within law.

ART. 95. A special law, applicable only to one local public entity, cannot be enacted by the Diet without the consent of the majority of the voters of the local public entity concerned, obtained in accordance with law.

CHAPTER IX / AMENDMENTS

ARTICLE 96. Amendments to the Constitution shall be initiated by the Diet, through a concurring vote of two-thirds or more of all the members of each House, and shall thereupon be submitted to the people for ratification, which shall require the affirmative vote of a majority of all votes cast thereon, at a special referendum or at such election as the Diet shall specify.

Amendments when so ratified shall immediately be promulgated by the Emperor in the name of the people, as an integral part of this Constitution.

CHAPTER X / SUPREME LAW

ARTICLE 97. The fundamental human rights by this Constitution guaranteed to the people of Japan are fruits of the age-old struggle of man to be free; they have survived the many exacting tests for durability and are conferred upon this and future generations in trust, to be held for all time inviolate.

ART. 98. This Constitution shall be the supreme law of the nation, and no law, ordinance, imperial rescript, or other act of government, or part thereof, contrary to the provisions hereof, shall have legal force or validity.

The treaties concluded by Japan and established laws of nations shall be faithfully observed.

ART. 99. The Emperor or Regent as well as Ministers of State, members of the Diet, judges, and all other public officials have the obligation to respect and uphold this Constitution.

CHAPTER XI / SUPPLEMENTARY PROVISIONS

ARTICLE 100. This Constitution shall be enforced as from the day when the period of six months will have elapsed, counting from the day of its promulgation.

The enactment of laws necessary for the enforcement of this Constitution, the election of members of the House of Councillors, and the procedure for the convocation of the Diet and other preparatory procedures necessary for the enforcement of this Constitution may be executed before the day prescribed in the preceding paragraph.

ART. 101. If the House of Councillors is not constituted before the effective date of this Constitution, the House of Representatives shall function as the Diet until such time as the House of Councillors shall be constituted.

ART. 102. The term of office for half the members of the House of Councillors serving in the first term under this Constitution shall be three years. Members falling under this category shall be determined in accordance with law.

ART. 103. The Ministers of State, members of the House of Representatives, and judges in office on the effective date of this Constitution, and all other public officials who occupy positions corresponding to such positions as are recognized by this Constitution, shall not forfeit their positions automatically on account of the enforcement of this Constitution unless otherwise specified by law. When, however, successors are elected or appointed under the provisions of this Constitution, they shall forfeit their positions as a matter of course.

APPENDIX 5

Chronologies

Chronology / PART *

CHINA	JAPAN

1523–1028 Shang Dynasty: tribal society, city states

1028–771 Chou (Western) Dynasty: feudal society, petty states

Jomon Culture

770–221 Chou (Eastern) Dynasty: Period of the Warring States

Confucius (551–479)
Mencius (371–289)
Chuang Tzu (died ca. 300)
Hsun Tzu (298–238)
Legalists

Yayoi Culture

221–206 Ch'in Dynasty: unification of China; reign of Shih Huang Ti

206 B.C.–8 A.D. Former Han Dynasty: reign of Wu Ti (140–87); triumph of Confucianism; Tung Chung-shu (179–104); menace of the Hsiung-nu

Uji Society

8–23 Reign of Wang Mang

23–220 Later Han Dynasty: Wang Ch'ung (27–100); peasant rebellions; nomad menace

220–589 Period of Division: nomad states in north China; spread of Buddhism

---

ca. 3500–2700 Upper and Lower Kingdoms in Egypt united under rule of the Pharaohs

2600 Pyramids built in Egypt

1800 Hammurabi; early law code; first Babylonian Empire

1170 Trojan War: stage in Greek conquest of Aegean Civilization

950 Solomon: peak of ancient Jewish political power

590 Independence of the Roman Republic

490 Battle of Marathon: Athens victorious over Persia; dawn of the Athenian golden age

431 Outbreak of the Peloponnesian War; waning of the Age of Pericles and of Athenian leadership

323 Death of Alexander the Great; beginning of the Hellenistic Epoch

27 B.C. Augustus as emperor of Rome; beginning of Pax Romana

29 A.D. Crucifixion of Christ

180 Death of Marcus Aurelius; beginning of Roman decline

ca. 400 Emergence of the imperial clan

589–618 Sui Dynasty: reunion of the empire; patronage of Buddhism; Grand Canal

552 Beginning of Chinese influence; introduction of Buddhism from Korea

618–906 T'ang Dynasty: cosmopolitan empire; Golden Age; Han Yu (768–824); persecution of Buddhism (842–845)

645 Elimination of the Soga family; beginning of the Taika Reform

710 Founding of Nara

712 "Kojiki"

720 "Nihongi"

794 Founding of Kyoto

814 Establishment of Minamoto clan

838 Last mission to China

889 Establishment of the Taira clan

906–960 Period of Division

960–1279 Sung and Southern Sung dynasties: Popular Buddhism at peak; economic and social changes; system of separate military and civil administrations ended

995 Height of Fujiwara supremacy

1039 Armed "monks" attack Kyoto and are driven off by the Taira

Neo-Confucianism: Chu Hsi (1130–1200)

1160–1181 Supremacy of the Taira

1185 Establishment of the supremacy of the Minamoto; the Kamakura Shogunate founded by Minamoto Yoritomo

325 Council of Nicaea: milestone in development of Christianity

378 Battle of Adrianople: beginning of the final German breakthrough into the Roman Empire

527 Justinian, emperor at Byzantium: Santa Sophia and law code

622 Hegira of Mohammed

717 Unsuccessful Arab siege of Byzantium: high point of Moslem expansion toward eastern Europe

732 Battle of Tours: high point of Moslem expansion toward western Europe

800 Charlemagne crowned emperor at Rome

962 Otto the Great of Germany crowned at Rome: "Holy Roman Empire"
982 Hugh Capet becomes king of France

1054 Formal schism between Greek and Roman Churches

1066 Conquest of England by William and the Normans

1075 Opening of the Investiture Controversy between Pope Gregory VII and Henry IV

1095 First Crusade preached by Urban II

1226 Establishment of the Hojo Regency; Popular Buddhism and Zen

1279–1368 Yuan Dynasty: extension of Grand Canal; Marco Polo; Catholic missionaries in China

1274–81 Mongol invasion attempts

1368–1644 Ming Dynasty: reintegration of the empire

1336 Establishment of two imperial courts; the Ashikaga Shogunate

1392 Reunion of the imperial courts

1467–1477 The Onin War, typical of the Age of Warfare

1520–1521 Portuguese mission to China

1557 Establishment of Macao as Portuguese base

1542 Portuguese at Tanegashima; Jesuits in Japan

1582–1610 Matteo Ricci: Jesuit penetration of China

1582 Nobunaga military master of half of Japan

1590 Hideyoshi imposes suzerainty on the daimyo

1600 Tokugawa Ieyasu victor at Sekigahara

1603 Ieyasu becomes shogun

1624–1625 Dutch base on Formosa

1636 Rise of the Manchus; capital of the Ta Ch'ing Dynasty at Mukden

1638 Completion of the seclusion policy imposed by the bakufu

1215 Magna Charta in England; Fourth Lateran Council: medieval papacy at height under Innocent III

1272 Death of St. Thomas Aquinas, greatest of medieval schoolmen

ca. 1300 Dante and Giotto: dawn of the Renaissance

1303 Philip IV of France against Pope Boniface VIII: prelude to the "Babylonian Captivity" of the Papacy

1453 Close of the Hundred Years War (France victorious); Capture of Byzantium by the Ottoman Turks

1485 Henry VII (Tudor) becomes King of England

1492 Capture of Granada by Ferdinand and Isabella: end of Moslem Spain and first voyage of Columbus

1517 Luther's "95 Theses": beginning of the Protestant Reformation

1529 Unsuccessful siege of Vienna by the Ottoman Turks: high point of their expansion into Europe

1543 "The Revolutions of Heavenly Bodies" of Copernicus

1588 Defeat of the Spanish Armada

1589 Henry IV king of France: waning of civil and religious strife

1608 Founding of Jamestown

1613 First Romanov czar in Russia

1644–1912 Ch'ing Dynasty

1662–1722 Reign of K'ang Hsi

1689 Treaty of Nerchinsk

1727 Treaty of Kiakhta

1716–1745 Reforms of Yoshimune

1736–1796 Reign of Ch'ien Lung

1793 Macartney mission to Peking

1796–1820 Reign of Chia Ching; increasing number of revolts; ban on opium trade and cultivation

1798 Motoori's commentary on the "Kojiki"; Shinto revival

1804 Resanov mission to Nagasaki fails to end seclusion

1821–1850 Reign of Tao Kuang; "Do-nothing" policy

1837 Osaka riot

1841–1843 Bakufu reforms

1849 Commodore Glynn succeeds in securing American castaways at Nagasaki

1648 Peace of Westphalia: end of the Thirty Years War

1649 Execution of Charles I: climax of the English revolution

1661 Beginning of the personal rule of Louis XIV in France

1687 Publication of Newton's "Principia"
1688–1689 Glorious Revolution in England: parliamentary supremacy confirmed

1709 Battle of Poltava: Peter the Great victorious over Sweden; Russia emerging as a great power

1713 Peace of Utrecht

1740 Accession of Maria Theresa in Austria and of Frederick the Great in Prussia: War of the Austrian Succession

1765 End of the Seven Years War: Britain victorious; Prussia holds her own; and France loses in North America and India

1776 American Declaration of Independence; "The Wealth of Nations" by Adam Smith

1787 U.S. Constitution drawn up

1789 Beginning of the French Revolution

1799 Napoleon in power in France

1815 Battle of Waterloo; Vienna settlement reshapes Europe

1823 Monroe Doctrine set forth

1830 Revolutions in France, Belgium, and Poland

1832 First Reform Bill in Britain: initial step toward British political democracy

Chronology/ PART 〓

CHINA

1796–1820 Reign of Chia Ching; increasing number of revolts; ban on opium trade and cultivation

1821–1850 Reign of Tao Kuang; "Do-nothing" policy

1851–1861 Reign of Hsien Feng

Taiping Rebellion (1850–1864)
Nien Rebellion (1853–1868)
Moslem Rebellion (1855–1873)

1862–1874 Reign of T'ung Chih; Tz'u Hsi as co-regent until 1873

Period of "Self-strengthening": Tseng Kuo-fan, Li Hung-chang, Tso Tsung-t'ang, Chang Chih-tung

JAPAN

1798 Motoori's commentary on the "Kojiki": Shinto revival

1837 Osaka riot

1841–1843 Bakufu reforms

1858 Iemochi becomes shogun: victory of Ii Naosuke in the succession struggle

1861 Bakufu adopts policy of the unification of the imperial court and the shogunate

1863 Expulsion of Choshu forces from Kyoto

1864 Choshu coup at Kyoto fails

1866 Bakufu punitive expedition against Choshu; formation of anti-Tokugawa alliance by Western han; death of Iemochi and accession of Tokugawa Keiki

INTERNATIONAL	WESTERN WORLD

1793 Macartney mission to Peking
1804 Resanov mission to Nagasaki fails to end seclusion
1816 Failure of the Amherst mission to Peking

1833 End of English East India Company trade monopoly; Napier at Canton

1839 Commissioner Lin Tse-hsu at Canton

1840–1842 Anglo-Chinese War
1842 Treaty of Nanking
1844 Treaties of Wanghsia and Whampoa

1853–1854 Commodore Perry and the Treaty of Kanagawa

1858 Townsend Harris and the commercial treaty with Japan; Anglo-French expedition to north China; the Treaties of Tientsin; the Treaty of Aigun

1860 Conventions of Peking; the Treaty of Peking

1863 British bombard Kagoshima

1864 Allied expedition destroys Choshu forts at Shimonoseki

1865 Allied naval expedition at Osaka secures imperial ratification of the treaties

---

1799 Napoleon in power in France

1815 Battle of Waterloo; Vienna settlement reshapes Europe

1823 Monroe Doctrine set forth

1830 Revolution in France, Belgium, and Poland

1832 First Reform Bill in Britain

1848 "Communist Manifesto" by Marx and Engels; wave of liberal and nationalistic revolutions in Europe

1858 Darwin's "Origin of Species": landmark in nineteenth-century scientific and intellectual revolution

1861 Outbreak of Civil War in U.S.; emancipation of Russian serfs by Czar Alexander II

1866 Austro-Prussian War: Bismarck unifying Germany under Prussia

1870 Tientsin massacre

1872–1881 Educational experiment of Yung Wing

1875–1908 Reign of Kuang Hsu (regency until 1889)

1875–1878 Suppression of the rebellion of Yakub Beg

1867 Death of Emperor Komei and accession of Emperor Meiji; resignation of Keiki as shogun

1868 The Meiji Restoration

1871 Abolition of the han; antifeudal and modernization reforms

1873 Decision against the war policy

1874 Beginning of samurai uprisings; agitation for representative government

1875 Reorganization of the government

1877 Satsuma Rebellion; broadening of the "democratic movement"

1881 Imperial rescript regarding establishment of parliament; formation of political parties; economic stabilization program

1884 Dissolution of political parties
1885 Establishment of cabinet system

1889 The Meiji Constitution

1890 First general elections for the Diet

1891 Matsukata replaces Yamagata as prime minister
1892 Ito replaces Matsukata as prime minister

1894 Sun Yat-sen organizes secret revolutionary society

1895 K'ang Yu-wei's reform memorial

1894 Beginning of substantial industrialization

1896 Matsukata replaces Ito as prime minister

1898 The One Hundred Days of Reform

1898 Ito replaces Matsukata as prime minister; the Okuma-Itagaki ministry; Yamagata becomes prime minister

1868–1870 Burlingame mission to the Western powers

1869 Alcock Convention

1871 Treaty of Tientsin between China and Japan as equals

1871–1873 Iwakura mission to the Western powers

1874 Japanese expedition to Formosa

1876 Chefoo Convention; Treaty of Kanghua

1881 Treaty of St. Petersburg

1885 Treaty of Tientsin recognizes French protectorate over Annam; Li-Ito Convention regarding Korea

1886 British protectorate over Burma

1894 Outbreak of Sino-Japanese War; Aoki-Kimberly Treaty to abolish extraterritoriality in 1898

1895 Treaty of Shimonoseki; Triple Intervention

1895–1898 Development of spheres of interest in China

1896 Yamagata-Lobanov Protocol
1898 Nishi-Rosen Agreement

1899 Hay's First Open-Door Notes

1870 Franco-Prussian War: leads to completion of German and Italian unification and to the Third Republic of France

1882 Triple Alliance of Germany, Austria, and Italy

1898 Spanish-American War: U.S. emerging as a world power

697

1900 Boxer Rebellion reaches its climax

1902–1911 Manchu reform program—political, economic, and social

1905 Sun Yat-sen forms T'ung Meng Hui

1909 Dismissal of Yuan Shih-k'ai and death of Chang Chih-tung

1911 Outbreak of the Chinese Revolution

1912 Establishment of the Chinese Republic; Sun Yat-sen forms the Kuomintang; the parliamentary elections

1913 Yuan Shih-k'ai suppresses the "second revolution"

1914 Yuan Shih-k'ai promulgates Constitional Compact

1915 Yuan's enthronement plan

1916 Yuan cancels enthronement; Yuan's death; beginning of the warlord era

1917–1920 Domination by the Anfu clique

1900 Ito forms Seiyukai and replaces Yamagata as prime minister

1901 Formation and dissolution of the Social Democratic Party; Katsura replaces Ito as prime minister

1904–1905 Acceleration of industrialization

1906 Saionji replaces Katsura as prime minister

1906–1907 Formation and dissolution of the Japan Socialist Party

1908 Katsura replaces Saionji as prime minister

1911 Saionji replaces Katsura as prime minister

1912 Death of the Emperor Meiji and accession of the Emperor Taisho; Katsura replaces Saionji as prime minister: beginning of the Taisho Change

1913 Yamamoto replaces Katsura as prime minister; naval scandals

1914 Okuma replaces Yamamoto as prime minister; wartime industrial boom

1916 Terauchi replaces Okuma as prime minister

1918 Rice riots; Hara replaces Terauchi as prime minister

1900 Hay's Second Open-Door Notes

1901 The Boxer Protocol

1902 Anglo-Japanese Alliance

1904 Outbreak of Russo-Japanese War

1905 Renewal of the Anglo-Japanese Alliance; Treaty of Portsmouth; Taft-Katsura notes

1907 Japanese protectorate over Korea; Russo-Japanese Treaty

1908–1911 The consortium and investment in China

1908 Gentlemen's Agreement; Root-Takahira notes

1909 Knox's "neutralization scheme"

1910 Japanese annexation of Korea; Russo-Japanese Treaty

1911 Renewal of the Anglo-Japanese Alliance; American-Japanese Commercial Treaty (tariff autonomy)

1913 Consortium support of Yuan Shih-k'ai; China recognizes autonomy of Outer Mongolia

1914 Japan declares war on Germany; capture of Tsingtao

1915 The Twenty-one Demands

1917 China declares war on Germany; Lansing-Ishii notes

1918 Siberian intervention

1904 Entente Cordiale between Britain and France

1914 Outbreak of World War I

1917 The Russian Revolutions

699

1919 Nationalism and the May 4th movement: an aspect of the Chinese Renaissance

1919 Debate over universal suffrage; dissolution of the diet; Reform Act doubles electorate; economic recession; industrial unrest and strikes

1920–1921 The Socialist League (formation and dissolution)

1921 Assassination of Hara; Takahashi succeeds as prime minister

1922 Establishment of Japanese Communist Party

1919 Establishment of Mongolian People's Revolutionary Government

1919 Treaty of Versailles

1921 Washington Conference

Chronology / PART III

1920–1922 Chang Tso-lin dominant at Peking; Sun Yat-sen and Ch'en Hsiung-ming co-operate at Canton

1921 Formation of Chinese Communist Party with help of Comintern

1921 Assassination of Hara; Takahashi succeeds as prime minister

1922 Wu Pei-fu drives Chang Tso-lin from Peking; Sun breaks with Ch'en and returns to Shanghai

1922 Admiral Kato replaces Takahashi as prime minister; formation of Japanese Communist Party

1923 Sun-Joffre Agreement; Sun returns to Canton

1923 Yamamoto replaces Kato as prime minister; the Great Earthquake; Kiyoura replaces Yamamoto as prime minister

1924 Borodin and the transformation of the Kuomintang; Feng Yu-hsiang, Chang Tso-lin, and Tuan Chi-jui dominant at Peking

1924 Kato Takaaki replaces Kiyoura as prime minister; Shidehara policy toward China

1925 Death of Sun Yat-sen; Wang Ching-wei and the left wing control the Kuomintang; anti-imperialism reaches peak

1925 Universal Manhood Suffrage Act increases electorate from 3 to 14 million; Peace Preservation Law

1926 Chiang K'ai-shek seizes control of the Kuomintang at Canton; beginning of the Northern March; Chang Tso-lin dominant at Peking; transfer of Kuomintang regime to Hankow: beginning of the split among the revolutionary forces

1926 Death of the Taisho emperor; Hirohito succeeds as the Showa emperor; death of Kato; Wakatsuki becomes prime minister; formation of various left-wing parties

1927 Chiang K'ai-shek establishes separate regime at Nanking; Hankow breaks with the Chinese Communists; consolidation of Hankow and Nanking regimes; dominance of Chiang K'ai-shek

1927 Bank crisis; Tanaka replaces Wakatsuki as prime minister; positive policy toward China

1928 Conclusion of the Northern March; Chang Tso-lin, driven from Peking, is killed by Japanese; the Chinese Republic with its capital at Nanking; the beginning of Political Tutelage

1928 First Universal Manhood Suffrage election; suppression of the extreme left wing

INTERNATIONAL	WESTERN WORLD

1920 Second Congress of the Comintern: Lenin's "Theses on the National and Colonial Question"

1921 Washington Conference; Russian-Mongolian Treaty

1922 Last Japanese troops withdraw from Siberia

1922 Mussolini in power in Italy

1924 U.S. Immigration Act abrogates Gentlemen's Agreement; Soviet-Peking Treaty; establishment of Mongolian People's Republic

1925 Restoration of Russian-Japanese relations

1925 Locarno Agreements guaranteeing Germany's western frontiers: high point of the brief "era of fulfillment"

1927–1928 Intervention by Japan in Shantung; Tsinan incident

1928–1930 China regains tariff autonomy

1928 Stalin issues First Five-Year Plan: rapid transformation of the Russian economy begins

1929 Hamaguchi replaces Tanaka as prime minister; Shidehara resumes office as foreign minister

1930 Hamaguchi shot by an assassin; Wakatsuki becomes prime minister; increasing ultranationalistic activity

1931 Establishment of Chinese Soviet Republic in Kiangsi Province

1931 Inukai replaces Wakatsuki as prime minister; Araki becomes army minister

1932 Establishment of Chiang K'ai-shek's General Headquarters for Bandit Suppression

1932 May 15 incident and assassination of Inukai; formation of nonparty cabinet by Saito; increasing pressure of the military

1934 New Life Movement; beginning of the Chinese Communists' Long March; supremacy of Mao Tse-tung

1934 Okada replaces Saito as prime minister; abrogation of naval agreements; factional struggle in the army

1935 National Salvation Movement

1936 The Sian incident: Chiang Hsueh-liang's mutiny

1936 February 26 incident; formation of the Hirota cabinet dominated by Terauchi, army minister

1937 Kuomintang–Chinese Communist Party "united front"

1937 Hayashi replaces Hirota as prime minister; Konoye replaces Hayashi and forms "national union" cabinet

1938 Kuomintang regime at Chungking; formation of the People's Political Council

1938 National Mobilization Bill

1939 Hiranuma replaces Konoye as prime minister; Abe succeeds Hiranuma

1940 Yonai replaces Abe as prime minister; Konoye succeeds Yonai; establishment of the Imperial Rule Assistance Association

1929 Chinese-Soviet hostilities in north Manchuria

1930 London Naval Agreement

1931 Mukden incident; Kwantung Army occupies Manchuria

1932 Stimson's nonrecognition doctrine; Sino-Japanese hostilities at Shanghai; establishment of Manchukuo

1933 Japan withdraws from the League of Nations; invasion of Jehol by Kwantung Army; Tangku Truce

1933 Hitler in power in Germany; Franklin Roosevelt president of the United States

1934 Amau statement regarding China

1935 Ho-Umezu Agreement; Hirota 3-point policy for China; Seventh Congress of the Comintern and the united-front policy; U.S. Neutrality Act

1935 Italy attacks Ethiopia

1936 Anti-Comintern Pact

1936 Outbreak of Spanish Civil War

1937 Sino-Japanese war; Brussels Conference; Italy joins Anti-Comintern Pact

1938 Sino-Japanese war reaches stalemate

1938 Munich Agreements dismember Czechoslovakia

1939 Nomohan incident; U.S. abrogates 1911 Commercial Treaty with Japan

1939 Stalin-Hitler nonaggression pacı; outbreak of World War II

1940 Japan in northern Indochina; U.S. embargoes; Japanese pressure on the Indies; Tripartite Pact

1940 Mao Tse-tung's "On New Democracy"; New Fourth Army incident: beginning of the end of the "united front"

1941 Reorganization of the Konoye cabinet; Tojo replaces Konoye as prime minister

1944 Wallace mission; Hurley as special representative in China; the Stilwell crisis

1944 Koiso replaces Tojo as prime minister; establishment of the Supreme Council for the Direction of the War

1945 Kuomintang and Chinese Communist Party agree to form Political Consultative Conference

1945 Suzuki replaces Koiso as prime minister; the surrender; beginning of the occupation under SCAP: political, economic, and social reforms

1946 Marshall mission

1946 Promulgation of the new constitution; continuation of reforms

1947 Outbreak of civil war

1949 Victory of the Chinese Communists: establishment of the People's Republic of China; Chiang and the Kuomintang retire to Formosa

1950 Purge of the Japanese Communist Party; beginning of rearmament

1951 Peace Treaty and American-Japanese Security Treaty

1952 End of the occupation; Yoshida as prime minister

1953 First Five-Year Plan

1954 Constitution of the People's Republic of China

1954 Hatoyama replaces Yoshida as prime minister

1955 Formation of united Socialist and Liberal Democratic parties

1956 Ishibashi replaces Hatoyama as prime minister

1957 Beginning of the Second Five-Year Plan: the Great Leap Forward
1958 Formation of communes

1957 Kishi replaces Ishibashi as prime minister

1959 Intervention in Tibet

1960 Ikeda replaces Kishi as prime minister

1941 U.S. Lend-Lease Act; Japanese-Russian Neutrality Pact; Hull-Nomura talks; Japan moves into southern Indochina; U.S. freezes Japanese assets

1941 German attack on the Soviet Union

1943 Cairo and Teheran conferences; extraterritoriality terminated in China

1944 Opening of the Burma campaign

1945 Yalta Agreement; Potsdam ultimatum; Sino-Soviet Treaty

1945 End of World War II; conference at San Francisco draws up Charter of the United Nations

1948 Cold War: beginning of the formation of the Communist and Western alliances

1950 Sino-Soviet agreements; outbreak of hostilities in Korea

1953 Korean Truce

1954 Geneva Agreement; Sino-Indian Treaty; formation of SEATO; U.S.-Taiwan Mutual Defense Treaty

1955 Bandung Conference

1956 Normalization of Japanese-Russian relations

1958 Sputnik

1960 Revision of American-Japanese Security Treaty; Chinese-Soviet ideological split

Glossary

bakufu "Tent" or "camp" government, a term referring to the basically feudal-military regimes of the Kamakura and Tokugawa periods.

bodhisattva One who defers entrance into nirvana because of a compassionate feeling of spiritual unity with others and makes over to them whatever merit he may possess. This term is often confused with buddha, as in the case of Amida.

buddha This word has various meanings: (1) an "enlightened one," in the sense of one who achieves understanding, hence salvation; (2) the historical buddha or Gotama, who founded Buddhism after his enlightenment; (3) "enlightened" beings who have become objects of devotion and prayer, e.g., Amida; (4) in pantheistic or cosmotheistic sects, the ultimate divine reality.

buke The military nobles (or families) of Japan who began to emerge as a result of the breakdown of the Taika Reform; a term used to distinguish the military nobility from the kuge, or civil nobility, of the imperial court.

bushi A Japanese warrior, often synonymous with the term samurai.

bushido "The way of the warrior"; the ethics of the Japanese military class. Having evolved with the development of feudalism, it became a feature of modern Japanese militarism.

chihokankaigi The meetings of Japanese prefectural governors that were inaugurated in the 1870's.

cho A Japanese unit of land measurement equal to approximately 2.45 acres.

co-hong The monopoly group of Chinese merchants that came into being in the eighteenth century, through whom the Europeans and Americans traded at Canton.

daimyo "Great name," or feudal lord, who usually controlled a large contiguous landed estate (han).

dainagon The deputies of the dajodaijin, or chancellor, in the imperial government of Japan.

daishinin The judicial office of Japanese government that was established in 1875.

dajodaijin The chancellor (chief minister) and head of the dajokan, the highest organ of the imperial government of Japan.

dajokan The highest organ of the imperial government of Japan and comparable to a council of state. It was important administratively in the Nara and early Heian periods and later during the first two decades of the Meiji era.

eta The "outcasts" in Japanese society, discriminated against because of their occupational roles. Before the end of World War II they generally lived in segregated villages or areas.

fu The three urban areas of Tokyo, Osaka, and Kyoto, all of which had administrations on a level of equality with the prefectures.

genro The "elder statesmen," a term that came into being in Japan in the 1890's to refer to the dominant political leaders of the central government.

genroin The senate that was established in Japan as a quasilegislative body in 1875.

han The territorial estate or domain of a Japanese feudal lord (daimyo). During the Tokugawa period there were between 250 and 300 han.

harakiri   Japanese ceremonial suicide by means of disembowelment with a knife and usually decapitation by a friend.

hoppo   The commissioner of customs at Canton.

hsien   The district or county, the lowest unit of imperial administration in China. The number of hsien was usually between 1,000 and 1,500.

jomon   A term referring to a type of Neolithic culture in Japan characterized by hand-molded pottery with a rope pattern.

jito   Manorial stewards used in Japan by the Taira, Minamoto, and Hojo families for the guarantee of tax obligations and revenue rights.

kempeitai   The military secret police of the Japanese army, established in the 1880's.

ken   Prefectures established in Japan following the Meiji Restoration of 1868; the largest unit of local administration in Japan.

kogisho   A quasilegislative advisory body, representing on the whole the interests of the han, which was established in Japan in the spring of 1869.

koku   The Japanese measurement of weight, equal to 4.96 lbs.

kokutai   The abstract concept of the national polity or fundamental character of the Japanese state; the foundation of imperial rule, or tennosei.

kotogakko   The higher school in the pre–World War II Japanese system of education, which was based on six years of grammar school, five years of middle school, three years of higher school, and three years of university.

kuge   The civil nobles of the imperial court of Japan.

likin   The internal-transit taxes that were first applied in China during the Taiping Rebellion.

nirvana   The spiritual goal of some Buddhist sects; the state achieved by the conquest of craving; release from the process of transmigration.

pao chia   The Chinese system of mutual responsibility and local control, used also at times for local military purposes. It was based on units of 10 (p'ai), 100 (chia), and 1,000 (pao) families.

ronin   Generally, retainers of a Japanese feudal lord whose lands have been confiscated, thus depriving the retainers of income.

sain   The left board (legislative) of the dajokan in the reorganization of the Japanese central government after the abolition of the han in 1871.

sake   Japanese rice wine, usually served warm.

samurai   This term has two meanings. (1) Originally, in the development of Japanese feudalism, any warrior, whether lord or vassal, but generally the latter. (2) The class, or members of a class, of military retainers of the daimyo. The special rights and privileges of the samurai were abolished after the downfall of feudalism in 1871.

sangi   Councilors in the governments of the first two decades of the Meiji period.

sankin kotai   The practice whereby the Tokugawa bakufu required the alternate residence of daimyo in the han and at Edo, the bakufu capital.

seiin   The central board (executive) of the dajokan in the reorganization of the Japanese central government after the abolition of the han in 1871.

shogun   The highest military-political leader in feudal Japan, a title derived from that held by the commanders of the forces that fought the Ainu.

shugiin   The Japanese quasilegislative advisory body that succeeded the kogisho in August, 1869.

709

shugo A constable or provincial military governor during the Kamakura period in Japan.

sosai The highest minister of the first Japanese government after the Meiji Restoration.

tael A name for the Chinese "ounce"; a weight measurement of silver, the value of which fluctuated with the price of the metal.

tao A Chinese word meaning "the way." It was used by Confucianists to describe what they regarded as an essentially moral, harmonious order of the universe and by the Taoists to describe a natural order ("natural" meaning "being so of itself").

tozama The so-called "outside," or enemy, daimyo during the Tokugawa period. The term was applied to those feudal lords who opposed Tokugawa Ieyasu at the Battle of Sekigahara.

tsungli yamen The special office in the Chinese imperial government created in the 1860's for foreign relations purposes. Later it was made responsible for more general administrative policies, including reform.

uin The right board (administrative) of the dajokan in the reorganization of the Japanese central government after the abolition of the han in 1871.

yamen The residence and office of a local official in imperial China, e.g., the viceroy's yamen.

yang In Chinese cosmology and philosophy, the principle of activity, light, heat, masculinity, etc.

yayoi A term referring to a type of Neolithic culture in Japan characterized by wheel-turned pottery of simple design.

yin In Chinese cosmology and philosophy, the principle of quiescence, darkness, cold, femininity, etc.

yuan The five branches of the Chinese central government—executive, legislative, judicial, control, and examination—as proposed by Sun Yat-sen and instituted by the Kuomintang.

zaibatsu The "financial clique," a term referring to the major Japanese economic trusts or holding companies like Mitsui or Mitsubishi.

Indexes

Index of Persons

Hu Feng, 521
Hu Han-min, 213, 220, 422, 425, 453–54
Hu Shih, 234
Hu Tsung-nan, 478
Huai Ta-pu, 184
Huang Hsing, 211, 220, 221, 223
Hughes, Charles Evans, 376–81, 382, 383
Hull, Cordell, 476, 492, 569–70, 583, 589–91, 605–11, 614–15
Hung Fu, 145
Hung Hsiu-ch'uan, 132–35, 136, 137, 143, 145
Hurley, Patrick, 494–98, 501, 506

Ichikawa Shoichi, 550–51, 556, 565
Iemitsu, Tokugawa, 94, 106
Iemochi, Tokugawa, 248, 249, 251, 252, 253, 255
Ieyasu, Tokugawa, 92–94, 99, 100–101
Ignatiev, General, 164
Ii Naosuke, 248–50
Ikeda Hayato, 638, 639, 644
Inouye Junnosuke, 552, 562, 565
Inouye Kaoru, 266, 284–85, 295–96, 299, 301, 309, 315, 318, 321
Inouye Kowashi, 292, 293, 300
Inouye Tetsujiro, 349
Inukai Tsuyoshi, 359, 544, 559, 563, 566
Ishibashi Tanzan, 638
Ishii Kikujiro, 360
Itagaki Taisuke, 265, 269, 270, 277–78, 280, 281–83, 285, 294, 296, 299, 301, 311, 317, 321
Ito Hirobumi, 169, 172–73, 202, 265, 278, 282–83, 284–85, 289–93, 295, 304–5, 306, 309, 310–13, 317–22, 328–29, 342, 347
Ito Myoji, 298, 300, 565
Ivan IV (the Terrible), 60
Iwakura Tomomi, 255, 258, 259, 265–66, 276–78, 282, 289–90, 292–93, 298, 303
Iwasaki Yanosuke, 345
Iwasaki Yotaro, 274, 291, 317

Jao Shu-shih, 518
Jardine, William, 126
Jiu Ch'eng, 212
Joffre, Adolphe, 402, 403–4, 406–7
Jung Lu, 184, 185–86, 189, 192, 198, 200

Kabayama, Admiral, 317
Kalmykov, 364
Kamenev, Lev B., 417
Kaneko Kentaro, 299, 300
K'ang Hsi, Emperor, 54, 55, 56, 59, 62, 129

K'ang Yu-wei, 179–86, 187, 188, 198, 229, 232
Kanin, Prince, 567
Kao Kang, 465, 518
Karakhan, Leo, 383–84, 404, 418
Katayama Sen, 346–48, 388
Katayama Tetsu, 628, 633
Kato Hiroyuki, 280–81
Kato Takaaki, 173, 321–22, 344, 345, 350, 351, 353–54, 355, 357, 358–59, 370, 375, 544–47, 551–52
Kato Tomosaburo, 369, 377–81, 543
Katsu Awa, 278
Katsura Taro, 304, 305, 319, 320–22, 328, 335, 342–45, 347, 368
Kawakami Jotaro, 637
Kawamoto, Colonel, 428
Kazama Jokichi, 564
Kearney, Lawrence, 127, 177
Keiki, Tokugawa, 248, 251, 254, 255, 257–58, 259–60
Kerensky, Alexander, 365
Ketteler, Baron von, 192, 197
Khabarov, 60
Khrushchev, Nikita, 530, 532
Khubilai, 88–89
Kido Koichi, 615, 624
Kido Koin (Takayoshi), 253, 259, 260, 262, 264–68, 276–79, 281–83, 284, 291, 299, 304
Kimberley, Lord, 173
Kishi Nobusuke, 532, 636, 638, 639, 641, 643
Kiso Yoshinaka, 84
Kita, General, 473
Kita Ikki, 557–58, 570, 574–75
Kiyomori, Taira, 83–84, 92
Kiyoura Keigo, 350, 544, 615
Knox, Philander, 336–37
Kobayashi Ichizo, 598
Kodama Gentaro, 326
Koiso Kuniaki, 561, 621, 624
Kokuryo Goichiro, 565
Kolchak, Alexander, 364–65, 375
Komatsu Tateki, 258
Komei, Emperor (Mutsuhito), 251, 253, 255
Komura Jutaro, 327, 330
Kondo Eizo, 388
Kono Hironaka, 317
Kono Ichiro, 638
Kono Togama, 312
Konoye Fumimaro, 470, 472–73, 474, 580–83, 586, 588, 594–600, 602, 606, 610–15, 621, 627
Koo, Wellington, 372
Kotoku Shusui, 346–48

715

717

719

General Index

Aigun, Treaty of, 163–64
Aikokukoto (Public Society of Patriots), 280
Aikokusha (Society of Patriots), 281, 286, 294
Ainu, the, 71, 80, 82
All-China Federation of Labor, 408–9, 419
All-China Federation of Trade Unions, 525
Allied Council for Japan, 623
Amaterasu, 73, 74
American-Japanese Commercial Treaty
of 1894, 333
of 1911, 319, 586, 589, 591
American-Japanese Mutual Defense Assistance Agreement, 642
American-Japanese Security Treaty of 1951, 635, 642
Amida, 45, 47, 87–88
Ancestor worship
Chinese, 7–8, 12, 23, 43
Japanese, 76–77
Anfu Clique, 230, 361, 397, 401
Anglo-Chinese War of 1840, 125–26
Anglo-Japanese Alliance, 216, 321–23, 328, 352, 374, 378–79
Anglo-Japanese Treaty of 1894, 313
Anti-Comintern Pact, 577–79, 587–88
"Arrow" Incident, 140
Ashikaga shogunate, 90–92

Bandung Conference, 531
Bank of China, 457
Bank of Japan, 293–94, 367, 560
Bank of Taiwan, 552
Boxer Protocol, 196–97, 205, 449
Boxer Rebellion, 179, 190–93, 196–97
Brahmanism, 38–39, 40
Brussels Conference, 584
Buddhism
Chinese, 42–47, 48, 49, 136, 190
Japanese, 74–75, 76, 77–80, 86–88, 99, 110, 269–70
origins of, 38–42
Burma, 41, 57, 161, 489–91, 493, 498, 530, 586, 603, 635
Bushido, 82, 269

Cairo Conference, 492–93, 503, 532
Canton trade, 59–60, 120–21
Ch'an sects, 44–45, 47
"Charter Oath," 260–61, 279, 285

Chefoo Convention, 161–62
Ch'iang Hsueh Hui ("Reform Club"), 180
Chichibu Uprising, 296
Chihli Faction, 230, 397
Ch'in dynasty, 16–18, 29, 33
China Incident (1937), 470–74
China Merchants Steam Navigation Company, 152, 153
Chinese Communist Party, 237, 396–97, 400, 405–410, 415–17, 419–25, 433–37, 462–69, 471, 480, 483–89, 491–97, 499–512, 514–15, 515–32
Chinese Eastern Railway, 175–76, 193, 330, 331, 335–36, 365–66, 402, 404, 406, 440–41, 497, 500, 578
Chinputang (Progressive Party), 223
Choshu, 92, 94–95, 244, 250, 251–56, 262–67, 268, 270, 278, 284, 291, 299, 317, 318, 343, 368
Chou dynasty, 5–10, 16
Christianity
in China, 61–63, 128, 133–34, 136–37, 141–43, 154, 160, 186, 190–91, 204, 233
in Japan, 99–101, 270, 275
in Korea, 166
Co-hong, the, 120, 122, 127
Comintern
in China, 399–400, 401, 405, 408, 410, 412, 417, 420, 421, 424, 433–34, 440, 466–67
in Japan, 388–89, 548, 550, 564–65
Confucianism
Chinese, 10–14, 16, 19–21, 23, 24, 30–31, 32, 34, 43, 45–46, 48–51, 52, 58–59, 62, 118, 136, 147–49, 153, 158, 167, 169, 174, 180–82, 232–33, 234, 461–62
Japanese, 76–77, 79, 93, 97–99, 110–11, 269, 272, 307–8
Consortium, the, 205–7, 221–22, 225, 336–37, 360–62
"Constitutional Compact," 224, 228
Constitutions
Chinese Constitution (1954), 516–17
Draft Constitution (China—1913), 397
Draft Constitution (China—1917), 397
Draft Constitution (China—1936), 455
Genroin draft constitutions, 288–90
Japanese Constitution (1947), 626–28, 635